P9-DBO-612

Houghton
Mifflin
Harcourt

CALIFORNIA

GO MATH!

© Houghton Mifflin Harcourt Publishing Company • Cover and Title Image Credits:

(fg) Fox ©Ocean/Corbis; (bg) Redwood Trees ©James Randklev/Getty Images

Made in the United States
Text printed on 90%
recycled paper

THIS BOOK IS THE PROPERTY OF:

STATE _____	Book No. _____
PROVINCE _____	Enter information in spaces to the left as instructed
COUNTY _____	
PARISH _____	
SCHOOL DISTRICT _____	
OTHER _____	

ISSUED TO	Year Used	CONDITION	
		ISSUED	RETURNED
_____	_____	_____	_____

Copyright © 2015 by Houghton Mifflin Harcourt Publishing Company

All rights reserved. No part of this work may be reproduced or transmitted in any form or by any means, electronic or mechanical, including photocopying or recording, or by any information storage and retrieval system, without the prior written permission of the copyright owner unless such copying is expressly permitted by federal copyright law. Requests for permission to make copies of any part of the work should be addressed to Houghton Mifflin Harcourt Publishing Company, Attn: Contracts, Copyrights, and Licensing, 9400 Southpark Center Loop, Orlando, Florida 32819-8647.

Common Core State Standards © Copyright 2010. National Governors Association Center for Best Practices and Council of Chief State School Officers. All rights reserved. This product is not sponsored or endorsed by the Common Core State Standards Initiative of the National Governors Association Center for Best Practices and the Council of Chief State School Officers.

Printed in the U.S.A.

ISBN 978-0-544-20397-6

11 12 13 14 15 0029 23 22 21 20 19 18

4500742716   F G

If you have received these materials as examination copies free of charge, Houghton Mifflin Harcourt Publishing Company retains title to the materials and they may not be resold. Resale of examination copies is strictly prohibited.

Possession of this publication in print format does not entitle users to convert this publication, or any portion of it, into electronic format.

Dear Students and Families,

Welcome to **California Go Math!**, Grade 3! In this exciting mathematics program, there are hands-on activities to do and real-world problems to solve. Best of all, you will write your ideas and answers right in your book. In **California Go Math!**, writing and drawing on the pages helps you think deeply about what you are learning, and you will really understand math!

By the way, all of the pages in your **California Go Math!** book are made using recycled paper. We wanted you to know that you can Go Green with **California Go Math!**

Sincerely,

The Authors

Made in the United States
Text printed on 90% recycled paper

© Houghton Mifflin Harcourt Publishing Company • Image Credits: (bg) ©Randall J Hodges/SuperStock/Corbis; (l) ©All Canada Photos/Getty Images; (c) ©Mark Mirror/Shutterstock; (r) ©Joseph Sohm/Visions of America/Corbis

CALIFORNIA

GO MATH!

Authors

Juli K. Dixon, Ph.D.
Professor, Mathematics Education
University of Central Florida
Orlando, Florida

Edward B. Burger, Ph.D.
President, Southwestern University
Georgetown, Texas

Steven J. Leinwand
Principal Research Analyst
American Institutes for
    Research (AIR)
Washington, D.C.

Contributor

Rena Petrello
Professor, Mathematics
Moorpark College
Moorpark, CA

Matthew R. Larson, Ph.D.
K-12 Curriculum Specialist for
    Mathematics
Lincoln Public Schools
Lincoln, Nebraska

Martha E. Sandoval-Martinez
Math Instructor
El Camino College
Torrance, California

English Language Learners Consultant

Elizabeth Jiménez
CEO, GEMAS Consulting
Professional Expert on English
    Learner Education
Bilingual Education and
    Dual Language
Pomona, California

© Houghton Mifflin Harcourt Publishing Company • Image Credits: (bg) ©Jeff Oishan/Getty Images; (t) ©Mark Karrass/Corbis; (b) ©Allan Vernon/Flickr/Getty Images

Whole Number Operations

 COMMON CORE **Critical Area** Developing understanding of multiplication and division and strategies for multiplication and division within 100

1 Addition and Subtraction Within 1,000   3

Domains Operations and Algebraic Thinking
Number and Operations in Base Ten
CALIFORNIA COMMON CORE STANDARDS 3.OA.8, 3.OA.9, 3.NBT.1, 3.NBT.2

2 Represent and Interpret Data   61

Domain Measurement and Data
CALIFORNIA COMMON CORE STANDARDS 3.MD.3, 3.MD.4

 GO DIGITAL

Go online! Your math lessons are interactive. Use *i*Tools, Animated Math Models, the Multimedia *e*Glossary, and more.

Chapter 1 Overview

In this chapter, you will explore and discover answers to the following **Essential Questions**:

• How can you add and subtract whole numbers and decide if an answer is reasonable?

• How do you know when an estimate will be close to an exact answer?

• When do you regroup to add or subtract whole numbers?

• How might you decide which strategy to use to add or subtract?

Chapter 2 Overview

In this chapter, you will explore and discover answers to the following **Essential Questions**:

• How can you represent and interpret data?

• What are some ways to organize data so it is easy to use?

• How can analyzing data in graphs help you solve problems?

© Houghton Mifflin Harcourt Publishing Company

Chapter 3 Overview

In this chapter, you will explore and discover answers to the following **Essential Questions**:

• How can you use multiplication to find how many in all?
• What models can help you multiply?
• How can you use skip counting to help you multiply?
• How can multiplication properties help you find products?
• What types of problems can be solved by using multiplication?

Chapter 4 Overview

In this chapter, you will explore and discover answers to the following **Essential Questions**:

• What strategies can you use to multiply?
• How are patterns and multiplication related?
• How can multiplication properties help you find products?
• What types of problems can be solved by using multiplication?

© Houghton Mifflin Harcourt Publishing Company

Chapter 5 Overview
In this chapter, you will explore and discover answers to the following **Essential Questions**:
- How can you use multiplication facts, place value, and properties to solve multiplication problems?
- How are patterns and multiplication related?
- How can multiplication properties help you find products?
- What types of problems can be solved by using multiplication?

Chapter 6 Overview
In this chapter, you will explore and discover answers to the following **Essential Questions**:
- How can you use division to find how many in each group or how many equal groups?
- How are multiplication and division related?
- What models can help you divide?
- How can subtraction help you divide?

© Houghton Mifflin Harcourt Publishing Company

Chapter 7 Overview

In this chapter, you will explore and discover answers to the following **Essential Questions:**

• What strategies can you use to divide?

• How can you use a related multiplication fact to divide?

• How can you use factors to divide?

• What types of problems can be solved by using division?

7 Division Facts and Strategies 263

Domain Operations and Algebraic Thinking
CALIFORNIA COMMON CORE STANDARDS 3.OA.3, 3.OA.4, 3.OA.7, 3.OA.8

© Houghton Mifflin Harcourt Publishing Company

Fractions

COMMON CORE **Critical Area** Developing understanding of fractions, especially unit fractions (fractions with numerator 1)

GO DIGITAL

Go online! Your math lessons are interactive. Use *i*Tools, Animated Math Models, the Multimedia eGlossary, and more.

Essential Question
What are equal parts of a whole?

Chapter 8 Overview

In this chapter, you will explore and discover answers to the following **Essential Questions**:

• How can you use fractions to describe how much or how many?

• Why do you need to have equal parts for fractions?

• How can you solve problems that involve fractions?

Chapter 9 Overview

In this chapter, you will explore and discover answers to the following **Essential Questions**:

• How can you compare fractions?

• What models can help you compare and order fractions?

• How can you use the size of the pieces to help you compare and order fractions?

• How can you find equivalent fractions?

© Houghton Mifflin Harcourt Publishing Company

Critical Area

GO DIGITAL

Go online! Your math lessons are interactive. Use *i*Tools, Animated Math Models, the Multimedia *e*Glossary, and more.

Chapter 10 Overview

In this chapter, you will explore and discover answers to the following **Essential Questions**:

- How can you tell time and use measurement to describe the size of something?

- How can you tell time and find the elapsed time, starting time, or ending time of an event?

- How can you measure the length of an object to the nearest half or fourth inch?

Chapter 11 Overview

In this chapter, you will explore and discover answers to the following **Essential Questions**:

- How can you solve problems involving perimeter and area?

- How can you find perimeter?

- How can you find area?

- What might you need to estimate or measure perimeter and area?

Measurement

 **COMMON CORE** **Critical Area** Developing understanding of the structure of rectangular arrays and of area

© Houghton Mifflin Harcourt Publishing Company

Geometry

COMMON CORE **Critical Area** Describing and analyzing two-dimensional shapes

12. Two-Dimensional Shapes 503

Domain Geometry
CALIFORNIA COMMON CORE STANDARDS 3.G.1, 3.G.2

GO DIGITAL

Go online! Your math lessons are interactive. Use *i*Tools, Animated Math Models, the Multimedia eGlossary, and more.

Chapter **12** Overview

In this chapter, you will explore and discover answers to the following **Essential Questions**:

- What are some ways to describe and classify two-dimensional shapes?
- How can you describe the angles and sides in polygons?
- How can you use sides and angles to describe quadrilaterals and triangles?
- How can you use properties of shapes to classify them?
- How can you divide shapes into equal parts and use unit fractions to describe the parts?

© Houghton Mifflin Harcourt Publishing Company

Whole Number Operations

 CRITICAL AREA Developing understanding of multiplication and division and strategies for multiplication and division within 100

Some Baby Abuelita dolls sing Spanish rhymes and lullabies.

© Houghton Mifflin Harcourt Publishing Company

Inventing Toys

The dolls in the picture are called Abuelitos. Some of them are grandmother and grandfather dolls that were designed to sing lullabies. They and the grandchildren dolls have music boxes inside them. You squeeze their hands to start them singing!

Get Started

Suppose you and a partner work in a toy store. You want to order enough dolls to fill two shelves in the store. Each shelf is 72 inches long. How many cartons of dolls will fill the two shelves? Use the Important Facts to help you.

Important Facts

- Each Abuelita doll comes in a box that is 8 inches wide.
  8 in.
- There are 4 boxes in 1 carton.
- Abuelita Rosa sings 6 songs.
- Abuelito Pancho sings 4 songs.
- Javier sings 5 songs.
- Baby Andrea and Baby Tita each sing 5 songs.
- Baby Mimi plays music but does not sing.

_____

_____

_____

_____

_____

_____

Completed by _____

© Houghton Mifflin Harcourt Publishing Company

Show What You Know ✔

Check your understanding of important skills.

Name _____

▶ **Think Addition to Subtract** Write the missing numbers.

1. $9 - 4 = \blacksquare$

Think: $4 + \blacksquare = 9$

$4 + \underline{} = 9$

So, $9 - 4 = \underline{}$.

2. $13 - 7 = \blacksquare$

Think: $7 + \blacksquare = 13$

$7 + \underline{} = 13$

So, $13 - 7 = \underline{}$.

3. $17 - 9 = \blacksquare$

Think: $9 + \blacksquare = 17$

$9 + \underline{} = 17$

So, $17 - 9 = \underline{}$.

▶ **Addition Facts** Find the sum.

4. $\begin{array}{r} 4 \\ +\ 3 \\ \hline \end{array}$

5. $\begin{array}{r} 2 \\ +\ 7 \\ \hline \end{array}$

6. $\begin{array}{r} 8 \\ +\ 6 \\ \hline \end{array}$

7. $\begin{array}{r} 9 \\ +\ 4 \\ \hline \end{array}$

8. $\begin{array}{r} 7 \\ +\ 9 \\ \hline \end{array}$

▶ **Subtraction Facts** Find the difference.

9. $\begin{array}{r} 8 \\ -\ 5 \\ \hline \end{array}$

10. $\begin{array}{r} 11 \\ -\ 2 \\ \hline \end{array}$

11. $\begin{array}{r} 10 \\ -\ 6 \\ \hline \end{array}$

12. $\begin{array}{r} 18 \\ -\ 9 \\ \hline \end{array}$

13. $\begin{array}{r} 15 \\ -\ 7 \\ \hline \end{array}$

Manuel's puppy chewed part of this homework paper. Two of the digits in his math problem are missing. Be a Math Detective to help Manuel figure out the missing digits. What digits are missing?

$\begin{array}{r} 3\square \\ +\ 2\square \\ \hline 72 \end{array}$

© Houghton Mifflin Harcourt Publishing Company

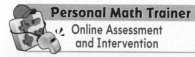

Personal Math Trainer
Online Assessment and Intervention

Vocabulary Builder

▶ **Visualize It** ••

Sort the review words with a ✓ into the Venn diagram.

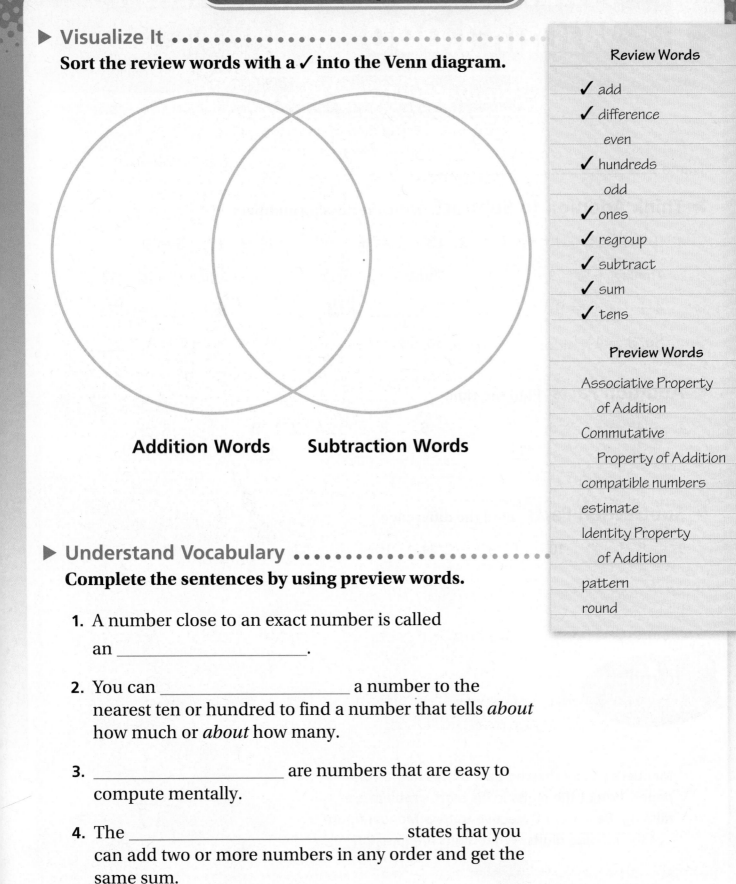

Addition Words   **Subtraction Words**

Review Words

✓ add
✓ difference
  even
✓ hundreds
  odd
✓ ones
✓ regroup
✓ subtract
✓ sum
✓ tens

Preview Words

Associative Property
  of Addition
Commutative
  Property of Addition
compatible numbers
estimate
Identity Property
  of Addition
pattern
round

▶ **Understand Vocabulary** ••••••••••••••••••••••••••••

Complete the sentences by using preview words.

1. A number close to an exact number is called
   an _____.

2. You can _____ a number to the
   nearest ten or hundred to find a number that tells *about*
   how much or *about* how many.

3. _____ are numbers that are easy to
   compute mentally.

4. The _____ states that you
   can add two or more numbers in any order and get the
   same sum.

© Houghton Mifflin Harcourt Publishing Company

 GO DIGITAL
• **Interactive Student Edition**
• **Multimedia eGlossary**

Number Patterns

Essential Question How can you use properties to explain patterns on the addition table?

 Operations and Algebraic Thinking—3.OA.9

MATHEMATICAL PRACTICES
MP.1, MP.2, MP.7

Unlock the Problem

A **pattern** is an ordered set of numbers or objects. The order helps you predict what will come next.

You can use the addition table to explore patterns.

Activity 1

Materials ■ orange and green crayons

- Look across each row and down each column. What pattern do you see?

  _____

  _____

- Shade the row and column orange for the addend 0. Compare the shaded squares to the yellow row and the blue column. What pattern do you see?

  _____

  What happens when you add 0 to a number?

  _____

- Shade the row and column green for the addend 1. What pattern do you see?

  _____

  What happens when you add 1 to a number?

  _____

  _____

+	0	1	2	3	4	5	6	7	8	9	10
0	0	1	2	3	4	5	6	7	8	9	10
1	1	2	3	4	5	6	7	8	9	10	11
2	2	3	4	5	6	7	8	9	10	11	12
3	3	4	5	6	7	8	9	10	11	12	13
4	4	5	6	7	8	9	10	11	12	13	14
5	5	6	7	8	9	10	11	12	13	14	15
6	6	7	8	9	10	11	12	13	14	15	16
7	7	8	9	10	11	12	13	14	15	16	17
8	8	9	10	11	12	13	14	15	16	17	18
9	9	10	11	12	13	14	15	16	17	18	19
10	10	11	12	13	14	15	16	17	18	19	20

The **Identity Property of Addition** states that the sum of any number and zero is that number.

$$7 + 0 = 7$$

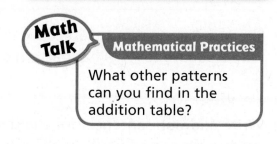

Math Talk
Mathematical Practices

What other patterns can you find in the addition table?

© Houghton Mifflin Harcourt Publishing Company

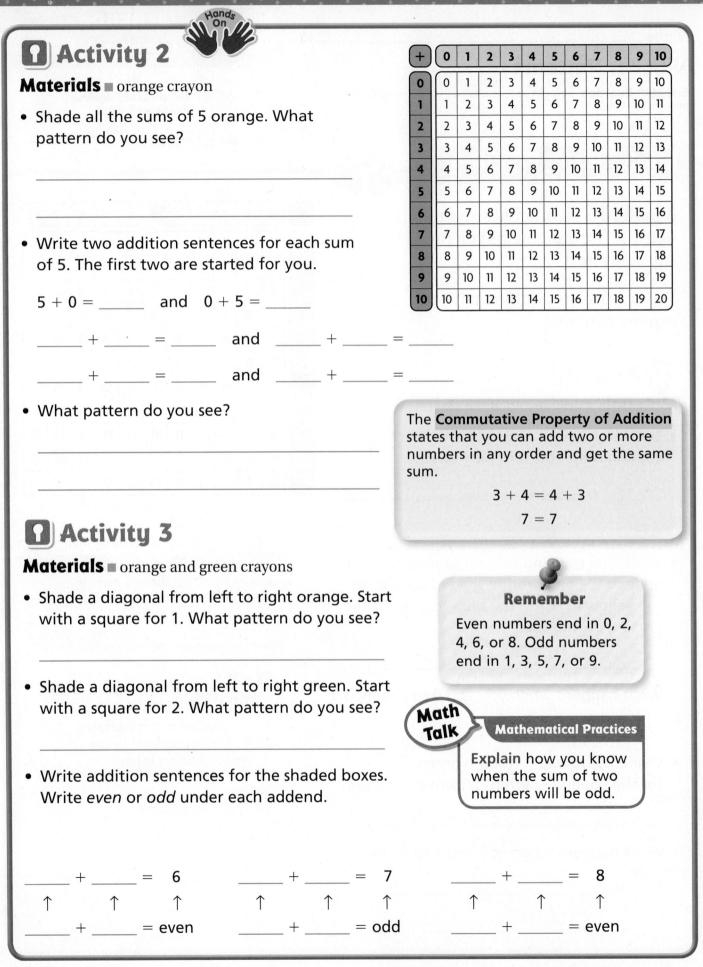

Activity 2

Materials ■ orange crayon

- Shade all the sums of 5 orange. What pattern do you see?

  _____

  _____

- Write two addition sentences for each sum of 5. The first two are started for you.

  5 + 0 = _____   and   0 + 5 = _____

  _____ + _____ = _____   and   _____ + _____ = _____

  _____ + _____ = _____   and   _____ + _____ = _____

- What pattern do you see?

  _____

  _____

+	0	1	2	3	4	5	6	7	8	9	10
0	0	1	2	3	4	5	6	7	8	9	10
1	1	2	3	4	5	6	7	8	9	10	11
2	2	3	4	5	6	7	8	9	10	11	12
3	3	4	5	6	7	8	9	10	11	12	13
4	4	5	6	7	8	9	10	11	12	13	14
5	5	6	7	8	9	10	11	12	13	14	15
6	6	7	8	9	10	11	12	13	14	15	16
7	7	8	9	10	11	12	13	14	15	16	17
8	8	9	10	11	12	13	14	15	16	17	18
9	9	10	11	12	13	14	15	16	17	18	19
10	10	11	12	13	14	15	16	17	18	19	20

The **Commutative Property of Addition** states that you can add two or more numbers in any order and get the same sum.

$$3 + 4 = 4 + 3$$
$$7 = 7$$

Activity 3

Materials ■ orange and green crayons

- Shade a diagonal from left to right orange. Start with a square for 1. What pattern do you see?

  _____

- Shade a diagonal from left to right green. Start with a square for 2. What pattern do you see?

  _____

- Write addition sentences for the shaded boxes. Write *even* or *odd* under each addend.

Remember

Even numbers end in 0, 2, 4, 6, or 8. Odd numbers end in 1, 3, 5, 7, or 9.

Math Talk — **Mathematical Practices**

Explain how you know when the sum of two numbers will be odd.

_____ + _____ = 6   _____ + _____ = 7   _____ + _____ = 8
  ↑   ↑   ↑   ↑   ↑   ↑   ↑   ↑   ↑
_____ + _____ = even   _____ + _____ = odd   _____ + _____ = even

© Houghton Mifflin Harcourt Publishing Company

Name _____

Share and Show

MATH BOARD

Use the addition table on page 6 for 1–15.

1. Complete the addition sentences to show the Commutative Property of Addition.

   $3 + $ _____ $ = $ _____ $4 + $ _____ $ = $ _____

Math Talk **Mathematical Practices**

Explain why you can use the Commutative Property of Addition to write a related addition sentence.

Find the sum. Then use the Commutative Property of Addition to write the related addition sentence.

✓ 2. $8 + 5 = $ _____

   _____ $+$ _____ $=$ _____

3. $7 + 9 = $ _____

   _____ $+$ _____ $=$ _____

4. $10 + 4 = $ _____

   _____ $+$ _____ $=$ _____

Is the sum even or odd? Write *even* or *odd*.

5. $8 + 1$ _____

6. $3 + 9$ _____

✓ 7. $4 + 8$ _____

Problem Solving • Applications Real World

8. **THINK SMARTER** Look back at the shaded diagonals in Activity 2. Why does the orange diagonal show only odd numbers? Explain.

   _____

   _____

9. **GO DEEPER** Find the sum $15 + 0$. Then write the name of the property that you used to find the sum.

   _____

10. **THINK SMARTER** Select the number sentences that show the Commutative Property of Addition. Mark all that apply.

    (A) $27 + 4 = 31$

    (B) $27 + 4 = 4 + 27$

    (C) $27 + 0 = 0 + 27$

    (D) $27 + (4 + 0) = (27 + 4) + 0$

© Houghton Mifflin Harcourt Publishing Company

Sense or Nonsense?

11. **MATHEMATICAL PRACTICE 3** **Make Arguments** Whose statement makes sense? Whose statement is nonsense? Explain your reasoning.

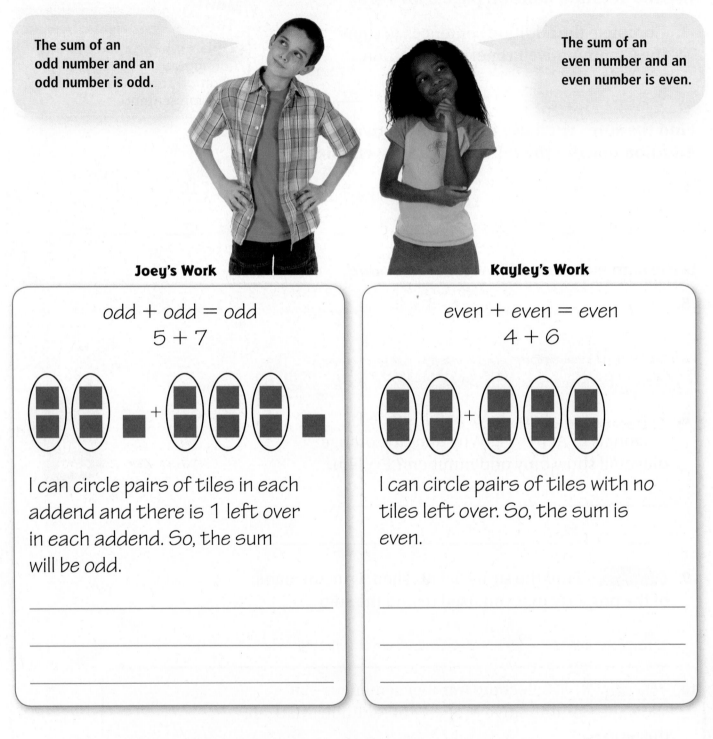

The sum of an odd number and an odd number is odd.

The sum of an even number and an even number is even.

Joey's Work

odd + odd = odd
5 + 7

I can circle pairs of tiles in each addend and there is 1 left over in each addend. So, the sum will be odd.

_____

_____

_____

Kayley's Work

even + even = even
4 + 6

I can circle pairs of tiles with no tiles left over. So, the sum is even.

_____

_____

_____

• For the statement that is nonsense, correct the statement.

_____

© Houghton Mifflin Harcourt Publishing Company

FOR MORE PRACTICE:
Standards Practice Book

Round to the Nearest Ten or Hundred

Essential Question How can you round numbers?

Number and Operations in Base Ten—
3.NBT.1
MATHEMATICAL PRACTICES
MP.5, MP.7, MP.8

🔑 Unlock the Problem (Real World)

When you **round** a number, you find a number that tells you *about* how much or *about* how many.

Mia's baseball bat is 32 inches long. What is its length rounded to the nearest ten inches?

🔒 One Way Use a number line to round.

A Round 32 to the nearest ten.

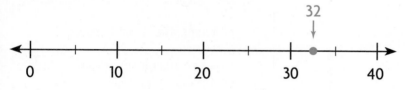

32

Find which tens the number is between.

32 is between _____ and _____.

32 is closer to _____ than it is to _____.

32 rounded to the nearest ten is _____.

So, the length of Mia's bat rounded to the

nearest ten inches is _____ inches.

B Round 174 to the nearest hundred.

174

Find which hundreds the number is between.

174 is between _____ and _____.

174 is closer to _____ than it is to _____.

So, 174 rounded to the nearest hundred is _____.

Math Talk **Mathematical Practices**

Name three other numbers that round to 30 when rounded to the nearest ten. **Explain.**

© Houghton Mifflin Harcourt Publishing Company • Image Credits: ©Design Pics Inc./Alamy Images

Try This! Round 718 to the nearest ten and hundred.
Locate and label 718 on the number lines.

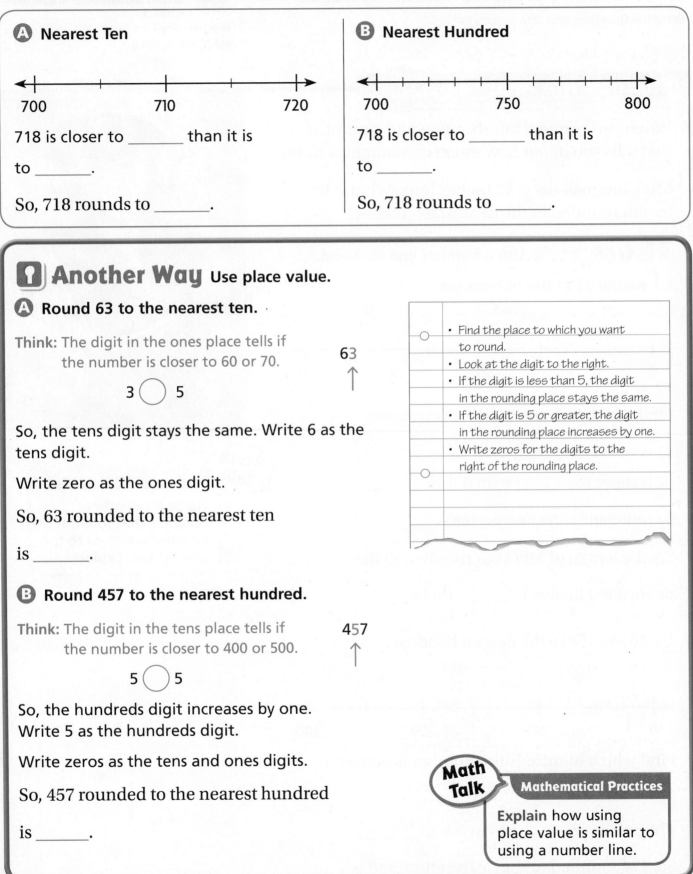

Ⓐ Nearest Ten

700   710   720

718 is closer to _____ than it is

to _____.

So, 718 rounds to _____.

Ⓑ Nearest Hundred

700   750   800

718 is closer to _____ than it is

to _____.

So, 718 rounds to _____.

🔓 Another Way Use place value.

Ⓐ Round 63 to the nearest ten.

Think: The digit in the ones place tells if
the number is closer to 60 or 70.

3 ◯ 5

63
↑

So, the tens digit stays the same. Write 6 as the
tens digit.

Write zero as the ones digit.

So, 63 rounded to the nearest ten

is _____.

• Find the place to which you want
  to round.
• Look at the digit to the right.
• If the digit is less than 5, the digit
  in the rounding place stays the same.
• If the digit is 5 or greater, the digit
  in the rounding place increases by one.
• Write zeros for the digits to the
  right of the rounding place.

Ⓑ Round 457 to the nearest hundred.

Think: The digit in the tens place tells if
the number is closer to 400 or 500.

5 ◯ 5

457
↑

So, the hundreds digit increases by one.
Write 5 as the hundreds digit.

Write zeros as the tens and ones digits.

So, 457 rounded to the nearest hundred

is _____.

Math Talk   **Mathematical Practices**

Explain how using
place value is similar to
using a number line.

© Houghton Mifflin Harcourt Publishing Company

Name _____

Share and Show MATH BOARD

Math Talk **Mathematical Practices**

What is the greatest number that rounds to 50 when rounded to the nearest ten? What is the least number? **Explain.**

Locate and label 46 on the number line. Round to the nearest ten.

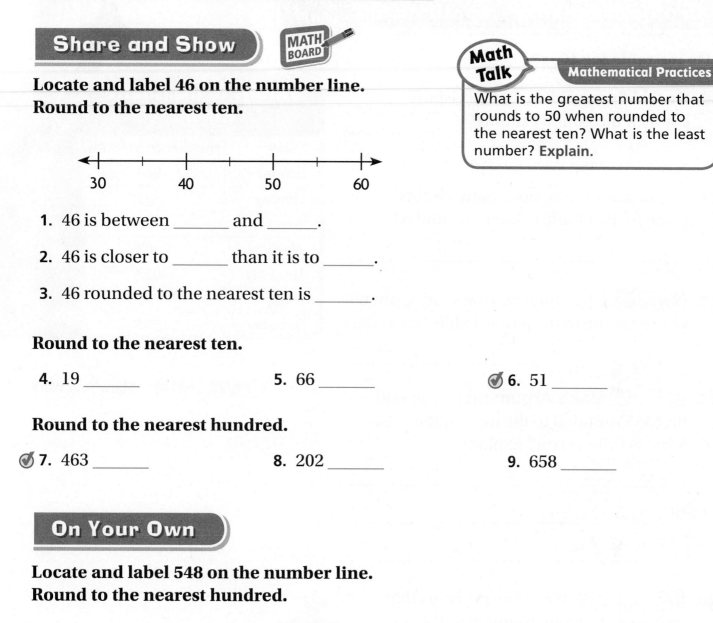

1. 46 is between _____ and _____.

2. 46 is closer to _____ than it is to _____.

3. 46 rounded to the nearest ten is _____.

Round to the nearest ten.

4. 19 _____

5. 66 _____

6. 51 _____

Round to the nearest hundred.

7. 463 _____

8. 202 _____

9. 658 _____

On Your Own

Locate and label 548 on the number line. Round to the nearest hundred.

10. 548 is between _____ and _____.

11. 548 is closer to _____ than it is to _____.

12. 548 rounded to the nearest hundred is _____.

Round to the nearest ten and hundred.

13. 576 _____

_____

14. 298 _____

_____

15. 844 _____

_____

© Houghton Mifflin Harcourt Publishing Company

Chapter 1 • Lesson 2 11

Problem Solving • Applications (Real World)

Use the table for 16–18.

16. On which day did about 900 visitors come to the giraffe exhibit?

_____

17. To the nearest ten, how many visitors came to the giraffe exhibit on Sunday?

_____

18. GO DEEPER On which two days did about 800 visitors come to the giraffe exhibit each day?

_____

Visitors to the Giraffe Exhibit	
Day	**Number of Visitors**
Sunday	894
Monday	793
Tuesday	438
Wednesday	362
Thursday	839
Friday	725
Saturday	598

19. MATHEMATICAL PRACTICE ③ **Make Arguments** Cole said that 555 rounded to the nearest ten is 600. What is Cole's error? Explain.

_____

_____

_____

WRITE ▸ Math • Show Your Work

20. THINK SMARTER Write five numbers that round to 360 when rounded to the nearest ten.

_____

_____

21. THINK SMARTER Select the numbers that round to 100. Select all that apply.

Ⓐ 38   Ⓒ 109

Ⓑ 162   Ⓓ 83

FOR MORE PRACTICE:
Standards Practice Book

© Houghton Mifflin Harcourt Publishing Company • Image Credits: ©Peter Barritt/Alamy Images

Estimate Sums

Essential Question How can you use compatible numbers and rounding to estimate sums?

🔑 Unlock the Problem (Real World)

The table shows how many dogs went to Pine Lake Dog Park during the summer months. About how many dogs went to the park during June and August?

You can estimate to find *about* how many or *about* how much. An **estimate** is a number close to an exact amount.

Pine Lake Dog Park	
Month	**Number of Dogs**
June	432
July	317
August	489

🔒 One Way Use compatible numbers.

Compatible numbers are numbers that are easy to compute mentally and are close to the real numbers.

$$
\begin{array}{rcr}
432 & \to & 425 \\
+\ 489 & \to & +\ 475 \\
\hline
\end{array}
$$

So, about _____ dogs went to Pine Lake Dog Park during June and August.

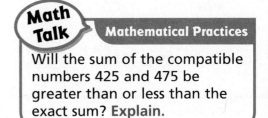

Math Talk **Mathematical Practices**

Will the sum of the compatible numbers 425 and 475 be greater than or less than the exact sum? **Explain.**

1. What other compatible numbers could you have used?

_____

2. About how many dogs went to the park during July and August? What compatible numbers could you use to estimate?

_____

© Houghton Mifflin Harcourt Publishing Company • Image Credits: (tr) ©Getty Images

🔒 Another Way Use place value to round.

432 + 489 = ■

First, find the place to which you want to round.
Round both numbers to the same place.
The greatest place value of 432 and 489 is
hundreds. So, round to the nearest hundred.

> **Remember**
> When you round a number,
> you find a number that tells
> *about* how many or *about*
> how much.

STEP 1 Round 432 to the nearest hundred.

- Look at the digit to the right of the
  hundreds place.

- Since 3 < 5, the digit 4 stays the same.

- Write zeros for the tens and ones digits.

$$4\ 3\ 2$$
$$\uparrow$$

$$\begin{array}{r} 4\ 3\ 2 \\ +\ 4\ 8\ 9 \end{array} \rightarrow \quad \begin{array}{r} \\ +\ \underline{} \end{array}$$

STEP 2 Round 489 to the nearest hundred.

- Look at the digit to the right of the
  hundreds place.

- Since 8 > 5, the digit 4 increases by one.

- Write zeros for the tens and ones digits.

$$4\ 8\ 9$$
$$\uparrow$$

$$\begin{array}{r} 4\ 3\ 2 \\ +\ 4\ 8\ 9 \end{array} \begin{array}{c} \rightarrow \\ \rightarrow \end{array} \begin{array}{r} 4\ 0\ 0 \\ +\ \underline{} \end{array}$$

STEP 3 Find the sum of the rounded numbers.

$$\begin{array}{r} 4\ 3\ 2 \\ +\ 4\ 8\ 9 \end{array} \begin{array}{c} \rightarrow \\ \rightarrow \end{array} \begin{array}{r} 4\ 0\ 0 \\ +\ 5\ 0\ 0 \\ \hline \end{array}$$

So, 432 + 489 is about _____.

> **Math Talk** Mathematical Practices
>
> How would you round 432
> and 489 to the nearest ten?
> What would be the estimated
> sum? **Explain.**

Try This! **Estimate the sum.**

Ⓐ Use compatible numbers.

$$\begin{array}{r} 47 \\ +\ 23 \end{array} \begin{array}{c} \rightarrow \\ \rightarrow \end{array} \begin{array}{r} \\ +\ 25 \\ \hline \end{array}$$

Ⓑ Use rounding.

$$\begin{array}{r} 304 \\ +\ 494 \end{array} \begin{array}{c} \rightarrow \\ \rightarrow \end{array} \begin{array}{r} 300 \\ +\ \\ \hline \end{array}$$

© Houghton Mifflin Harcourt Publishing Company

Name _____

Share and Show

1. Use compatible numbers to complete
   the problem. Then estimate the sum.

$$
\begin{array}{r}
428 \\
+286
\end{array}
\quad
\begin{array}{r}
\rightarrow \\
\rightarrow \quad +
\end{array}
$$

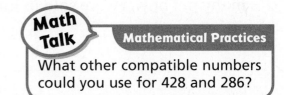

Math Talk · **Mathematical Practices**

What other compatible numbers could you use for 428 and 286?

Use rounding or compatible numbers to estimate the sum.

2. $\begin{array}{r} 65 \\ +23 \end{array}$ $+ \underline{}$

☑ 3. $\begin{array}{r} 421 \\ +218 \end{array}$ $+ \underline{}$

☑ 4. $\begin{array}{r} 369 \\ +480 \end{array}$ $+ \underline{}$

On Your Own

Use rounding or compatible numbers to estimate the sum.

5. $\begin{array}{r} 19 \\ +54 \end{array}$ $+ \underline{}$

6. $\begin{array}{r} 39 \\ +42 \end{array}$ $+ \underline{}$

7. $\begin{array}{r} 327 \\ +581 \end{array}$ $+ \underline{}$

8. $\begin{array}{r} 27 \\ +78 \end{array}$ $+ \underline{}$

9. $\begin{array}{r} 267 \\ +517 \end{array}$ $+ \underline{}$

10. $\begin{array}{r} 465 \\ +478 \end{array}$ $+ \underline{}$

11. $\begin{array}{r} 186 \\ +460 \end{array}$ $+ \underline{}$

12. $\begin{array}{r} 817 \\ +118 \end{array}$ $+ \underline{}$

13. $\begin{array}{r} 632 \\ +244 \end{array}$ $+ \underline{}$

14. $278 + 369$

$\underline{} + \underline{} = \underline{}$

15. $523 + 195$

$\underline{} + \underline{} = \underline{}$

© Houghton Mifflin Harcourt Publishing Company

Problem Solving • Applications

Use the table for 16–18.

Dan's Pet Supplies Sold		
Month	Pet Bowls	Bags of Pet Food
June	91	419
July	57	370
August	76	228

16. **MATHEMATICAL PRACTICE ②** **Use Reasoning** About how many pet bowls were sold in June and July altogether?

_____

17. **GO DEEPER** Would you estimate there were more pet bowls sold in June or in July and August combined? Explain.

_____

_____

18. **THINK SMARTER** Dan estimated the lowest monthly sales of both pet bowls and bags of pet food to be about 300. What month had the lowest sales? Explain.

_____

_____

_____

19. **THINK SMARTER** Write each number sentence in the box below the better estimate of the sum.

263 + 189 = ■ 305 + 72 = ■ 195 + 238 = ■ 215 + 289 = ■

400	500

© Houghton Mifflin Harcourt Publishing Company • Image Credits: ©Image Source/Alamy Images

FOR MORE PRACTICE: Standards Practice Book

Name _____

Mental Math Strategies for Addition

Essential Question What mental math strategies can you use to find sums?

Number and Operations in Base Ten—
3.NBT.2
MATHEMATICAL PRACTICES
MP.2, MP.7, MP.8

🔑 Unlock the Problem (Real World)

The table shows how many musicians are in each section of a symphony orchestra. How many musicians play either string or woodwind instruments?

Orchestra Musicians	
Section	**Number**
Brass	12
Percussion	13
String	57
Woodwind	15

🔑 One Way Count by tens and ones to find 57 + 15.

A Count on to the nearest ten. Then count by tens and ones.

Think: 3 + ■ = 15

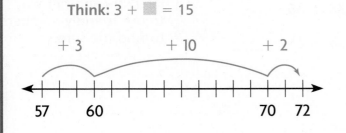

57 + 15 = _____

So, _____ musicians play either string or woodwind instruments.

B Count by tens. Then count by ones.

Think: 10 + 5 = 15

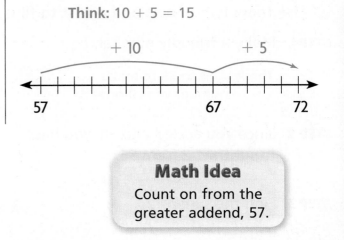

Math Idea
Count on from the greater addend, 57.

Try This! Find 43 + 28. Draw jumps and label the number line to show your thinking.

So, 43 + 28 = _____.

Math Talk

Mathematical Practices

Explain another way you can draw the jumps.

© Houghton Mifflin Harcourt Publishing Company

🔑 Other Ways

Ⓐ Use compatible numbers to find 178 + 227.

STEP 1 Break apart the addends to make them compatible.

Think: $178 = 175 + 3$
$227 = 225 + 2$

175 and 225 are compatible numbers.

Remember
Compatible numbers are easy to compute mentally and are close to the real numbers.

STEP 2 Find the sums.

$$178 \quad \rightarrow \quad 175 \quad + \quad 3$$
$$+\,227 \quad \rightarrow \quad 225 \quad + \quad 2$$
$$\underline{} \quad + \quad \underline{}$$

STEP 3 Add the sums.

_____ + _____ = _____

So, 178 + 227 = _____.

Ⓑ Use friendly numbers and adjust to find 38 + 56.

STEP 1 Make a friendly number.

$38 + 2 =$ _____

Think: Add to 38 to make a number with 0 ones.

Math Talk **Mathematical Practices**

Describe another way to use friendly numbers to find the sum.

STEP 2 Since you added 2 to 38, you have to subtract 2 from 56.

$56 - 2 =$ _____

STEP 3 Find the sum.

_____ + _____ = _____

So, 38 + 56 = _____.

Share and Show

1. Count by tens and ones to find 63 + 27. Draw jumps and label the number line to show your thinking.

Think: Count by tens and ones from 63.

63

63 + 27 = _____

© Houghton Mifflin Harcourt Publishing Company

Name _____

2. Use compatible numbers to find $26 + 53$.

Think: $26 = 25 + 1$
$\quad\quad\quad 53 = 50 + 3$

$26 + 53 =$ _____

Math Talk **Mathematical Practices**

Explain how you could use friendly numbers to find $26 + 53$.

Count by tens and ones to find the sum.
Use the number line to show your thinking.

3. $34 + 18 =$ _____

4. $22 + 49 =$ _____

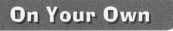

On Your Own

Use mental math to find the sum.
Draw or describe the strategy you use.

5. $116 + 203 =$ _____

6. $18 + 57 =$ _____

7. **MATHEMATICAL PRACTICE ⑥ Explain a Method** On Friday, 376 people attended the school concert. On Saturday, 427 people attended. Explain how can you use mental math to find how many people attended the concert.

_____

_____

_____

8. **THINK SMARTER** There are 14 more girls than boys in the school orchestra. There are 19 boys. How many students are in the school orchestra?

_____

© Houghton Mifflin Harcourt Publishing Company

Problem Solving • Applications Real World

Use the table for 9–12

9. **MATHEMATICAL PRACTICE ①** **Analyze** How many girls attended school on Monday and Tuesday?

_____

10. **What's the Question?** The answer is 201 students.

_____

_____

Harrison School Attendance

Day	Boys	Girls
Monday	92	104
Tuesday	101	96
Wednesday	105	93
Thursday	99	102
Friday	97	103

11. **THINK SMARTER** How many students attended school on Tuesday and Wednesday? Explain how you can find your answer.

_____

_____

_____

_____

12. **GO DEEPER** On which day did the most students attend school?

_____

13. **THINK SMARTER** On Monday, 46 boys and 38 girls bought lunch at school. How many students bought lunch? Explain one way to solve the problem.

_____

_____

© Houghton Mifflin Harcourt Publishing Company • Image Credits: © Creatas/Jupiterimages/Getty Images

FOR MORE PRACTICE:
Standards Practice Book

Use Properties to Add

Essential Question How can you add more than two addends?

Number and Operations in Base Ten—
3.NBT.2
MATHEMATICAL PRACTICES
MP.2, MP.7, MP.8

CONNECT You have learned the Commutative Property of Addition. You can add two or more numbers in any order and get the same sum.

$$16 + 9 = 9 + 16$$

The **Associative Property of Addition** states that you can group addends in different ways and still get the same sum. It is also called the Grouping Property.

$$(16 + 7) + 23 = 16 + (7 + 23)$$

Math Idea
You can change the order or the grouping of the addends to make combinations that are easy to add.

Unlock the Problem

Mrs. Gomez sold 23 cucumbers, 38 tomatoes, and 42 peppers at the Farmers' Market. How many vegetables did she sell in all?

Find 23 + 38 + 42.

• Will the sum be closer to 90 or 100?

_____

Look for an easy way to add.

STEP 1 Line up the numbers by place value.

```
  2 3
  3 8
+ 4 2
```

STEP 2 Group the ones to make them easy to add.

Think: Make a ten.

```
  ¹
  2 3
  3 8  ⟩ 10
+ 4 2
  3
```

STEP 3 Group the tens to make them easy to add.

Think: Make doubles.

```
        ¹
    5 ⟨ 5 ⟨ 2 3
          3 8
        + 4 2
        1 0 3
```

23 + 38 + 42 = _____

So, Mrs. Gomez sold _____ vegetables in all.

Math Talk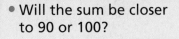

Mathematical Practices

Explain how to group the digits to make them easy to add.

© Houghton Mifflin Harcourt Publishing Company • Image Credits: (tr) ©Digital Vision/Getty Images

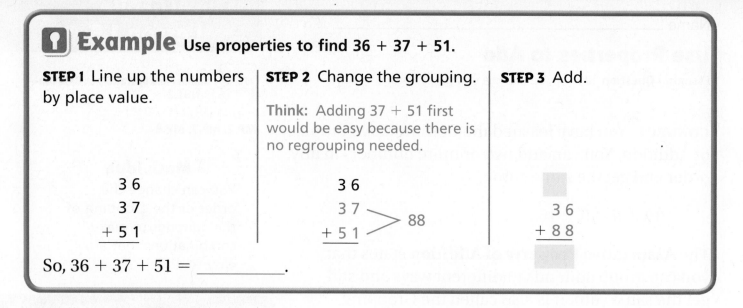

Example Use properties to find 36 + 37 + 51.

STEP 1 Line up the numbers by place value.

$$
\begin{array}{r}
3\ 6 \\
3\ 7 \\
+\ 5\ 1 \\
\hline
\end{array}
$$

STEP 2 Change the grouping.

Think: Adding 37 + 51 first would be easy because there is no regrouping needed.

$$
\begin{array}{r}
3\ 6 \\
3\ 7 \\
+\ 5\ 1 \\
\end{array} \Big\rangle 88
$$

STEP 3 Add.

$$
\begin{array}{r}
3\ 6 \\
+\ 8\ 8 \\
\hline
\end{array}
$$

So, 36 + 37 + 51 = _____.

Try This! Use properties to add.

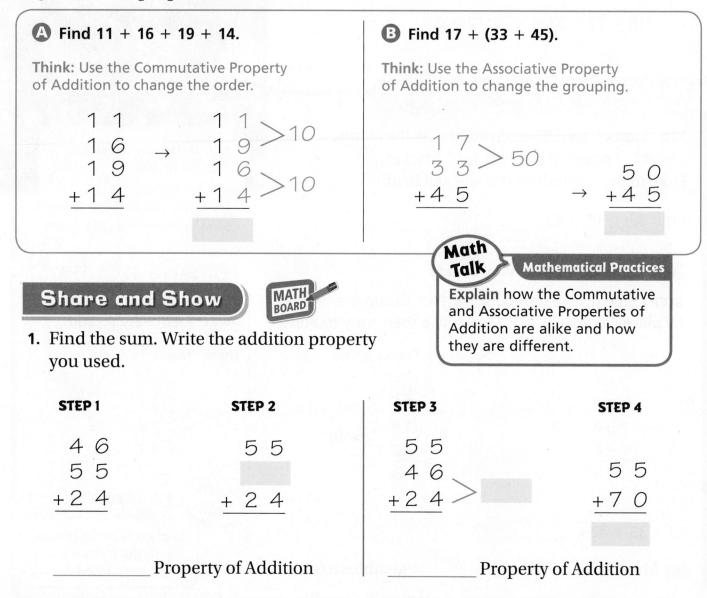

A Find 11 + 16 + 19 + 14.

Think: Use the Commutative Property of Addition to change the order.

$$
\begin{array}{r}
1\ 1 \\
1\ 6 \\
1\ 9 \\
+\ 1\ 4 \\
\hline
\end{array} \rightarrow
\begin{array}{r}
1\ 1 \\
1\ 9 \\
1\ 6 \\
+\ 1\ 4 \\
\hline
\end{array}
\begin{array}{l} \rangle 10 \\ \rangle 10 \end{array}
$$

B Find 17 + (33 + 45).

Think: Use the Associative Property of Addition to change the grouping.

$$
\begin{array}{r}
1\ 7 \\
3\ 3 \\
+\ 4\ 5 \\
\hline
\end{array} \Big\rangle 50 \rightarrow
\begin{array}{r}
5\ 0 \\
+\ 4\ 5 \\
\hline
\end{array}
$$

Share and Show MATH BOARD

Math Talk — **Mathematical Practices**

Explain how the Commutative and Associative Properties of Addition are alike and how they are different.

1. Find the sum. Write the addition property you used.

STEP 1

$$
\begin{array}{r}
4\ 6 \\
5\ 5 \\
+\ 2\ 4 \\
\hline
\end{array}
$$

STEP 2

$$
\begin{array}{r}
5\ 5 \\
\\
+\ 2\ 4 \\
\hline
\end{array}
$$

_____ Property of Addition

STEP 3

$$
\begin{array}{r}
5\ 5 \\
4\ 6 \\
+\ 2\ 4 \\
\hline
\end{array} \Big\rangle
$$

STEP 4

$$
\begin{array}{r}
5\ 5 \\
+\ 7\ 0 \\
\hline
\end{array}
$$

_____ Property of Addition

© Houghton Mifflin Harcourt Publishing Company

Name _____

Use addition properties and strategies to find the sum.

✓ 2. $13 + 26 + 54 =$ _____

✓ 3. $57 + 62 + 56 + 43 =$ _____

Use addition properties and strategies to find the sum.

4. $18 + 39 + 32 =$ _____

5. $13 + 49 + 87 =$ _____

6. $15 + 76 + 125 =$ _____

7. $33 + 71 + 56 + 29 =$ _____

8. Change the order and the grouping of the addends so that
you can use mental math to find the sum. Then find the sum.

$43 + 39 + 43 + 11 =$ _____

_____ + _____ + _____ + _____ = _____

© Houghton Mifflin Harcourt Publishing Company

Problem Solving • Applications (Real World)

9. **GO DEEPER** Mr. Arnez bought 32 potatoes, 29 onions, 31 tomatoes, and 28 peppers to make salads for his deli. How many vegetables did he buy?

_____

10. Ms. Chang is baking for the school bake sale. She bought 16 apples, 29 peaches, and 11 bananas at the Farmers' Market. How many pieces of fruit did she buy?

_____

11. **MATHEMATICAL PRACTICE ②** **Reason Abstractly** What is the unknown number? Which property did you use?

$$(\blacksquare + 8) + 32 = 49$$

_____

12. **THINK SMARTER** Change the order or grouping to find the sum. Explain how you used properties to find the sum.

$$63 + 86 + 77$$

_____

_____

_____

13. **THINK SMARTER** For numbers 13a–13d, choose Yes or No to tell whether the number sentence shows the Associative Property of Addition.

13a. $(86 + 7) + 93 = 86 + (7 + 93)$ ○ Yes ○ No

13b. $86 + 7 = 7 + 86$ ○ Yes ○ No

13c. $86 + 0 = 86$ ○ Yes ○ No

13d. $86 = 80 + 6$ ○ Yes ○ No

FOR MORE PRACTICE:
Standards Practice Book

© Houghton Mifflin Harcourt Publishing Company • Image Credits: ©Brand X Pictures/Getty Images

Name _____

Use the Break Apart Strategy to Add

Essential Question How can you use the break apart strategy to add 3-digit numbers?

Number and Operations in Base Ten— 3.NBT.2 Also 3.NBT.1, 3.OA.8
MATHEMATICAL PRACTICES
MP.2, MP.7, MP.8

🔑 Unlock the Problem (Real World)

There are more zoos in Germany than in any other country. At one time, there were 355 zoos in the United States and 414 zoos in Germany. How many zoos were there in the United States and Germany altogether?

You can use the break apart strategy to find sums.

🔑 Example 1 Add. 355 + 414

STEP 1 Estimate. 400 + 400 = _____

STEP 2 Break apart the addends.
Start with the hundreds.
Then add each place value.

STEP 3 Add the sums.

    700 + 60 + 9 = _____

So, there were _____ zoos in the United States and Germany altogether.

Math Talk

Mathematical Practices

Do you think the sum will be greater than or less than 800? **Explain.**

$$
\begin{array}{rcl}
355 & = & 300 + \boxed{} + 5 \\
+\ 414 & = & \boxed{} + 10 + 4 \\
\hline
 & & 700 + 60 + 9
\end{array}
$$

🔑 Example 2 Add. 467 + 208

STEP 1 Estimate. 500 + 200 = _____

STEP 2 Break apart the addends.
Start with the hundreds.
Then add each place value.

$$
\begin{array}{rcl}
467 & = & 400 + \boxed{} + \boxed{} \\
+\ 208 & = & \boxed{} + 0 + 8 \\
\hline
 & & 600 + 60 + 15
\end{array}
$$

STEP 3 Add the sums.

    600 + 60 + 15 = _____

So, 467 + 208 = _____.

© Houghton Mifflin Harcourt Publishing Company • Image Credits: ©Michael Halberstadt/Alamy Images

Try This! Use the break apart strategy to find 343 + 259.

Estimate. 300 + 300 = _____

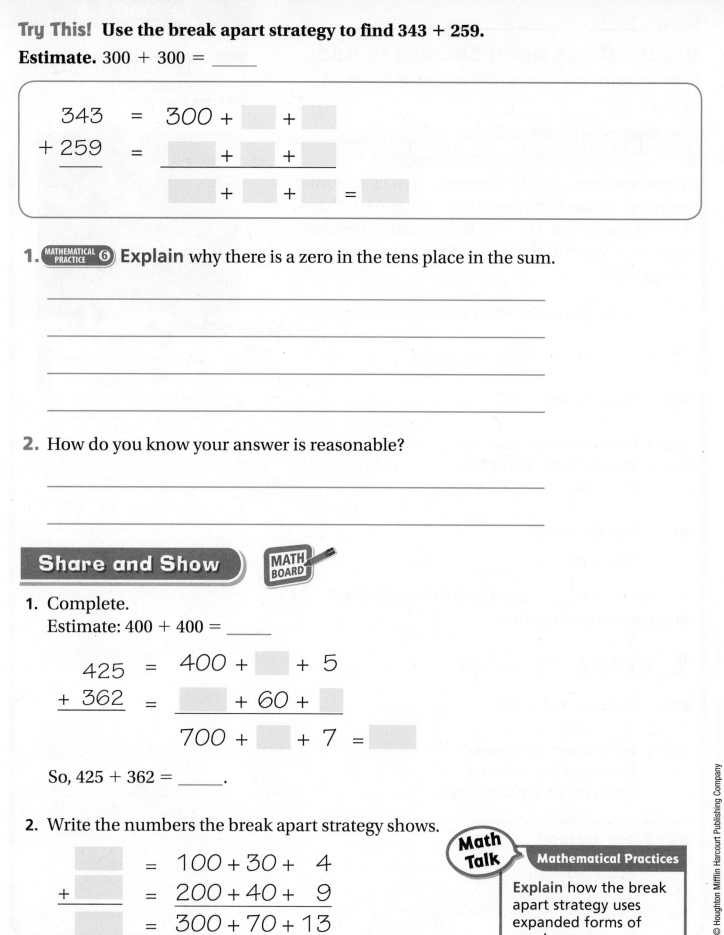

343 = $300 +$ ⬜ $+$ ⬜
$+\ 259$ = ⬜ $+$ ⬜ $+$ ⬜
⬜ $+$ ⬜ $+$ ⬜ = ⬜

1. **MATHEMATICAL PRACTICE ⑥ Explain** why there is a zero in the tens place in the sum.

_____

_____

_____

_____

2. How do you know your answer is reasonable?

_____

_____

Share and Show **MATH BOARD**

1. Complete.

Estimate: 400 + 400 = _____

425 = $400 +$ ⬜ $+ 5$
$+\ 362$ = ⬜ $+ 60 +$ ⬜
$700 +$ ⬜ $+ 7$ = ⬜

So, 425 + 362 = _____.

2. Write the numbers the break apart strategy shows.

⬜ = $100 + 30 + 4$
$+$ ⬜ = $200 + 40 + 9$
⬜ = $300 + 70 + 13$

Math Talk **Mathematical Practices**

Explain how the break apart strategy uses expanded forms of numbers.

© Houghton Mifflin Harcourt Publishing Company

Estimate. Then use the break apart strategy to find the sum.

3. Estimate: _____

$$142 =$$
$$+436 =$$

4. Estimate: _____

$$459 =$$
$$+213 =$$

5. Estimate: _____

$$291 =$$
$$+420 =$$

6. Estimate: _____

$$654 =$$
$$+243 =$$

On Your Own

Estimate. Then use the break apart strategy to find the sum.

7. Estimate: _____

$$435 =$$
$$+312 =$$

8. Estimate: _____

$$163 =$$
$$+205 =$$

9. Estimate: _____

$$634 =$$
$$+251 =$$

10. Estimate: _____

$$526 =$$
$$+357 =$$

Practice: Copy and Solve **Estimate. Then solve.**

11. $163 + 205$ **12.** $543 + 215$ **13.** $213 + 328$ **14.** $372 + 431$

15. $152 + 304$ **16.** $268 + 351$ **17.** $413 + 257$ **18.** $495 + 312$

© Houghton Mifflin Harcourt Publishing Company

Problem Solving • Applications Real World

Use the table for 19–20.

Number of Students	
School	Number
Harrison	304
Montgomery	290
Bryant	421

19. **GO DEEPER** Which two schools together have fewer than 600 students? Explain.

_____

_____

_____

20. **THINK SMARTER** The number of students in Collins School is more than double the number of students in Montgomery School. What is the least number of students that could attend Collins School?

_____

21. **What's the Error?** Lexi used the break apart strategy to find 145 + 203. Describe her error. What is the correct sum?

$$
\begin{array}{r}
100 + 40 + 5 \\
+\ 200 + 30 + 0 \\
\hline
300 + 70 + 5 = 375
\end{array}
$$

_____

22. **MATHEMATICAL PRACTICE ⑤** **Communicate** Is the sum of 425 and 390 less than or greater than 800? How do you know?

_____

_____

23. **THINK SMARTER** What is the sum of 421 and 332? Show your work.

_____

© Houghton Mifflin Harcourt Publishing Company

FOR MORE PRACTICE:
Standards Practice Book

Use Place Value to Add

Essential Question How can you use place value to add 3-digit numbers?

Number and Operations in Base Ten—3.NBT.2

MATHEMATICAL PRACTICES
MP.2, MP.7, MP.8

Unlock the Problem Real World

Dante is planning a trip to Illinois. His airplane leaves from Dallas, Texas, and stops in Tulsa, Oklahoma. Then it flies from Tulsa to Chicago, Illinois. How many miles does Dante fly?

Chicago

585 miles

Tulsa

236 miles

Dallas

Use place value to add two addends.

Add. 236 + 585

Estimate. 200 + 600 = _____

STEP 1

Add the ones. Regroup the ones as tens and ones.

$$\begin{array}{r} \overset{1}{2\ 3\ 6} \\ +\ 5\ 8\ 5 \\ \hline \end{array}$$

STEP 2

Add the tens. Regroup the tens as hundreds and tens.

$$\begin{array}{r} \overset{1}{2}\ \overset{1}{3}\ 6 \\ +\ 5\ 8\ 5 \\ \hline 1 \end{array}$$

STEP 3

Add the hundreds.

$$\begin{array}{r} \overset{1}{2}\ \overset{1}{3}\ 6 \\ +\ 5\ 8\ 5 \\ \hline 2\ 1 \end{array}$$

236 + 585 = _____

So, Dante flies _____ miles.

Since _____ is close to the estimate of _____ , the answer is reasonable.

> **! ERROR Alert**
>
> Remember to add the regrouped ten and hundred.

- You can also use the Commutative Property of Addition to check your work. Change the order of the addends and find the sum.

$$\begin{array}{r} 5\ 8\ 5 \\ +\ 2\ 3\ 6 \\ \hline \end{array}$$

© Houghton Mifflin Harcourt Publishing Company

Try This! Find 563 + 48 in two ways.

Estimate. 550 + 50 = _____

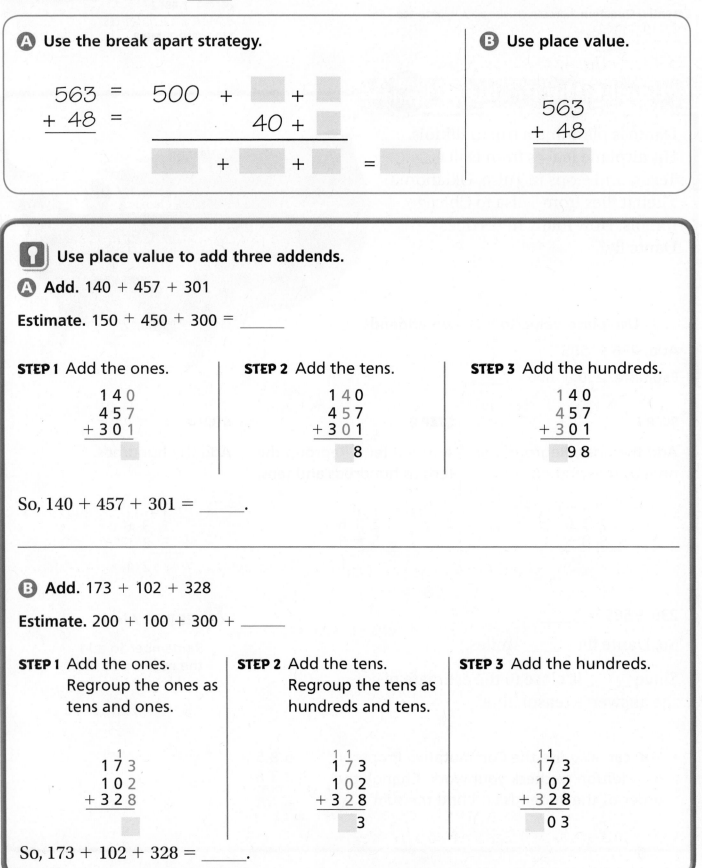

A Use the break apart strategy.

563 = 500 + ▢ + ▢
+ 48 =   40 + ▢
_____
      ▢ + ▢ + ▢ = ▢

B Use place value.

563
+ 48
▢

🔑 Use place value to add three addends.

A Add. 140 + 457 + 301

Estimate. 150 + 450 + 300 = _____

STEP 1 Add the ones.

1 4 0
4 5 7
+ 3 0 1
▢

STEP 2 Add the tens.

1 4 0
4 5 7
+ 3 0 1
▢ 8

STEP 3 Add the hundreds.

1 4 0
4 5 7
+ 3 0 1
▢ 9 8

So, 140 + 457 + 301 = _____.

B Add. 173 + 102 + 328

Estimate. 200 + 100 + 300 + _____

STEP 1 Add the ones.
Regroup the ones as tens and ones.

  1
1 7 3
1 0 2
+ 3 2 8
▢

STEP 2 Add the tens.
Regroup the tens as hundreds and tens.

1 1
1 7 3
1 0 2
+ 3 2 8
▢ 3

STEP 3 Add the hundreds.

1 1
1 7 3
1 0 2
+ 3 2 8
▢ 0 3

So, 173 + 102 + 328 = _____.

© Houghton Mifflin Harcourt Publishing Company

Share and Show 📝 MATH BOARD

1. **Circle the problem in which you need to regroup. Use the strategy that is easier to find the sum.**

   a. 496 + 284

   b. 482 + 506

Estimate. Then find the sum.

✓ 2. Estimate: _____

$$\begin{array}{r} 251 \\ +345 \\ \hline \end{array}$$

3. Estimate: _____

$$\begin{array}{r} 479 \\ +395 \\ \hline \end{array}$$

✓ 4. Estimate: _____

$$\begin{array}{r} 686 \\ +314 \\ \hline \end{array}$$

5. Estimate: _____

$$\begin{array}{r} 231 \\ 410 \\ +158 \\ \hline \end{array}$$

Math Talk **Mathematical Practices**

Explain how you can compute 403 + 201 mentally.

On Your Own

Practice: Copy and Solve **Estimate. Then solve.**

6. 253 + 376

7. 654 + 263

8. 321 + 439 + 112

9. 182 + 321

10. 701 + 108

11. 543 + 372 + 280

MATHEMATICAL PRACTICE ② **Use Reasoning** **Algebra** **Find the unknown digits.**

12.
$$\begin{array}{r} 1\ \square\ 4 \\ +\ \square\ 3\ \square \\ \hline 2\ 5\ 7 \end{array}$$

13.
$$\begin{array}{r} \square\ 7\ \square \\ +6\ \square\ 4 \\ \hline 9\ 8\ 6 \end{array}$$

14.
$$\begin{array}{r} 2\ \square\ \square \\ +\ \square\ 2\ 9 \\ \hline 6\ 8\ 2 \end{array}$$

15.
$$\begin{array}{r} 3\ \square\ \square \\ +\ \square\ 1\ 7 \\ \hline 9\ 0\ 3 \end{array}$$

16. **GO DEEPER** There are 431 crayons in a box and 204 crayons on the floor. About how many fewer than 1,000 crayons are there? Estimate. Then solve.

© Houghton Mifflin Harcourt Publishing Company

Unlock the Problem (Real World)

17. **THINK SMARTER** A plane flew 187 miles from New York City, New York, to Boston, Massachusetts. It then flew 273 miles from Boston to Philadelphia, Pennsylvania. The plane flew the same distance on the return trip. How many miles did the plane fly?

Boston
273 miles
187 miles
New York City
Philadelphia

Math on the Spot

a. What do you need to find?

_____

b. What is an estimate of the total distance?

_____

c. Show the steps you used to solve the problem.

d. How do you know your answer is reasonable?

_____

_____

e. The total distance is _____ miles round trip.

---

18. **THINK SMARTER** Help Max find the sum of the problem.

$$\begin{array}{r} 4\ 5\ 1 \\ 2\ 4\ 6 \\ +\ 2\ 2\ 2 \\ \hline \end{array}$$

For numbers 18a–18d, choose Yes or No to tell if Max should regroup.

18a. Regroup the ones.　　　　　○ Yes　　○ No

18b. Add the regrouped ten.　　　○ Yes　　○ No

18c. Regroup the tens.　　　　　○ Yes　　○ No

18d. Add the regrouped hundred.　○ Yes　　○ No

© Houghton Mifflin Harcourt Publishing Company

FOR MORE PRACTICE:
Standards Practice Book

Name _____

 **Mid-Chapter Checkpoint**

© Houghton Mifflin Harcourt Publishing Company

Vocabulary

Choose the best term from the box.

Vocabulary
Commutative Property of Addition
compatible numbers
Identity Property of Addition
pattern

1. A _____ is an ordered set of numbers or objects in which the order helps you predict what comes next. (p. 5)

2. The _____ states that when you add zero to any number, the sum is that number. (p. 5)

Concepts and Skills

Is the sum even or odd? Write *even* or *odd*. (3.OA.9)

3. $8 + 5$ _____

4. $9 + 7$ _____

5. $4 + 6$ _____

Use rounding or compatible numbers to estimate the sum. (3.NBT.1)

6.
```
  56
+ 32
```
+ _____

7.
```
  271
+ 425
```
+ _____

8.
```
  328
+ 127
```
+ _____

Use mental math to find the sum. (3.NBT.2)

9. $46 + 14 +$ _____

10. $39 + 243 +$ _____

11. $326 + 402 +$ _____

Estimate. Then find the sum. (3.NBT.2)

12. Estimate: _____
```
  356
+ 442
```

13. Estimate: _____
```
  164
+ 230
```

14. Estimate: _____
```
  545
+ 139
```

15. Estimate: _____
```
  437
+ 184
```

16. Nancy planted 77 daisies, 48 roses, and 39 tulips. About how many more roses and tulips did she plant than daisies? (3.NBT.1)

_____

17. Tomas collected 139 cans for recycling on Monday, and twice that number on Tuesday. How many cans did he collect on Tuesday? (3.NBT.2)

_____

18. There are 294 boys and 332 girls in the Hill School. How many students are in the school? (3.NBT.2)

_____

19. On Monday, 76 students played soccer. On Tuesday, 62 students played soccer. On Wednesday, 68 students played soccer. How many more students played soccer on Tuesday and Wednesday combined than on Monday? (3.NBT.2)

_____

© Houghton Mifflin Harcourt Publishing Company

Estimate Differences

Essential Question How can you use compatible numbers and rounding to estimate differences?

Number and Operations in Base Ten—3.NBT.1 *Also 3.NBT.2*
MATHEMATICAL PRACTICES
MP.5, MP.7, MP.8

Unlock the Problem Real World

The largest yellowfin tuna caught by fishers weighed 387 pounds. The largest grouper caught weighed 436 pounds. About how much more did the grouper weigh than the yellowfin tuna?

You can estimate to find *about* how much more.

- Does the question ask for an exact answer? How do you know?

  _____

  _____

- Circle the numbers you need to use.

One Way Use compatible numbers.

Think: Compatible numbers are numbers that are easy to compute mentally and are close to the real numbers.

$$\begin{array}{r} 436 \\ -387 \end{array} \rightarrow \begin{array}{r} 425 \\ -375 \\ \hline \end{array}$$

So, the grouper weighed about

_____ pounds more than the yellowfin tuna.

Yellowfin tuna

Grouper

- What other compatible numbers could you have used?

_____

Try This! Estimate. Use compatible numbers.

Ⓐ
$$\begin{array}{r} 73 \\ -22 \end{array} \rightarrow \begin{array}{r} 75 \\ - \\ \hline \end{array}$$

Ⓑ
$$\begin{array}{r} 376 \\ -148 \end{array} \rightarrow \begin{array}{r} \\ -150 \\ \hline \end{array}$$

© Houghton Mifflin Harcourt Publishing Company • Image Credits: (bcr) ©PhotoLink/Photodisc/Getty Images, (tcr) ©Jeff Rotman/ImageBank/Getty Images

🔑 Another Way Use place value to round.

436 − 387 = ▇

STEP 1 Round 436 to the nearest ten.

Think: Find the place to which you want to round. Look at the digit to the right.

- Look at the digit in the ones place.
- Since 6 > 5, the digit 3 increases by one.
- Write a zero for the ones place.

4 3 6   4 3 6 →
   ↑   − 3 8 7   −_____

STEP 2 Round 387 to the nearest ten.

- Look at the digit in the ones place.
- Since 7 > 5, the digit 8 increases by one.
- Write a zero for the ones place.

            4 3 6 →   4 4 0
3 8 7   − 3 8 7 →   −▇▇▇
      ↑

STEP 3 Find the difference of the rounded numbers.

4 3 6 →   4 4 0
− 3 8 7 →   − 3 9 0
            ▇▇▇

So, 436 − 387 is about _____.

Try This! Estimate. Use place value to round.

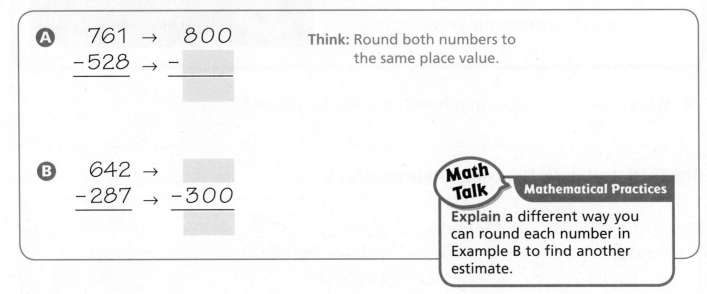

Ⓐ   761 →   800
   −528 → − ▇

Think: Round both numbers to the same place value.

Ⓑ   642 → ▇
   −287 → −300
           ▇

Math Talk **Mathematical Practices**

Explain a different way you can round each number in Example B to find another estimate.

© Houghton Mifflin Harcourt Publishing Company

Name _____

1. Use compatible numbers to complete the problem. Then estimate the difference.

546 → 550
−209 → − _____
_____

Use rounding or compatible numbers to estimate the difference.

Math Talk **Mathematical Practices**

Explain another way you can estimate 546 − 209.

2. 57
−21 − _____
_____

✓ 3. 642
−137 − _____
_____

✓ 4. 374
−252 − _____
_____

On Your Own

Use rounding or compatible numbers to estimate the difference.

5. 67
− 24 − _____
_____

6. 81
−39 − _____
_____

7. 936
−421 − _____
_____

8. 804
−259 − _____
_____

9. 584
−208 − _____
_____

10. 442
− 36 − _____
_____

11. 429 − 51

_____ − _____ = _____

12. 491 − 270

_____ − _____ = _____

13. **GO DEEPER** There are 262 students in the 2nd grade and 298 students in the 3rd grade. If 227 students take the bus to school, about how many students do not take the bus?

_____

© Houghton Mifflin Harcourt Publishing Company

Problem Solving • Applications Real World

Use the table for 14–16.

Largest Saltwater Fish Caught	
Type of Fish	**Weight in Pounds**
Pacific Halibut	459
Conger	133
Yellowfin Tuna	387

14. **MATHEMATICAL PRACTICE ③** **Use Counterexamples** Melissa said the estimated difference between the weight of the Pacific halibut and the yellowfin tuna is zero. Do you agree or disagree? Explain.

_____

_____

_____

WRITE ▸ *Math* • **Show Your Work**

15. **What's the Question?** The answer is about 500 pounds.

_____

_____

16. **THINK SMARTER** About how much more is the total weight of the Pacific halibut and conger than the weight of the yellowfin tuna? Explain.

_____

_____

_____

Personal Math Trainer

17. **THINK SMARTER +** A total of 907 people went to a fishing tournament. Of these people, 626 arrived before noon. Alina estimates that fewer than 300 people arrived in the afternoon. How did she estimate? Explain.

_____

_____

© Houghton Mifflin Harcourt Publishing Company

FOR MORE PRACTICE:
Standards Practice Book

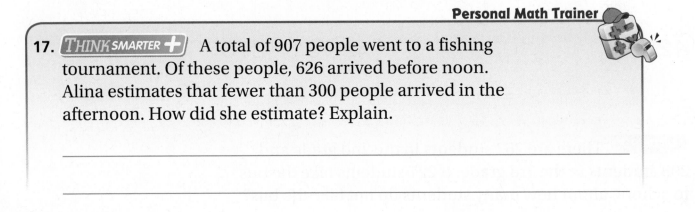

Mental Math Strategies for Subtraction

Essential Question What mental math strategies can you use to find differences?

Number and Operations in Base Ten—
3.NBT.2
MATHEMATICAL PRACTICES
MP.2, MP.7, MP.8

Unlock the Problem Real World

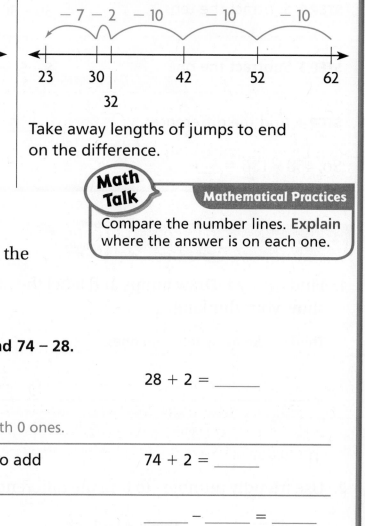

A sunflower can grow to be very tall. Dylan is 39 inches tall. She watered a sunflower that grew to be 62 inches tall. How many inches shorter was Dylan than the sunflower?

One Way Use a number line to find 62 − 39.

A Count up by tens and then ones.

Think: Start at 39. Count up to 62.

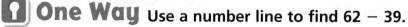

$+ 10 \qquad + 10 \qquad + 3$

39   49   59 62

Add the lengths of the jumps to find the difference.

$$10 + 10 + 3 = \underline{\hspace{1cm}}$$

$$62 - 39 = \underline{\hspace{1cm}}$$

So, Dylan was _____ inches shorter than the sunflower.

B Take away tens and ones.

Think: Start at 62. Count back 39.

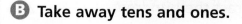

$-7 -2 \quad -10 \qquad -10 \qquad -10$

23   30 | 42   52   62
         32

Take away lengths of jumps to end on the difference.

Math Talk Mathematical Practices

Compare the number lines. **Explain** where the answer is on each one.

Other Ways

A Use friendly numbers and adjust to find 74 − 28.

STEP 1 Make the number you subtract a friendly number.

Think: Add to 28 to make a number with 0 ones.

$28 + 2 = \underline{\hspace{1cm}}$

STEP 2 Since you added 2 to 28, you have to add 2 to 74.

$74 + 2 = \underline{\hspace{1cm}}$

STEP 3 Find the difference.

$\underline{\hspace{1cm}} - \underline{\hspace{1cm}} = \underline{\hspace{1cm}}$

So, $74 - 28 = \underline{\hspace{1cm}}$.

© Houghton Mifflin Harcourt Publishing Company • Image Credits: ©Echo/Getty Images

Try This! **Use friendly numbers to subtract 9 and 99.**

- **Find 36 − 9.**

  Think: 9 is 1 less than 10.

  Subtract 10.   36 − 10 = _____

  Then add 1.   _____ + 1 = _____

  So, 36 − 9 = _____ .

- **Find 423 − 99.**

  Think: 99 is 1 less than 100.

  Subtract 100.   423 − 100 = _____

  Then add 1.   _____ + 1 = _____

  So, 423 − 99 = _____ .

B **Use the break apart strategy to find 458 − 136.**

STEP 1 Subtract the hundreds.   400 − 100 = _____

_____

STEP 2 Subtract the tens.   50 − 30 = _____

_____

STEP 3 Subtract the ones.   8 − 6 = _____

_____

STEP 4 Add the differences.   _____ + _____ + _____ = _____

So, 458 − 136 = _____ .

Share and Show

1. Find 61 − 24. Draw jumps and label the number line to show your thinking.

   Think: Take away tens and ones.

   <————————————————————————————|—►

   61

   61 − 24 = _____

2. Use friendly numbers to find the difference.

   86 − 42 = _____   **Think:** 42 − 2 = 40

   86 − 2 = 84

Math Talk

Mathematical Practices

Explain how you can use the break apart strategy to find 86 − 42.

© Houghton Mifflin Harcourt Publishing Company

Name _____

Use mental math to find the difference.
Draw or describe the strategy you use.

3. $56 - 38 =$ _____

4. $435 - 121 =$ _____

Problem Solving • Applications (Real World)

5. **MATHEMATICAL PRACTICE ③ Make Arguments** Erica used friendly numbers to find $43 - 19$. She added 1 to 19 and subtracted 1 from 43. What is Erica's error? Explain.

_____

_____

6. **THINK SMARTER** The farm shop had 68 small bags of bird treats and 39 large bags of bird treats on a shelf. If Jill buys 5 small bags and 1 large bag, how many more small bags than large bags of bird treats are left on the shelf?

_____

_____

_____

Math on the Spot

7. **THINK SMARTER** There were 87 sunflowers at the flower shop in the morning. There were 56 sunflowers left at the end of the day. How many sunflowers were sold? Explain a way to solve the problem.

_____

_____

© Houghton Mifflin Harcourt Publishing Company

Compare and Contrast

Emus and ostriches are the world's largest birds. They are alike in many ways and different in others.

When you compare things, you decide how they are alike. When you contrast things, you decide how they are different.

The table shows some facts about emus and ostriches. Use the information on this page to compare and contrast the birds.

Facts About Emus and Ostriches		
	Emus	**Ostriches**
Can they fly?	No	No
Where do they live?	Australia	Africa
How much do they weigh?	About 120 pounds	About 300 pounds
How tall are they?	About 72 inches	About 108 inches
How fast can they run?	About 40 miles per hour	About 40 miles per hour

Ostrich

Emu

8. How are emus and ostriches alike? How are they different?

    Alike: 1. _____

                2. _____

    Different: 1. _____

                2. _____

                3. _____

9. **GO DEEPER** What if two emus weigh 117 pounds and 123 pounds, and an ostrich weighs 338 pounds. How much more does the ostrich weigh than the two emus?

_____

© Houghton Mifflin Harcourt Publishing Company • Image Credits: (br) ©Picture Press/Alamy, (cr) ©Peter Arnold, Inc./Alamy

Name _____

Use Place Value to Subtract

Essential Question How can you use place value to subtract
3-digit numbers?

**Number and Operations in Base Ten—
3.NBT.2** *Also 3.NBT.1*
MATHEMATICAL PRACTICES
MP.2, MP.7, MP.8

 ## Unlock the Problem Real World

Ava sold 473 tickets for the school
play. Kim sold 294 tickets. How many
more tickets did Ava sell than Kim?

🔑 **Use place value to subtract.**

Subtract. 473 − 294

Estimate. 475 − 300 = _____

• Do you need to combine or compare
the number of tickets sold?

_____

• Circle the numbers you will need
to use.

STEP 1

Subtract the ones.
3 < 4, so regroup.

7 tens 3 ones =

6 tens _____ ones

$$\begin{array}{r} {}^{6\,13} \\ 4\cancel{7}\cancel{3} \\ -294 \\ \hline \end{array}$$

STEP 2

Subtract the tens.
6 < 9, so regroup.

4 hundreds 6 tens =

3 hundreds _____ tens

$$\begin{array}{r} {}^{16} \\ 3\,\cancel{6}\,13 \\ 4\cancel{7}\cancel{3} \\ -294 \\ \hline 9 \end{array}$$

STEP 3

Subtract the hundreds.
Add to check your answer.

$$\begin{array}{r} {}^{16} \\ 3\,\cancel{6}\,13 \\ 4\cancel{7}\cancel{3} \\ -294 \\ \hline 79 \end{array}$$ $$\begin{array}{r} {}^{1\ 1} \\ 179 \\ +294 \\ \hline 473 \end{array}$$

So, Ava sold _____ more tickets than Kim.

Since _____ is close to the estimate of _____, the
answer is reasonable.

> **Math Idea**
> Addition and subtraction
> undo each other. So you
> can use addition to check
> subtraction.

Try This! **Use place value to subtract.**
Use addition to check your work.

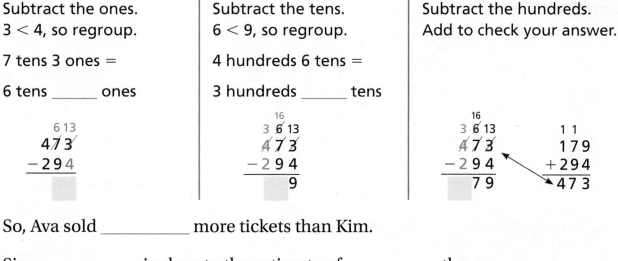

$$\begin{array}{r} 631 \\ -258 \\ \hline \end{array}$$ $$\begin{array}{r} \\ + \\ \hline \end{array}$$

© Houghton Mifflin Harcourt Publishing Company

Example Use place value to find 890 − 765.

Estimate. 900 − 750 = _____

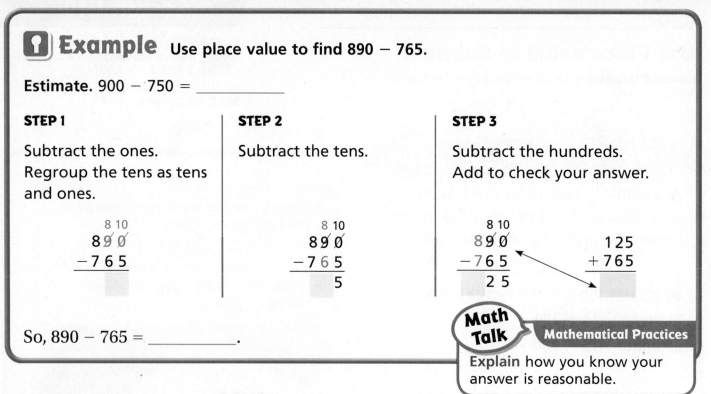

STEP 1

Subtract the ones. Regroup the tens as tens and ones.

```
   8 10
  8 9 0
 −7 6 5
```

STEP 2

Subtract the tens.

```
   8 10
  8 9 0
 −7 6 5
      5
```

STEP 3

Subtract the hundreds. Add to check your answer.

```
   8 10
  8 9 0      1 2 5
 −7 6 5     +7 6 5
    2 5
```

So, 890 − 765 = _____ .

Math Talk **Mathematical Practices**

Explain how you know your answer is reasonable.

Try This! Circle the problem in which you need to regroup. Find the difference.

A
```
  8 9 4
 −5 8 3
```

B
```
  5 2 1
 −3 0 1
```

C
```
  9 1 8
 −4 2 7
```

Share and Show MATH BOARD

1. Estimate. Then use place value to find 627 − 384. Add to check your answer.

Estimate. _____ − _____ = _____

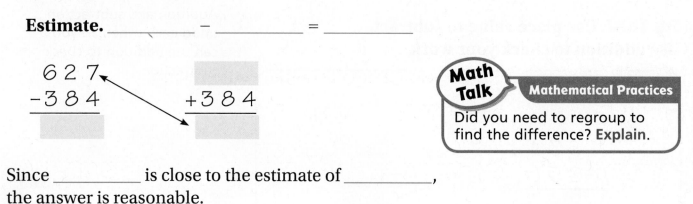

```
  6 2 7
 −3 8 4
```
```
 +3 8 4
```

Math Talk **Mathematical Practices**

Did you need to regroup to find the difference? **Explain.**

Since _____ is close to the estimate of _____, the answer is reasonable.

44

© Houghton Mifflin Harcourt Publishing Company

Name _____

Estimate. Then find the difference.

2. Estimate: _____
$$386$$
$$-123$$

3. Estimate: _____
$$519$$
$$-205$$

4. Estimate: _____
$$456$$
$$-217$$

☑5. Estimate: _____
$$642$$
$$-159$$

☑6. Estimate: _____
$$242$$
$$-220$$

7. Estimate: _____
$$870$$
$$-492$$

8. Estimate: _____
$$654$$
$$-263$$

9. Estimate: _____
$$937$$
$$-618$$

Math Talk **Mathematical Practices**

Which exercises can you compute mentally? **Explain** why.

On Your Own

Estimate. Then find the difference.

10. Estimate: _____
$$435$$
$$-312$$

11. Estimate: _____
$$617$$
$$-501$$

12. Estimate: _____
$$893$$
$$-268$$

13. Estimate: _____
$$750$$
$$-276$$

Practice: Copy and Solve **Estimate. Then solve.**

14. $568 - 276$ 15. $761 - 435$ 16. $829 - 765$ 17. $974 - 285$

MATHEMATICAL PRACTICE ② **Use Reasoning** **Algebra** **Find the unknown number.**

18.
$$86$$
$$-\ \boxed{}$$
$$62$$

19.
$$372$$
$$-\ \boxed{}$$
$$240$$

20.
$$537$$
$$-\ \boxed{}$$
$$172$$

21.
$$629$$
$$-\ \boxed{}$$
$$335$$

© Houghton Mifflin Harcourt Publishing Company

Problem Solving • Applications (Real World)

Use the table for 22–23.

22. **THINK SMARTER** Alicia sold 59 fewer tickets than Jenna and Matt sold together. How many tickets did Alicia sell? Explain.

_____

_____

_____

School Play Tickets Sold	
Student	**Number of Tickets**
Jenna	282
Matt	178
Sonja	331

23. **GO DEEPER** How many more tickets would each student need to sell so that each student sells 350 tickets?

_____

_____

24. Nina says to check subtraction, add the difference to the number you subtracted from. Does this statement make sense? Explain.

_____

_____

_____

25. **MATHEMATICAL PRACTICE ⑤ Communicate** Do you have to regroup to find 523 − 141? Explain. Then solve.

_____

_____

Personal Math Trainer

26. **THINK SMARTER +** Students want to sell 400 tickets to the school talent show. They have sold 214 tickets. How many more tickets do they need to sell to reach their goal? Show your work.

_____

© Houghton Mifflin Harcourt Publishing Company

FOR MORE PRACTICE:
Standards Practice Book

Name _____

Combine Place Values to Subtract

Essential Question How can you use the combine place values strategy to subtract 3-digit numbers?

Number and Operations in Base Ten—
3.NBT.2 *Also 3.NBT.1, 3.OA.8*
MATHEMATICAL PRACTICES
MP.2, MP.7, MP.8

Unlock the Problem (Real World)

Elena collected 431 bottles for recycling. Pete collected 227 fewer bottles than Elena. How many bottles did Pete collect?

- What do you need to find?
_____
- Circle the numbers you need to use.

Combine place values to find the difference.

A **Subtract.** 431 – 227

Estimate. 400 – 200 = _____

STEP 1 Look at the ones place. Since 7 > 1, combine place values. Combine the tens and ones places. There are 31 ones and 27 ones. Subtract the ones. Write 0 for the tens.

$$\begin{array}{r} 4\;\boxed{3\;1} \\ -\,2\;\boxed{2\;7} \end{array}$$ Think: 31 – 27

STEP 2 Subtract the hundreds.

So, Pete collected _____ bottles.

Since _____ is close to the estimate

of _____, the answer is reasonable.

$$\begin{array}{r} 4\,3\,1 \\ -\,2\,2\,7 \\ \hline 0\,4 \end{array}$$

Math Talk

Mathematical Practices

Explain why there is a zero in the tens place.

B **Subtract.** 513 – 482

Estimate. 510 – 480 = _____

STEP 1 Subtract the ones.

$$\begin{array}{r} 5\,1\,3 \\ -\,4\,8\,2 \end{array}$$

STEP 2 Look at the tens place. Since 8 > 1, combine place values. Combine the hundreds and tens places. There are 51 tens and 48 tens. Subtract the tens.

$$\begin{array}{r} \boxed{5\,1}\,3 \\ -\,\boxed{4\,8}\,2 \\ \hline 1 \end{array}$$ Think: 51 – 48

So, 513 – 482 = _____.

© Houghton Mifflin Harcourt Publishing Company

🔒 Example Combine place values to find 500 − 173.

Estimate. 500 − 175 = _____

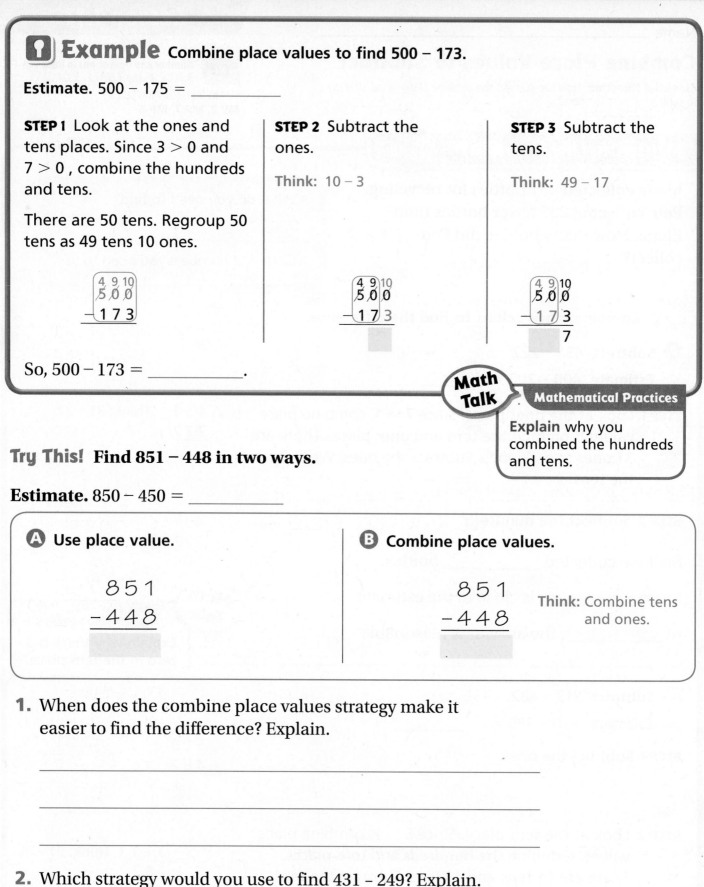

STEP 1 Look at the ones and tens places. Since 3 > 0 and 7 > 0 , combine the hundreds and tens.

There are 50 tens. Regroup 50 tens as 49 tens 10 ones.

STEP 2 Subtract the ones.

Think: 10 − 3

STEP 3 Subtract the tens.

Think: 49 − 17

So, 500 − 173 = _____.

Math Talk

Mathematical Practices

Explain why you combined the hundreds and tens.

Try This! Find 851 − 448 in two ways.

Estimate. 850 − 450 = _____

A Use place value.

$$851$$
$$-448$$

B Combine place values.

$$851$$
$$-448$$

Think: Combine tens and ones.

1. When does the combine place values strategy make it easier to find the difference? Explain.

_____

_____

_____

2. Which strategy would you use to find 431 − 249? Explain.

_____

_____

© Houghton Mifflin Harcourt Publishing Company

Name _____

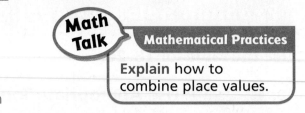

1. Combine place values to find 406 − 274.

$$\begin{array}{r} 406 \\ -274 \\ \hline \end{array}$$

Think: Subtract the ones. Then combine the hundreds and tens places.

Math Talk Mathematical Practices

Explain how to combine place values.

Estimate. Then find the difference.

2. Estimate: _____
$$\begin{array}{r} 595 \\ -286 \\ \hline \end{array}$$

3. Estimate: _____
$$\begin{array}{r} 728 \\ -515 \\ \hline \end{array}$$

4. Estimate: _____
$$\begin{array}{r} 543 \\ -307 \\ \hline \end{array}$$

5. Estimate: _____
$$\begin{array}{r} 600 \\ -453 \\ \hline \end{array}$$

On Your Own

Estimate. Then find the difference.

6. Estimate: _____
$$\begin{array}{r} 438 \\ -257 \\ \hline \end{array}$$

7. Estimate: _____
$$\begin{array}{r} 706 \\ -681 \\ \hline \end{array}$$

8. Estimate: _____
$$\begin{array}{r} 839 \\ -754 \\ \hline \end{array}$$

9. Estimate: _____
$$\begin{array}{r} 916 \\ -558 \\ \hline \end{array}$$

10. Estimate: _____
$$\begin{array}{r} 537 \\ -428 \\ \hline \end{array}$$

11. Estimate: _____
$$\begin{array}{r} 528 \\ -297 \\ \hline \end{array}$$

12. Estimate: _____
$$\begin{array}{r} 734 \\ -327 \\ \hline \end{array}$$

13. Estimate: _____
$$\begin{array}{r} 800 \\ -789 \\ \hline \end{array}$$

Practice: Copy and Solve **Estimate. Then solve.**

14. 457 − 364

15. 652 − 341

16. 700 − 648

17. 963 − 256

© Houghton Mifflin Harcourt Publishing Company

Problem Solving • Applications (Real World)

Use the table for 18–20.

Roller Coaster Heights		
Roller Coaster	**State**	**Height in Feet**
Titan	Texas	245
Kingda Ka	New Jersey	456
Intimidator 305	Virginia	305
Top Thrill Dragster	Ohio	420

18. **MATHEMATICAL PRACTICE 5** **Use Appropriate Tools** The table shows the heights of some roller coasters in the United States. How much taller is Kingda Ka than Titan?

_____

19. **GO DEEPER** Jason rode two roller coasters with a difference in height of 115 feet. Which roller coasters did Jason ride?

_____

WRITE ▸ Math • Show Your Work

20. **THINK SMARTER** What if another roller coaster was 500 feet tall? Which roller coaster would be 195 feet shorter?

_____

21. **THINK SMARTER** Owen solves this problem. He says the difference is 127. Explain the mistake Owen made. What is the correct difference?

$$\begin{array}{r} 335 \\ -218 \\ \hline \end{array}$$

_____

_____

_____

_____

© Houghton Mifflin Harcourt Publishing Company

Name _____

Problem Solving •
Model Addition and Subtraction

Essential Question How can you use the strategy *draw a diagram* to solve one- and two-step addition and subtraction problems?

Operations and Algebraic Thinking—
3.OA.8 *Also 3.NBT.2*
MATHEMATICAL PRACTICES
MP.1, MP.4, MP.5

Unlock the Problem · Real World

Sami scored 84 points in the first round of a new computer game. He scored 21 more points in the second round than in the first round. What was Sami's total score?

You can use a bar model to solve the problem.

Read the Problem

What do I need to find?	**What information do I need to use?**	**How will I use the information?**
I need to find _____.	Sami scored _____ points in the first round. He scored _____ more points than that in the second round.	I will draw a bar model to show the number of points Sami scored in each round. Then I will use the bar model to decide which operation to use.

Solve the Problem

• Complete the bar model to show the number of points Sami scored in the second round.

_____ points	_____ points

■ points

_____ + _____ = ■

_____ = ■

• Complete another bar model to show Sami's total score.

_____ points	_____ points

▲ points

_____ + _____ = ▲

_____ = ▲

1. How many points did Sami score in the second round? _____

2. What was Sami's total score? _____

© Houghton Mifflin Harcourt Publishing Company • Image Credits: ©Jose Luis Pelaez Inc/Blend Images/Getty Images

🔓 Try Another Problem

Anna scored 265 points in a computer game. Greg scored 142 points. How many more points did Anna score than Greg?

You can use a bar model to solve the problem.

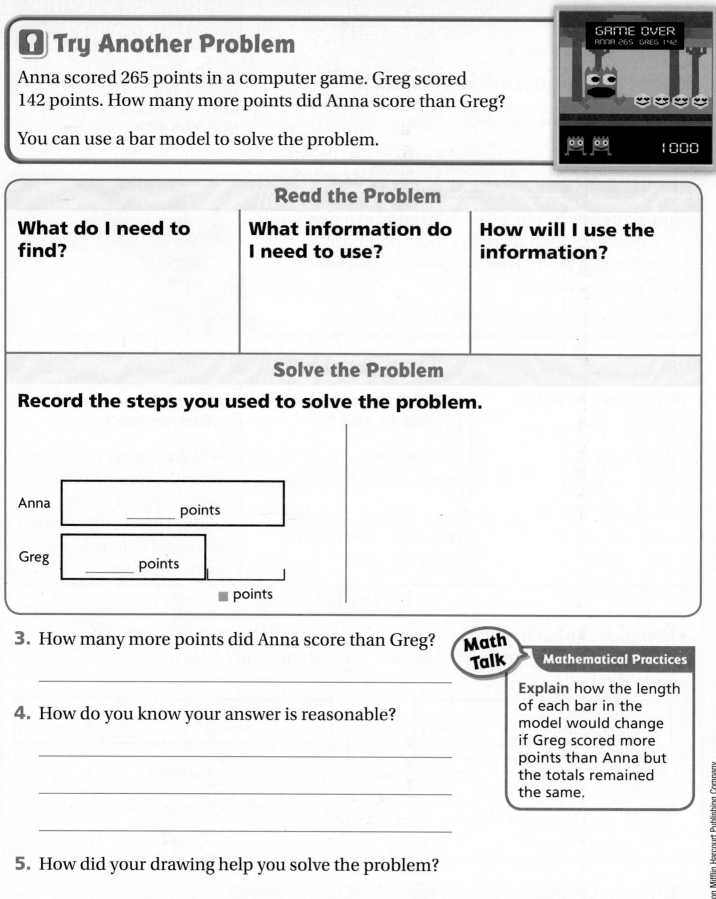

Read the Problem

What do I need to find?	What information do I need to use?	How will I use the information?

Solve the Problem

Record the steps you used to solve the problem.

Anna
_____ points

Greg
_____ points

■ points

3. How many more points did Anna score than Greg?

_____

4. How do you know your answer is reasonable?

_____

_____

_____

5. How did your drawing help you solve the problem?

_____

_____

Math Talk

Mathematical Practices

Explain how the length of each bar in the model would change if Greg scored more points than Anna but the totals remained the same.

© Houghton Mifflin Harcourt Publishing Company

Name _____

Share and Show

1. Sara received 73 votes in the school election. Ben received 25 fewer votes than Sara. How many students voted?

First, find how many students voted for Ben.

Think: $73 - 25 = \blacksquare$

Write the numbers in the bar model.

So, Ben received _____ votes.

Next, find the total number of votes.

Think: $73 + 48 = \blacktriangle$

Write the numbers in the bar model.

So, _____ students voted.

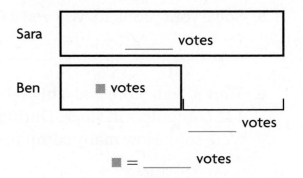

Sara _____ votes

Ben ▨ votes _____ votes

$\blacksquare =$ _____ votes

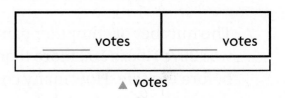

_____ votes _____ votes

▲ votes

$\blacktriangle =$ _____ votes

2. If Ben received 73 votes and Sara received 25 fewer votes than Ben, how would your bar models change? Would the total votes be the same? Explain.

_____

_____

_____

On Your Own

3. THINK SMARTER What if there were 3 students in another election and the total number of votes was the same? What would the bar model for the total number of votes look like? How many votes might each student get?

Math on the Spot

_____

_____

© Houghton Mifflin Harcourt Publishing Company

4. **Pose a Problem** Use the bar model at the right. Write a problem to match it.

89	▪

157

_____

_____

5. Solve your problem. Will you add or subtract?

_____

6. Tony's Tech Store had a big sale. The store had 142 computers in stock. During the sale, 91 computers were sold. How many computers were not sold?

_____

7. The number of computer games sold during the sale was 257. This is 162 more than the number sold the week before the sale. How many computer games were sold the week before the sale?

_____

8. **Go DEEPER** In one week, 128 cell phones were sold. The following week, 37 more cell phones were sold than the week before. How many cell phones were sold in those two weeks?

_____

9. **MATHEMATICAL PRACTICE 6** On Monday, the number of customers in the store, rounded to the nearest hundred, was 400. What is the greatest number of customers that could have been in the store? **Explain.**

_____

_____

10. **THINK SMARTER** There are 306 people at the fair on Saturday. There are 124 fewer people on Sunday. How many people are at the fair on the two days?

_____

© Houghton Mifflin Harcourt Publishing Company

FOR MORE PRACTICE:
Standards Practice Book

✓ Chapter 1 Review/Test

1. For numbers 1a–1d, choose Yes or No to tell whether the sum is even.

   1a. $5 + 8$ ○ Yes   ● No

   1b. $9 + 3$ ● Yes   ○ No

   1c. $6 + 7$ ○ Yes   ● No

   1d. $9 + 5$ ● Yes   ○ No

2. Select the number sentences that show the Commutative Property of Addition. Mark all that apply.

   Ⓐ $14 + 8 = 22$

   Ⓑ $8 + 14 = 14 + 8$

   Ⓒ $8 + (13 + 1) = (8 + 13) + 1$

   Ⓓ $(5 + 9) + 8 = (9 + 5) + 8$

3. Select the numbers that round to 300 when rounded to the nearest hundred. Mark all that apply.

   Ⓐ 238

   Ⓑ 250

   Ⓒ 283

   Ⓓ 342

   Ⓔ 359

4. There are 486 books in the classroom library. Complete the chart to show 486 rounded to the nearest 10.

Hundreds	Tens	Ones
4	9	0

© Houghton Mifflin Harcourt Publishing Company

GO DIGITAL Assessment Options
Chapter Test

5. Write each number sentence in the box below the better estimate of the sum.

$$393 + 225 = \blacksquare \qquad 481 + 215 = \blacksquare$$

$$352 + 328 = \blacksquare \qquad 309 + 335 = \blacksquare$$

600	700
309 + 335	

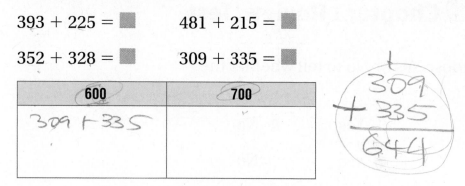

309
+ 335
644

6. Diana sold 336 muffins at the bake sale. Bob sold 287 muffins. Bob estimates that he sold 50 fewer muffins than Diana. How did he estimate? Explain.

7. The table shows how many books each class read.

Reading Contest	
Class	**Number of Books**
Mr. Lopez	273
Ms. Martin	402
Mrs. Wang	247

273
402
247
922

For numbers 7a–7d, select True or False for each statement.

7a. Ms. Martin's class read about 100 more books than Mr. Lopez's class. ● True ○ False

7b. The 3 classes read over 900 books altogether. ○ True ○ False

7c. Mrs. Wang's class read about 50 fewer books than Mr. Lopez's class. ○ True ○ False

273
− 247
26

7d. Ms. Martin's and Mrs. Wang's class read about 700 books. ○ True ● False

402
+ 247
649

© Houghton Mifflin Harcourt Publishing Company

Name _____

8. Janna buys 2 bags of dog food for her dogs. One bag weighs 37 pounds. The other bag weighs 15 pounds. How many pounds do both bags weigh? Explain how you solved the problem.

$$\begin{array}{r} 37 \\ +15 \\ \hline 52 \end{array}$$

9. Choose the property that makes the statement true.

| Identity |
| Commutative |
| Associative |

The Commutative Property of addition states that you can group addends in different ways and get the same sum.

Use the table for 10–12.

Susie's Sweater Shop	
Month	**Number of Sweaters Sold**
January	402
February	298
March	171

10. The table shows the number of sweaters sold online in three months. How many sweaters were sold in January and February?

_____700_____ sweaters

11. How many more sweaters were sold in January than March?

_____231_____ sweaters

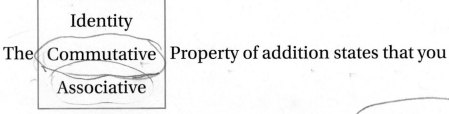

$$\begin{array}{r} 3 \\ \cancel{4}02 \\ -171 \\ \hline 231 \end{array}$$

12. How many more sweaters were sold in February and March than in January?

_____469_____ sweaters

Step 1. Add
$$\begin{array}{r} +298 \\ +171 \\ \hline 469 \end{array}$$

$$\begin{array}{r} 469 \\ -402 \\ \hline 67 \end{array}$$

67

© Houghton Mifflin Harcourt Publishing Company

13. Help Dana find the sum.

$$346$$
$$421$$
$$+\ 152$$

For numbers 13a–13d, select Yes or No to tell Dana when to regroup.

13a. Regroup the ones.   ○ Yes   ○ No

13b. Add the regrouped
      ten.   ○ Yes   ○ No

13c. Regroup the tens.   ○ Yes   ○ No

13d. Add the regrouped
      hundred.   ○ Yes   ○ No

14. Alexandra has 78 emails in her inbox. She deletes 47 emails. How many emails are left in her inbox? Draw jumps and label the number line to show your thinking.

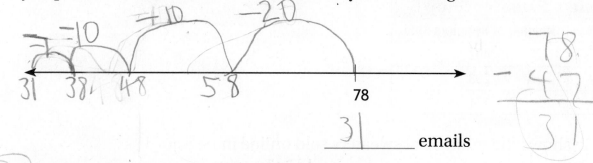

_____31_____ emails

15. Daniel has 402 pieces in a building set. He uses 186 pieces to build a house. How many pieces does he have left? Show your work.

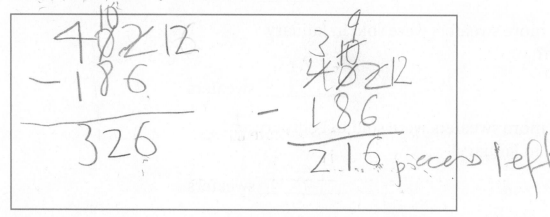

© Houghton Mifflin Harcourt Publishing Company

16. Luke solves this problem. He says the difference is 214. Explain the mistake Luke made. What is the correct difference?

2 3̶5̶2 12
− 148
2̶4̶

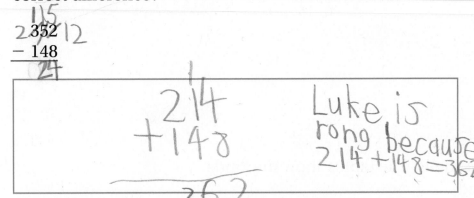

214
+148
362

Luke is rong because 214+148=362

4
3̶5̶212
− 148
2 0 4

4   12
3̶5̶2̶
− 1 4 8
2 1 4

9
3̶6̶2

17. Sunnyday Elementary School is having its annual Read-a-thon. The third graders have read 573 books so far. Their goal is to read more than 900 books. What is the least number of books they need to read to reach their goal? Explain.

18. There are 318 fiction books in the class library. The number of nonfiction books is 47 less than the number of fiction books.

Part A

About how many nonfiction books are there in the class library? Explain.

Part B

How many fiction and nonfiction books are there in the class library altogether? Show your work.

© Houghton Mifflin Harcourt Publishing Company

19. Alia used $67 + 38 = 105$ to check her subtraction.
Which math problem could she be checking?
Mark all that apply.

Ⓐ $67 - 38 = \blacksquare$

Ⓑ $105 - 67 = \blacksquare$

Ⓒ $105 + 38 = \blacksquare$

Ⓓ $105 - 38 = \blacksquare$

20. Alex and Erika collect shells. The tables show the kinds of shells they collected.

Alex's Shells	
Shell	Number of Shells
Scallop	36
Jingle	95
Clam	115

Erika's Shells	
Shell	Number of Shells
Scallop	82
Clam	108
Whelk	28

Part A

Who collected more shells? How many did she collect?
About how many more is that? Explain how you solved the problem.

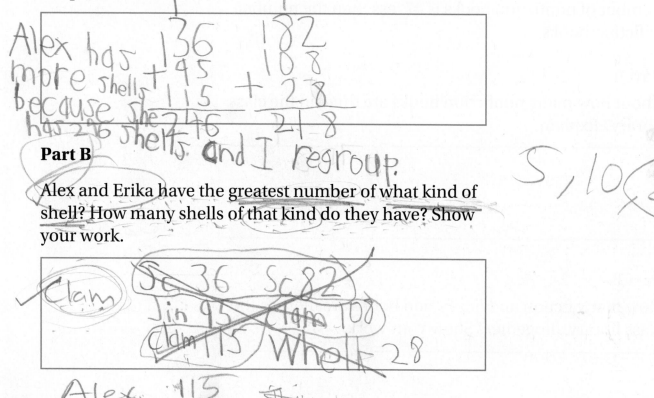

Alex has more shells because she has 246 shells and I regroup.

$\begin{array}{r} 36 \\ + 95 \\ \underline{115} \\ 246 \end{array}$ $\begin{array}{r} 82 \\ 108 \\ + 28 \\ \underline{218} \end{array}$

Part B

Alex and Erika have the greatest number of what kind of shell? How many shells of that kind do they have? Show your work.

Clam

Sc 36   Sc 82
Jin 95   Clam 108
Clam 115   Whelk 28

$\begin{array}{r} \text{Alex} \quad 115 \\ \text{Erika} + 108 \\ \hline 223 \end{array}$ Clam shells

60

© Houghton Mifflin Harcourt Publishing Company

Show What You Know

Check your understanding of important skills.

Name _____

▶ **Numbers to 20** Circle the number word. Write the number.

1. [ten frames showing 14 dots] _____

fourteen

fifteen

2. [ten frames showing 17 dots] _____

seventeen

eighteen

▶ **Skip Count** Skip count to find the missing numbers.

3. Count by twos. 2, 4, _____, _____, 10, _____, _____, 16

4. Count by fives. 5, 10, _____, _____, _____, 30, _____

▶ **Addition and Subtraction Facts** Find the sum or difference.

5. $12 - 4 =$ _____

6. $9 + 8 =$ _____

7. $11 - 7 =$ _____

Paige helps to sell supplies in the school store. Each month she totals all the sales and makes a bar graph. The graph shows sales through December. Be a Math Detective to find the month during which the hundredth sale was made.

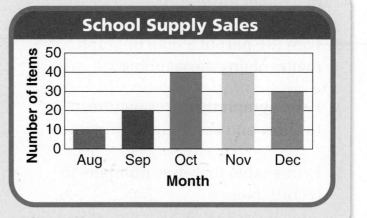

© Houghton Mifflin Harcourt Publishing Company

Personal Math Trainer

Online Assessment and Intervention

Vocabulary Builder

▶ **Visualize It** •

Complete the bubble map by using the words with a ✓.

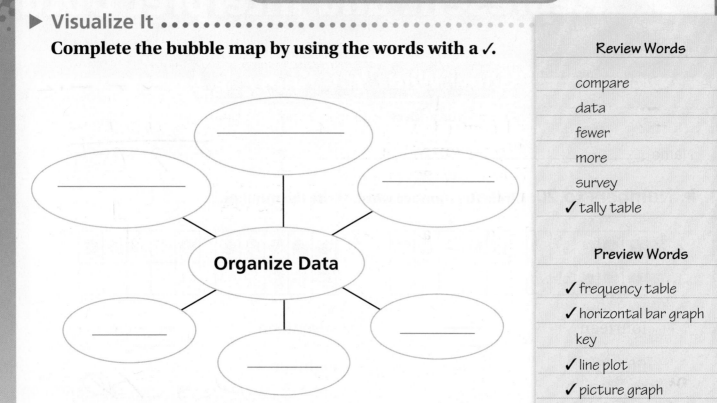

Organize Data

Review Words

compare

data

fewer

more

survey

✓ tally table

Preview Words

✓ frequency table

✓ horizontal bar graph

key

✓ line plot

✓ picture graph

scale

✓ vertical bar graph

▶ **Understand Vocabulary** • • • • • • • • • • • • • •

Write the review word or preview word that answers the riddle.

1. I am a graph that records each piece of data above a number line. _____

2. I am the numbers that are placed at fixed distances on a graph to help label the graph. _____

3. I am the part of a map or graph that explains the symbols. _____

4. I am a graph that uses pictures to show and compare information. _____

5. I am a table that uses numbers to record data. _____

© Houghton Mifflin Harcourt Publishing Company

 GO DIGITAL • Interactive Student Edition
• Multimedia eGlossary

Name _____

Problem Solving • Organize Data

Essential Question How can you use the strategy *make a table* to organize data and solve problems?

Measurement and Data—3.MD.3
Also 3.NBT.2

MATHEMATICAL PRACTICES
MP.1, MP.5, MP.6

Unlock the Problem (Real World)

The students in Alicia's class voted for their favorite yogurt flavor. They organized the data in this tally table. How many more students chose chocolate than strawberry?

Another way to show the data is in a frequency table. A **frequency table** uses numbers to record data.

Favorite Yogurt Flavor	
Flavor	**Tally**
Vanilla	卌 ‖
Chocolate	卌 ‖‖
Strawberry	‖‖‖

Read the Problem

What do I need to find?

How many more students chose

_____ than _____ yogurt
as their favorite?

What information do I need to use?

the data about favorite _____
in the tally table

How will I use the information?

I will count the _____. Then I will put the numbers in a frequency table and compare the number of students

who chose _____ to the number of

students who chose _____.

Solve the Problem

Favorite Yogurt Flavor	
Flavor	**Number**
Vanilla	

Count the tally marks. Record _____ for vanilla. Write the other flavors and record the number of tally marks.

To compare the number of students who chose strawberry and the number of students who chose chocolate, subtract.

_____ − _____ = _____

So, _____ more students chose chocolate as their favorite flavor.

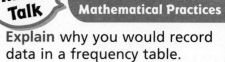

Math Talk **Mathematical Practices**

Explain why you would record data in a frequency table.

© Houghton Mifflin Harcourt Publishing Company

Chapter 2 63

🔓 Try Another Problem

Two classes in Carter's school grew bean plants for a science project. The heights of the plants after six weeks are shown in the tally table. The plants were measured to the nearest inch. How many fewer bean plants were 9 inches tall than 7 inches and 8 inches combined?

Bean Plant Heights

Height in Inches	Tally
7	卌 IIII
8	卌 III
9	卌 卌 II
10	卌 IIII

Read the Problem

What do I need to find?

What information do I need to use?

How will I use the information?

Solve the Problem

Record the steps you used to solve the problem.

• Suppose the number of 3-inch plants was half the number of 8-inch plants. How many 3-inch bean plants were there?

_____

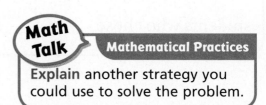

Math Talk — Mathematical Practices

Explain another strategy you could use to solve the problem.

© Houghton Mifflin Harcourt Publishing Company

Name _____

© Houghton Mifflin Harcourt Publishing Company

Share and Show

 MATH BOARD

Use the Shoe Lengths table for 1–3.

1. The students in three third-grade classes recorded the lengths of their shoes to the nearest centimeter. The data are in the tally table. How many more shoes were 18 or 22 centimeters long combined than 20 centimeters long?

First, count the tally marks and record the data in a frequency table.

To find the number of shoes that were 18 or 22 centimeters long, add

6 + _____ + _____ + _____ = _____.

To find the number of shoes that were

20 centimeters long, add _____ + _____ = _____.

To find the difference between the shoes that were 18 or 22 centimeters long and the shoes that were 20 centimeters long, subtract the sums.

_____ – _____ = _____

So, _____ more shoes were 18 or 22 centimeters long than 20 centimeters long.

Shoe Lengths		
Length in Centimeters	Tally	
	Boys	Girls
18	卌 l	llll
19	卌	llll
20	卌 lll	卌 llll
21	卌 ll	卌
22	卌 llll	卌 ll

Shoe Lengths		
Length in Centimeters	Number	
	Boys	Girls
18		
19		
20		
21		
22		

2. How many fewer girls' shoes than boys' shoes

were measured? _____

On Your Own

3. **THINK SMARTER** What if the length of 5 more boys' shoes measured 21 centimeters? Explain how the table would change.

Math on the Spot

_____

_____

4. **MATHEMATICAL PRACTICE ② Use Reasoning** Isabel is thinking of an even number between 234 and 250. The sum of the digits is double the digit in the ones place. What is Isabel's number?

_____

5. **GO DEEPER** Heather has 6 dimes and 10 pennies. Jason has 3 quarters. Who has more money? Explain your answer.

_____

6. **THINK SMARTER** Andrew has 10 more goldfish than Todd. Together, they have 50 goldfish. How many goldfish does each boy have?

_____

7. **THINK SMARTER** Jade made this tally table to record how many students have different types of pets.

Students' Pets	
Type of Pet	**Tally**
Dog	卌 卌 IIII
Rabbit	III
Hamster	卌
Cat	卌 II

For numbers 7a–7d, select True or False for each statement.

7a. Nine fewer students have hamsters than have dogs. ○ True ○ False

7b. Seven students have cats. ○ True ○ False

7c. Fewer students have cats than hamsters. ○ True ○ False

7d. More students have dogs than other animals combined. ○ True ○ False

© Houghton Mifflin Harcourt Publishing Company

FOR MORE PRACTICE:
Standards Practice Book

Name _____

Use Picture Graphs

Essential Question How can you read and interpret data in a picture graph?

Measurement and Data—3.MD.3
Also 3.NBT.2
MATHEMATICAL PRACTICES
MP.1, MP.2, MP.4, MP.8

Unlock the Problem Real World

A **picture graph** uses small pictures or symbols to show and compare information.

Nick has a picture graph that shows how some students get to school. How many students ride the bus?

- Underline the words that tell you where to find the information to answer the question.

- How many ☺ are shown for Bus?

_____

Each row has a label that names one way students get to school.

How We Get to School	
Walk	☺ ☺ ☺
Bike	☺ ☺ ☺ ☺
Bus	☺ ☺ ☺ ☺ ☺ ☺ ☺ ☺
Car	☺ ☺ ☺ ☺ ☺ ☺

Key: Each ☺ = 10 students.

The title says that the picture graph is about how some students get to school.

The **key** tells that each picture or symbol stands for the way 10 students get to school.

To find the number of students who ride the bus, count each ☺ as 10 students.

10, 20, _____, _____, _____, _____, _____, _____

So, _____ students ride the bus to school.

1. How many fewer students walk than ride the bus? _____

2. How many students were surveyed? _____

3. What if the symbol stands for 5 students? How many symbols will you need to show the number of students who walk to school? _____

© Houghton Mifflin Harcourt Publishing Company

Use a Half Symbol

How many students chose an orange as their favorite fruit?

Math Idea

Half of the picture stands for half the value of the whole picture.

☺ = 2 students

◖ = 1 student

Our Favorite Fruit	
Banana	☺ ☺ ☺ ☺ ☺
Apple	☺ ☺ ☺
Pear	☺ ☺
Orange	☺ ☺ ☺ ☺ ◖

Key: Each ☺ = 2 students.

Count the ☺ in the orange row by twos. Then add 1 for the half symbol.

2, 4, _____, _____   _____ + _____ = _____

So, _____ students chose an orange as their favorite fruit.

Share and Show

Use the Number of Books Students Read picture graph for 1–3.

1. What does 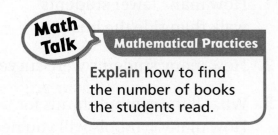 stand for?

   Think: Half of 2 is 1.

   _____

2. How many books did the students read in September?

   _____

3. How many more books did the students read in October than in November?

   _____

Number of Books Students Read	
September	📖 📖 📖 📖
October	📖 📖 📖 📖 📖 📖
November	📖 📖 📖 📖

Key: Each 📖 = 2 books.

Math Talk

Mathematical Practices

Explain how to find the number of books the students read.

© Houghton Mifflin Harcourt Publishing Company

Name _____

Use the Favorite Game picture graph for 4–10.

4. How many students chose puzzles?

_____

Favorite Game	
Puzzles	🂠 🂠 🂠 🂠 🂠
Card Games	🂠 🂠 🂠 🂠
Board Games	🂠 🂠 🂠 🂠 🂠 🂠

Key: Each 🂠 = 4 students.

5. How many fewer students chose card games than board games?

_____

6. **MATHEMATICAL PRACTICE ❽ Draw Conclusions** Which two types of games did a total of 34 students choose?

_____

7. **Go DEEPER** How many students were surveyed?

_____

8. How many students did not choose card games?

_____

9. **WRITE ▸ Math What's the Error?** Jacob said one more student chose board games than puzzles. Explain his error.

_____

_____

_____

10. **Go DEEPER** What if computer games were added as a choice and more students chose it than puzzles, but fewer students chose it than board games? How many students would choose computer games?

_____

© Houghton Mifflin Harcourt Publishing Company

🔑 Unlock the Problem (Real World)

Use the picture graph for 11–12.

11. *THINK SMARTER* The students who went to summer camp voted for their favorite activity. Which two activities received a total of 39 votes?

Favorite Camp Activity	
Biking	☀️ ☀️ ☀️ ☄️
Hiking	☀️ ☀️ ☀️ ☀️
Boating	☀️ ☀️ ☀️
Fishing	☀️ ☄️

Key: Each ☀️ = 6 students.

Math on the Spot

a. What do you need to find?

_____

b. What steps will you use to solve the problem?

_____

c. Show the steps you used to solve the problem.

d. Complete the sentences.

Each ☀️ = _____ students.

Each ☄️ = _____ students.

votes for biking + hiking = _____

votes for hiking + boating = _____

votes for biking + boating = _____

votes for fishing + hiking = _____

So, _____ received a total of 39 votes.

Personal Math Trainer

12. *THINK SMARTER +* Choose the word from each box that makes the sentence true.

Fifteen fewer students voted for

| hiking |
| boating |
| fishing |

than for

| hiking |
| boating |
| fishing |

.

FOR MORE PRACTICE:
Standards Practice Book

© Houghton Mifflin Harcourt Publishing Company

Name _____

Make Picture Graphs

Essential Question How can you draw a picture graph to show data in a table?

Measurement and Data—3.MD.3
Also 3.NBT.2
MATHEMATICAL PRACTICES
MP.2, MP.4, MP.6

Unlock the Problem

Delia made the table at the right. She used it to record the places the third grade classes would like to go during a field trip. How can you show the data in a picture graph?

 Make a picture graph.

Field Trip Choices	
Place	**Number**
Museum	6
Science Center	15
Aquarium	12
Zoo	9

STEP 1

Write the title at the top of the picture graph. Write the name of a place in each row.

STEP 2

Look at the numbers in the table. Choose a picture for the key, and tell how many students each picture represents. Write the key at the bottom of the graph.

STEP 3

Draw the correct number of pictures for each field trip choice.

Museum	

Key: Each ____ = ____ students.

- How did you decide how many pictures to draw for the Science Center?

_____

_____

© Houghton Mifflin Harcourt Publishing Company

Try This! Make a picture graph from data you collect. Take a survey or observe a subject that interests you. Collect and record the data in a frequency table. Then make a picture graph. Decide on a symbol and a key. Include a title and labels.

Key:	

Jeremy pulled marbles from a bag one at a time, recorded their color, and then put them back. Make a picture graph of the data. Use this key:

Each = 2 marbles.

Jeremy's Marble Experiment

Color	Number
Blue	4
Green	11
Red	8

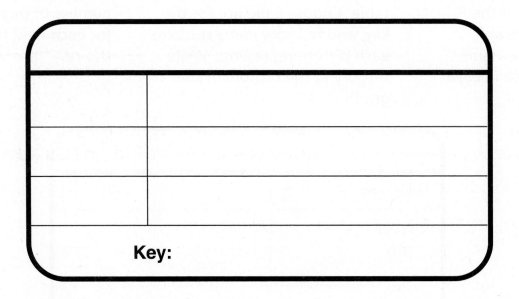

Key:	

Use your picture graph above for 1–2.

✓ 1. How many more times did Jeremy pull out a red marble than a blue marble?

_____

✓ 2. How many fewer times did Jeremy pull out green marbles than blue and red marbles combined?

_____

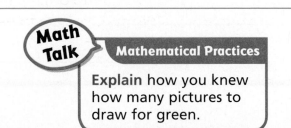

Math Talk **Mathematical Practices**

Explain how you knew how many pictures to draw for green.

© Houghton Mifflin Harcourt Publishing Company

On Your Own

Favorite Exhibit

Exhibit	Tally
Nature	卌 I
Solar System	卌 III
Light and Sound	卌 卌 IIII
Human Body	卌 III

3. Two classes from Delia's school visited the Science Center. They recorded their favorite exhibit in the tally table. Use the data in the table to make a picture graph. Use this key:

Each ☼ = 4 votes.

Key:

Use your picture graph above for 4–6.

4. Which exhibits received the same number of votes?

_____

5. MATHEMATICAL PRACTICE ④ **Model Mathematics** What if a weather exhibit received 22 votes? Explain how many pictures you would draw.

_____

6. THINK SMARTER What if the Solar System exhibit received 15 votes? Would it make sense to use the key Each ☼ = 4 votes to represent 15 votes? Explain.

_____

© Houghton Mifflin Harcourt Publishing Company

Problem Solving • Applications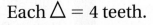

Teeth in Mammals	
Animal	Number
Hamster	16
Cat	30
Dog	42
Cow	32

7. While at the Science Center, Delia's classmates learned how many teeth some mammals have. Use the data in the table to make a picture graph. Use this key:

   Each $\triangle$ = 4 teeth.

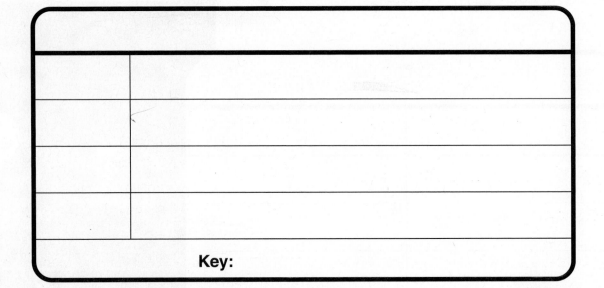

Key:

Use your picture graph above for 8–10.

8. *THINK SMARTER* **Pose a Problem** Write a problem that can be solved by using the data in your picture graph. Then solve the problem.

_____

9. *GO DEEPER* How many fewer teeth do cats and hamsters have combined than dogs and cows combined?

_____

10. *THINK SMARTER* How many pictures would you draw for Cat if each $\triangle$ = 5 teeth? Explain your reasoning.

   _____

   _____

FOR MORE PRACTICE:
Standards Practice Book

© Houghton Mifflin Harcourt Publishing Company

 **Mid-Chapter Checkpoint**

Vocabulary

Choose the best term from the box.

Vocabulary
frequency table
key
picture graph

1. A _____ uses numbers to record data. (p. 63)

2. A _____ uses small pictures or symbols to show and compare information. (p. 67)

Concepts and Skills

Use the Favorite Season table for 3–6. (3.MD.3)

Favorite Season	
Season	**Number**
Spring	19
Summer	28
Fall	14
Winter	22

3. Which season got the most votes?

_____

4. Which season got 3 fewer votes than winter?

_____

5. How many more students chose summer than fall?

14 students

6. How many students chose a favorite season?

_____

Use the Our Pets picture graph for 7–9. (3.MD.3)

Our Pets	
Bird	🐾🐾🐾🐾
Cat	🐾🐾🐾🐾🐾
Dog	🐾🐾🐾🐾🐾🐾
Fish	🐾🐾🐾

Key: Each 🐾 = 2 students.

7. How many students have cats as pets?

_____

8. Five more students have dogs than which other pet? Bird

9. How many pets in all do students have?

_____

© Houghton Mifflin Harcourt Publishing Company

Use the Favorite Summer Activity picture graph for 10–14.

Favorite Summer Activity	
Camping	☺☺☺☺☺
Biking	☺☺☺☺
Swimming	☺☺☺☺☺☺
Canoeing	☺☺☺

Key: Each ☺ = 10 students.

10. Some students in Brooke's school chose their favorite summer activity. The results are in the picture graph at the right. How many students chose camping? (3.MD.3)

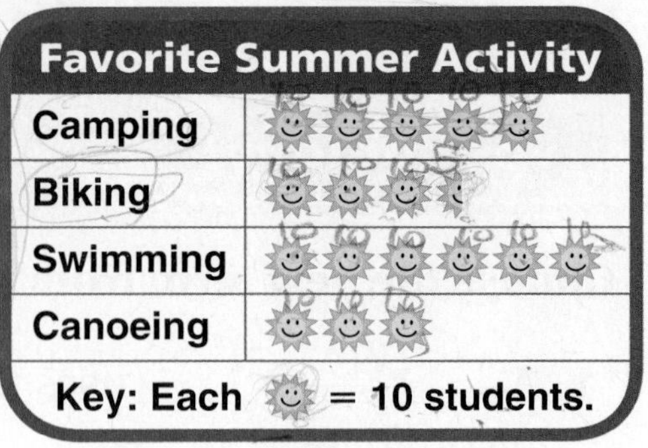

50 st

11. How many more students chose swimming than canoeing? (3.MD.3)

30 st

12. Which activity did 15 fewer students choose than camping? (3.MD.3)

4̶5̶ 10
− 15
35

Biking

35

13. How many pictures would you draw for biking if each ☺ = 5 students? (3.MD.3)

0 0 0 0 0 0 0

7 pictures

14. How many more students chose biking and canoeing combined than swimming? (3.MD.3)

35
+ 30
65

65
− 60
5

5 students

© Houghton Mifflin Harcourt Publishing Company

Use Bar Graphs

Essential Question How can you read and interpret data in a bar graph?

 Measurement and Data—3.MD.3
Also 3.NBT.2
MATHEMATICAL PRACTICES
MP.1, MP.6, MP.7

🔑 Unlock the Problem Real World

A **bar graph** uses bars to show data. A **scale** of equally spaced numbers helps you read the number each bar shows.

The students in the reading group made a bar graph to record the number of books they read in October. How many books did Seth read?

• Underline the words that tell you where to find the information to answer the question.

The title tells what the bar graph is about.

The length of a bar tells how many books each student read.

Each bar is labeled with a student's name.

The scale is 0–16 by twos.

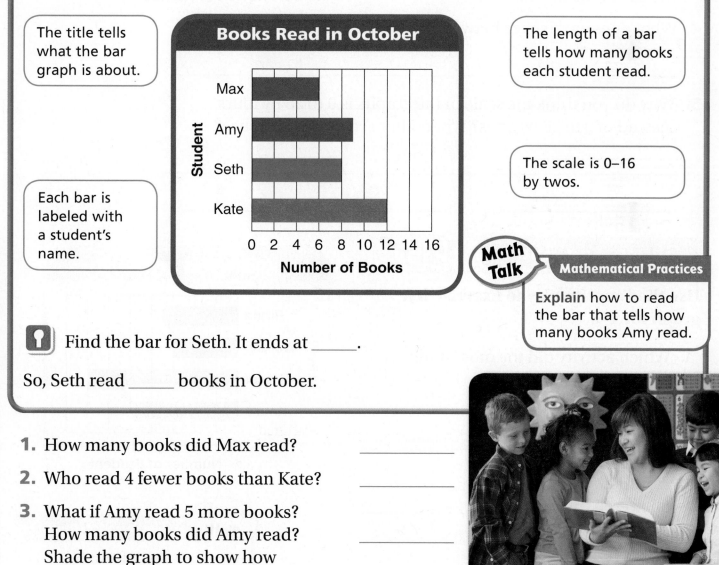

Books Read in October

Student: Max, Amy, Seth, Kate
Number of Books: 0 2 4 6 8 10 12 14 16

Math Talk — Mathematical Practices

Explain how to read the bar that tells how many books Amy read.

🔑 Find the bar for Seth. It ends at _____.

So, Seth read _____ books in October.

1. How many books did Max read? _____

2. Who read 4 fewer books than Kate? _____

3. What if Amy read 5 more books?
How many books did Amy read? _____
Shade the graph to show how
many she read.

© Houghton Mifflin Harcourt Publishing Company • Image Credits: ©Blend Images/Alamy Images

More Examples These bar graphs show the same data.

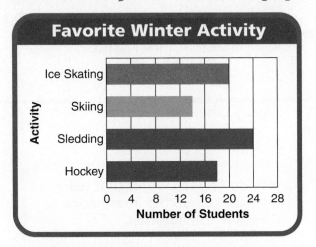

Favorite Winter Activity

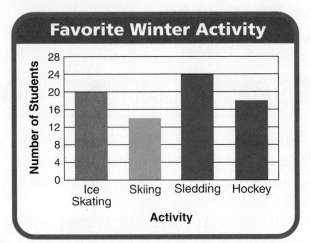

Favorite Winter Activity

In a **horizontal bar graph**, the bars go across from left to right. The length of the bar shows the number.

In a **vertical bar graph**, the bars go up from the bottom. The height of the bar shows the number.

4. What does each space between two numbers represent?

_____

5. Why do you think the scale in the graphs is 0 to 28 by fours instead of 0 to 28 by ones? What other scale could you use?

_____

_____

Share and Show

Use the Favorite Way to Exercise bar graph for 1–3.

1. Which activity did the most students choose?

Think: Which bar is the longest?

_____

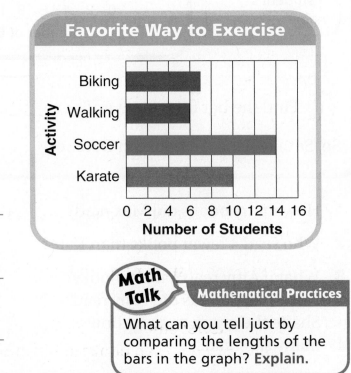

Favorite Way to Exercise

2. How many students answered the survey? _____

3. Which activity received 7 fewer votes than soccer? _____

Math Talk **Mathematical Practices**

What can you tell just by comparing the lengths of the bars in the graph? **Explain.**

© Houghton Mifflin Harcourt Publishing Company

Name _____

Problem Solving • Applications *Real World*

Use the Favorite Kind of Book bar graph for 4–8.

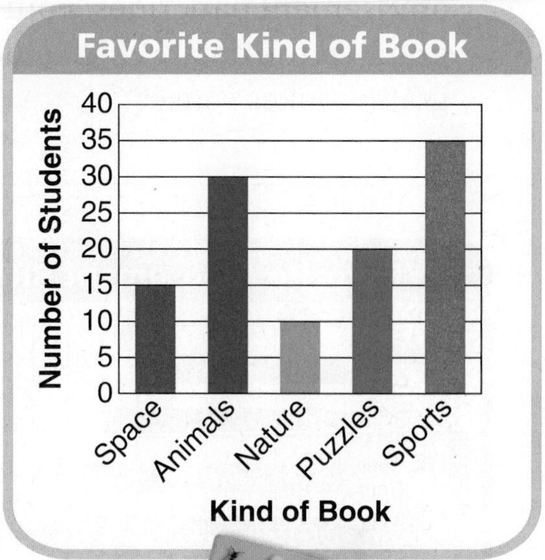

Favorite Kind of Book

4. Which kind of book was chosen by half the number of students as books about animals?

_____

5. **GO DEEPER** Which two kinds of books combined were chosen as often as books about sports?

_____

6. **MATHEMATICAL PRACTICE ④ Use Graphs** Write and solve a problem that matches the data in the graph.

_____

_____

7. **THINK SMARTER** What if 10 more students were asked and they chose books about animals? Describe what the bar graph would look like.

_____

_____

8. **THINK SMARTER** For numbers 8a–8d, select True or False for each statement.

8a. More students chose books about sports than any other kind of book. ○ True ○ False

8b. Five more students chose books about puzzles than books about space. ○ True ○ False

8c. Thirty more students chose books about animals than books about nature. ○ True ○ False

8d. Fifteen fewer students chose books about puzzles than books about sports. ○ True ○ False

© Houghton Mifflin Harcourt Publishing Company

Sense or Nonsense?

9. **THINK SMARTER** The table shows data about some students' favorite amusement park rides. Four students graphed the data. Which student's bar graph makes sense?

Favorite Amusement Ride	
Ride	**Number of Students**
Super Slide	11
Ferris Wheel	14
Bumper Cars	18
Roller Coaster	23

_____

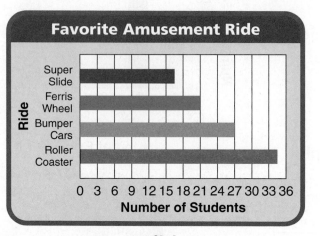

Alicia

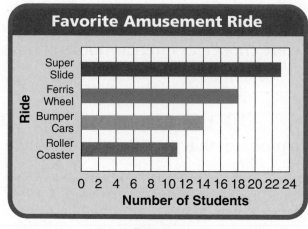

Spencer

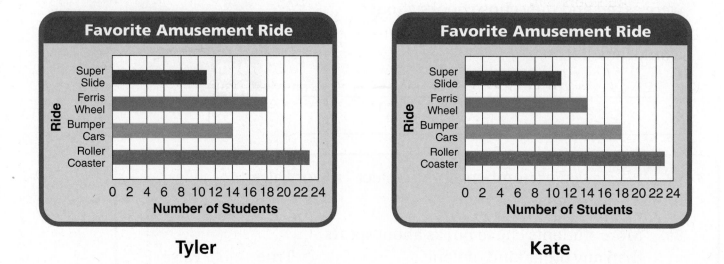

Tyler

Kate

• Explain why the other bar graphs do not make sense.

_____

_____

_____

FOR MORE PRACTICE:
Standards Practice Book

© Houghton Mifflin Harcourt Publishing Company

Name _____

Make Bar Graphs

Essential Question How can you draw a bar graph to show data in a table or picture graph?

 Measurement and Data—3.MD.3
Also 3.NBT.2
MATHEMATICAL PRACTICES
MP.2, MP.4, MP.5

Unlock the Problem (Real World)

Jordan took a survey of his classmates' favorite team sports. He recorded the results in the table at the right. How can he show the results in a bar graph?

Favorite Team Sport

Sport		Tally
Soccer	⚽	卌 卌 ll
Basketball	🏀	llll
Baseball	⚾	卌 卌 llll
Football	🏈	卌 llll

🔒 **Make a bar graph.**

STEP 1

Write a title at the top to tell what the graph is about. Label the side of the graph to tell about the bars. Label the bottom of the graph to explain what the numbers tell.

STEP 2

Choose numbers for the bottom of the graph so that most of the bars will end on a line. Since the least number is 4 and the greatest number is 14, make the scale 0–16. Mark the scale by twos.

STEP 3

Draw and shade a bar to show the number for each sport.

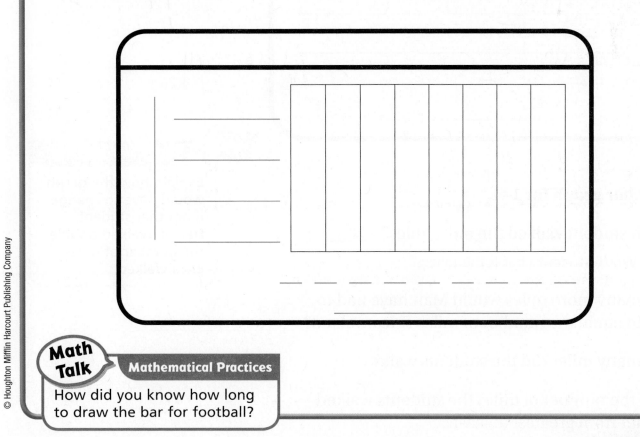

Math Talk **Mathematical Practices**

How did you know how long to draw the bar for football?

© Houghton Mifflin Harcourt Publishing Company

Share and Show

Matt's school is having a walk-a-thon to raise money for the school library. Matt made a picture graph to show the number of miles some students walked. Make a bar graph of Matt's data. Use a scale of 0–_____ , and mark the scale by _____ .

School Walk-a-Thon					
Sam	👕	👕	👕	👕	👕
Matt	👕	👕	🧍		
Ben	👕				
Erica	👕	👕	👕	👕	

Key: Each 👕 = 2 miles.

Use your bar graph for 1–4.

1. Which student walked the most miles? _____

   Think: Which student's bar is the tallest?

2. How many more miles would Matt have had to walk to equal the number of miles Erica walked? _____

3. How many miles did the students walk? _____

4. Write the number of miles the students walked in order from greatest to least. _____

Math Talk — Mathematical Practices

Explain how the graph would have to change if another student, Daniel, walked double the number of miles Erica walked.

© Houghton Mifflin Harcourt Publishing Company • Image Credits: (cr) ©Steve Debenport/Getty Images

Name _____

5. Lydia and Joey did an experiment with a spinner. Lydia recorded the result of each spin in the table at the right. Use the data in the table to make a bar graph. Choose numbers and a scale and decide how to mark your graph.

Spinner Results	
Color	**Tally**
Red	卌 卌 卌 l
Yellow	卌 lll
Blue	卌 卌 ll
Green	卌 卌

! ERROR Alert

Be sure to draw the bars correctly when you transfer data from a table.

Use your bar graph for 6–8.

6. The pointer stopped on _____ half the number of times that it stopped on _____.

7. The pointer stopped on green _____ fewer times than it stopped on blue.

8. **MATHEMATICAL PRACTICE ⑥** **Explain** why you chose the scale you did.

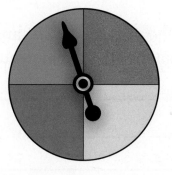

_____

_____

© Houghton Mifflin Harcourt Publishing Company

Problem Solving • Applications Real World

9. **MATHEMATICAL PRACTICE 4** **Use Graphs** Susie recorded the number of points some basketball players scored. Use the data in the table to make a bar graph. Choose numbers so that most of the bars will end on a line.

Points Scored	
Player	**Number of Points**
Billy	10
Dwight	30
James	15
Raul	25
Sean	10

Use your bar graph for 10–12.

10. **GO DEEPER** Which player scored more points than James but fewer points than Dwight? _____

11. **THINK SMARTER** Write and solve a new question that matches the data in your bar graph.

_____

_____

12. **THINK SMARTER** Which player scored 10 more points than James?

_____

FOR MORE PRACTICE: Standards Practice Book

© Houghton Mifflin Harcourt Publishing Company • Image Credits: ©D. Hurst/Alamy Images

Name _____

Solve Problems Using Data

Essential Question How can you solve problems using data represented in bar graphs?

Measurement and Data—3.MD.3
Also 3.NBT.2, 3.OA.8
MATHEMATICAL PRACTICES
MP.1, MP.3, MP.7

🔑 Unlock the Problem · Real World

CONNECT Answering questions about data helps you better understand the information.

Derek's class voted on a topic for the school bulletin board. The bar graph shows the results. How many more votes did computers receive than space?

🔓 One Way Use a model.

Count back along the scale to find the difference between the bars.

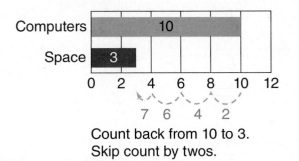

Count back from 10 to 3.
Skip count by twos.

The difference is _____ votes.

🔓 Another Way Write a number sentence.

Think: There are 10 votes for computers. There are 3 votes for space. Subtract to compare the number of votes.

_____

So, computers received _____ more votes than space.

• **How do you know you need to subtract?**

_____

_____

Votes for School Bulletin Board Topic

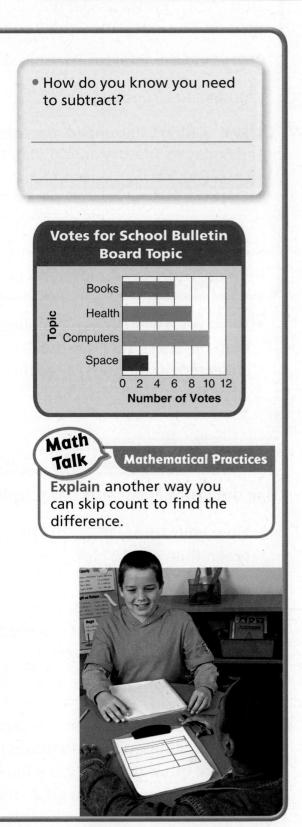

Math Talk **Mathematical Practices**

Explain another way you can skip count to find the difference.

© Houghton Mifflin Harcourt Publishing Company

Example

Brooke's school collected cans of food. The bar graph at the right shows the number of cans. How many fewer cans were collected on Tuesday than on Thursday and Friday combined?

STEP 1 Find the total for Thursday and Friday.

_____

STEP 2 Subtract to compare the total for Thursday and Friday to Tuesday and to find the difference.

_____

So, _____ fewer cans were collected on Tuesday than on Thursday and Friday combined.

Cans of Food Collected

- What if 4 fewer cans were collected on Monday than on Tuesday? How many cans were collected on Monday? Explain.

Share and Show

MATH BOARD

Use the Spinner Results bar graph for 1–3.

1. How many more times did the pointer stop on green than on purple?

   _____ more times

✓ 2. How many fewer times did the pointer stop on blue than on red and green combined?

   _____ fewer times

✓ 3. What if there were 15 more spins and the pointer stopped 10 more times on green and 5 more times on blue? How many more times did the pointer stop on green than blue?

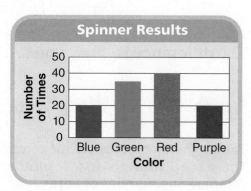

Spinner Results

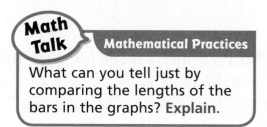

Math Talk

Mathematical Practices

What can you tell just by comparing the lengths of the bars in the graphs? **Explain.**

© Houghton Mifflin Harcourt Publishing Company

Name _____

Use the Diego's DVDs bar graph for 4–6.

4. Diego has 5 fewer of this kind of DVD than comedy. Which kind of DVD is this?

_____

5. Is the number of comedy and action DVDs greater than or less than the number of animated and drama DVDs? Explain.

_____

_____

6. **THINK SMARTER** How many DVDs does Diego have that are NOT comedy DVDs?

_____

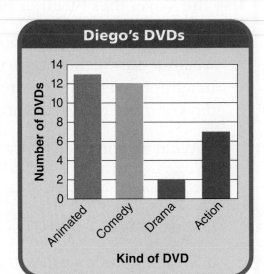

Problem Solving • Applications *Real World*

Use the Science Fair Projects bar graph for 7–9.

7. How many more students would have to do a project on plants to equal the number of projects on space?

_____

8. **WRITE** ▸Math **What's the Question?** The answer is animals, space, rocks, oceans, and plants.

_____

_____

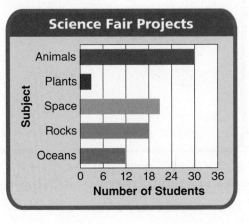

9. **MATHEMATICAL PRACTICE ①** What if 3 fewer students did a project on weather than did a project on rocks? **Describe** what the bar graph would look like.

_____

_____

© Houghton Mifflin Harcourt Publishing Company

Unlock the Problem · Real World

Use the November Weather bar graph for 10–12.

10. **GO DEEPER** Lacey's class recorded the kinds of weather during the month of November in a bar graph. Were there more cloudy and sunny days or more rainy and snowy days?

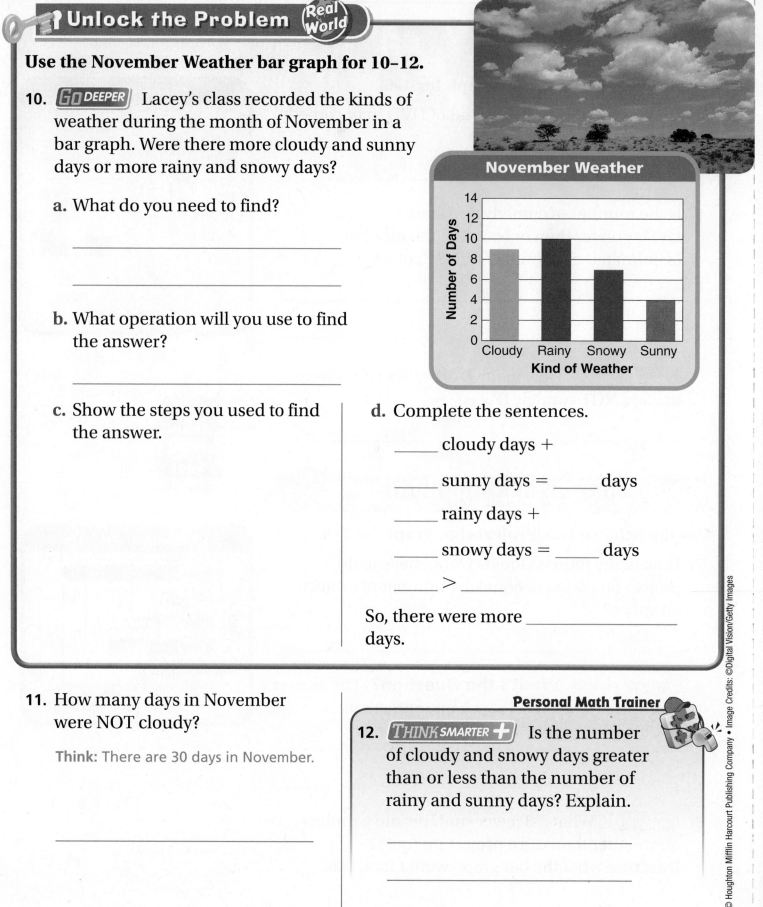

November Weather

a. What do you need to find?

_____

_____

b. What operation will you use to find the answer?

_____

c. Show the steps you used to find the answer.

d. Complete the sentences.

_____ cloudy days +

_____ sunny days = _____ days

_____ rainy days +

_____ snowy days = _____ days

_____ > _____

So, there were more _____ days.

11. How many days in November were NOT cloudy?

Think: There are 30 days in November.

_____

Personal Math Trainer

12. **THINK SMARTER +** Is the number of cloudy and snowy days greater than or less than the number of rainy and sunny days? Explain.

_____

_____

© Houghton Mifflin Harcourt Publishing Company • Image Credits: ©Digital Vision/Getty Images

FOR MORE PRACTICE:
Standards Practice Book

Use and Make Line Plots

Essential Question How can you read and interpret data in a line plot and use data to make a line plot?

Measurement and Data—3.MD.4
Also 3.NBT.2
MATHEMATICAL PRACTICES
MP.1, MP.4, MP.5, MP.6

Unlock the Problem Real World

A **line plot** uses marks to record each piece of data above a number line. It helps you see groups in the data.

Some students took a survey of the number of letters in their first names. Then they recorded the data in a line plot.

How many students have 6 letters in their first names?

> Each ✗ stands for 1 student.

→

```
                    ✗
              ✗     ✗
              ✗     ✗     ✗
              ✗     ✗     ✗
        ✗     ✗     ✗     ✗           ✗
        ✗     ✗     ✗     ✗     ✗     ✗
        ┼─────┼─────┼─────┼─────┼─────┼
        3     4     5     6     7     8
```

Number of Letters in Our First Names

← The numbers show the number of letters in a name.

🔑 Find 6 on the number line. The 6 stands for 6 _____.

There are _____ ✗s above the 6.

So, _____ students have 6 letters in their first names.

1. Which number of letters was found most often? _____

2. Write a sentence to describe the data. _____

_____

3. How many letters are in your first name? _____

4. Put an ✗ above the number of letters in your first name.

Math Talk **Mathematical Practices**

What does the shape of the data show you?

© Houghton Mifflin Harcourt Publishing Company

Activity Make a line plot.

Materials ■ ruler ■ measuring tape

Measure the height of four classmates to the nearest inch. Combine your data with other groups. Make a line plot to show the data you collected.

STEP 1 Record the heights in the table.

STEP 2 Write a title below the number line to describe your line plot.

STEP 3 Write the number of inches in order from left to right above the title.

STEP 4 Draw *X*s above the number line to show each student's height.

Heights in Inches	
Number of Inches	Tally

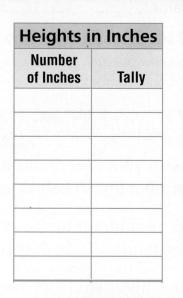

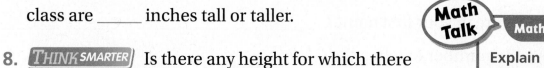

5. Which height appears most often? _____

   Think: Which height has the most *X*s?

6. Which height appears least often? _____

7. Complete the sentence. Most of the students in the

   class are _____ inches tall or taller.

8. [THINK SMARTER] Is there any height for which there are no data? Explain.

_____

_____

Math Talk **Mathematical Practices**

Explain what the shape of the data tells you.

© Houghton Mifflin Harcourt Publishing Company • Image Credits: Comstock/Getty Images

Name _____

1. Measure the length of three drawing tools from your desk to the nearest inch. Combine your data with several other classmates. Record the lengths in the table.

✓ 2. Make a line plot to show the data you collected.

Lengths in Inches	
Number of Inches	Tally

```
+---+---+---+---+---+
___   ___   ___   ___   ___

_____
```

✓ 3. Which length appears most often? _____

Problem Solving • Applications

Use the line plot at the right for 4–6.

4. **MATHEMATICAL PRACTICE ⑤ Use Appropriate Tools** Garden club members recorded the height of their avocado plants to the nearest inch in a line plot. Write a sentence to describe what the line plot shows.

_____

_____

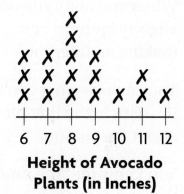

Height of Avocado Plants (in Inches)

5. **THINK SMARTER** How many more plants are 8 or 9 inches tall than are 6 or 7 inches tall? Explain.

_____

_____

6. **THINK SMARTER** How many plants are taller than 8 inches?

_____ plants

© Houghton Mifflin Harcourt Publishing Company

GO DEEPER **Make an Inference**

Addison made the line plot below to show the high temperature every day for one month. What *inference* can you make about what season this is?

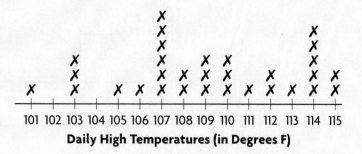

Daily High Temperatures (in Degrees F)

When you combine what you see with what you already know to come up with an idea, you are making an inference.

You can use what you know about weather and the data in the line plot to make an inference about the season.

You know that the numbers in the line plot are the high temperatures recorded during the month.

The highest temperature recorded was _____.

The lowest temperature recorded was _____.

The temperature recorded most often was _____.

Since all the high temperatures are greater than 100, you know the days were hot. This will help you make an inference about the season.

So, you can infer that the season is _____.

> **Remember**
>
> **The Four Seasons**
>
> spring
>
> summer
>
> fall
>
> winter

© Houghton Mifflin Harcourt Publishing Company

Name _____

1. Mia made a tally table to record the different types of birds she saw at the bird feeder in the garden.

Birds at the Feeder	
Name	**Tally**
Jay	IIII
Sparrow	卌 卌 II
Finch	卌 III
Blackbird	卌 I

For numbers 1a–1c, select True or False for each statement.

1a. Mia saw twice as many
sparrows as blackbirds.　　　○ True　　　○ False

1b. Mia saw 8 finches.　　　○ True　　　○ False

1c. Mia saw 4 fewer jays
than blackbirds.　　　○ True　　　○ False

2. Jake asked 25 students in his class how close they live to school. The frequency table shows the results.

Miles to School	Boys	Girls
about 1 mile	4	5
about 2 miles		4
about 3 miles	3	2

Part A

Complete the table and explain how you found the answer.

```


```

Part B

How many more students live about 2 miles or less from school than students who live about 3 miles from school? Show your work.

```


```

© Houghton Mifflin Harcourt Publishing Company

Use the picture graph for 3–6.

Students at Barnes School are performing in a play. The picture graph shows the number of tickets each class has sold so far.

3. How many tickets were sold altogether? Explain how you found the total.

Number of Tickets Sold	
Ms. Brown's Class	✓ ✓ ✓ ✓ ✓ ✓ ✓ ✓
Mrs. Gold's Class	✓ ✓ ✓ ✓ ✓
Mr. Castro's Class	✓ ✓ ✓ ✓ ✓ ✓

Key: Each ✓ = 5 tickets.

4. Choose the name from each box that makes the sentence true.

Five fewer tickets were sold by
| Ms. Brown's |
| Mrs. Gold's | class
| Mr. Castro's |

than
| Ms. Brown's |
| Mrs. Gold's | class.
| Mr. Castro's |

5. How many more tickets were sold by Ms. Brown's class than Mr. Castro's class?

_____ tickets

6. What if Mrs. Gold's class sold 20 more tickets? Draw a picture to show how the graph would change.

94

© Houghton Mifflin Harcourt Publishing Company

Use the frequency table for 7–8.

7. The Pet Shop keeps track of the number of fish it has for sale. The frequency table shows how many fish are in three tanks.

Fish in Tanks	
Tank	**Number of Fish**
Tank 1	16
Tank 2	9
Tank 3	12

Part A

Use the data in the table to complete the picture graph.

Tank 1	◯◯

Key: Each ◯ = 2 fish.

Part B

How many pictures did you draw for Tank 2? Explain.

8. Each tank can hold up to 20 fish. How many more fish can the Pet Shop put in the three tanks?

Ⓐ 60 fish   Ⓒ 20 fish

Ⓑ 23 fish   Ⓓ 13 fish

© Houghton Mifflin Harcourt Publishing Company

Use the bar graph for 9–12.

9. Three more students play piano than which other instrument?

_____

10. The same number of students play which two instruments?

_____

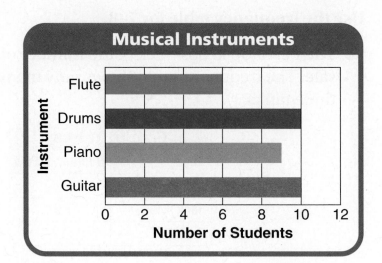

Musical Instruments

Instrument

Flute
Drums
Piano
Guitar

0 2 4 6 8 10 12
Number of Students

11. For numbers 11a–11d, select True or False for each statement.

11a. Ten more students play guitar than play flute. ○ True   ○ False

11b. Nine students play piano. ○ True   ○ False

11c. Six fewer students play flute and piano combined than play drums and guitar combined. ○ True   ○ False

11d. Nine more students play piano and guitar combined than play drums. ○ True   ○ False

12. There are more students who play the trumpet than play the flute, but fewer students than play the guitar. Explain how you would change the bar graph to show the number of students who play the trumpet.

© Houghton Mifflin Harcourt Publishing Company

Name _____

Use the frequency table for 13–14.

13. Karen asks students what vegetables they would like to have in the school cafeteria. The table shows the results of her survey.

Favorite Vegetables	
Vegetable	Number of Votes
broccoli	15
carrots	40
corn	20
green beans	10

Part A

Use the data in the table to complete the bar graph.

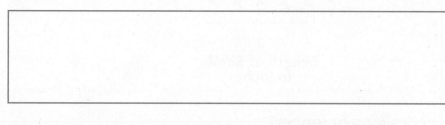

Part B

How do you know how long to make the bars on your graph? How did you show 15 votes for broccoli? Explain.

14. How many more votes did the two most popular vegetables get than the two least popular vegetables? Explain how you solved the problem.

_____

_____

© Houghton Mifflin Harcourt Publishing Company

Use the line plot for 15–16.

The line plot shows the number of goals the players on Scot's team scored.

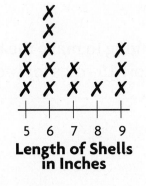

X
X X
X X X
X X X X X
+---+---+---+---+
0   1   2   3   4
**Number of Goals
Scored**

15. For numbers 15a–15d, select True or False for each statement.

15a.   Three players
scored 2 goals.   ○ True   ○ False

15b.   Six players scored
fewer than 2 goals.   ○ True   ○ False

15c.   There are 8 players
on the team.   ○ True   ○ False

15d.   Five players scored
more than 1 goal.   ○ True   ○ False

16. What if two more people played and each scored 3 goals? Describe what the line plot would look like.

```
+------------------------------------------------------------+
|                                                            |
|                                                            |
|                                                            |
+------------------------------------------------------------+
```

Use the line plot for 17–18.

Robin collected shells during her vacation. She measured the length of each shell to the nearest inch and recorded the data in a line plot.

X
X
X X   X
X X X   X
X X X X X
+---+---+---+---+
5   6   7   8   9
**Length of Shells
in Inches**

17. How many shells were 6 inches long or longer?

_____ shells

18. How many more shells did Robin collect that were 5 inches long than 8 inches long?

_____ shells

© Houghton Mifflin Harcourt Publishing Company

Understand Multiplication

Show What You Know ✓

Check your understanding of important skills.

Name _____

▶ **Count On to Add** Use the number line. Write the sum.

0 1 2 3 4 5 6 7 8 9 10

1. $6 + 2 =$ _____

2. $3 + 7 =$ _____

▶ **Skip Count by Twos and Fives** Skip count. Write the missing numbers.

3. 2, 4, 6, _____, _____, _____

4. 5, 10, 15, _____, _____, _____

▶ **Model with Arrays** Use the array. Complete.

5.

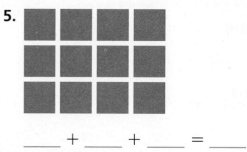

___ + ___ + ___ = ___

6.

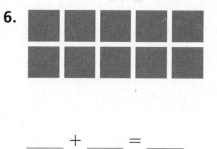

___ + ___ = ___

Math Detective

Ryan's class went on a field trip to a farm. They saw 5 cows and 6 chickens. Be a Math Detective to find how many legs were on all the animals they saw.

© Houghton Mifflin Harcourt Publishing Company • Image Credits: ©David Frazier/Corbis

Personal Math Trainer

Online Assessment and Intervention

Vocabulary Builder

► **Visualize It** ••

Complete the tree map by using the review words.

```
                    ┌─────────────────────┐
                    │    Related Facts     │
                    └──────────┬──────────┘
                    ┌──────────┴──────────┐
                    │                     │
                    └──┬───────────────┬──┘
            ┌──────────┴──┐       ┌────┴──────────┐
            │   addition   │       │               │
            └──────┬──────┘       └───────────────┘
            ┌──────┴──────┐
            │             │
            └──────┬──────┘
            ┌──────┴──────┐
            │             │
            └─────────────┘
```

Review Words

addend
addition
difference
number sentences
related facts
subtraction
sum

Preview Words

array
equal groups
factor
multiply
product

► **Understand Vocabulary** ••••••••••••••••••••••••••••

Read the definition. Write the preview word that matches it.

1. A set of objects arranged in rows and columns _____

2. The answer in a multiplication problem _____

3. When you combine equal groups to find how many in all _____

4. A number that is multiplied by another number to find a product _____

© Houghton Mifflin Harcourt Publishing Company

• **Interactive Student Edition**
• **Multimedia eGlossary**

Name _____

Count Equal Groups

Essential Question How can you use equal groups to find how many in all?

**Operations and Algebraic Thinking—
3.OA.1** *Also 3.OA.3*
MATHEMATICAL PRACTICES
MP.2, MP.4, MP.5

⚷ Unlock the Problem (Real World)

Equal groups have the same number of objects in each group.

Tim has 6 toy cars. Each car has 4 wheels. How many wheels are there in all?

- How many wheels are on each car?

  _____

- How many equal groups of wheels are there?

  _____

- How can you find how many wheels in all?

  _____

🔒 Activity Use counters to model the equal groups.

Materials ■ counters

STEP 1 Draw 4 counters in each group.

_____

STEP 2 Skip count to find how many wheels in all.
Skip count by 4s until you say 6 numbers.

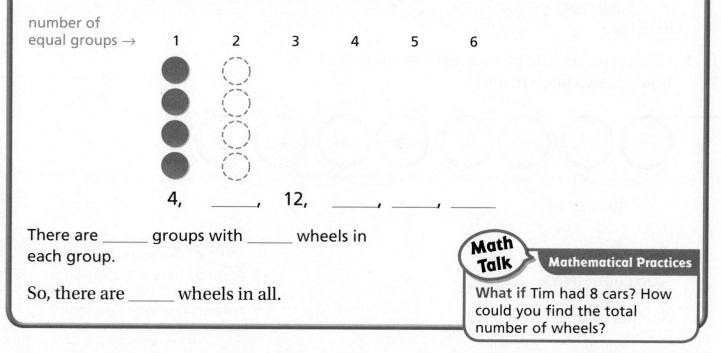

number of
equal groups →   1   2   3   4   5   6

4, _____, 12, _____, _____, _____

There are _____ groups with _____ wheels in each group.

So, there are _____ wheels in all.

Math Talk Mathematical Practices

What if Tim had 8 cars? How could you find the total number of wheels?

© Houghton Mifflin Harcourt Publishing Company

☐ Example Count equal groups to find the total.

Sam, Kyla, and Tia each have 5 pennies.
How many pennies do they have in all?

How many pennies does each person have? _____

How many equal groups of pennies are there? _____

Draw 5 counters in each group.

Think: There are _____ groups of 5 pennies.

Think: There are _____ fives.

5¢   5¢   5¢

Skip count to find how many pennies.

So, they have _____ pennies.

_____ , _____ , _____

• THINK SMARTER Explain why you can skip count by 5s to find how many.

_____

Share and Show MATH BOARD

1. Complete. Use the picture. Skip count to find
   how many wheels in all.

_____ groups of 2

_____ twos

Skip count by 2s.   2, 4, _____ , _____

So, there are _____ wheels.

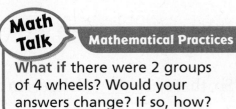

Math Talk   Mathematical Practices

What if there were 2 groups
of 4 wheels? Would your
answers change? If so, how?

© Houghton Mifflin Harcourt Publishing Company

Name _____

Draw equal groups. Skip count to find how many.

2. 2 groups of 6 _____

☑ 3. 3 groups of 2 _____

Count equal groups to find how many.

☑ 4.

_____ groups of _____

_____ in all

5.

_____ groups of _____

_____ in all

On Your Own

Draw equal groups. Skip count to find how many.

6. 3 groups of 3 _____

7. 2 groups of 9 _____

8. **GO DEEPER** A toy car costs $3. A toy truck costs $4. Which costs more—4 cars or 3 trucks? Explain.

_____

_____

9. **MATHEMATICAL PRACTICE ③ Make Arguments** Elliott has a collection of 20 toy cars. Will he be able to put an equal number of toy cars on 3 shelves? Explain your answer.

_____

_____

© Houghton Mifflin Harcourt Publishing Company

🔑 Unlock the Problem 🌐 Real World

10. **THINK SMARTER** Tina, Charlie, and Amber have toy cars. Each car has 4 wheels. How many wheels do their cars have altogether?

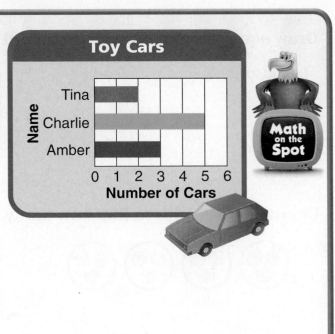

a. What do you need to find?

_____

b. What information will you use from the graph to solve the problem?

_____

c. Show the steps you used to solve the problem.

d. So, the cars have _____ wheels.

11. **THINK SMARTER** A bookcase has 4 shelves. Each shelf holds 5 books. How many books are in the bookcase?

Draw counters to model the problem. Then explain how you solved the problem.

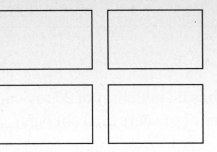

_____

_____

© Houghton Mifflin Harcourt Publishing Company

FOR MORE PRACTICE:
Standards Practice Book

Relate Addition and Multiplication

Essential Question How is multiplication like addition?
How is it different?

Operations and Algebraic Thinking—
3.OA.1 Also 3.OA.3, 3.OA.7, 3.NBT.2
MATHEMATICAL PRACTICES
MP.1, MP.4, MP.7

Unlock the Problem Real World

Tomeka needs 3 apples to make one loaf of apple bread. Each loaf has the same number of apples. How many apples does Tomeka need to make 4 loaves?

- How many loaves is Tomeka making?
  _____
- How many apples are in each loaf?
  _____
- How can you solve the problem?
  _____

One Way Add equal groups.

Use the 4 circles to show the 4 loaves.

Draw 3 counters in each circle to show the apples Tomeka needs for each loaf.

Find the number of counters.
Complete the addition sentence.

3 + _____ + _____ + _____ = _____

So, Tomeka needs _____ apples to

make _____ loaves of apple bread.

Math Talk **Mathematical Practices**

How is the picture you drew like the addition sentence you wrote?

© Houghton Mifflin Harcourt Publishing Company

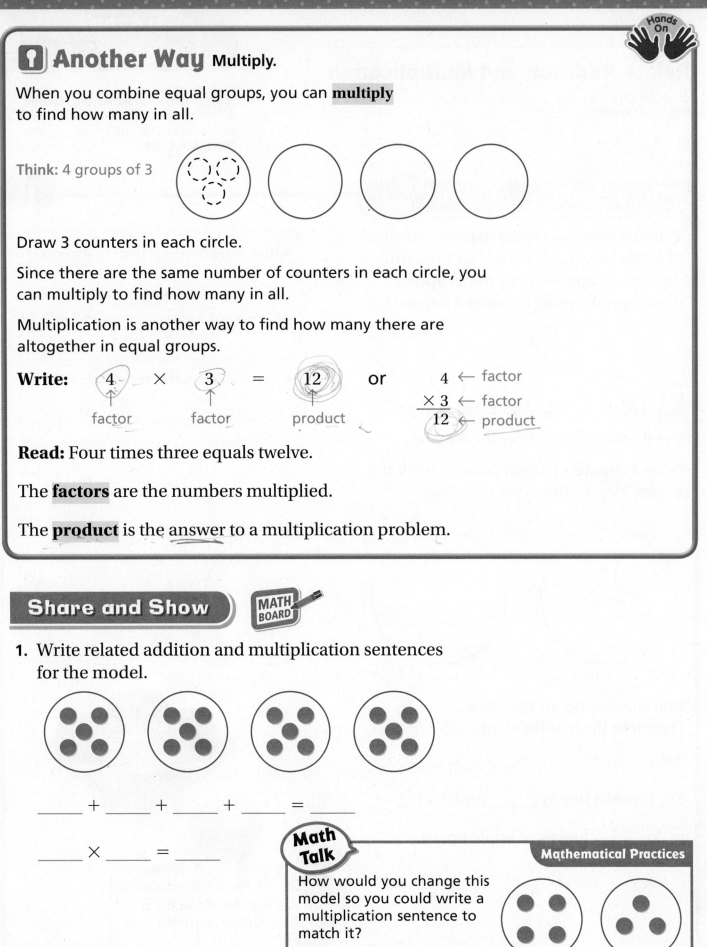

🔓 Another Way Multiply.

When you combine equal groups, you can **multiply** to find how many in all.

Think: 4 groups of 3

Draw 3 counters in each circle.

Since there are the same number of counters in each circle, you can multiply to find how many in all.

Multiplication is another way to find how many there are altogether in equal groups.

Write:

4 × 3 = 12   or

factor factor product

$$4 \leftarrow \text{factor}$$
$$\underline{\times\ 3} \leftarrow \text{factor}$$
$$12 \leftarrow \text{product}$$

Read: Four times three equals twelve.

The **factors** are the numbers multiplied.

The **product** is the answer to a multiplication problem.

Share and Show   MATH BOARD

1. Write related addition and multiplication sentences for the model.

____ + ____ + ____ + ____ = ____

____ × ____ = ____

Math Talk

Mathematical Practices

How would you change this model so you could write a multiplication sentence to match it?

© Houghton Mifflin Harcourt Publishing Company

Name _____

Draw a quick picture to show the equal groups. Then write related addition and multiplication sentences.

2. 3 groups of 6

___ + ___ + ___ = ___

___ × ___ = ___

3. 2 groups of 3

___ + ___ = ___

___ × ___ = ___

On Your Own

Draw a quick picture to show the equal groups. Then write related addition and multiplication sentences.

4. 4 groups of 2

___ + ___ + ___ + ___ = ___

___ × ___ = ___

5. 5 groups of 4

___ + ___ + ___ + ___ + ___ = ___

___ × ___ = ___

Complete. Write a multiplication sentence.

6.

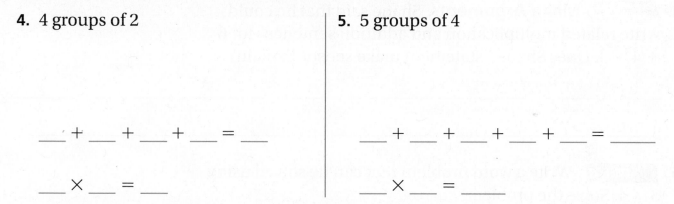

___ × ___ = ___

7.

___ × ___ = ___

8.

___ × ___ = ___

9. 2 + 2 + 2 + 2 = ___

___ × ___ = ___

10. 4 + 4 + 4 + 4 = ___

___ × ___ = ___

11. 9 + 9 + 9 = ___

___ × ___ = ___

© Houghton Mifflin Harcourt Publishing Company

Problem Solving • Applications Real World

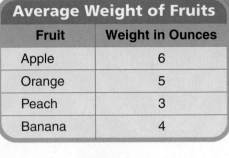

Use the table for 12–13.

Average Weight of Fruits	
Fruit	Weight in Ounces
Apple	6
Orange	5
Peach	3
Banana	4

12. Morris bought 4 peaches. How much do the peaches weigh? Write a multiplication sentence to find the weight of the peaches.

_____ × _____ = _____ ounces

13. *THINK SMARTER* Thomas bought 2 apples. Sydney bought 4 bananas. Which weighed more—the 2 apples or the 4 bananas? How much more? Explain how you know.

_____

_____

_____

14. *MATHEMATICAL PRACTICE ③* **Make Arguments** Shane said that he could write related multiplication and addition sentences for 6 + 4 + 3. Does Shane's statement make sense? Explain.

_____

_____

15. *GO DEEPER* Write a word problem that can be solved using 3 × 4. Solve the problem.

_____

_____

16. *THINK SMARTER* Select the number sentences that represent the model at the right. Mark all that apply.

(A) 3 + 6 = 9   (C) 3 × 6 = 18

(B) 6 + 6 + 6 = 18   (D) 6 + 3 = 9

FOR MORE PRACTICE:
Standards Practice Book

© Houghton Mifflin Harcourt Publishing Company

Name _____

Skip Count on a Number Line

Operations and Algebraic Thinking—
3.OA.3 *Also 3.OA.1*
MATHEMATICAL PRACTICES
MP.1, MP.4, MP.7

Essential Question How can you use a number line to skip count and find how many in all?

Unlock the Problem (Real World)

Caleb wants to make 3 balls of yarn for his cat to play with. He uses 6 feet of yarn to make each ball. How many feet of yarn does Caleb need in all?

Use a number line to count equal groups.

How many feet of yarn does Caleb

need for each ball? _____

How many equal lengths of yarn does he need? _____

Begin at 0. Skip count by 6s by drawing jumps on the number line.

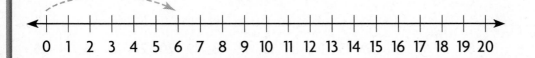

0 1 2 3 4 5 6 7 8 9 10 11 12 13 14 15 16 17 18 19 20

How many jumps did you make? _____

How long is each jump? _____

Multiply. $3 \times 6 =$ _____

So, Caleb needs _____ feet of yarn in all.

- **How many equal groups of yarn will Caleb make?**

  _____

- **How many feet of yarn will be in each group?**

  _____

- **What do you need to find?**

  _____

Math Talk **Mathematical Practices**

What if Caleb made 4 balls of yarn with 5 feet of yarn in each ball? What would you do differently to find the total number of feet of yarn needed?

- **MATHEMATICAL PRACTICE ① Analyze** Why did you jump by 6s on the number line?

_____

© Houghton Mifflin Harcourt Publishing Company • Image Credits: ©Roman Milert/Alamy Images

1. Skip count by drawing jumps on the number line. Find how many in 5 jumps of 4. Then write the product.

Think: 1 jump of 4 shows 1 group of 4.

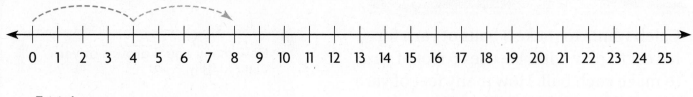

5 × 4 = _____

Draw jumps on the number line to show equal groups. Find the product.

2. 3 groups of 8

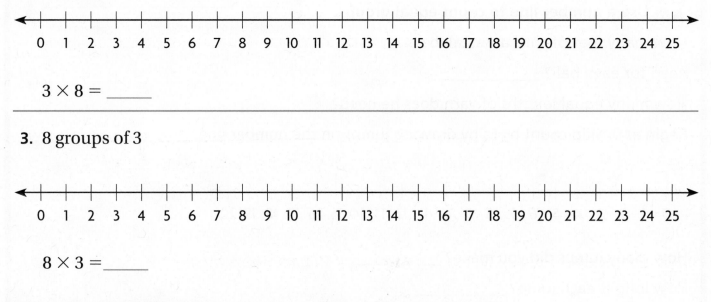

3 × 8 = _____

3. 8 groups of 3

8 × 3 = _____

Write the multiplication sentence shown by the number line.

4.

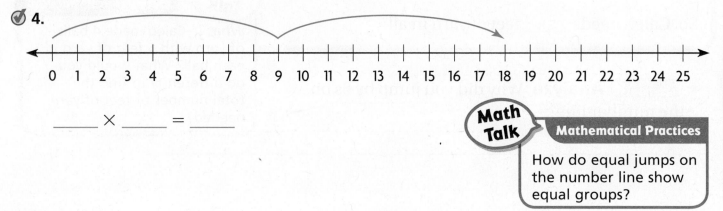

_____ × _____ = _____

Math Talk **Mathematical Practices**

How do equal jumps on the number line show equal groups?

© Houghton Mifflin Harcourt Publishing Company

Name _____

On Your Own

Draw jumps on the number line to show equal groups. Find the product.

5. 6 groups of 4

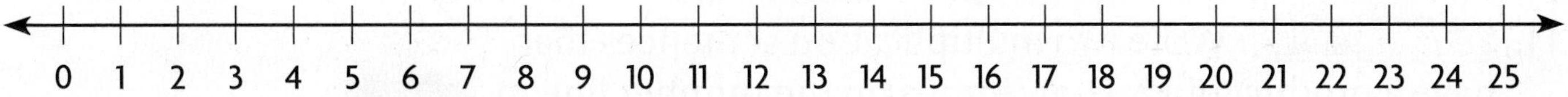

6 × 4 = _____

6. 7 groups of 3

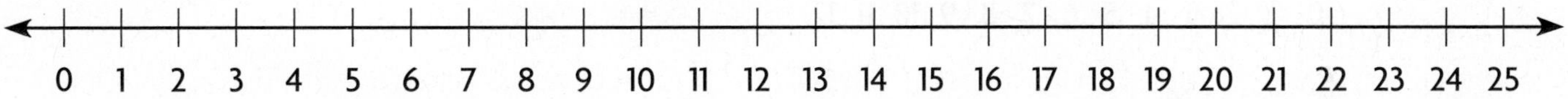

7 × 3 = _____

7. 2 groups of 10

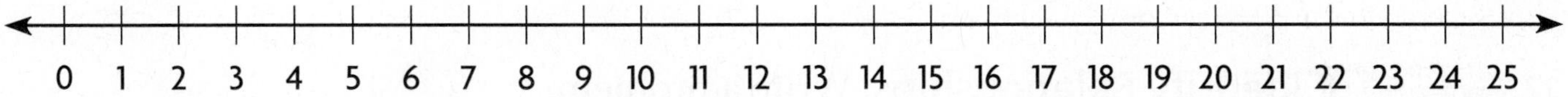

2 × 10 = _____

Write the multiplication sentence shown by the number lines.

8.

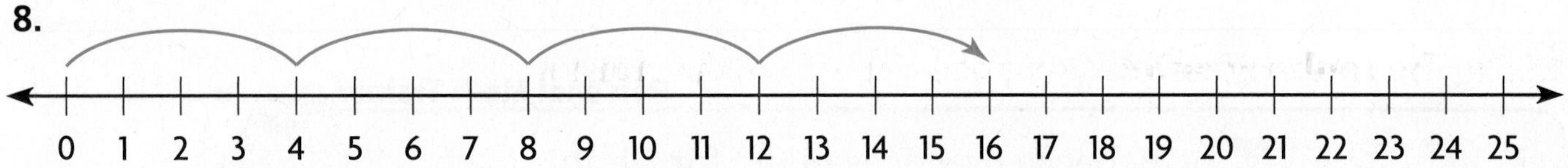

_____ × _____ = _____

9.

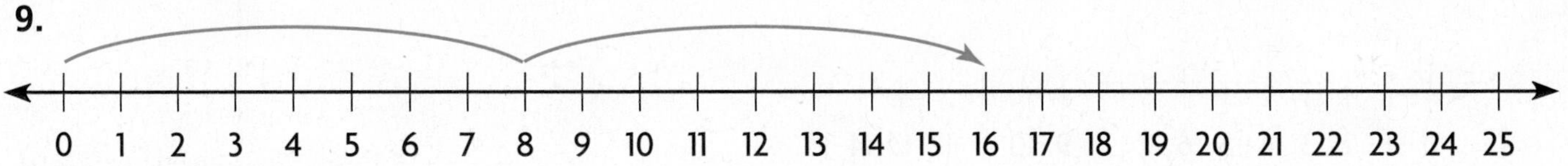

_____ × _____ = _____

© Houghton Mifflin Harcourt Publishing Company

Problem Solving • Applications

10. **Go DEEPER** Erin displays her toy cat collection on 3 shelves. She puts 8 cats on each shelf. If she collects 3 more cats, how many cats will she have?

_____

11. **THINK SMARTER** Write two multiplication sentences that have a product of 12. Draw jumps on the number line to show the multiplication.

____ × ____ = ◯

```
←+—+—+—+—+—+—+—+—+—+—+—+—+→
  0  1  2  3  4  5  6  7  8  9  10 11 12
```

____ × ____ = ____

12. **MATHEMATICAL PRACTICE ⑦** **Identify Relationships** Write a problem that can be solved by finding 8 groups of 5. Write a multiplication sentence to solve the problem. Then solve.

_____

_____

Personal Math Trainer

13. **THINK SMARTER +** Rebecca practices piano for 3 hours each week. How many hours does she practice in 4 weeks?

Draw jumps and label the number line to show your thinking.

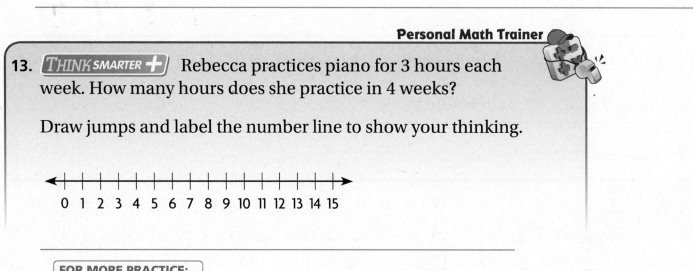

```
←+—+—+—+—+—+—+—+—+—+—+—+—+—+—+—+→
  0  1  2  3  4  5  6  7  8  9  10 11 12 13 14 15
```

© Houghton Mifflin Harcourt Publishing Company

_____

FOR MORE PRACTICE:
Standards Practice Book

Name _____

 ☑Mid-Chapter Checkpoint

Vocabulary

Choose the best term from the box.

Vocabulary
equal groups
factors
multiply
product

1. When you combine equal groups, you can **multiply** to find how many in all. (p. 106)

2. The answer in a multiplication problem is called the **factors** ~~product~~. (p. 106)

   factors

3. The numbers you multiply are called the **product**. (p. 106)

Concepts and Skills

Count equal groups to find how many. (3.OA.1)

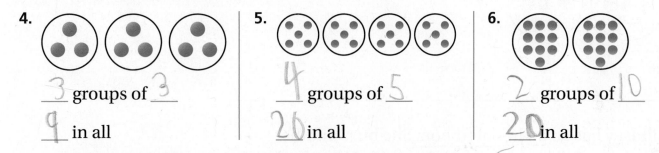

4. **3** groups of **3**
   9 in all

5. **4** groups of **5**
   20 in all

6. **2** groups of **10**
   20 in all

Write related addition and multiplication sentences. (3.OA.1)

7. 3 groups of 9

   $9 + 9 + 9 = 27$

   $3 \times 9 = 27$

8. 5 groups of 7

   $7 + 7 + 7 + 7 + 7 = 31$

   $5 \times 7 = 31$

Draw jumps on the number line to show equal groups.
Find the product. (3.OA.3)

9. 6 groups of 3

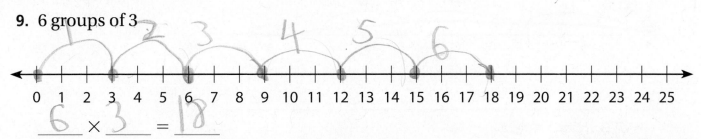

   $6 \times 3 = 18$

© Houghton Mifflin Harcourt Publishing Company

10. Beth's mother cut some melons into equal slices. She put 4 slices each on 8 plates. Write a multiplication sentence to show the total number of melon slices she put on the plates. (3.OA.1)

$8 \times 4 = 32$ melon slices

11. Avery had 125 animal stickers. She gave 5 animal stickers to each of her 10 friends. How many animal stickers did she have left? What number sentences did you use to solve? (3.OA.3)

125
$\underline{50}$

$10 \times 5 = 50$

$125 - 10 - 5 = $ 75 animal stickers

12. Matt made 2 equal groups of marbles. Write a multiplication sentence to show the total number of marbles. (3.OA.1)

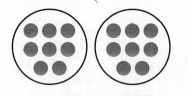

$2 \times 8 = 16$ marbles

13. Lindsey has 10 inches of ribbon. She buys another 3 lengths of ribbon, each 5 inches long. How much ribbon does she have now? (3.OA.3)

$5 \times 3 = 15$

$\begin{array}{r} 10 \\ + 15 \\ \hline 25 \end{array}$ 325 inches of ribbon + 3 inches

14. Jack's birthday is in 4 weeks. How many days is it until Jack's birthday? Describe how you could use a number line to solve. (3.OA.3)

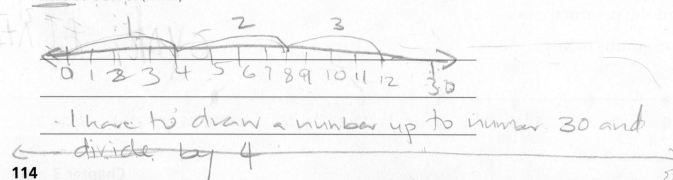

I have to draw a number up to number 30 and divide by 4

© Houghton Mifflin Harcourt Publishing Company

Name _____

Problem Solving • Model Multiplication

Essential Question How can you use the strategy *draw a diagram* to solve one- and two-step problems?

Operations and Algebraic Thinking—
3.OA.8 *Also 3.OA.1, 3.OA.3*
MATHEMATICAL PRACTICES
MP.1, MP.4, MP.5, MP.6

Unlock the Problem *Real World*

Three groups of students are taking drum lessons. There are 8 students in each group. How many students are taking drum lessons?

Read the Problem

What do I need to find?

I need to find how many _____

are taking drum lessons.

What information do I need to use?

There are _____ groups of students

taking drum lessons. There are

_____ students in each group.

How will I use the information?

I will draw a bar model to help me see

_____

_____ .

Solve the Problem

Complete the bar model to show the drummers.

Write 8 in each box to show the 8 students in each of the 3 groups.

8	_____	_____

▪ students

Since there are equal groups, I can multiply to find the number of students taking drum lessons.

_____ × _____ = ▪

_____ = ▪

So, there are _____ students in all.

Math Talk

Mathematical Practices

How would the bar model change if there were 6 groups of 4 students? Solve.

© Houghton Mifflin Harcourt Publishing Company • Image Credits: (t) ©Ben Molyneux People/Alamy Images

🚩 Try Another Problem

Twelve students in Mrs. Taylor's class want to start a band. Seven students each made a drum. The rest of the students made 2 shakers each. How many shakers were made?

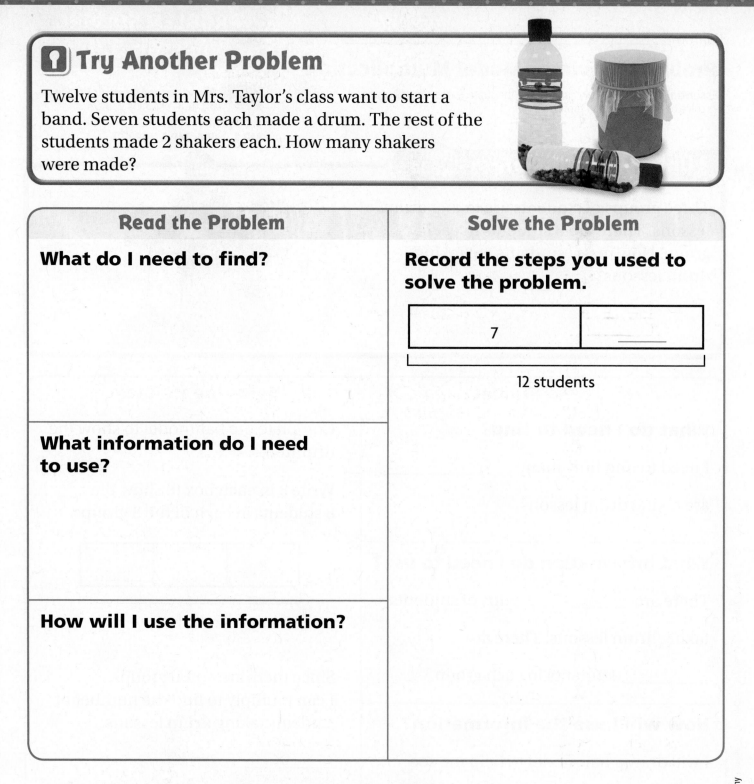

Read the Problem	Solve the Problem
What do I need to find?	**Record the steps you used to solve the problem.**
What information do I need to use?	
How will I use the information?	

Solve the Problem table:

7	_____

12 students

1. How many shakers in all did the students make? _____

2. How do you know your answer is reasonable? _____

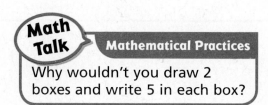

Math Talk **Mathematical Practices**

Why wouldn't you draw 2 boxes and write 5 in each box?

© Houghton Mifflin Harcourt Publishing Company

Name _____

✓**1.** There are 6 groups of 4 students who play the trumpet in the marching band. How many students play the trumpet in the band?

First, draw a bar model to show each group of students.

Draw _____ boxes and write _____ in each box.

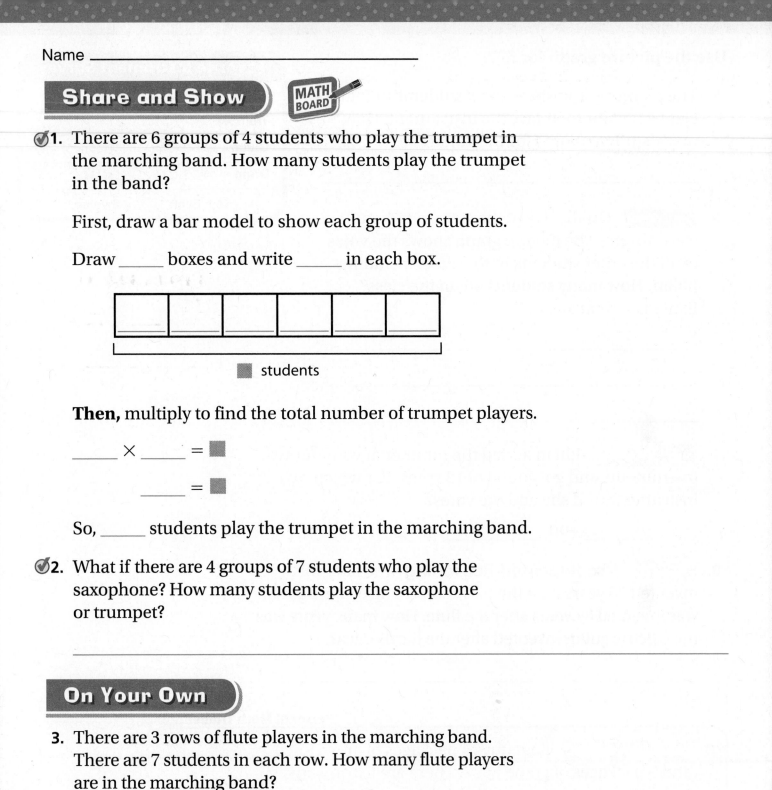

■ students

Then, multiply to find the total number of trumpet players.

_____ × _____ = ■

_____ = ■

So, _____ students play the trumpet in the marching band.

✓**2.** What if there are 4 groups of 7 students who play the saxophone? How many students play the saxophone or trumpet?

_____

3. There are 3 rows of flute players in the marching band. There are 7 students in each row. How many flute players are in the marching band?

_____

4. THINK SMARTER Suppose there are 5 groups of 4 trumpet players. In front of the trumpet players are 18 saxophone players. How many students play the trumpet or saxophone?

Math on the Spot

_____

© Houghton Mifflin Harcourt Publishing Company

Use the picture graph for 5–7.

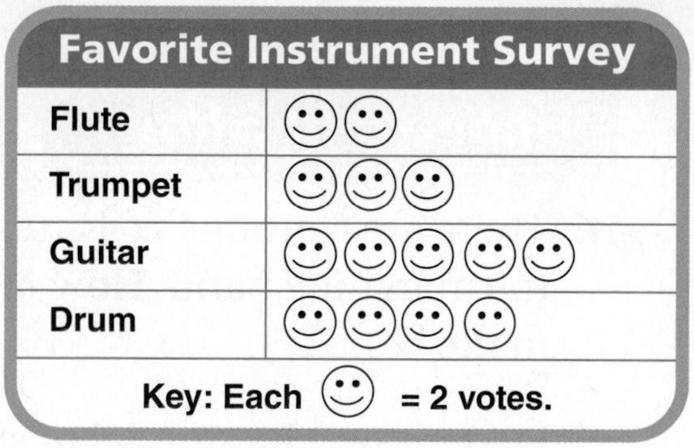

Favorite Instrument Survey

Flute	🙂 🙂
Trumpet	🙂 🙂 🙂
Guitar	🙂 🙂 🙂 🙂 🙂
Drum	🙂 🙂 🙂 🙂

Key: Each 🙂 = 2 votes.

5. The picture graph shows how students in Jillian's class voted for their favorite instrument. How many students voted for the guitar?

_____

6. **Go DEEPER** On the day of the survey, two students were absent. The picture graph shows the votes of all the other students in the class, including Jillian. How many students are in the class? Explain your answer.

_____

_____

_____

7. **THINK SMARTER** Jillian added the number of votes for two instruments and got a total of 12 votes. For which two instruments did she add the votes?

_____ and _____

8. **MATHEMATICAL PRACTICE ⑧ Use Repeated Reasoning** The flute was invented 26 years after the harmonica. The electric guitar was invented 84 years after the flute. How many years was the electric guitar invented after the harmonica?

_____

Personal Math Trainer

9. **THINK SMARTER ➕** Raul buys 4 packages of apple juice and 3 packages of grape juice. There are 6 drink boxes in each package. How many drink boxes does Raul buy? Show your work.

_____

FOR MORE PRACTICE:
Standards Practice Book

© Houghton Mifflin Harcourt Publishing Company

Name _____

Model with Arrays

Essential Question How can you use arrays to model multiplication and find factors?

Operations and Algebraic Thinking—3.OA.3 *Also 3.OA.1*
MATHEMATICAL PRACTICES
MP.1, MP.2, MP.4, MP.6

Unlock the Problem (Real World)

Many people grow tomatoes in their gardens. Lee plants 3 rows of tomato plants with 6 plants in each row. How many tomato plants are there?

▲ Tomatoes are a great source of vitamins.

Activity 1

Materials ■ square tiles ■ MathBoard

- You make an **array** by placing the same number of tiles in each row. Make an array with 3 rows of 6 tiles to show the tomato plants.

- Now draw the array you made.

- Find the total number of tiles.

Multiply.   3   ×   6 = _____
                  ↑   ↑
               number   number
               of rows   in each row

So, there are _____ tomato plants.

Math Talk
Mathematical Practices

Does the number of tiles change if you turn the array to show 6 rows of 3? **Explain.**

© Houghton Mifflin Harcourt Publishing Company • Image Credits: (cr) ©Getty Images/Photodisc

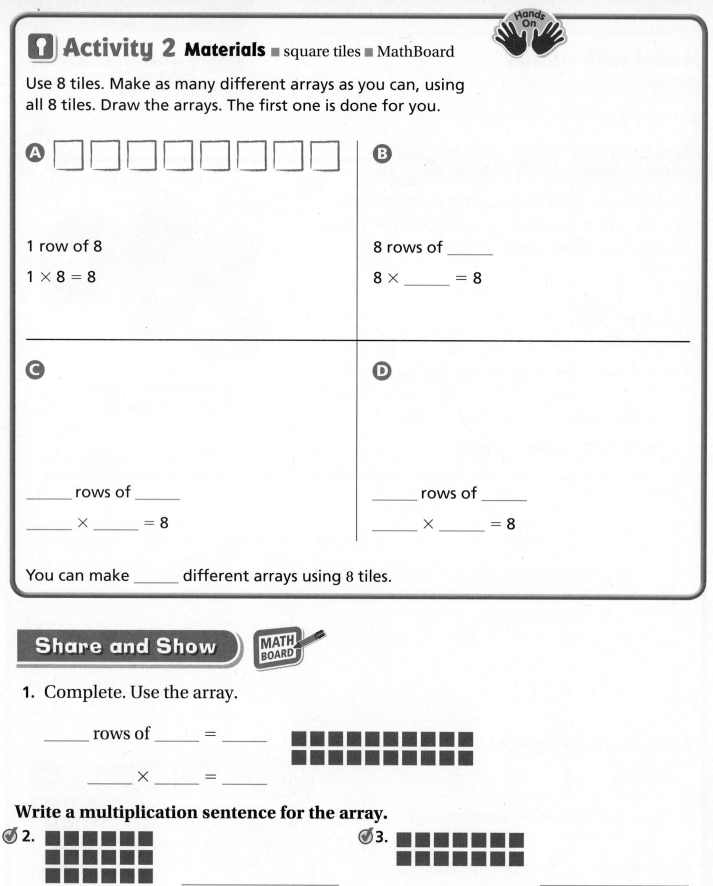

🔑 Activity 2 Materials ▪ square tiles ▪ MathBoard

Use 8 tiles. Make as many different arrays as you can, using all 8 tiles. Draw the arrays. The first one is done for you.

A

1 row of 8

$1 \times 8 = 8$

B

8 rows of _____

$8 \times$ _____ $= 8$

C

_____ rows of _____

_____ $\times$ _____ $= 8$

D

_____ rows of _____

_____ $\times$ _____ $= 8$

You can make _____ different arrays using 8 tiles.

Share and Show

MATH BOARD

1. Complete. Use the array.

_____ rows of _____ = _____

_____ $\times$ _____ = _____

Write a multiplication sentence for the array.

✓ 2.

_____

✓ 3.

_____

© Houghton Mifflin Harcourt Publishing Company

Name _____

Write a multiplication sentence for the array.

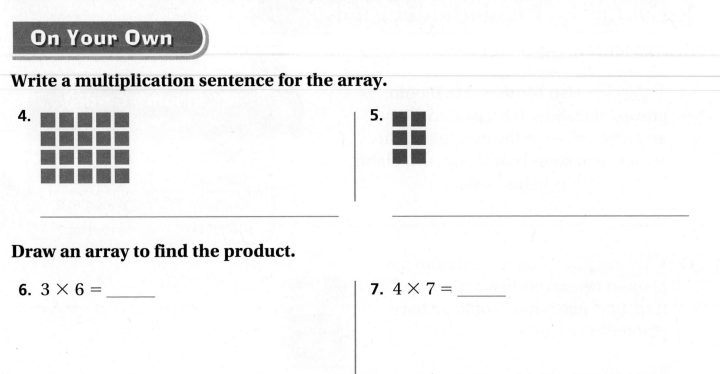

4.

_____

5.

_____

Draw an array to find the product.

6. $3 \times 6 =$ _____

7. $4 \times 7 =$ _____

8. $3 \times 5 =$ _____

9. $4 \times 4 =$ _____

10. **GO DEEPER** Use 6 tiles. Make as many different arrays as you can using all the tiles. Draw the arrays. Then write a multiplication sentence for each array.

_____

_____

© Houghton Mifflin Harcourt Publishing Company

Problem Solving • Applications  Real World

Use the table to solve 11–12.

| Mr. Bloom's Garden ||
Vegetable	**Planted In**
Beans	4 rows of 6
Carrots	2 rows of 8
Corn	5 rows of 9
Beets	4 rows of 7

11. **MATHEMATICAL PRACTICE 4 Use Models** Mr. Bloom grows vegetables in his garden. Draw an array and write the multiplication sentence to show how many corn plants Mr. Bloom has in his garden.

_____

12. **THINK SMARTER** Could Mr. Bloom have planted his carrots in equal rows of 4? If so, how many rows could he have planted? Explain.

_____

_____

_____

13. **MATHEMATICAL PRACTICE 5 Communicate** Mr. Bloom has 12 strawberry plants. Describe all of the different arrays that Mr. Bloom could make using all of his strawberry plants. The first one is done for you.

2 rows of 6; _____

_____

14. **THINK SMARTER** Elizabeth ran 3 miles each day for 5 days. How many miles did she run in all? Shade the array to represent the problem. Then solve.

_____

© Houghton Mifflin Harcourt Publishing Company

Name _____

Commutative Property of Multiplication

Essential Question How can you use the Commutative Property of Multiplication to find products?

 Operations and Algebraic Thinking—3.OA.5 *Also 3.OA.1, 3.OA.3, 3.OA.7*

MATHEMATICAL PRACTICES
MP.2, MP.4, MP.7, MP.8

🔑 Unlock the Problem (Real World)

Dave works at the Bird Store. He arranges 15 boxes of birdseed in rows on the shelf. What are two ways he can arrange the boxes in equal rows?

• Circle the number that is the product.

🔑 Activity **Make an array.**

Materials ■ square tiles ■ MathBoard

Arrange 15 tiles in 5 equal rows.
Draw a quick picture of your array.

How many tiles are in each row? _____

What multiplication sentence does your array show? _____

Suppose Dave arranges the boxes in 3 equal rows.
Draw a quick picture of your array.

How many tiles are in each row? _____

What multiplication sentence does your array show? _____

So, two ways Dave can arrange the 15 boxes are

in _____ rows of 3 or in 3 rows of _____.

Math Talk **Mathematical Practices**

Why do 5 rows of 3 and 3 rows of 5 both equal the same number?

© Houghton Mifflin Harcourt Publishing Company

Multiplication Property The **Commutative Property of Multiplication** states that when you change the order of the factors, the product stays the same. You can think of it as the Order Property of Multiplication.

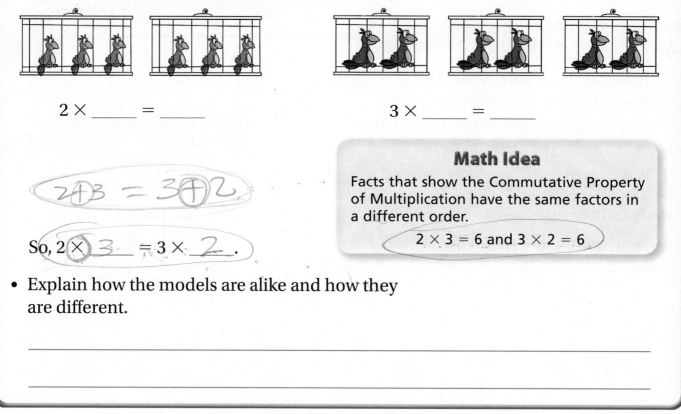

2 × _____ = _____   3 × _____ = _____

2 AB = 3 A 2

So, 2 × 3 = 3 × 2.

> **Math Idea**
>
> Facts that show the Commutative Property of Multiplication have the same factors in a different order.
>
> 2 × 3 = 6 and 3 × 2 = 6

- Explain how the models are alike and how they are different.

_____

_____

Try This! Draw a quick picture on the right that shows the Commutative Property of Multiplication. Then complete the multiplication sentences.

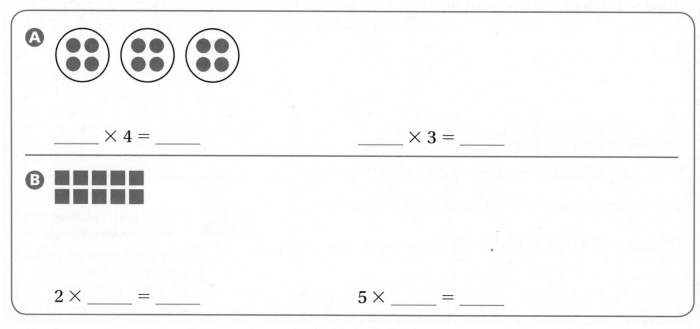

A

_____ × 4 = _____   _____ × 3 = _____

B

2 × _____ = _____   5 × _____ = _____

© Houghton Mifflin Harcourt Publishing Company

Name _____

Share and Show

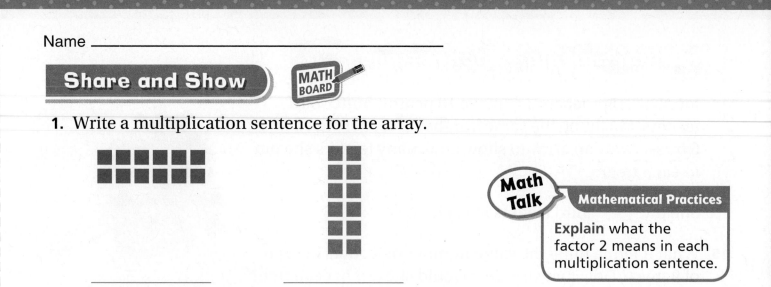

1. Write a multiplication sentence for the array.

_____   _____

Math Talk **Mathematical Practices**

Explain what the factor 2 means in each multiplication sentence.

Write a multiplication sentence for the model. Then use the Commutative Property of Multiplication to write a related multiplication sentence.

2.   ⊘**3.**   ⊘**4.**

___ × ___ = ___   ___ × ___ = ___   ___ × ___ = ___

___ × ___ = ___   ___ × ___ = ___   ___ × ___ = ___

On Your Own

Write a multiplication sentence for the model. Then use the Commutative Property of Multiplication to write a related multiplication sentence.

5.   **6.**   **7.**

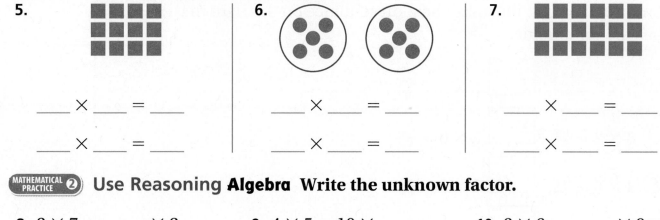

___ × ___ = ___   ___ × ___ = ___   ___ × ___ = ___

___ × ___ = ___   ___ × ___ = ___   ___ × ___ = ___

MATHEMATICAL PRACTICE ② Use Reasoning **Algebra** Write the unknown factor.

8. $3 \times 7 =$ _____ $\times 3$ **9.** $4 \times 5 = 10 \times$ _____   **10.** $3 \times 6 =$ _____ $\times 9$

11. $6 \times$ _____ $= 4 \times 9$ **12.** _____ $\times 8 = 4 \times 6$ **13.** $5 \times 8 = 8 \times$ _____

© Houghton Mifflin Harcourt Publishing Company

Problem Solving • Applications (Real World)

14. Jenna used pinecones to make 18 peanut butter bird feeders. She hung the same number of feeders in each of 6 trees. Draw an array to show how many feeders she put in each tree.

She put _____ bird feeders in each tree.

15. What if Jenna hung the same number of feeders in each of 9 trees? How many feeders would she put in each tree?

_____

16. **GO DEEPER** Write two different word problems about 12 birds to show 2 × 6 and 6 × 2. Solve each problem.

_____

_____

_____

17. **THINK SMARTER** There are 4 rows of 6 bird stickers in Don's sticker album. There are 7 rows of 5 bird stickers in Lindsey's album. How many bird stickers do they have?

_____

18. **THINK SMARTER** Write the letter for each multiplication sentence on the left next to the multiplication sentence on the right that has the same value.

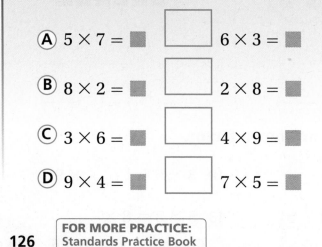

Ⓐ 5 × 7 = ▪   [ ]   6 × 3 = ▪

Ⓑ 8 × 2 = ▪   [ ]   2 × 8 = ▪

Ⓒ 3 × 6 = ▪   [ ]   4 × 9 = ▪

Ⓓ 9 × 4 = ▪   [ ]   7 × 5 = ▪

© Houghton Mifflin Harcourt Publishing Company

Name _____

Multiply with 1 and 0

Essential Question What happens when you multiply a number by 0 or 1?

Operations and Algebraic Thinking—
3.OA.5 Also 3.OA.1,
3.OA.3, 3.OA.7
MATHEMATICAL PRACTICES
MP.2, MP.3, MP.7, MP.8

Unlock the Problem Real World

Luke sees 4 birdbaths. Each birdbath has 2 birds in it. What multiplication sentence tells how many birds there are?

🔒 **Draw a quick picture to show the birds in the birdbaths.**

- How many birdbaths are there?

  _____

- How many birds does Luke see in

  each birdbath? _____

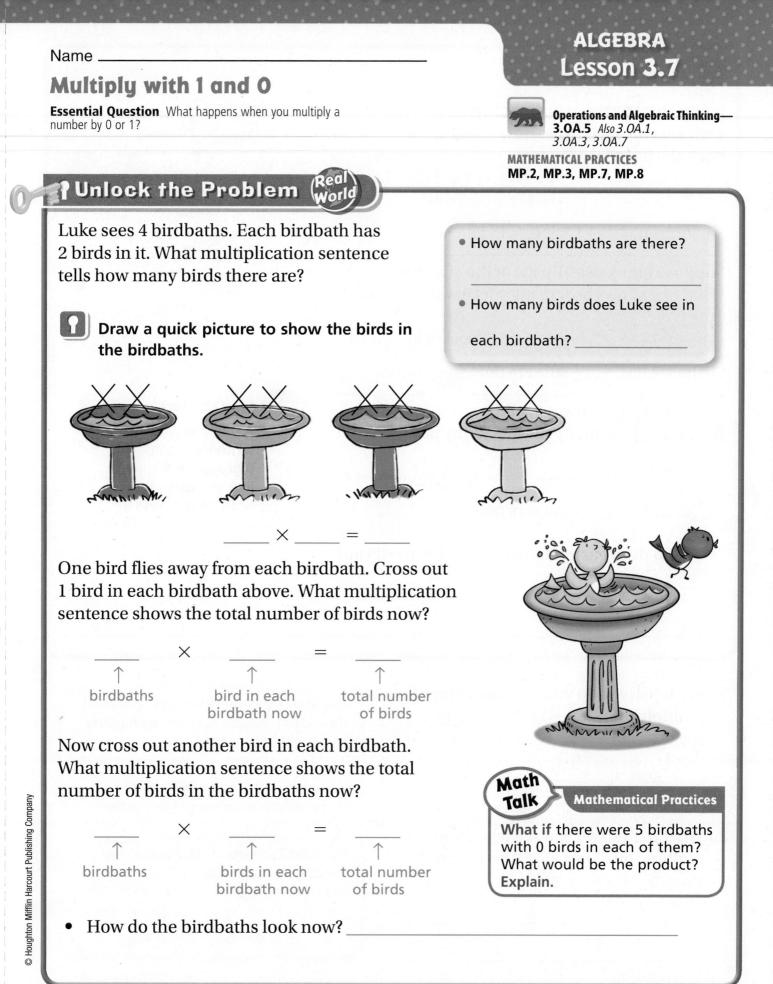

_____ × _____ = _____

One bird flies away from each birdbath. Cross out 1 bird in each birdbath above. What multiplication sentence shows the total number of birds now?

_____ × _____ = _____
   ↑   ↑   ↑
birdbaths   bird in each   total number
            birdbath now   of birds

Now cross out another bird in each birdbath. What multiplication sentence shows the total number of birds in the birdbaths now?

_____ × _____ = _____
   ↑   ↑   ↑
birdbaths   birds in each   total number
            birdbath now   of birds

- How do the birdbaths look now? _____

Math Talk **Mathematical Practices**

What if there were 5 birdbaths with 0 birds in each of them? What would be the product? Explain.

© Houghton Mifflin Harcourt Publishing Company

🔑 Example

Jenny has 2 pages of bird stickers. There are 4 stickers on each page. How many stickers does she have in all?

$2 \times 4 = $ _____   **Think:** 2 groups of 4

So, Jenny has _____ stickers in all.

Suppose Jenny uses 1 page of the stickers. What fact shows how many stickers she has now?

_____ $\times$ _____ $=$ _____   **Think:** 1 group of 4

So, Jenny has _____ stickers now.

Then, Jenny uses the rest of the stickers. What fact shows how many stickers Jenny has now?

_____ $\times$ _____ $=$ _____   **Think:** 0 groups of 4

So, Jenny has _____ stickers now.

⚠️ **ERROR Alert**

A 0 in a multiplication sentence means 0 groups or 0 things in a group, so the product is always 0.

- What does each number in $0 \times 4 = 0$ tell you?

_____

_____

---

1. What pattern do you see when you multiply numbers with 1 as a factor?

   Think: $1 \times 2 = 2$ $1 \times 3 = 3$ $1 \times 4 = 4$

   _____

   _____

The **Identity Property of Multiplication** states that the product of any number and 1 is that number.

$$7 \times 1 = 7 \qquad 6 \times 1 = 6$$
$$1 \times 7 = 7 \qquad 1 \times 6 = 6$$

2. What pattern do you see when you multiply numbers with 0 as a factor?

   Think: $0 \times 1 = 0$ $0 \times 2 = 0$ $0 \times 5 = 0$

   _____

   _____

The **Zero Property of Multiplication** states that the product of zero and any number is zero.

$$0 \times 5 = 0 \qquad 0 \times 8 = 0$$
$$5 \times 0 = 0 \qquad 8 \times 0 = 0$$

© Houghton Mifflin Harcourt Publishing Company

Name _____

1. What multiplication sentence matches this picture? Find the product.

_____

Find the product.

2. $5 \times 1 =$ ____

3. $0 \times 2 =$ ____

✅ **4.** $4 \times 0 =$ ____

✅ **5.** $1 \times 6 =$ ____

6. $3 \times 0 =$ ____

7. $1 \times 2 =$ ____

8. $0 \times 6 =$ ____

9. $8 \times 1 =$ ____

Math Talk **Mathematical Practices**

Explain how 3×1 and $3 + 1$ are different.

On Your Own

Find the product.

10. $3 \times 1 =$ ____

11. $8 \times 0 =$ ____

12. $1 \times 9 =$ ____

13. $0 \times 7 =$ ____

14. $0 \times 4 =$ ____

15. $10 \times 1 =$ ____

16. $1 \times 3 =$ ____

17. $6 \times 1 =$ ____

18. $1 \times 0 =$ ____

19. $1 \times 7 =$ ____

20. $6 \times 0 =$ ____

21. $1 \times 4 =$ ____

MATHEMATICAL PRACTICE 2 **Use Reasoning Algebra** Complete the multiplication sentence.

22. ____ $\times 1 = 15$

23. $1 \times 28 =$ ____

24. $0 \times 46 =$ ____

25. $36 \times 0 =$ ____

26. ____ $\times 5 = 5$

27. $19 \times$ ____ $= 0$

28. ____ $\times 0 = 0$

29. $7 \times$ ____ $= 7$

30. **GO DEEPER** Each box holds 6 black markers and 4 red markers. Derek has 0 boxes of markers. Write a number sentence that shows how many markers Derek has. Explain how you found your answer.

_____

_____

© Houghton Mifflin Harcourt Publishing Company

Problem Solving • Applications

Use the table for 31–33.

Circus Vehicles	
Type of Vehicle	Number of Wheels
Car	4
Tricycle	3
Bicycle	2
Unicycle	1

31. At the circus Jon saw 5 unicycles. How many wheels are on the 5 unicycles? Write a multiplication sentence.

   _____ × _____ = _____

32. **What's the Question?** Julia used multiplication with 1 and the information in the table. The answer is 3.

   _____

   _____

33. THINK SMARTER Brian saw some circus vehicles. He saw 17 wheels in all. If 2 of the vehicles are cars, how many vehicles are bicycles and tricycles?

   _____

34. WRITE ▸Math Write a word problem that uses multiplying with 1 or 0. Show how to solve your problem.

   _____

   _____

35. THINK SMARTER For numbers 35a–35d, select True or False for each multiplication sentence.

   35a. $6 \times 0 = 0$ ○ True   ○ False

   35b. $0 \times 9 = 9 \times 0$ ○ True   ○ False

   35c. $1 \times 0 = 1$ ○ True   ○ False

   35d. $3 \times 1 = 3$ ○ True   ○ False

© Houghton Mifflin Harcourt Publishing Company

FOR MORE PRACTICE:
Standards Practice Book

Chapter 3 Review/Test

1. There are 3 boats on the lake. Six people ride in each boat. How many people ride in the boats? Draw equal groups to model the problem and explain how to solve it.

_____ people

2. Nadia has 4 sheets of stickers. There are 8 stickers on each sheet. She wrote this number sentence to represent the total number of stickers.

$$4 \times 8 = 32$$

What is a related number sentence that also represents the total number of stickers she has?

Ⓐ $8 + 4 = \blacksquare$

Ⓑ $4 + 4 + 4 + 4 = \blacksquare$

Ⓒ $8 \times 8 = \blacksquare$

Ⓓ $8 \times 4 = \blacksquare$

3. Lindsay went hiking for two days in Yellowstone National Park. The first jump on the number line shows how many birds she saw the first day. She saw the same number of birds the next day.

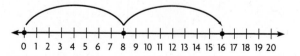

Write the multiplication sentence that is shown on the number line.

_____ × _____ = _____

© Houghton Mifflin Harcourt Publishing Company

 Assessment Options
Chapter Test

4. Paco drew an array to show the number of desks in his classroom.

Write a multiplication sentence for the array.

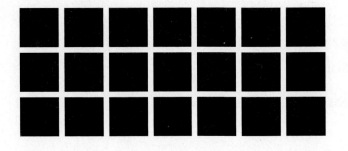

---

5. Alondra makes 4 necklaces. She uses 5 beads on each necklace.

For numbers 5a–5d, choose Yes or No to tell if the number sentence could be used to find the number of beads Alondra uses.

5a. $4 \times 5 = \blacksquare$ ○ Yes   ○ No

5b. $4 + 4 + 4 + 4 = \blacksquare$ ○ Yes   ○ No

5c. $5 + 5 + 5 + 5 = \blacksquare$ ○ Yes   ○ No

5d. $5 + 4 = \blacksquare$ ○ Yes   ○ No

6. John sold 3 baskets of apples at the market. Each basket contained 9 apples. How many apples did John sell? Make a bar model to solve the problem.

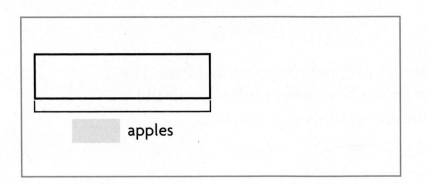

apples

© Houghton Mifflin Harcourt Publishing Company

7. Select the number sentences that show the Commutative Property of Multiplication. Mark all that apply.

    Ⓐ $3 \times 2 = 2 \times 3$

    Ⓑ $4 \times 9 = 4 \times 9$

    Ⓒ $5 \times 0 = 0$

    Ⓓ $6 \times 1 = 1 \times 6$

    Ⓔ $7 \times 2 = 14 \times 1$

8. A waiter carried 6 baskets with 5 dinner rolls in each basket. How many dinner rolls did he carry? Show your work.

_____ dinner rolls

9. Sonya needs 3 equal lengths of wire to make 3 bracelets. The jump on the number line shows the length of one wire in inches. How many inches of wire will Sonya need to make the 3 bracelets?

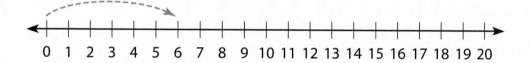

_____ inches

10. Josh has 4 dogs. Each dog gets 2 dog biscuits every day. How many biscuits will Josh need for all of his dogs for Saturday and Sunday?

_____ biscuits

© Houghton Mifflin Harcourt Publishing Company

11. Jorge displayed 28 cans of paint on a shelf in his store.

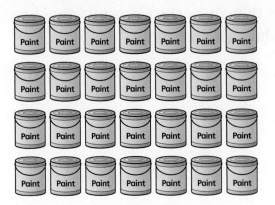

Select other ways Jorge could arrange the same number of cans. Mark all that apply.

Ⓐ   2 rows of 14   Ⓓ   8 rows of 3

Ⓑ   1 row of 28   Ⓔ   7 rows of 4

Ⓒ   6 rows of 5

12. Choose the number that makes the statement true.

The product of any number and $\boxed{\begin{array}{c} 0 \\ 1 \\ 10 \end{array}}$ is zero.

13. James made this array to show that $3 \times 5 = 15$.

Part A

James says that $5 \times 3 = 15$. Is James correct? Draw an array to explain your answer.

_____

Part B

Which number property supports your answer?

_____

_____

© Houghton Mifflin Harcourt Publishing Company

14. Julio has a collection of coins. He puts the coins in 2 equal groups. There are 6 coins in each group. How many coins does Julio have? Use the number line to show your work.

```
←+—+—+—+—+—+—+—+—+—+—+—+—+—+—+—+→
  0  1  2  3  4  5  6  7  8  9 10 11 12 13 14 15
```

_____ coins

15. Landon collects trading cards.

Part A

Yesterday, Landon sorted his trading cards into 4 groups. Each group had 7 cards. Draw a bar model to show Landon's cards. How many cards does he have?

Part B   _____ trading cards

Landon buys 3 more packs of trading cards today. Each pack has 8 cards. Write a multiplication sentence to show how many cards Landon buys today. Then find how many cards Landon has now. Show your work.

_____

16. A unicycle has only 1 wheel. Write a multiplication sentence to show how many wheels there are on 9 unicycles.

_____ × _____ = _____

17. Carlos spent 5 minutes working on each of 8 math problems. He can use 8×5 to find the total amount of time he spent on the problems.

For numbers 17a–17d, choose Yes or No to show which are equal to 8×5.

17a. $8 + 5$ ○ Yes   ○ No

17b. $5 + 5 + 5 + 5 + 5$ ○ Yes   ○ No

17c. $8 + 8 + 8 + 8 + 8$ ○ Yes   ○ No

17d. $5 + 5 + 5 + 5 + 5 + 5 + 5 + 5$ ○ Yes   ○ No

© Houghton Mifflin Harcourt Publishing Company

18. Lucy and her mother made tacos. They put 2 tacos on each of 7 plates.

Select the number sentences that show all the tacos Lucy and her mother made. Mark all that apply.

(A) $2 + 2 + 2 + 2 + 2 + 2 + 2 = 14$

(B) $2 + 7 = 9$

(C) $7 + 7 = 14$

(D) $8 + 6 = 14$

(E) $2 \times 7 = 14$

19. Jayson is making 5 sock puppets. He glues 2 buttons on each puppet for its eyes. He glues 1 pompom on each puppet for its nose.

Part A

Write the total number of buttons and pompoms he uses. Write a multiplication sentence for each.

Eyes   **Noses**

_____ buttons   _____ pompoms

_____ × _____ = _____   _____ × _____ = _____

Part B

After making 5 puppets, Jayson has 4 buttons and 3 pompoms left. What is the greatest number of puppets he can make with those items if he wants all his puppets to look the same? Draw models and use them to explain.

At most, he can make _____ more puppets.

_____

_____

_____

© Houghton Mifflin Harcourt Publishing Company

Chapter 4

Multiplication Facts and Strategies

Show What You Know ✓

Check your understanding of important skills.

Name _____

▶ **Doubles and Doubles Plus One** Write the doubles and doubles plus one facts.

1.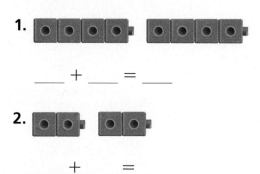

___ + ___ = ___   ___ + ___ = ___

2. ___ + ___ = ___   ___ + ___ = ___

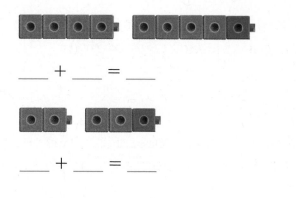

▶ **Equal Groups** Complete.

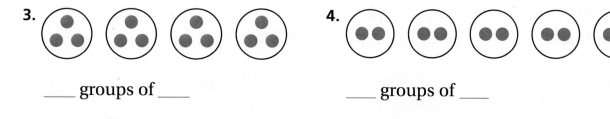

3. ____ groups of ____

____ in all

4. ____ groups of ____

____ in all

Math Detective

Stephen needs to use these clues to find a buried time capsule.
• Start with a number that is the product of 3 and 4.
• Double the product and go to that number.
• Add 2 tens and find the number that is 1 less than the sum.
Be a Math Detective to help Stephen find the time capsule.

14	12	22
24	33	15
21	43	32

© Houghton Mifflin Harcourt Publishing Company

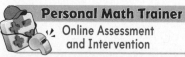

Personal Math Trainer
Online Assessment
and Intervention

Vocabulary Builder

▶ **Visualize It** ••••••••••••••••••••••••••••••••

Complete the tree map by using the words with a ✓.

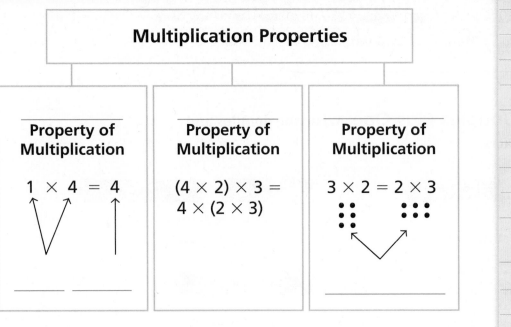

Multiplication Properties

_____ Property of Multiplication	_____ Property of Multiplication	_____ Property of Multiplication
$1 \times 4 = 4$	$(4 \times 2) \times 3 = 4 \times (2 \times 3)$	$3 \times 2 = 2 \times 3$

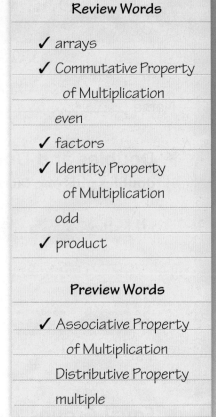

Review Words

✓ arrays

✓ Commutative Property
   of Multiplication

even

✓ factors

✓ Identity Property
   of Multiplication

odd

✓ product

Preview Words

✓ Associative Property
   of Multiplication

Distributive Property

multiple

▶ **Understand Vocabulary** •••••••••••••••••••••••••••

Complete the sentences by using the preview words.

1. The _____ Property of Multiplication states that when the grouping of factors is changed, the product is the same.

2. A _____ of 5 is any product that has 5 as one of its factors.

3. The _____ Property states that multiplying a sum by a number is the same as multiplying each addend by the number and then adding the products.

   Example: $2 \times 8 = 2 \times (4 + 4)$
   $2 \times 8 = (2 \times 4) + (2 \times 4)$
   $2 \times 8 = 8 + 8$
   $2 \times 8 = 16$

© Houghton Mifflin Harcourt Publishing Company

GO DIGITAL • Interactive Student Edition
• Multimedia eGlossary

Multiply with 2 and 4

Essential Question How can you multiply with 2 and 4?

Operations and Algebraic Thinking—3.OA.3
Also 3.OA.1, 3.OA.7

MATHEMATICAL PRACTICES
MP.1, MP.4, MP.5, MP.7

Unlock the Problem (Real World)

Hands On

Two students are in a play. Each of the students has 3 costumes. How many costumes do they have in all?

Multiplying when there are two equal groups is like adding doubles.

- What does the word "each" tell you?

  _____

- How can you find the number of costumes the 2 students have?

  _____

 Find 2 × 3.

MODEL	THINK	RECORD
Draw counters to show the costumes.	2 groups of 3 3 + 3 6	2 × 3 = 6 ↑ ↑ ↑ how many groups how many in each group how many in all

So, the 2 students have ____ costumes in all.

Try This!

$2 \times 1 = 1 + 1 = 2$

$2 \times 2 = 2 + 2 = 4$

$2 \times \underline{} = 3 + \underline{} = 6$

$2 \times \underline{} = 4 + \underline{} = 8$

$2 \times \underline{} = 5 + \underline{} = \underline{}$

$2 \times \underline{} = 6 + \underline{} = \underline{}$

$2 \times \underline{} = 7 + \underline{} = \underline{}$

$2 \times \underline{} = 8 + \underline{} = \underline{}$

$2 \times \underline{} = 9 + \underline{} = \underline{}$

Math Talk **Mathematical Practices**

What do you notice about the product when you multiply by 2?

© Houghton Mifflin Harcourt Publishing Company

⚡ Count by 2s.

When there are 2 in each group, you can count by 2s to find how many there are in all.

There are 4 students with 2 costumes each. How many costumes do they have in all?

Skip count by drawing the jumps on the number line.

0 1 2 3 4 5 6 7 8 9 10

So, the 4 students have _____ in all.

- How can you decide whether to count by 2s or double?

_____

⚡ **Example** Use doubles to find 4 × 5.

When you multiply with 4, you can multiply with 2 and then double the product.

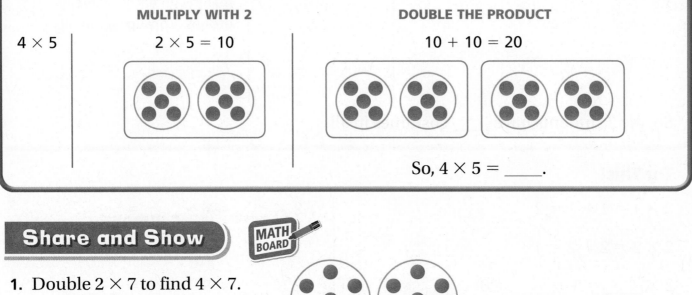

MULTIPLY WITH 2

4 × 5 | 2 × 5 = 10

DOUBLE THE PRODUCT

10 + 10 = 20

So, 4 × 5 = ____.

Share and Show MATH BOARD

1. Double 2 × 7 to find 4 × 7.

   Multiply with 2. 2 × 7 = ____

   Double the product. 14 + 14 = ____

   So, 4 × 7 = ____.

Math Talk **Mathematical Practices**

Explain how knowing the product for 2 × 8 helps you find the product for 4 × 8.

© Houghton Mifflin Harcourt Publishing Company

Name _____

Write a multiplication sentence for the model.

2.

____ × ____ = ____

☑**3.**

____ × ____ = ____

Find the product.

4. 6
    ×2

5. 9
    ×4

6. 2
    ×7

7. 8
    ×4

☑**8.** 5
    ×2

Find the product. Use your MathBoard.

9. 10
    × 4

10. 2
    ×9

11. 4
    ×6

12. 7
    ×2

13. 2
    ×0

14. 4
    ×3

15. 2
    ×8

16. 4
    ×4

17. 10
    × 2

18. 4
    ×5

MATHEMATICAL PRACTICE ⑦ **Look for Structure** **Algebra** Complete the table for the factors 2 and 4.

	×	1	2	3	4	5	6	7	8	9	10
19.	2										
20.	4										

MATHEMATICAL PRACTICE ② **Reason Quantitatively** **Algebra** Write the unknown number.

21. $4 \times 8 = 16 +$ ____

22. $20 = 2 \times$ ____

23. $8 \times 2 = 10 +$ ____

24. 𝕋ℍ𝕀ℕ𝕂 SMARTER Lindsey, Louis, Sally, and Matt each brought 5 guests to the school play. How many guests were at the school play? Explain.

_____

© Houghton Mifflin Harcourt Publishing Company

Unlock the Problem (Real World)

25. **GO DEEPER** Ms. Peterson's class sold tickets for the class play. How many tickets in all did Brandon and Haylie sell?

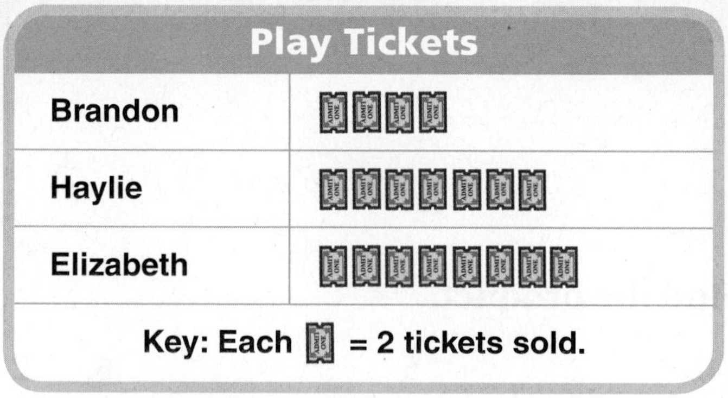

Play Tickets	
Brandon	🎟🎟🎟🎟
Haylie	🎟🎟🎟🎟🎟🎟
Elizabeth	🎟🎟🎟🎟🎟🎟🎟

Key: Each 🎟 = 2 tickets sold.

a. What do you need to find?

_____

_____

b. Why should you multiply to find the number of tickets shown? Explain.

_____

_____

c. Show the steps you used to solve the problem.

d. Complete the sentences.

Brandon sold _____ tickets. Haylie sold

_____ tickets. So, Brandon and Haylie

sold _____ tickets.

26. **MATHEMATICAL PRACTICE ❶** **Analyze** Suppose Sam sold 20 tickets to the school play. How many tickets should be on the picture graph above to show his sales? Explain.

_____

_____

27. **THINK SMARTER** Alex exchanges some dollar bills for quarters at the bank. He receives 4 quarters for each dollar bill. Select the numbers of quarters that Alex could receive. Mark all that apply.

Ⓐ 16   Ⓓ 32

Ⓑ 18   Ⓔ 50

Ⓒ 24

© Houghton Mifflin Harcourt Publishing Company

FOR MORE PRACTICE:
Standards Practice Book

Name _____

Multiply with 5 and 10

Essential Question How can you multiply with 5 and 10?

Operations and Algebraic Thinking—3.OA.3
Also 3.OA.1, 3.OA.7
MATHEMATICAL PRACTICES
MP.1, MP.4, MP.7

Unlock the Problem

Marcel is making 6 toy banjos. He needs 5 strings for each banjo. How many strings does he need in all?

Use skip counting.

Skip count by 5s until you say 6 numbers.

5, _____, _____, _____, _____, _____

6 × 5 = _____

So, Marcel needs _____ strings in all.

- How many banjos is Marcel making? _____
- How many strings does each banjo have? _____

Example 1 Use a number line.

Each string is 10 inches long. How many inches of string will Marcel use for each banjo?

Think: 1 jump = 10 inches

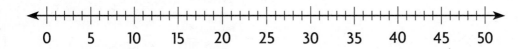

| 0 | 5 | 10 | 15 | 20 | 25 | 30 | 35 | 40 | 45 | 50 |

- Draw 5 jumps for the 5 strings. Jump 10 spaces at a time for the length of each string.

- You land on 10, _____, _____, _____, and _____.   5 × 10 = _____

The numbers 10, 20, 30, 40, and 50 are multiples of 10.

So, Marcel will use _____ inches of string for each banjo.

A **multiple** of 10 is any product that has 10 as one of its factors.

Math Talk Mathematical Practices

What do you notice about the multiples of 10?

Example 2 Use a bar model.

Marcel bought 3 packages of strings.
Each package cost 10¢. How much did
the packages cost in all?

MODEL	THINK	RECORD
	1 unit → 10¢	
10¢ | 10¢ | 10¢	3 units → _____ × _____	_____ × _____ = _____

So, the packages of strings cost _____ in all.

Share and Show

MATH BOARD

1. How can you use this number line to find 8×5?

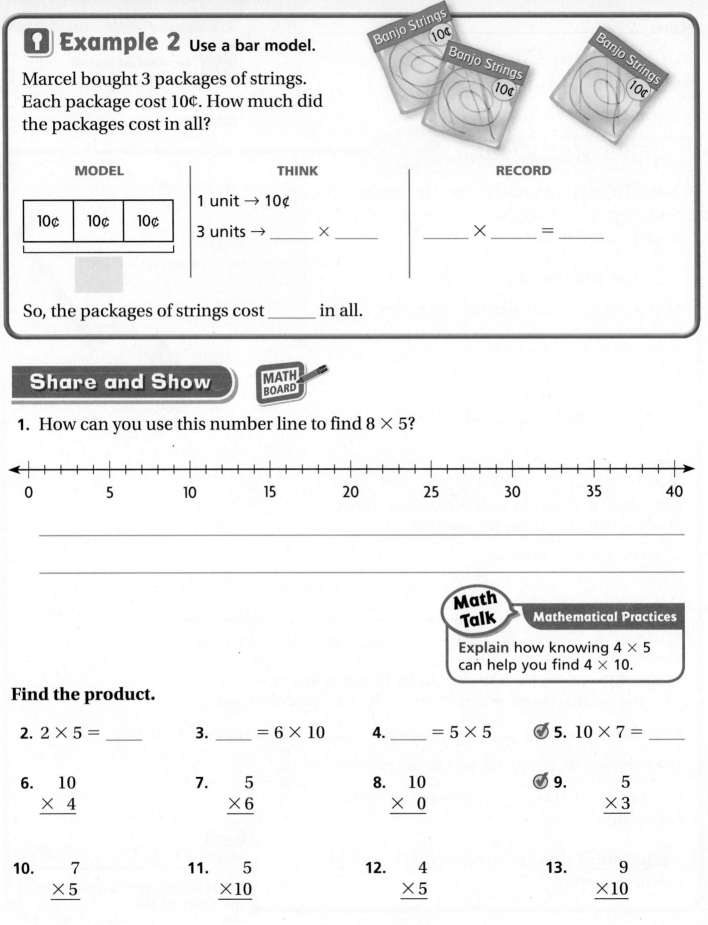

_____

_____

Math Talk **Mathematical Practices**

Explain how knowing 4×5 can help you find 4×10.

Find the product.

2. $2 \times 5 =$ _____

3. _____ $= 6 \times 10$

4. _____ $= 5 \times 5$

5. $10 \times 7 =$ _____

6. $\begin{array}{r} 10 \\ \times\ 4 \\ \hline \end{array}$

7. $\begin{array}{r} 5 \\ \times 6 \\ \hline \end{array}$

8. $\begin{array}{r} 10 \\ \times\ 0 \\ \hline \end{array}$

9. $\begin{array}{r} 5 \\ \times 3 \\ \hline \end{array}$

10. $\begin{array}{r} 7 \\ \times 5 \\ \hline \end{array}$

11. $\begin{array}{r} 5 \\ \times 10 \\ \hline \end{array}$

12. $\begin{array}{r} 4 \\ \times 5 \\ \hline \end{array}$

13. $\begin{array}{r} 9 \\ \times 10 \\ \hline \end{array}$

© Houghton Mifflin Harcourt Publishing Company

Name _____

On Your Own

Find the product.

14. $5 \times 1 =$ _____

15. _____ $= 10 \times 2$

16. _____ $= 4 \times 5$

17. $10 \times 10 =$ _____

18. $10 \times 0 =$ _____

19. $10 \times 5 =$ _____

20. _____ $= 1 \times 5$

21. _____ $= 5 \times 9$

22. $\begin{array}{r} 3 \\ \times 4 \\ \hline \end{array}$

23. $\begin{array}{r} 5 \\ \times 0 \\ \hline \end{array}$

24. $\begin{array}{r} 4 \\ \times 8 \\ \hline \end{array}$

25. $\begin{array}{r} 10 \\ \times 5 \\ \hline \end{array}$

26. $\begin{array}{r} 10 \\ \times 9 \\ \hline \end{array}$

27. $\begin{array}{r} 10 \\ \times 1 \\ \hline \end{array}$

28. $\begin{array}{r} 10 \\ \times 8 \\ \hline \end{array}$

29. $\begin{array}{r} 9 \\ \times 2 \\ \hline \end{array}$

30. $\begin{array}{r} 4 \\ \times 10 \\ \hline \end{array}$

31. $\begin{array}{r} 5 \\ \times 9 \\ \hline \end{array}$

32. $\begin{array}{r} 5 \\ \times 0 \\ \hline \end{array}$

33. $\begin{array}{r} 5 \\ \times 7 \\ \hline \end{array}$

MATHEMATICAL PRACTICE ⑦ Identify Relationships Algebra Use the pictures to find the unknown numbers.

34.

$3 \times$ _____ $=$ _____

35.

_____ $\times 3 =$ _____

MATHEMATICAL PRACTICE ④ Use a Diagram Complete the bar model to solve.

36. Marcel played 5 songs on the banjo. If each song lasted 8 minutes, how long did he play?

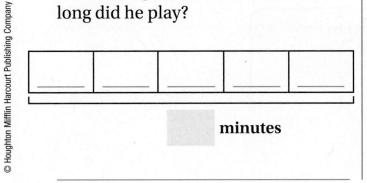

_____ minutes

37. There are 6 banjo players. If each player needs 10 sheets of music, how many sheets of music are needed?

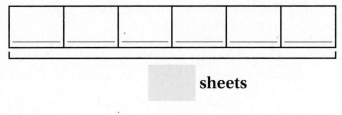

_____ sheets

© Houghton Mifflin Harcourt Publishing Company

Problem Solving • Applications Real World

Use the table for 38–40.

Stringed Instruments	
Instrument	Strings
Guitar	6
Banjo	5
Mandolin	8
Violin	4

38. John and his dad own 7 banjos. They want to replace the strings on all of them. How many strings should they buy? Write a multiplication sentence to solve.

_____

39. **GO DEEPER** Mr. Lemke has 5 guitars, 4 banjos, and 2 mandolins. What is the total number of strings on Mr. Lemke's instruments?

_____

40. **THINK SMARTER** The orchestra has 5 violins and 3 guitars that need new strings. What is the total number of strings that need to be replaced? Explain.

_____

_____

_____

41. **WRITE** ▸*Math* **What's the Error?** Mr. James has 3 banjos. Mr. Lewis has 5 times the number of banjos Mr. James has. Riley says Mr. Lewis has 12 banjos. Describe her error.

_____

_____

42. **THINK SMARTER** Circle the number that makes the multiplication sentence true.

$$5 \times \begin{array}{|c|} \hline 7 \\ \hline 8 \\ \hline 9 \\ \hline \end{array} = 45$$

© Houghton Mifflin Harcourt Publishing Company

Name _____

Multiply with 3 and 6

Essential Question What are some ways to multiply with 3 and 6?

Operations and Algebraic Thinking—3.OA.3 *Also 3.OA.1, 3.OA.7, 3.OA.9*

MATHEMATICAL PRACTICES
MP.1, MP.4, MP.6, MP.7

Unlock the Problem Real World

Sabrina is making triangles with toothpicks. She uses 3 toothpicks for each triangle. She makes 4 triangles. How many toothpicks does Sabrina use?

- Why does Sabrina need 3 toothpicks for each triangle?

_____

_____

Draw a picture. Hands On

STEP 1

Complete the 4 triangles.

STEP 2

Skip count by the number of sides. _____, _____, _____, _____

How many triangles are there in all? _____

How many toothpicks are in each triangle? _____

How many toothpicks are there in all?

4 × _____ = _____

4 triangles have _____ toothpicks.

So, Sabrina uses _____ toothpicks.

Math Talk **Mathematical Practices**

How can you use what you know about the number of toothpicks needed for 4 triangles to find the number of toothpicks needed for 8 triangles? **Explain.**

Try This! **Find the number of toothpicks needed for 6 triangles.**

Draw a quick picture to help you. How did you find the answer?

_____

_____

_____

© Houghton Mifflin Harcourt Publishing Company

Jessica is using craft sticks to make 6 octagons.
How many craft sticks will she use?

One Way Use 5s facts and addition.

▲ An octagon has 8 sides.

To multiply a factor by 6, multiply the factor
by 5, and then add the factor.

$6 \times 7 = 5 \times 7 + 7 = 42$

$6 \times 6 = 5 \times 6 +$ _____ $=$ _____

$6 \times 8 = 5 \times$ _____ $+$ _____ $=$ _____

$6 \times 9 =$ _____ $\times$ _____ $+$ _____ $=$ _____

So, Jessica will use _____ craft sticks.

5×8

$+ 8$

Other Ways

A Use doubles.

When at least one factor is an even number,
you can use doubles.

$6 \times 8 = \blacksquare$

First multiply with half of an even number.

$3 \times 8 =$ _____

After you multiply, double the product.

_____ $+ 24 =$ _____

$6 \times 8 =$ _____

B Use a multiplication table.

Hands
On

Find the product 6×8 where
row 6 and column 8 meet.

$6 \times 8 =$ _____

• Shade the row for 3 in the table. Then,
compare the rows for 3 and 6. What do
you notice about their products?

_____

_____

×	0	1	2	3	4	5	6	7	8	9	10
0	0	0	0	0	0	0	0	0	0	0	0
1	0	1	2	3	4	5	6	7	8	9	10
2	0	2	4	6	8	10	12	14	16	18	20
3	0	3	6	9	12	15	18	21	24	27	30
4	0	4	8	12	16	20	24	28	32	36	40
5	0	5	10	15	20	25	30	35	40	45	50
6	0	6	12	18	24	30	36	42	48	54	60
7	0	7	14	21	28	35	42	49	56	63	70
8	0	8	16	24	32	40	48	56	64	72	80
9	0	9	18	27	36	45	54	63	72	81	90
10	0	10	20	30	40	50	60	70	80	90	100

© Houghton Mifflin Harcourt Publishing Company

Name _____

Share and Show

1. Use 5s facts and addition to find $6 \times 4 = $ ▪ .

$6 \times 4 = $ _____ $\times$ _____ $+$ _____ $=$ _____

$6 \times 4 = $ _____

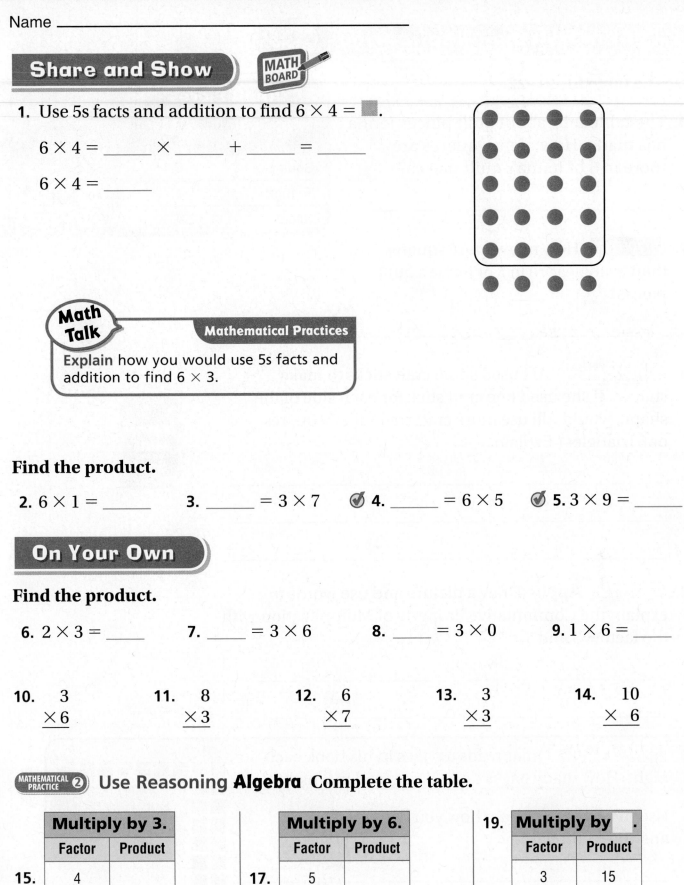

Math Talk **Mathematical Practices**

Explain how you would use 5s facts and addition to find 6×3.

Find the product.

2. $6 \times 1 = $ _____   **3.** _____ $= 3 \times 7$ ✓ **4.** _____ $= 6 \times 5$ ✓ **5.** $3 \times 9 = $ _____

On Your Own

Find the product.

6. $2 \times 3 = $ _____   **7.** _____ $= 3 \times 6$ **8.** _____ $= 3 \times 0$ **9.** $1 \times 6 = $ _____

10. $\begin{array}{r} 3 \\ \times 6 \\ \hline \end{array}$ **11.** $\begin{array}{r} 8 \\ \times 3 \\ \hline \end{array}$ **12.** $\begin{array}{r} 6 \\ \times 7 \\ \hline \end{array}$ **13.** $\begin{array}{r} 3 \\ \times 3 \\ \hline \end{array}$ **14.** $\begin{array}{r} 10 \\ \times \ 6 \\ \hline \end{array}$

MATHEMATICAL PRACTICE ② **Use Reasoning Algebra** Complete the table.

Multiply by 3.	
Factor	Product
15. 4	
16.	18

Multiply by 6.	
Factor	Product
17. 5	
18. 7	

19. Multiply by ▢.	
Factor	Product
3	15
20. 2	

© Houghton Mifflin Harcourt Publishing Company

Problem Solving • Applications Real World

Use the table for 21–22.

Quilt Pieces	
Shape	**Number in One Quilt Piece**
Square	6
Triangle	4
Circle	4

21. The table tells about quilt pieces Jenna has made. How many squares are there in 6 of Jenna's quilt pieces?

_____

22. **GO DEEPER** How many more squares than triangles are in 3 of Jenna's quilt pieces?

_____

23. **THINK SMARTER** Alli used some craft sticks to make shapes. If she used one craft stick for each side of the shape, would Alli use more craft sticks for 5 squares or 6 triangles? Explain.

_____

_____

_____

24. **MATHEMATICAL PRACTICE ③** **Apply** Draw a picture and use words to explain the Commutative Property of Multiplication with the factors 3 and 4.

_____

_____

25. **THINK SMARTER** Omar reads 6 pages in his book each night. How many pages does Omar read in 7 nights?

Use the array to explain how you know your answer is correct.

_____

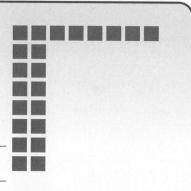

FOR MORE PRACTICE:
Standards Practice Book

© Houghton Mifflin Harcourt Publishing Company • Image Credits: ©Index Stock/Alamy Images

Distributive Property

Essential Question How can you use the Distributive Property to find products?

Operations and Algebraic Thinking—3.OA.5 *Also 3.OA.1, 3.OA.3, 3.OA.4, 3.OA.7*

MATHEMATICAL PRACTICES
MP.4, MP.7, MP.8

Unlock the Problem Real World

Mark bought 6 new fish for his aquarium. He paid $7 for each fish. How much money did he spend in all?

Find 6 × $7.

You can use the Distributive Property to solve the problem.

The **Distributive Property** states that multiplying a sum by a number is the same as multiplying each addend by the number and then adding the products.

- Describe the groups in this problem.

  _____

- Circle the numbers you will use to solve the problem.

Remember

sum—the answer to an addition problem

addends—the numbers being added

Activity Materials ■ square tiles

Make an array with tiles to show 6 rows of 7.

6 × 7 = ■

Break apart the array to make two smaller arrays for facts you know.

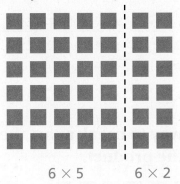

6 × 5   6 × 2

6 × 7 = ■
6 × 7 = 6 × (5 + 2)   **Think:** 7 = 5 + 2
6 × 7 = (6 × 5) + (6 × 2)   Multiply each addend by 6.

6 × 7 = _____ + _____   Add the products.

6 × 7 = _____

So, Mark spent $_____ for his new fish.

Math Talk Mathematical Practices

What other ways could you break apart the 6 × 7 array?

© Houghton Mifflin Harcourt Publishing Company

Try This!

Suppose Mark bought 9 fish for $6 each.

You can break apart a 9 × 6 array into two smaller arrays for facts you know. One way is to think of 9 as 5 + 4. Draw a line to show this way. Then find the product.

9 × 6 = (_____ × _____) + (_____ × _____)

9 × 6 = _____ + _____

So, Mark spent $_____ for 9 fish.

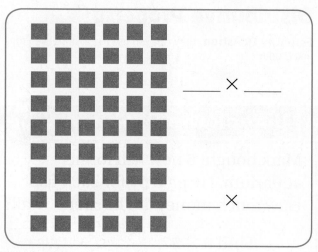

_____ × _____

_____ × _____

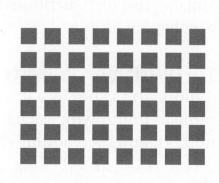

Share and Show MATH BOARD Hands On

1. Draw a line to show how you could break apart this 6 × 8 array into two smaller arrays for facts you know.

- What numbers do you multiply? _____ and _____

  _____ and _____

- What numbers do you add? _____ + _____

6 × 8 = 6 × (_____ + _____)

6 × 8 = (_____ × _____) + (_____ × _____)

6 × 8 = _____ + _____

6 × 8 = _____

Math Talk Mathematical Practices

Why do you have to add to find the total product when you use the Distributive Property?

Write one way to break apart the array. Then find the product.

✓ 2.

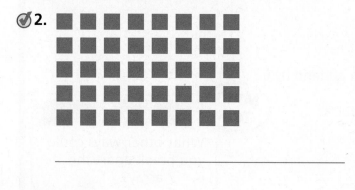

_____

_____

✓ 3.

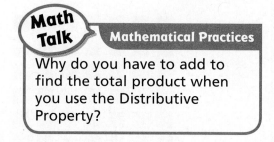

_____

_____

© Houghton Mifflin Harcourt Publishing Company

Name _____

On Your Own

4. **GO DEEPER** Shade tiles to make an array that shows a fact with 7, 8, or 9 as a factor. Write the fact. Explain how you found the product.

_____

_____

_____

_____

5. **THINK SMARTER** Robin says, "I can find 8×7 by multiplying 3×7 and doubling it." Does her statement make sense? Justify your answer.

_____

_____

6. **THINK SMARTER** For numbers 6a–6d, choose Yes or No to indicate whether the sum or product is equal to 7×5.

6a. $7 + (3 + 2) = $ ▨   ○ Yes   ○ No

6b. $7 \times (3 + 2) = $ ▨   ○ Yes   ○ No

6c. $(5 \times 4) + (5 \times 3) = $ ▨   ○ Yes   ○ No

6d. $(7 \times 2) + (7 \times 5) = $ ▨   ○ Yes   ○ No

© Houghton Mifflin Harcourt Publishing Company

Problem Solving • Applications (Real World)

What's the Error?

7. **MATHEMATICAL PRACTICE 3** **Verify the Reasoning of Others**
Brandon needs 8 boxes of spinners for his fishing club. The cost of each box is $9. How much will Brandon pay?

$8 \times \$9 = $

Look at how Brandon solved the problem.
Find and describe his error.

$8 \times 9 = (4 \times 9) + (5 \times 9)$

$8 \times 9 = 36 + 45$

$8 \times 9 = 81$

_____

_____

Use the array to help solve the problem
and correct his error.

$8 \times 9 = (4 + 4) \times 9$

$8 \times 9 = (\underline{\quad} \times \underline{\quad}) + (\underline{\quad} \times \underline{\quad})$

$8 \times 9 = \underline{\quad} + \underline{\quad}$

$8 \times 9 = \underline{\quad}$

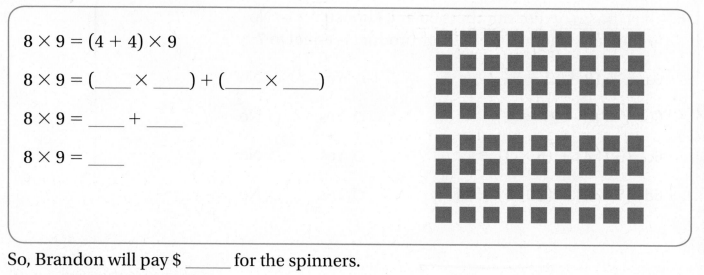

So, Brandon will pay $ _____ for the spinners.

© Houghton Mifflin Harcourt Publishing Company

Multiply with 7

Essential Question What strategies can you use to multiply with 7?

Operations and Algebraic Thinking—3.OA.7 *Also 3.OA.1, 3.OA.3, 3.OA.4, 3.OA.5*

MATHEMATICAL PRACTICES
MP.2, MP.7, MP.8

Unlock the Problem Real World

Jason's family has a new puppy. Jason takes a turn walking the puppy once a day. How many times will Jason walk the puppy in 4 weeks?

Find 4×7.

- How often does Jason walk the puppy?
  _____
- How many days are in 1 week?
  _____

One Way Use the Commutative Property of Multiplication.

If you know 7×4, you can use that fact to find 4×7.

You can change the order of the factors and the product is the same.

$7 \times 4 =$ _____, so $4 \times 7 =$ _____.

So, Jason will walk the puppy _____ times in 4 weeks.

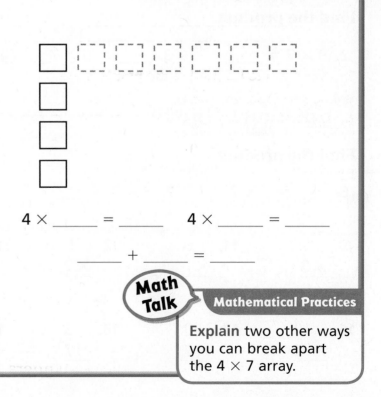

Other Ways

A Use the Distributive Property.

STEP 1 Complete the array to show 4 rows of 7.

STEP 2 Draw a line to break the array into two smaller arrays for facts you know.

STEP 3 Multiply the facts for the smaller arrays. Add the products.

$4 \times$ _____ = _____ $4 \times$ _____ = _____

_____ + _____ = _____

So, $4 \times 7 =$ _____.

Math Talk   **Mathematical Practices**

Explain two other ways you can break apart the 4×7 array.

© Houghton Mifflin Harcourt Publishing Company • Image Credits: ©Geostock/Getty Images/PhotoDisc

B Use a fact you know.

Multiply. $4 \times 7 = $ ▨

- Start with a fact you know.

  $2 \times 7 = $ _____

- Add a group of 7 for 3×7.

  $2 \times 7 + 7 = $ _____

- Then add 7 more for 4×7.

  $3 \times 7 + 7 = $ _____

So, $4 \times 7 = $ _____.

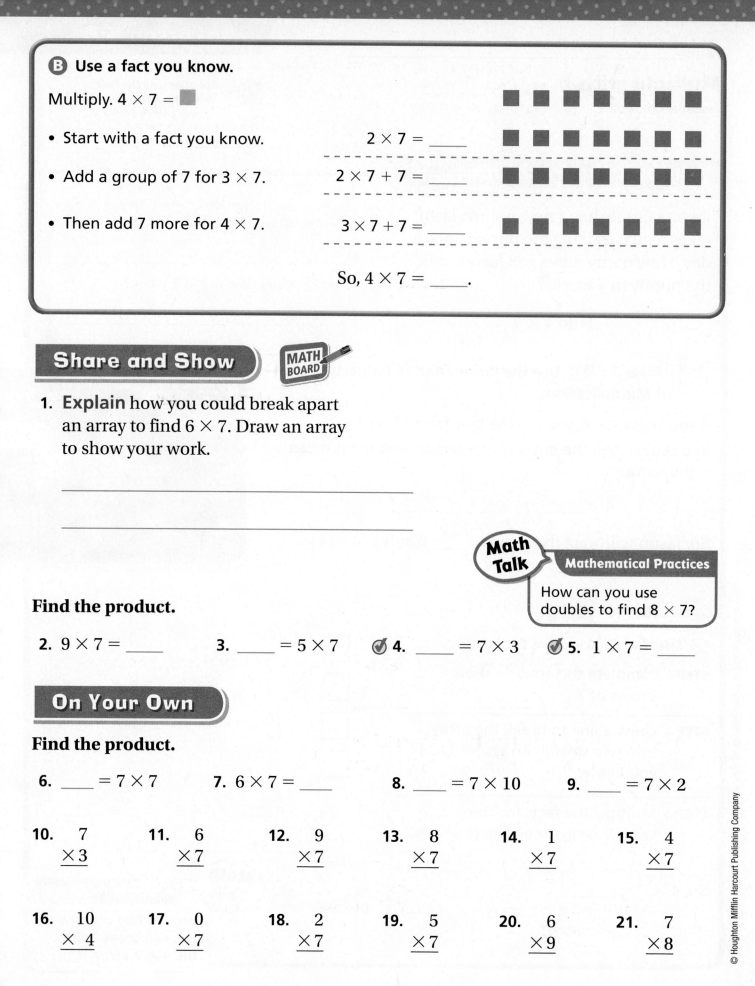

Share and Show

MATH BOARD

1. **Explain** how you could break apart an array to find 6×7. Draw an array to show your work.

_____

_____

Math Talk — **Mathematical Practices**

How can you use doubles to find 8×7?

Find the product.

2. $9 \times 7 = $ _____

3. _____ $= 5 \times 7$

✓ 4. _____ $= 7 \times 3$

✓ 5. $1 \times 7 = $ _____

On Your Own

Find the product.

6. _____ $= 7 \times 7$

7. $6 \times 7 = $ _____

8. _____ $= 7 \times 10$

9. _____ $= 7 \times 2$

10. $\begin{array}{r} 7 \\ \times 3 \\ \hline \end{array}$

11. $\begin{array}{r} 6 \\ \times 7 \\ \hline \end{array}$

12. $\begin{array}{r} 9 \\ \times 7 \\ \hline \end{array}$

13. $\begin{array}{r} 8 \\ \times 7 \\ \hline \end{array}$

14. $\begin{array}{r} 1 \\ \times 7 \\ \hline \end{array}$

15. $\begin{array}{r} 4 \\ \times 7 \\ \hline \end{array}$

16. $\begin{array}{r} 10 \\ \times 4 \\ \hline \end{array}$

17. $\begin{array}{r} 0 \\ \times 7 \\ \hline \end{array}$

18. $\begin{array}{r} 2 \\ \times 7 \\ \hline \end{array}$

19. $\begin{array}{r} 5 \\ \times 7 \\ \hline \end{array}$

20. $\begin{array}{r} 6 \\ \times 9 \\ \hline \end{array}$

21. $\begin{array}{r} 7 \\ \times 8 \\ \hline \end{array}$

© Houghton Mifflin Harcourt Publishing Company

Use the table for 22–24.

Rusty's Care	
Food	3 cups a day
Water	4 cups a day
Bath	2 times a month

22. Lori has a dog named Rusty. How many baths will Rusty have in 7 months?

_____

23. **THINK SMARTER** How many more cups of water than food will Rusty get in 1 week?

_____

24. **GO DEEPER** Tim's dog, Midnight, eats 28 cups of food in a week. Midnight eats the same amount each day. In one day, how many more cups of food will Midnight eat than Rusty? Explain.

_____

_____

_____

_____

WRITE ▸ *Math* • **Show Your Work**

25. José walks his dog 10 miles every week. How many miles do they walk in 7 weeks?

_____

26. **MATHEMATICAL PRACTICE ⑦ Look for Structure** Dave takes Zoey, his dog, for a 3-mile walk twice a day. How many miles do they walk in one week?

_____

27. **THINK SMARTER** Alia arranges some playing cards in 7 equal rows with 7 cards in each row. How many cards does Alia arrange?

_____

© Houghton Mifflin Harcourt Publishing Company • Image Credits: (tr) ©Martin Harvey/Getty Images

Summarize

To help you stay healthy, you should eat a balanced diet and exercise every day.

The table shows the recommended daily servings for third graders. You should eat the right amounts of the food groups.

Suppose you want to share with your friends what you learned about healthy eating. How could you summarize what you learned?

When you *summarize,* you restate the most important information in a shorter way to help you understand what you have read.

Recommended Daily Servings	
Food Group	**Servings**
Whole Grains (bread, cereal)	6 ounces
Vegetables (beans, corn)	2 cups
Fruits (apples, oranges)	1 cup
Dairy Products (milk, cheese)	3 cups
Meat, Beans, Fish, Eggs, Nuts	5 ounces
8 ounces = 1 cup	

- To stay healthy, you should eat a balanced

  _____ and _____ every day.

- A third grader should eat 3 cups of _____, such as milk and cheese, each day.

- A third grader should eat _____ of vegetables and fruits each day.

  How many cups of vegetables and fruits should a third

  grader eat in 1 week? _____

  Remember: 1 week = 7 days

- A third grader should eat _____ of whole grains, such as bread and cereal, each day.

  How many ounces of whole grains should a third grader

  eat in 1 week? _____

FOR MORE PRACTICE: Standards Practice Book

© Houghton Mifflin Harcourt Publishing Company

Name _____

Vocabulary

Choose the best term from the box to complete the sentence.

Vocabulary
Commutative Property of Multiplication
Distributive Property
multiple

1. A ___multiple___ of 4 is any product that has 4 as one of its factors. (p. 143)

2. This is an example of the ___Distributive___ property Property.

$$3 \times 8 = (3 \times 6) + (3 \times 2)$$

This property states that multiplying a sum by a number is the same as multiplying each addend by the number and then adding the products. (p. 151)

Concepts and Skills

Write one way to break apart the array.
Then find the product. (3.OA.5)

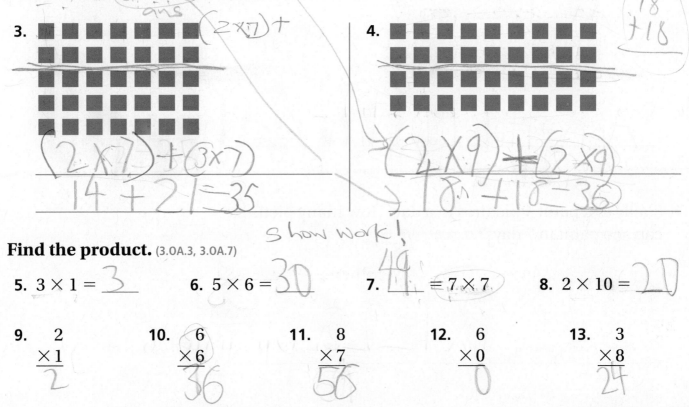

3. $(2 \times 7) + (3 \times 7)$
$14 + 21 = 35$

4. $(2 \times 9) + (2 \times 9)$
$18 + 18 = 36$

Show work!

Find the product. (3.OA.3, 3.OA.7)

5. $3 \times 1 = $ 3

6. $5 \times 6 = $ 30

7. 4 $= 7 \times 7$

8. $2 \times 10 = $ 20

9. $\begin{array}{r} 2 \\ \times 1 \\ \hline 2 \end{array}$

10. $\begin{array}{r} 6 \\ \times 6 \\ \hline 36 \end{array}$

11. $\begin{array}{r} 8 \\ \times 7 \\ \hline 56 \end{array}$

12. $\begin{array}{r} 6 \\ \times 0 \\ \hline 0 \end{array}$

13. $\begin{array}{r} 3 \\ \times 8 \\ \hline 24 \end{array}$

© Houghton Mifflin Harcourt Publishing Company

14. Lori saw 6 lightning bugs. They each had 6 legs. How many legs did the lightning bugs have in all?

(3.OA.3)

6 12 18 24 30 36

6 × 6 = 36 legs

15. Zach walked his dog twice a day, for 7 days. Moira walked her dog three times a day for 5 days. Whose dog was walked more times? How many more? (3.OA.3)

Z   2 × 7 = 14
M   3 × 5 = 15

Moira's dog was walked more times, 1 more times

16. Annette buys 4 boxes of pencils. There are 8 pencils in each box. Jordan buys 3 boxes of pencils with 10 pencils in each box. Who buys more pencils? How many more?

(3.OA.3)

8 16 24 32

A 4 × 8 = 32
J 3 × 10 = 30

Annette buys more pencils, 2 more pencils.

17. Shelly can paint 4 pictures in a day. How many pictures can she paint in 7 days? (3.OA.7)

7 14 21 28

Show work ans. label

4 × 7 = 28 pictures

© Houghton Mifflin Harcourt Publishing Company

Name _____

Associative Property of Multiplication

Essential Question How can you use the Associative Property of Multiplication to find products?

Operations and Algebraic Thinking—3.OA.5 *Also 3.OA.1, 3.OA.3, 3.OA.4, 3.OA.7*

MATHEMATICAL PRACTICES
MP.1, MP.4, MP.7, MP.8

CONNECT You have learned the Associative Property of Addition. When the grouping of the addends is changed, the sum stays the same.

$$(2 + 3) + 4 = 2 + (3 + 4)$$

The **Associative Property of Multiplication** states that when the grouping of the factors is changed, the product is the same. It is also called the Grouping Property of Multiplication.

$$2 \times (3 \times 4) = (2 \times 3) \times 4$$

> **Math Idea**
> Always multiply the numbers inside the parentheses first.

Unlock the Problem (Real World)

Each car on the roller coaster has 2 rows of seats. Each row has 2 seats. There are 3 cars in each train. How many seats are on each train?

- Underline what you need to find.
- Describe the grouping of the seats.

_____

Use an array.

You can use an array to show $3 \times (2 \times 2)$.

$3 \times (2 \times 2) = \blacksquare$

$3 \times$ _____ = _____

So, there are 3 cars with 4 seats in each car.

There are _____ seats on each roller coaster train.

You can change the grouping with parentheses and the product is the same.

$(3 \times 2) \times 2 = \blacksquare$

_____ $\times 2 =$ _____

Math Talk **Mathematical Practices**

Explain why the products $3 \times (2 \times 2)$ and $(3 \times 2) \times 2$ are the same.

© Houghton Mifflin Harcourt Publishing Company

Example Use the Commutative and Associative Properties.

You can also change the order of the factors.
The product is the same.

$(4 \times 3) \times 2 =$ ▢

$4 \times (3 \times 2) =$ ▢   Associative Property

$4 \times$ _____ = _____

$4 \times (3 \times 2) =$ ▢

$4 \times (2 \times 3) =$ ▢   Commutative Property

$(4 \times 2) \times 3 =$ ▢   Associative Property

_____ $\times 3 =$ _____

Share and Show MATH BOARD

1. Find the product of 5, 2, and 3. Write another way to group the factors. Is the product the same? Why?

_____

_____

Write another way to group the factors. Then find the product.

2. $(2 \times 1) \times 7$

_____

_____

3. $3 \times (3 \times 4)$

_____

_____

✓ 4. $5 \times (2 \times 5)$

_____

_____

✓ 5. $3 \times (2 \times 6)$

_____

_____

6. $2 \times (2 \times 5)$

_____

_____

7. $(1 \times 3) \times 6$

_____

_____

Math Talk **Mathematical Practices**

Choose one answer from Exercises 2–7. **Explain** why you multiplied those factors first.

© Houghton Mifflin Harcourt Publishing Company

Name _____

Write another way to group the factors. Then find the product.

8. $(2 \times 3) \times 3$

_____

_____

9. $(8 \times 3) \times 2$

_____

_____

10. $2 \times (5 \times 5)$

_____

_____

11. $(3 \times 2) \times 4$

_____

_____

12. $(6 \times 1) \times 4$

_____

_____

13. $2 \times (2 \times 6)$

_____

_____

14. $2 \times (4 \times 2)$

_____

_____

15. $5 \times (2 \times 4)$

_____

_____

16. $9 \times (1 \times 2)$

_____

_____

Practice: Copy and Solve Use parentheses and multiplication properties. Then, find the product.

17. $6 \times 5 \times 2$

18. $2 \times 3 \times 5$

19. $3 \times 1 \times 6$

20. $2 \times 5 \times 6$

21. $2 \times 0 \times 8$

22. $1 \times 9 \times 4$

23. $2 \times 2 \times 2$

24. $4 \times 2 \times 2$

25. $2 \times 4 \times 5$

26. $2 \times 6 \times 1$

27. $2 \times 9 \times 3$

28. $2 \times 7 \times 2$

THINK SMARTER **Algebra** Find the unknown factor.

29. $7 \times (2 \times \underline{\quad}) = 56$

30. $30 = 6 \times (5 \times \underline{\quad})$

31. $\underline{\quad} \times (2 \times 2) = 32$

32. $42 = 7 \times (2 \times \underline{\quad})$

33. $8 \times (5 \times \underline{\quad}) = 40$

34. $0 = \underline{\quad} \times (25 \times 1)$

35. $(2 \times 9) \times \underline{\quad} = 18$

36. $60 = (2 \times \underline{\quad}) \times 6$

37. $4 \times (3 \times \underline{\quad}) = 24$

© Houghton Mifflin Harcourt Publishing Company

Problem Solving • Applications Real World

Use the graph for 38–39.

38. **MATHEMATICAL PRACTICE ②** **Represent a Problem**
Each car on the Steel Force train has 3 rows with 2 seats in each row. How many seats are on the train? Draw a quick picture.

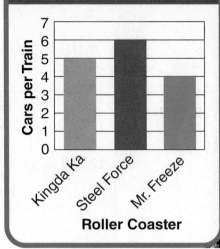

Roller Coasters

Cars per Train (vertical axis, 0–7)

- Kingda Ka: 5
- Steel Force: 6
- Mr. Freeze: 4

Roller Coaster (horizontal axis)

_____

39. **THINK SMARTER** A Kingda Ka train has 4 seats per car, but the last car has only 2 seats. How many seats are on one Kingda Ka train?

_____

40. **GO DEEPER** **Sense or Nonsense?** Each week, Kelly works 2 days for 4 hours each day and earns $5 an hour. Len works 5 days for 2 hours each day and earns $4 an hour. Kelly says they both earn the same amount. Does this statement make sense? Explain.

_____

_____

WRITE ▸ *Math*
Show Your Work

41. **THINK SMARTER** Clayton packs 3 boxes. He puts 3 lunch bags in each box. There are 4 sandwiches in each lunch bag. How many sandwiches does Clayton pack? Show your work.

_____

© Houghton Mifflin Harcourt Publishing Company • Image Credits: (tr) ©Joel Rogers Photography

Patterns on the Multiplication Table

Essential Question How can you use properties to explain patterns on the multiplication table?

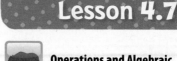

Operations and Algebraic Thinking—3.OA.9 *Also 3.OA.5*
MATHEMATICAL PRACTICES
MP.1, MP.3, MP.7

Unlock the Problem Real World

You can use a multiplication table to explore number patterns.

Activity 1

Materials ■ MathBoard

- Write the products for the green squares. What do you notice about the products?

_____

_____

Write the multiplication sentences for the products on your MathBoard. What do you notice about the factors?

_____

- Will this be true in the yellow squares? **Explain** using a property you know.

_____

Write the products for the yellow squares.

- Complete the columns for 1, 5, and 6. Look across each row and compare the products. What do you notice?

_____

What property does this show?

_____

×	0	1	2	3	4	5	6	7	8	9	10
0											
1											
2											
3											
4											
5											
6											
7											
8											
9											
10											

Math Talk

Mathematical Practices

Explain how you can use these patterns to find other products.

© Houghton Mifflin Harcourt Publishing Company

Activity 2

Materials ■ yellow and blue crayons

×	0	1	2	3	4	5	6	7	8	9	10
0	0	0	0	0	0	0	0	0	0	0	0
1	0	1	2	3	4	5	6	7	8	9	10
2	0	2	4	6	8	10	12	14	16	18	20
3	0	3	6	9	12	15	18	21	24	27	30
4	0	4	8	12	16	20	24	28	32	36	40
5	0	5	10	15	20	25	30	35	40	45	50
6	0	6	12	18	24	30	36	42	48	54	60
7	0	7	14	21	28	35	42	49	56	63	70
8	0	8	16	24	32	40	48	56	64	72	80
9	0	9	18	27	36	45	54	63	72	81	90
10	0	10	20	30	40	50	60	70	80	90	100

- Shade the rows for 0, 2, 4, 6, 8, and 10 yellow.

- What pattern do you notice about each shaded row? _____

  _____

- Compare the rows for 2 and 4. What do you notice about the products?

  _____

- Shade the columns for 1, 3, 5, 7, and 9 blue.

- What do you notice about the products for each shaded column?

  _____

- Compare the products for the green squares. What do you notice? What do you notice about the factors?

  _____

- What other patterns do you see?

  _____

Share and Show

1. Use the table to write the products for the row for 2.

   _____, _____, _____, _____, _____,

   _____, _____, _____, _____, _____, _____

   Describe a pattern you see.

   _____

> **Math Talk**
> **Mathematical Practices**
> What do you notice about the product of any number and 2?

Is the product even or odd? Write *even* or *odd*.

2. 5×8 _____   **3.** 6×3 _____   **4.** 3×5 _____   ✓**5.** 4×4 _____

© Houghton Mifflin Harcourt Publishing Company

Name _____

Use the multiplication table. Describe a pattern you see.

6. in the column for 10

_____

_____

✓ **7.** in the column for 8

_____

_____

On Your Own

Is the product even or odd? Write *even* or *odd*.

8. 4×8 _____

9. 5×5 _____

10. 7×4 _____

11. 2×9 _____

12. **GO DEEPER** Use the multiplication table. Rewrite the pattern correctly.

6, 12, 18, 22, 30, 36 _____

Problem Solving • Applications Real World

Complete the table. Then describe a pattern you see in the products.

13.

×	2	4	6	8	10
5					

_____

_____

14.

×	1	3	5	7	9
5					

_____

_____

15. **THINK SMARTER** **Explain** how patterns of the ones digits in the products relate to the factors in Exercises 13 and 14.

_____

_____

Personal Math Trainer

16. **THINK SMARTER +** Helene selected an odd number to multiply by the factors in this table. Write *even* or *odd* to describe each product.

×	1	2	3	4	5
odd number					

© Houghton Mifflin Harcourt Publishing Company

Sense or Nonsense?

17. (MATHEMATICAL PRACTICE ③) **Make Arguments** Whose statement makes sense? Whose statement is nonsense? Explain your reasoning.

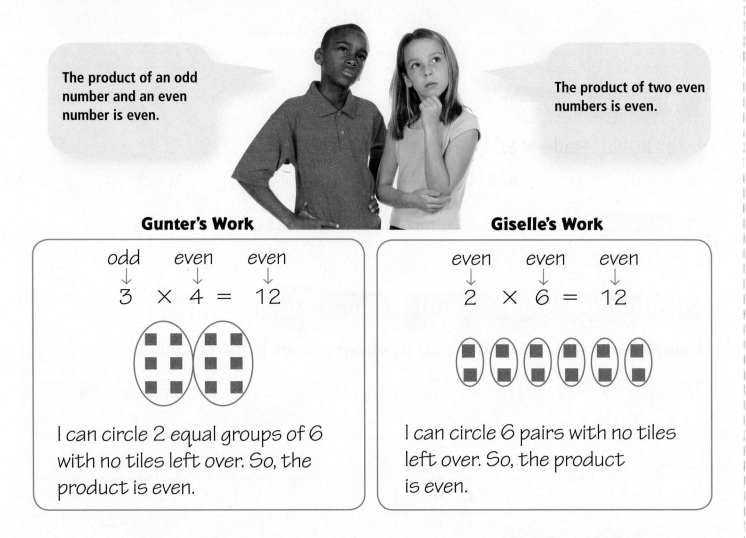

The product of an odd number and an even number is even.

The product of two even numbers is even.

Gunter's Work

odd   even   even
↓   ↓   ↓
3 × 4 = 12

I can circle 2 equal groups of 6 with no tiles left over. So, the product is even.

Giselle's Work

even   even   even
↓   ↓   ↓
2 × 6 = 12

I can circle 6 pairs with no tiles left over. So, the product is even.

_____

_____

18. **GO DEEPER** Write a statement about the product of two odd numbers. Give an example to show why your statement is true.

_____

_____

_____

© Houghton Mifflin Harcourt Publishing Company

Name _____

Multiply with 8

Essential Question What strategies can you use to multiply with 8?

Operations and Algebraic Thinking—3.OA.7 *Also 3.OA.1, 3.OA.3, 3.OA.4, 3.OA.5, 3.OA.9*

MATHEMATICAL PRACTICES
MP.2, MP.7, MP.8

Unlock the Problem Real World

A scorpion has 8 legs. How many legs do 5 scorpions have?

Find 5×8.

One Way Use doubles.

$5 \times 8 = $ ▇
$\swarrow \searrow$
$4 + 4$

Think: The factor 8 is an even number. $4 + 4 = 8$

$5 \times 4 = $ _____

20 doubled is _____.

$5 \times 8 = $ _____

So, 5 scorpions have _____ legs.

- How many legs does one scorpion have?

  _____

- What are you asked to find?

  _____

  _____

Another Way Use a number line.

Use the number line to show 5 jumps of 8.

0 2 4 6 8 10 12 14 16 18 20 22 24 26 28 30 32 34 36 38 40

So, 5 jumps of 8 is _____.   _____ × _____ = _____

! ERROR Alert

Be sure to count the spaces between the tick marks, not the tick marks.

- **Describe** two different ways you can use doubles to find 6×8.

  _____

  _____

© Houghton Mifflin Harcourt Publishing Company • Image Credits: ©David Aubrey/Photo Researchers, Inc.

Example Use the Associative Property of Multiplication.

Scorpions have two eyes on the top of the head, and usually two to five pairs along the front corners of the head. If each scorpion has 6 eyes, how many eyes would 8 scorpions have?

$8 \times 6 = \blacksquare$

$8 \times 6 = (2 \times 4) \times 6$ Think: $8 = 2 \times 4$

$8 \times 6 = 2 \times (4 \times 6)$ Use the Associative Property.

$8 \times 6 = 2 \times$ _____   Multiply. 4×6

$8 \times 6 =$ _____ + _____   Double the product.

$8 \times 6 =$ _____

Math Talk **Mathematical Practices**

When you multiply with 8, will the product always be even? Explain.

Share and Show MATH BOARD

1. **Explain** one way you can find 4×8.

_____

Find the product.

2. $3 \times 8 =$ _____   3. _____ $= 8 \times 2$ ✓4. _____ $= 7 \times 8$ ✓5. $9 \times 8 =$ _____

On Your Own

Find the product.

6. _____ $= 6 \times 8$ 7. $10 \times 8 =$ _____   8. _____ $= 8 \times 3$ 9. $1 \times 8 =$ _____

10. $4 \times 8 =$ _____   11. $5 \times 8 =$ _____   12. $0 \times 8 =$ _____   13. $8 \times 8 =$ _____

14. $\begin{array}{r} 6 \\ \times 8 \\ \hline \end{array}$ 15. $\begin{array}{r} 8 \\ \times 2 \\ \hline \end{array}$ 16. $\begin{array}{r} 5 \\ \times 8 \\ \hline \end{array}$ 17. $\begin{array}{r} 3 \\ \times 8 \\ \hline \end{array}$ 18. $\begin{array}{r} 10 \\ \times 8 \\ \hline \end{array}$ 19. $\begin{array}{r} 7 \\ \times 8 \\ \hline \end{array}$

20. A chef is making 5 batches of potato salad. He needs 8 cups of dressing for each salad. How many cups of dressing does he need?

_____

© Houghton Mifflin Harcourt Publishing Company

Name _____

Problem Solving • Applications

Use the table for 21–24.

21. About how much rain falls in the Chihuahuan Desert in 6 years? **Explain** how you can use doubles to find the answer.

_____

_____

Average Yearly Rainfall in North American Deserts

Desert	Inches
Chihuahuan	8
Great Basin	9
Mojave	4
Sonoran	9

22. **GO DEEPER** In 2 years, about how many more inches of rain will fall in the Sonoran Desert than in the Chihuahuan Desert? **Explain**.

_____

_____

23. **MATHEMATICAL PRACTICE 6 Describe a Method** Look back at Exercise 22. Write and show how to solve a similar problem by comparing two different deserts.

_____

_____

24. **THINK SMARTER** How can you find about how many inches of rain will fall in the Mohave Desert in 20 years?

_____

_____

25. **THINK SMARTER** For numbers 25a–25d, select True or False for each multiplication sentence.

25a. $3 \times (2 \times 4) = 24$ ○ True ○ False

25b. $4 \times 8 = 32$ ○ True ○ False

25c. $7 \times 8 = 72$ ○ True ○ False

25d. $2 \times (5 \times 8) = 80$ ○ True ○ False

© Houghton Mifflin Harcourt Publishing Company

There are 90 species of scorpions that live in the United States. Only 3 species of scorpions live in Arizona. They are the Arizona bark scorpion, the Desert hairy scorpion, and the Stripe-tailed scorpion.

Facts About Scorpions

Scorpions:

- are between 1 and 4 inches long
- mostly eat insects
- glow under ultraviolet light

They have:

- 8 legs for walking
- 2 long, claw-like pincers used to hold their food
- a curled tail held over their body with a stinger on the tip

▲ Scorpions glow under ultraviolet light.

26. How many species of scorpions do *not* live in Arizona?

27. Students saw 8 scorpions. What multiplication sentences can help you find how many pincers and legs the 8 scorpions had?

28. **GO DEEPER** Three scorpions were in a display with ultraviolet light. Eight groups of 4 students saw the display. How many students saw the glowing scorpions?

© Houghton Mifflin Harcourt Publishing Company • Image Credits: (cr) ©Raul Gonzalez Perez/Photo Researchers, Inc.

Name _____

Multiply with 9

Essential Question What strategies can you use to multiply with 9?

Operations and Algebraic Thinking—3.OA.7 Also 3.OA.1, 3.OA.3, 3.OA.4, 3.OA.5, 3.OA.9

MATHEMATICAL PRACTICES
MP.2, MP.7, MP.8

Unlock the Problem Real World

Olivia's class is studying the solar system. Seven students are making models of the solar system. Each model has 9 spheres (eight for the planets and one for Pluto, a dwarf planet). How many spheres do the 7 students need for all the models?

Find 7 × 9.

- What are you asked to find?

  _____

  _____

- How many students are making

  models? _____

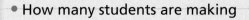

One Way Use the Distributive Property.

A **With multiplication and addition**

$$7 \times 9 = \blacksquare$$

Think: 9 = 3 + 6 $7 \times 9 = 7 \times (3 + 6)$

Multiply each addend by 7. $7 \times 9 = (7 \times 3) + (7 \times 6)$

Add the products. $7 \times 9 = $ _____ + _____

$7 \times 9 = $ _____

B **With multiplication and subtraction**

$$7 \times 9 = \blacksquare$$

Think: 9 = 10 − 1 $7 \times 9 = 7 \times (10 - 1)$

Multiply each number by 7. $7 \times 9 = (7 \times 10) - (7 \times 1)$

Subtract the products. $7 \times 9 = $ _____ − _____

$7 \times 9 = $ _____

So, 7 students need _____ spheres for all the models.

© Houghton Mifflin Harcourt Publishing Company

Another Way Use patterns of 9.

The table shows the 9s facts.

Multiply by 9.	
Factors	Product
1 × 9	9
2 × 9	18
3 × 9	27
4 × 9	36
5 × 9	45
6 × 9	54
7 × 9	
8 × 9	
9 × 9	

- What do you notice about the tens digit in the product?

  The tens digit is _____ less than the factor that is multiplied by 9.

- What do you notice about the sum of the digits in the product?

  The sum of the digits in the product is always _____.

  So, to multiply 7 × 9, think the tens digit is _____

  and the ones digit is _____. The product is _____.

Try This! **Complete the table above.**

Use the patterns to find 8 × 9 and 9 × 9.

Share and Show
MATH BOARD

Math Talk **Mathematical Practices**

Explain how you know the ones digit in the product 3 × 9.

1. What is the tens digit in the product

   3 × 9? _____

   Think: What number is 1 less than 3?

Find the product.

2. 9 × 8 = _____ 3. _____ = 2 × 9 ✓ 4. _____ = 6 × 9 ✓ 5. 9 × 1 = _____

On Your Own

Find the product.

6. 4 × 9 = _____ 7. 5 × 9 = _____ 8. 10 × 9 = _____ 9. 1 × 9 = _____

10. $\begin{array}{r} 9 \\ \times 5 \\ \hline \end{array}$
11. $\begin{array}{r} 9 \\ \times 3 \\ \hline \end{array}$
12. $\begin{array}{r} 6 \\ \times 9 \\ \hline \end{array}$
13. $\begin{array}{r} 7 \\ \times 9 \\ \hline \end{array}$
14. $\begin{array}{r} 4 \\ \times 9 \\ \hline \end{array}$

15. A beetle has 6 legs. How many legs do 9 beetles have? _____

© Houghton Mifflin Harcourt Publishing Company

MATHEMATICAL PRACTICE ② **Reason Quantitatively** **Algebra** Compare. Write $<$, $>$, or $=$.

16. $2 \times 9 \bigcirc 3 \times 6$ **17.** $5 \times 9 \bigcirc 6 \times 7$ **18.** $1 \times 9 \bigcirc 3 \times 3$

19. $9 \times 4 \bigcirc 7 \times 5$ **20.** $9 \times 0 \bigcirc 2 \times 3$ **21.** $5 \times 8 \bigcirc 3 \times 9$

Problem Solving • Applications (Real World)

Use the table for 22–25.

22. The number of moons for one of the planets can be found by multiplying 7×9. Which planet is it?

_____

23. **GO DEEPER** This planet has 9 times the number of moons that Mars and Earth have together. Which planet is it? **Explain** your answer.

_____

_____

_____

Moons	
Planet	**Number of Moons**
Earth	1
Mars	2
Jupiter	63
Saturn	47
Uranus	27
Neptune	13

24. **THINK SMARTER** Uranus has 27 moons. What multiplication fact with 9 has a product of 27? Describe how you can find the fact.

_____

_____

_____

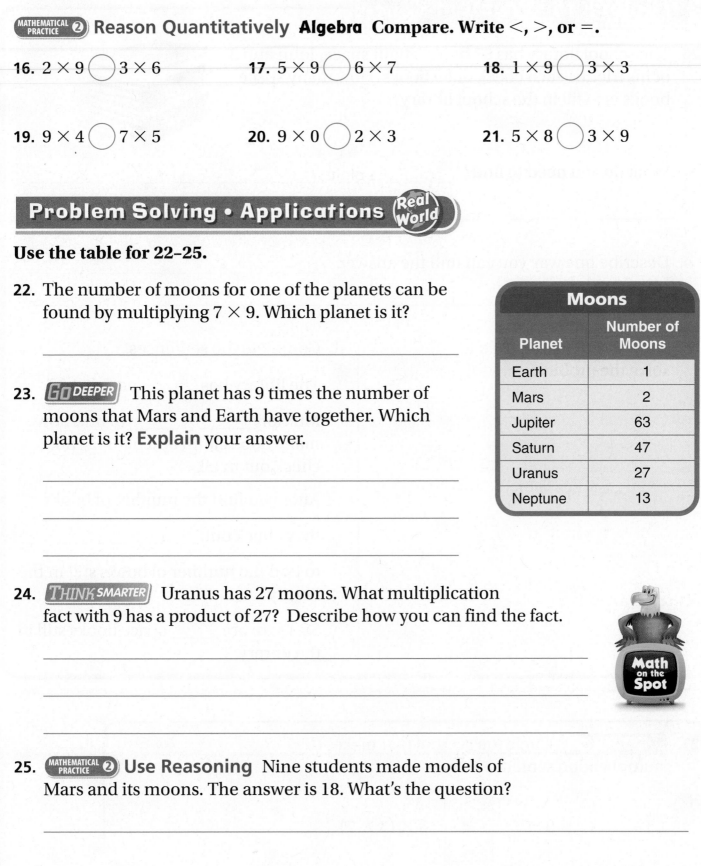

Math on the Spot

25. **MATHEMATICAL PRACTICE ②** **Use Reasoning** Nine students made models of Mars and its moons. The answer is 18. What's the question?

_____

© Houghton Mifflin Harcourt Publishing Company

🔑 Unlock the Problem (Real World)

26. The school library has 97 books about space. John and 3 of his friends each check out 9 books. How many space books are still in the school library?

a. What do you need to find? _____

_____

b. Describe one way you can find the answer. _____

_____

c. Show the steps you used to solve the problem.

d. Complete the sentences.

The library has _____ space books.

Multiply _____ × _____ to find how many books John and his 3 friends check out in all.

After you find the number of books

they check out, _____

to find the number of books still in the library.

So, there are _____ space books still in the library.

---

27. ⬛ THINK SMARTER Circle the symbol that makes the multiplication sentence true.

$$9 \times 7 \quad \boxed{\begin{matrix} > \\ < \\ = \end{matrix}} \quad 3 \times (3 \times 7)$$

© Houghton Mifflin Harcourt Publishing Company

Problem Solving • Multiplication

Essential Question How can you use the strategy *make a table* to solve multiplication problems?

Operations and Algebraic Thinking—3.OA.8, 3.OA.9
Also 3.OA.3, 3.OA.7

MATHEMATICAL PRACTICES
MP.1, MP.4, MP.5

Unlock the Problem

Scott has a stamp album. Some pages have 1 stamp on them, and other pages have 2 stamps on them. If Scott has 18 stamps, show how many different ways he could put them in the album. Use the graphic organizer below to solve the problem.

Read the Problem	Solve the Problem

Read the Problem

What do I need to find?

_____

_____

_____

What information do I need to use?

Scott has _____ stamps. Some of the

pages have _____ stamp on them, and

the other pages have _____ stamps.

How will I use the information?

I will make a _____ showing all the different ways of arranging the stamps in the album.

Solve the Problem

Make a table to show the number of pages with 1 stamp and with 2 stamps. Each row must equal

_____, the total number of stamps.

Pages with 2 Stamps	Pages with 1 Stamp	Total Stamps
8	2	18
7	4	18
6	6	18
5		18
	10	18
3	12	
2		

So, there are _____ different ways.

1. What number patterns do you see in the table?

_____

_____

© Houghton Mifflin Harcourt Publishing Company

🔑 Try Another Problem

What if Scott bought 3 more stamps and now has 21 stamps? Some album pages have 1 stamp and some pages have 2 stamps. Show how many different ways he could put the odd number of stamps in the album.

Read the Problem	Solve the Problem
What do I need to find?	
What information do I need to use?	
How will I use the information?	So, there are _____ different ways.

2. What patterns do you see in this table? _____

_____

3. How are these patterns different from the patterns in

   the table on page 177? _____

_____

© Houghton Mifflin Harcourt Publishing Company

Name _____

1. Aaron's mother is making lemonade. For each pitcher, she uses 1 cup of lemon juice, 1 cup of sugar, and 6 cups of water. What is the total number of cups of ingredients she will use to make 5 pitchers of lemonade?

   First, make a table to show the number of cups of lemon juice, sugar, and water that are in 1 pitcher of lemonade.

   Next, multiply to find the number of cups of water needed for each pitcher of lemonade.

   Last, use the table to solve the problem.

Think: For every pitcher, the number of cups of water increases by 6.

Number of Pitchers	1	2	3		5
Cups of Lemon Juice	1		3		
Cups of Sugar	1	2			
Cups of Water	6	12		24	
Total Number of Cups of Ingredients	8				

So, in 5 pitchers of lemonade, there are _____ cups of

lemon juice, _____ cups of sugar, and _____ cups of water.

This makes a total of _____ cups of ingredients.

✓ 2. What if it takes 4 lemons to make 1 cup of lemon juice? How many lemons would it take to make 5 pitchers? Explain how you can use the table to help you find the answer.

_____

_____

✓ 3. What pattern do you see in the total number of cups of ingredients?

_____

_____

© Houghton Mifflin Harcourt Publishing Company

On Your Own

4. Julie saw 3 eagles each day she went bird-watching. How many eagles did Julie see in 6 days?

_____

5. **MATHEMATICAL PRACTICE ②** **Use Reasoning** Greg has a dollar bill, quarters, and dimes. How many ways can he make $1.75?

Name the ways. _____

_____

_____

6. **THINK SMARTER** Cammi needs 36 postcards. She buys 4 packages of 10 postcards. How many postcards will Cammi have left over? Explain.

_____

_____

_____

Math on the Spot

7. **GO DEEPER** Phillip has 8 books on each of 3 bookshelves. His aunt gives him 3 new books. How many books does Phillip have now?

_____

Personal Math Trainer

8. **THINK SMARTER +** Stuart has some 2-ounce, 3-ounce, and 4-ounce weights. How many different ways can Stuart combine the weights to make a total of 12 ounces? List the ways.

_____

_____

_____

_____

FOR MORE PRACTICE:
Standards Practice Book

© Houghton Mifflin Harcourt Publishing Company

Name _____

1. Mrs. Ruiz sorted spools of thread into 4 boxes.
   Each box holds 5 spools. How many spools of thread
   does Mrs. Ruiz have?

   Draw circles to model the problem. Then solve.

   _____

   _____

2. For numbers 2a–2d, select True or False for each
   multiplication sentence.

   2a. $2 \times 8 = 16$ ○ True   ○ False

   2b. $5 \times 8 = 40$ ○ True   ○ False

   2c. $6 \times 8 = 56$ ○ True   ○ False

   2d. $8 \times 8 = 64$ ○ True   ○ False

3. Bella is planning to write in a journal. Some pages will have
   one journal entry on them, and other pages will have two
   journal entries on them. If Bella wants to make 10 entries,
   how many different ways can she write them in her journal?

4. There are 7 days in 1 week. How many days are there
   in 4 weeks?

   _____ days

© Houghton Mifflin Harcourt Publishing Company

5. Circle groups to show $3 \times (2 \times 3)$.

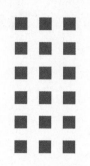

6. Dale keeps all of his pairs of shoes in his closet. Select the number of shoes that Dale could have in his closet. Mark all that apply.

(A) 3

(B) 4

(C) 6

(D) 7

(E) 8

7. Lisa completed the table to describe the product of a mystery one-digit factor and each number.

$\times$	1	2	3	4	5
?	even	even	even	even	even

Part A

Give all of the possible numbers that could be Lisa's mystery one-digit factor.

_____

Part B

Explain how you know that you have selected all of the correct possibilities.

_____

_____

_____

© Houghton Mifflin Harcourt Publishing Company

8. Kate drew 7 octagons. An octagon has 8 sides.
How many sides did Kate draw?

_____ sides

9. José buys 6 bags of flour. Each bag weighs 5 pounds. How
many pounds of flour did José buy?

_____ pounds

10. Break apart the array to show $8 \times 6 = (4 \times 6) + (4 \times 6)$.

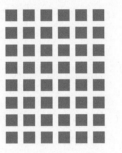

11. Circle the symbol that makes the multiplication sentence
true.

$$9 \times 6 \quad \boxed{\begin{array}{c} > \\ < \\ = \end{array}} \quad 3 \times (3 \times 9)$$

12. Roberto wants to make $2.00 using dollars, half
dollar, and quarters. How many different ways can
he make $2.00?

_____ different ways

© Houghton Mifflin Harcourt Publishing Company

13. A carpenter builds stools that have 3 legs each. How many legs does the carpenter use to build 5 stools? Use the array to explain how you know your answer is correct.

_____

_____

14. Etta buys some ribbon and cuts it into 7 pieces that are the same length. Each piece is 9 inches long. How long was the ribbon that Etta bought?

_____ inches

15. Antoine and 3 friends divide some pennies evenly among themselves. Each friend separates his pennies into 3 equal stacks with 5 pennies in each stack.

Write a multiplication sentence that shows the total number of pennies.

_____

16. Luke is making 4 first-aid kits. He wants to put 3 large and 4 small bandages in each kit. How many bandages does he need for the kits? Show your work.

_____ bandages

© Houghton Mifflin Harcourt Publishing Company

Name _____

17. For numbers 17a–17d, select True or False for each equation.

17a. $3 \times 7 = 21$ ○ True   ○ False

17b. $5 \times 7 = 28$ ○ True   ○ False

17c. $8 \times 7 = 49$ ○ True   ○ False

17d. $9 \times 7 = 63$ ○ True   ○ False

18. Circle the number that makes the multiplication sentence true.

$$10 \times \boxed{\begin{array}{c} 4 \\ 5 \\ 8 \end{array}} = 40$$

19. For numbers 19a–19d, select Yes or No to indicate whether the number sentence has the same value as 8×6.

19a. $8 + (4 \times 2) = \blacksquare$ ○ Yes   ○ No

19b. $(8 \times 4) + (8 \times 2) = \blacksquare$ ○ Yes   ○ No

19c. $(6 \times 4) + (6 \times 2) = \blacksquare$ ○ Yes   ○ No

19d. $6 \times (4 + 4) = \blacksquare$ ○ Yes   ○ No

20. Chloe bought 4 movie tickets. Each ticket cost $6. What was the total cost of the movie tickets?

$ _____

21. Write a multiplication sentence using the following numbers and symbols.

_____

© Houghton Mifflin Harcourt Publishing Company

22. Louis started a table showing a multiplication pattern.

Part A

Complete the table. Describe a pattern you see in the products.

×	1	2	3	4	5	6	7	8	9	10
3	3	6	9							

_____

_____

Part B

If you multiplied 3 × 37, would the product be an even number or an odd number? Use the table to explain your reasoning.

_____

_____

_____

_____

_____

23. Use the number line to show the product of 4 × 8.

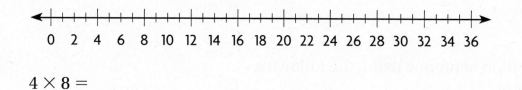

4 × 8 = _____

© Houghton Mifflin Harcourt Publishing Company

Show What You Know ✓

Check your understanding of important skills.

Name _____

▶ **Add Tens** **Write how many tens. Then add.**

1. 30 + 30 = ■

_____ tens + _____ tens =

_____ tens

30 + 30 = _____

2. 40 + 50 = ■

_____ tens + _____ tens =

_____ tens

40 + 50 = _____

▶ **Regroup Tens as Hundreds** **Write the missing numbers.**

3. 35 tens = _____ hundreds _____ tens

4. 52 tens = _____ hundreds _____ tens

5. 97 tens = _____ hundreds _____ tens

▶ **Multiplication Facts Through 9** **Find the product.**

6. 3 × 9 = _____   **7.** 4 × 5 = _____   **8.** 7 × 6 = _____   **9.** 8 × 2 = _____

Math Detective

The butterfly exhibit at the museum will display 60 different butterfly species arranged in an array. Each row has 6 butterflies. Be a Math Detective to find the number of rows in the butterfly exhibit.

The butterfly exhibit will open soon.

© Houghton Mifflin Harcourt Publishing Company

Personal Math Trainer
Online Assessment and Intervention

► **Visualize It** ••

Complete the tree map by using the words with a ✓.

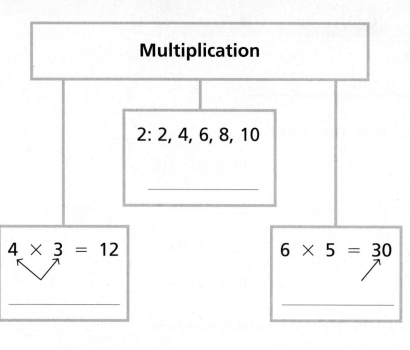

Multiplication

2: 2, 4, 6, 8, 10

_____

4 × 3 = 12

_____

6 × 5 = 30

_____

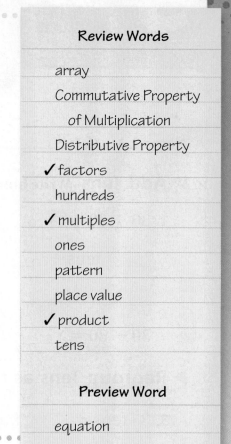

Review Words

array

Commutative Property
of Multiplication

Distributive Property

✓ factors

hundreds

✓ multiples

ones

pattern

place value

✓ product

tens

Preview Word

equation

► **Understand Vocabulary** ••••••••••••••••••••••••••••

**Read the definition. Write the preview word
or review word that matches it.**

1. An ordered set of numbers or objects
   in which the order helps you predict
   what will come next.

   _____

2. A set of objects arranged in rows
   and columns.

   _____

3. A number sentence that uses the equal
   sign to show that two amounts are equal.

   _____

4. The property that states that multiplying
   a sum by a number is the same as
   multiplying each addend by the number
   and then adding the products.

   _____

5. The value of each digit in a number, based
   on the location of the digit.

   _____

© Houghton Mifflin Harcourt Publishing Company

GO DIGITAL
• **Interactive Student Edition**
• **Multimedia eGlossary**

Name _____

Describe Patterns

Essential Question What are some ways you can describe a pattern in a table?

**Operations and Algebraic Thinking—
3.OA.9** *Also 3.OA.3, 3.OA.7*
MATHEMATICAL PRACTICES
MP.4, MP.6, MP.7

🔑 Unlock the Problem Real World

The outdoor club is planning a camping trip. Each camper will need a flashlight. One flashlight uses 4 batteries. How many batteries are needed for 8 flashlights?

You can describe a pattern in a table.

Flashlights	1	2	3	4	5	6	7	8	Think: Count by 1s.
Batteries	4	8	12	16	20	24	28	■	Think: Count by 4s.

🔓 One Way Describe a pattern across the rows.

STEP 1 Look for a pattern to complete the table. As you look across the rows, you can see that the number of batteries increases by 4 for each flashlight.

So, for every flashlight add _____ batteries.

STEP 2 Use the pattern to find the number of batteries in 8 flashlights.

Add _____ to 28 batteries. $28 + 4 =$ _____

So, _____ batteries are needed for 8 flashlights.

> **! ERROR Alert**
> Check that your pattern will work for all the numbers in the table.

🔓 Another Way Describe a pattern in the columns.

STEP 1 Look for a pattern by comparing the columns in the table. You can multiply the number of flashlights by 4 to find the number of batteries that are needed.

STEP 2 Use the pattern to find how many batteries are needed for 8 flashlights.

$8 \times 4 =$ _____

Math Talk **Mathematical Practices**

Why is it important to know how many batteries are needed for 1 flashlight?

© Houghton Mifflin Harcourt Publishing Company • Image Credits: ©Sonya Farrell/Getty Images

Try This! Describe a pattern. Then complete the table.

The campers need 5 packs of batteries. If there are 8 batteries in each pack, how many batteries will be in 5 packs?

Packs of Batteries	Number of Batteries
1	8
2	16
3	
4	32
5	

Use addition.

Describe a pattern.

Add _____ batteries for each pack.

Use multiplication.

Describe a pattern.

Multiply the number of packs of batteries

by _____.

So, there will be _____ batteries in 5 packs.

Share and Show MATH BOARD

1. How can you describe a pattern to find the cost of 4 packs of batteries?

_____

Packs of Batteries	1	2	3	4
Cost	$3	$6	$9	

Describe a pattern in the table. Then complete the table.

2.

Tents	Lanterns
2	4
3	6
4	8
5	10
6	
7	

3.

Adults	1	2	3	4	5
Campers	6	12	18		

_____

Math Talk **Mathematical Practices**

Explain how you use your description for a pattern to complete a table.

© Houghton Mifflin Harcourt Publishing Company

On Your Own

Describe a pattern in the table. Then complete the table.

4.

Hours	1	2	3	4	5
Miles Hiked	2	4	6		

_____

5.

Cabins	3	4	5	6	7
Campers	27	36	45		

_____

6.

Cabins	Beds
1	5
2	10
3	
4	20
5	
6	

_____

7.

Adults	Students
2	12
3	18
4	
5	30
6	
7	

_____

8.

Canoes	4	5	6	7	8
Campers	12	15	18		

_____

9.

Canoes	2	3	4	5	6
Paddles	4	6	8		

_____

10. **THINK SMARTER** Students made a craft project at camp. They used 2 small pine cone patterns and 1 large pine cone pattern. Complete the table to find how many patterns were used for the different numbers of projects.

Math on the Spot

Projects	1	2	3						
Small Pattern	2								
Large Pattern	1								

© Houghton Mifflin Harcourt Publishing Company

Problem Solving • Applications Real World

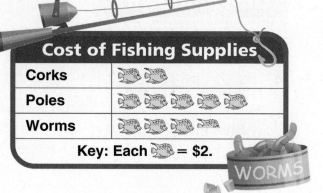

Cost of Fishing Supplies

Corks	🐟🐟
Poles	🐟🐟🐟🐟🐟
Worms	🐟🐟🐟🐟

Key: Each 🐟 = $2.

WORMS

MATHEMATICAL PRACTICE ④ Use Graphs Use the picture graph for 11–13.

11. Jena bought 3 fishing poles. How much money did she spend?

_____

12. Noah bought 1 fishing pole, 2 corks, and 1 carton of worms. What was the total cost?

_____

13. **WRITE** ▸*Math* Ryan bought 8 corks. Explain how you can use the Commutative Property to find the cost.

_____

_____

14. **GO DEEPER** The cost to rent a raft is $7 per person. A raft can hold up to 6 people. There is a $3 launch fee per raft. What is the total cost for a group of 6? Explain.

_____

15. Taylor bought 4 boxes of granola bars. There are 6 bars in each box. How many granola bars did Taylor buy?

_____

Personal Math Trainer

16. **THINK SMARTER ✚** Complete the table. Amir said a rule for the pattern shown in this table is "Multiply by 4." Is he correct? Explain how you know your answer is reasonable.

Cans	2	3	4		6
Peaches	8	12		20	

_____

_____

FOR MORE PRACTICE: Standards Practice Book

© Houghton Mifflin Harcourt Publishing Company

Find Unknown Numbers

Essential Question How can you use an array or a multiplication table to find an unknown factor or product?

**Operations and Algebraic Thinking—
3.OA.4** *Also 3.OA.1, 3.OA.3, 3.OA.7*
MATHEMATICAL PRACTICES
MP.2, MP.4, MP.5, MP.6

Unlock the Problem (Real World)

Tanisha plans to invite 24 people to a picnic. The invitations come in packs of 8. How many packs of invitations does Tanisha need to buy?

An **equation** is a number sentence that uses the equal sign to show that two amounts are equal.

A symbol or letter can stand for an unknown factor. You can write the equation, $n \times 8 = 24$, to find how many packs of invitations Tanisha needs. Find the number, n, that makes the equation true.

- How many people is Tanisha inviting? _____
- How many invitations are in 1 pack? _____

You Are Invited

Use an array.

- Show an array of 24 tiles with 8 tiles in each row by completing the drawing.

Math Talk

Mathematical Practices

Explain how the array represents the problem. How do the factors relate to the array?

$$
\begin{array}{ccccc}
n & \times & 8 & = & 24 \\
\uparrow & & \uparrow & & \uparrow \\
\text{factor} & & \text{factor} & & \text{product} \\
\text{number of} & & \text{number in} & & \text{total} \\
\text{rows} & & \text{each row} & & \text{number}
\end{array}
$$

- Count how many rows of 8 tiles there are. **Think:** What number times 8 equals 24?

There are _____ rows of 8 tiles. The unknown factor is _____. $n =$ _____

_____ $\times 8 = 24$ Check.

_____ $= 24$ ✓ The equation is true.

So, Tanisha needs _____ packs of invitations.

© Houghton Mifflin Harcourt Publishing Company

Use a multiplication table.

$3 \times 8 = \blacksquare$

Think: The symbol, $\blacksquare$, stands for the unknown product.

Find the product 3×8 where row 3 and column 8 meet.

The unknown product is _____.

$\blacksquare$ = _____

$3 \times 8 =$ _____   Check.

$24 =$ _____ ✓ The equation is true.

×	0	1	2	3	4	5	6	7	8	9	10
0	0	0	0	0	0	0	0	0	0	0	0
1	0	1	2	3	4	5	6	7	8	9	10
2	0	2	4	6	8	10	12	14	16	18	20
3	0	3	6	9	12	15	18	21	24	27	30
4	0	4	8	12	16	20	24	28	32	36	40
5	0	5	10	15	20	25	30	35	40	45	50
6	0	6	12	18	24	30	36	42	48	54	60
7	0	7	14	21	28	35	42	49	56	63	70
8	0	8	16	24	32	40	48	56	64	72	80
9	0	9	18	27	36	45	54	63	72	81	90
10	0	10	20	30	40	50	60	70	80	90	100

Share and Show   MATH BOARD

1. What is the unknown factor shown by this array?

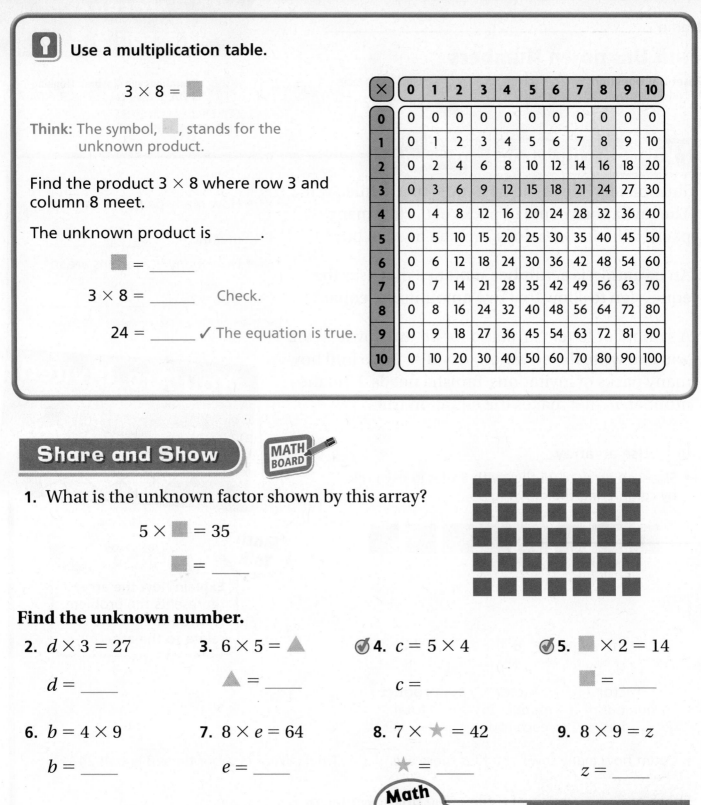

$5 \times \blacksquare = 35$

$\blacksquare =$ _____

Find the unknown number.

2. $d \times 3 = 27$

$d =$ _____

3. $6 \times 5 = \blacktriangle$

$\blacktriangle =$ _____

✓4. $c = 5 \times 4$

$c =$ _____

✓5. $\blacksquare \times 2 = 14$

$\blacksquare =$ _____

6. $b = 4 \times 9$

$b =$ _____

7. $8 \times e = 64$

$e =$ _____

8. $7 \times \bigstar = 42$

$\bigstar =$ _____

9. $8 \times 9 = z$

$z =$ _____

Math Talk   **Mathematical Practices**

Explain how you know if you are looking for the number of rows or the number in each row when you make an array to find an unknown factor.

© Houghton Mifflin Harcourt Publishing Company

On Your Own

Find the unknown number.

10. $\blacksquare = 9 \times 2$

$\blacksquare = $ _____

11. $28 = 4 \times m$

$m = $ _____

12. $y \times 3 = 9$

$y = $ _____

13. $7 \times 9 = g$

$g = $ _____

14. $5 \times p = 40$

$p = $ _____

15. $w = 8 \times 7$

$w = $ _____

16. $36 = \blacklozenge \times 6$

$\blacklozenge = $ _____

17. $8 \times e = 72$

$e = $ _____

18. $9 \times \bigstar = 27$

$\bigstar = $ _____

19. $a = 6 \times 10$

$a = $ _____

20. $2 \times 5 = d$

$d = $ _____

21. $32 = 8 \times n$

$n = $ _____

22. $a = 6 \times 4$

$a = $ _____

23. $7 = 7 \times n$

$n = $ _____

24. $w \times 3 = 15$

$w = $ _____

25. $\bigstar = 8 \times 6$

$\bigstar = $ _____

MATHEMATICAL PRACTICE ② Reason Quantitatively **Algebra** **Find the unknown number.**

26. $3 \times 6 = k \times 9$

$k = $ _____

27. $4 \times y = 2 \times 6$

$y = $ _____

28. $5 \times g = 36 - 6$

$g = $ _____

29. $6 \times 4 = \blacksquare \times 3$

$\blacksquare = $ _____

30. $9 \times d = 70 + 2$

$d = $ _____

31. $8 \times h = 60 - 4$

$h = $ _____

32. **GO DEEPER** Invitations cost \$3 for a pack of 8. Lori gives the cashier \$20 to buy invitations and gets \$11 in change. How many packs of invitations does Lori buy? Explain.

_____

_____

© Houghton Mifflin Harcourt Publishing Company

Problem Solving • Applications (Real World)

Use the table for 33–36.

Picnic Supplies		
Item	Number in 1 Pack	Cost
Bowls	6	$10
Cups	8	$3
Tablecloth	1	$2
Napkins	36	$2
Forks	50	$3

33. Tanisha needs 40 cups for the picnic. How many packs of cups should she buy?

_____

34. **GO DEEPER** Ms. Hill buys 3 tablecloths and 2 packs of napkins. How much money does she spend?

_____

35. **THINK SMARTER** What if Tanisha needs 40 bowls for the picnic? Explain how to write an equation with a letter for an unknown factor to find the number of packs she should buy. Then find the unknown factor.

_____

_____

_____

36. **MATHEMATICAL PRACTICE ① Analyze** What if Randy needs an equal number of bowls and cups for his picnic? How many packs of each will he need to buy?

_____

_____

37. **THINK SMARTER** For numbers 37a–37d, choose Yes or No to show whether the unknown factor is 8.

37a. $8 \times \blacksquare = 64$ ○ Yes ○ No

37b. $\blacksquare \times 3 = 27$ ○ Yes ○ No

37c. $6 \times \blacksquare = 42$ ○ Yes ○ No

37d. $\blacksquare \times 7 = 56$ ○ Yes ○ No

FOR MORE PRACTICE: Standards Practice Book

© Houghton Mifflin Harcourt Publishing Company

✓ Mid-Chapter Checkpoint

Vocabulary

Choose the best term from the box.

Vocabulary
array
equation

1. An _**equation**_ is a number sentence that uses the equal sign to show that two amounts are equal. (p. 193)

Concepts and Skills

Describe a pattern in the table. Then complete the table. (3.OA.9)

2.

Weeks	1	2	3	4	5
Days	7	14	21	28	35

Multiply the number of weeks by 7

3.

Tickets	2	3	4	5	6
Cost	$8	$12	$16	20	24

Multiply the number of tickets by 4

4.

Project Teams	Members
3	9
4	12
5	15
6	18
7	21

Multiply the number of project teams by 3

5.

Tables	Chairs
1	8
2	16
3	24
4	32
5	40

Multiply the number of tables by 8

Find the unknown number. (3.OA.4)

6. $m \times 5 = 30$

   $m =$ _6_

7. ■ $\times 6 = 48$

   ■ $=$ _8_

8. $n = 2 \times 10$

   $n =$ _20_

9. $4 \times 8 = p$

   $p =$ _32_

10. $25 = y \times 5$

    $y =$ _5_

11. ◆ $\times 10 = 10$

    ◆ $=$ _1_

© Houghton Mifflin Harcourt Publishing Company

12. Describe a pattern in the table. (3.OA.9)

Packages	1	2	3	4	5
Stickers	6	12	18	24	30

Multiply the number of packages by 6.

13. What number makes the equation true? (3.OA.4)

$$a \times 8 = 72$$

a = 9

14. Mia bought 2 copies of the same book. She spent $18. What was the cost of one book? (3.OA.4)

18 ÷ 2 = 9

$9

15. Kyle saves $10 every week for 6 weeks. How much money will Kyle have in Week 6? (3.OA.9)

Weeks	1	2	3	4	5	6
Amount	$10	$20	$30			

$60

16. There are 24 students in the class. They arrange their desks in rows with 6 desks in each row. How many rows are there? (3.OA.4)

24 ÷ 6 = 4

4 rows

© Houghton Mifflin Harcourt Publishing Company

Name _____

Problem Solving •
Use the Distributive Property

Essential Question How can you use the strategy *draw a diagram* to multiply with multiples of 10?

**Number and Operations in Base Ten—
3.NBT.3** *Also 3.OA.3, 3.OA.5, 3.OA.7*
MATHEMATICAL PRACTICES
MP.1, MP.3, MP.4, MP.7

Unlock the Problem Real World

The school assembly room has 5 rows of chairs with 20 chairs in each row. If the third-grade classes fill 3 rows of chairs, how many third graders are at the assembly?

Read the Problem

What do I need to find?

I need to find how many _____ are at the assembly.

What information do I need to use?

There are _____ chairs in each row.

The third graders fill _____ rows of chairs.

How will I use the information?

The Distributive Property tells me I can

_____ the factor 20 to multiply.

$3 \times 20 = 3 \times (10 + \underline{\quad})$

Solve the Problem

Draw a diagram. Finish the shading to show 3 rows of 20 chairs.

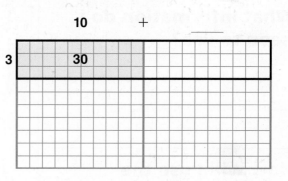

I can use the sum of the products of the smaller rectangles to find how many third graders are at the assembly.

$3 \times 10 = \underline{\quad}$ $3 \times 10 = \underline{\quad}$

$\underline{\quad} + \underline{\quad} = \underline{\quad}$

$3 \times 20 = \underline{\quad}$

So, _____ third graders are at the assembly.

1. Explain how breaking apart the factor 20 makes finding the

product easier. _____

© Houghton Mifflin Harcourt Publishing Company

🔒 Try Another Problem

Megan is watching a marching band practice. The band marches by with 4 rows of people playing instruments. She counts 30 people in each row. How many people march in the band?

Read the Problem	Solve the Problem
What do I need to find?	**Record the steps you used to solve the problem.** 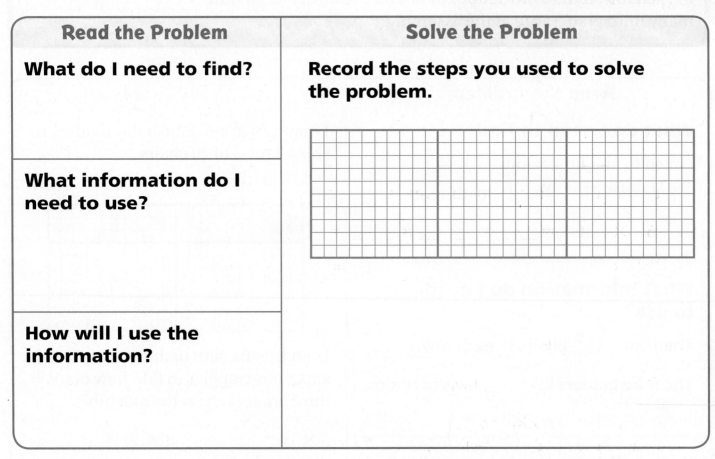
What information do I need to use?	
How will I use the information?	

2. How can you check to see if your answer is reasonable?

_____

_____

3. Explain how you can use the Distributive Property to help you find a product.

_____

_____

© Houghton Mifflin Harcourt Publishing Company • Image Credits: ©Visions of America, LLC/Alamy Images

Name _____

Unlock the Problem

√ Circle the numbers you will use.

√ Use the Distributive Property and break apart a greater factor to use facts you know.

√ Draw a diagram to help you solve the problem.

1. People filled all the seats in the front section of the theater. The front section has 6 rows with 40 seats in each row. How many people are in the front section of the theater?

   First, draw and label a diagram to break apart the problem into easier parts to solve.

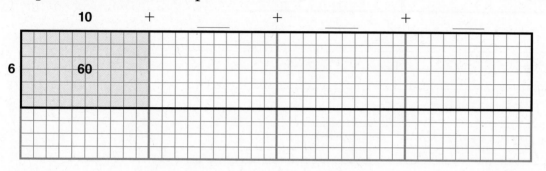

   Next, find the products of the smaller rectangles.

   $6 \times 10 =$ _____   _____ $\times$ _____ $=$ _____

   _____ $\times$ _____ $=$ _____   _____ $\times$ _____ $=$ _____

   Then, find the sum of the products.

   _____ $+$ _____ $+$ _____ $+$ _____ $=$ _____

   So, there are _____ people in the front section of the theater.

2. What if seats are added to the front section of the theater so that there are 6 rows with 50 seats in each row? How many seats are in the front section?

   _____

On Your Own

3. **THINK SMARTER** Tova sewed 60 pieces of blue ribbon together to make a costume. Each piece of ribbon was 2 meters long. She also sewed 40 pieces of red ribbon together that were each 3 meters long. Did Tova use more blue ribbon or red ribbon? Explain.

   _____

© Houghton Mifflin Harcourt Publishing Company

4. **MATHEMATICAL PRACTICE 3** **Verify the Reasoning of Others**
Carina draws this diagram to show that $8 \times 30 = 210$.
Explain her error.

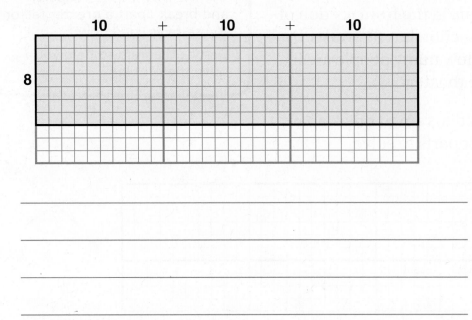

_____

_____

_____

_____

5. **WRITE** ▸*Math* Tamika wants to display 10 trophies on a
table in a rectangular array. How many different ways can
Tamika arrange the trophies? Explain your answer.

_____

_____

6. **GO DEEPER** The drama club has 350 tickets to sell. They
sell 124 tickets on Monday and 98 tickets on Tuesday.
How many tickets does the drama club have left to sell?

_____

7. **THINK SMARTER** Select the equations that show the
Distributive Property. Mark all that apply.

Ⓐ $3 \times 20 = (3 \times 10) + (3 \times 10)$

Ⓑ $(7 + 3) + 8 = 7 + (3 + 8)$

Ⓒ $(5 \times 10) + (5 \times 10) = 5 \times 20$

Ⓓ $(9 \times 2) + (9 \times 4) = 9 \times 6$

© Houghton Mifflin Harcourt Publishing Company

FOR MORE PRACTICE:
Standards Practice Book

Name _____

Multiplication Strategies with Multiples of 10

Essential Question What strategies can you use to multiply with multiples of 10?

Number and Operations in Base Ten— 3.NBT.3
Also 3.OA.3, 3.OA.5, 3.OA.7
MATHEMATICAL PRACTICES
MP.2, MP.4, MP.5, MP.7

Unlock the Problem Real World

You can use models and place value to multiply with multiples of 10.

> • What is a product of 10 and the counting numbers 1, 2, 3, and so on?
>
> _____

Activity Model multiples of 10.

Materials ■ base-ten blocks

Model the first nine multiples of 10.

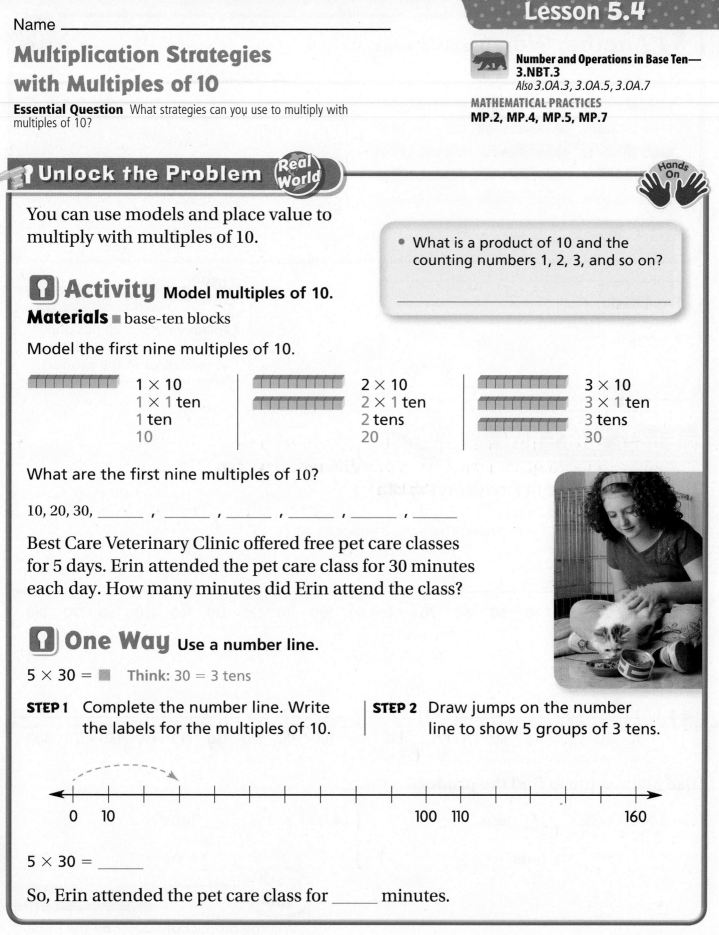

1×10	2×10	3×10
1×1 ten	2×1 ten	3×1 ten
1 ten	2 tens	3 tens
10	20	30

What are the first nine multiples of 10?

10, 20, 30, _____ , _____ , _____ , _____ , _____ , _____

Best Care Veterinary Clinic offered free pet care classes for 5 days. Erin attended the pet care class for 30 minutes each day. How many minutes did Erin attend the class?

One Way Use a number line.

$5 \times 30 =$ ■ **Think:** 30 = 3 tens

STEP 1 Complete the number line. Write the labels for the multiples of 10.

STEP 2 Draw jumps on the number line to show 5 groups of 3 tens.

0   10   100   110   160

$5 \times 30 =$ _____

So, Erin attended the pet care class for _____ minutes.

© Houghton Mifflin Harcourt Publishing Company

Another Way Use place value.

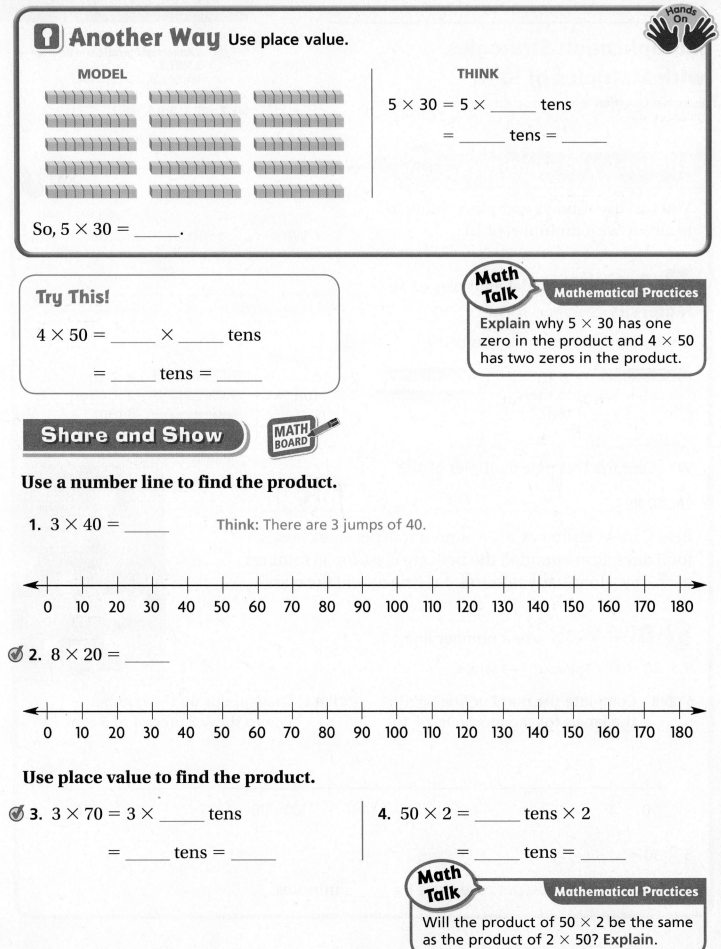

MODEL

THINK

$5 \times 30 = 5 \times$ _____ tens

= _____ tens = _____

So, $5 \times 30 =$ _____ .

Try This!

$4 \times 50 =$ _____ $\times$ _____ tens

= _____ tens = _____

Math Talk **Mathematical Practices**

Explain why 5×30 has one zero in the product and 4×50 has two zeros in the product.

Share and Show

MATH BOARD

Use a number line to find the product.

1. $3 \times 40 =$ _____   **Think:** There are 3 jumps of 40.

0 10 20 30 40 50 60 70 80 90 100 110 120 130 140 150 160 170 180

2. $8 \times 20 =$ _____

0 10 20 30 40 50 60 70 80 90 100 110 120 130 140 150 160 170 180

Use place value to find the product.

3. $3 \times 70 = 3 \times$ _____ tens

= _____ tens = _____

4. $50 \times 2 =$ _____ tens $\times$ 2

= _____ tens = _____

Math Talk **Mathematical Practices**

Will the product of 50×2 be the same as the product of 2×50? **Explain.**

204

© Houghton Mifflin Harcourt Publishing Company

Name _____

On Your Own

Use a number line to find the product.

5. $7 \times 20 =$ _____

0 10 20 30 40 50 60 70 80 90 100 110 120 130 140 150 160 170 180

6. $3 \times 50 =$ _____

0 10 20 30 40 50 60 70 80 90 100 110 120 130 140 150 160 170 180

Use place value to find the product.

7. $6 \times 60 = 6 \times$ _____ tens

  $=$ _____ tens $=$ _____

8. $50 \times 7 =$ _____ tens $\times 7$

  $=$ _____ tens $=$ _____

Problem Solving • Applications (Real World)

Use the table for 9–11.

9. The cost of a bottle of shampoo is $9. If the clinic sells their entire supply of shampoo, how much money will they receive?

_____

10. What's the Question? Each bag of treats has 30 treats. The answer is 240.

_____

11. THINK SMARTER There are 4 bottles of vitamins in each box of vitamins. Each bottle of vitamins has 20 vitamins. If the clinic wants to have a supply of 400 vitamins, how many more boxes should they order?

_____

Best Care Clinic Pet Supplies	
Item	**Amount**
Cat toys	10 packs
Treats	8 bags
Shampoo	20 bottles
Vitamins	3 boxes

Math on the Spot

© Houghton Mifflin Harcourt Publishing Company

Unlock the Problem Real World

12. **MATHEMATICAL PRACTICE 1** **Make Sense of Problems** Hiromi needs to set up chairs for 155 people to attend the school career day program. So far she has set up 6 rows with 20 chairs in each row. How many more chairs does Hiromi need to set up?

a. What do you need to find?

_____

b. What operations will you use to find how many more chairs Hiromi needs to set up?

_____

c. Write the steps you will use to solve the problem.

d. Complete the sentences.

Hiromi needs to set up _____ chairs for people to attend the program.

She has set up _____ rows with _____ chairs in each row.

So, Hiromi needs to set up _____ more chairs.

13. **GO DEEPER** Last week, Dr. Newman examined the paws of 30 dogs at her clinic. She examined the paws of 20 cats. What is the total number of paws Dr. Newman examined last week?

_____

14. **THINK SMARTER** Nick made this multiplication model. Complete the equation that represents the model.

_____ × _____ = _____

© Houghton Mifflin Harcourt Publishing Company • Image Credits: ©Comstock Images/Getty Images

FOR MORE PRACTICE:
Standards Practice Book

Name _____

Multiply 1-Digit Numbers by Multiples of 10

Number and Operations in Base Ten—
3.NBT.3
Also 3.OA.3, 3.OA.7
MATHEMATICAL PRACTICES
MP.4, MP.5, MP.7, MP.8

Essential Question How can you model and record multiplying 1-digit whole numbers by multiples of 10?

🔑 Unlock the Problem *Real World*

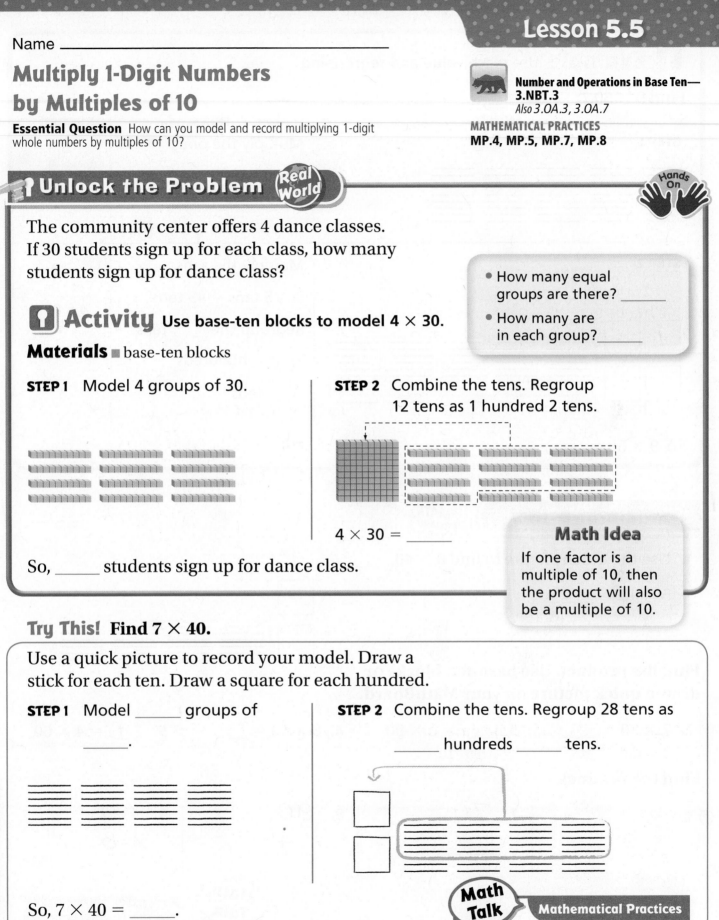

The community center offers 4 dance classes. If 30 students sign up for each class, how many students sign up for dance class?

- How many equal groups are there? _____
- How many are in each group? _____

🔓 Activity Use base-ten blocks to model 4 × 30.

Materials ■ base-ten blocks

STEP 1 Model 4 groups of 30.

STEP 2 Combine the tens. Regroup 12 tens as 1 hundred 2 tens.

4 × 30 = _____

So, _____ students sign up for dance class.

Math Idea

If one factor is a multiple of 10, then the product will also be a multiple of 10.

Try This! Find 7 × 40.

Use a quick picture to record your model. Draw a stick for each ten. Draw a square for each hundred.

STEP 1 Model _____ groups of _____.

STEP 2 Combine the tens. Regroup 28 tens as _____ hundreds _____ tens.

So, 7 × 40 = _____.

Math Talk **Mathematical Practices**

Will the product of 7 × 40 be the same as 4 × 70? **Explain**.

© Houghton Mifflin Harcourt Publishing Company

🔑 Example Use place value and regrouping.

Find 9×50.

MODEL	THINK	RECORD
STEP 1	Multiply the ones.	$\begin{array}{r} 5\,0 \\ \times\ \ 9 \\ \hline 0 \end{array}$
	9×0 ones = _____ ones	
STEP 2	Multiply the tens.	$\begin{array}{r} 5\,0 \\ \times\ \ 9 \\ \hline 4\,5\,0 \end{array}$
	9×5 tens = 45 tens	
	Regroup the _____ tens	
	as _____ hundreds	
	_____ tens.	

So, $9 \times 50 =$ _____.

Share and Show 🖊 MATH BOARD

1. Use the quick picture to find 5×40.

$5 \times 40 =$ _____

Find the product. Use base-ten blocks or draw a quick picture on your MathBoard.

✓ **2.** $7 \times 30 =$ _____   **3.** _____ $= 2 \times 90$ **4.** $8 \times 40 =$ _____   **5.** _____ $= 4 \times 60$

Find the product.

✓ **6.** $\begin{array}{r} 80 \\ \times\ 9 \\ \hline \end{array}$ **7.** $\begin{array}{r} 70 \\ \times\ 7 \\ \hline \end{array}$ **8.** $\begin{array}{r} 90 \\ \times\ 4 \\ \hline \end{array}$ **9.** $\begin{array}{r} 60 \\ \times\ 8 \\ \hline \end{array}$

Math Talk **Mathematical Practices**

Explain how you can use place value to solve Exercise 9.

© Houghton Mifflin Harcourt Publishing Company

Name _____

**Find the product. Use base-ten blocks or draw a
quick picture on your MathBoard.**

10. $2 \times 70 =$ _____   **11.** $8 \times 50 =$ _____   **12.** _____ $= 3 \times 90$ **13.** $2 \times 80 =$ _____

Find the product.

14. $\begin{array}{r} 80 \\ \times\ 3 \\ \hline \end{array}$ **15.** $\begin{array}{r} 60 \\ \times\ 9 \\ \hline \end{array}$ **16.** $\begin{array}{r} 90 \\ \times\ 8 \\ \hline \end{array}$ **17.** $\begin{array}{r} 80 \\ \times\ 8 \\ \hline \end{array}$

Practice: Copy and Solve Find the product.

18. 6×70 **19.** 9×90 **20.** 70×8 **21.** 90×7

MATHEMATICAL PRACTICE ② Reason Quantitatively Algebra Find the unknown factor.

22. $a \times 80 = 480$ **23.** $b \times 30 = 30$ **24.** $7 \times \blacksquare = 420$ **25.** $50 \times \blacktriangle = 0$

$a =$ _____ $b =$ _____ $\blacksquare =$ _____ $\blacktriangle =$ _____

Problem Solving • Applications Real World

26. THINK SMARTER Ava's class bought 6 packages of balloons for a school
celebration. Each package had 30 balloons. If 17 balloons were left
over, how many balloons were used for the party?

Math on the Spot

_____

27. Sense or Nonsense? Lori says that 8 is not a factor of 80 because
8 does not end in zero. Does Lori's statement make sense? Explain.

_____

28. MATHEMATICAL PRACTICE ④ **Model Mathematics** The book club members read
200 books in all. Each member read 5 books. Write an equation to
find the number of members in the book club. Use a letter to stand
for the unknown factor.

_____

© Houghton Mifflin Harcourt Publishing Company

Unlock the Problem

29. **GO DEEPER** Frank has a 2-digit number on his baseball uniform. The number is a multiple of 10 and has 3 for one of its factors. What three numbers could Frank have on his uniform?

a. What do you need to find?

_____

b. What information do you need to use?

_____

c. How can you solve the problem?

d. Complete the sentences.

Frank has a _____ on his uniform.

The number is a multiple of _____.

One factor of the number is _____.

Frank could have _____, _____, or

_____ on his uniform.

Personal Math Trainer

30. **THINK SMARTER ➕** Baker Farm grows and sells carrots to local grocery stores. The stores bundle the carrots to sell. Which grocery store bought the greatest number of carrots from Baker Farm? How many carrots did the store buy?

Grocery Store	Number of Carrots in 1 Bundle	Number of Bundles
Buy–More Foods	6	90
Lower Price Foods	8	60
Yummy Foods	7	80
Healthy Foods	9	70

© Houghton Mifflin Harcourt Publishing Company • Image Credits: ©George Doyle/Getty Images

FOR MORE PRACTICE:
Standards Practice Book

Name _____

1. The camping club wants to rent rafts. Each raft can hold 8 people. Which equation could be used to find how many rafts are needed for 32 people?

   (A) $8 \times 32 = \blacksquare$

   (B) $32 \times \blacksquare = 8$

   (C) $\blacksquare \times 8 = 32$

   (D) $32 \times 8 = \blacksquare$

2. Select the equations that show the Distributive Property. Mark all that apply.

   (A) $8 \times 20 = 8 \times (10 + 10)$

   (B) $5 \times 60 = 5 \times (20 + 40)$

   (C) $30 \times 6 = 6 \times 30$

   (D) $9 \times (4 + 3) = 9 \times 7$

3. Choose the number from the box that makes the sentence true.

   A library has 48 shelves of fiction books. There are 6 shelves in each cabinet.

   | 7 |
   | 8 |
   | 9 |

   There are [8] cabinets of fiction books in the library.

© Houghton Mifflin Harcourt Publishing Company

4. For numbers 4a–4d, choose True or False for each equation.

4a. $5 \times (4 + 4) = 8 \times 5$ ○ True   ○ False

4b. $8 \times (3 + 3) = 8 \times 5$ ○ True   ○ False

4c. $(3 \times 5) + (5 \times 5) = 8 \times 5$ ○ True   ○ False

4d. $(3 \times 2) + (8 \times 3) = 8 \times 5$ ○ True   ○ False

5. Alya planted 30 trays of flowers. Each tray held 8 flowers. Javon planted 230 flowers. Did Alya plant more flowers than Javon, the same number of flowers as Javon, or fewer flowers than Javon?

(A)   She planted more flowers than Javon.

(B)   She planted the exact same number of flowers as Javon.

(C)   She planted fewer flowers than Javon.

6. For numbers 6a–6d, choose Yes or No to show whether the unknown number is 6.

6a. $4 \times \blacksquare = 32$ ○ Yes   ○ No

6b. $\blacksquare \times 6 = 36$ ○ Yes   ○ No

6c. $8 \times \blacksquare = 49$ ○ Yes   ○ No

6d. $\blacksquare \times 30 = 180$ ○ Yes   ○ No

7. Each train can carry 20 cars. Use the number line to find how many cars 6 trains can carry.

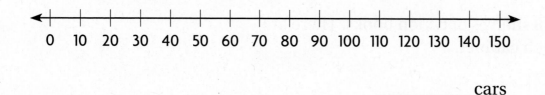

_____ cars

© Houghton Mifflin Harcourt Publishing Company

8. Samantha made this multiplication model. Complete the equation that represents the model.

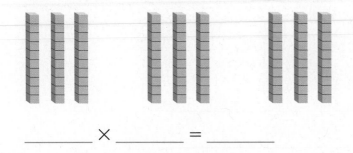

_____ × _____ = _____

9. A printer prints newsletters for many groups every month. Which group uses the greatest number of pieces of paper?

Group	Number of pieces of paper in newsletter	Number of copies of newsletter printed
Garden Ladies	5	70
Book Lovers Club	6	80
Model Train Fans	7	60
Travel Club	8	50

_____

10. A store has 30 boxes of melons. Each box holds 4 bags. Each bag holds 2 melons. What is the total number of melons in the store?

_____ melons

11. Heather's puppy weighs 23 pounds. He has been gaining 3 pounds every month as he grows. If this pattern continues, how much will the puppy weigh 5 months from now?

_____

© Houghton Mifflin Harcourt Publishing Company

12. Tim describes a pattern. He says the rule for the pattern shown in the table is "Add 3." Is his rule correct? Explain how you know.

Packages	1	2	3	4	5
Markers	4	8	12	16	20

_____

_____

_____

13. This shows a part of a multiplication table. Find the missing numbers. Explain how you found the numbers.

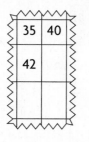

35	40
42	

_____

_____

_____

_____

_____

14. Find a rule for this table.

Tanks	3	4	5	6	7
Fish	240	320	400	480	560

Rule: _____

How would the table change if the rule was "Multiply by 8"? Explain.

_____

_____

© Houghton Mifflin Harcourt Publishing Company

15. Devon has 80 books to pack in boxes. She packs 20 books in each box. How many boxes does she need?

Write an equation using the letter *n* to stand for the unknown factor. Explain how to find the unknown factor.

_____

_____

_____

16. The bookstore has 6 shelves of books about animals. There are 30 books on each shelf. How many books about animals does the bookstore have?

Shade squares to make a diagram to show how you can use the Distributive Property to find the number of books about animals in the bookstore.

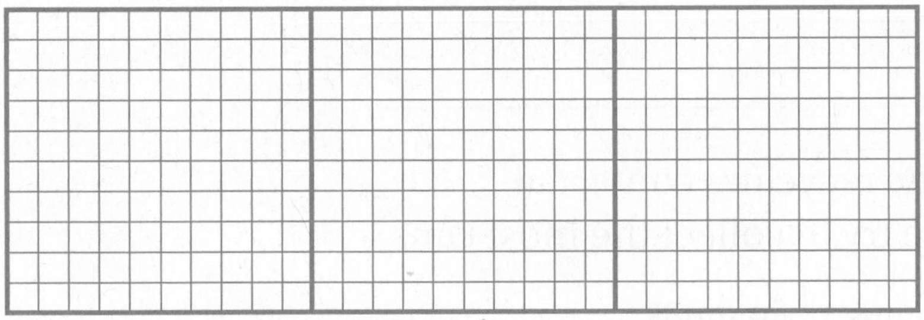

_____ animal books

© Houghton Mifflin Harcourt Publishing Company

17. Cody saves all his nickels. Today he is getting them out of his piggy bank and wrapping them to take to the bank. He finds he has 360 nickels. It takes 40 nickels to fill each paper wrapper and make a roll. How many wrappers does he need?

Part A

Write an equation using *n* for the unknown number. Find the number of wrappers needed.

_____ × _____ = _____

Part B

Explain how you solved this problem and how you know your answer is correct.

_____

_____

_____

_____

18. Ruben is collecting cans for the recycling contest at school. He makes two plans to try to collect the most cans.

Plan A: Collect 20 cans each week for 9 weeks.

Plan B: Collect 30 cans each week for 7 weeks.

Part A

Which plan should Ruben choose? _____

Part B

Explain how you made your choice.

_____

_____

_____

_____

_____

© Houghton Mifflin Harcourt Publishing Company

Show What You Know ✓

Check your understanding of important skills.

Name _____

▶ **Count Back to Subtract** **Use the number line. Write the difference.**

1. 8 − 5 = _____

     0 1 2 3 4 5 6 7 8 9 10

2. 9 − 4 = _____

     0 1 2 3 4 5 6 7 8 9 10

▶ **Count Equal Groups** **Complete.**

3.

_____ groups

_____ in each group

4.

_____ groups

_____ in each group

▶ **Multiplication Facts Through 9** **Find the product.**

5. 8 × 5 = _____   **6.** _____ = 7 × 7   **7.** 3 × 9 = _____

The table shows 3 different ways you can score points in basketball. Corina scored 12 points in a basketball game. Be a Math Detective to find the greatest number of field goals she could have scored. Then find the greatest number of 3-pointers she could have scored.

Scoring Points in Basketball	
free throw	1 point
field goal	2 points
3-pointer	3 points

© Houghton Mifflin Harcourt Publishing Company • ©D. Hurst/Alamy Images

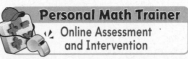

Personal Math Trainer
Online Assessment
and Intervention

Vocabulary Builder

▶ **Visualize It** • • • • • • • • • • • • • • • • • •

Complete the bubble map by using the words with a ✓ .

What is it like?   What are some examples?

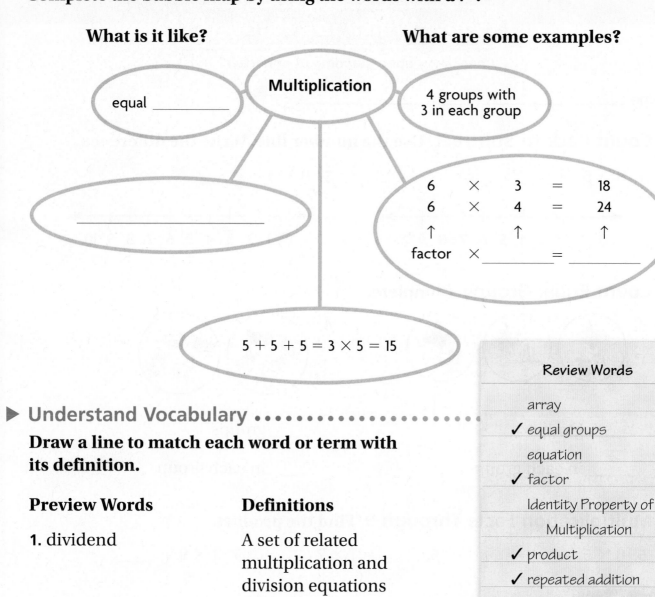

Multiplication

equal _____

4 groups with
3 in each group

_____

6	×	3	=	18
6	×	4	=	24
↑		↑		↑
factor	×	_____	=	_____

5 + 5 + 5 = 3 × 5 = 15

▶ **Understand Vocabulary** •

**Draw a line to match each word or term with
its definition.**

Preview Words	Definitions
1. dividend	A set of related multiplication and division equations
2. related facts	The number that divides the dividend
3. divisor	The number that is to be divided in a division problem

Review Words

array
✓ equal groups
equation
✓ factor
Identity Property of
   Multiplication
✓ product
✓ repeated addition

Preview Words

divide
dividend
divisor
inverse operations
quotient
related facts

• Interactive Student Edition
• Multimedia eGlossary

© Houghton Mifflin Harcourt Publishing Company

Name _____

Problem Solving • Model Division

Essential Question How can you use the strategy *act it out* to solve problems with equal groups?

Operations and Algebraic Thinking—3.OA.3 *Also 3.OA.2*

MATHEMATICAL PRACTICES
MP.1, MP.4, MP.5, MP.7

Unlock the Problem Real World

Stacy has 16 flowers. She puts an equal number of flowers in each of 4 vases. How many flowers does Stacy put in each vase?

Use the graphic organizer below to solve the problem.

Read the Problem	Solve the Problem
What do I need to find? I need to find the number of _____ Stacy puts in each _____. **What information do I need to use?** Stacy has _____ flowers. She puts an equal number of flowers in each of _____ vases. **How will I use the information?** I will act out the problem by making equal _____ with counters.	**Describe how to act out the problem to solve.** $16 \div 4 = 4$ First, count out __16__ counters. Next, make __4__ equal groups. Place 1 counter at a time in each group until all 16 counters are used. Last, draw the equal groups by completing the picture below. 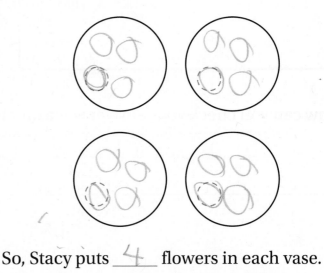 So, Stacy puts __4__ flowers in each vase.

© Houghton Mifflin Harcourt Publishing Company • Image Credits: ©Texas Department of Transportation (TxDOT)

🔑 Try Another Problem

Jamal is at the pet store. He buys 21 dog treats. If he plans to give each dog 3 treats, how many dogs does he feed?

Read the Problem	Solve the Problem
What do I need to find?	**Describe how to act out the problem to solve.**
What information do I need to use?	
How will I use the information?	

● How can you check your answer is reasonable? _____

_____

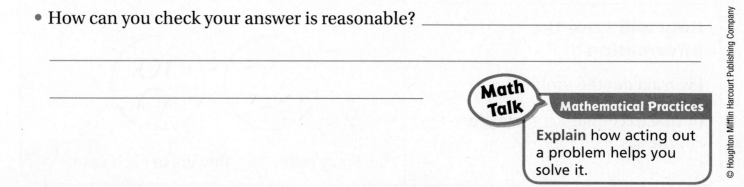

Math Talk

Mathematical Practices

Explain how acting out a problem helps you solve it.

© Houghton Mifflin Harcourt Publishing Company

Name _____

Unlock the Problem

✓ Use the Problem Solving MathBoard
✓ Underline important facts.
✓ Choose a strategy you know.

Share and Show

1. Mariana is having a party. She has 16 cups. She puts them in 2 equal stacks. How many cups are in each stack?

   First, decide how to act out the problem.

   You can use counters to represent the _____.

   You can draw _____ to represent the stacks.

   Then, draw to find the number of _____ in each stack.

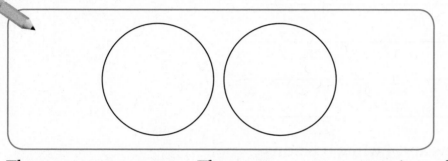

   There are _____ groups. There are _____ counters in each group.

   So, there are _____ cups in each stack.

2. **MATHEMATICAL PRACTICE ①** **Make Sense of Problems** What if Mariana has 24 cups and puts 4 cups in each stack? If she already made 4 stacks, how many more stacks can she make with the remaining cups?

   _____

On Your Own

3. **THINK SMARTER** At Luke's school party, the children get into teams of 5 to play a game. If there are 20 boys and 15 girls, how many teams are there?

   _____

4. **GO DEEPER** Anne put 20 party hats and 20 balloons on 4 tables. If she put the same number on each one, how many hats and balloons did she put on each table?

   _____

© Houghton Mifflin Harcourt Publishing Company

Use the table for 5–6.

5. Sadie's plates came in packages of 5. How many packages of plates did she buy?

_____

6. **MATHEMATICAL PRACTICE 6 Explain a Method** Sadie bought 4 packages of napkins and 3 packages of cups. Which item had more in each package? How many more? Explain how you found your answer.

_____

_____

_____

_____

Sadie's Party Supplies

Item	Number
Plates	30
Napkins	28
Cups	24

7. Megan put 3 red balloons and 4 white balloons at each of 4 tables. How many balloons are at the tables?

_____

WRITE ▸ Math
Show Your Work

Personal Math Trainer

8. **THINK SMARTER ➕** Miguel bought 18 party favors. He gave 2 party favors to each of the children at his party. How many children were at Miguel's party?

● ● ● ● ● ●
● ● ● ● ● ●
● ● ● ● ● ●

Ring equal groups to model the problem.

_____ children

© Houghton Mifflin Harcourt Publishing Company

Name _____

Size of Equal Groups

Essential Question How can you model a division problem to find how many in each group?

Unlock the Problem · Real World · Hands On

Hector has 12 rocks from a nearby state park. He puts an equal number of his rocks in each of 3 boxes. How many rocks are in each box?

When you multiply, you put equal groups together. When you **divide**, you separate into equal groups.

You can divide to find the number in each group.

- What do you need to find?

_____

- Circle the numbers you need to use.

Activity Use counters to model the problem.

Materials ■ counters ■ MathBoard

STEP 1

Use 12 counters.

STEP 2

Draw 3 circles on your MathBoard. Place 1 counter at a time in each circle until all 12 counters are used. Draw the rest of the counters to show your work.

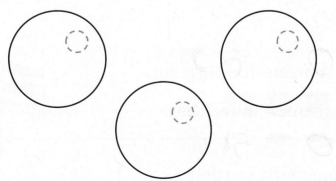

There are _____ counters in each group.

So, there are _____ rocks in each box.

Try This!

Madison has 15 rocks. She puts an equal number of rocks in each of 5 boxes. How many rocks are in each box?

STEP 1

Draw 5 squares to show 5 boxes.

STEP 2

Draw 1 counter in each square to show the rocks. Continue drawing 1 counter at a time in each box until all 15 counters are drawn.

There are _____ counters in each group.

So, there are _____ rocks in each box.

Math Talk

Mathematical Practices

Describe another way to arrange 15 counters to make equal groups.

1. How many counters did you draw? _____

2. How many equal groups did you make? _____

3. How many counters are in each group? _____

224

© Houghton Mifflin Harcourt Publishing Company

Name _____

1. Jon has 8 counters. He makes 4 equal groups. Draw a picture to show the number of counters in each group.

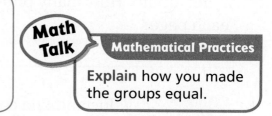

Math Talk — **Mathematical Practices**

Explain how you made the groups equal.

Use counters or draw a quick picture on your MathBoard. Make equal groups. Complete the table.

	Counters	Number of Equal Groups	Number in Each Group
✓ 2.	10	2	
✓ 3.	24	6	

On Your Own

Use counters or draw a quick picture on your MathBoard. Make equal groups. Complete the table.

	Counters	Number of Equal Groups	Number in Each Group
4.	14	7	
5.	21	3	

6. **GO DEEPER** Cameron and Jody collected 20 stamps. Cameron says they can put an equal number of stamps on 5 pages of their album. Jody says they can put an equal number on 4 pages. Whose statement makes sense? Explain.

_____

_____

© Houghton Mifflin Harcourt Publishing Company

Problem Solving • Applications Real World

Use the table for 7–8.

Photos	
Name	**Number of Photos**
Madison	28
Joe	25
Ella	15

7. Madison puts all of her photos in a photo album. She puts an equal number of photos on each of 4 pages in her album. How many photos are on each page?

_____

8. **THINK SMARTER** Joe and Ella combine their photos. Then they put an equal number on each page of an 8-page photo album. How many photos are on each page?

_____

9. **MATHEMATICAL PRACTICE ❸** **Make Arguments** Rebekah found 28 sea shells. Can she share the sea shells equally among the 6 people in her family? Explain.

_____

_____

_____

10. **THINK SMARTER** Zana has 9 rocks from a trip. She puts an equal number of rocks in each of 3 bags. How many rocks are in each bag?

Circle the amount to complete the sentence.

There are
$\begin{array}{c} 3 \\ 6 \\ 12 \\ 27 \end{array}$
rocks in each bag.

© Houghton Mifflin Harcourt Publishing Company

FOR MORE PRACTICE:
Standards Practice Book

Name _____

Number of Equal Groups

Essential Question How can you model a division problem to find how many equal groups?

Operations and Algebraic Thinking—3.OA.2
Also 3.OA.3
MATHEMATICAL PRACTICES
MP.1, MP.4, MP.5, MP.7

CONNECT You have learned how to divide to find the number in each group. Now you will learn how to divide to find the number of equal groups.

Unlock the Problem Real World

Juan has 12 shells and some boxes. He wants to put his shells in groups of 3. How many boxes does he need for his shells?

- Underline what you need to find.
- How many shells does Juan want to put in each group?

_____

🔑 **Make equal groups.**

- Look at the 12 counters.
- Circle a group of 3 counters.
- Continue circling groups of 3 until all 12 counters are in groups.

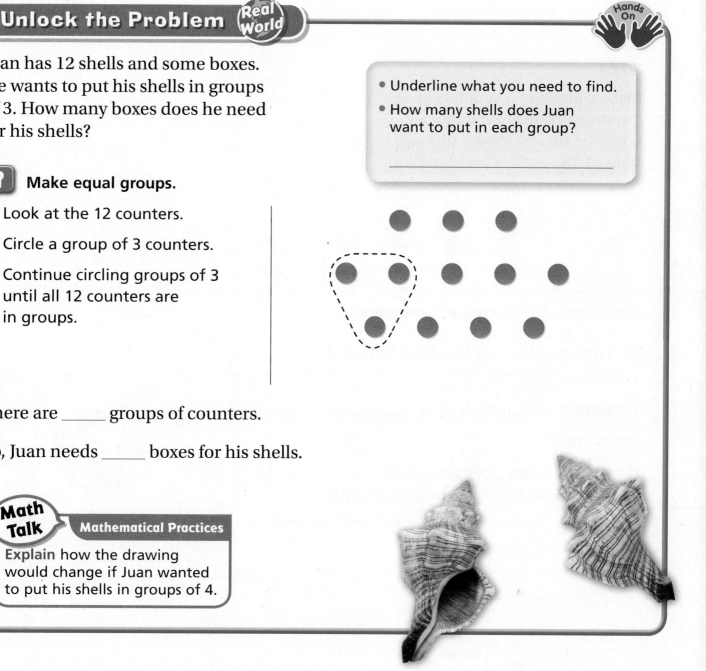

There are _____ groups of counters.

So, Juan needs _____ boxes for his shells.

Math Talk *Mathematical Practices*

Explain how the drawing would change if Juan wanted to put his shells in groups of 4.

© Houghton Mifflin Harcourt Publishing Company • Image Credits: Eyewire/Getty Images

Try This!

Sarah has 15 shells. She wants to put each group of 5 shells in a box.
How many boxes does she need for her shells?

STEP 1

Draw 15 counters.

STEP 2

Make a group of 5 counters by
drawing a circle around them.
Continue circling groups of 5
until all 15 counters are in groups.

There are _____ groups of 5 counters.

So, Sarah needs _____ boxes for her shells.

• **THINK SMARTER** What if Sarah puts her 15 shells in
groups of 3?

How many boxes does she need? _____
Draw a quick picture to show your work.

© Houghton Mifflin Harcourt Publishing Company

Name _____

1. Tamika has 12 counters. She puts them in groups of 2. Draw a picture to show the number of groups.

Math Talk
Mathematical Practices

Explain how you find the number of equal groups when you divide.

Draw counters on your MathBoard. Then circle equal groups. Complete the table.

	Counters	Number of Equal Groups	Number in Each Group
✓2.	20		4
✓3.	24		3

On Your Own

Draw counters on your MathBoard. Then circle equal groups. Complete the table.

	Counters	Number of Equal Groups	Number in Each Group
4.	18		2
5.	16		8

6. **THINK SMARTER** A store has 18 red beach balls and 17 green beach balls in boxes of 5 beach balls each. How many boxes of beach balls are at the store?

_____

© Houghton Mifflin Harcourt Publishing Company

Unlock the Problem Real World

7. **MATHEMATICAL PRACTICE 1** **Make Sense of Problems** A store has 24 beach towels in stacks of 6 towels each. How many stacks of beach towels are at the store?

a. What do you need to find? _____

_____

b. How will you use what you know about making equal groups

to solve the problem? _____

_____

c. Draw equal groups to find how many stacks of beach towels there are at the store.

d. Complete the sentences.

The store has _____ beach towels.

There are _____ towels in each stack.

So, there are _____ stacks of beach towels at the store.

8. **GO DEEPER** Write a problem about dividing beach toys into equal groups. Then solve the problem.

_____

_____

_____

9. **THINK SMARTER** Dan's train is 27 inches long. If each train car is 3 inches long, how many train cars are there?

Choose a number from the box to complete the sentence.

| 6 |
| 7 |
| 8 |
| 9 |

There are _____ train cars.

© Houghton Mifflin Harcourt Publishing Company • Image Credits: ©Kitch Bain/Alamy Images

FOR MORE PRACTICE:
Standards Practice Book

Name _____

Model with Bar Models

Essential Question How can you use bar models to solve division problems?

Operations and Algebraic Thinking—3.OA.2
Also 3.OA.3
MATHEMATICAL PRACTICES
MP.1, MP.4, MP.5, MP.7

🔑 Unlock the Problem 🌎 Real World

A dog trainer has 20 dog treats for 5 dogs in his class. If each dog gets the same number of treats, how many treats will each dog get?

• What do you need to find?

_____

🔓 Activity 1 Use counters to find how many in each group.

Materials ■ counters ■ MathBoard

• Use 20 counters.

• Draw 5 circles on your MathBoard.

• Place 1 counter at a time in each circle until all 20 counters are used.

• Draw the rest of the counters to show your work.

There are _____ counters in each of the 5 groups.

A bar model can show how the parts of a problem are related.

• Complete the bar model to show 20 dog treats divided into 5 equal groups.

20 dog treats

So, each dog will get _____ treats.

© Houghton Mifflin Harcourt Publishing Company • Image Credits: (cr) ©Juniors Bildarchiv/Alamy

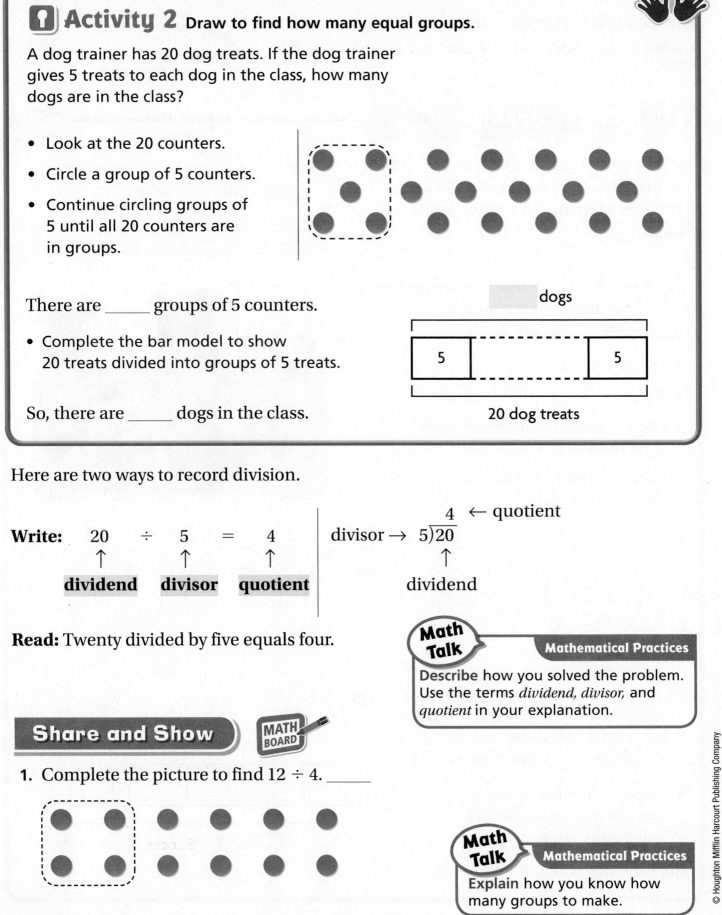

Activity 2 Draw to find how many equal groups.

A dog trainer has 20 dog treats. If the dog trainer gives 5 treats to each dog in the class, how many dogs are in the class?

- Look at the 20 counters.
- Circle a group of 5 counters.
- Continue circling groups of 5 until all 20 counters are in groups.

There are _____ groups of 5 counters.

- Complete the bar model to show 20 treats divided into groups of 5 treats.

So, there are _____ dogs in the class.

_____ dogs

| 5 | | 5 |

20 dog treats

Here are two ways to record division.

Write: 20 ÷ 5 = 4 $\quad$ 4 ← quotient

↑   ↑   ↑   divisor → 5)‾20‾

dividend   divisor   quotient   ↑

dividend

Read: Twenty divided by five equals four.

Math Talk   **Mathematical Practices**

Describe how you solved the problem. Use the terms *dividend, divisor,* and *quotient* in your explanation.

Share and Show

MATH BOARD

1. Complete the picture to find 12 ÷ 4. _____

Math Talk   **Mathematical Practices**

Explain how you know how many groups to make.

© Houghton Mifflin Harcourt Publishing Company

Name _____

Write a division equation for the picture.

2.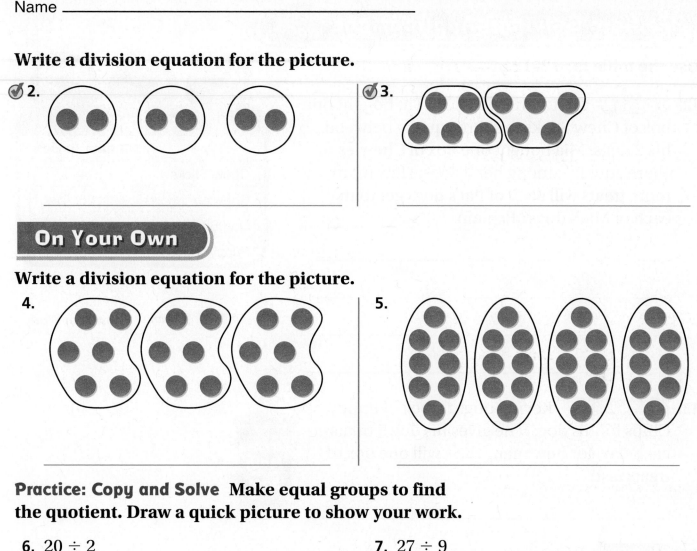

3.

_____

On Your Own

Write a division equation for the picture.

4.

5.

_____

Practice: Copy and Solve Make equal groups to find the quotient. Draw a quick picture to show your work.

6. $20 \div 2$

7. $27 \div 9$

8. $20 \div 5$

9. $18 \div 3$

Complete the bar model to solve. Then write a division equation for the bar model.

10. There are 24 books in 4 equal stacks. How many books are in each stack?

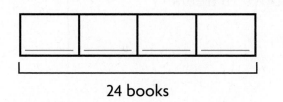

24 books

_____

11. There are 8 matching socks. How many pairs of socks can you make?

pairs

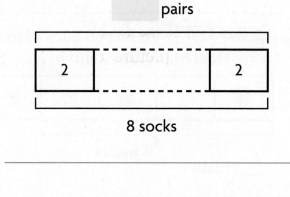

| 2 | | | 2 |

8 socks

_____

© Houghton Mifflin Harcourt Publishing Company

Problem Solving • Applications Real World

Use the table for 12–13.

Dog Treats

Type	Number in Box
Chew Sticks	14
Chewies	25
Dog Bites	30
Puppy Chips	45

12. **MATHEMATICAL PRACTICE 4** **Write an Equation** Pat bought one box of Chew Sticks to share equally between his 2 dogs. Mia bought one box of Chewies to share equally among her 5 dogs. How many more treats will each of Pat's dogs get than each of Mia's dogs? Explain.

_____

_____

_____

_____

WRITE ▸ *Math* • **Show Your Work** • • • • •

13. **THINK SMARTER** Kevin bought a box of Puppy Chips for his dog. If he gives his dog 5 treats each day, for how many days will one box of treats last?

_____

14. **GO DEEPER** Write and solve a problem for $42 \div 7$ in which the quotient is the number of groups.

_____

_____

_____

15. **THINK SMARTER** Ed buys 5 bags of treats. He buys 15 treats in all. How many treats are in each bag?

■	■	■	■	■

15 treats

_____ treats

FOR MORE PRACTICE:
Standards Practice Book

© Houghton Mifflin Harcourt Publishing Company • Image Credits: (tr) ©Lawrence Manning/Corbis

Name _____

Relate Subtraction and Division

Essential Question How is division related to subtraction?

🔑 Another Way Count back on a number line.

- Start at 12.
- Count back by 2s as many times as you can. Draw the rest of the jumps on the number line.
- Count the number of times you jumped back 2.

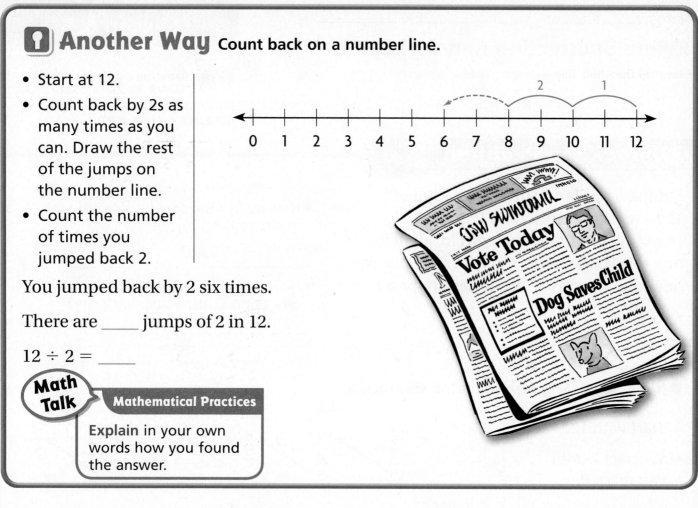

You jumped back by 2 six times.

There are _____ jumps of 2 in 12.

$12 \div 2 =$ _____

Math Talk **Mathematical Practices**

Explain in your own words how you found the answer.

- What do your jumps of 2 represent? _____

_____

Share and Show MATH BOARD

1. Draw the rest of the jumps on the number line to complete the division equation. $12 \div 4 =$ _____

Math Talk **Mathematical Practices**

Explain how counting back on a number line is like using repeated subtraction.

Write a division equation.

✓ 2.
```
  10        5
 - 5       - 5
 ----      ----
   5         0
```

✓ 3.

_____   _____

© Houghton Mifflin Harcourt Publishing Company

On Your Own

Write a division equation.

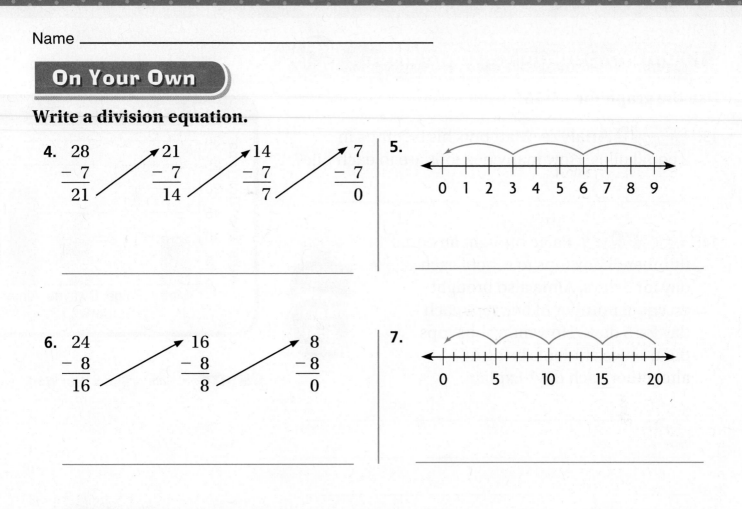

4.
$$\begin{array}{r} 28 \\ -\ 7 \\ \hline 21 \end{array} \qquad \begin{array}{r} 21 \\ -\ 7 \\ \hline 14 \end{array} \qquad \begin{array}{r} 14 \\ -\ 7 \\ \hline 7 \end{array} \qquad \begin{array}{r} 7 \\ -\ 7 \\ \hline 0 \end{array}$$

_____

5.

_____

6.
$$\begin{array}{r} 24 \\ -\ 8 \\ \hline 16 \end{array} \qquad \begin{array}{r} 16 \\ -\ 8 \\ \hline 8 \end{array} \qquad \begin{array}{r} 8 \\ -\ 8 \\ \hline 0 \end{array}$$

_____

7.

_____

8. **THINK SMARTER** Write a word problem that can be solved by using one of the division equations above.

_____

_____

Use repeated subtraction or a number line to solve.

9. $18 \div 6 =$ _____

10. $14 \div 7 =$ _____

11. $9\overline{)27}$

12. $3\overline{)24}$

© Houghton Mifflin Harcourt Publishing Company

Problem Solving • Applications

Use the graph for 13–15.

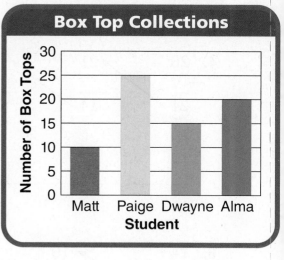

Box Top Collections

13. **MATHEMATICAL PRACTICE ① Analyze** Matt puts his box tops in 2 equal piles. How many box tops are in each pile?

_____

14. **THINK SMARTER** Paige brought an equal number of box tops to school each day for 5 days. Alma also brought an equal number of box tops each day for 5 days. How many box tops did the two students bring in altogether each day? Explain.

_____

_____

_____

WRITE ▸ Math • Show Your Work • • • •

15. **GO DEEPER** Dwayne collects another 15 box tops and puts all his box tops into bins. He puts an equal number in each bin. The answer is 5. What's the question?

_____

_____

$\overline{)25}$

Personal Math Trainer

16. **THINK SMARTER +** Maya collected 4 box tops each day. She collected 20 box tops in all. For how many days did Maya collect box tops?

Draw jumps on the number line to model the problem.

0   5   10   15   20   _____ days

FOR MORE PRACTICE:
Standards Practice Book

© Houghton Mifflin Harcourt Publishing Company

Name _____

 **Mid-Chapter Checkpoint**

Vocabulary

Vocabulary
divide
divisor

Choose the best term from the box to complete the sentence.

1. You __divide__ when you separate into equal groups. (p. 223)

Concepts and Skills

Use counters or draw a quick picture on your MathBoard.
Make or circle equal groups. Complete the table. (3.OA.2)

	Counters	Number of Equal Groups	Number in Each Group
2.	6	2	3
3.	30	6	5
4.	28	7	4

Write a division equation for the picture. (3.OA.2)

5.
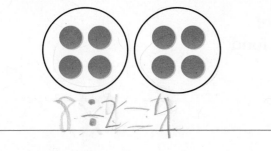

$8 \div 2 = 4$

6.
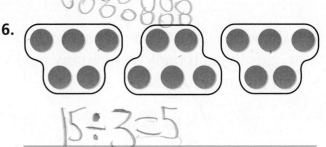

$15 \div 3 = 5$

Write a division equation. (3.OA.3)

7.
$$
\begin{array}{cccc}
36 & 27 & 18 & 9 \\
-9 & -9 & -9 & -9 \\
\hline
27 & 18 & 9 & 0
\end{array}
$$

$36 \div 9 = 4$

8.
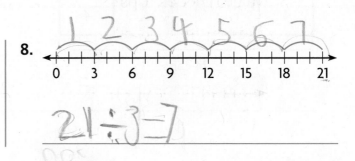

$21 \div 3 = 7$

© Houghton Mifflin Harcourt Publishing Company

9. Victor plants 14 seeds in some flowerpots. If he puts 2 seeds in each pot, how many flowerpots does he use? (3.OA.2)

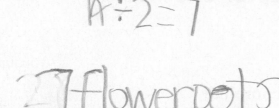

14 ÷ 2 = 7

7 flowerpots

10. Desiree has 20 stickers. She gives the same number of stickers to each of 5 friends. What equation can be used to find the number of stickers each friend receives? (3.OA.3)

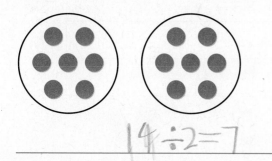

20 ÷ 5 = 4 stickers

11. Jayden modeled a division equation with some counters. What division equation matches the model? (3.OA.2)

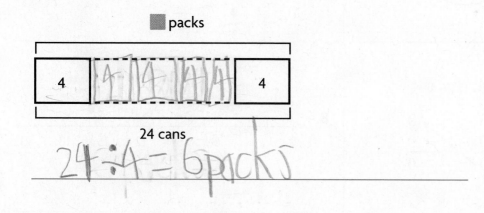

14 ÷ 2 = 7

12. Lillian bought 24 cans of cat food. There were 4 cans in each pack. How many packs of cat food did Lillian buy? (3.OA.2)

■ packs

| 4 | | | | | | 4 |

24 cans

24 ÷ 4 = 6 packs

© Houghton Mifflin Harcourt Publishing Company

Model with Arrays

Essential Question How can you use arrays to solve division problems?

Operations and Algebraic Thinking—3.OA.3 *Also 3.OA.2*
MATHEMATICAL PRACTICES
MP.4, MP.6, MP.7, MP.8

Investigate

Materials ■ square tiles

You can use arrays to model division and find equal groups.

A. Count out 30 tiles. Make an array to find how many rows of 5 are in 30.

B. Make a row of 5 tiles.

C. Continue to make as many rows of 5 tiles as you can.

How many rows of 5 did you make? _____

Draw Conclusions

1. Explain how you used the tiles to find the number of rows of 5 in 30.

_____

_____

2. What multiplication equation could you write for the array? Explain.

_____

_____

3. Tell how to use an array to find how many rows of 6 are in 30.

_____

_____

© Houghton Mifflin Harcourt Publishing Company

Make Connections

You can write a division equation to show how many rows of 5 are in 30. Show the array you made in Investigate by completing the drawing below.

> **Math Idea**
>
> You can divide to find the number of equal rows or to find the number in each row.

$30 \div 5 = \blacksquare$

There are _____ rows of 5 tiles in 30.

So, $30 \div 5 =$ _____.

Try This!

Count out 24 tiles. Make an array with the same number of tiles in 4 rows. Place 1 tile in each of the 4 rows. Then continue placing 1 tile in each row until you use all the tiles. Draw your array below.

> **Math Talk**
>
> **Mathematical Practices**
>
> **Explain** how making an array helps you divide.

- How many tiles are in each row? _____

- What division equation can you write for your array? _____

242

© Houghton Mifflin Harcourt Publishing Company

Name _____

Use square tiles to make an array. Solve.

1. How many rows of 3 are in 18?

   _____

2. How many rows of 6 are in 12?

   _____

3. How many rows of 7 are in 21?

   _____

4. How many rows of 8 are in 32?

   _____

Make an array. Then write a division equation.

5. 25 tiles in 5 rows

   _____

6. 14 tiles in 2 rows

   _____

7. 28 tiles in 4 rows

   _____

8. 27 tiles in 9 rows

   _____

Problem Solving • Applications

9. THINK SMARTER Tell how to use an array to find how many rows of 8 are in 40.

   _____

   _____

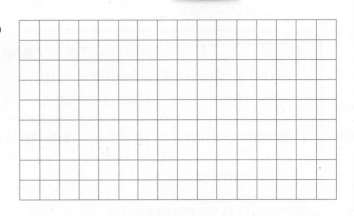

10. MATHEMATICAL PRACTICE ④ Model Mathematics Show two ways you could make an array with tiles for $18 \div 6$. Shade squares on the grid to record the arrays.

© Houghton Mifflin Harcourt Publishing Company

Unlock the Problem · Real World

11. **MATHEMATICAL PRACTICE ⑦ Look for Structure** Thomas has 28 tomato seedlings to plant in his garden. He wants to plant 4 seedlings in each row. How many rows of tomato seedlings will Thomas plant?

a. What do you need to find? _____

_____

b. What operation could you use to solve the problem? _____

_____

c. Draw an array to find the number of rows of tomato seedlings.

e. Complete the sentences.

Thomas has _____ tomato seedlings.

He wants to plant _____

seedlings in each _____.

So, Thomas will plant _____ rows of tomato seedlings.

d. What is another way you could have solved the problem?

_____

_____

12. **Go DEEPER** There were 20 plants sold at a store on Saturday, and 30 plants sold at the store on Sunday. Customers bought 5 plants each. How many customers in all bought the plants?

_____

13. **THINK SMARTER** Paige walked her dog 15 times in 5 days. She walked him the same number of times each day. How many times did Paige walk her dog each day?

Shade squares to make an array to model the problem.

_____ times

FOR MORE PRACTICE: Standards Practice Book

© Houghton Mifflin Harcourt Publishing Company

Relate Multiplication and Division

Essential Question How can you use multiplication to divide?

Operations and Algebraic Thinking—3.OA.6 Also 3.OA.2, 3.OA.3, 3.OA.4, 3.OA.7

MATHEMATICAL PRACTICES
MP.2, MP.4, MP.7, MP.8

🔑 Unlock the Problem (Real World)

Pam went to the fair. She went on the same ride 6 times and used the same number of tickets each time. She used 18 tickets. How many tickets did she use each time she went on the ride?

• What do you need to find?

_____

_____

• Circle the numbers you need to use.

🔓 One Way Use bar models.

You can use bar models to understand how multiplication and division are related.

Complete the bar model to show 18 tickets divided into 6 equal groups.

18 tickets

Write: 18 ÷ 6 = _____

So, Pam used _____ tickets each time she went on the ride.

What if the problem said Pam went on the ride 6 times and used 3 tickets each time? How many tickets did Pam use in all?

Complete the bar model to show 6 groups of 3 tickets.

3	3	3	3	3	3

_____ tickets

Write: 6 × 3 = _____

Multiplication and division are opposite operations, or **inverse operations**.

You can think about multiplication to solve a division problem.

To solve 18 ÷ 6 = ■, think 6 × ■ = 18.

Since 6 × 3 = 18, then 18 ÷ 6 = 3.

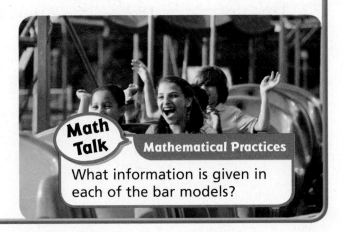

Math Talk **Mathematical Practices**

What information is given in each of the bar models?

© Houghton Mifflin Harcourt Publishing Company • Image Credits: ©kali9/Getty Images

🔑 Another Way Use an array.

You can use an array to see how multiplication and division are related.

Show an array with 18 counters in 3 equal rows by completing the drawing.

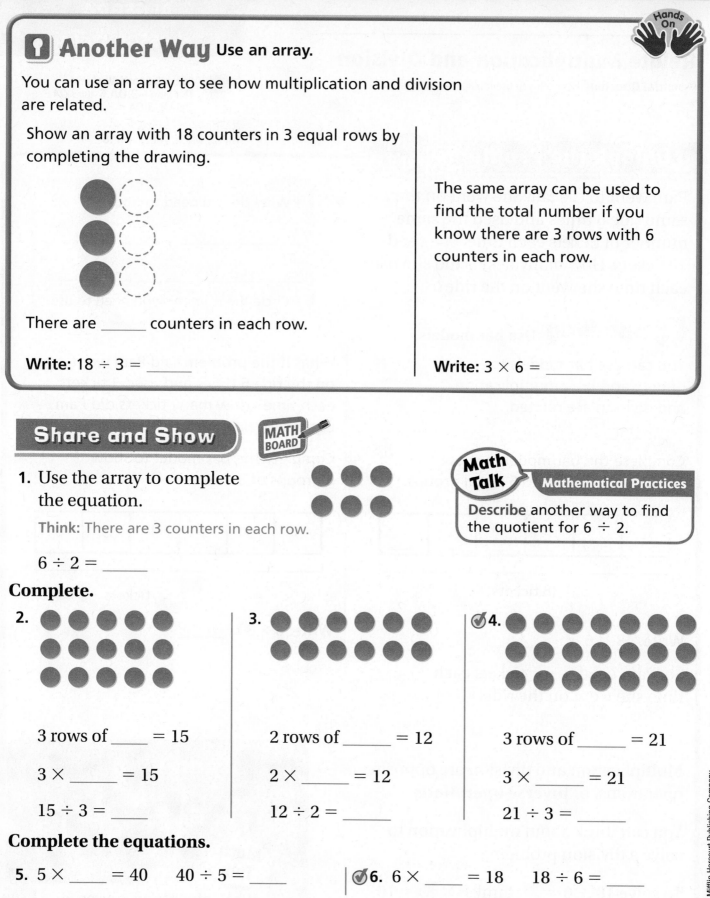

There are _____ counters in each row.

Write: 18 ÷ 3 = _____

The same array can be used to find the total number if you know there are 3 rows with 6 counters in each row.

Write: 3 × 6 = _____

Share and Show

MATH BOARD

1. Use the array to complete the equation.

   Think: There are 3 counters in each row.

   6 ÷ 2 = _____

Math Talk   **Mathematical Practices**

Describe another way to find the quotient for 6 ÷ 2.

Complete.

2.
   3 rows of _____ = 15

   3 × _____ = 15

   15 ÷ 3 = _____

3.
   2 rows of _____ = 12

   2 × _____ = 12

   12 ÷ 2 = _____

✓4.
   3 rows of _____ = 21

   3 × _____ = 21

   21 ÷ 3 = _____

Complete the equations.

5. 5 × _____ = 40   40 ÷ 5 = _____

✓6. 6 × _____ = 18   18 ÷ 6 = _____

© Houghton Mifflin Harcourt Publishing Company

On Your Own

Complete.

7.

5 rows of ____ = 30

5 × ____ = 30

30 ÷ 5 = ____

8.

4 rows of ____ = 20

4 × ____ = 20

20 ÷ 4 = ____

9.

4 rows of ____ = 28

4 × ____ = 28

28 ÷ 4 = ____

Complete the equations.

10. 7 × ____ = 21   21 ÷ 7 = ____

11. 8 × ____ = 16   16 ÷ 8 = ____

12. 4 × ____ = 32   32 ÷ 4 = ____

13. 6 × ____ = 24   24 ÷ 6 = ____

MATHEMATICAL PRACTICE 6 **Attend to Precision** **Algebra** **Complete.**

14. 3 × 3 = 27 ÷ ____

15. 16 ÷ 2 = ____ × 2

16. 9 = ____ ÷ 4

17. 5 = ____ ÷ 7

18. 42 ÷ 7 = ____ × 2

19. 30 ÷ ____ = 2 × 3

20. Justin and Ivan went to the fair when all rides were $2 each. Each boy went on the same number of rides, and spent $10. How many rides did each boy go on?

_____

© Houghton Mifflin Harcourt Publishing Company

Problem Solving • Applications

Use the table for 21–22.

Ventura County Fair	
Price of Admission	
Adults	$6
Students	$3
Children 5 and under free	

21. Mr. Jerome paid $24 for some students to get into the fair. How many students did Mr. Jerome pay for?

_____

22. **THINK SMARTER** Garrett is 8 years old. He and his family are going to the county fair. What is the price of admission for Garrett, his 2 parents, and baby sister?

_____

23. **MATHEMATICAL PRACTICE ④ Use a Diagram** There are 20 seats on the Wildcat ride. The number of seats in each car is the same. If there are 5 cars on the ride, how many seats are in each car? Complete the bar model to show the problem. Then answer the question.

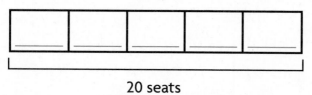

20 seats

_____

24. **GO DEEPER** How many days are there in 2 weeks? Write and solve a related word problem to represent the inverse operation.

_____

25. **THINK SMARTER** There are 35 prizes in 5 equal rows. How many prizes are in each row?

Complete each equation to represent the problem.

$5 \times$ _____ $= 35$ $35 \div 5 =$ _____

_____ prizes

FOR MORE PRACTICE:
Standards Practice Book

248

© Houghton Mifflin Harcourt Publishing Company

Write Related Facts

Essential Question How can you write a set of related multiplication and division facts?

**Operations and Algebraic Thinking—
3.OA.7** *Also 3.OA.2, 3.OA.3*
MATHEMATICAL PRACTICES
MP.2, MP.6, MP.7, MP.8

Unlock the Problem

Related facts are a set of related multiplication and division equations. What related facts can you write for 2, 4, and 8?

Activity

Materials ■ square tiles

• What model can you use to show how multiplication and division are related?

_____

STEP 1

Use 8 tiles to make an array with 2 equal rows.

Draw the rest of the tiles.

How many tiles are in each row? _____

Write a division equation for the array using the total number of tiles as the dividend and the number of rows as the divisor.

_____ ÷ _____ = _____

Write a multiplication equation for the array.

_____ × _____ = _____

STEP 2

Now, use 8 tiles to make an array with 4 equal rows.

Draw the rest of the tiles.

How many tiles are in each row? _____

Write a division equation for the array using the total number of tiles as the dividend and the number of rows as the divisor.

_____ ÷ _____ = _____

So, $8 ÷ 2 =$ _____, $2 × 4 =$ _____,

$8 ÷ 4 =$ _____, and $4 × 2 =$ _____ are related facts.

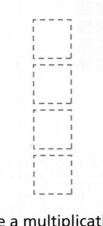

Write a multiplication equation for the array.

_____ × _____ = _____

© Houghton Mifflin Harcourt Publishing Company

Try This! Draw an array with 4 rows of 4 tiles.

Your array shows the related facts for 4, 4, and 16.

$4 \times 4 =$ _____ $16 \div 4 =$ _____

Since both factors are the same, there are only two equations in this set of related facts.

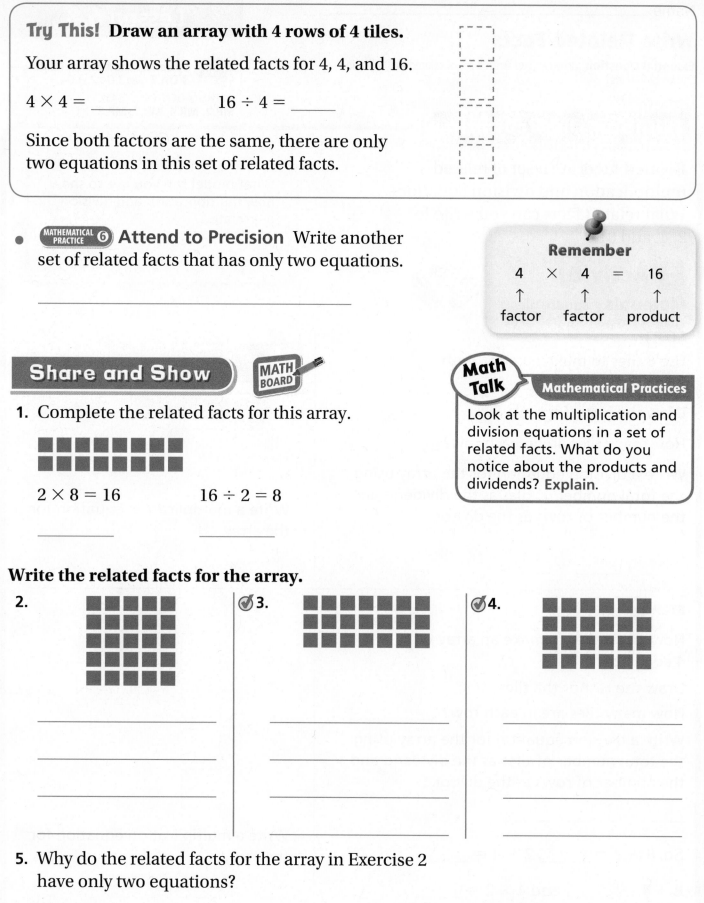

• **MATHEMATICAL PRACTICE ⑥** **Attend to Precision** Write another set of related facts that has only two equations.

_____

Remember

$$4 \quad \times \quad 4 \quad = \quad 16$$
↑   ↑   ↑
factor   factor   product

Share and Show

MATH BOARD

1. Complete the related facts for this array.

$2 \times 8 = 16$ $16 \div 2 = 8$

_____   _____

Math Talk **Mathematical Practices**

Look at the multiplication and division equations in a set of related facts. What do you notice about the products and dividends? **Explain**.

Write the related facts for the array.

2.

_____
_____
_____
_____

✓3.

_____
_____
_____
_____

✓4.

_____
_____
_____
_____

5. Why do the related facts for the array in Exercise 2 have only two equations?

_____

© Houghton Mifflin Harcourt Publishing Company

Name _____

Write the related facts for the array.

6.

_____

_____

_____

7.

_____

_____

_____

8.

_____

_____

_____

Write the related facts for the set of numbers.

9. 2, 5, 10

_____

_____

_____

10. 3, 8, 24

_____

_____

_____

11. 6, 6, 36

_____

_____

_____

Complete the related facts.

12. $4 \times 7 =$ _____

$7 \times$ _____ $= 28$

$28 \div$ _____ $= 4$

$28 \div 4 =$ _____

13. $5 \times$ _____ $= 30$

$6 \times$ _____ $= 30$

$30 \div 6 =$ _____

$30 \div 5 =$ _____

14. _____ $\times 9 = 27$

_____ $\times 3 = 27$

_____ $\div 9 = 3$

$27 \div$ _____ $= 9$

15. Write a set of related facts that has only
two equations. Draw an array to show the facts.

_____

© Houghton Mifflin Harcourt Publishing Company

Problem Solving • Applications (Real World)

Use the table for 16–17.

Clay Supplies	
Item	**Number in Package**
Clay	12 sections
Clay tool set	11 tools
Glitter dough	36 sections

16. **MATHEMATICAL PRACTICE ③** **Verify the Reasoning of Others** Ty has a package of glitter dough. He says he can give 9 friends 5 equal sections. Describe his error. What is the correct answer?

_____

_____

_____

_____

WRITE ▸ *Math*
Show Your Work

17. **THINK SMARTER** Mr. Lee divides 1 package of clay and 1 package of glitter dough equally among 4 students. How many more glitter dough sections than clay sections does each student get?

_____

18. **GO DEEPER** Write a word problem that can be solved by using $35 \div 5$. Solve your problem.

_____

_____

_____

19. **THINK SMARTER** Select the equations that represent the array. Mark all that apply.

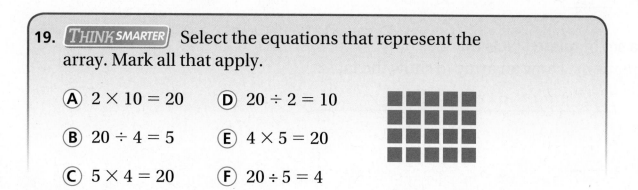

   Ⓐ $2 \times 10 = 20$ Ⓓ $20 \div 2 = 10$

   Ⓑ $20 \div 4 = 5$ Ⓔ $4 \times 5 = 20$

   Ⓒ $5 \times 4 = 20$ Ⓕ $20 \div 5 = 4$

FOR MORE PRACTICE:
Standards Practice Book

© Houghton Mifflin Harcourt Publishing Company

Name _____

Division Rules for 1 and 0

Essential Question What are the rules for dividing with 1 and 0?

**Operations and Algebraic Thinking—
3.OA.5** *Also 3.OA.2, 3.OA.3, 3.OA.7*
MATHEMATICAL PRACTICES
MP.1, MP.2, MP.4, MP.7

Unlock the Problem (Real World)

What rules for division can help you divide with 1 and 0?

If there is only 1 fishbowl, then all the fish must go in that fishbowl.

$$4 \div 1 = 4$$

number of fish   number of bowls   number in each bowl

Rule A: Any number divided by 1 equals that number.

Try This! There are 3 fish and 1 fishbowl. Draw a quick picture to show the fish in the fishbowl.

Write the equation your picture shows.

_____ ÷ _____ = _____

Math Talk   **Mathematical Practices**

Explain how Rule A is related to the Identity Property of Multiplication.

If there is the same number of fish and fishbowls, then 1 fish goes in each fishbowl.

$$4 \div 4 = 1$$

number of fish   number of bowls   number in each bowl

Rule B: Any number (except 0) divided by itself equals 1.

Try This! There are 3 fish and 3 fishbowls. Draw a quick picture to show the fish divided equally among the fishbowls.

Write the equation your picture shows.

_____ ÷ _____ = _____

© Houghton Mifflin Harcourt Publishing Company

If there are 0 fish and 4 fishbowls, there will not be any fish in the fishbowls.

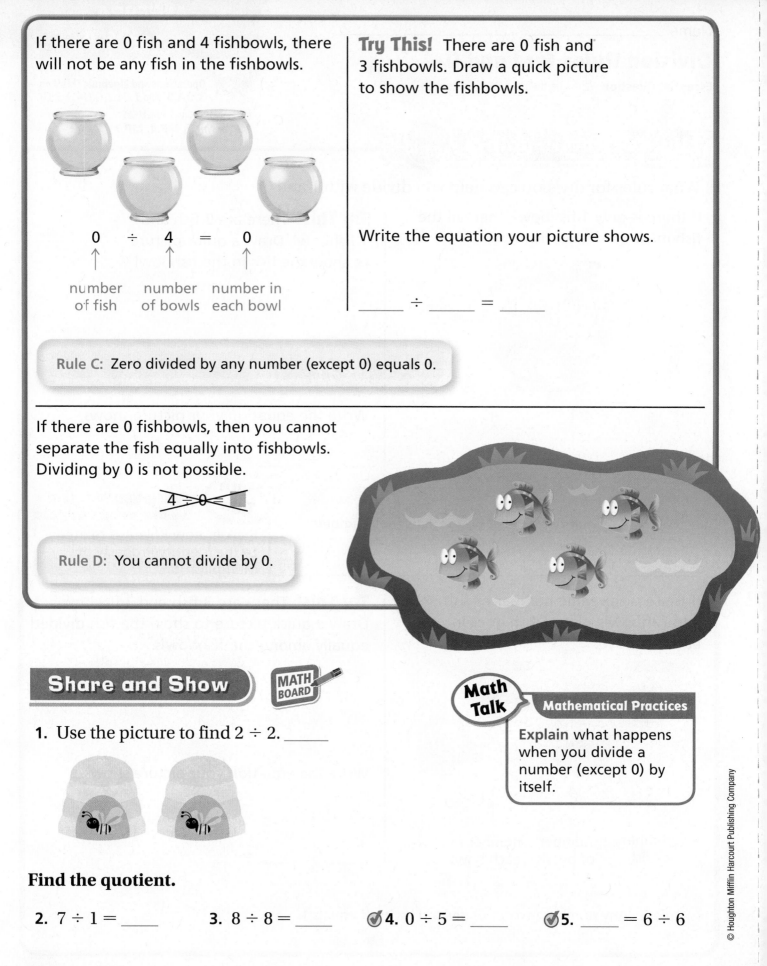

$$0 \div 4 = 0$$

number of fish   number of bowls   number in each bowl

Rule C: Zero divided by any number (except 0) equals 0.

If there are 0 fishbowls, then you cannot separate the fish equally into fishbowls. Dividing by 0 is not possible.

4 ÷ 0

Rule D: You cannot divide by 0.

Try This! There are 0 fish and 3 fishbowls. Draw a quick picture to show the fishbowls.

Write the equation your picture shows.

_____ ÷ _____ = _____

Share and Show

MATH BOARD

1. Use the picture to find 2 ÷ 2. _____

Math Talk Mathematical Practices

Explain what happens when you divide a number (except 0) by itself.

Find the quotient.

2. 7 ÷ 1 = _____   3. 8 ÷ 8 = _____   ✓ 4. 0 ÷ 5 = _____   ✓ 5. _____ = 6 ÷ 6

© Houghton Mifflin Harcourt Publishing Company

Name _____

Find the quotient.

6. $0 \div 8 =$ _____

7. $5 \div 5 =$ _____

8. $2 \div 1 =$ _____

9. $0 \div 7 =$ _____

10. $5 \overline{)0}$

11. $1 \overline{)9}$

12. $7 \overline{)7}$

13. $10 \overline{)10}$

Practice: Copy and Solve **Find the quotient.**

14. $6 \div 1$

15. $25 \div 5$

16. $0 \div 6$

17. $18 \div 3$

18. $14 \div 2$

19. $9 \div 9$

20. $28 \div 4$

21. $8 \div 1$

22. $3 \overline{)27}$

23. $5 \overline{)10}$

24. $3 \overline{)0}$

25. $1 \overline{)0}$

Problem Solving • Applications

26. **THINK SMARTER** Claire has 7 parakeets. She puts 4 of them in a cage. She divides the other parakeets equally among 3 friends to hold. How many parakeets does each friend get to hold?

_____

27. **GO DEEPER** Lena has 5 parrots. She gives each parrot 1 grape in the morning and 1 grape in the evening. How many grapes does she give to her parrots each day?

_____

28. **MATHEMATICAL PRACTICE 6** Suppose a pet store has 21 birds that are in 21 cages. Use what you know about division rules to find the number of birds in each cage. **Explain** your answer.

_____

_____

© Houghton Mifflin Harcourt Publishing Company

29. **THINK SMARTER** For numbers 29a–29c, select True or False for each equation.

29a. $4 \div 4 = 1$ ○ True ○ False

29b. $6 \div 1 = 1$ ○ True ○ False

29c. $1 \div 5 = 1$ ○ True ○ False

Connect to Reading

Compare and Contrast

You have learned the rules for division with 1. Compare and contrast them to help you learn how to use the rules to solve problems.

Compare the rules. Think about how they are *alike*.

Contrast the rules. Think about how they are *different*.

Read: Rule A: Any number divided by 1 equals that number.

Rule B: Any number (except 0) divided by itself equals 1.

Compare: How are the rules alike?

- Both are division rules for 1.

Contrast: How are the rules different?

- Rule A is about dividing a number by 1. The quotient is that number.

- Rule B is about dividing a number (except 0) by itself. The quotient is always 1.

Read the problem. Write an equation. Solve.
Write *Rule A* or *Rule B* to tell which rule you used.

30. Jamal bought 7 goldfish at the pet store. He put them in 1 fishbowl. How many goldfish did he put in the fishbowl?

31. Ava has 6 turtles. She divides them equally among 6 aquariums. How many turtles does she put in each aquarium?

© Houghton Mifflin Harcourt Publishing Company • Image Credits: ©Georgette Douwma/Getty Images

FOR MORE PRACTICE:
Standards Practice Book

Name _____

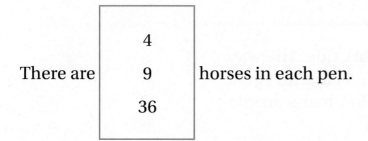
1. For numbers 1a–1d, select True or False for each equation.

    1a. $3 \div 1 = 1$ ○ True   ○ False

    1b. $0 \div 4 = 0$ ○ True   ○ False

    1c. $7 \div 7 = 1$ ○ True   ○ False

    1d. $6 \div 1 = 6$ ○ True   ○ False

2. Elizabeth has 12 horses on her farm. She puts an equal number of horses in each of 3 pens. How many horses are in each pen?

   Circle a number that makes the sentence true.

   There are
4
9
36
   horses in each pen.

3. Chris plants 25 pumpkins seeds in 5 equal rows. How many seeds does Chris plant in each row?

   Make an array to represent the problem. Then solve the problem.

   _____ seeds

© Houghton Mifflin Harcourt Publishing Company

4. Becca spent 24 minutes walking around a track. It took her 3 minutes to walk each time around the track. How many times did Becca walk around the track?

Make equal groups to model the problem. Then explain how you solved the problem.

_____

_____

5. There are 7 cars in an amusement park ride. There are 42 people divided equally among the 7 cars. An equal number of people ride in each car. How many people ride in one car?

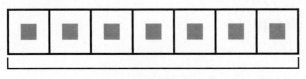

42 people

_____ people

6. Select the equations that represent the array. Mark all that apply.

(A) 3 × 5 = ▥

(B) 2 × ▥ = 12

(C) ▥ ÷ 3 = 5

(D) 5 × ▥ = 15

(E) 12 ÷ 3 = ▥

(F) 15 ÷ 5 = ▥

258

© Houghton Mifflin Harcourt Publishing Company

7. Eduardo visited his cousin for 28 days over the summer. There are 7 days in each week. How long, in weeks, was Eduardo's visit?

Part A
Draw jumps on the number line to model the problem.

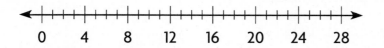

0   4   8   12   16   20   24   28

Part B
Write a division equation to represent the model.

_____

_____ weeks

8. A workbook is 64 pages long. If each chapter is 8 pages long, how many chapters are there?

_____ chapters

9. There are 56 apples packed in 7 baskets with the same number of apples in each basket. How many apples are in each basket?

For numbers 9a–9d, choose Yes or No to tell whether the equation represents the problem.

9a. $56 + 7 = $ ■   ○ Yes   ○ No

9b. $7 \times $ ■ $ = 56$ ○ Yes   ○ No

9c. $56 \div $ ■ $ = 8$ ○ Yes   ○ No

9d. $56 - $ ■ $ = 8$ ○ Yes   ○ No

10. Stefan has 24 photos to display on some posters. Select a way that he could display the photos in equal groups on the posters. Mark all that apply.

Ⓐ 6 photos on each of 4 posters   Ⓓ 5 photos on each of 5 posters

Ⓑ 7 photos on each of 3 posters   Ⓔ 3 photos on each of 8 posters

Ⓒ 4 photos on each of 6 posters   Ⓕ 7 photos on each of 4 posters

© Houghton Mifflin Harcourt Publishing Company

11. Debbie made this array to model a division equation. Which equation did Debbie model? Mark all that apply.

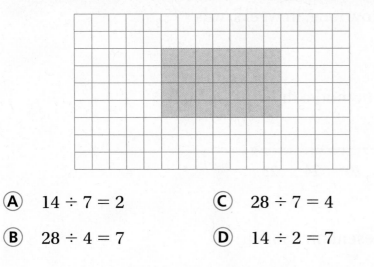

(A) $14 \div 7 = 2$ (C) $28 \div 7 = 4$

(B) $28 \div 4 = 7$ (D) $14 \div 2 = 7$

12. Mrs. Edwards made a total of 40 fingers on some gloves she knitted. How many gloves did Mrs. Edwards knit?

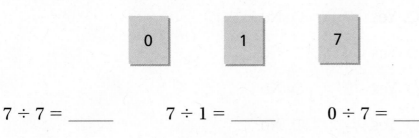

40 fingers

_____ gloves

13. Make true equations. Select a number to complete the equation.

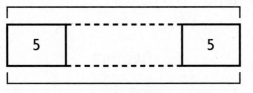

$7 \div 7 =$ _____ $7 \div 1 =$ _____ $0 \div 7 =$ _____

14. The coach separated the 18 players at lacrosse practice into 3 different groups. How many players were in each group?

_____ players

© Houghton Mifflin Harcourt Publishing Company

15. Write a division equation to represent the repeated subtraction.

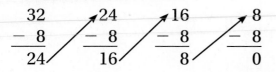

_____

16. Write related facts for the array. Explain why there are not more related facts.

_____

_____

17. Darius bakes 18 muffins for his friends. He gives each of his friends an equal number of muffins and has none left over.

Part A

Draw a picture to show how Darius divided the muffins and complete the sentence.

_____

Darius gave muffins to _____

_____ friends.

Part B

Could Darius have given all of his muffins equally to 4 of his friends? Explain why or why not.

_____

_____

© Houghton Mifflin Harcourt Publishing Company

18. Circle numbers to complete the related facts.

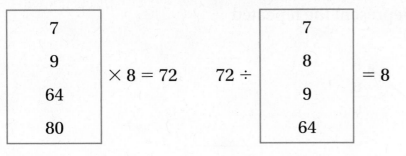

$$
\boxed{\begin{matrix} 7 \\ 9 \\ 64 \\ 80 \end{matrix}} \times 8 = 72 \qquad 72 \div \boxed{\begin{matrix} 7 \\ 8 \\ 9 \\ 64 \end{matrix}} = 8
$$

19. Use the numbers to write a related multiplication and division facts.

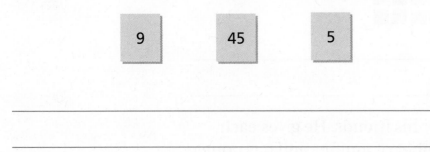

9   45   5

_____

_____

20. Tyrone took 16 pennies from his bank and put them in 4 equal stacks. How many pennies did Tyrone put in each stack? Show your work.

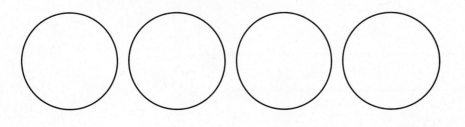

_____ pennies

© Houghton Mifflin Harcourt Publishing Company

Division Facts and Strategies

Show What You Know ✓

Check your understanding of important skills.

Name _____

▶ **Think Addition to Subtract** **Write the missing numbers.**

1. $10 - 3 = \blacksquare$

Think: $3 + \blacksquare = 10$

$3 + \underline{\quad} = 10$
So, $10 - 3 = \underline{\quad}$.

2. $12 - 8 = \blacksquare$

Think: $8 + \blacksquare = 12$

$8 + \underline{\quad} = 12$
So, $12 - 8 = \underline{\quad}$.

▶ **Missing Factors** **Write the missing factor.**

3. $2 \times \underline{\quad} = 10$

4. $42 = \underline{\quad} \times 7$

5. $\underline{\quad} \times 6 = 18$

▶ **Multiplication Facts Through 9** **Find the product.**

6. $\underline{\quad} = 6 \times 9$

7. $3 \times 8 = \underline{\quad}$

8. $4 \times 4 = \underline{\quad}$

On Monday, the students in Mr. Carson's class worked in pairs. On Tuesday, the students worked in groups of 3. On Wednesday, the students worked in groups of 4. Each day the students made equal groups with no student left out of a group. Be a Math Detective to find how many students could be in Mr. Carson's class.

© Houghton Mifflin Harcourt Publishing Company • Image Credits: ©Radius Images/Alamy Images

Personal Math Trainer
Online Assessment and Intervention

▶ **Visualize It** ●●●●●●●●●●●●●●●●●●●●●●●●●●●●●●●

Sort the review words into the Venn diagram.

Multiplication Words   **Division Words**

Review Words
divide
dividend
divisor
equation
factor
inverse operations
multiply
product
quotient
related facts

Preview Word

order of operations

▶ **Understand Vocabulary** ●●●●●●●●●●●●●●●●●●●●●●●

Complete the sentences by using the review and preview words.

1. An _____ is a number sentence that uses the equal sign to show that two amounts are equal.

2. The _____ is a special set of rules that gives the order in which calculations are done to solve a problem.

3. _____ are a set of related multiplication and division equations.

© Houghton Mifflin Harcourt Publishing Company

GO DIGITAL
• **Interactive Student Edition**
• **Multimedia eGlossary**

Name _____

Divide by 2

Essential Question What does dividing by 2 mean?

**Operations and Algebraic Thinking—
3.OA.3** *Also 3.OA.2, 3.OA.7*
MATHEMATICAL PRACTICES
MP.4, MP.5, MP.6

🔑 Unlock the Problem

There are 10 hummingbirds and 2 feeders in Marissa's backyard. If there are an equal number of birds at each feeder, how many birds are at each one?

- **What do you need to find?**

  _____

- **Circle the numbers you need to use.**
- **What can you use to help solve the problem?** _____

🔑 Activity 1

Use counters to find how many in each group.

Materials ▪ counters ▪ MathBoard

MODEL

- Use 10 counters.
- Draw 2 circles on your MathBoard.
- Place 1 counter at a time in each circle until all 10 counters are used.
- Draw the rest of the counters to show your work.

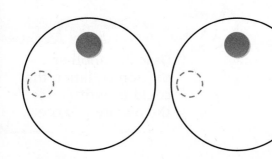

THINK

_____ in all

_____ equal groups

_____ in each group

RECORD

$$10 \div 2 = 5 \text{ or } 2\overline{)10}^{\;5}$$

Read: Ten divided by two equals five.

There are _____ counters in each of the 2 groups.

So, there are _____ hummingbirds at each feeder.

▶ A hummingbird can fly right, left, up, down, forward, backward, and even upside down!

Math Talk
Mathematical Practices

Explain what each number in $10 \div 2 = 5$ represents from the word problem.

© Houghton Mifflin Harcourt Publishing Company • Image Credits: ©Visuals Unlimited/Corbis

Activity 2 Draw to find how many equal groups.

There are 10 hummingbirds in Tyler's backyard. If there are 2 hummingbirds at each feeder, how many feeders are there?

Math Idea

You can divide to find the number in each group or to find the number of equal groups.

MODEL

- Look at the 10 counters.
- Circle a group of 2 counters.
- Continue circling groups of 2 until all 10 counters are in groups.

THINK

_____ in all

_____ in each group

_____ equal groups

RECORD

$$10 \div 2 = 5 \text{ or } 2\overline{)10}^{\,5}$$

Read: Ten divided by two equals five.

There are _____ groups of 2 counters.

So, there are _____ feeders.

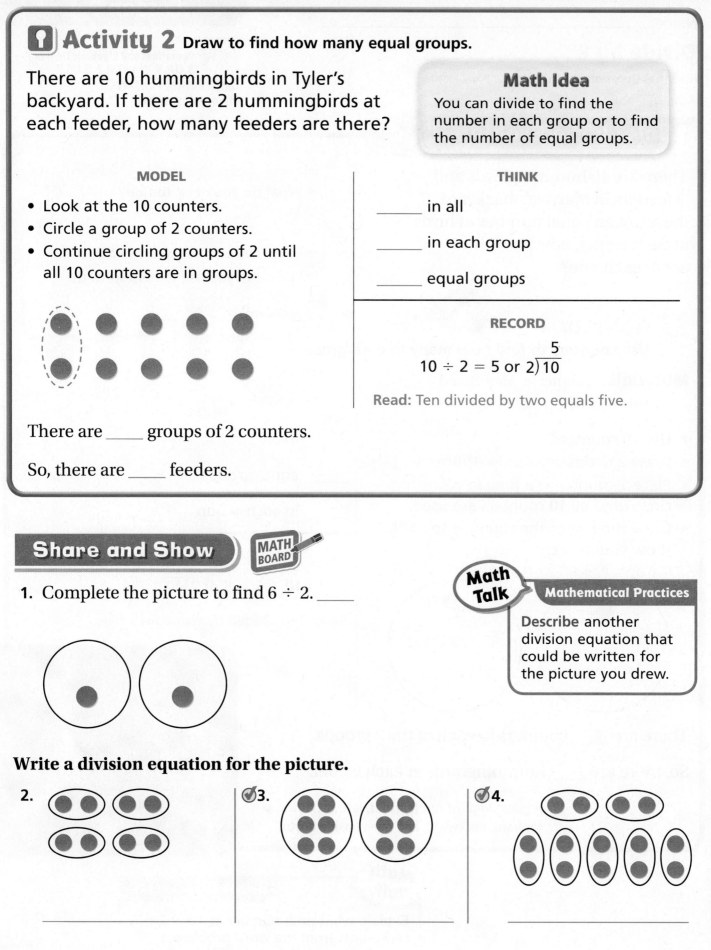

Share and Show

MATH BOARD

1. Complete the picture to find $6 \div 2$. _____

Math Talk — **Mathematical Practices**

Describe another division equation that could be written for the picture you drew.

Write a division equation for the picture.

2.

3.

4.

© Houghton Mifflin Harcourt Publishing Company

Name _____

Write a division equation for the picture.

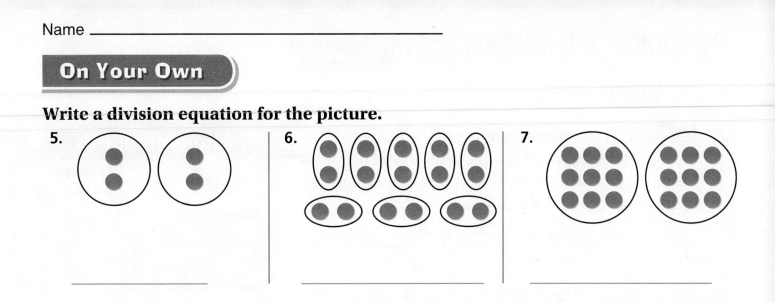

5. _____

6. _____

7. _____

Find the quotient. You may want to draw a quick picture to help.

8. $2 \div 2 =$ _____

9. _____ $= 10 \div 2$

10. _____ $= 14 \div 2$

11. _____ $= 18 \div 2$

12. $16 \div 2 =$ _____

13. _____ $= 0 \div 2$

14. $2\overline{)8}$

15. $2\overline{)12}$

16. $2\overline{)20}$

MATHEMATICAL PRACTICE ② **Reason Abstractly** **Algebra** Find the unknown number.

17. _____ $\div 2 = 5$

18. _____ $\div 2 = 2$

19. _____ $\div 2 = 3$

20. _____ $\div 2 = 8$

© Houghton Mifflin Harcourt Publishing Company

Problem Solving • Applications

Use the table for 21–22.

21. **GO DEEPER** Two hummingbirds of the same type have a total mass of 10 grams. Which type of hummingbird are they? Write a division equation to show how to find the answer.

_____

Hummingbirds

Type	Mass (in grams)
Magnificent	7
Ruby-throated	3
Violet-crowned	5

22. **THINK SMARTER** There are 3 Ruby-throated hummingbirds and 2 of another type of hummingbird at a feeder. The birds have a mass of 23 grams in all. What other type of hummingbird is at the feeder? **Explain.**

WRITE ▶ *Math* • **Show Your Work**

Math on the Spot

_____

_____

_____

_____

23. **THINK SMARTER** Ryan has 18 socks.

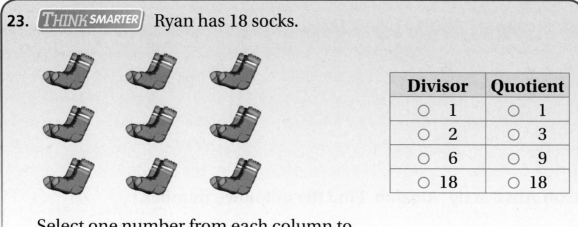

Divisor	Quotient
○ 1	○ 1
○ 2	○ 3
○ 6	○ 9
○ 18	○ 18

Select one number from each column to show the division equation represented by the picture.

$$18 \div \frac{?}{\text{(divisor)}} = \frac{?}{\text{(quotient)}}$$

© Houghton Mifflin Harcourt Publishing Company • Image Credits: (tr) ©PhotoDisc/Getty Images; (tc) Tim Davis/Corbis

Name _____

Divide by 10

Essential Question What strategies can you use to divide by 10?

Operations and Algebraic Thinking—3.OA.7 *Also 3.OA.2, 3.OA.3, 3.OA.4, 3.OA.6*

MATHEMATICAL PRACTICES
MP.1, MP.2, MP.5, MP.8

🔑 Unlock the Problem *Real World*

There are 50 students going on a field trip to the Philadelphia Zoo. The students are separated into equal groups of 10 students each. How many groups of students are there?

- What do you need to find?

  _____

- Circle the numbers you need to use.

🔓 One Way Use repeated subtraction.

- Start with 50.

- Subtract 10 until you reach 0.

- Count the number of times you subtract 10.

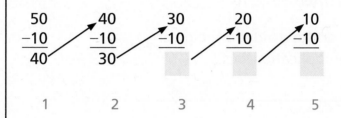

You subtracted 10 five times. $50 \div 10 =$ _____

So, there are _____ groups of 10 students.

🔓 Other Ways

Ⓐ Use a number line.

- Start at 50 and count back by 10s until you reach 0.

- Count the number of times you jumped back 10.

You jumped back by 10 five times.

$50 \div 10 =$ _____

Math Talk **Mathematical Practices**

How is counting on a number line to divide by 10 different from counting on a number line to multiply by 10?

© Houghton Mifflin Harcourt Publishing Company • Image Credits: ©Stephen Meese/Alamy Images

Chapter 7 **269**

B **Use a multiplication table.**

Divide. 50 ÷ 10 = ▨

Since division is the opposite of multiplication, you can use a multiplication table to find a quotient.

Think of a related multiplication fact.

▨ × 10 = 50

STEP 1 Find the factor, 10, in the top row.

STEP 2 Look down to find the product, 50.

STEP 3 Look left to find the unknown

factor, ____.

Since ____ × 10 = 50, then 50 ÷ 10 = ____.

In Step 1, is the divisor or the dividend the given factor in the related multiplication fact?

_____

In Step 2, is the divisor or the dividend the product in the related multiplication fact?

_____

The quotient is the unknown factor.

×	0	1	2	3	4	5	6	7	8	9	10
0	0	0	0	0	0	0	0	0	0	0	0
1	0	1	2	3	4	5	6	7	8	9	10
2	0	2	4	6	8	10	12	14	16	18	20
3	0	3	6	9	12	15	18	21	24	27	30
4	0	4	8	12	16	20	24	28	32	36	40
5	0	5	10	15	20	25	30	35	40	45	50
6	0	6	12	18	24	30	36	42	48	54	60
7	0	7	14	21	28	35	42	49	56	63	70
8	0	8	16	24	32	40	48	56	64	72	80
9	0	9	18	27	36	45	54	63	72	81	90
10	0	10	20	30	40	50	60	70	80	90	100

Share and Show

MATH BOARD

Math Talk **Mathematical Practices**

Describe two other ways to find 30 ÷ 10.

1. Use repeated subtraction to find 30 ÷ 10. ____

Think: How many times do you subtract 10?

$$\begin{array}{r} 30 \\ -10 \\ \hline 20 \end{array} \qquad \begin{array}{r} 20 \\ -10 \\ \hline 10 \end{array} \qquad \begin{array}{r} 10 \\ -10 \\ \hline \end{array}$$

Find the unknown factor and quotient.

2. 10 × ____ = 40   ____ = 40 ÷ 10

3. 10 × ____ = 60   60 ÷ 10 = ____

Find the quotient.

4. ____ = 20 ÷ 10

5. 10)‾50‾

6. 10)‾70‾

7. 90 ÷ 10 = ____

270

© Houghton Mifflin Harcourt Publishing Company

On Your Own

Find the unknown factor and quotient.

8. $10 \times \underline{\quad} = 70$ $70 \div 10 = \underline{\quad}$

9. $10 \times \underline{\quad} = 10$ $10 \div 10 = \underline{\quad}$

10. $10 \times \underline{\quad} = 80$ $80 \div 10 = \underline{\quad}$

11. $\underline{\quad} \times 2 = 12$ $\underline{\quad} = 12 \div 2$

Find the quotient.

12. $50 \div 10 = \underline{\quad}$

13. $\underline{\quad} = 60 \div 10$

14. $16 \div 2 = \underline{\quad}$

15. $90 \div 10 = \underline{\quad}$

16. $10 \div 2 = \underline{\quad}$

17. $30 \div 10 = \underline{\quad}$

18. $\underline{\quad} = 20 \div 2$

19. $\underline{\quad} = 0 \div 10$

20. $10\overline{)20}$

21. $10\overline{)100}$

22. $10\overline{)40}$

23. $10\overline{)80}$

MATHEMATICAL PRACTICE ② Reason Quantitatively Algebra Write $<$, $>$, or $=$.

24. $10 \div 1 \bigcirc 4 \times 10$

25. $17 - 6 \bigcirc 18 \div 2$

26. $4 \times 4 \bigcirc 8 + 8$

27. $23 + 14 \bigcirc 5 \times 8$

28. $70 \div 10 \bigcirc 23 - 16$

29. $9 \times 0 \bigcirc 9 + 0$

© Houghton Mifflin Harcourt Publishing Company

Problem Solving • Applications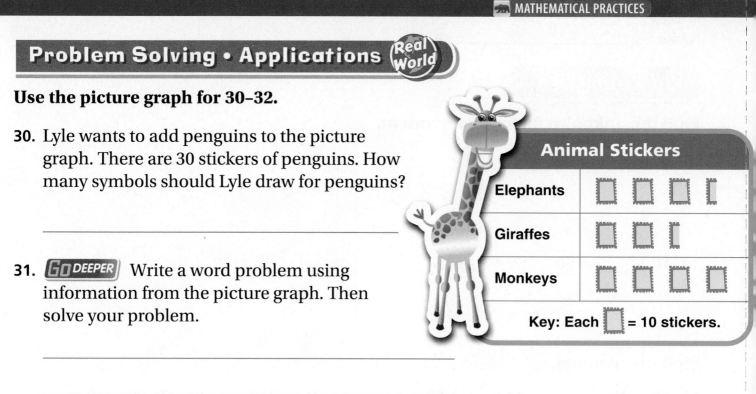

Use the picture graph for 30–32.

30. Lyle wants to add penguins to the picture graph. There are 30 stickers of penguins. How many symbols should Lyle draw for penguins?

_____

31. **Go DEEPER** Write a word problem using information from the picture graph. Then solve your problem.

_____

_____

Animal Stickers

Elephants	▢	▢	▢	▯
Giraffes	▢	▢	▯	
Monkeys	▢	▢	▢	▢

Key: Each ▢ = 10 stickers.

32. **THINK SMARTER** **Sense or Nonsense?** Lena wants to put the monkey stickers in an album. She says she will use more pages if she puts 5 stickers on a page instead of 10 stickers on a page. Is she correct? Explain.

WRITE ▸ *Math* • **Show Your Work** • • •

_____

_____

_____

33. **MATHEMATICAL PRACTICE ⑥** **Explain** how a division problem is like an unknown factor problem.

_____

_____

_____

34. **THINK SMARTER** Lilly found 40 seashells. She put 10 seashells in each bucket. How many buckets did Lilly use? Show your work.

_____ buckets

FOR MORE PRACTICE:
Standards Practice Book

© Houghton Mifflin Harcourt Publishing Company

Name _____

Divide by 5

Essential Question What does dividing by 5 mean?

Operations and Algebraic Thinking—
3.OA.3 *Also 3.OA.2, 3.OA.7*
MATHEMATICAL PRACTICES
MP.1, MP.2, MP.5, MP.7

⚷ Unlock the Problem Real World

Kaley wants to buy a new cage for Coconut, her guinea pig. She has saved 35¢. If she saved a nickel each day, for how many days has she been saving?

• How much is a nickel worth?

_____

1 One Way Count up by 5s.

• Begin at 0.

• Count up by 5s until you reach 35.   5, 10, _____, _____, _____, _____, _____

• Count the number of times you count up.   1   2   3   4   5   6   7

You counted up by 5 seven times. 35 ÷ 5 = _____

So, Kaley has been saving for _____ days.

2 Another Way

Count back on a number line.

• Start at 35.

• Count back by 5s until you reach 0. Complete the jumps on the number line.

• Count the number of times you jumped back 5.

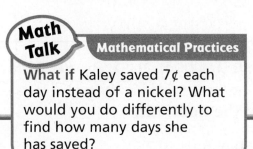

You jumped back by 5 _____ times.

35 ÷ 5 = _____

Math Talk **Mathematical Practices**

What if Kaley saved 7¢ each day instead of a nickel? What would you do differently to find how many days she has saved?

© Houghton Mifflin Harcourt Publishing Company • Image Credits: ©Peter Cade/Getty Images

Strategies for Multiplying and Dividing with 5

You have learned how to use doubles to multiply. Now you will learn how to use doubles to divide by 5.

🔑 Use 10s facts, and then take half to multiply with 5.

When one factor is 5, you can use a 10s fact.

$5 \times 2 = $ ■

First, multiply by 10.

$10 \times 2 = $ _____

After you multiply, take half of the product.

$20 \div 2 = $ _____

So, $5 \times 2 = $ _____.

🔑 Divide by 10, and then double to divide by 5.

When the divisor is 5 and the dividend is even, you can use a 10s fact.

$30 \div 5 = $ ■

First, divide by 10.

$30 \div 10 = $ _____

After you divide, double the quotient.

$3 + $ _____ $ = $ _____

So, $30 \div 5 = $ _____.

Share and Show | MATH BOARD

1. Count back on the number line to find $15 \div 5$. _____

Use count up or count back on a number line to solve.

Math Talk **Mathematical Practices**

Explain how counting up to solve a division problem is like counting back on a number line.

2. $10 \div 2 = $ _____

✓ 3. $20 \div 5 = $ _____

Find the quotient.

4. $50 \div 5 = $ _____   5. $5 \div 5 = $ _____   ✓ 6. $45 \div 5 = $ _____

274

© Houghton Mifflin Harcourt Publishing Company

On Your Own

Use count up or count back on a number line to solve.

7. $30 \div 5 =$ _____

0 5 10 15 20 25 30

8. $25 \div 5 =$ _____

0 5 10 15 20 25

Find the quotient.

9. ___ $= 20 \div 5$

10. $40 \div 5 =$ ___

11. ___ $= 18 \div 2$

12. $0 \div 5 =$ ___

13. $35 \div 5 =$ ___

14. ___ $= 10 \div 5$

15. $40 \div 10 =$ ___

16. ___ $= 4 \div 2$

17. $10\overline{)30}$

18. $2\overline{)16}$

19. $5\overline{)45}$

20. $5\overline{)15}$

MATHEMATICAL PRACTICE ⑦ Look for a Pattern **Algebra** **Complete the table.**

21.

$\times$	1	2	3	4	5
10					
5					

22.

$\div$	10	20	30	40	50
10					
5					

Problem Solving • Applications (Real World)

23. **MATHEMATICAL PRACTICE ① Evaluate** Guinea pigs eat hay, pellets, and vegetables. If Wonder Hay comes in a 5-pound bag and costs $15, how much does 1 pound of hay cost?

_____

24. Guinea pigs sleep about 45 hours every 5 days with their eyes open. About how many hours a day do guinea pigs sleep?

_____

25. **GO DEEPER** The clerk at the pet supply store works 45 hours a week. He works an equal number of hours on Monday through Friday. He works an extra 5 hours on Saturday. How many hours does he work on each weekday?

_____

© Houghton Mifflin Harcourt Publishing Company

26. **THINK SMARTER** **Pose a Problem** Maddie went to a veterinary clinic. She saw the vet preparing some carrots for the guinea pigs.

Write a division problem that can be solved using the picture of carrots. Draw circles to group the carrots for your problem.

Pose a problem.

Solve your problem.

- Group the carrots in a different way. Then write a problem for the new groups. Solve your problem.

27. **THINK SMARTER** Circle the unknown factor and quotient.

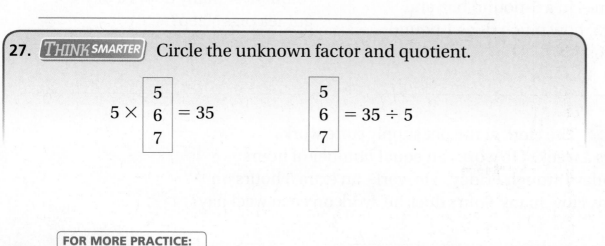

$$5 \times \begin{array}{|c|} 5 \\ 6 \\ 7 \end{array} = 35 \qquad \begin{array}{|c|} 5 \\ 6 \\ 7 \end{array} = 35 \div 5$$

FOR MORE PRACTICE: Standards Practice Book

© Houghton Mifflin Harcourt Publishing Company • Image Credits: ©Adams Picture Library t/a apl/Alamy Images

Name _____

Divide by 3

Essential Question What strategies can you use to divide by 3?

Operations and Algebraic Thinking—3.OA.7 *Also 3.OA.2, 3.OA.3, 3.OA.4, 3.OA.6*

MATHEMATICAL PRACTICES
MP.1, MP.4, MP.5, MP.6

Unlock the Problem

For field day, 18 students have signed up for the relay race. Each relay team needs 3 students. How many teams can be made?

One Way Make equal groups.

- Look at the 18 counters below.
- Circle as many groups of 3 as you can.
- Count the number of groups.

- What do you need to find?

_____

_____

- Circle the numbers you need to use.

There are _____ groups of 3.

So, _____ teams can be made.

You can write $18 \div 3 =$ _____ or $3\overline{)18}$.

Math Talk **Mathematical Practices**

Suppose the question asked how many students would be on 3 equal teams. How would you model 3 equal teams? Would the quotient be the same?

© Houghton Mifflin Harcourt Publishing Company

🔐 Other Ways

Ⓐ Count back on a number line.

- Start at 18.

- Count back by 3s as many times as you can.
  Complete the jumps on the number line.

- Count the number of times you jumped back 3.

⚠️ **ERROR Alert**

Be sure to count back the same number of spaces each time you jump back on the number line.

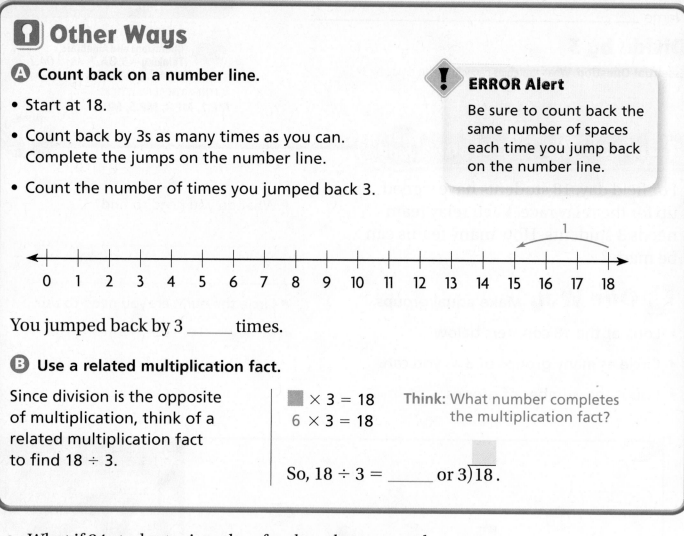

You jumped back by 3 _____ times.

Ⓑ Use a related multiplication fact.

Since division is the opposite of multiplication, think of a related multiplication fact to find 18 ÷ 3.

⬛ × 3 = 18
6 × 3 = 18

Think: What number completes the multiplication fact?

So, 18 ÷ 3 = _____ or 3)‾1‾8‾ .

- What if 24 students signed up for the relay race and there were 3 students on each team? What related multiplication fact would you use to find the number of teams?

_____

Share and Show 📝 MATH BOARD

1. Circle groups of 3 to find 12 ÷ 3. _____

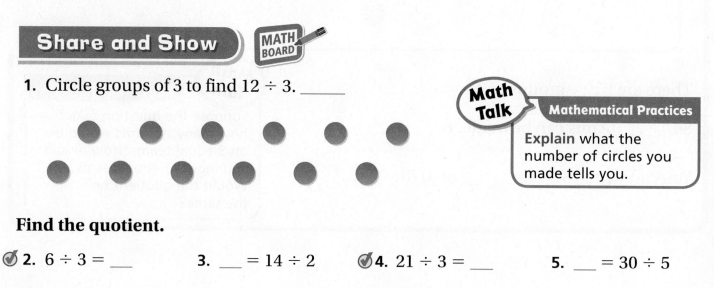

Math Talk **Mathematical Practices**

Explain what the number of circles you made tells you.

Find the quotient.

✓ **2.** 6 ÷ 3 = ___

3. ___ = 14 ÷ 2

✓ **4.** 21 ÷ 3 = ___

5. ___ = 30 ÷ 5

© Houghton Mifflin Harcourt Publishing Company

Name _____

Practice: Copy and Solve **Find the quotient. Draw a quick picture to help.**

6. $9 \div 3$ **7.** $10 \div 5$ **8.** $18 \div 2$ **9.** $24 \div 3$

Find the quotient.

10. ___ $= 12 \div 2$ **11.** $40 \div 5 =$ ___   **12.** $60 \div 10 =$ ___   **13.** ___ $= 20 \div 10$

14. $27 \div 3 =$ ___   **15.** ___ $= 0 \div 3$ **16.** $12 \div 3 =$ ___   **17.** ___ $= 8 \div 2$

18. $3\overline{)15}$ **19.** $2\overline{)4}$ **20.** $5\overline{)20}$ **21.** $3\overline{)18}$

22. $2\overline{)16}$ **23.** $3\overline{)12}$ **24.** $3\overline{)6}$ **25.** $5\overline{)35}$

26. $3\overline{)3}$ **27.** $10\overline{)70}$ **28.** $3\overline{)30}$ **29.** $10\overline{)50}$

MATHEMATICAL PRACTICE 2 **Use Reasoning** **Algebra** Write $+$, $-$, $\times$, or $\div$.

30. $25 \bigcirc 5 = 10 \div 2$ **31.** $3 \times 3 = 6 \bigcirc 3$ **32.** $16 \bigcirc 2 = 24 - 16$

33. $13 + 19 = 8 \bigcirc 4$ **34.** $14 \bigcirc 2 = 6 \times 2$ **35.** $21 \div 3 = 5 \bigcirc 2$

© Houghton Mifflin Harcourt Publishing Company

Problem Solving • Applications

Use the table for 36–37.

Field Day Events	
Activity	Number of Students
Relay race	25
Beanbag toss	18
Jump-rope race	27

36. **GO DEEPER** There are 5 equal teams in the relay race. How many students are on each team? Write a division equation that shows the number of students on each team.

_____

37. **THINK SMARTER** Students doing the jump-rope race and the beanbag toss compete in teams of 3. How many more teams participate in the jump-rope race than in the beanbag toss? **Explain** how you know.

WRITE ▸ Math
Show Your Work

_____

_____

38. **MATHEMATICAL PRACTICE ①** **Make Sense of Problems** Michael puts 21 sports cards into stacks of 3. The answer is 7 stacks. What's the question?

_____

_____

39. **THINK SMARTER** Jorge made $24 selling water at a baseball game. He wants to know how many bottles of water he sold. Jorge used this number line to help him.

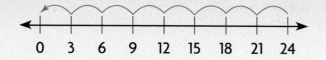

0   3   6   9   12   15   18   21   24

Write the division equation that the number line represents.

_____ ÷ _____ = _____

FOR MORE PRACTICE:
Standards Practice Book

© Houghton Mifflin Harcourt Publishing Company

Divide by 4

Essential Question What strategies can you use to divide by 4?

Operations and Algebraic Thinking—
3.OA.7 *Also 3.OA.2, 3.OA.3, 3.OA.4,*
3.OA.5, 3.OA.6
MATHEMATICAL PRACTICES
MP.3, MP.4, MP.7, MP.8

Unlock the Problem Real World

A tree farmer plants 12 red maple trees in 4 equal rows. How many trees are in each row?

• What strategy could you use to solve the problem?

_____

One Way Make an array.

• Look at the array.

• Continue the array by drawing 1 tile in each of the 4 rows until all 12 tiles are drawn.

• Count the number of tiles in each row.

There are _____ tiles in each row.

So, there are _____ trees in each row.

Write: _____ ÷ _____ = _____ or $4\overline{)12}$

Read: Twelve divided by four equals three.

Other Ways

A Make equal groups.

• Draw 1 counter in each group.

• Continue drawing 1 counter at a time until all 12 counters are drawn.

There are _____ counters in each group.

Math Talk **Mathematical Practices**

Explain how making an array to solve the problem is like making equal groups.

© Houghton Mifflin Harcourt Publishing Company • Image Credits: ©Todd Muskopf/Alamy Images

B Use factors to find $12 \div 4$.

The factors of 4 are 2 and 2.

$$2 \times 2 = 4$$

factors   product

To divide by 4, use the factors.

$12 \div 4 = n$

Divide by 2. $12 \div 2 = 6$

Then divide by 2 again. $6 \div 2 = 3$

$12 \div 4 = $ _____

C Use a related multiplication fact.

$12 \div 4 = n$

$4 \times n = 12$

$4 \times 3 = 12$

Think: What number completes the multiplication fact?

$12 \div 4 = $ _____ or $4\overline{)12}$

Remember
A letter or symbol, like n, can stand for an unknown number.

Try This! Use factors of 4 to find $16 \div 4$.

The factors of 4 are 2 and 2. $16 \div 4 = \blacksquare$

Divide by 2. $16 \div 2 = $ _____

Then divide by 2 again. $8 \div 2 = $ _____

So, $16 \div 4 = $ _____.

Think: Dividing by the factors of the divisor is the same as dividing by the divisor.

Share and Show MATH BOARD

Math Talk **Mathematical Practices**

Explain how you used the array to find the quotient.

1. Use the array to find $28 \div 4$. _____

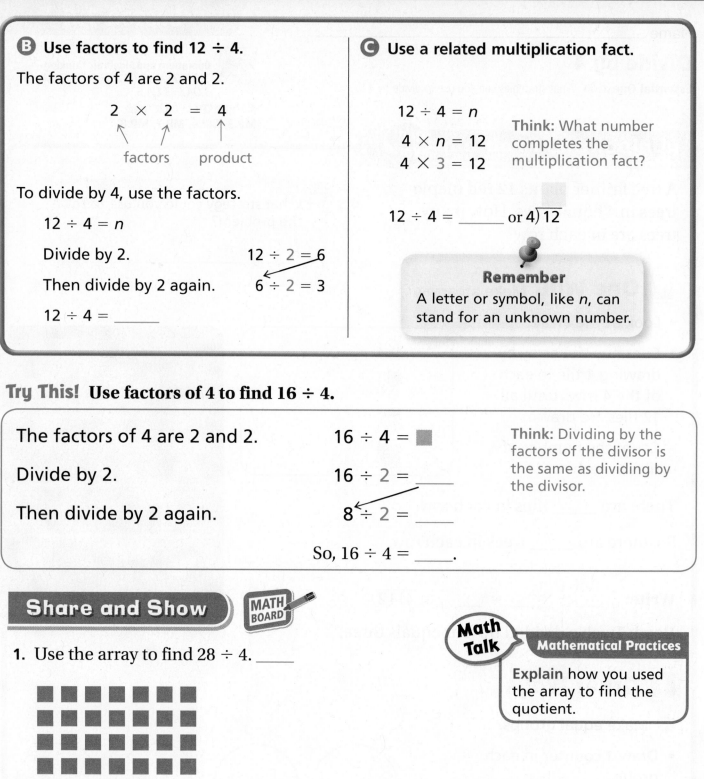

Find the quotient.

2. _____ $= 21 \div 3$

3. $8 \div 4 = $ _____

4. _____ $= 40 \div 5$

✓5. $24 \div 4 = $ _____

Find the unknown number.

6. $20 \div 4 = a$

$a = $ _____

7. $12 \div 2 = p$

$p = $ _____

8. $27 \div 3 = \blacktriangle$

$\blacktriangle = $ _____

✓9. $12 \div 4 = t$

$t = $ _____

© Houghton Mifflin Harcourt Publishing Company

On Your Own

Practice: Copy and Solve Draw tiles to make an array.
Find the quotient.

10. $30 \div 10$ **11.** $15 \div 5$ **12.** $40 \div 4$ **13.** $16 \div 2$

Find the quotient.

14. $12 \div 3 =$ ___   **15.** $20 \div 4 =$ ___   **16.** ___ $= 0 \div 4$ **17.** ___ $= 36 \div 4$

18. $4\overline{)28}$ **19.** $2\overline{)18}$ **20.** $4\overline{)16}$ **21.** $5\overline{)25}$

Find the unknown number.

22. $45 \div 5 = b$

$b =$ ___

23. $20 \div 10 = e$

$e =$ ___

24. $8 \div 2 = \blacksquare$

$\blacksquare =$ ___

25. $24 \div 3 = h$

$h =$ ___

26. $4 \div 4 = p$

$p =$ ___

27. $24 \div 4 = t$

$t =$ ___

28. $16 \div 4 = s$

$s =$ ___

29. $32 \div 4 = \blacksquare$

$\blacksquare =$ ___

Algebra Complete the table.

30.

÷	9	12	15	18
3				

31.

÷	20	24	28	32
4				

MATHEMATICAL PRACTICE ② **Use Reasoning** **Algebra** Find the unknown number.

32. $14 \div$ ___ $= 7$ **33.** $30 \div$ ___ $= 6$ **34.** $8 \div$ ___ $= 2$ **35.** $24 \div$ ___ $= 8$

36. $36 \div$ ___ $= 9$ **37.** $40 \div$ ___ $= 4$ **38.** $3 \div$ ___ $= 1$ **39.** $35 \div$ ___ $= 7$

© Houghton Mifflin Harcourt Publishing Company

Problem Solving • Applications

Use the table for 40–41.

40. **GO DEEPER** Douglas planted the birch trees in 4 equal rows. Then he added 2 more birch trees to each row. How many birch trees did he plant in each row?

_____

41. **THINK SMARTER** Mrs. Banks planted the oak trees in 4 equal rows. Mr. Webb planted the dogwood trees in 3 equal rows. Who planted more trees in each row? How many more? Explain how you know.

_____

_____

Trees Planted	
Type	**Number Planted**
Dogwood	24
Oak	28
Birch	16

WRITE ▸ *Math*
Show Your Work

42. **MATHEMATICAL PRACTICE ⑥ Use Math Vocabulary** Bryan earns $40 mowing lawns each week. He earns the same amount of money for each lawn. If he mows 4 lawns, how much does Bryan earn for each lawn? Explain how you found your answer.

_____

_____

43. **THINK SMARTER** For numbers 43a–43d, select True or False for each equation.

43a. $0 \div 4 = 4$ ○ True   ○ False

43b. $4 \div 4 = 1$ ○ True   ○ False

43c. $20 \div 4 = 6$ ○ True   ○ False

43d. $24 \div 4 = 8$ ○ True   ○ False

FOR MORE PRACTICE:
Standards Practice Book

© Houghton Mifflin Harcourt Publishing Company • Image Credits: ©James Randklev/Getty Images

Name _____

Divide by 6

Essential Question What strategies can you use to divide by 6?

Operations and Algebraic Thinking—
3.OA.7 *Also 3.OA.2, 3.OA.3, 3.OA.4,*
3.OA.5, 3.OA.6
MATHEMATICAL PRACTICES
MP.2, MP.4, MP.5, MP.6

Unlock the Problem (Real World)

Ms. Sing needs to buy 24 juice boxes for the class picnic. Juice boxes come in packs of 6. How many packs does Ms. Sing need to buy?

- Circle the number that tells you how many juice boxes come in a pack.
- How can you use the information to solve the problem?

_____

_____

_____

One Way Make equal groups.

- Draw 24 counters.
- Circle as many groups of 6 as you can.
- Count the number of groups.

There are _____ groups of 6.

So, Ms. Sing needs to buy _____ packs of juice boxes.

You can write ____ ÷ ____ = ____ or 6)‾2‾4‾ .

Math Talk **Mathematical Practices**

If you divided the 24 counters into groups of 4, how many groups would there be? **Explain** how you know.

© Houghton Mifflin Harcourt Publishing Company

🔓 Other Ways

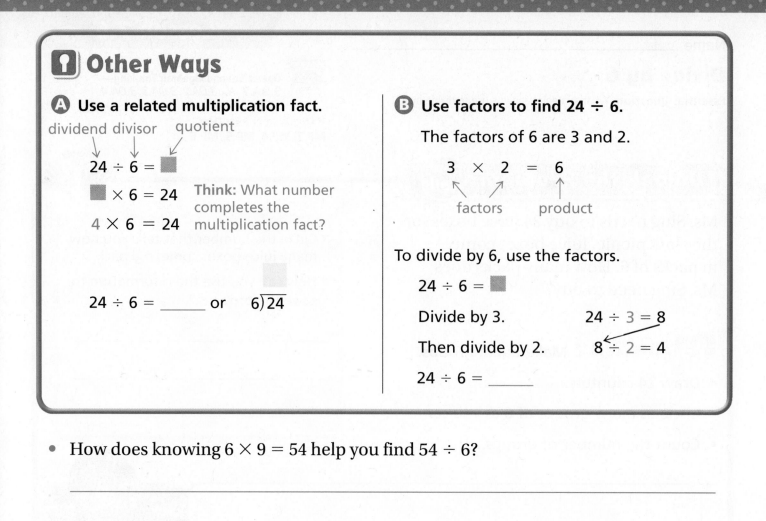

A Use a related multiplication fact.

dividend divisor quotient

$$24 \div 6 = \blacksquare$$

$\blacksquare \times 6 = 24$ **Think:** What number completes the multiplication fact?

$4 \times 6 = 24$

$24 \div 6 = \underline{\hspace{1cm}}$ or $6\overline{)24}$

B Use factors to find $24 \div 6$.

The factors of 6 are 3 and 2.

$$3 \times 2 = 6$$

factors   product

To divide by 6, use the factors.

$24 \div 6 = \blacksquare$

Divide by 3. $24 \div 3 = 8$

Then divide by 2. $8 \div 2 = 4$

$24 \div 6 = \underline{\hspace{1cm}}$

• How does knowing $6 \times 9 = 54$ help you find $54 \div 6$?

_____

_____

Share and Show   MATH BOARD

1. Continue making equal groups to find $18 \div 6$. _____

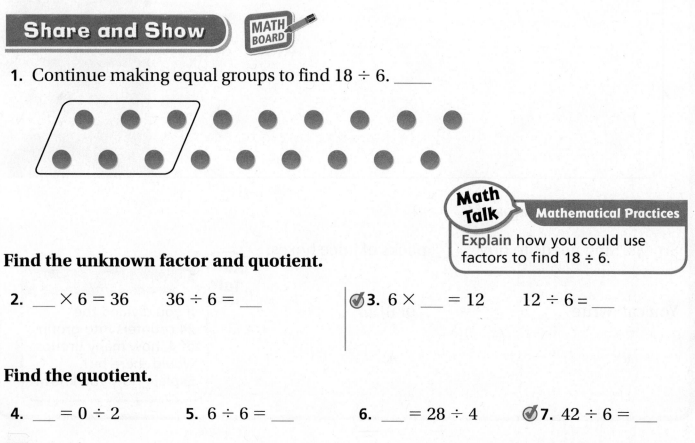

Math Talk   **Mathematical Practices**

Explain how you could use factors to find $18 \div 6$.

Find the unknown factor and quotient.

2. $\underline{\hspace{0.5cm}} \times 6 = 36$ $36 \div 6 = \underline{\hspace{0.5cm}}$

✓**3.** $6 \times \underline{\hspace{0.5cm}} = 12$ $12 \div 6 = \underline{\hspace{0.5cm}}$

Find the quotient.

4. $\underline{\hspace{0.5cm}} = 0 \div 2$

5. $6 \div 6 = \underline{\hspace{0.5cm}}$

6. $\underline{\hspace{0.5cm}} = 28 \div 4$

✓**7.** $42 \div 6 = \underline{\hspace{0.5cm}}$

© Houghton Mifflin Harcourt Publishing Company

Name _____

Find the unknown factor and quotient.

8. $6 \times$ ____ $= 30$ $30 \div 6 =$ ____

9. ____ $\times 6 = 48$ $48 \div 6 =$ ____

10. $2 \times$ ____ $= 16$ ____ $= 16 \div 2$

11. $5 \times$ ____ $= 45$ ____ $= 45 \div 5$

Find the quotient.

12. $12 \div 6 =$ ____

13. ____ $= 6 \div 1$

14. ____ $= 60 \div 6$

15. $27 \div 3 =$ ____

16. $5\overline{)35}$

17. $6\overline{)42}$

18. $6\overline{)6}$

19. $2\overline{)10}$

Find the unknown number.

20. $24 \div 6 = n$

$n =$ ____

21. $40 \div 5 = \triangle$

$\triangle =$ ____

22. $60 \div 10 = m$

$m =$ ____

23. $18 \div 6 = \blacksquare$

$\blacksquare =$ ____

MATHEMATICAL PRACTICE ② **Use Reasoning** **Algebra** **Find the unknown number.**

24. $20 \div$ ____ $= 4$

25. $24 \div$ ____ $= 8$

26. $16 \div$ ____ $= 4$

27. $3 \div$ ____ $= 3$

28. $42 \div$ ____ $= 7$

29. $30 \div$ ____ $= 10$

30. $10 \div$ ____ $= 2$

31. $32 \div$ ____ $= 4$

32. **THINK SMARTER** Derek has 2 boxes of fruit snacks. There are 12 fruit snacks in each box. If he eats 6 fruit snacks each day, how many days will the fruit snacks last? Explain.

_____

_____

© Houghton Mifflin Harcourt Publishing Company

Problem Solving • Applications

33. **Go DEEPER** Cody baked 12 muffins. He keeps 6 muffins. How many muffins can he give to each of his 6 friends if each friend gets the same number of muffins?

_____

34. **MATHEMATICAL PRACTICE ③** **Make Arguments** Mary has 36 stickers to give to 6 friends. She says she can give each friend only 5 stickers. Use a division equation to describe Mary's error.

_____

_____

_____

WRITE ▸Math · **Show Your Work** · · · ·

35. **WRITE** ▸Math **Pose a Problem** Write and solve a word problem for the bar model.

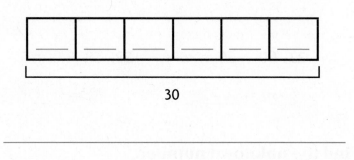

30

_____

_____

_____

Personal Math Trainer

36. **THINK SMARTER ✚** Each van can transport 6 people. How many vans are needed to transport 48 people to an event? Explain the strategy you used to solve the problem.

_____ vans

FOR MORE PRACTICE:
Standards Practice Book

© Houghton Mifflin Harcourt Publishing Company

✓ Mid-Chapter Checkpoint

Concepts and Skills

1. **Explain** how to find 20 ÷ 4 by making an array.
(3.OA.3)

OOOOO so, 20÷4=5
OOOOO
OOOOO
OOOOO

2. **Explain** how to find 30 ÷ 6 by making equal groups.
(3.OA.3)

so, 30÷6=5

Find the unknown factor and quotient. (3.OA.7)

3. $10 \times \underline{5} = 50$ $\underline{5} = 50 \div 10$

4. $2 \times \underline{8} = 16$ $\underline{8} = 16 \div 2$

5. $2 \times \underline{10} = 20$ $\underline{10} = 20 \div 2$

6. $5 \times \underline{4} = 20$ $\underline{4} = 20 \div 5$

4, 8, 12, 16, 20, 24, 28, 32, 36

Find the quotient. (3.OA.3, 3.OA.7)

7. $\underline{1} = 6 \div 6$

8. $21 \div 3 = \underline{7}$

9. $\underline{0} = 0 \div 3$

10. $36 \div 4 = \underline{9}$

6 12 18 24 30 36 42 48 54

11. $5\overline{)35}$ → 7

12. $4\overline{)24}$ → 6

13. $6\overline{)54}$ → 9

14. $3\overline{)9}$ → 3

© Houghton Mifflin Harcourt Publishing Company

15. Carter has 18 new books. He plans to read 3 of them each week. How many weeks will it take Carter to read all of his new books? (3.OA.7)

Show work

$18 \div 3 = \boxed{6}$ weeks

16. Gabriella made 5 waffles for breakfast. She has 25 strawberries and 15 blueberries to put on top of the waffles. She will put an equal number of berries on each waffle. How many berries will Gabriella put on each waffle? (3.OA.3)

8 berries

17. There are 60 people at the fair waiting in line for a ride. Each car in the ride can hold 10 people. Write an equation that could be used to find the number of cars needed to hold all 60 people. (3.OA.7)

$60 \div 10 = 6$ cars

18. Alyssa has 4 cupcakes. She gives 2 cupcakes to each of her cousins. How many cousins does Alyssa have? (3.OA.3)

$4 \div 2 = 2$ cousins

© Houghton Mifflin Harcourt Publishing Company

Name _____

Divide by 7

Essential Question What strategies can you use to divide by 7?

**Operations and Algebraic Thinking—
3.OA.7** *Also 3.OA.2, 3.OA.3, 3.OA.4, 3.OA.6*

MATHEMATICAL PRACTICES
MP.2, MP.4, MP.6, MP.8

🔑 Unlock the Problem Real World

Yasmin used 28 large apples to make 7 loaves of apple bread. She used the same number of apples for each loaf. How many apples did Yasmin use for each loaf?

- Do you need to find the number of equal groups or the number in each group?

  _____

- What label will your answer have?

  _____

🔒 One Way Make an array.

- Draw 1 tile in each of 7 rows.

- Continue drawing 1 tile in each of the 7 rows until all 28 tiles are drawn.

- Count the number of tiles in each row.

There are _____ tiles in each row.

So, Yasmin used _____ for each loaf.

You can write 28 ÷ 7 = _____ or 7)‾28‾ .

Math Talk **Mathematical Practices**

Why can you use division to solve the problem? **Explain.**

© Houghton Mifflin Harcourt Publishing Company

Other Ways

A **Use a related multiplication fact.**

$28 \div 7 = a$ $7 \times a = 28$ **Think:** What number completes the multiplication fact? $28 \div 7 = $ _____ or $7\overline{)28}$

$7 \times 4 = 28$

B **Make equal groups.**

- Draw 7 circles to show 7 groups.

- Draw 1 counter in each group.

- Continue drawing 1 counter at a time until all 28 counters are drawn.

There are ____ counters in each group.

Share and Show

1. Use the related multiplication fact to find $42 \div 7$.
   $6 \times 7 = 42$

   $42 \div 7 = $ ____

Math Talk **Mathematical Practices**

Explain why you can use a related multiplication fact to solve a division problem.

Find the unknown factor and quotient.

2. $7 \times$ ____ $= 7$ $7 \div 7 = $ ____   ✔ 3. $7 \times$ ____ $= 35$ $35 \div 7 = $ ____

Find the quotient.

4. $4 \div 2 = $ ____   5. $56 \div 7 = $ ____   6. ____ $= 20 \div 5$ ✔ 7. ____ $= 21 \div 7$

© Houghton Mifflin Harcourt Publishing Company

On Your Own

Find the unknown factor and quotient.

8. $3 \times$ _____ $= 9$ _____ $= 9 \div 3$

9. $7 \times$ _____ $= 49$ $49 \div 7 =$ _____

10. _____ $\times 7 = 63$ $63 \div 7 =$ _____

11. $4 \times$ _____ $= 32$ _____ $= 32 \div 4$

Find the quotient.

12. $48 \div 6 =$ _____

13. $7 \div 1 =$ _____

14. _____ $= 42 \div 6$

15. _____ $= 18 \div 2$

16. $7\overline{)56}$

17. $1\overline{)9}$

18. $7\overline{)21}$

19. $2\overline{)8}$

Find the unknown number.

20. $60 \div 10 = \blacksquare$

$\blacksquare =$ _____

21. $70 \div 7 = k$

$k =$ _____

22. $m = 63 \div 9$

$m =$ _____

23. $r = 12 \div 6$

$r =$ _____

MATHEMATICAL PRACTICE ⑥ Make Connections Algebra Complete the table.

24.

÷	18	30	24	36
6				

25.

÷	56	42	49	35
7				

26. Clare bought 35 peaches to make peach jam. She used 7 peaches for each jar of jam. How many jars did Clare make?

_____

27. There are 49 jars of peach salsa packed into 7 gift boxes. If each box has the same number of jars of salsa, how many jars are in each box?

_____

© Houghton Mifflin Harcourt Publishing Company

Unlock the Problem (Real World)

28. **THINK SMARTER** Gavin sold 21 bagels to 7 different people. Each person bought the same number of bagels. How many bagels did Gavin sell to each person?

a. What do you need to find? _____

_____

b. How can you use a bar model to help you decide which

operation to use to solve the problem? _____

_____

_____

c. Complete the bar model to help you find the number of bagels Gavin sold to each person.

__	__	__	__	__	__	__

21 bagels

d. What is another way you could have solved the problem?

_____

_____

e. Complete the sentences.

Gavin sold _____ bagels to _____ different people.

Each person bought the same number

of _____.

So, Gavin sold _____ bagels to each person.

---

29. **GO DEEPER** There are 35 plain bagels and 42 wheat bagels on 7 shelves in the bakery. Each shelf has the same number of plain bagels and the same number of wheat bagels. How many bagels are on each shelf?

_____

30. **THINK SMARTER** Write the correct symbol that makes the equations true.

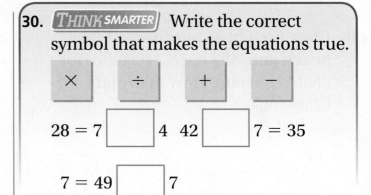

×	÷	+	−

$28 = 7 \boxed{} 4$ $42 \boxed{} 7 = 35$

$7 = 49 \boxed{} 7$

FOR MORE PRACTICE:
Standards Practice Book

© Houghton Mifflin Harcourt Publishing Company

Name _____

Divide by 8

Essential Question What strategies can you use to divide by 8?

**Operations and Algebraic Thinking—
3.OA.3, 3.OA.4** *Also 3.OA.2,
3.OA.6, 3.OA.7*

MATHEMATICAL PRACTICES
MP.2, MP.4, MP.6, MP.7

🔑 Unlock the Problem (Real World)

At Stephen's camping store, firewood is sold in bundles of 8 logs. He has 32 logs to put in bundles. How many bundles of firewood can he make?

- What will Stephen do with the 32 logs?

_____

_____

🔒 One Way **Use repeated subtraction.**

- Start with 32.

- Subtract 8 until you reach 0.

- Count the number of times you subtract 8.

⚠️ **ERROR Alert**
Continue to subtract the divisor, 8, until the difference is less than 8.

$$
\begin{array}{cccc}
32 & 24 & & \\
-\ 8 & -\ 8 & -\ 8 & -\ 8 \\
\hline
24 & & & \\
\end{array}
$$

Number of times
you subtract 8:   1   2   3   4

You subtracted 8 _____ times.

So, Stephen can make _____ bundles of firewood.

You can write $32 \div 8 =$ _____ or $8 \overline{)32}$.

🔒 Another Way **Use a related multiplication fact.**

$32 \div 8 =$ ■   ■ $\times\ 8 = 32$

                    $4 \times 8 = 32$

Think: What number completes the multiplication fact?

$32 \div 8 =$ _____ or $8 \overline{)32}$

Math Talk **Mathematical Practices**

How does knowing $4 \times 8 = 32$ help you find $32 \div 8$?

© Houghton Mifflin Harcourt Publishing Company

Example Find the unknown divisor.

Stephen has a log that is 16 feet long. If he cuts the log into pieces that are 2 feet long, how many pieces will Stephen have?

Divide. $16 \div \blacksquare = 2$

You can also use a multiplication table to find the divisor in a division problem.

Think: $\blacksquare \times 2 = 16$

STEP 1 Find the factor, 2, in the top row.

STEP 2 Look down to find the product, 16.

STEP 3 Look left to find the unknown factor.

The unknown factor is _____.

$$\blacksquare = \_\_\_\_\_$$

$$\_\_\_\_\_ \times 2 = 16 \qquad \text{Check.}$$

$$\_\_\_\_\_ = 16 \checkmark \qquad \text{The equation is true.}$$

So, Stephen will have _____ pieces.

×	0	1	2	3	4	5	6	7	8	9	10
0	0	0	0	0	0	0	0	0	0	0	0
1	0	1	2	3	4	5	6	7	8	9	10
2	0	2	4	6	8	10	12	14	16	18	20
3	0	3	6	9	12	15	18	21	24	27	30
4	0	4	8	12	16	20	24	28	32	36	40
5	0	5	10	15	20	25	30	35	40	45	50
6	0	6	12	18	24	30	36	42	48	54	60
7	0	7	14	21	28	35	42	49	56	63	70
8	0	8	16	24	32	40	48	56	64	72	80
9	0	9	18	27	36	45	54	63	72	81	90
10	0	10	20	30	40	50	60	70	80	90	100

Math Talk Mathematical Practices

Explain how to use the multiplication table to find the unknown dividend for $\blacksquare \div 8 = 5$.

Share and Show MATH BOARD

1. Use repeated subtraction to find $24 \div 8$. _____

$$
\begin{array}{ccc}
24 & 16 & 8 \\
-\ 8 & -\ 8 & -8 \\
\hline
16 & 8 & 0 \\
\end{array}
$$

Think: How many times do you subtract 8?

Math Talk Mathematical Practices

Explain why you subtract 8 from 24 to find $24 \div 8$.

Find the unknown factor and quotient.

2. $8 \times \_\_\_\_ = 56$ $56 \div 8 = \_\_\_\_$ ☑ 3. $\_\_\_\_ \times 8 = 40$ $40 \div 8 = \_\_\_\_$

Find the quotient.

4. $18 \div 3 = \_\_\_\_$ 5. $\_\_\_\_ = 48 \div 8$ 6. $56 \div 7 = \_\_\_\_$ ☑ 7. $\_\_\_\_ = 32 \div 8$

© Houghton Mifflin Harcourt Publishing Company

On Your Own

Find the unknown factor and quotient.

8. $8 \times$ ____ $= 8$ $8 \div 8 =$ ____

9. ____ $\times 5 = 35$ ____ $= 35 \div 5$

10. $6 \times$ ____ $= 18$ $18 \div 6 =$ ____

11. $8 \times$ ____ $= 72$ ____ $= 72 \div 8$

Find the quotient.

12. $28 \div 4 =$ ____

13. $42 \div 7 =$ ____

14. ____ $= 3 \div 3$

15. ____ $= 28 \div 7$

16. $8 \overline{)0}$

17. $6 \overline{)24}$

18. $8 \overline{)64}$

19. $1 \overline{)8}$

Find the unknown number.

20. $72 \div \bigstar = 9$

$\bigstar =$ ____

21. $t \div 8 = 2$

$t =$ ____

22. $64 \div \blacktriangle = 8$

$\blacktriangle =$ ____

23. $m \div 8 = 10$

$m =$ ____

24. $\blacktriangle \div 2 = 10$

$\blacktriangle =$ ____

25. $40 \div \blacksquare = 8$

$\blacksquare =$ ____

26. $25 \div k = 5$

$k =$ ____

27. $54 \div n = 9$

$n =$ ____

28. **MATHEMATICAL PRACTICE ②** **Connect Symbols and Words** Write a word problem that can be solved by using one of the division facts above.

_____

_____

MATHEMATICAL PRACTICE ④ **Use Symbols** **Algebra** Write $+$, $-$, $\times$, or $\div$.

29. $6 \times 6 = 32 \bigcirc 4$

30. $12 \bigcirc 3 = 19 - 15$

31. $40 \div 8 = 35 \bigcirc 7$

© Houghton Mifflin Harcourt Publishing Company

Problem Solving • Applications Real World

Use the table for 32–33.

Tent Sizes	
Type	**Number of People**
Cabin	10
Vista	8
Trail	4

32. **GO DEEPER** There are 32 people who plan to camp over the weekend. Describe two different ways the campers can sleep using 4 tents.

_____

_____

_____

33. **THINK SMARTER** There are 36 people camping at Max's family reunion. They have cabin tents and vista tents. How many of each type of tent do they need to sleep exactly 36 people if each tent is filled? Explain.

_____

_____

_____

_____

WRITE ▸Math · **Show Your Work**

34. Josh is dividing 64 bags of trail mix equally among 8 campers. How many bags of trail mix will each camper get?

_____

35. **THINK SMARTER** Circle the unknown factor and quotient.

$$8 \times \boxed{\begin{array}{c} 6 \\ 7 \\ 8 \end{array}} = 48 \qquad \boxed{\begin{array}{c} 6 \\ 7 \\ 8 \end{array}} = 48 \div 8$$

© Houghton Mifflin Harcourt Publishing Company

Name _____

Divide by 9

Essential Question What strategies can you use to divide by 9?

Operations and Algebraic Thinking—3.OA.7 *Also 3.OA.2, 3.OA.3, 3.OA.4, 3.OA.5, 3.OA.6*

MATHEMATICAL PRACTICES
MP.2, MP.4, MP.6

⚷ Unlock the Problem (Real World)

Becket's class goes to the aquarium. The 27 students from the class are separated into 9 equal groups. How many students are in each group?

- Do you need to find the number of equal groups or the number in each group?

_____

🔒 One Way. Make equal groups.

- Draw 9 circles to show 9 groups.

- Draw 1 counter in each group.

- Continue drawing 1 counter at a time until all 27 counters are drawn.

There are _____ counters in each group.

So, there are _____ in each group.

You can write $27 \div 9 =$ _____ or $9\overline{)27}$.

Math Talk

Mathematical Practices

What is another way you could solve the problem? **Explain.**

© Houghton Mifflin Harcourt Publishing Company • Image Credits: ©Francisco Martinez/Alamy

🔓 Other Ways

A Use factors to find $27 \div 9$.

The factors of 9 are 3 and 3.

$$3 \quad \times \quad 3 \quad = \quad 9$$

factors   product

To divide by 9, use the factors.

$27 \div 9 = s$

Divide by 3. $27 \div 3 = 9$

Then divide by 3 again. $9 \div 3 = 3$

$27 \div 9 = \underline{\hspace{2em}}$

B Use a related multiplication fact.

$27 \div 9 = s$

$9 \times s = 27$ **Think:** What number completes the multiplication fact?

$9 \times 3 = 27$

$27 \div 9 = \underline{\hspace{2em}}$ or $9\overline{)27}$

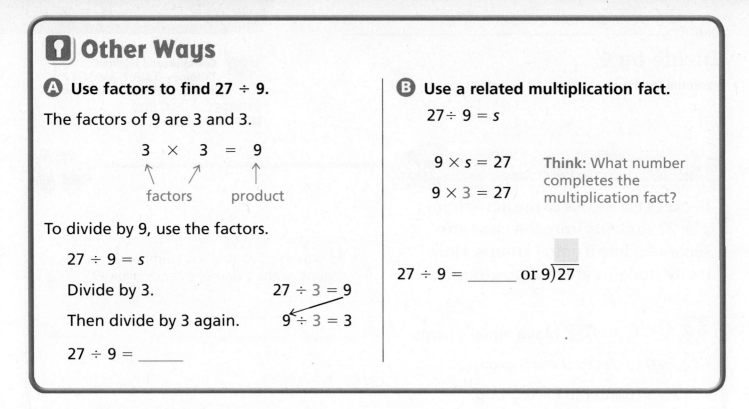

- What multiplication fact can you use to find $63 \div 9$? _____

Share and Show   MATH BOARD

1. Draw counters in the groups to find $18 \div 9.$ _____

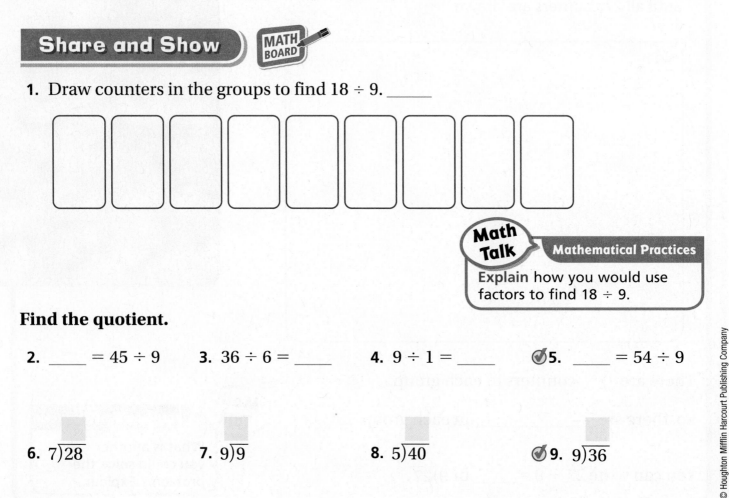

Math Talk   **Mathematical Practices**

Explain how you would use factors to find $18 \div 9$.

Find the quotient.

2. _____ $= 45 \div 9$ 3. $36 \div 6 = $ _____   4. $9 \div 1 = $ _____   ✅5. _____ $= 54 \div 9$

6. $7\overline{)28}$ 7. $9\overline{)9}$ 8. $5\overline{)40}$ ✅9. $9\overline{)36}$

© Houghton Mifflin Harcourt Publishing Company

Name ____________________

On Your Own

10. $8 \div 2 =$ ____ 11. ____ $= 72 \div 9$ 12. $56 \div 8 =$ ____ 13. ____ $= 27 \div 9$

14. ____ $= 5 \div 1$ 15. ____ $= 36 \div 4$ 16. $81 \div 9 =$ ____ 17. $30 \div 5 =$ ____

18. $4\overline{)12}$ 19. $9\overline{)63}$ 20. $2\overline{)16}$ 21. $5\overline{)25}$

Find the unknown number.

22. $64 \div 8 = e$ 23. $0 \div 9 = g$ 24. ■ $= 20 \div 4$ 25. $s = 9 \div 9$

$e =$ ____ $g =$ ____ ■ $=$ ____ $s =$ ____

MATHEMATICAL PRACTICE 2 **Use Reasoning** **Algebra** **Complete the table.**

26.

÷	24	40	32	48
8				

27.

÷	54	45	72	63
9				

28. GO DEEPER Sophie has two new fish. She feeds one fish 4 pellets and the other fish 5 pellets each day. If Sophie has fed her fish 72 pellets, for how many days has she had her fish? Explain.

____

____

29. MATHEMATICAL PRACTICE 4 **Write an Equation** Each van going to the aquarium carries 9 students. If 63 third-grade students go to the aquarium, what multiplication fact can you use to find the number of vans that will be needed?

____

© Houghton Mifflin Harcourt Publishing Company

Unlock the Problem Real World

30. THINK SMARTER Carlos has 28 blue tang fish and 17 yellow tang fish in one large fish tank. He wants to separate the fish so that there are the same number of fish in each of 9 smaller tanks. How many tang fish will Carlos put in each smaller tank?

Math on the Spot

a. What do you need to find? _____

_____

b. Why do you need to use two operations to solve the problem? _____

_____

c. Write the steps to find how many tang fish Carlos will put in each smaller tank.

d. Complete the sentences.

Carlos has _____ blue tang fish

and _____ yellow tang fish in one large fish tank.

He wants to separate the fish so that there are the same number

of fish in each of _____ smaller tanks.

So, Carlos will put _____ fish in each smaller tank.

31. THINK SMARTER Complete the chart to show the quotients.

÷	27	18	45	36
9				

© Houghton Mifflin Harcourt Publishing Company • Image Credits: ©Medioimages/Getty Images

FOR MORE PRACTICE:
Standards Practice Book

Name _____

Problem Solving • Two-Step Problems

Essential Question How can you use the strategy *act it out* to solve two-step problems?

Operations and Algebraic Thinking—3.OA.8
Also 3.OA.2, 3.OA.3, 3.OA.7

MATHEMATICAL PRACTICES
MP.4, MP.5, MP.6

Unlock the Problem (Real World)

Madilyn bought 2 packs of pens and a notebook for $11. The notebook cost $3. Each pack of pens cost the same amount. What is the price of 1 pack of pens?

Read the Problem	Solve the Problem
What do I need to find? I need to find the price of 1 pack of _____.	**Describe how to act out the problem.** Start with 11 counters. Take away 3 counters.

Solve the Problem

Describe how to act out the problem.

Start with 11 counters. Take away 3 counters.

total cost		cost of notebook		p, cost of 2 packs of pens
↓		↓		↓
_____	−	_____	=	p
		_____	=	p

Now I know that 2 packs of pens cost _____.

Next, make _____ equal groups with the 8 remaining counters.

p, cost of 2 packs of pens		number of packs		c, cost of 1 pack of pens
↓		↓		↓
$8	÷	_____	=	c
		_____	=	c

So, the price of 1 pack of pens is _____.

Read the Problem

What do I need to find?

I need to find the price of

1 pack of _____.

What information do I need to use?

Madilyn spent _____ in all.

She bought _____ packs of

pens and _____ notebook.

The notebook cost _____.

How will I use the information?

I will use the information to

_____ out the problem.

Math Talk Mathematical Practices

Why do you need to use two operations to solve the problem? **Explain.**

🔓 Try Another Problem

Chad bought 4 packs of T-shirts. He gave 5 T-shirts to his brother. Now Chad has 19 shirts. How many T-shirts were in each pack?

Read the Problem	Solve the Problem
What do I need to find?	**Describe how to act out the problem.**
What information do I need to use?	
How will I use the information?	

- How can you use multiplication and subtraction to check your answer?

_____

_____

_____

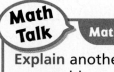

Math Talk **Mathematical Practices**

Explain another strategy you could use to solve this problem.

© Houghton Mifflin Harcourt Publishing Company • Image Credits: ©C Squared Studios/Getty Images

Name _____

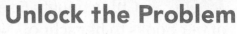

Share and Show

Unlock the Problem

✓ Circle the question.
✓ Underline the important facts.
✓ Choose a strategy you know.

1. Mac bought 4 packs of toy cars. Then his friend gave him 9 cars. Now Mac has 21 cars. How many cars were in each pack?

Act out the problem by using counters or the picture and by writing equations.

First, subtract the cars Mac's friend gave him.

total cars		cars given to Mac		c, cars in 4 packs
↓		↓		↓
21	−	_____	=	c
		_____	=	c

Then, divide to find the number of cars in each pack.

c, cars in 4 packs		number of packs		p, number in each pack
↓		↓		↓
12	÷	_____	=	p
		_____	=	p

So, there were _____ cars in each pack.

2. **THINK SMARTER** What if Mac bought 8 packs of cars and then he gave his friend 3 cars? If Mac has 13 cars now, how many cars were in each pack?

_____

On Your Own

3. **THINK SMARTER** Ryan gave 7 of his model cars to a friend. Then he bought 6 more cars. Now Ryan has 13 cars. How many cars did Ryan start with?

_____

© Houghton Mifflin Harcourt Publishing Company

4. **GO DEEPER** Chloe bought 5 sets of books. She donated 9 of her books to her school. Now she has 26 books. How many books were in each set?

_____

5. Raul bought 2 packs of erasers. He found 2 erasers in his backpack. Now Raul has 8 erasers. How many erasers were in each pack?

_____

6. Hilda cuts a ribbon into 2 equal pieces. Then she cuts 4 inches off one piece. That piece is now 5 inches long. What was the length of the original ribbon?

_____

WRITE ▸ *Math*
Show Your Work

7. **MATHEMATICAL PRACTICE 6** Rose saw a movie, shopped, and ate at a restaurant. She did not see the movie first. She shopped right after she ate. In what order did Rose do these activities? **Explain** how you know.

_____

_____

_____

_____

_____

Personal Math Trainer

8. **THINK SMARTER +** Eleni bought 3 packs of crayons. She then found 3 crayons in her desk. Eleni now has 24 crayons. How many crayons were in each pack she bought? Explain how you solved the problem.

_____

_____

© Houghton Mifflin Harcourt Publishing Company

FOR MORE PRACTICE:
Standards Practice Book

Order of Operations

Essential Question Why are there rules such as the order of operations?

Operations and Algebraic Thinking—
3.OA.8 *Also 3.OA.1, 3.OA.2, 3.OA.3, 3.OA.7*

MATHEMATICAL PRACTICES
MP.2, MP.4, MP.6

Investigate

CONNECT You can use what you know about acting out a two-step problem to write one equation to describe and solve a two-step problem.

- If you solved a two-step problem in a different order, what do you think might happen?

_____

Use different orders to find $4 + 16 \div 2$.

A. Make a list of all the possible orders you can use to find the answer to $4 + 16 \div 2$.

_____

B. Use each order in your list to find the answer. Show the steps you used.

_____

_____

Draw Conclusions

1. Did following different orders change the answer? _____

2. **MATHEMATICAL PRACTICE ⑧ Draw Conclusions** If a problem has more than one type of operation, how does the order in which you perform the operations affect the answer?

_____

3. Explain the need for setting an order of operations that everyone follows.

_____

_____

© Houghton Mifflin Harcourt Publishing Company

Make Connections

When solving problems with more than one type of operation, you need to know which operation to do first. A special set of rules, called the **order of operations**, gives the order in which calculations are done in a problem.

First, multiply and divide from left to right.

Then, add and subtract from left to right.

Meghan buys 2 books for $4 each. She pays with a $10 bill. How much money does she have left?

You can write $\$10 - 2 \times \$4 = c$ to describe and solve the problem.

Use the order of operations to solve $\$10 - 2 \times \$4 = c$.

STEP 1

Multiply from left to right.
$$\$10 - 2 \times \$4 = c$$
$$\$10 - \quad \$8 \quad = c$$

STEP 2

Subtract from left to right.
$$\$10 - \$8 = c$$
$$\$2 \quad = c$$

So, Meghan has _____ left.

- Does your answer make sense? Explain.

_____

_____

_____

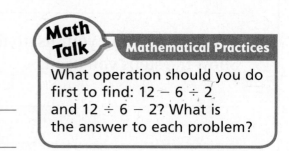

Math Talk   **Mathematical Practices**

What operation should you do first to find: $12 - 6 \div 2$ and $12 \div 6 - 2$? What is the answer to each problem?

Share and Show

Write *correct* if the operations are listed in the correct order. If not correct, write the correct order of operations.

1. $4 + 5 \times 2$ multiply, add

_____

2. $8 \div 4 \times 2$ multiply, divide

_____

3. $12 + 16 \div 4$ add, divide ✗

divide, add

4. $9 + 2 \times 3$ add, multiply ✗

multiply, add

5. $4 + 6 \div 3$ divide, add

_____

6. $36 - 7 \times 3$ multiply, subtract

_____

© Houghton Mifflin Harcourt Publishing Company

Name _____

Follow the order of operations to find the unknown number.
Use your MathBoard.

7. $63 \div 9 - 2 = f$

$f =$ _____

8. $7 - 5 + 8 = y$

$y =$ _____

9. $3 \times 6 - 2 = h$

$h =$ _____

10. $80 - 64 \div 8 = n$

$n =$ _____

11. $3 \times 4 + 6 = a$

$a =$ _____

12. $2 \times 7 \div 7 = c$

$c =$ _____

Problem Solving • Applications

MATHEMATICAL PRACTICE ④ Write an Equation **Algebra** Use the numbers listed to make the equation true.

13. 2, 6, and 5

_____ + _____ × _____ = 16

14. 4, 12, and 18

_____ − _____ ÷ _____ = 15

15. 8, 9, and 7

_____ × _____ − _____ = 47

16. 2, 4, and 9

_____ ÷ _____ + _____ = 11

17. **WRITE** ▸ *Math* **Pose a Problem** Write a word problem that can be solved by using $2 \times 5 \div 5$. Solve your problem.

_____

_____

_____

_____

18. **THINK SMARTER** Is $4 + 8 \times 3$ equal to $4 + 3 \times 8$? Explain how you know without finding the answers.

_____

_____

_____

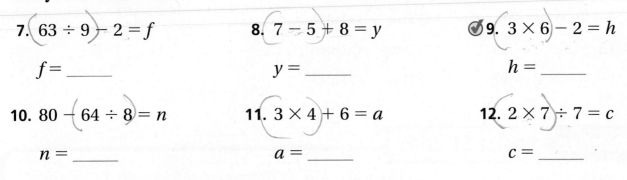

Math on the Spot

© Houghton Mifflin Harcourt Publishing Company

19. **THINK SMARTER** For numbers 19a–19d, select True or False for each equation.

19a. $24 \div 3 + 5 = 13$ ○ True   ○ False

19b. $5 + 2 \times 3 = 21$ ○ True   ○ False

19c. $15 - 3 \div 3 = 14$ ○ True   ○ False

19d. $18 \div 3 \times 2 = 12$ ○ True   ○ False

Connect to Social Studies

Picture Book Art

The Eric Carle Museum of Picture Book Art in Amherst, Massachusetts, is the first museum in the United States that is devoted to picture book art. Picture books introduce literature to young readers.

The museum has 3 galleries, a reading library, a café, an art studio, an auditorium, and a museum shop. The exhibits change every 3 to 6 months, depending on the length of time the picture art is on loan and how fragile it is.

The table shows prices for some souvenirs in the bookstore in the museum.

Souvenir Prices	
Souvenir	Price
Firefly Picture Frame	$25
Exhibition Posters	$10
Caterpillar Note Cards	$8
Caterpillar Pens	$4
Sun Note Pads	$3

20. Kallon bought 3 Caterpillar note cards and 1 Caterpillar pen. How much did he spend on souvenirs?

_____

21. **GO DEEPER** Raya and 4 friends bought their teacher 1 Firefly picture frame. They shared the cost equally. Then Raya bought an Exhibition poster. How much money did Raya spend in all? Explain.

_____

_____

_____

© Houghton Mifflin Harcourt Publishing Company

FOR MORE PRACTICE:
Standards Practice Book

Chapter 7 Review/Test

1. Ming divided 35 marbles between 7 different friends.
   Each friend received the same number of marbles. How
   many marbles did Ming give to each friend?

$$35 \div 7 = a$$
$$7 \times a = 35$$

   (A) 4   (C) 6

   (B) 5   (D) 7

2. Mrs. Conner has 16 shoes.

   Select one number from each column to show the
   division equation represented by the picture.

$$16 \div \frac{?}{(\text{divisor})} = \frac{?}{(\text{quotient})}$$

Divisor	Quotient
○ 1	○ 1
○ 2	○ 4
○ 4	○ 8
○ 16	○ 16

3. Twenty boys are going camping. They brought 5 tents.
   An equal number of boys sleep in each tent. How many
   boys will sleep in each tent?

   _____ boys

© Houghton Mifflin Harcourt Publishing Company

GO DIGITAL Assessment Options
Chapter Test

4. Circle a number for the unknown factor and quotient that makes the equation true.

$$4 \times \boxed{\begin{matrix} 6 \\ 7 \\ 8 \end{matrix}} = 28 \qquad \boxed{\begin{matrix} 6 \\ 7 \\ 8 \end{matrix}} = 28 \div 4$$

5. Mrs. Walters has 30 markers. She gives each student 10 markers. How many students received the markers?

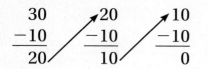

Write a division equation to represent the repeated subtraction.

_____ ÷ _____ = _____

6. Complete the chart to show the quotients.

÷	27	36	45	54
9				

7. For numbers 7a–7e, select True or False for each equation.

7a. $12 \div 6 = 2$ ○ True   ○ False

7b. $24 \div 6 = 3$ ○ True   ○ False

7c. $30 \div 6 = 6$ ○ True   ○ False

7d. $42 \div 6 = 7$ ○ True   ○ False

7e. $48 \div 6 = 8$ ○ True   ○ False

© Houghton Mifflin Harcourt Publishing Company

8. Alicia says that $6 \div 2 + 5$ is the same as $5 + 6 \div 2$.
Is Alicia correct or incorrect? Explain.

_____

_____

_____

_____

9. Keith arranged 40 toy cars in 8 equal rows. How many
toy cars are in each row?

_____ toy cars

10. Bella made $21 selling bracelets. She wants to know how
many bracelets she sold. Bella used this number line.

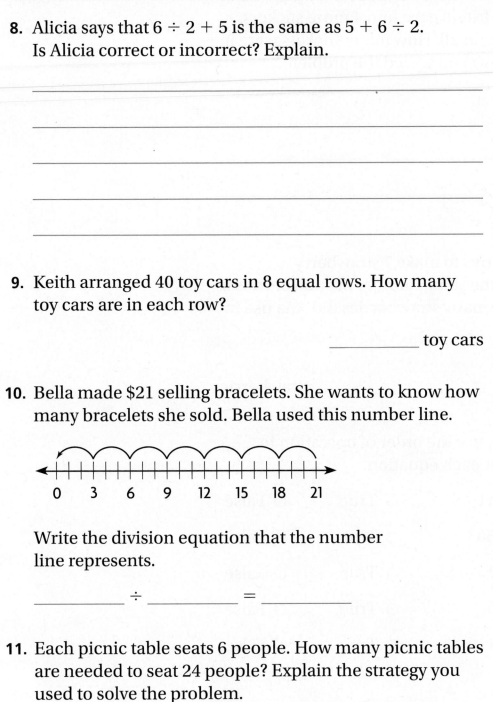

Write the division equation that the number
line represents.

_____ ÷ _____ = _____

11. Each picnic table seats 6 people. How many picnic tables
are needed to seat 24 people? Explain the strategy you
used to solve the problem.

_____

_____

_____

© Houghton Mifflin Harcourt Publishing Company

12. Finn bought 2 packs of stickers. Each pack had the same number of stickers. A friend gave him 4 more stickers. Now he has 24 stickers in all. How many stickers were in each pack? Explain how you solved the problem.

_____

_____

_____

13. Ana used 49 strawberries to make 7 strawberry smoothies. She used the same number of strawberries in each smoothies. How many strawberries did Ana use in each smoothie?

_____ strawberries

14. For numbers 14a–14e, use the order of operation to select True or False for each equation.

14a.	$81 \div 9 + 2 = 11$	○ True	○ False
14b.	$6 + 4 \times 5 = 50$	○ True	○ False
14c.	$10 + 10 \div 2 = 15$	○ True	○ False
14d.	$12 - 3 \times 2 = 6$	○ True	○ False
14e.	$20 \div 4 \times 5 = 1$	○ True	○ False

15. A flower shop sells daffodils in bunches of 9. It sells 27 daffodils. How many bunches of daffodils does the shop sell?

_____ bunches

© Houghton Mifflin Harcourt Publishing Company

Name _____

16. Aviva started a table showing a division pattern.

÷	20	30	40	50
10				
5				

Part A

Complete the table.

Compare the quotients when dividing by 10 and when dividing by 5. Describe a pattern you see in the quotients.

_____

_____

Part B

Find the quotient, *a*.

$70 \div 10 = a$

$a = $ _____

How could you use *a* to find the value of *n*? Find the value of *n*.

$70 \div 5 = n$

$n = $ _____

_____

_____

17. Ben needs 2 oranges to make a glass of orange juice. If oranges come in bags of 10, how many glasses of orange juice can he make using one bag of oranges?

_____ glasses

© Houghton Mifflin Harcourt Publishing Company

18. For numbers 18a–18e, select True or False for each equation.

18a. $0 \div 9 = 0$ ○ True   ○ False

18b. $9 \div 9 = 1$ ○ True   ○ False

18c. $27 \div 9 = 4$ ○ True   ○ False

18d. $54 \div 9 = 6$ ○ True   ○ False

18e. $90 \div 9 = 9$ ○ True   ○ False

19. Ellen is making gift baskets for four friends. She has 16 prizes she wants to divide equally among the baskets. How many prizes should she put in each basket?

_____ prizes

20. Emily is buying a pet rabbit. She needs to buy items for her rabbit at the pet store.

Part A

Emily buys a cage and 2 bowls for $54. The cage costs $40. Each bowl costs the same amount. What is the price of 1 bowl? Explain the steps you used to solve the problem.

_____

_____

_____

Part B

Emily also buys food and toys for her rabbit. She buys a bag of food for $20. She buys 2 toys for $3 each. Write one equation to describe the total amount Emily spends on food and toys. Explain how to use the order of operations to solve the equation.

_____

_____

_____

© Houghton Mifflin Harcourt Publishing Company

CRITICAL AREA Developing understanding of fractions, especially unit fractions (fractions with numerator 1)

MISSOURI
1821
CORPS OF DISCOVERY
1804   2004
2003
E PLURIBUS UNUM

The Missouri quarter shows explorers Lewis and Clark traveling down the Missouri River. The Gateway Arch is in the background.

© Houghton Mifflin Harcourt Publishing Company • Image Credits: ©Department of the Treasury/United States Mint

Coins in the U.S.

Many years ago, a coin called a *piece of eight* was sometimes cut into 8 equal parts. Each part was equal to one eighth ($\frac{1}{8}$) of the whole. Now, U.S. coin values are based on the dollar. Four quarters are equal in value to 1 dollar. So, 1 quarter is equal to one fourth ($\frac{1}{4}$) of a dollar.

Get Started

Work with a partner. In which year were the Missouri state quarters minted? Use the Important Facts to help you. Then write fractions to answer these questions:

1. 2 quarters are equal to what part of a dollar?
2. 1 nickel is equal to what part of a dime?
3. 2 nickels are equal to what part of a dime?

Important Facts

- The U.S. government minted state quarters every year from 1999 to 2008 in the order that the states became part of the United States.
- 1999—Delaware, Pennsylvania, New Jersey, Georgia, Connecticut
- 2000—Massachusetts, Maryland, South Carolina, New Hampshire, Virginia
- 2001—New York, North Carolina, Rhode Island, Vermont, Kentucky
- 2002—Tennessee, Ohio, Louisiana, Indiana, Mississippi
- 2003—Illinois, Alabama, Maine, Missouri, Arkansas
- 2004—Michigan, Florida, Texas, Iowa, Wisconsin
- 2005—California, Minnesota, Oregon, Kansas, West Virginia
- 2006—Nevada, Nebraska, Colorado, North Dakota, South Dakota
- 2007—Montana, Washington, Idaho, Wyoming, Utah
- 2008—Oklahoma, New Mexico, Arizona, Alaska, Hawaii

Completed by _____

© Houghton Mifflin Harcourt Publishing Company • Image Credits: (tl) ©Garry Gay/Alamy

8 Understand Fractions

Show What You Know ✓

Check your understanding of important skills.

Name _____

▶ **Equal Parts** Circle the shape that has equal parts.

1.

2.

▶ **Combine Plane Shapes** Write the number of needed to cover the shape.

3. _____ triangles

4. _____ triangles

5. _____ triangles

▶ **Count Equal Groups** Complete.

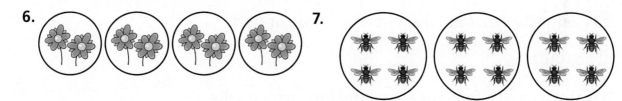

6. _____ groups

_____ in each group

7. _____ groups

_____ in each group

Math Detective

Casey shared a pizza with some friends. They each ate $\frac{1}{3}$ of the pizza. Be a Math Detective to find how many people shared the pizza.

© Houghton Mifflin Harcourt Publishing Company • Image Credits: ©PhotoDisc / Getty Images

 Personal Math Trainer
Online Assessment
and Intervention

Vocabulary Builder

▶ **Visualize It** ·

Complete the bubble map by using the words with a ✓.

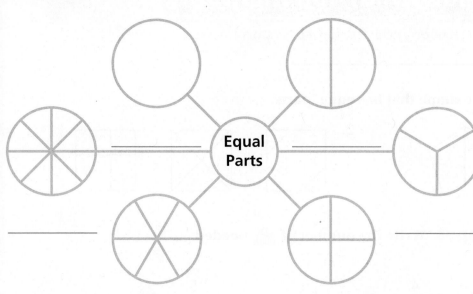

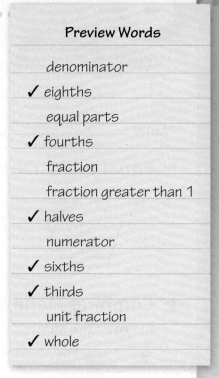

Preview Words

denominator

✓ eighths

   equal parts

✓ fourths

   fraction

   fraction greater than 1

✓ halves

   numerator

✓ sixths

✓ thirds

   unit fraction

✓ whole

▶ **Understand Vocabulary** ·

Read the description. Write the preview word.

1. It is a number that names part of a whole or part of a group. _____

2. It is the part of a fraction above the line, which tells how many parts are being counted.

   _____

3. It is the part of a fraction below the line, which tells how many equal parts there are in the whole or in the group. _____

4. It is a number that names 1 equal part of a whole and has 1 as its numerator. _____

• **Interactive Student Edition**
• **Multimedia eGlossary**

© Houghton Mifflin Harcourt Publishing Company

Equal Parts of a Whole

Essential Question What are equal parts of a whole?

Number and Operations—
Fractions—3.NF.1 *Also 3.G.2*
MATHEMATICAL PRACTICES
MP.2, MP.4, MP.5

Unlock the Problem Real World

Lauren shares a sandwich with her brother. They each get an equal part. How many equal parts are there?

🔑 Each whole shape below is divided into equal parts. A **whole** is all of the parts of one shape or group. **Equal parts** are exactly the same size.

- What do you need to find?

_____

_____

- How many people share the sandwich? _____

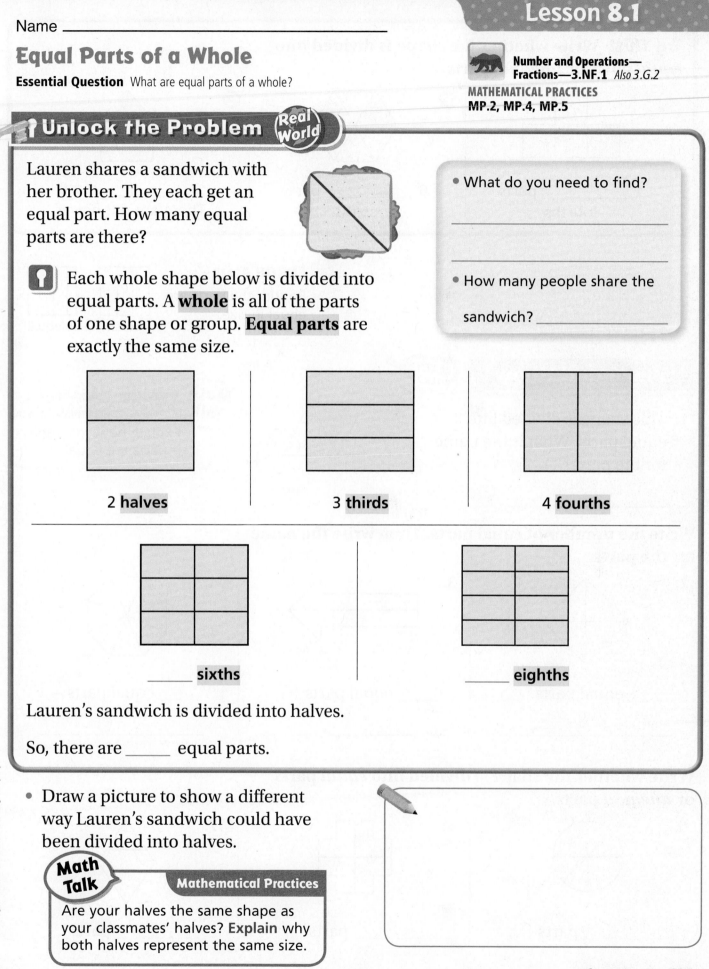

2 halves   **3 thirds**   **4 fourths**

_____ **sixths**   _____ **eighths**

Lauren's sandwich is divided into halves.

So, there are _____ equal parts.

- Draw a picture to show a different way Lauren's sandwich could have been divided into halves.

Math Talk
Mathematical Practices
Are your halves the same shape as your classmates' halves? **Explain** why both halves represent the same size.

© Houghton Mifflin Harcourt Publishing Company

Try This! Write whether the shape is divided into *equal* parts or *unequal* parts.

Ⓐ

4 _____ parts
fourths

Ⓑ

6 _____ parts
sixths

Ⓒ

2 _____ parts
These are not halves.

> ⚠ **ERROR Alert**
> Be sure the parts are equal in size.
>
> equal   unequal

Share and Show MATH BOARD

1. This shape is divided into 3 equal parts. What is the name for the parts?

_____

> **Math Talk** **Mathematical Practices**
> **Explain** how you know if parts are equal.

Write the number of equal parts. Then write the name for the parts.

2.

_____ equal parts

_____

3.

_____ equal parts

_____

✓4.

_____ equal parts

_____

Write whether the shape is divided into *equal* parts or *unequal* parts.

5.

_____ parts

6.

_____ parts

✓7.

_____ parts

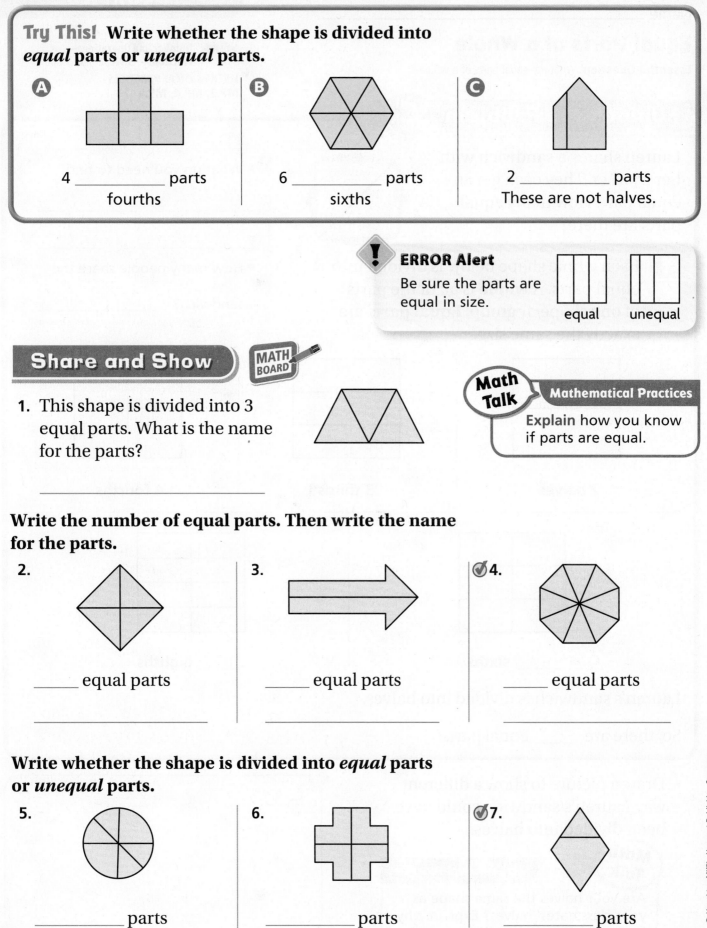

© Houghton Mifflin Harcourt Publishing Company

Name _____

Write the number of equal parts. Then write the name for the parts.

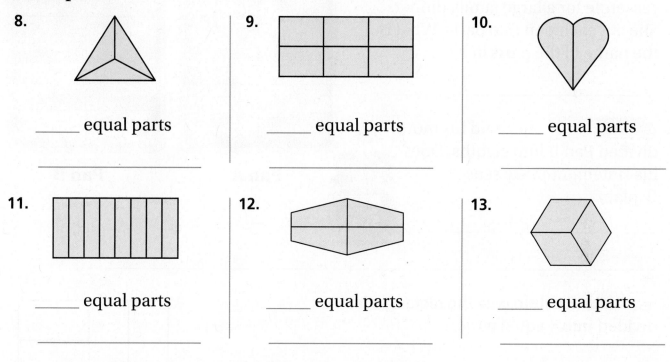

8.

_____ equal parts

_____

9.

_____ equal parts

_____

10.

_____ equal parts

_____

11.

_____ equal parts

_____

12.

_____ equal parts

_____

13.

_____ equal parts

_____

Write whether the shape is divided into *equal* parts or *unequal* parts.

14.

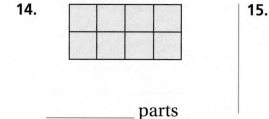

_____ parts

15.

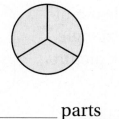

_____ parts

16.

_____ parts

17. Draw lines to divide the circle into 8 eighths.

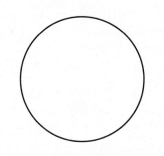

18. **GO DEEPER** Thomas wants to divide a square piece of paper into 4 equal parts. Draw two different quick pictures to show what his paper could look like.

© Houghton Mifflin Harcourt Publishing Company

Problem Solving • Applications Real World

Use the pictures for 19–20.

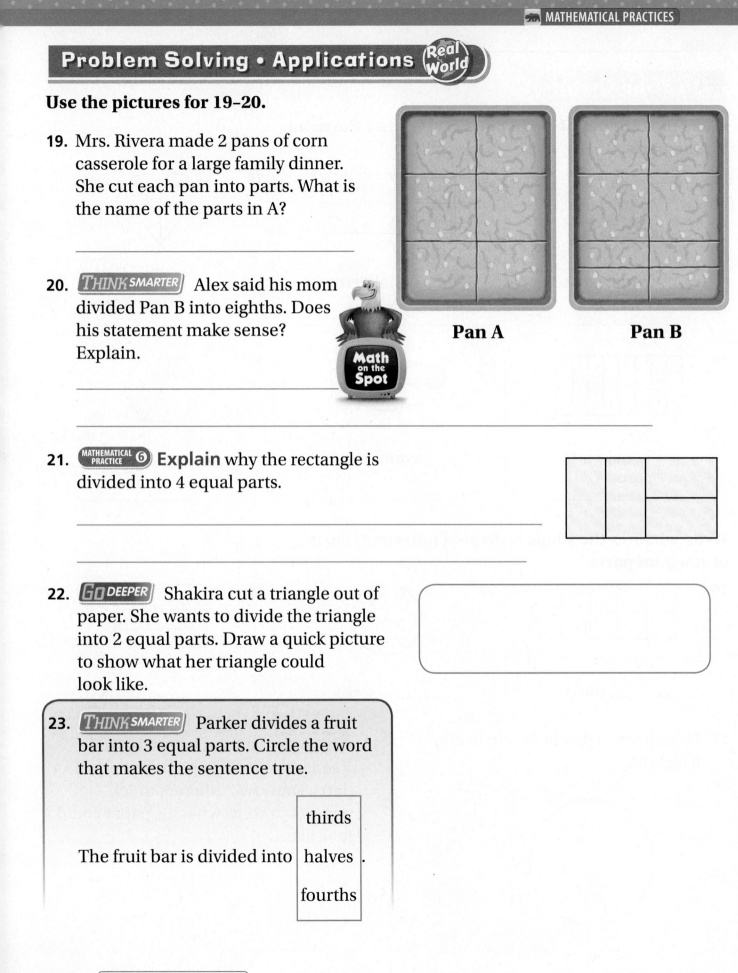

19. Mrs. Rivera made 2 pans of corn casserole for a large family dinner. She cut each pan into parts. What is the name of the parts in A?

_____

20. THINK SMARTER Alex said his mom divided Pan B into eighths. Does his statement make sense? Explain.

_____

Pan A   Pan B

_____

21. MATHEMATICAL PRACTICE 6 **Explain** why the rectangle is divided into 4 equal parts.

_____

_____

22. GO DEEPER Shakira cut a triangle out of paper. She wants to divide the triangle into 2 equal parts. Draw a quick picture to show what her triangle could look like.

23. THINK SMARTER Parker divides a fruit bar into 3 equal parts. Circle the word that makes the sentence true.

The fruit bar is divided into | thirds |
| halves | .
| fourths |

© Houghton Mifflin Harcourt Publishing Company

FOR MORE PRACTICE:
Standards Practice Book

Name _____

Equal Shares

Essential Question Why do you need to know how to make equal shares?

 Number and Operations— Fractions—3.NF.1 *Also 3.G.2*
MATHEMATICAL PRACTICES
MP.1, MP.4, MP.7

 Unlock the Problem

Four friends share 2 small pizzas equally. What are two ways the pizza could be divided equally? How much pizza will each friend get?

Draw to model the problem.

Draw 2 circles to show the pizzas.

• How might the two ways be different?

_____

_____

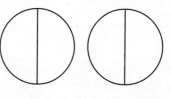

One Way

There are ____ friends.

So, divide each pizza into 4 slices.

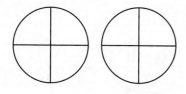

There are ____ equal parts.

Each friend can have 2 equal parts. Each friend will get 2 eighths of all the pizza.

Another Way

There are ____ friends.

So, divide all the pizza into 4 slices.

There are ____ equal parts.

Each friend can have 1 equal part. Each friend will get 1 half of a pizza.

Math Talk **Mathematical Practices**

Explain why both ways let the friends have an equal share.

Try This! Four girls share 3 oranges equally. Draw a quick picture to find out how much each girl gets.

• Draw 3 circles to show the oranges.

• Draw lines to divide the circles equally.

• Shade the part 1 girl gets.

• Describe what part of an orange each girl gets.

_____

© Houghton Mifflin Harcourt Publishing Company • Image Credits: ©Getty Images

1 Example

Melissa and Kyle are planning to share one pan of lasagna with 6 friends. They do not agree on the way to cut the pan into equal parts. Will each friend get an equal share using Melissa's way? Using Kyle's way?

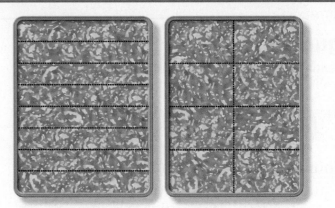

Melissa's Way   **Kyle's Way**

- Will Melissa's shares and Kyle's shares have the same shape? _____

- Will their shares using either way be the same size? _____

So, each friend will get an _____ share using either way.

- Explain why both ways let the friends have the same amount.

_____

_____

Share and Show

MATH BOARD

1. Two friends share 4 oranges equally. Use the picture to find how much each friend gets.

Think: There are more oranges than friends.

_____

Math Talk   **Mathematical Practices**

Explain another way the oranges could have been divided. Tell how much each friend will get.

Draw lines to show how much each person gets.
Write the answer.

✓ 2. 8 sisters share 3 eggrolls equally.

_____

✓ 3. 6 students share 4 bagels equally.

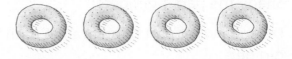

_____

© Houghton Mifflin Harcourt Publishing Company

Name _____

Draw lines to show how much each person gets. Write the answer.

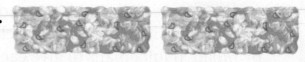

4. 3 classmates share 2 granola bars equally.

_____

5. 4 brothers share 2 sandwiches equally.

_____

Draw to show how much each person gets. Shade the amount that one person gets. Write the answer.

6. 8 friends share 4 sheets of construction paper equally.

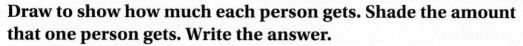

7. **MATHEMATICAL PRACTICE ④** **Model Mathematics** 4 sisters share 3 muffins equally.

8. **GO DEEPER** Maria prepared 5 quesadillas. She wants to share them equally among 8 of her neighbors. How much of a quesadilla will each neighbor get?

_____

© Houghton Mifflin Harcourt Publishing Company

🔑 Unlock the Problem (Real World)

9. THINK SMARTER Julia holds a bread-baking class. She has 4 adults and 3 children in the class. The class will make 2 round loaves of bread. If Julia plans to give each person, including herself, an equal part of the baked breads, how much bread will each person get?

Math on the Spot

a. What do you need to find? _____

_____

b. How will you use what you know about drawing equal

shares to solve the problem? _____

_____

c. Draw a quick picture to find the share
of bread each person will get.

d. So, each person will get

_____ of a loaf of bread.

---

10. THINK SMARTER Lara and three girl friends share three sandwiches equally.

☐ ☐ ☐

How much does each girl get? Mark all that apply.

A 3 fifths of a sandwich   **C** 1 whole sandwich

B 3 fourths of a sandwich   **D** one half and 1 fourth of a sandwich

© Houghton Mifflin Harcourt Publishing Company

Name _____

Unit Fractions of a Whole

Essential Question What do the top and bottom numbers of a fraction tell?

Number and Operations—Fractions—3.NF.1 Also 3.G.2

MATHEMATICAL PRACTICES
MP.2, MP.4, MP.7

A **fraction** is a number that names part of a whole or part of a group.

In a fraction, the top number tells how many equal parts are being counted.

The bottom number tells how many equal parts are in the whole or in the group.

$$\longrightarrow \frac{1}{6}$$

A **unit fraction** names 1 equal part of a whole. It has 1 as its top number. $\frac{1}{6}$ is a unit fraction.

Unlock the Problem · Real World

Luke's family picked strawberries. They put the washed strawberries in one part of a fruit platter. The platter had 6 equal parts. What fraction of the fruit platter had strawberries?

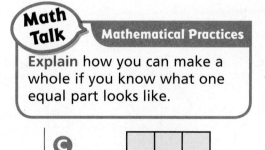

Find part of a whole.

Shade 1 of the 6 equal parts.

Read: one sixth   **Write:** $\frac{1}{6}$

So, _____ of the platter had strawberries.

Use a fraction to find a whole.

This shape ☐ is $\frac{1}{4}$ of the whole. Here are examples of what the whole could look like.

Math Talk · **Mathematical Practices**

Explain how you can make a whole if you know what one equal part looks like.

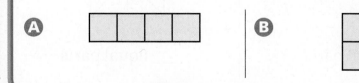

Ⓐ   Ⓑ   Ⓒ

© Houghton Mifflin Harcourt Publishing Company

Try This! Look again at the examples at the bottom of page 329. Draw two other pictures of how the whole might look.

Share and Show MATH BOARD

Math Talk **Mathematical Practices**

Explain how you knew what number to write as the bottom number of the fraction in Exercise 1.

1. What fraction names the shaded part? _____

Think: 1 out of 3 equal parts is shaded.

Write the number of equal parts in the whole.
Then write the fraction that names the shaded part.

2.

_____ equal parts

_____

3.

_____ equal parts

_____

4.

_____ equal parts

_____

5.

_____ equal parts

_____

6.

_____ equal parts

_____

7.

_____ equal parts

_____

© Houghton Mifflin Harcourt Publishing Company

Name _____

On Your Own

Write the number of equal parts in the whole.
Then write the fraction that names the shaded part.

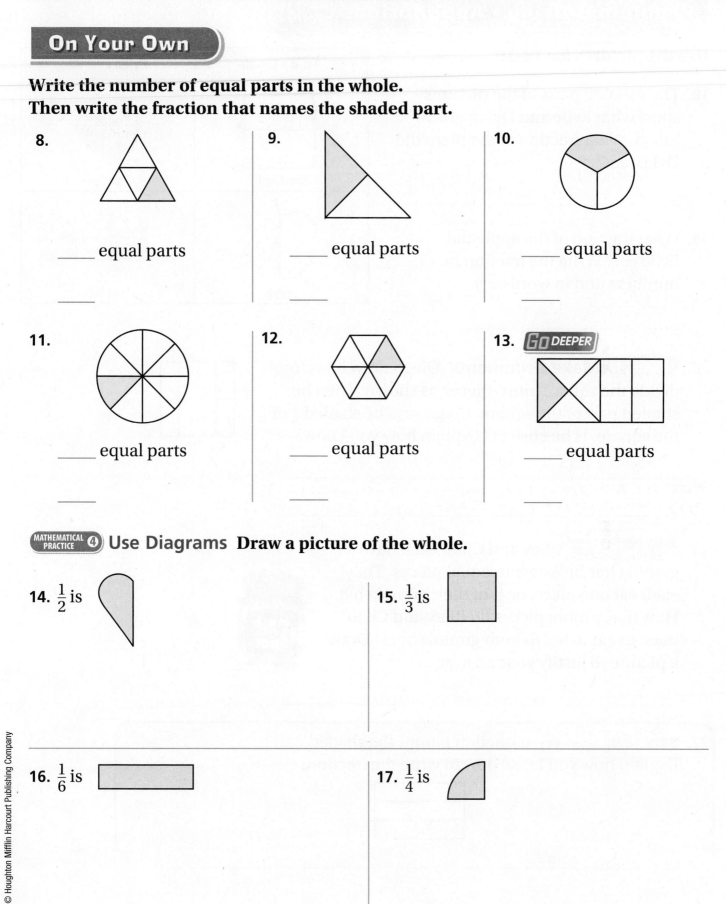

8.

_____ equal parts

_____

9.

_____ equal parts

_____

10.

_____ equal parts

_____

11.

_____ equal parts

_____

12.

_____ equal parts

_____

13. **Go DEEPER**

_____ equal parts

_____

MATHEMATICAL PRACTICE ④ Use Diagrams Draw a picture of the whole.

14. $\frac{1}{2}$ is

15. $\frac{1}{3}$ is

16. $\frac{1}{6}$ is

17. $\frac{1}{4}$ is

© Houghton Mifflin Harcourt Publishing Company

Problem Solving • Applications

Use the pictures for 18–19.

Kylie's Lunch	Dylan's Lunch
sandwich	pizza
apple	fruit bar

18. The missing parts of the pictures show what Kylie and Dylan ate for lunch. What fraction of the pizza did Dylan eat?

_____

19. What fraction of the apple did Kylie eat? Write the fraction in numbers and in words.

_____ _____

20. MATHEMATICAL PRACTICE ❸ **Make Arguments** Diego drew lines to divide the square into 6 pieces as shown. Then he shaded part of the square. Diego says he shaded $\frac{1}{6}$ of the square. Is he correct? Explain how you know.

_____

_____

21. THINK SMARTER Riley and Chad each have a granola bar broken into equal pieces. They each eat one piece, or $\frac{1}{4}$, of their granola bar. How many more pieces do Riley and Chad need to eat to finish both granola bars? Draw a picture to justify your answer.

_____

22. THINK SMARTER What fraction names the shaded part? Explain how you know how to write the fraction.

_____

_____

© Houghton Mifflin Harcourt Publishing Company

Fractions of a Whole

Essential Question How does a fraction name part of a whole?

 **Number and Operations—
Fractions—3.NF.1** *Also 3.G.2*
MATHEMATICAL PRACTICES
MP.2, MP.4, MP.7

Unlock the Problem Real World

The first pizzeria in America opened in New York in 1905. The pizza recipe came from Italy. Look at Italy's flag. What fraction of the flag is not red?

🔑 **Name equal parts of a whole.**

A fraction can name more than 1 equal part of a whole.

The flag is divided into 3 equal parts, and 2 parts are not red.

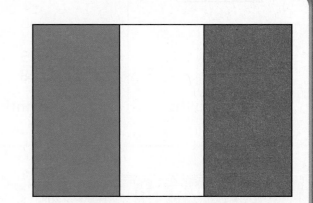

▲ Italy's flag has three equal parts.

2 parts not red → **2** ← numerator
3 equal parts in all → **3** ← denominator

Read: two thirds or two parts out of three equal parts

Write: $\frac{2}{3}$

So, _____ of the flag is not red.

Math Idea

When all the parts are shaded, one whole shape is equal to all of its parts. It represents the whole number 1.

$$\frac{3}{3} = 1$$

The **numerator** tells how many parts are being counted.

The **denominator** tells how many equal parts are in the whole or in the group.

You can count equal parts, such as sixths, to make a whole.

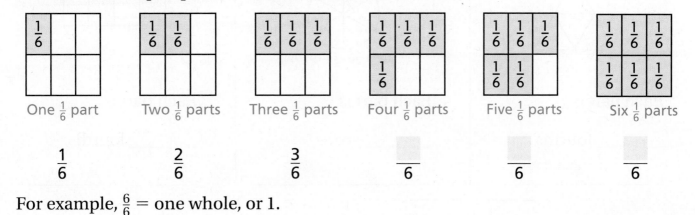

One $\frac{1}{6}$ part   Two $\frac{1}{6}$ parts   Three $\frac{1}{6}$ parts   Four $\frac{1}{6}$ parts   Five $\frac{1}{6}$ parts   Six $\frac{1}{6}$ parts

$\frac{1}{6}$ $\frac{2}{6}$ $\frac{3}{6}$ $\frac{}{6}$ $\frac{}{6}$ $\frac{}{6}$

For example, $\frac{6}{6}$ = one whole, or 1.

© Houghton Mifflin Harcourt Publishing Company

Try This! Write the missing word or number to name the shaded part.

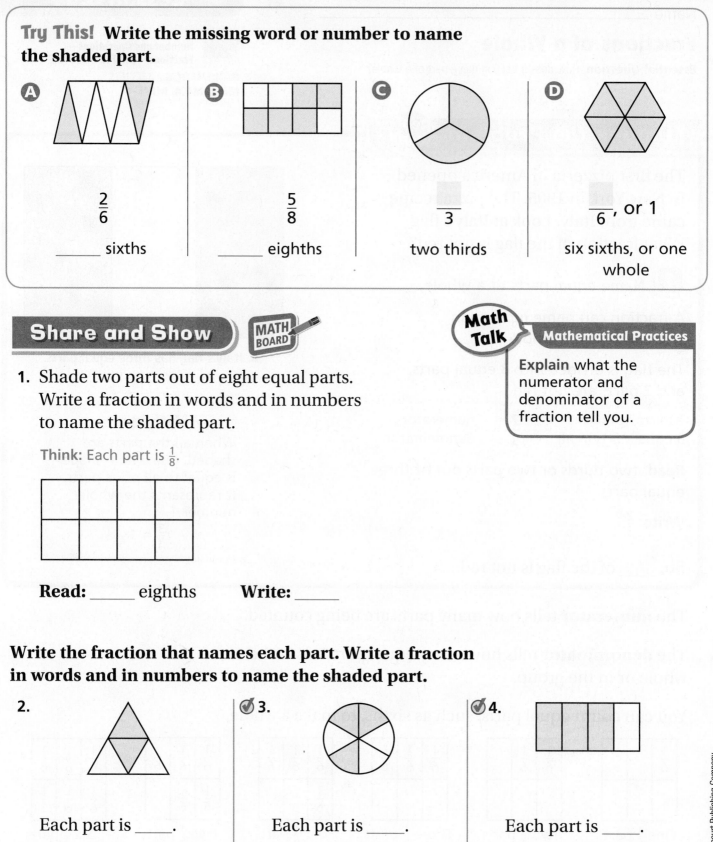

Ⓐ

$\dfrac{2}{6}$

_____ sixths

Ⓑ

$\dfrac{5}{8}$

_____ eighths

Ⓒ

$\dfrac{}{3}$

two thirds

Ⓓ

$\dfrac{}{6}$, or 1

six sixths, or one whole

Share and Show

MATH BOARD

Math Talk **Mathematical Practices**

Explain what the numerator and denominator of a fraction tell you.

1. Shade two parts out of eight equal parts. Write a fraction in words and in numbers to name the shaded part.

Think: Each part is $\frac{1}{8}$.

Read: _____ eighths   **Write:** _____

Write the fraction that names each part. Write a fraction in words and in numbers to name the shaded part.

2.

Each part is _____.

_____ fourths

_____

✓ 3.

Each part is _____.

_____ sixths

_____

✓ 4.

Each part is _____.

_____ fourths

_____

© Houghton Mifflin Harcourt Publishing Company

On Your Own

**Write the fraction that names each part. Write a fraction
in words and in numbers to name the shaded part.**

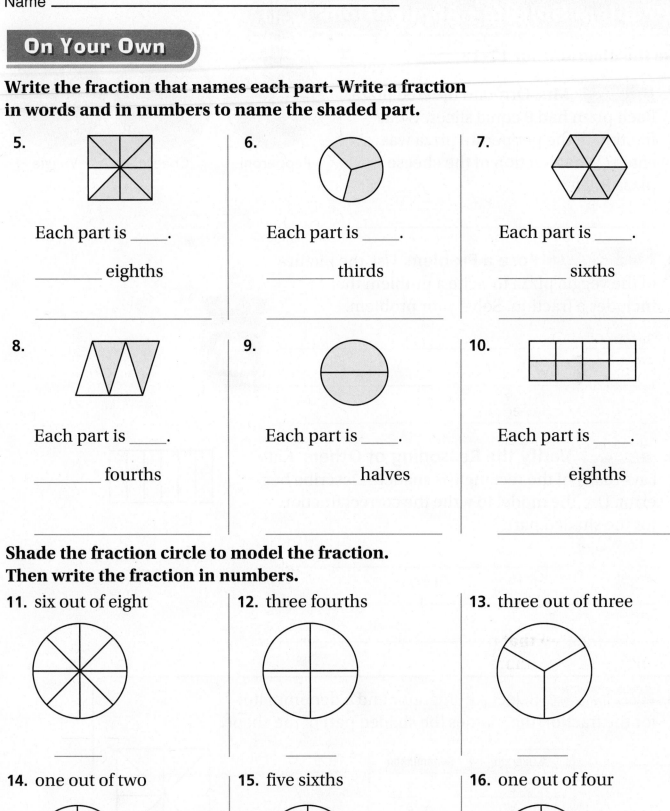

5.

Each part is ____.

_____ eighths

_____

6.

Each part is ____.

_____ thirds

_____

7.

Each part is ____.

_____ sixths

_____

8.

Each part is ____.

_____ fourths

_____

9.

Each part is ____.

_____ halves

_____

10.

Each part is ____.

_____ eighths

_____

**Shade the fraction circle to model the fraction.
Then write the fraction in numbers.**

11. six out of eight

_____

12. three fourths

_____

13. three out of three

_____

14. one out of two

_____

15. five sixths

_____

16. one out of four

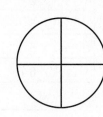

_____

© Houghton Mifflin Harcourt Publishing Company

Problem Solving • Applications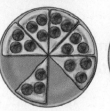

Use the diagrams for 17–18.

17. **Go DEEPER** Mrs. Ormond ordered pizza. Each pizza had 8 equal slices. What fraction of the pepperoni pizza was eaten? What fraction of the cheese pizza is left?

Pepperoni   Cheese   Veggie

_____

18. **THINK SMARTER** **Pose a Problem** Use the picture of the veggie pizza to write a problem that includes a fraction. Solve your problem.

_____

_____

_____

19. **MATHEMATICAL PRACTICE ③** **Verify the Reasoning of Others** Kate says that $\frac{2}{4}$ of the rectangle is shaded. Describe her error. Use the model to write the correct fraction for the shaded part.

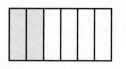

_____

_____

_____

20. **THINK SMARTER** Select a numerator and a denominator for the fraction that names the shaded part of the shape.

Numerator	Denominator
○ 2	○ 3
○ 3	○ 5
○ 5	○ 6
○ 6	○ 8

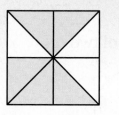

© Houghton Mifflin Harcourt Publishing Company

FOR MORE PRACTICE:
Standards Practice Book

Name _____

Fractions on a Number Line

Essential Question How can you represent and locate fractions on a number line?

Number and Operations—Fractions—3.NF.2a, 3.NF.2b
Also 3.NF.2
MATHEMATICAL PRACTICES
MP.1, MP.4, MP.7

Unlock the Problem Real World

Hands On

Billy's family is traveling from his house to his grandma's house. They stop at gas stations when they are $\frac{1}{4}$ and $\frac{3}{4}$ of the way there. How can you represent those distances on a number line?

You can use a number line to show fractions. The length from one whole number to the next whole number represents one whole. The line can be divided into any number of equal parts, or lengths.

> **Math Idea**
>
> A point on a number line shows the endpoint of a length, or distance, from zero. A number or fraction can name the distance.

Activity Locate fractions on a number line.

Materials ■ fraction strips

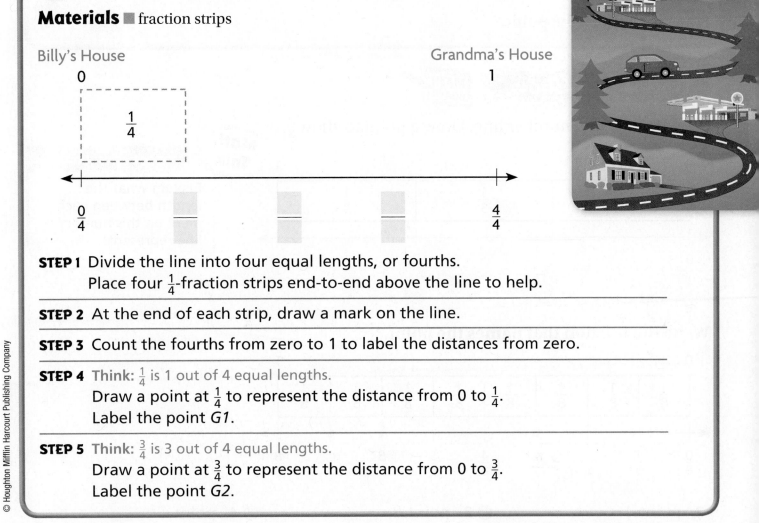

STEP 1 Divide the line into four equal lengths, or fourths.
Place four $\frac{1}{4}$-fraction strips end-to-end above the line to help.

STEP 2 At the end of each strip, draw a mark on the line.

STEP 3 Count the fourths from zero to 1 to label the distances from zero.

STEP 4 Think: $\frac{1}{4}$ is 1 out of 4 equal lengths.
Draw a point at $\frac{1}{4}$ to represent the distance from 0 to $\frac{1}{4}$.
Label the point *G1*.

STEP 5 Think: $\frac{3}{4}$ is 3 out of 4 equal lengths.
Draw a point at $\frac{3}{4}$ to represent the distance from 0 to $\frac{3}{4}$.
Label the point *G2*.

© Houghton Mifflin Harcourt Publishing Company

🔒 Example Complete the number line to name the point.

Materials ■ color pencils

Write the fraction that names the point on the number line.

Think: This number line is divided into six equal lengths, or sixths.

The length of one equal part is _____.

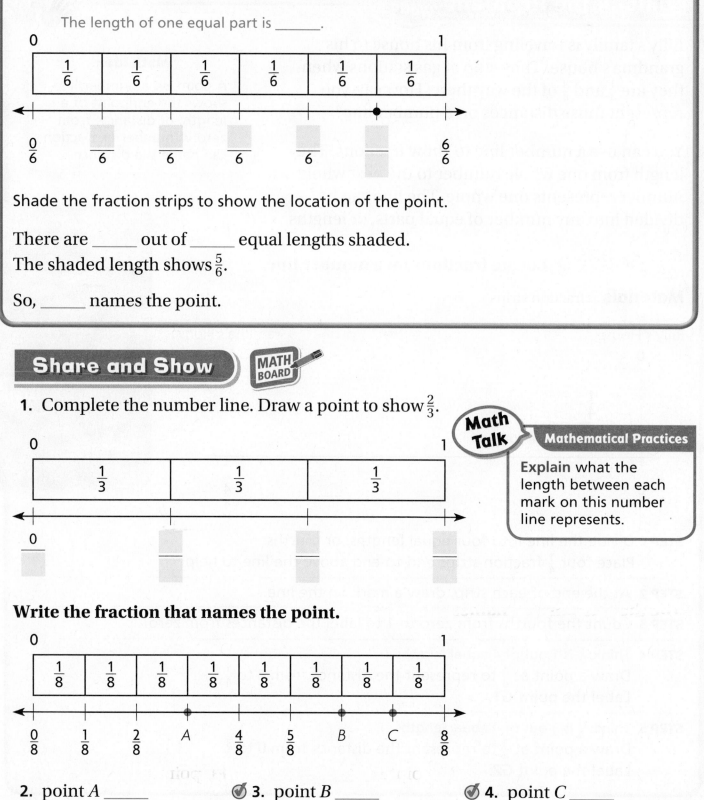

Shade the fraction strips to show the location of the point.

There are _____ out of _____ equal lengths shaded.

The shaded length shows $\frac{5}{6}$.

So, _____ names the point.

Share and Show MATH BOARD

1. Complete the number line. Draw a point to show $\frac{2}{3}$.

Math Talk **Mathematical Practices**

Explain what the length between each mark on this number line represents.

Write the fraction that names the point.

2. point A _____   ✓ 3. point B _____   ✓ 4. point C _____

© Houghton Mifflin Harcourt Publishing Company

Name _____

Use fraction strips to help you complete the number line. Then locate and draw a point for the fraction.

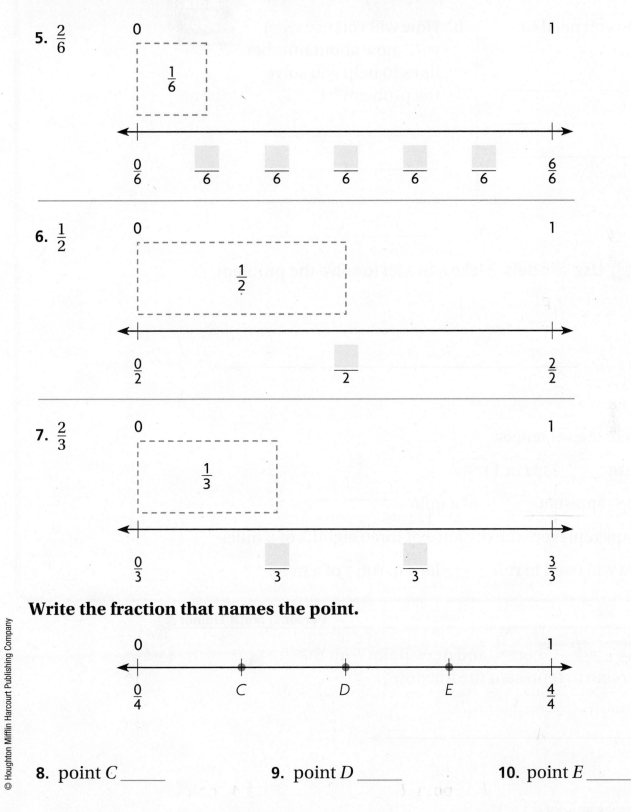

5. $\frac{2}{6}$

0   1

$\frac{1}{6}$

$\frac{0}{6}$ $\frac{}{6}$ $\frac{}{6}$ $\frac{}{6}$ $\frac{}{6}$ $\frac{}{6}$ $\frac{6}{6}$

6. $\frac{1}{2}$

0   1

$\frac{1}{2}$

$\frac{0}{2}$ $\frac{}{2}$ $\frac{2}{2}$

7. $\frac{2}{3}$

0   1

$\frac{1}{3}$

$\frac{0}{3}$ $\frac{}{3}$ $\frac{}{3}$ $\frac{3}{3}$

Write the fraction that names the point.

0   1

$\frac{0}{4}$ C   D   E $\frac{4}{4}$

© Houghton Mifflin Harcourt Publishing Company

8. point C _____

9. point D _____

10. point E _____

🔑 Unlock the Problem (Real World)

11. THINK SMARTER | Javia ran 8 laps around a track to run a total of 1 mile on Monday. How many laps will she need to run on Tuesday to run $\frac{3}{8}$ of a mile?

a. What do you need to find?

_____

_____

_____

b. How will you use what you know about number lines to help you solve the problem?

_____

_____

_____

_____

c. MATHEMATICAL PRACTICE ④ **Use Models** Make a model to solve the problem.

←————————————————————————→

d. Complete the sentences.

There are _____ laps in 1 mile.

Each lap represents _____ of a mile.

_____ laps represent the distance of three eighths of a mile.

So, Javia will need to run _____ laps to run $\frac{3}{8}$ of a mile.

Personal Math Trainer

12. THINK SMARTER ➕ | Locate and draw point *F* on the number line to represent the fraction $\frac{2}{4}$.

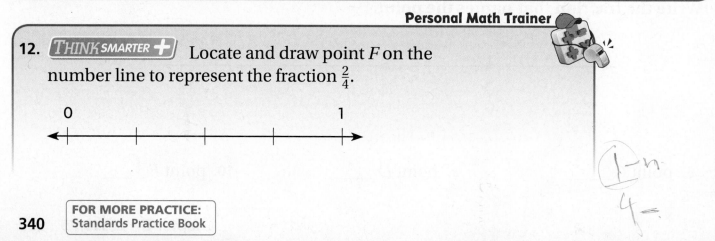

FOR MORE PRACTICE:
Standards Practice Book

© Houghton Mifflin Harcourt Publishing Company

✓ **Mid-Chapter Checkpoint**

Vocabulary

Choose the best term from the box to complete the sentence.

Vocabulary
denominator
fraction
numerator

1. A ___numerator___ is a number that names part of a whole or part of a group. (p. 329)

2. The ___denominator___ tells how many equal parts are in the whole or in the group. (p. 333)

Concepts and Skills

Write the number of equal parts. Then write the name for the parts. (3.NF.1)

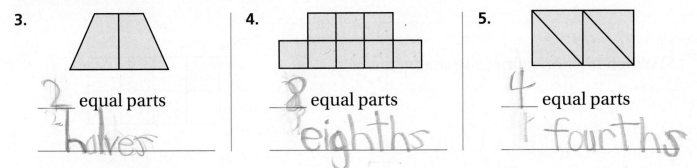

3. _2_ equal parts

   halves

4. _8_ equal parts

   eighths

5. _4_ equal parts

   fourths

Write the number of equal parts in the whole. Then write the fraction that names the shaded part. (3.NF.1)

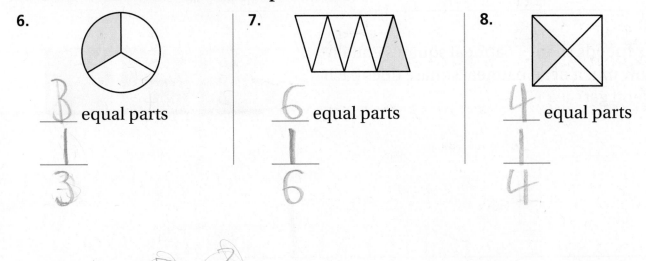

6. _3_ equal parts

   $\frac{1}{3}$

7. _6_ equal parts

   $\frac{1}{6}$

8. _4_ equal parts

   $\frac{4}{4}$

© Houghton Mifflin Harcourt Publishing Company

Write the fraction that names the point. (3.NF.2a, 3.NF.2b)

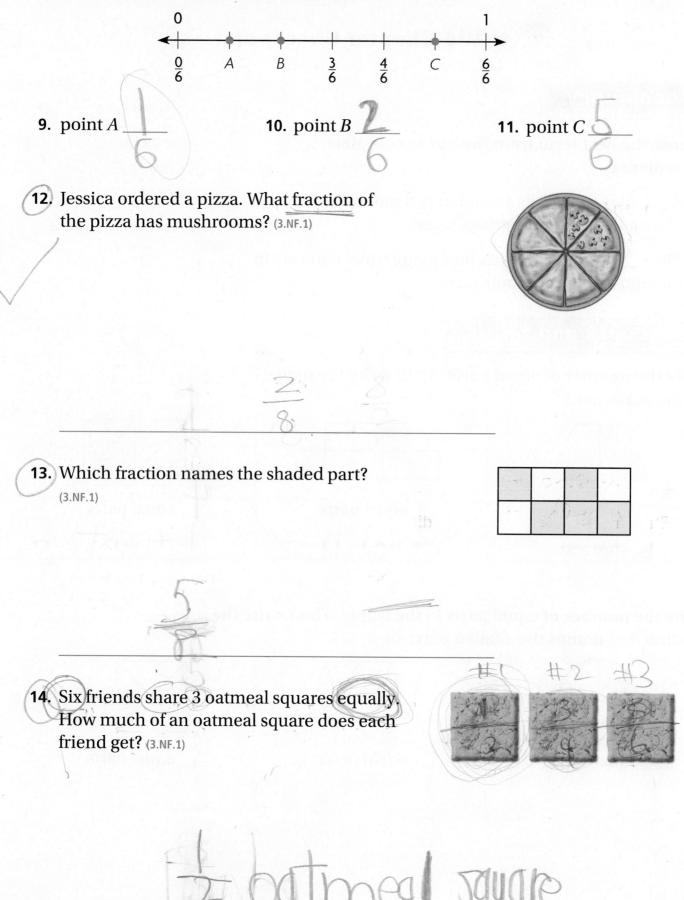

0   1

$\frac{0}{6}$ *A*   *B* $\frac{3}{6}$ $\frac{4}{6}$ *C* $\frac{6}{6}$

9. point *A* $\frac{1}{6}$

10. point *B* $\frac{2}{6}$

11. point *C* $\frac{5}{6}$

12. Jessica ordered a pizza. What fraction of the pizza has mushrooms? (3.NF.1)

$\frac{2}{8}$

13. Which fraction names the shaded part?

(3.NF.1)

$\frac{5}{8}$

14. Six friends share 3 oatmeal squares equally. How much of an oatmeal square does each friend get? (3.NF.1)

#1   #2   #3

$1\frac{1}{2}$ oatmeal square

© Houghton Mifflin Harcourt Publishing Company

Name _____

Relate Fractions and Whole Numbers

Essential Question When might you use a fraction greater than 1 or a whole number?

Number and Operations—Fractions—3.NF.3c *Also 3.NF.2, 3.NF.2b, 3.G.2*

MATHEMATICAL PRACTICES
MP.1, MP.4, MP.6, MP.7

Unlock the Problem Real World

Steve ran 1 mile and Jenna ran $\frac{4}{4}$ of a mile.
Did Steve and Jenna run the same distance?

Locate 1 and $\frac{4}{4}$ on a number line.

- Shade 4 lengths of $\frac{1}{4}$ and label the number line.

- Draw a point at 1 and $\frac{4}{4}$.

> **Math Idea**
> If two numbers are located at the same point on a number line, then they are equal and represent the same distance.

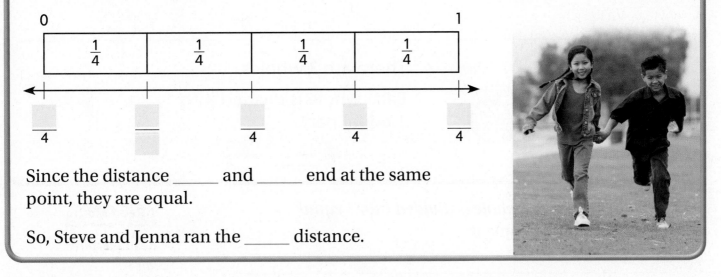

Since the distance _____ and _____ end at the same point, they are equal.

So, Steve and Jenna ran the _____ distance.

Try This! Complete the number line. Locate and draw points at $\frac{3}{6}$, $\frac{6}{6}$, and 1.

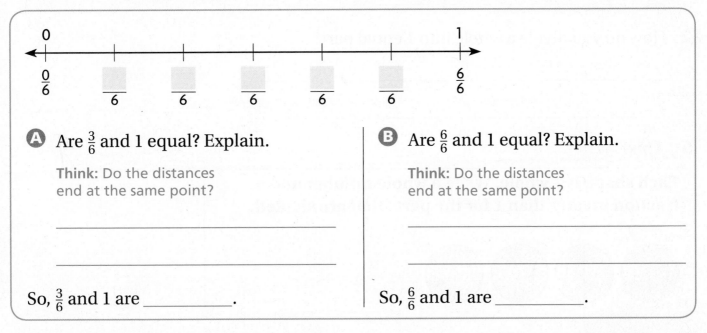

A Are $\frac{3}{6}$ and 1 equal? Explain.

Think: Do the distances end at the same point?

_____

_____

So, $\frac{3}{6}$ and 1 are _____.

B Are $\frac{6}{6}$ and 1 equal? Explain.

Think: Do the distances end at the same point?

_____

_____

So, $\frac{6}{6}$ and 1 are _____.

© Houghton Mifflin Harcourt Publishing Company • Image Credits: (cr) ©Stockbyte/Getty Images

CONNECT The number of equal parts the whole is divided into is the denominator of a fraction. The number of parts being counted is the numerator. A **fraction greater than 1** has a numerator greater than its denominator.

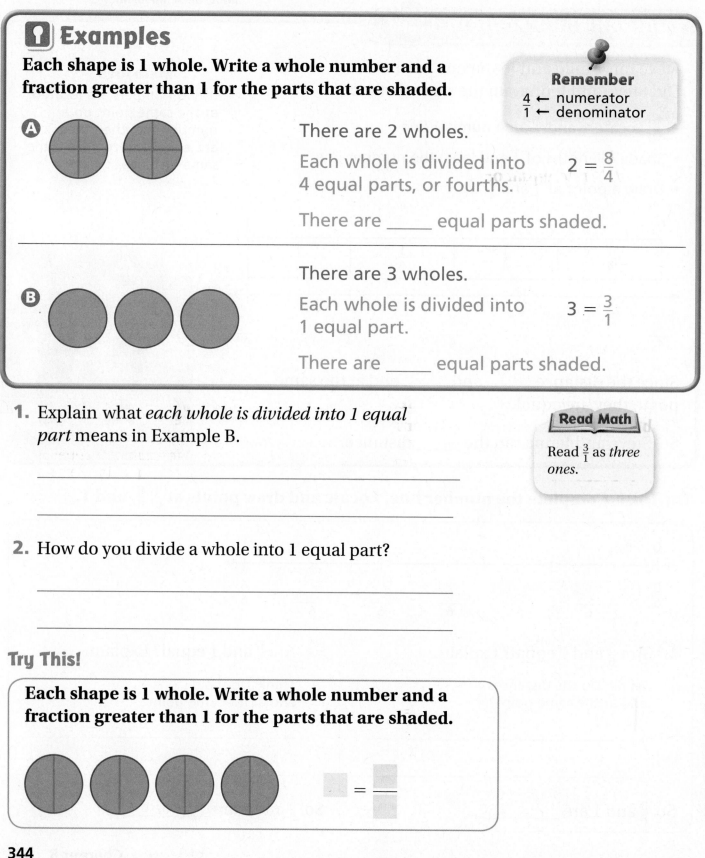

1 Examples

Each shape is 1 whole. Write a whole number and a fraction greater than 1 for the parts that are shaded.

Remember

$\frac{4}{1}$ ← numerator
  ← denominator

A

There are 2 wholes.

Each whole is divided into 4 equal parts, or fourths. $2 = \frac{8}{4}$

There are _____ equal parts shaded.

B

There are 3 wholes.

Each whole is divided into 1 equal part. $3 = \frac{3}{1}$

There are _____ equal parts shaded.

1. Explain what *each whole is divided into 1 equal part* means in Example B.

_____

_____

Read Math

Read $\frac{3}{1}$ as *three ones*.

2. How do you divide a whole into 1 equal part?

_____

_____

Try This!

Each shape is 1 whole. Write a whole number and a fraction greater than 1 for the parts that are shaded.

$\boxed{} = \frac{\boxed{}}{\boxed{}}$

© Houghton Mifflin Harcourt Publishing Company

Name _____

1. Each shape is 1 whole. Write a whole number and a fraction greater than 1 for the parts that are shaded.

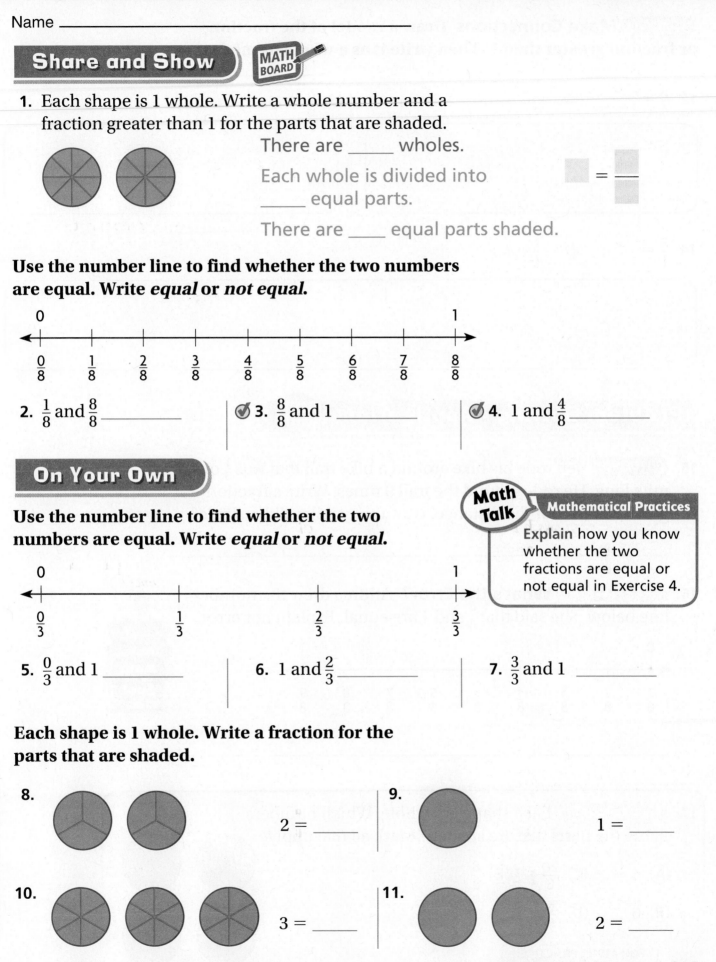

There are _____ wholes.

Each whole is divided into _____ equal parts.

There are _____ equal parts shaded.

☐ = ⎯

Use the number line to find whether the two numbers are equal. Write *equal* or *not equal*.

0   1

$\frac{0}{8}$ $\frac{1}{8}$ $\frac{2}{8}$ $\frac{3}{8}$ $\frac{4}{8}$ $\frac{5}{8}$ $\frac{6}{8}$ $\frac{7}{8}$ $\frac{8}{8}$

2. $\frac{1}{8}$ and $\frac{8}{8}$ _____

✓ 3. $\frac{8}{8}$ and 1 _____

✓ 4. 1 and $\frac{4}{8}$ _____

On Your Own

Use the number line to find whether the two numbers are equal. Write *equal* or *not equal*.

0   1

$\frac{0}{3}$ $\frac{1}{3}$ $\frac{2}{3}$ $\frac{3}{3}$

Math Talk **Mathematical Practices**

Explain how you know whether the two fractions are equal or not equal in Exercise 4.

5. $\frac{0}{3}$ and 1 _____

6. 1 and $\frac{2}{3}$ _____

7. $\frac{3}{3}$ and 1 _____

Each shape is 1 whole. Write a fraction for the parts that are shaded.

8.   2 = _____

9.   1 = _____

10.   3 = _____

11.   2 = _____

© Houghton Mifflin Harcourt Publishing Company

MATHEMATICAL PRACTICE 6 Make Connections Draw a model of the fraction or fraction greater than 1. Then write it as a whole number.

12. $\frac{8}{4} = $ _____

13. $\frac{6}{6} = $ _____

14. $\frac{5}{1} = $ _____

Problem Solving • Applications Real World

15. **GO DEEPER** Jeff rode his bike around a bike trail that was $\frac{1}{3}$ of a mile long. He rode around the trail 9 times. Write a fraction greater than 1 for the distance. How many miles did Jeff ride?

_____

16. **THINK SMARTER** What's the Error? Andrea drew the number line below. She said that $\frac{9}{8}$ and 1 are equal. Explain her error.

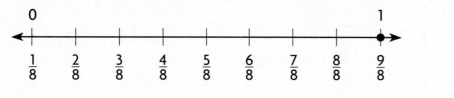

0   1

$\frac{1}{8}$ $\frac{2}{8}$ $\frac{3}{8}$ $\frac{4}{8}$ $\frac{5}{8}$ $\frac{6}{8}$ $\frac{7}{8}$ $\frac{8}{8}$ $\frac{9}{8}$

_____

17. **THINK SMARTER** Each shape is 1 whole. Which numbers name the parts that are shaded? Mark all that apply.

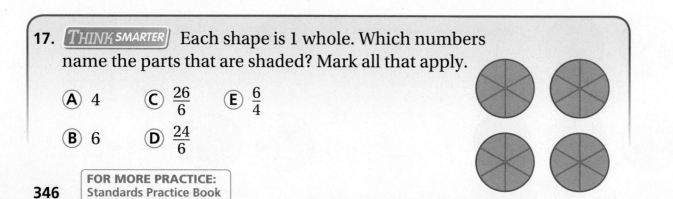

(A) 4   (C) $\frac{26}{6}$ (E) $\frac{6}{4}$

(B) 6   (D) $\frac{24}{6}$

FOR MORE PRACTICE:
Standards Practice Book

© Houghton Mifflin Harcourt Publishing Company

Fractions of a Group

Essential Question How can a fraction name part of a group?

**Number and Operations—
Fractions—3.NF.1**

MATHEMATICAL PRACTICES
MP.1, MP.4, MP.5

Unlock the Problem (Real World)

Jake and Emma each have a collection of marbles.
What fraction of each collection is blue?

You can use a fraction to name part of a group.

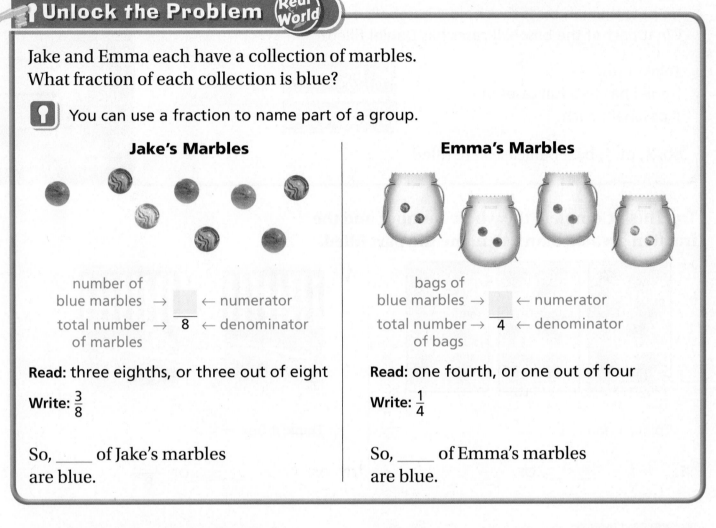

Jake's Marbles

number of
blue marbles → ☐ ← numerator
total number → 8 ← denominator
of marbles

Read: three eighths, or three out of eight

Write: $\frac{3}{8}$

So, _____ of Jake's marbles
are blue.

Emma's Marbles

bags of
blue marbles → ☐ ← numerator
total number → 4 ← denominator
of bags

Read: one fourth, or one out of four

Write: $\frac{1}{4}$

So, _____ of Emma's marbles
are blue.

Try This! **Name part of a group.**

Draw 2 red counters and 6 yellow
counters.

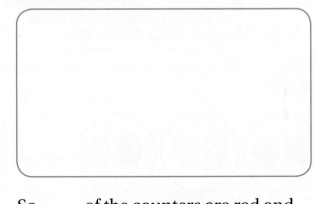

Write the fraction of counters that are red.

☐ ← number of red counters
── ← total number of counters

Write the fraction of counters that are
not red.

☐ ← number of yellow counters
── ← total number of counters

So, _____ of the counters are red and _____ are not red.

© Houghton Mifflin Harcourt Publishing Company

Fractions Greater Than 1

Sometimes a fraction can name more than a whole group.

Daniel collects baseballs. He has collected 8 so far. He puts them in cases that hold 4 baseballs each. What part of the baseball cases has Daniel filled?

Think: 1 case = 1

Daniel has two full cases of 4 baseballs each.

So, 2, or $\frac{8}{4}$, baseball cases are filled.

Try This! **Complete the whole number and the fraction greater than 1 to name the part filled.**

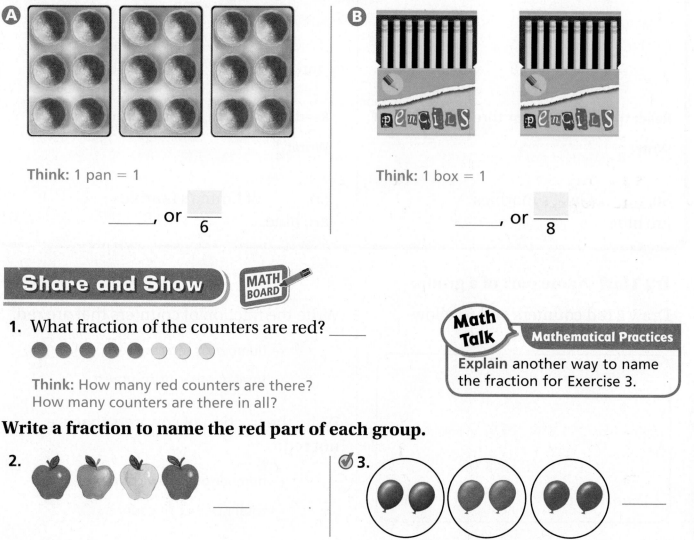

A

Think: 1 pan = 1

_____, or $\dfrac{}{6}$

B

Think: 1 box = 1

_____, or $\dfrac{}{8}$

Share and Show

MATH BOARD

1. What fraction of the counters are red? _____

Think: How many red counters are there? How many counters are there in all?

Write a fraction to name the red part of each group.

2. _____

Math Talk

Mathematical Practices

Explain another way to name the fraction for Exercise 3.

☑ 3. _____

© Houghton Mifflin Harcourt Publishing Company

Name _____

Write a whole number and a fraction greater than 1 to name the part filled.

4.

Think: 1 carton = 1

_____ _____

5.

Think: 1 container = 1

_____ _____

On Your Own

Write a fraction to name the blue part of each group.

6.

_____

7.

_____

8.

_____

9.

_____

Write a whole number and a fraction greater than 1 to name the part filled.

10.

Think: 1 container = 1

_____ _____

11. THINK SMARTER

Think: 1 carton = 1

_____ _____

Draw a quick picture on your MathBoard. Then write a fraction to name the shaded part of the group.

12. Draw 8 circles.
Shade 8 circles.

_____

13. Draw 8 triangles.
Make 4 groups.
Shade 1 group.

_____

14. Draw 4 rectangles.
Shade 2 rectangles.

_____

© Houghton Mifflin Harcourt Publishing Company

Problem Solving • Applications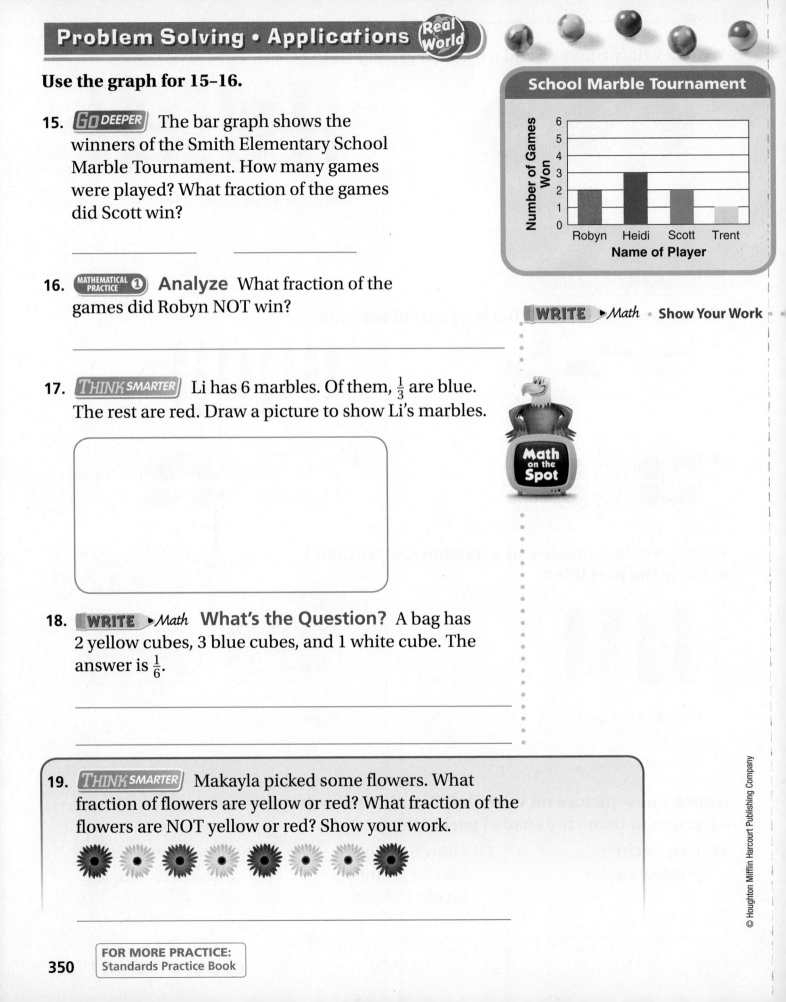

Use the graph for 15–16.

15. **GO DEEPER** The bar graph shows the winners of the Smith Elementary School Marble Tournament. How many games were played? What fraction of the games did Scott win?

_____ _____

School Marble Tournament

16. **MATHEMATICAL PRACTICE ①** **Analyze** What fraction of the games did Robyn NOT win?

_____

WRITE ▶Math ・ Show Your Work

17. **THINK SMARTER** Li has 6 marbles. Of them, $\frac{1}{3}$ are blue. The rest are red. Draw a picture to show Li's marbles.

18. **WRITE ▶Math What's the Question?** A bag has 2 yellow cubes, 3 blue cubes, and 1 white cube. The answer is $\frac{1}{6}$.

_____

19. **THINK SMARTER** Makayla picked some flowers. What fraction of flowers are yellow or red? What fraction of the flowers are NOT yellow or red? Show your work.

FOR MORE PRACTICE:
Standards Practice Book

© Houghton Mifflin Harcourt Publishing Company

Find Part of a Group Using Unit Fractions

Essential Question How can a fraction tell how many are in part of a group?

Number and Operations—Fractions—3.NF.1
MATHEMATICAL PRACTICES
MP.4, MP.5

🔑 Unlock the Problem (Real World)

Audrey buys a bouquet of 12 flowers. One third of them are red. How many of the flowers are red?

- How many flowers does Audrey buy in all? _____
- What fraction of the flowers are red? _____

🔑 Activity

Materials ■ two-color counters ■ MathBoard

- Put 12 counters on your MathBoard.

- Since you want to find $\frac{1}{3}$ of the group, there should be _____ equal groups. Draw the counters below.

- Circle one of the groups to show _____.

  Then count the number of counters in that group.

There are _____ counters in 1 group. $\frac{1}{3}$ of 12 = _____

So, _____ of the flowers are red.

- What if Audrey buys a bouquet of 9 flowers and one third of them are yellow? Use your MathBoard and counters to find how many of the flowers are yellow.

  _____

Math Talk

Mathematical Practices

Explain how you can use the numerator and denominator in a fraction to find part of a group.

© Houghton Mifflin Harcourt Publishing Company

Try This! Find part of a group.

Raul picks 20 flowers from his mother's garden. One fourth of them are purple. How many of the flowers are purple?

STEP 1 Draw a row of 4 counters.

Think: To find $\frac{1}{4}$, make 4 equal groups.

_____

○   ○   ○   ○

STEP 2 Continue to draw as many rows of 4 counters as you can until you have 20 counters.

_____

STEP 3 Then circle _____ equal groups.

Think: Each group represents $\frac{1}{4}$ of the flowers.

$\frac{1}{4}$ $\frac{1}{4}$ $\frac{1}{4}$ $\frac{1}{4}$

There are _____ counters in 1 group.

$\frac{1}{4}$ of 20 = _____

So, _____ of the flowers are purple.

Share and Show

MATH BOARD

1. Use the model to find $\frac{1}{2}$ of 8. _____

   Think: How many counters are in 1 of the 2 equal groups?

   ● ●   ● ●
   ● ●   ● ●

Math Talk

Mathematical Practices

Explain why you count the number of counters in just one of the groups in Exercise 1.

Circle equal groups to solve. Count the number of flowers in 1 group.

2. $\frac{1}{4}$ of 8 = _____

3. $\frac{1}{3}$ of 6 = _____

4. $\frac{1}{6}$ of 12 = _____

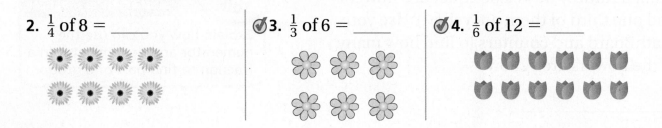

© Houghton Mifflin Harcourt Publishing Company

Name _____

Circle equal groups to solve. Count the number of flowers in 1 group.

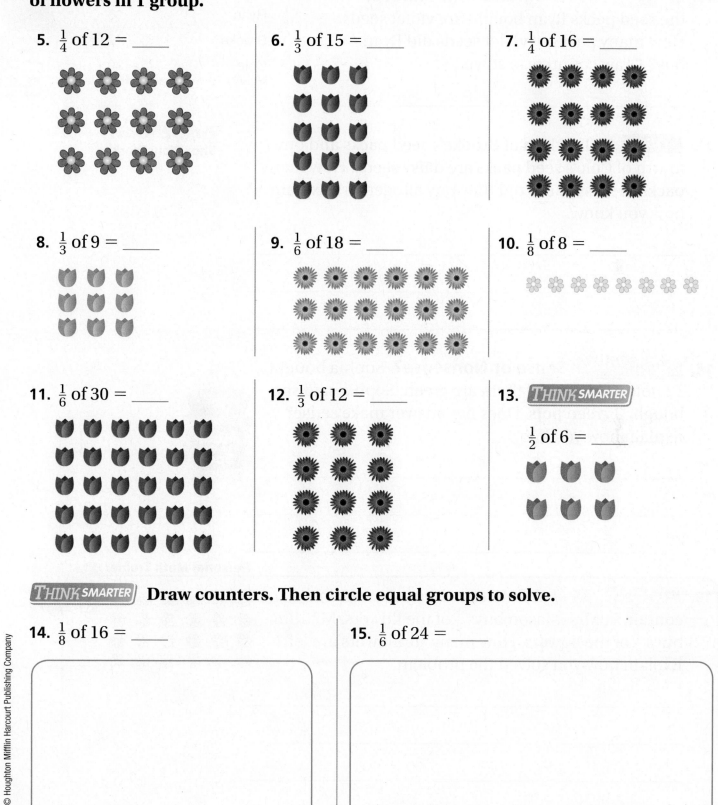

5. $\frac{1}{4}$ of 12 = _____

6. $\frac{1}{3}$ of 15 = _____

7. $\frac{1}{4}$ of 16 = _____

8. $\frac{1}{3}$ of 9 = _____

9. $\frac{1}{6}$ of 18 = _____

10. $\frac{1}{8}$ of 8 = _____

11. $\frac{1}{6}$ of 30 = _____

12. $\frac{1}{3}$ of 12 = _____

13. *THINK SMARTER*

$\frac{1}{2}$ of 6 = _____

THINK SMARTER **Draw counters. Then circle equal groups to solve.**

14. $\frac{1}{8}$ of 16 = _____

15. $\frac{1}{6}$ of 24 = _____

© Houghton Mifflin Harcourt Publishing Company

Problem Solving • Applications

Use the table for 16–17.

Flower Seeds Bought	
Name	**Number of Packs**
Ryan	8
Brooke	12
Cole	20

16. **MATHEMATICAL PRACTICE 4** **Use Diagrams** One fourth of the seed packs Ryan bought are violet seeds. How many packs of violet seeds did Ryan buy? Draw counters to solve.

_____

17. **GO DEEPER** One third of Brooke's seed packs and one fourth of Cole's seed packs are daisy seeds. How many packs of daisy seeds did they buy altogether? Explain how you know.

WRITE ▸ *Math*
Show Your Work

_____

_____

_____

18. **THINK SMARTER** **Sense or Nonsense?** Sophia bought 12 pots. One sixth of them are green. Sophia said she bought 2 green pots. Does her answer make sense? Explain how you know.

Math on the Spot

_____

_____

_____

Personal Math Trainer

19. **THINK SMARTER +** A florist has 24 sunflowers in a container. Mrs. Mason buys $\frac{1}{4}$ of the flowers. Mr. Kim buys $\frac{1}{3}$ of the flowers. How many sunflowers are left? Explain how you solved the problem.

❀ ❀ ❀ ❀ ❀ ❀
❀ ❀ ❀ ❀ ❀ ❀
❀ ❀ ❀ ❀ ❀ ❀
❀ ❀ ❀ ❀ ❀ ❀

_____

_____

© Houghton Mifflin Harcourt Publishing Company

FOR MORE PRACTICE:
Standards Practice Book

Name _____

Problem Solving • Find the Whole Group Using Unit Fractions

Essential Question How can you use the strategy *draw a diagram* to solve fraction problems?

 Number and Operations— Fractions—3.NF.1
MATHEMATICAL PRACTICES
MP.1, MP.4, MP.5, MP.6

🔑 Unlock the Problem (Real World)

Cameron has 4 clown fish in his fish tank. One third of the fish in the tank are clown fish. How many fish does Cameron have in his tank?

Use the graphic organizer to help you solve the problem.

Read the Problem	Solve the Problem
What do I need to find? I need to find _____ are in Cameron's fish tank.	**Describe how to draw a diagram to solve.** The denominator in $\frac{1}{3}$ tells you that there are _____ equal parts in the whole group. Draw 3 circles to show _____ equal parts. Since 4 fish are $\frac{1}{3}$ of the whole group,
What information do I need to use? Cameron has _____ clown fish. _____ of the fish in the tank are clown fish.	draw _____ counters in the first circle. Since there are _____ counters in the first circle, draw _____ counters in each of the remaining circles. Then find the total number of counters.
How will I use the information? I will use the information in the problem to draw a _____.	
	So, Cameron has _____ fish in his tank.

© Houghton Mifflin Harcourt Publishing Company • Image Credits: (tr) ©Getty Images

🔑 Try Another Problem

A pet store has 2 gray rabbits. One eighth of the rabbits at the pet store are gray. How many rabbits does the pet store have?

Read the Problem	Solve the Problem
What do I need to find?	
What information do I need to use?	
How will I use the information?	

1. **MATHEMATICAL PRACTICE 8** **Draw Conclusions** How do you know that your answer is reasonable?

_____

_____

2. How did your diagram help you solve the problem? _____

_____

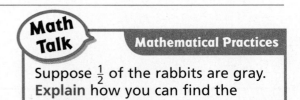

Math Talk **Mathematical Practices**

Suppose $\frac{1}{2}$ of the rabbits are gray. **Explain** how you can find the number of rabbits at the pet store.

© Houghton Mifflin Harcourt Publishing Company • Image Credits: (tr) ©Getty Images

Share and Show

Unlock the Problem

✓ Circle the question.
✓ Underline important facts.
✓ Put the problem in your own words.
✓ Choose a strategy you know.

1. Lily has 3 dog toys that are red. One fourth of all her dog toys are red. How many dog toys does Lily have?

First, draw _____ circles to show _____ equal parts.

Next, draw _____ toys in _____ circle since

_____ circle represents the number of red toys.

Last, draw _____ toys in each of the remaining circles. Find the total number of toys.

So, Lily has _____ dog toys.

2. **THINK SMARTER** What if Lily has 4 toys that are red? How many dog toys would she have?

_____

3. The pet store sells bags of pet food. There are 4 bags of cat food. One sixth of the bags of food are bags of cat food. How many bags of pet food does the pet store have?

_____

4. Rachel owns 2 parakeets. One fourth of all her birds are parakeets. How many birds does Rachel own?

_____

© Houghton Mifflin Harcourt Publishing Company

On Your Own

5. THINK SMARTER Before lunchtime, Abigail and Teresa each read some pages from different books. Abigail read 5, or one fifth, of the pages in her book. Teresa read 6, or one sixth, of the pages in her book. Whose book had more pages? How many more pages?

Math on the Spot

WRITE ▸ *Math* · **Show Your Work**

_____

6. MATHEMATICAL PRACTICE ② **Represent a Problem** Six friends share 5 meat pies. Each friend first eats half of a meat pie. How much more meat pie does each friend need to eat to finish all the meat pies and share them equally? Draw a quick picture to solve.

_____

7. GO DEEPER Braden bought 4 packs of dog treats. He gave 4 treats to his neighbor's dog. Now Braden has 24 treats left for his dog. How many dog treats were in each pack? Explain how you know.

_____

_____

_____

_____

8. THINK SMARTER Two hats are $\frac{1}{3}$ of the group. How many hats are in the whole group?

_____ hats

FOR MORE PRACTICE:
Standards Practice Book

© Houghton Mifflin Harcourt Publishing Company

Chapter 8 Review/Test

1. Each shape is divided into equal parts. Select the shapes that show thirds. Mark all that apply.

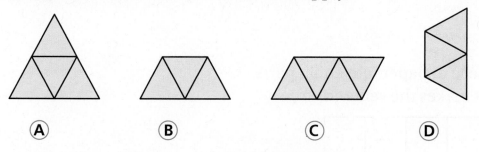

   Ⓐ   Ⓑ   Ⓒ   Ⓓ

2. What fraction names the shaded part of the shape?

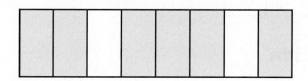

  Ⓐ   8 sixths

  Ⓑ   8 eighths

  Ⓒ   6 eighths

  Ⓓ   2 sixths

3. Omar shaded a model to show the part of the lawn that he finished mowing. What fraction names the shaded part? Explain how you know how to write the fraction.

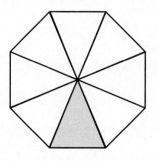

_____

_____

© Houghton Mifflin Harcourt Publishing Company

Assessment Options
Chapter Test

4. What fraction names point *A* on the number line?

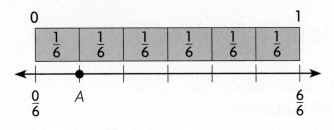

_____

5. Jamal folded this piece of paper into equal parts.
Circle the word that makes the sentence true.

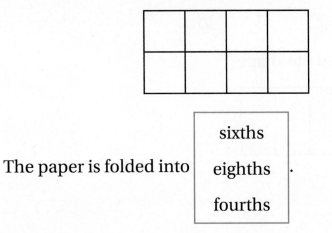

The paper is folded into | sixths
eighths
fourths | .

6. Caleb took 18 photos at the zoo. One sixth of his
photos are of giraffes. How many of Caleb's photos are
of giraffes?

_____ photos

7. Three teachers share 2 packs of paper equally.

☐ ☐

How much paper does each teacher get? Mark all
that apply.

Ⓐ 3 halves of a pack

Ⓑ 2 thirds of a pack

Ⓒ 3 sixths of a pack

Ⓓ 1 half of a pack

Ⓔ 1 third of a pack

© Houghton Mifflin Harcourt Publishing Company

8. Lilly shaded this design.

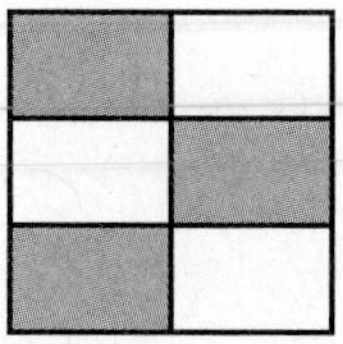

Select one number from each column to show
the part of the design that Lilly shaded.

Numerator	Denominator
○ 1	○ 3
○ 3	○ 4
○ 5	○ 5
○ 6	○ 6

9. Marcus baked a loaf of banana bread for a party.
He cut the loaf into equal size pieces. At the end of the
party, there were 6 pieces left. Explain how you can find
the number of pieces in the whole loaf if Marcus told you
that $\frac{1}{3}$ of the loaf was left. Use a drawing to show your
work.

_____

_____

_____

_____

© Houghton Mifflin Harcourt Publishing Company

10. The model shows one whole. What fraction of the model is NOT shaded?

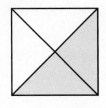

_____

11. Together, Amy and Thea make up $\frac{1}{4}$ of the midfielders on the soccer team. How many midfielders are on the team? Show your work.

_____ midfielders

12. Six friends share 4 apples equally. How much apple does each friend get?

_____

13. Each shape is 1 whole.

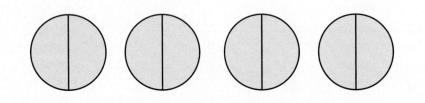

For numbers 13a–13e, choose Yes or No to show whether the number names the parts that are shaded.

13a. 4   ○ Yes   ○ No

13b. 8   ○ Yes   ○ No

13c. $\frac{8}{2}$ ○ Yes   ○ No

13d. $\frac{8}{4}$ ○ Yes   ○ No

13e. $\frac{2}{8}$ ○ Yes   ○ No

© Houghton Mifflin Harcourt Publishing Company

14. Alex has 3 baseballs. He brings 2 baseballs to school. What fraction of his baseballs does Alex bring to school?

_____

15. Janeen and Nicole each made fruit salad for a school event.

Part A

Janeen used 16 pieces of fruit to make her salad. If $\frac{1}{4}$ of the fruits were peaches, how many peaches did she use? Make a drawing to show your work.

_____ peaches

Part B

Nicole used 24 pieces of fruit. If $\frac{1}{6}$ of them were peaches, how many peaches in all did Janeen and Nicole use to make their fruit salads? Explain how you found your answer.

_____

_____

16. There are 8 rows of chairs in the auditorium. Three of the rows are empty. What fraction of the rows are empty?

_____

© Houghton Mifflin Harcourt Publishing Company

17. Tara ran 3 laps around her neighborhood for a total of 1 mile yesterday. Today she wants to run $\frac{2}{3}$ of a mile. How many laps will she need to run around her neighborhood?

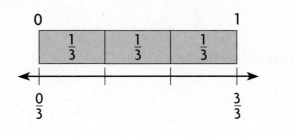

_____ laps

18. Gary painted some shapes.

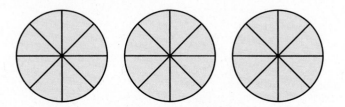

Select one number from each column to show a fraction greater than 1 that names the parts Gary painted.

Numerator	Denominator
○ 3	○ 3
○ 4	○ 4
○ 8	○ 8
○ 24	○ 24

19. Angelo rode his bike around a bike trail that was $\frac{1}{4}$ of a mile long. He rode his bike around the trail 8 times. Angelo says he rode a total of $\frac{8}{4}$ miles. Teresa says he is wrong and that he actually rode 2 miles. Who is correct? Use words and drawings to explain how you know.

_____

_____

_____

_____

_____

© Houghton Mifflin Harcourt Publishing Company

Compare Fractions

Show What You Know ✓

Check your understanding of important skills.

Name _____

▶ Halves and Fourths

1. Find the shape that is divided into 2 equal parts. Color $\frac{1}{2}$.

2. Find the shape that is divided into 4 equal parts. Color $\frac{1}{4}$.

▶ Parts of a Whole   Write the number of shaded parts and the number of equal parts.

3. 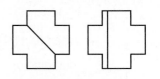   _____ shaded parts

_____ equal parts

4. _____ shaded parts

_____ equal parts

▶ Fractions of a Whole

Write the fraction that names the shaded part of each shape.

5. _____

6. 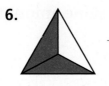 _____

7. _____

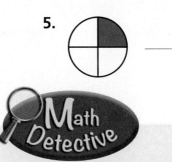

Hannah keeps her marbles in bags with 4 marbles in each bag. She writes $\frac{3}{4}$ to show the number of red marbles in each bag. Be a Math Detective to find another fraction to name the number of red marbles in 2 bags.

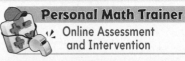

Personal Math Trainer

Online Assessment and Intervention

© Houghton Mifflin Harcourt Publishing Company

Vocabulary Builder

▶ **Visualize It** •

Complete the flow map by using the words with a ✓.

Fractions and Whole Numbers

What is it?		What are some examples?
_____	→	$\frac{2}{3} > \frac{1}{3}$
_____	→	$\frac{1}{4} < \frac{2}{4}$
_____	→	$\frac{1}{2} = \frac{2}{4}$
_____	→	$\frac{1}{3}, \frac{1}{4}$
_____	→	$\frac{2}{2}, \frac{4}{2}$

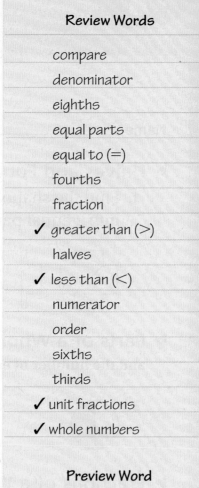

Review Words

compare

denominator

eighths

equal parts

equal to (=)

fourths

fraction

✓ greater than (>)

halves

✓ less than (<)

numerator

order

sixths

thirds

✓ unit fractions

✓ whole numbers

Preview Word

✓ equivalent

fractions

▶ **Understand Vocabulary** •

Write the review word or preview word that
answers the riddle.

1. We are two fractions that name the same amount.

   _____

2. I am the part of a fraction above the line. I tell how
   many parts are being counted.

   _____

3. I am the part of a fraction below the line. I tell how
   many equal parts are in the whole or in the group.

   _____

© Houghton Mifflin Harcourt Publishing Company

 GO DIGITAL
• **Interactive Student Edition**
• **Multimedia eGlossary**

Name _____

Problem Solving • Compare Fractions

Essential Question How can you use the strategy *act it out* to solve comparison problems?

Number and Operations—
Fractions—3.NF.3d Also 3.NF.1
MATHEMATICAL PRACTICES
MP.1, MP.3, MP.4, MP.5

🔑 Unlock the Problem (Real World)

Mary and Vincent climbed up a rock wall at the park. Mary climbed $\frac{3}{4}$ of the way up the wall. Vincent climbed $\frac{3}{8}$ of the way up the wall. Who climbed higher?

You can act out the problem by using manipulatives to help you compare fractions.

Remember

< is less than

> is greater than

= is equal to

Read the Problem

What do I need to find?

_____

What information do I need to use?

Mary climbed _____ of the way.

Vincent climbed _____ of the way.

How will I use the information?

I will use _____

and _____ the lengths of

the models to find who climbed

_____.

Solve the Problem

Record the steps you used to solve the problem.

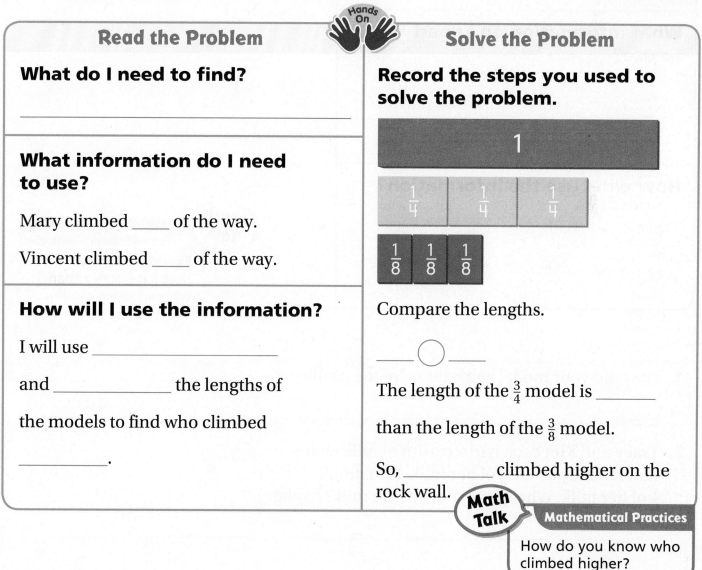

Compare the lengths.

____ ◯ ____

The length of the $\frac{3}{4}$ model is _____

than the length of the $\frac{3}{8}$ model.

So, _____ climbed higher on the rock wall.

Math Talk Mathematical Practices

How do you know who climbed higher?

© Houghton Mifflin Harcourt Publishing Company • Image Credits: (tr) ©The Photolibrary Wales/Alamy Images

Chapter 9 **367**

Try Another Problem

Students at day camp are decorating paper circles for placemats. Tracy finished $\frac{3}{6}$ of her placemat. Kim finished $\frac{5}{6}$ of her placemat. Who finished more of her placemat?

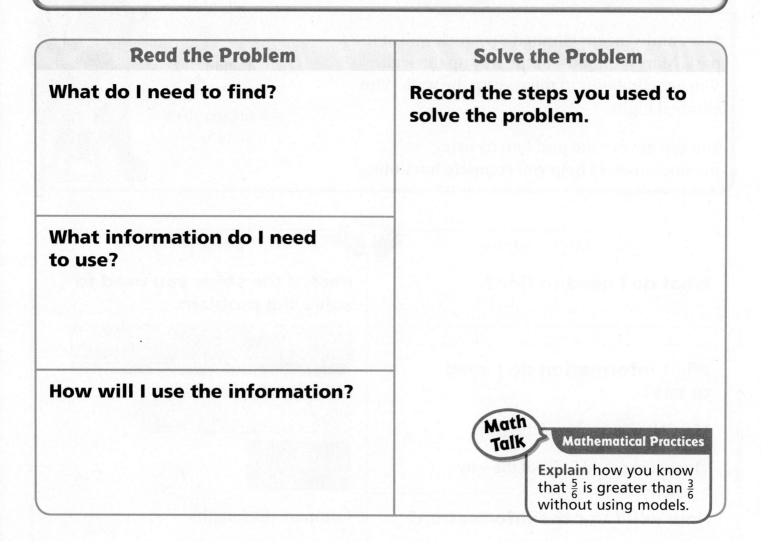

Read the Problem	Solve the Problem
What do I need to find?	**Record the steps you used to solve the problem.**
What information do I need to use?	
How will I use the information?	

Math Talk

Mathematical Practices

Explain how you know that $\frac{5}{6}$ is greater than $\frac{3}{6}$ without using models.

1. How did your model help you solve the problem? _____

_____

2. Tracy and Kim each had a carton of milk with lunch. Tracy drank $\frac{5}{8}$ of her milk. Kim drank $\frac{7}{8}$ of her milk. Who drank more of her milk? Explain.

_____

_____

© Houghton Mifflin Harcourt Publishing Company

Name _____

Share and Show

1. At the park, people can climb a rope ladder to its top. Rosa climbed $\frac{2}{8}$ of the way up the ladder. Justin climbed $\frac{2}{6}$ of the way up the ladder. Who climbed higher on the rope ladder?

First, what are you asked to find?

_____

Then, model and compare the fractions. **Think:** Compare $\frac{2}{8}$ and $\frac{2}{6}$.

Last, find the greater fraction.

____ ◯ ____

So, _____ climbed higher on the rope ladder.

2. What if Cara also tried the rope ladder and climbed $\frac{2}{4}$ of the way up? Who climbed highest on the rope ladder: Rosa, Justin, or Cara? Explain how you know.

_____

_____

_____

On Your Own

3. **MATHEMATICAL PRACTICE ⑤ Use a Concrete Model** Ted walked $\frac{2}{3}$ mile to his soccer game. Then he walked $\frac{1}{3}$ mile to his friend's house. Which distance is shorter? Explain how you know.

_____

_____

© Houghton Mifflin Harcourt Publishing Company

Use the table for 4–5.

4. **GO DEEPER** Suri is spreading jam on 8 biscuits for breakfast. The table shows the fraction of biscuits spread with each jam flavor. Which flavor did Suri use on the most biscuits?

   Hint: Use 8 counters to model the biscuits.

   _____

Suri's Biscuits	
Jam Flavor	Fraction of Biscuits
Peach	$\frac{3}{8}$
Raspberry	$\frac{4}{8}$
Strawberry	$\frac{1}{8}$

5. **WRITE** ▸*Math* **What's the Question?** The answer is strawberry.

   _____

   _____

6. **THINK SMARTER** Suppose Suri had also used plum jam on the biscuits. She frosted $\frac{1}{2}$ of the biscuits with peach jam, $\frac{1}{4}$ with raspberry jam, $\frac{1}{8}$ with strawberry jam, and $\frac{1}{8}$ with plum jam. Which flavor of jam did Suri use on the most biscuits?

   _____

Math on the Spot

7. Ms. Gordon has many snack bar recipes. One recipe uses $\frac{1}{3}$ cup oatmeal and $\frac{1}{2}$ cup flour. Will Ms. Gordon use more oatmeal or more flour? Explain.

   _____

8. **THINK SMARTER** Rick lives $\frac{4}{6}$ mile from school. Noah lives $\frac{3}{6}$ mile from school.

   Use the fractions and symbols to show which distance is longer.

   $\boxed{\frac{3}{6}}$, $\boxed{\frac{4}{6}}$, $\boxed{<}$ and $\boxed{>}$ $\boxed{} \bigcirc \boxed{}$

© Houghton Mifflin Harcourt Publishing Company

FOR MORE PRACTICE: Standards Practice Book

Name _____

Compare Fractions with the Same Denominator

Essential Question How can you compare fractions with the same denominator?

Number and Operations—Fractions—3.NF.3d *Also 3.NF.1, 3.NF.2b*

MATHEMATICAL PRACTICES
MP.2, MP.3, MP.5, MP.8

🔑 Unlock the Problem Real World

Jeremy and Christina are each making quilt blocks. Both blocks are the same size and both are made of 4 equal-size squares. $\frac{2}{4}$ of Jeremy's squares are green. $\frac{1}{4}$ of Christina's squares are green. Whose quilt block has more green squares?

Compare fractions of a whole.

- Shade $\frac{2}{4}$ of Jeremy's quilt block.
- Shade $\frac{1}{4}$ of Christina's quilt block.
- Compare $\frac{2}{4}$ and $\frac{1}{4}$.

The greater fraction will have the larger amount of the whole shaded.

$$\frac{2}{4} \bigcirc \frac{1}{4}$$

So, _____ quilt block has more green squares.

- Circle the two fractions you need to compare.
- How are the two fractions alike?

_____

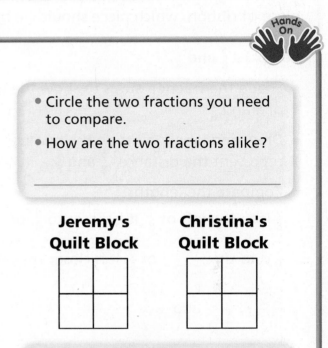

Jeremy's Quilt Block   **Christina's Quilt Block**

Math Idea
You can compare two fractions when they refer to the same whole or to groups that are the same size.

Compare fractions of a group.
Jen and Maggie each have 6 buttons.

- Shade 3 of Jen's buttons to show the number of buttons that are red. Shade 5 of Maggie's buttons to show the number that are red.

- Write a fraction to show the number of red buttons in each group. Compare the fractions.

There are the same number of buttons in each group, so you can count the number of red buttons to compare the fractions.

$$3 < \text{\_\_\_\_\_}, \text{ so } \frac{}{6} < \frac{}{6}.$$

So, _____ has a greater fraction of red buttons.

Jen's Buttons

Maggie's Buttons

© Houghton Mifflin Harcourt Publishing Company

🔑 Use fraction strips and a number line.

At the craft store, one piece of ribbon is $\frac{2}{8}$ yard long. Another piece of ribbon is $\frac{7}{8}$ yard long. If Sean wants to buy the longer piece of ribbon, which piece should he buy?

- On a number line, a fraction farther to the right is greater than a fraction to its left.
- On a number line, a fraction farther to the left is _____ a fraction to its right.

Compare $\frac{2}{8}$ and $\frac{7}{8}$.

- Shade the fraction strips to show the locations of $\frac{2}{8}$ and $\frac{7}{8}$.

- Draw and label points on the number line to represent the distances $\frac{2}{8}$ and $\frac{7}{8}$.

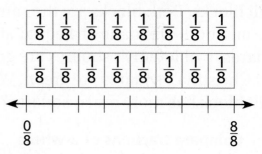

- Compare the lengths.

  $\frac{2}{8}$ is to the left of $\frac{7}{8}$. It is closer to $\frac{0}{8}$, or _____.

  $\frac{7}{8}$ is to the _____ of $\frac{2}{8}$. It is closer to —, or _____.

  ⬛/⬛ < ⬛/⬛ and ⬛/⬛ > ⬛/⬛

So, Sean should buy the piece of ribbon that is ⬛/⬛ yard long.

🔑 Use reasoning.

Ana and Omar are decorating same-size bookmarks. Ana covers $\frac{3}{3}$ of her bookmark with glitter. Omar covers $\frac{1}{3}$ of his bookmark with glitter. Whose bookmark is covered with more glitter?

Compare $\frac{3}{3}$ and $\frac{1}{3}$.

- When the denominators are the same, the whole is divided into same-size pieces. You can look at the _____ to compare the number of pieces.

- Both fractions involve third-size pieces. _____ pieces are more than _____ piece. 3 > _____, so ⬛/⬛ > ⬛/⬛.

So, _____ bookmark is covered with more glitter.

Math Talk — **Mathematical Practices**

Explain how you can use reasoning to compare fractions with the same denominator.

© Houghton Mifflin Harcourt Publishing Company • Image Credits: (cr) ©Deborah Waters – Studio/Alamy Images

Name _____

1. Draw points on the number line to show $\frac{1}{6}$ and $\frac{5}{6}$. Then compare the fractions.

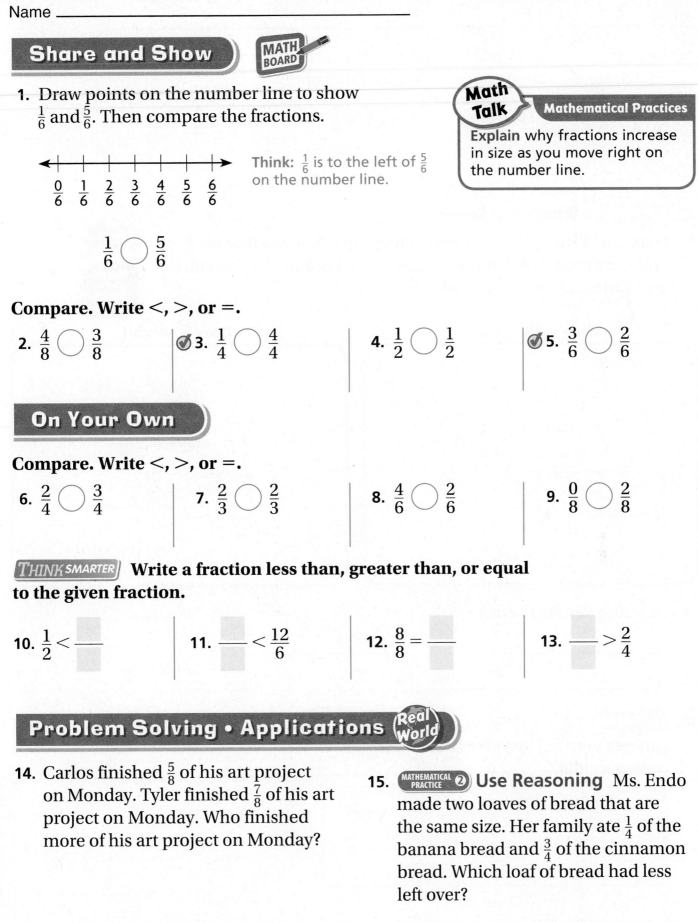

Think: $\frac{1}{6}$ is to the left of $\frac{5}{6}$ on the number line.

Math Talk **Mathematical Practices**

Explain why fractions increase in size as you move right on the number line.

$$\frac{1}{6} \bigcirc \frac{5}{6}$$

Compare. Write <, >, or =.

2. $\frac{4}{8} \bigcirc \frac{3}{8}$ ✓3. $\frac{1}{4} \bigcirc \frac{4}{4}$ 4. $\frac{1}{2} \bigcirc \frac{1}{2}$ ✓5. $\frac{3}{6} \bigcirc \frac{2}{6}$

On Your Own

Compare. Write <, >, or =.

6. $\frac{2}{4} \bigcirc \frac{3}{4}$ 7. $\frac{2}{3} \bigcirc \frac{2}{3}$ 8. $\frac{4}{6} \bigcirc \frac{2}{6}$ 9. $\frac{0}{8} \bigcirc \frac{2}{8}$

THINK SMARTER Write a fraction less than, greater than, or equal to the given fraction.

10. $\frac{1}{2} < \underline{\quad}$ 11. $\underline{\quad} < \frac{12}{6}$ 12. $\frac{8}{8} = \underline{\quad}$ 13. $\underline{\quad} > \frac{2}{4}$

Problem Solving • Applications Real World

14. Carlos finished $\frac{5}{8}$ of his art project on Monday. Tyler finished $\frac{7}{8}$ of his art project on Monday. Who finished more of his art project on Monday?

15. **MATHEMATICAL PRACTICE ② Use Reasoning** Ms. Endo made two loaves of bread that are the same size. Her family ate $\frac{1}{4}$ of the banana bread and $\frac{3}{4}$ of the cinnamon bread. Which loaf of bread had less left over?

© Houghton Mifflin Harcourt Publishing Company

16. THINK SMARTER Todd and Lisa are comparing fraction strips. Which statements are correct? Mark all that apply.

(A) $\frac{1}{4} < \frac{4}{4}$ (B) $\frac{5}{6} < \frac{4}{6}$ (C) $\frac{2}{3} > \frac{1}{3}$ (D) $\frac{5}{8} > \frac{4}{8}$

THINK SMARTER **What's the Error?**

17. Gary and Vanessa are comparing fractions. Vanessa models $\frac{2}{4}$ and Gary models $\frac{3}{4}$. Vanessa writes $\frac{3}{4} < \frac{2}{4}$. Look at Gary's model and Vanessa's model and describe her error.

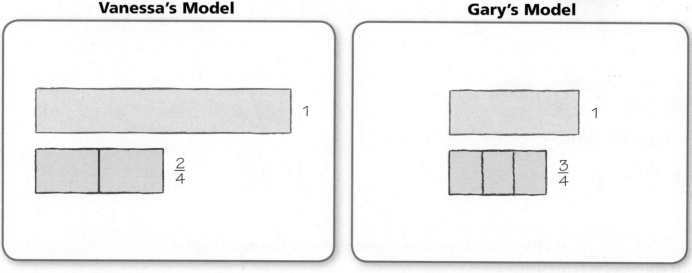

Vanessa's Model

1

$\frac{2}{4}$

Gary's Model

1

$\frac{3}{4}$

• Describe Vanessa's error.

_____

_____

18. GO DEEPER Explain how to correct Vanessa's error. Then show the correct model.

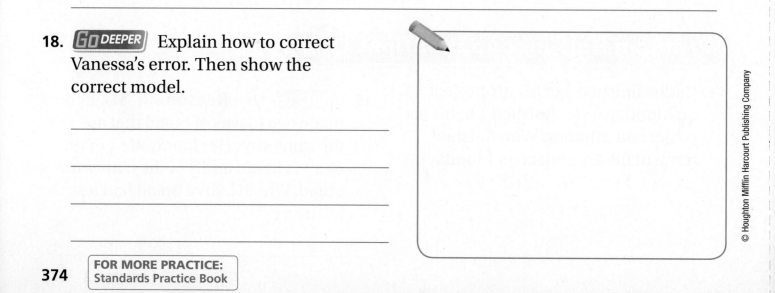

_____

_____

_____

_____

© Houghton Mifflin Harcourt Publishing Company

FOR MORE PRACTICE:
Standards Practice Book

Name _____

Compare Fractions with the Same Numerator

Essential Question How can you compare fractions with the same numerator?

Number and Operations—Fractions—3.NF.3d *Also 3.NF.1*

MATHEMATICAL PRACTICES
MP.1, MP.2, MP.4, MP.7

Unlock the Problem Real World

Markos is at Athena's Cafe. He can sit at a table with 5 of his friends or at a different table with 7 of his friends. The same-size spinach pie is shared equally among the people at each table. At which table should Markos sit to get more pie?

- Including Markos, how many friends will be sharing pie at each table?

_____

- What will you compare?

_____

_____

Model the problem.

There will be 6 friends sharing Pie A or 8 friends sharing Pie B.

So, Markos will get either $\frac{1}{6}$ or $\frac{1}{8}$ of a pie.

- Shade $\frac{1}{6}$ of Pie A.
- Shade $\frac{1}{8}$ of Pie B.
- Which piece of pie is larger?
- Compare $\frac{1}{6}$ and $\frac{1}{8}$.

$$\frac{1}{6} \bigcirc \frac{1}{8}$$

So, Markos should sit at the table with _____ friends to get more pie.

Pie A

$\frac{1}{6}$ $\frac{1}{6}$ $\frac{1}{6}$ $\frac{1}{6}$ $\frac{1}{6}$ $\frac{1}{6}$

Pie B

$\frac{1}{8}$ $\frac{1}{8}$ $\frac{1}{8}$ $\frac{1}{8}$ $\frac{1}{8}$ $\frac{1}{8}$ $\frac{1}{8}$ $\frac{1}{8}$

1. Which pie has more pieces? _____
   The *more* pieces a whole is divided into,

   the _____ the pieces are.

2. Which pie has fewer pieces? _____
   The *fewer* pieces a whole is divided into,

   the _____ the pieces are.

Math Talk **Mathematical Practices**

Suppose Markos wants two pieces of one of the pies above. Is $\frac{2}{6}$ or $\frac{2}{8}$ of the pie a greater amount? **Explain** how you know.

© Houghton Mifflin Harcourt Publishing Company

🔑 **Use fraction strips.**

On Saturday, the campers paddled $\frac{2}{8}$ of their planned route down the river. On Sunday, they paddled $\frac{2}{3}$ of their route down the river. On which day did the campers paddle farther?

Compare $\frac{2}{8}$ and $\frac{2}{3}$.

- Place a ✓ next to the fraction strips that show more parts in the whole.

- Shade $\frac{2}{8}$. Then shade $\frac{2}{3}$. Compare the shaded parts.

- $\frac{2}{8}$ ◯ $\frac{2}{3}$

1							
$\frac{1}{8}$	$\frac{1}{8}$	$\frac{1}{8}$	$\frac{1}{8}$	$\frac{1}{8}$	$\frac{1}{8}$	$\frac{1}{8}$	$\frac{1}{8}$

$\frac{1}{3}$	$\frac{1}{3}$	$\frac{1}{3}$

Think: $\frac{1}{8}$ is less than $\frac{1}{3}$, so $\frac{2}{8}$ is less than $\frac{2}{3}$.

So, the campers paddled farther on _____.

🔑 **Use reasoning.**

For her class party, Felicia baked two trays of snacks that were the same size. After the party, she had $\frac{3}{4}$ of the carrot snack and $\frac{3}{6}$ of the apple snack left over. Was more carrot snack or more apple snack left over?

Compare $\frac{3}{4}$ and $\frac{3}{6}$.

- Since the numerators are the same, look at the denominators to compare the size of the pieces. $\frac{3}{4}$ $\frac{3}{6}$

  - The *more* pieces a whole is divided into,

    the _____ the pieces are.
  - The *fewer* pieces a whole is divided into,

    the _____ the pieces are.

⚠ **ERROR Alert**

When comparing fractions with the same numerator, be sure the symbol shows that the fraction with fewer pieces in the whole is the greater fraction.

- $\frac{1}{4}$ is _____ than $\frac{1}{6}$ because there are

  _____ pieces.

- $\frac{3}{4}$ ◯ $\frac{3}{6}$

So, there was more of the _____ snack left over.

© Houghton Mifflin Harcourt Publishing Company

Name _____

1. Shade the models to show $\frac{1}{6}$ and $\frac{1}{4}$.

Then compare the fractions.

$\frac{1}{6} \bigcirc \frac{1}{4}$

Compare. Write <, >, or =.

✓2. $\frac{1}{8} \bigcirc \frac{1}{3}$

✓3. $\frac{3}{4} \bigcirc \frac{3}{8}$

4. $\frac{2}{6} \bigcirc \frac{2}{3}$

5. $\frac{4}{8} \bigcirc \frac{4}{4}$

6. $\frac{3}{6} \bigcirc \frac{3}{6}$

7. $\frac{8}{4} \bigcirc \frac{8}{8}$

Math Talk **Mathematical Practices**

Explain why $\frac{1}{2}$ is greater than $\frac{1}{4}$.

On Your Own

Compare. Write <, >, or =.

8. $\frac{1}{3} \bigcirc \frac{1}{4}$

9. $\frac{2}{3} \bigcirc \frac{2}{6}$

10. $\frac{4}{8} \bigcirc \frac{4}{2}$

11. $\frac{6}{8} \bigcirc \frac{6}{6}$

12. $\frac{1}{6} \bigcirc \frac{1}{2}$

13. $\frac{7}{8} \bigcirc \frac{7}{8}$

14. **GO DEEPER** James ate $\frac{3}{4}$ of his quesadilla. David ate $\frac{2}{3}$ of his quesadilla. Both are the same size. Who ate more of his quesadilla?

James said he knows he ate more because he looked at the amounts left. Does his answer make sense? Shade the models. Explain.

James   **David**

_____

_____

© Houghton Mifflin Harcourt Publishing Company

Unlock the Problem (Real World)

15. **MATHEMATICAL PRACTICE ① Make Sense of Problems** Quinton and Hunter are biking on trails in Katy Trail State Park. They biked $\frac{5}{6}$ mile in the morning and $\frac{5}{8}$ mile in the afternoon. Did they bike a greater distance in the morning or in the afternoon?

a. What do you need to know? _____

b. The numerator is 5 in both fractions, so compare $\frac{1}{6}$ and $\frac{1}{8}$. Explain.

_____

c. How can you solve the problem?

d. Complete the sentences.

In the morning, the boys biked

_____ mile. In the afternoon, they biked _____ mile.

So, the boys biked a greater distance

in the _____. $\frac{5}{6} \bigcirc \frac{5}{8}$

16. **THINK SMARTER** Zach has a piece of pie that is $\frac{1}{4}$ of a pie. Max has a piece of pie that is $\frac{1}{2}$ of a pie. Max's piece is smaller than Zach's piece. Explain how this could happen. Draw a picture to show your answer.

Math on the Spot

_____

_____

Personal Math Trainer

17. **THINK SMARTER +** Before taking a hike, Kate and Dylan each ate part of same-size granola bars. Kate ate $\frac{1}{3}$ of her bar. Dylan ate $\frac{1}{2}$ of his bar. Who ate more of the granola bar? Explain how you solved the problem.

_____

_____

© Houghton Mifflin Harcourt Publishing Company

FOR MORE PRACTICE:
Standards Practice Book

378

Compare Fractions

Essential Question What strategies can you use to compare fractions?

**Number and Operations—
Fractions—3.NF.3d** *Also 3.NF.1,
3.NF.3*

MATHEMATICAL PRACTICES
MP.1, MP.2, MP.4, MP.6

Unlock the Problem Real World

Luka and Ann are eating the same-size small pizzas. One plate has $\frac{3}{4}$ of Luka's cheese pizza. Another plate has $\frac{5}{6}$ of Ann's mushroom pizza. Whose plate has more pizza?

- Circle the numbers you need to compare.
- How many pieces make up each whole pizza?

_____

🔑 Compare $\frac{3}{4}$ and $\frac{5}{6}$. **Hands On**

Missing Pieces Strategy
- You can compare fractions by comparing pieces missing from a whole.

- Shade $\frac{3}{4}$ of Luka's pizza and $\frac{5}{6}$ of Ann's pizza. Each fraction represents a whole that is missing one piece.

- Since $\frac{1}{6}$ ◯ $\frac{1}{4}$, a smaller piece is missing from Ann's pizza.

- If a smaller piece is missing from Ann's pizza, she must have more pizza.

So, _____ plate has more pizza.

Luka

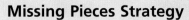

$\frac{3}{4}$

Ann

$\frac{5}{6}$

Math Talk **Mathematical Practices**

Explain how knowing that $\frac{1}{4}$ is less than $\frac{1}{3}$ helps you compare $\frac{3}{4}$ and $\frac{2}{3}$.

Morgan ran $\frac{2}{3}$ mile. Alexa ran $\frac{1}{3}$ mile. Who ran farther?

🔑 Compare $\frac{2}{3}$ and $\frac{1}{3}$.

$\frac{\square}{3} > \frac{\square}{3}$

Same Denominator Strategy
- When the denominators are the same, you can compare only the number of pieces, or the numerators.

So, _____ ran farther.

© Houghton Mifflin Harcourt Publishing Company

Ms. Davis is making a fruit salad with $\frac{3}{4}$ pound of cherries and $\frac{3}{8}$ pound of strawberries. Which weighs less, the cherries or the strawberries?

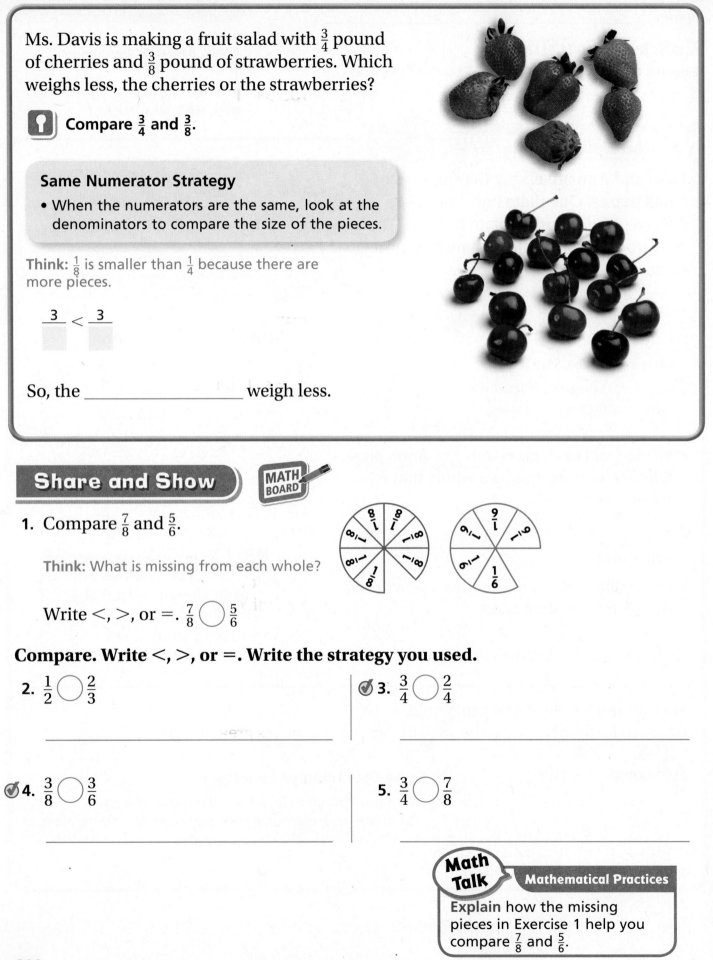

🔑 Compare $\frac{3}{4}$ and $\frac{3}{8}$.

Same Numerator Strategy
- When the numerators are the same, look at the denominators to compare the size of the pieces.

Think: $\frac{1}{8}$ is smaller than $\frac{1}{4}$ because there are more pieces.

$$\frac{3}{} < \frac{3}{}$$

So, the _____ weigh less.

Share and Show MATH BOARD

1. Compare $\frac{7}{8}$ and $\frac{5}{6}$.

   Think: What is missing from each whole?

   Write $<$, $>$, or $=$. $\frac{7}{8} \bigcirc \frac{5}{6}$

Compare. Write $<$, $>$, or $=$. Write the strategy you used.

2. $\frac{1}{2} \bigcirc \frac{2}{3}$

_____

✅ 3. $\frac{3}{4} \bigcirc \frac{2}{4}$

_____

✅ 4. $\frac{3}{8} \bigcirc \frac{3}{6}$

_____

5. $\frac{3}{4} \bigcirc \frac{7}{8}$

_____

Math Talk Mathematical Practices

Explain how the missing pieces in Exercise 1 help you compare $\frac{7}{8}$ and $\frac{5}{6}$.

© Houghton Mifflin Harcourt Publishing Company

Name _____

On Your Own

Compare. Write <, >, or =. Write the strategy you used.

6. $\frac{1}{2}$ ◯ $\frac{2}{2}$

_____

7. $\frac{1}{3}$ ◯ $\frac{1}{4}$

_____

8. $\frac{2}{3}$ ◯ $\frac{5}{6}$

_____

9. $\frac{4}{6}$ ◯ $\frac{4}{2}$

_____

Name a fraction that is less than or greater than the given fraction. Draw to justify your answer.

10. less than $\frac{5}{6}$ _____

11. greater than $\frac{3}{8}$ _____

12. **GO DEEPER** Luke, Seth, and Anja have empty glasses. Mr. Gabel pours $\frac{3}{6}$ cup of orange juice in Seth's glass. Then he pours $\frac{1}{6}$ cup of orange juice in Luke's glass and $\frac{2}{6}$ cup of orange juice in Anja's glass. Who gets the most orange juice?

_____

13. **THINK SMARTER** **What's the Error?** Jack says that $\frac{5}{8}$ is greater than $\frac{5}{6}$ because the denominator 8 is greater than the denominator 6. Describe Jack's error. Draw a picture to explain your answer.

_____

_____

_____

© Houghton Mifflin Harcourt Publishing Company

Unlock the Problem (Real World)

14. **MATHEMATICAL PRACTICE ① Analyze** Tracy is making blueberry
muffins. She is using $\frac{4}{4}$ cup of honey and $\frac{4}{2}$ cups of
flour. Does Tracy use more honey or more flour?

a. What do you need to know?

_____

b. What strategy will you use to compare
the fractions?

_____

c. Show the steps you used to solve
the problem.

d. Complete the comparison.

$$\frac{}{} > \frac{}{}$$

So, Tracy uses more _____.

15. **THINK SMARTER** Compare the fractions. Circle a symbol that
makes the statement true.

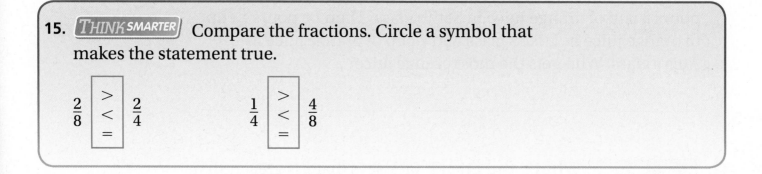

$$\frac{2}{8} \quad \begin{array}{c} > \\ < \\ = \end{array} \quad \frac{2}{4} \qquad\qquad \frac{1}{4} \quad \begin{array}{c} > \\ < \\ = \end{array} \quad \frac{4}{8}$$

© Houghton Mifflin Harcourt Publishing Company

FOR MORE PRACTICE:
Standards Practice Book

Mid-Chapter Checkpoint

Concepts and Skills

1. When two fractions refer to the same whole, explain why the fraction with a lesser denominator has larger pieces than the fraction with a greater denominator. (3.NF.3d)

The denominator had a small number and the other one had a big number the small number will be greater

2. When two fractions refer to the same whole and have the same denominators, explain why you can compare only the numerators. (3.NF.3d)

You can only compare the numerators because the numerators are the number of parts.

Compare. Write <, >, or =. (3.NF.3d)

3. $\frac{1}{6} \bigcirc \frac{1}{4}$ 4. $\frac{1}{8} \bigcirc \frac{1}{8}$ 5. $\frac{2}{8} \bigcirc \frac{2}{3}$

6. $\frac{4}{2} \bigcirc \frac{1}{2}$ 7. $\frac{7}{8} \bigcirc \frac{3}{8}$ 8. $\frac{5}{6} \bigcirc \frac{2}{3}$

9. $\frac{2}{4} \bigcirc \frac{3}{4}$ 10. $\frac{6}{6} \bigcirc \frac{6}{8}$ 11. $\frac{3}{4} \bigcirc \frac{7}{8}$

Name a fraction that is less than or greater than the given fraction. Draw to justify your answer. (3.NF.3d)

12. greater than $\frac{2}{6}$ _____

13. less than $\frac{2}{3}$ _____

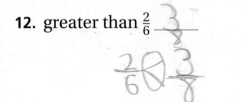

© Houghton Mifflin Harcourt Publishing Company

14. Two walls in Tiffany's room are the same size. Tiffany paints $\frac{1}{4}$ of one wall. Roberto paints $\frac{1}{8}$ of the other wall. Who painted a greater amount in Tiffany's room? (3.NF.3d)

Tiffany

15. Matthew ran $\frac{5}{8}$ mile during track practice. Pablo ran $\frac{5}{6}$ mile. Write a fraction that shows who ran farther. (3.NF.3d)

$$\frac{5}{6} \bigcirc \frac{5}{8}$$

Pablo

16. Mallory bought 6 roses for her mother. Two-sixths of the roses are red and $\frac{4}{6}$ are yellow. Write a fraction that correctly compares the amounts. (3.NF.3d)

$$\frac{2}{6} \bigcirc \frac{4}{6}$$

yellow

17. Lani used $\frac{2}{3}$ cup of raisins and $\frac{3}{4}$ cup of oatmeal to bake cookies. Did Lani use less oatmeal or less raisins? (3.NF.3d)

less raisins

© Houghton Mifflin Harcourt Publishing Company

Compare and Order Fractions

Essential Question How can you compare and order fractions?

Number and Operations—
Fractions—3.NF.3d *Also 3.NF.1*
MATHEMATICAL PRACTICES
MP.3, MP.4, MP.5, MP.6

Unlock the Problem

Sierra, Tad, and Dale ride their bikes to school. Sierra rides $\frac{3}{4}$ mile, Tad rides $\frac{3}{8}$ mile, and Dale rides $\frac{3}{6}$ mile. Compare and order the distances from least to greatest.

> • Circle the fractions you need to use.
>
> • Underline the sentence that tells you what you need to do.

Activity 1 Order fractions with the same numerator.

Materials ■ color pencil

You can order fractions by reasoning about the size of unit fractions.

1			
$\frac{1}{4}$	$\frac{1}{4}$	$\frac{1}{4}$	$\frac{1}{4}$

| $\frac{1}{8}$ | $\frac{1}{8}$ | $\frac{1}{8}$ | $\frac{1}{8}$ | $\frac{1}{8}$ | $\frac{1}{8}$ | $\frac{1}{8}$ | $\frac{1}{8}$ |

| $\frac{1}{6}$ | $\frac{1}{6}$ | $\frac{1}{6}$ | $\frac{1}{6}$ | $\frac{1}{6}$ | $\frac{1}{6}$ |

> **Remember**
> • The *more* pieces a whole is divided into, the smaller the pieces are.
> • The *fewer* pieces a whole is divided into, the larger the pieces are.

STEP 1 Shade one unit fraction for each fraction strip.

_____ is the longest unit fraction.

_____ is the shortest unit fraction.

STEP 2 Shade one more unit fraction for each fraction strip.

Are the shaded fourths still the longest? _____

Are the shaded eighths still the shortest? _____

STEP 3 Continue shading the fraction strips so that three unit fractions are shaded for each strip.

Are the shaded fourths still the longest? _____

Are the shaded eighths still the shortest? _____

$\frac{3}{4}$ mile is the _____ distance. $\frac{3}{8}$ mile is the _____ distance. $\frac{3}{6}$ mile is *between* the other two distances.

So, the distances in order from least to greatest are

_____ mile, _____ mile, _____ mile.

© Houghton Mifflin Harcourt Publishing Company

Try This! Order $\frac{2}{6}$, $\frac{2}{3}$, and $\frac{2}{4}$ from greatest to least.

Order the fractions $\frac{2}{6}$, $\frac{2}{3}$, and $\frac{2}{4}$ by thinking about the length of the unit fraction strip. Then label the fractions *shortest*, *between*, or *longest*.

Fraction	Unit Fraction	Length
$\frac{2}{6}$		
$\frac{2}{3}$		
$\frac{2}{4}$		

Math Talk **Mathematical Practices**

When ordering three fractions, what do you know about the third fraction when you know which fraction is the shortest and which fraction is the longest? **Explain** your answer.

- When the numerators are the same, think about the

  _____ of the pieces to compare and order fractions.

So, the order from greatest to least is _____, _____, _____ .

Hands On

🔓 Activity 2 Order fractions with the same denominator.

Materials ■ color pencil

Shade fraction strips to order $\frac{5}{8}$, $\frac{8}{8}$, and $\frac{3}{8}$ from least to greatest.

1

| $\frac{1}{8}$ | $\frac{1}{8}$ | $\frac{1}{8}$ | $\frac{1}{8}$ | $\frac{1}{8}$ | $\frac{1}{8}$ | $\frac{1}{8}$ | $\frac{1}{8}$ | Shade $\frac{5}{8}$. |

| $\frac{1}{8}$ | $\frac{1}{8}$ | $\frac{1}{8}$ | $\frac{1}{8}$ | $\frac{1}{8}$ | $\frac{1}{8}$ | $\frac{1}{8}$ | $\frac{1}{8}$ | Shade $\frac{8}{8}$. |

| $\frac{1}{8}$ | $\frac{1}{8}$ | $\frac{1}{8}$ | $\frac{1}{8}$ | $\frac{1}{8}$ | $\frac{1}{8}$ | $\frac{1}{8}$ | $\frac{1}{8}$ | Shade $\frac{3}{8}$. |

- When the denominators are the same, the size of the pieces is the _____.

  So, think about the _____ of pieces to compare and order fractions.

  _____ is the shortest. _____ is the longest.

  _____ is between the other two fractions.

So, the order from least to greatest is _____, _____, _____ .

© Houghton Mifflin Harcourt Publishing Company

Name _____

1. Shade the fraction strips to order $\frac{4}{6}$, $\frac{4}{4}$, and $\frac{4}{8}$ from least to greatest.

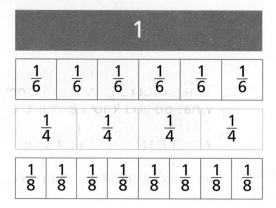

Math Talk Mathematical Practices

Explain how you would order the fractions $\frac{2}{3}$, $\frac{1}{3}$, and $\frac{3}{3}$ from greatest to least.

1

| $\frac{1}{6}$ | $\frac{1}{6}$ | $\frac{1}{6}$ | $\frac{1}{6}$ | $\frac{1}{6}$ | $\frac{1}{6}$ |

| $\frac{1}{4}$ | $\frac{1}{4}$ | $\frac{1}{4}$ | $\frac{1}{4}$ |

| $\frac{1}{8}$ | $\frac{1}{8}$ | $\frac{1}{8}$ | $\frac{1}{8}$ | $\frac{1}{8}$ | $\frac{1}{8}$ | $\frac{1}{8}$ | $\frac{1}{8}$ |

_____ is the shortest. _____ is the longest.

_____ is between the other two lengths. _____ , _____ , _____

Write the fractions in order from least to greatest.

2. $\frac{1}{2}$, $\frac{0}{2}$, $\frac{2}{2}$ ___ $\frac{0}{2}$, $\frac{1}{2}$, $\frac{2}{2}$

3. $\frac{1}{6}$, $\frac{1}{2}$, $\frac{1}{3}$ ___ $\frac{1}{6}$, $\frac{1}{3}$, $\frac{1}{2}$

Write the fractions in order from greatest to least.

4. $\frac{6}{6}$, $\frac{2}{6}$, $\frac{5}{6}$ ___ $\frac{6}{6}$, $\frac{5}{6}$, $\frac{2}{6}$

5. $\frac{1}{8}$, $\frac{1}{4}$, $\frac{1}{2}$ ___ , ___ , ___

Write the fractions in order from least to greatest.

6. THINK SMARTER
$\frac{6}{3}$, $\frac{6}{2}$, $\frac{6}{8}$ ___ $\frac{6}{8}$, $\frac{6}{3}$, $\frac{6}{2}$

7. THINK SMARTER
$\frac{4}{2}$, $\frac{2}{2}$, $\frac{8}{2}$ ___ , ___ , ___

8. MATHEMATICAL PRACTICE ⑥ **Compare** Pam is making biscuits. She needs $\frac{2}{6}$ cup of oil, $\frac{2}{3}$ cup of water, and $\frac{2}{4}$ cup of milk. Write the ingredients from greatest to least amount.

___ $\frac{2}{3}$, $\frac{2}{4}$, $\frac{2}{6}$

Problem Solving • Applications

9. In fifteen minutes, Greg's sailboat went $\frac{3}{6}$ mile, Gina's sailboat went $\frac{6}{6}$ mile, and Stuart's sailboat went $\frac{4}{6}$ mile. Whose sailboat went the longest distance in fifteen minutes?

_____

Whose sailboat went the shortest distance?

_____

10. **GO DEEPER** Look back at Problem 9. Write a similar problem by changing the fraction of a mile each sailboat traveled, so the answers are different from Problem 9. Then solve the problem.

_____

_____

_____

_____

WRITE *Math* • **Show Your Work**

11. **THINK SMARTER** Tom has three pieces of wood. The length of the longest piece is $\frac{3}{4}$ foot. The length of the shortest piece is $\frac{3}{8}$ foot. What might be the length of the third piece of wood?

_____

12. **THINK SMARTER** Jesse ran $\frac{2}{4}$ mile on Monday, $\frac{2}{3}$ mile on Tuesday, and $\frac{2}{8}$ mile on Wednesday. Order the fractions from least to greatest.

$\frac{2}{4}$, $\frac{2}{3}$ and $\frac{2}{8}$ $\boxed{\frac{2}{8}}$ $\boxed{\frac{2}{4}}$ $\boxed{\frac{2}{3}}$

© Houghton Mifflin Harcourt Publishing Company • Image Credits: (tr) ©Vince Streano/Corbis

FOR MORE PRACTICE:
Standards Practice Book

Name _____

Model Equivalent Fractions

Essential Question How can you use models to find equivalent fractions?

Number and Operations—Fractions—
3.NF.3a *Also 3.NF.1, 3.NF.2a, 3.NF.2b,*
3.NF.3, 3.NF.3b, 3.NF.3c, 3.G.2
MATHEMATICAL PRACTICES
MP.4, MP.5, MP.7

Investigate

Hands On

Materials ■ sheet of paper ■ crayon or color pencil

Two or more fractions that name the same amount are called **equivalent fractions**. You can use a sheet of paper to model fractions equivalent to $\frac{1}{2}$.

A. First, fold a sheet of paper into two equal parts. Open the paper and count the parts.

There are _____ equal parts. Each part is _____ of the paper.

Shade one of the halves. Write $\frac{1}{2}$ on each of the halves.

B. Next, fold the paper in half two times. Open the paper.

Now there are _____ equal parts. Each part is

_____ of the paper.

Write $\frac{1}{4}$ on each of the fourths.

Look at the shaded parts. $\frac{1}{2} \overset{\times 2}{\underset{\times 2}{=}} \frac{2}{4}$

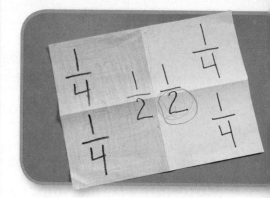

C. Last, fold the paper in half three times.

Now there are _____ equal parts. Each part is

_____ of the paper.

Write $\frac{1}{8}$ on each of the eighths.

Find the fractions equivalent to $\frac{1}{2}$ on your paper.

So, $\frac{1}{2}$, ____, and ____ are equivalent.

© Houghton Mifflin Harcourt Publishing Company

Draw Conclusions

1. Explain how many $\frac{1}{8}$ parts are equivalent to one $\frac{1}{4}$ part on your paper.

_____

_____

Math Idea

Two or more numbers that have the same value or name the same amount are *equivalent*.

2. **THINK SMARTER** What do you notice about how the numerators changed for the shaded part as you folded the paper? _____

What does this tell you about the change in the number of parts? _____

How did the denominators change for the shaded part as you folded? _____

What does this tell you about the change in the size of the parts? _____

Make Connections

Hands On

You can use a number line to find equivalent fractions.

Find a fraction equivalent to $\frac{2}{3}$.

Materials ■ fraction strips

Math Talk Mathematical Practices

Explain how the number of sixths in a distance on the number line is related to the number of thirds in the same distance.

$$\frac{0}{6} \quad \frac{1}{6} \quad \frac{2}{6} \quad \frac{3}{6} \quad \frac{4}{6} \quad \frac{5}{6} \quad \frac{6}{6}$$

$$\frac{0}{3} \quad \frac{1}{3} \quad \frac{2}{3} \quad \frac{3}{3}$$

STEP 1 Draw a point on the number line to represent the distance $\frac{2}{3}$.

_____

STEP 2 Use fraction strips to divide the number line into sixths. At the end of each strip, draw a mark on the number line and label the marks to show sixths.

_____

STEP 3 Identify the fraction that names the same point as $\frac{2}{3}$. _____

So, $\frac{2}{3} = \frac{4}{6}$.

© Houghton Mifflin Harcourt Publishing Company

Name _____

Shade the model. Then divide the pieces to find the equivalent fraction.

1.

$\frac{1 \times 2}{4 \times 2} = \frac{2}{8}$

✓2.

$\frac{2 \times 2}{3 \times 2} = \frac{4}{6}$

Use the number line to find the equivalent fraction.

3.

$$\frac{0}{6} \quad \frac{1}{6} \quad \frac{2}{6} \quad \frac{3}{6} \quad \frac{4}{6} \quad \frac{5}{6} \quad \frac{6}{6}$$

$$\frac{0}{2} \qquad \frac{1}{2} \qquad \frac{2}{2}$$

$\frac{1}{2} = \frac{}{6}$

✓4.

$$\frac{0}{8} \quad \frac{1}{8} \quad \frac{2}{8} \quad \frac{3}{8} \quad \frac{4}{8} \quad \frac{5}{8} \quad \frac{6}{8} \quad \frac{7}{8} \quad \frac{8}{8}$$

$$\frac{0}{4} \quad \frac{1}{4} \quad \frac{2}{4} \quad \frac{3}{4} \quad \frac{4}{4}$$

$\frac{3}{4} = \frac{6}{8}$

Problem Solving • Applications Real World

5. **MATHEMATICAL PRACTICE ⑥** **Explain** why $\frac{2}{2} = 1$. Write another fraction that is equal to 1. Draw to justify your answer.

_____

_____

_____

Personal Math Trainer

6. **THINK SMARTER +** For numbers 6a–6d, select True or False to tell whether the fractions are equivalent.

6a. $\frac{6}{6}$ and $\frac{3}{3}$ ● True   ○ False

6b. $\frac{4}{6}$ and $\frac{1}{3}$ ○ True   ● False

6c. $\frac{2}{3}$ and $\frac{3}{6}$ ○ True   ● False

6d. $\frac{1}{3}$ and $\frac{2}{6}$ ● True   ○ False

$$\frac{0}{6} \quad \frac{1}{6} \quad \frac{2}{6} \quad \frac{3}{6} \quad \frac{4}{6} \quad \frac{5}{6} \quad \frac{6}{6}$$

$$\frac{0}{3} \qquad \frac{1}{3} \qquad \frac{2}{3} \qquad \frac{3}{3}$$

© Houghton Mifflin Harcourt Publishing Company

Summarize

You can *summarize* the information in a problem by underlining it or writing the information needed to answer a question.

Read the problem. Underline the important information.

7. **THINK SMARTER** Mrs. Akers bought three sandwiches that were the same size. She cut the first one into thirds. She cut the second one into fourths and the third one into sixths. Marian ate 2 pieces of the first sandwich. Jason ate 2 pieces of the second sandwich. Marcos ate 3 pieces of the third sandwich. Which children ate the same amount of a sandwich? Explain.

Math on the Spot

The first sandwich was cut into _____.	The second sandwich was cut into _____.	The third sandwich was cut into _____.
Marian ate _____ pieces of the sandwich. Shade the part Marian ate.	Jason ate _____ pieces of the sandwich. Shade the part Jason ate.	Marcos ate _____ pieces of the sandwich. Shade the part Marcos ate.
Marian ate —— of the first sandwich.	Jason ate —— of the second sandwich.	Marcos ate —— of the third sandwich.

Are all the fractions equivalent? _____

Which fractions are equivalent? —— = ——

So, _____ and _____ ate the same amount of a sandwich.

FOR MORE PRACTICE:
Standards Practice Book

© Houghton Mifflin Harcourt Publishing Company

Name _____

Equivalent Fractions

Essential Question How can you use models to name
equivalent fractions?

**Number and Operations—
Fractions—3.NF.3b** *Also 3.NF.1,
3.NF.3, 3.NF.3a, 3.G.2*

MATHEMATICAL PRACTICES
MP.1, MP.3, MP.4, MP.8

🔑 Unlock the Problem 🌎

Cole brought a submarine sandwich to the picnic.
He shared the sandwich equally with 3 friends. The
sandwich was cut into eighths. What are two ways to
describe the part of the sandwich each friend ate?

Cole grouped the smaller pieces into twos. Draw circles
to show equal groups of two pieces to show what each
friend ate.

- How many people
shared the sandwich?

_____

There are 4 equal groups. Each group is $\frac{1}{4}$ of the whole
sandwich. So, each friend ate $\frac{1}{4}$ of the whole sandwich.

How many eighths did each friend eat? _____

$\frac{1}{4}$ and _____ are equivalent fractions since they both name

the _____ amount of the sandwich.

So, $\frac{1}{4}$ and _____ of the sandwich are two ways to describe
the part of the sandwich each friend ate.

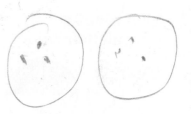

Try This! Circle equal groups. Write an equivalent
fraction for the shaded part of the whole.

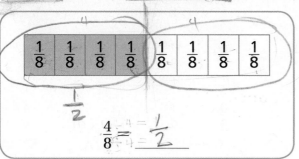

Math Talk

Mathematical Practices

Explain a different way
you could have circled
the equal groups.

© Houghton Mifflin Harcourt Publishing Company

Example Model the problem.

Heidi ate $\frac{3}{6}$ of her fruit bar. Molly ate $\frac{4}{8}$ of her fruit bar, which is the same size. Which girl ate more of her fruit bar?

Shade $\frac{3}{6}$ of Heidi's fruit bar and $\frac{4}{8}$ of Molly's fruit bar.

- Is $\frac{3}{6}$ greater than, less than, or equal to $\frac{4}{8}$? _____

So, both girls ate the _____ amount.

Heidi

$\frac{1}{6}$	$\frac{1}{6}$	$\frac{1}{6}$
$\frac{1}{6}$	$\frac{1}{6}$	$\frac{1}{6}$

Molly

$\frac{1}{8}$	$\frac{1}{8}$	$\frac{1}{8}$	$\frac{1}{8}$
$\frac{1}{8}$	$\frac{1}{8}$	$\frac{1}{8}$	$\frac{1}{8}$

Try This! Each shape is 1 whole. Write an equivalent fraction for the shaded part of the models.

$$\frac{6}{3} = \frac{\boxed{}}{6}$$

Share and Show

Math Talk **Mathematical Practices**

Explain why both fractions name the same amount.

1. Each shape is 1 whole. Use the model to find the equivalent fraction.

$\frac{2}{4}$

$\frac{2}{4} = \frac{4}{2}$

Each shape is 1 whole. Shade the model to find the equivalent fraction.

2.

$$\frac{2}{4} = \frac{4}{8}$$

3.

$$\frac{12}{6} = \frac{6}{3}$$

4. Andy swam $\frac{8}{8}$ mile in a race. Use the number line to find a fraction that is equivalent to $\frac{8}{8}$.

$$\frac{8}{8} = \frac{4}{4}$$

$\frac{0}{8}$ $\frac{1}{8}$ $\frac{2}{8}$ $\frac{3}{8}$ $\frac{4}{8}$ $\frac{5}{8}$ $\frac{6}{8}$ $\frac{7}{8}$ $\frac{8}{8}$

$\frac{0}{4}$ $\frac{1}{4}$ $\frac{2}{4}$ $\frac{3}{4}$ $\frac{4}{4}$

© Houghton Mifflin Harcourt Publishing Company

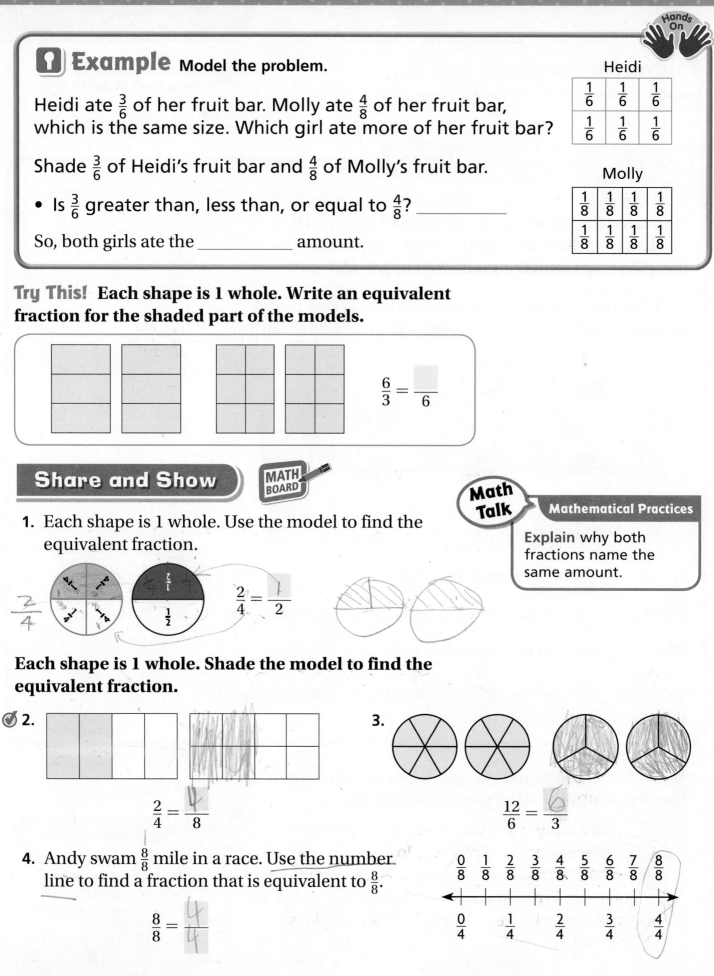

Name _____

Circle equal groups to find the equivalent fraction.

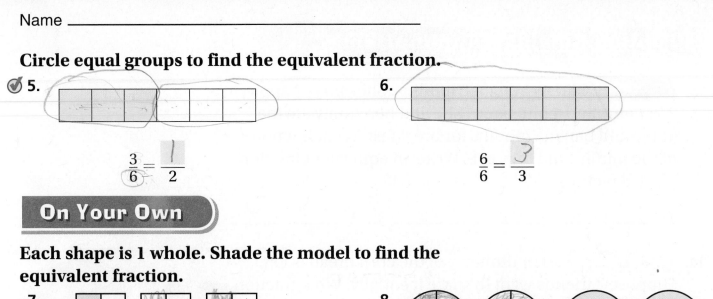

5.

$$\frac{3}{6} = \frac{1}{2}$$

6.

$$\frac{6}{6} = \frac{3}{3}$$

On Your Own

Each shape is 1 whole. Shade the model to find the equivalent fraction.

7.

$$\frac{1}{2} = \frac{2}{4} = \frac{4}{8}$$

8.

$$\frac{8}{4} = \frac{4}{2}$$

Circle equal groups to find the equivalent fraction.

9.

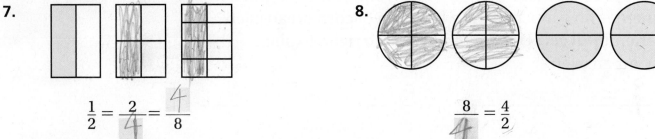

$$\frac{6}{8} = \frac{3}{4}$$

10.

$$\frac{2}{6} = \frac{1}{3}$$

11. Write the fraction that names the shaded part of each circle.

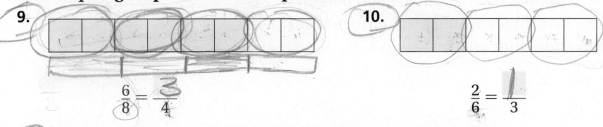

$$\frac{2}{6} \qquad \frac{1}{4} \qquad \frac{1}{3} \qquad \frac{2}{4} \qquad \frac{2}{8}$$

Which pairs of fractions are equivalent? _____

12. **MATHEMATICAL PRACTICE ③ Apply** Matt cut his small pizza into 6 equal pieces and ate 4 of them. Josh cut his small pizza, which is the same size, into 3 equal pieces and ate 2 of them. Write fractions for the amount they each ate. Are the fractions equivalent? Draw to explain.

_____

© Houghton Mifflin Harcourt Publishing Company

Problem Solving • Applications Real World

13. **GO DEEPER** Christy bought 8 muffins. She chose 2 apple, 2 banana, and 4 blueberry. She and her family ate the apple and banana muffins for breakfast. What fraction of the muffins did they eat? Write an equivalent fraction. Draw a picture.

_____

14. **THINK SMARTER** After dinner, $\frac{2}{3}$ of the corn bread is left. Suppose 4 friends want to share it equally. What fraction names how much of the whole pan of corn bread each friend will get? Use the model on the right. Explain your answer.

_____

_____

15. There are 16 people having lunch. Each person wants $\frac{1}{4}$ of a pizza. How many whole pizzas are needed? Draw a picture to show your answer.

_____

16. Lucy has 5 oatmeal bars, each cut in half. What fraction names all of the oatmeal bar halves? $\frac{}{2}$

   What if Lucy cuts each part of the oatmeal bar into 2 equal pieces to share with friends? What fraction names all of the oatmeal bar pieces now? $\frac{}{4}$

   $\frac{}{2}$ and $\frac{}{4}$ are equivalent fractions.

17. **THINK SMARTER** Mr. Peters made a pizza. There is $\frac{4}{8}$ of the pizza left over. Select the fraction that are equivalent to the part of the pizza that is left over. Mark all that apply.

   Ⓐ $\frac{5}{8}$ Ⓑ $\frac{3}{4}$ Ⓒ $\frac{2}{4}$ Ⓓ $\frac{1}{2}$

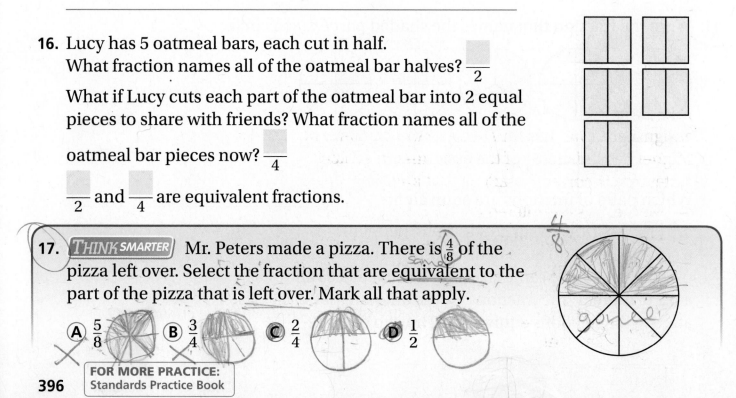

FOR MORE PRACTICE:
Standards Practice Book

396

© Houghton Mifflin Harcourt Publishing Company

Name _____

1. Alexa and Rose read books that have the same number of pages. Alexa's book is divided into 8 equal chapters. Rose's book is divided into 6 equal chapters. Each girl has read 3 chapters of her book.

   Write a fraction to describe what part of the book each girl read. Then tell who read more pages. Explain.

   _____

   _____

   _____

2. David, Maria, and Simone are shading same-sized index cards for a science project. David shaded $\frac{2}{4}$ of his index card. Maria shaded $\frac{2}{8}$ of her index card and Simone shaded $\frac{2}{6}$ of her index card.

   For 2a–2d, choose Yes or No to indicate whether the comparisons are correct.

   2a. $\frac{2}{4} > \frac{2}{8}$ ○ Yes   ○ No

   2b. $\frac{2}{8} > \frac{2}{6}$ ○ Yes   ○ No

   2c. $\frac{2}{6} < \frac{2}{4}$ ○ Yes   ○ No

   2d. $\frac{2}{8} = \frac{2}{4}$ ○ Yes   ○ No

3. Dan and Miguel are working on the same homework assignment. Dan has finished $\frac{1}{4}$ of the assignment. Miguel has finished $\frac{3}{4}$ of the assignment. Which statement is correct? Mark all that apply.

   Ⓐ Miguel has completed the entire assignment.

   Ⓑ Dan has not completed the entire assignment.

   Ⓒ Miguel has finished more of the assignment than Dan.

   Ⓓ Dan and Miguel have completed equal parts of the assignment.

© Houghton Mifflin Harcourt Publishing Company

 Assessment Options
Chapter Test

4. Bryan cut two peaches that were the same size for lunch. He cut one peach into fourths and the other into sixths. Bryan ate $\frac{3}{4}$ of the first peach. His brother ate $\frac{5}{6}$ of the second peach. Who ate more peach? Explain the strategy you used to solve the problem.

_____

_____

_____

5. A nature center offers 2 guided walks. The morning walk is $\frac{2}{3}$ mile. The evening walk is $\frac{3}{6}$ mile. Which walk is shorter? Explain how you can use the model to find the answer.

$\frac{1}{3}$		$\frac{1}{3}$		$\frac{1}{3}$	
$\frac{1}{6}$	$\frac{1}{6}$	$\frac{1}{6}$	$\frac{1}{6}$	$\frac{1}{6}$	$\frac{1}{6}$

_____

_____

6. Chun lives $\frac{3}{8}$ mile from school. Gail lives $\frac{5}{8}$ mile from school.

Use the fractions and symbols to show which distance is longer.

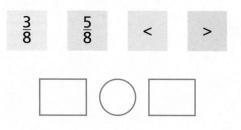

© Houghton Mifflin Harcourt Publishing Company

398

Name _____

7. Mrs. Reed baked four pans of lasagna for a family party.
Use the rectangles to represent the pans.

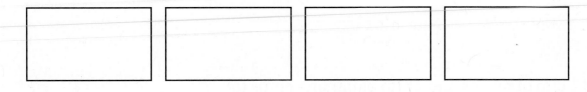

Part A

Draw lines to show how Mrs. Reed could cut one pan of
lasagna into thirds, one into fourths, one into sixths, and
one into eighths.

Part B

At the end of the dinner, equivalent amounts of lasagna
in two pans were left. Use the models to show the
lasagna that might have been left over. Write two pairs
of equivalent fractions to represent the models.

_____

8. Tom rode his horse for $\frac{4}{6}$ mile. Liz rode her horse for
an equal distance. What is an equivalent fraction that
describes how far Liz rode? Use the models to show
your work.

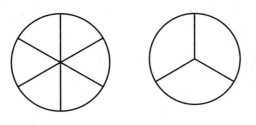

_____

9. Avery prepares 2 equal-size oranges for the bats at the
zoo. One dish has $\frac{3}{8}$ of an orange. Another dish has $\frac{1}{4}$
of an orange. Which dish has more orange? Show
your work.

_____

© Houghton Mifflin Harcourt Publishing Company

10. Jenna painted $\frac{1}{8}$ of one side of a fence. Mark painted $\frac{1}{6}$ of the other side of the same fence. Use $>$, $=$, or $<$ to compare the parts that they painted.

_____

11. Bill used $\frac{1}{3}$ cup of raisins and $\frac{2}{3}$ cup of banana chips to make a snack.

For 11a–11d, select True or False for each comparison.

11a. $\frac{1}{3} > \frac{2}{3}$ ○ True   ○ False

11b. $\frac{2}{3} = \frac{1}{3}$ ○ True   ○ False

11c. $\frac{1}{3} < \frac{2}{3}$ ○ True   ○ False

11d. $\frac{2}{3} > \frac{1}{3}$ ○ True   ○ False

12. Jorge, Lynne, and Crosby meet at the playground. Jorge lives $\frac{5}{6}$ mile from the playground. Lynne lives $\frac{4}{6}$ mile from the playground. Crosby lives $\frac{7}{8}$ mile from the playground.

Part A

Who lives closer to the playground, Jorge or Lynne? Explain how you know.

_____

_____

_____

Part B

Who lives closer to the playground, Jorge or Crosby? Explain how you know.

_____

_____

_____

© Houghton Mifflin Harcourt Publishing Company

13. Ming needs $\frac{1}{2}$ pint of red paint for an art project. He has 6 jars that have the following amounts of red paint in them. He wants to use only 1 jar of paint. Mark all of the jars of paints that Ming could use.

(A) $\frac{2}{3}$ pint

(D) $\frac{3}{4}$ pint

(B) $\frac{1}{4}$ pint

(E) $\frac{3}{8}$ pint

(C) $\frac{4}{6}$ pint

(F) $\frac{2}{6}$ pint

14. There are 12 people having lunch. Each person wants $\frac{1}{3}$ of a sub sandwich. How many whole sub sandwiches are needed? Use the models to show your answer.

_____ sub sandwiches

15. Mavis mixed $\frac{2}{4}$ quart of apple juice with $\frac{1}{2}$ quart of cranberry juice. Compare the fractions. Choose the symbol that makes the statement true.

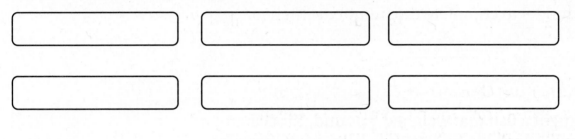

16. Pat has three pieces of fabric that measure $\frac{3}{6}$, $\frac{5}{6}$, and $\frac{2}{6}$ yards long. Write the lengths in order from least to greatest.

_____

© Houghton Mifflin Harcourt Publishing Company

17. Cora measures the heights of three plants. Draw a line to match each height on the left to the word on the right that describes its place in the order of heights.

$\frac{4}{6}$ foot •   • least

$\frac{4}{4}$ foot •   • between

$\frac{4}{8}$ foot •   • greatest

18. Danielle drew a model to show equivalent fractions.

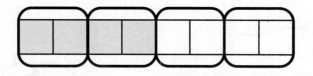

Use the model to complete the number sentence.

$\frac{1}{2} = $ _____ $=$ _____

19. Floyd caught a fish that weighed $\frac{2}{3}$ pound. Kira caught a fish that weighed $\frac{7}{8}$ pound. Whose fish weighed more? Explain the strategy you used to solve the problem.

_____

_____

_____

_____

20. Sam went for a ride on a sailboat. The ride lasted $\frac{3}{4}$ hour.

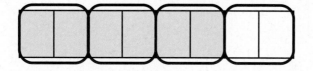

What fraction is equivalent to $\frac{3}{4}$?

_____

© Houghton Mifflin Harcourt Publishing Company

© Houghton Mifflin Harcourt Publishing Company • Image Credits: (b) ©Mischa Photo Ltd/Getty Images

CRITICAL AREA Developing understanding of the structure of rectangular arrays and of area

Critical Area Measurement

Measurement tools and data are used to design and build a safe and enjoyable playground.

Plan a Playground

Is there a playground at your school, in your neighborhood, or in a nearby park? Playgrounds provide a fun and safe outdoor space for you to climb, swing, slide, and play.

Important Facts

Playground Features

- Bench
- Jungle Gym
- Playhouse
- Sandbox
- Seesaw
- Slide
- Swing Set
- Water Fountain

Get Started

Suppose you want to help plan a playground for a block in your neighborhood.

- Draw a large rectangle on the grid paper to show a fence around your playground. Find the distance around your playground by counting the number of units on each side. Record the distance.

- Use the Important Facts to help you decide on features to have in your playground. Shade parts of your playground to show each feature's location. Then find the number of unit squares the feature covers and record it on your plan.

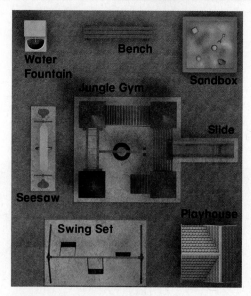

▲ This drawing shows a plan for a playground.

Completed by _____

© Houghton Mifflin Harcourt Publishing Company

Time, Length, Liquid Volume, and Mass

Show What You Know ✓

Check your understanding of important skills.

Name _____

▶ **Time to the Half Hour** Read the clock. Write the time.

1.  _____

2.  _____

▶ **Skip Count by Fives**

Skip count by fives. Write the missing numbers.

3. 5, 10, 15, ____, 25, ____, 35

4. 55, 60, ____, 70, ____, ____, 85

▶ **Inches** Use a ruler to measure the length to the nearest inch.

5.

6.

about _____ inches

about _____ inch

You can look at the time the sun rises and sets to find the amount of daylight each day. The table shows the time the sun rose and set from January 10 to January 14 in Philadelphia, Pennsylvania. Be a Math Detective to find which day had the least daylight and which day had the most daylight.

Sunrise and Sunset Times

Date	Sunrise	Sunset
Jan 10	7:22 A.M.	4:55 P.M.
Jan 11	7:22 A.M.	4:56 P.M.
Jan 12	7:22 A.M.	4:57 P.M.
Jan 13	7:21 A.M.	4:58 P.M.
Jan 14	7:21 A.M.	4:59 P.M.

© Houghton Mifflin Harcourt Publishing Company • Image Credits: (br) ©Ken Welsh/Alamy

 Personal Math Trainer
Online Assessment and Intervention

▶ **Visualize It** •

Complete the graphic organizer by using the
words with a ✓. Write the words in order from the
greatest to the least length of time.

_____

_____

_____

_____

_____

Review Words

analog clock

digital clock

fourth

half

✓ half hour

✓ hour (hr)

inch (in.)

✓ quarter hour

Preview Words

A.M.

elapsed time

gram (g)

kilogram (kg)

liquid volume

liter (L)

mass

midnight

✓ minute (min)

noon

P.M.

▶ **Understand Vocabulary** •

Write the word that answers the riddle.

1. I am written with times after midnight and
   before noon.   _____

2. I am the time when it is 12:00 in the daytime.   _____

3. I am the amount of liquid in a container.   _____

4. I am the time that passes from the start of
   an activity to the end of that activity.   _____

5. I am the amount of matter in an object.   _____

© Houghton Mifflin Harcourt Publishing Company

 GO DIGITAL   • Interactive Student Edition
• Multimedia eGlossary

Time to the Minute

Essential Question How can you tell time to the nearest minute?

Measurement and Data—3.MD.1

MATHEMATICAL PRACTICES
MP.2, MP.3, MP.6

🔑 Unlock the Problem Real World

Groundhog Day is February 2. People say that if a groundhog can see its shadow on that morning, winter will last another 6 weeks. The clock shows the time when the groundhog saw its shadow. What time was it?

- Underline the question.
- Where will you look to find the time?

_____

🔒 Example

Look at the time on this clock face.

- What does the hour hand tell you?

_____

- What does the minute hand tell you?

_____

In 1 **minute**, the minute hand moves from one mark to the next on a clock. It takes 5 minutes for the minute hand to move from one number to the next on a clock.

You can count on by fives to tell time to five minutes. Count zero at the 12.

0, 5, 10, 15, _____, _____, _____, _____

So, the groundhog saw its shadow at _____.

Write: 7:35

Read:

- seven _____

- thirty-five minutes after _____

Math Talk **Mathematical Practices**

How does skip counting by fives help you tell the time when the minute hand points to a number?

- Is 7:35 a reasonable answer? Explain. _____

© Houghton Mifflin Harcourt Publishing Company

Time to the Minute

Count by fives and ones to help you.

⬆️ One Way Find minutes after the hour.

Look at the time on this clock face.

- What does the hour hand tell you?

_____

- What does the minute hand tell you?

_____

Count on by fives and ones from the 12 on the clock to where the minute hand is pointing. Write the missing counting numbers next to the clock.

When a clock shows 30 or fewer minutes after the hour, you can read the time as a number of minutes *after* the hour.

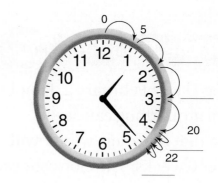

Write: _____

Read:

- twenty-three minutes after _____

- one _____

⬇️ Another Way Find minutes before the hour.

Look at the time on this clock face.

- What does the hour hand tell you?

_____

- What does the minute hand tell you?

_____

Now count by fives and ones from the 12 on the clock back to where the minute hand is pointing. Write the missing counting numbers next to the clock.

When a clock shows 31 or more minutes after the hour, you can read the time as a number of minutes *before* the next hour.

Write: 2:43

Read:

- seventeen _____ before three

- two _____

> ⚠️ **ERROR Alert**
>
> Remember that time *after* the hour uses the previous hour, and time *before* the hour uses the next hour.

© Houghton Mifflin Harcourt Publishing Company

Name _____

1. How would you use counting and the minute hand to find the time shown on this clock? Write the time.

_____

Write the time. Write one way you can read the time.

2.

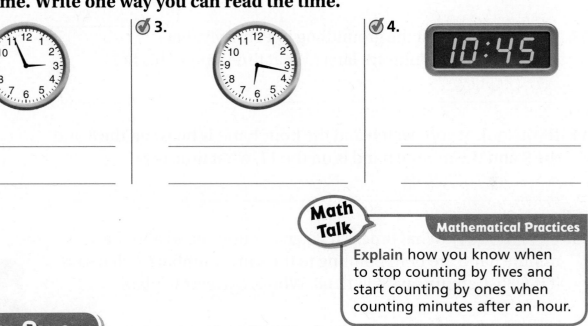

✓ 3.

✓ 4.

10:45

_____   _____   _____

_____   _____   _____

Math Talk **Mathematical Practices**

Explain how you know when to stop counting by fives and start counting by ones when counting minutes after an hour.

 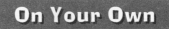
Write the time. Write one way you can read the time.

5.

3:12

6.

7.

_____   _____   _____

_____   _____   _____

MATHEMATICAL PRACTICE ② **Represent a Problem Write the time another way.**

8. 34 minutes after 5

9. 11 minutes before 6

_____   _____

10. 22 minutes after 11

11. 5 minutes before 12

_____   _____

© Houghton Mifflin Harcourt Publishing Company

Problem Solving • Applications Real World

Use the clocks for 12–13.

Time of Day the Groundhog Saw Its Shadow

NY   PA

12. How many minutes later in the day did the groundhog in Pennsylvania see its shadow than the groundhog in New York?

_____

13. **GO DEEPER** What if the groundhog in Pennsylvania saw its shadow 5 minutes later? What time would this be?

_____

14. If you look at your watch and the hour hand is between the 8 and the 9 and the minute hand is on the 11, what time is it?

_____

15. **THINK SMARTER** What time is it when the hour hand and the minute hand are both pointing to the same number? Aiden says it is 6:30. Camilla says it is 12:00. Who is correct? Explain.

_____

_____

Math on the Spot

16. **MATHEMATICAL PRACTICE ③** **Verify the Reasoning of Others** Lucy said the time is 4:46 on her digital watch. Explain where the hands on an analog clock are pointing when it is 4:46.

_____

_____

17. **THINK SMARTER** Write the time that is shown on the clock. Then write the time another way.

_____

FOR MORE PRACTICE:
Standards Practice Book

© Houghton Mifflin Harcourt Publishing Company

Name _____

A.M. and P.M.

Essential Question How can you tell when to use A.M. and P.M. with time?

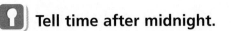

Measurement and Data—
3.MD.1
MATHEMATICAL PRACTICES
MP.1, MP.2, MP.4

? Unlock the Problem Real World

Lauren's family is going hiking tomorrow at 7:00. How should Lauren write the time to show that they are going in the morning, not in the evening?

You can use a number line to show the sequence or order of events. It can help you understand the number of hours in a day.

Think: The distance from one mark to the next mark represents one hour.

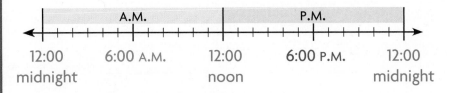

12:00 midnight   6:00 A.M.   12:00 noon   6:00 P.M.   12:00 midnight

• Circle the helpful information that tells about the hiking time.

• What do you need to find?

_____

_____

🔑 **Tell time after midnight.**

Midnight is 12:00 at night.

The times after midnight and before noon are written with **A.M.**

7:00 in the morning is written as

7:00 _____

After Midnight and Before Noon

A.M.

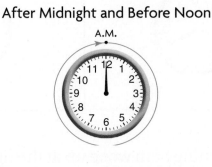

So, Lauren should write the hiking time as 7:00 _____

• Find the mark that shows 7:00 A.M. on the number line above. Circle the mark.

Math Talk   **Mathematical Practices**

How are the number line on this page and the clock face alike? How are they different?

© Houghton Mifflin Harcourt Publishing Company • Image Credits: ©Michael Halbersta ©Steve Mason/Photodisc/Getty Images

Chapter 10   **411**

🔑 **Tell time after noon.**

Callie's family is going for a canoe ride at 3:00 in the afternoon. How should Callie write the time?

Noon is 12:00 in the daytime.

The times after noon and before midnight are written with **P.M.**

3:00 in the afternoon is written as 3:00 _____

After Noon and Before Midnight

P.M.

So, Callie should write the time as 3:00 _____

Share and Show — MATH BOARD

1. Name two things you do in the A.M. hours.
   Name two things you do in the P.M. hours.

_____

_____

Write the time for the activity. Use A.M. or P.M.

2. ride a bicycle

3. make a sandwich

4. get ready for bed

8:12

_____   _____   _____

5. This morning Sam woke up at the time shown on this

   clock. Write the time using A.M. or P.M. _____

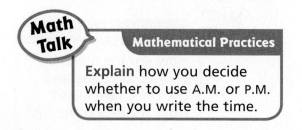

Math Talk

Mathematical Practices

Explain how you decide whether to use A.M. or P.M. when you write the time.

© Houghton Mifflin Harcourt Publishing Company • Image Credits: (c) ©Ariel Skelley/Blend Images/Getty Images

Name _____

On Your Own

Write the time for the activity. Use A.M. or P.M.

6. eat breakfast

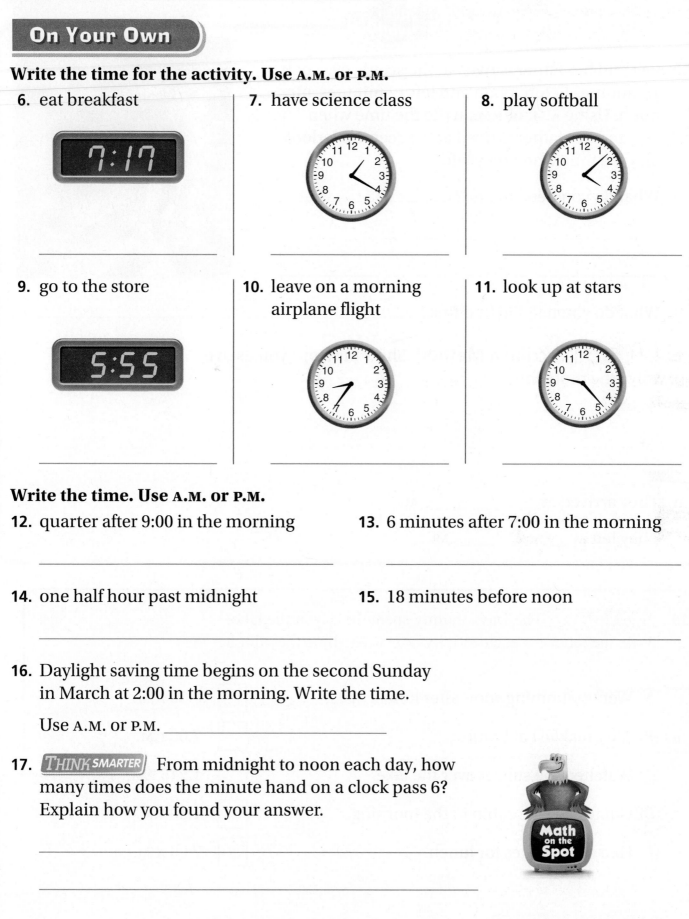

7:17

_____

7. have science class

_____

8. play softball

_____

9. go to the store

5:55

_____

10. leave on a morning airplane flight

_____

11. look up at stars

_____

Write the time. Use A.M. or P.M.

12. quarter after 9:00 in the morning

_____

13. 6 minutes after 7:00 in the morning

_____

14. one half hour past midnight

_____

15. 18 minutes before noon

_____

16. Daylight saving time begins on the second Sunday in March at 2:00 in the morning. Write the time.

Use A.M. or P.M. _____

17. THINK SMARTER From midnight to noon each day, how many times does the minute hand on a clock pass 6? Explain how you found your answer.

Math on the Spot

_____

_____

© Houghton Mifflin Harcourt Publishing Company

![key] Unlock the Problem (Real World)

18. Lea and her father arrived at the scenic overlook 15 minutes before noon and left 12 minutes after noon. Using A.M. or P.M., write the time when Lea and her father arrived at the scenic overlook and the time when they left.

a. What do you need to find? _____

_____

_____

b. What do you need to find first? _____

c. **MATHEMATICAL PRACTICE ⑥** **Describe a Method** Show the steps you used to solve the problem.

d. They arrived at _____ _____.M.

They left at _____ _____.M.

---

19. **THINK SMARTER** The Davis family spent the day at the lake. Write the letter for each activity next to the time they did it.

(A) Went swimming soon after lunch.   ☐ 9:50 A.M.

(B) Ate breakfast at home.   ☐ 7:00 P.M.

(C) Watched the sunset over the lake.   ☐ 12:15 P.M.

(D) Got to the lake cabin in the morning.   ☐ 1:30 P.M.

(E) Had sandwiches for lunch.   ☐ 7:00 A.M.

© Houghton Mifflin Harcourt Publishing Company • Image Credits: ©Andre Jenny/Alamy Images

Measure Time Intervals

Essential Question How can you measure elapsed time in minutes?

Measurement and Data—3.MD.1

MATHEMATICAL PRACTICES
MP.1, MP.3, MP.4, MP.8

Unlock the Problem Real World

Alicia and her family visited the Kennedy Space Center. They watched a movie that began at 4:10 P.M. and ended at 4:53 P.M. How long did the movie last?

- Circle the times the movie began and ended.
- Underline the question.

To find **elapsed time**, find the amount of time that passes from the start of an activity to the end of the activity.

One Way Use a number line.

STEP 1 Find the time on the number line that the movie began.

STEP 2 Count on to the ending time, 4:53. Count on by tens for each 10 minutes. Count on by ones for each minute. Write the times below the number line.

STEP 3 Draw the jumps on the number line to show the minutes from 4:10 to 4:53. Record the minutes. Then add them.

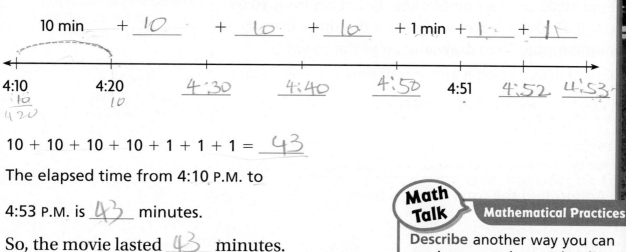

10 min + 10 + 10 + 10 + 1 min + 1 + 1

4:10   4:20   4:30   4:40   4:50   4:51   4:52   4:53
 10   10

10 + 10 + 10 + 10 + 1 + 1 + 1 = 43

The elapsed time from 4:10 P.M. to 4:53 P.M. is 43 minutes.

So, the movie lasted 43 minutes.

Math Talk **Mathematical Practices**

Describe another way you can use jumps on the number line to find the elapsed time from 4:10 P.M. to 4:53 P.M.

© Houghton Mifflin Harcourt Publishing Company • Image Credits: ©Richard Broadwell/Alamy Images

🔑 Other Ways

Start time: 4:10 P.M. End time: 4:53 P.M.

Ⓐ Use an analog clock.

STEP 1 Find the starting time on the clock.

STEP 2 Count the minutes by counting on by fives and ones to 4:53 P.M. Write the missing counting numbers next to the clock.

So, the elapsed time is _____ minutes.

Ⓑ Use subtraction.

STEP 1 Write the ending time. Then write the starting time so that the hours and minutes line up.

STEP 2 The hours are the same, so subtract the minutes.

$$4 : \boxed{} \quad \leftarrow \text{end time}$$
$$-4 : \boxed{} \quad \leftarrow \text{start time}$$
$$\overline{} \quad \leftarrow \text{elapsed time}$$

Try This! Find the elapsed time in minutes two ways.

Start time: 10:05 A.M. End time: 10:30 A.M.

Ⓐ Use a number line.

STEP 1 Find 10:05 on the number line. Count on from 10:05 to 10:30. Draw marks and record the times on the number line. Then draw and label the jumps.

Think: Count on using longer amounts of time that make sense.

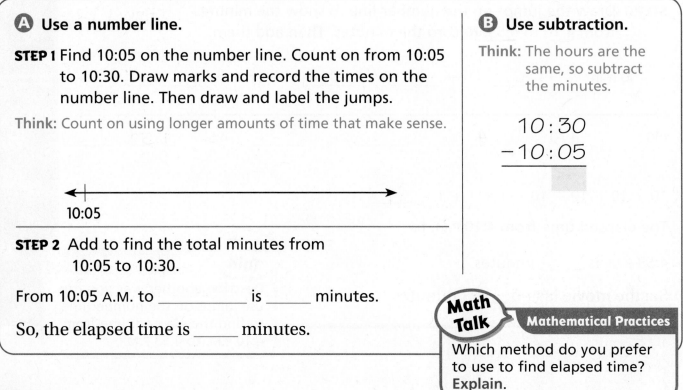

10:05

STEP 2 Add to find the total minutes from 10:05 to 10:30.

From 10:05 A.M. to _____ is _____ minutes.

So, the elapsed time is _____ minutes.

Ⓑ Use subtraction.

Think: The hours are the same, so subtract the minutes.

$$10 : 30$$
$$-10 : 05$$
$$\overline{\boxed{}}$$

Math Talk

Mathematical Practices

Which method do you prefer to use to find elapsed time? Explain.

© Houghton Mifflin Harcourt Publishing Company

Name _____

1. Use the number line to find the elapsed time

from 1:15 P.M. to 1:40 P.M. _____

1:15

Find the elapsed time.

☑ 2. Start: 11:35 A.M.   End: 11:54 A.M.

☑ 3. Start: 4:20 P.M.   End: 5:00 P.M.

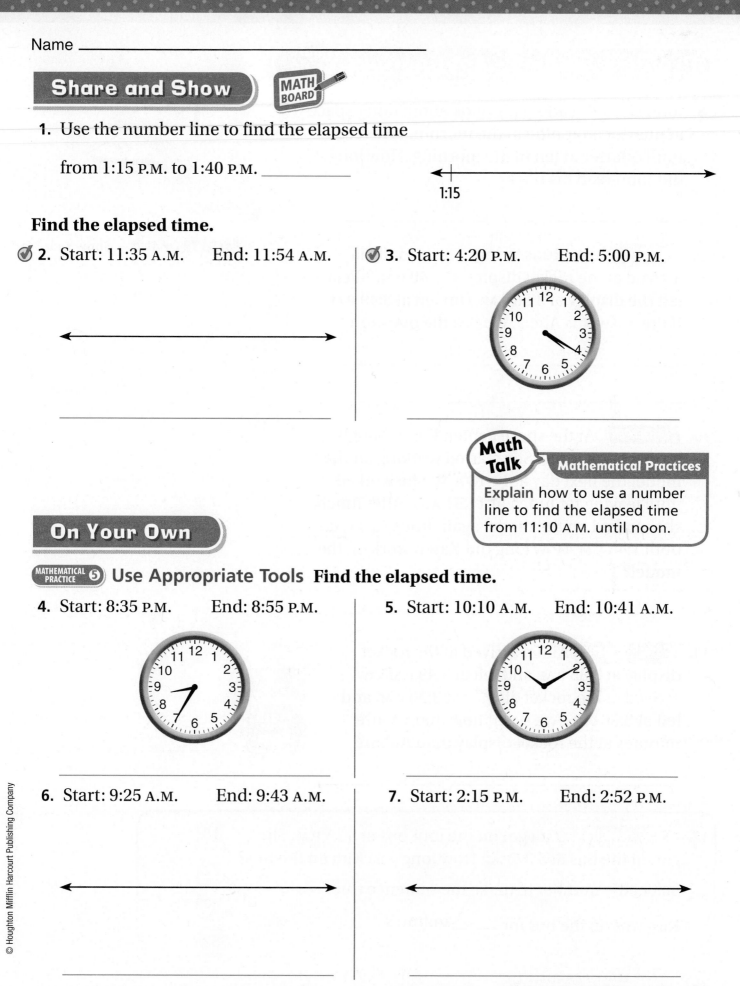

_____

_____

Math Talk **Mathematical Practices**

Explain how to use a number line to find the elapsed time from 11:10 A.M. until noon.

On Your Own

MATHEMATICAL PRACTICE ⑤ **Use Appropriate Tools** **Find the elapsed time.**

4. Start: 8:35 P.M.   End: 8:55 P.M.

5. Start: 10:10 A.M.   End: 10:41 A.M.

_____

_____

6. Start: 9:25 A.M.   End: 9:43 A.M.

7. Start: 2:15 P.M.   End: 2:52 P.M.

_____

_____

© Houghton Mifflin Harcourt Publishing Company

Problem Solving • Applications

8. John started reading his book about outer space at quarter after nine in the morning. He read until quarter to ten in the morning. How long did John read his book?

_____

WRITE ▸Math • Show Your Work

9. **MATHEMATICAL PRACTICE ②** **Use Reasoning** Tim and Alicia arrived at the rocket display at 3:40 P.M. Alicia left the display at 3:56 P.M. Tim left at 3:49 P.M. If the answer is Alicia, what is the question?

_____

_____

10. **GO DEEPER** At the space center, Karen bought a model of a shuttle. She started working on the model the next day at 11:13 A.M. She worked until leaving for lunch at 11:51 A.M. After lunch, she worked on the model again from 1:29 P.M. until 1:48 P.M. How long did Karen work on the model?

_____

11. **THINK SMARTER** Aiden arrived at the rocket display at 3:35 P.M. and left at 3:49 P.M. Ava arrived at the rocket display at 3:30 P.M. and left at 3:56 P.M. Ava spent how many more minutes at the rocket display than Aiden?

_____

12. **THINK SMARTER** Kira got on the tour bus at 5:15 P.M. She got off the bus at 5:37 P.M. How long was Kira on the bus? Select the number to make the sentence true.

Kira was on the bus for _____ minutes.

| 15 |
| 22 |
| 37 |
| 52 |

© Houghton Mifflin Harcourt Publishing Company

Name _____

Use Time Intervals

Essential Question How can you find a starting time or an ending time when you know the elapsed time?

Measurement and Data—
3.MD.1 *Also 3.NBT.2*
MATHEMATICAL PRACTICES
MP.1, MP.3, MP.4, MP.8

Unlock the Problem · Real World

Javier begins working on his oceans project at 1:30 P.M. He spends 42 minutes painting a model of Earth and labeling the oceans. At what time does Javier finish working on his project?

- Circle the information you need.
- What time do you need to find?

_____

_____

One Way Use a number line to find the ending time.

STEP 1 Find the time on the number line when Javier started working on the project.

STEP 2 Count forward on the number line to add the elapsed time. Draw and label the jumps to show the minutes.

Think: I can break apart 42 minutes into shorter amounts of time.

STEP 3 Write the times below the number line.

Math Talk Mathematical Practices

Explain how you decided what size jumps to make on the number line.

```
      5  5  5  5  5  5  5  5 1 1
   ◄───∩──∩──∩──∩──∩──∩──∩──∩─m──►
1:30 P.M. 1:35 1:40 1:45 1:50 1:55 2:00 2:05 2:10 2:11 2:12
```

The jumps end at _____

So, Javier finishes working on his project at _~~2:12 pm~~_

Another Way Use a clock to find the ending time.

STEP 1 Find the starting time on the clock.

STEP 2 Count on by fives and ones for the elapsed time of 42 minutes. Write the missing counting numbers next to the clock.

So, the ending time is _____

© Houghton Mifflin Harcourt Publishing Company

Find Starting Times

Whitney went swimming in the ocean for
25 minutes. She finished swimming at 11:15 A.M.
At what time did Whitney start swimming?

One Way Use a number line to find the starting time.

STEP 1 Find the time on the number line when Whitney finished
swimming in the ocean.

STEP 2 Count back on the number line to subtract the elapsed
time. Draw and label the jumps to show the minutes.

STEP 3 Write the times below the number line.

← ─── |
                                       11:15 A.M.

You jumped back to _____

So, Whitney started swimming at _____

> **Math Talk** **Mathematical Practices**
>
> **Explain** how the problem on this page is different from the problem on page 419.

Another Way Use a clock to find the starting time.

STEP 1 Find the ending time on the clock.

STEP 2 Count back by fives for the elapsed time of 25 minutes.
Write the missing counting numbers next to the clock.

So, the starting time is _____

> **Math Talk** **Mathematical Practices**
>
> **Explain** how to find the starting time when you know the ending time and the elapsed time.

1. Use the number line to find the starting time if the

   elapsed time is 35 minutes. _____

← ─────────────────────────────────────── |
                                   5:10 P.M.

© Houghton Mifflin Harcourt Publishing Company

Name _____

Find the ending time.

2. Starting time: 1:40 P.M.
   Elapsed time: 33 minutes

_____

3. Starting time: 9:55 A.M.
   Elapsed time: 27 minutes

_____

On Your Own

Find the starting time.

4. Ending time: 3:05 P.M.
   Elapsed time: 40 minutes

_____

5. Ending time: 8:06 A.M.
   Elapsed time: 16 minutes

_____

Problem Solving • Applications Real World

6. **THINK SMARTER** Suzi began fishing at 10:30 A.M.
   and fished until 11:10 A.M. James finished fishing
   at 11:45 A.M. He fished for the same length of time
   as Suzi. At what time did James start fishing? **Explain.**

   Math on the Spot

_____

_____

© Houghton Mifflin Harcourt Publishing Company

Personal Math Trainer

7. THINK SMARTER + Dante's surfing lesson began at 2:35 P.M. His lesson lasted 45 minutes.

Draw hands on the clock to show the time Dante's surfing lesson ended.

Connect to Science

Tides

If you have ever been to the beach, you have seen the water rise and fall along the shore every day. This change in water level is called the tide. Ocean tides are mostly caused by the pull of the moon and the sun's gravity. High tide is when the water is at its highest level. Low tide is when the water is at its lowest level. In most places on Earth, high tide and low tide each occur about twice a day.

Use the table for 8–9.

8. GO DEEPER The first morning, Courtney walked on the beach for 20 minutes. She finished her walk 30 minutes before high tide. At what time did Courtney start her walk?

_____

9. MATHEMATICAL PRACTICE ② Use Reasoning The third afternoon, Courtney started collecting shells at low tide. She collected shells for 35 minutes. At what time did Courtney finish collecting shells?

_____

Tide Times Atlantic City, NJ		
	Low Tide	High Tide
Day 1	2:12 A.M.	9:00 A.M.
	2:54 P.M.	9:00 P.M.
Day 2	3:06 A.M.	9:36 A.M.
	3:36 P.M.	9:54 P.M.
Day 3	4:00 A.M.	10:12 A.M.
	4:30 P.M.	10:36 P.M.

© Houghton Mifflin Harcourt Publishing Company • Image Credits: ©thenakedsnail/Getty Images

Name _____

Problem Solving • Time Intervals

Essential Question How can you use the strategy *draw a diagram* to solve problems about time?

**Measurement and Data—
3.MD.1** *Also 3.OA.8, 3.NBT.2*

MATHEMATICAL PRACTICES
MP.1, MP.3, MP.4, MP.6

🔑 Unlock the Problem 🌎 Real World

Zach and his family are going to New York City. Their airplane leaves at 9:15 A.M. They need to arrive at the airport 60 minutes before their flight. It takes 15 minutes to get to the airport. The family needs 30 minutes to get ready to leave. At what time should Zach's family start getting ready?

Read the Problem

What do I need to find?	**What information do I need to use?**	**How will I use the information?**
I need to find what _____ Zach's family should start _____.	the time the _____ leaves; the time the family needs to arrive at the _____ ; the time it takes to get to the _____ ; and the time the family needs to _____	I will use a number line to find the answer.

Solve the Problem

- Find 9:15 A.M. on the number line. Draw the jumps to show the time.

- Count back _____ minutes for the time they need to arrive at the airport.

$$\longleftarrow\underset{\text{9:15 A.M.}}{\overset{\displaystyle|}{}}\longrightarrow$$

- Count back _____ minutes for the time to get to the airport.

- Count back _____ minutes for the time to get ready.

So, Zach's family should start getting ready at _____ _____.M.

Math Talk **Mathematical Practices**

How can you check your answer by starting with the time the family starts getting ready?

© Houghton Mifflin Harcourt Publishing Company • Image Credits: © PhotoDisc/Getty Images

1 Try Another Problem

Bradley gets out of school at 2:45 P.M. It takes him 10 minutes to walk home. Then he spends 10 minutes eating a snack. He spends 8 minutes putting on his soccer uniform. It takes 20 minutes for Bradley's father to drive him to soccer practice. At what time does Bradley arrive at soccer practice?

Read the Problem

What do I need to find?	What information do I need to use?	How will I use the information?

Solve the Problem

Draw a diagram to help you explain your answer.

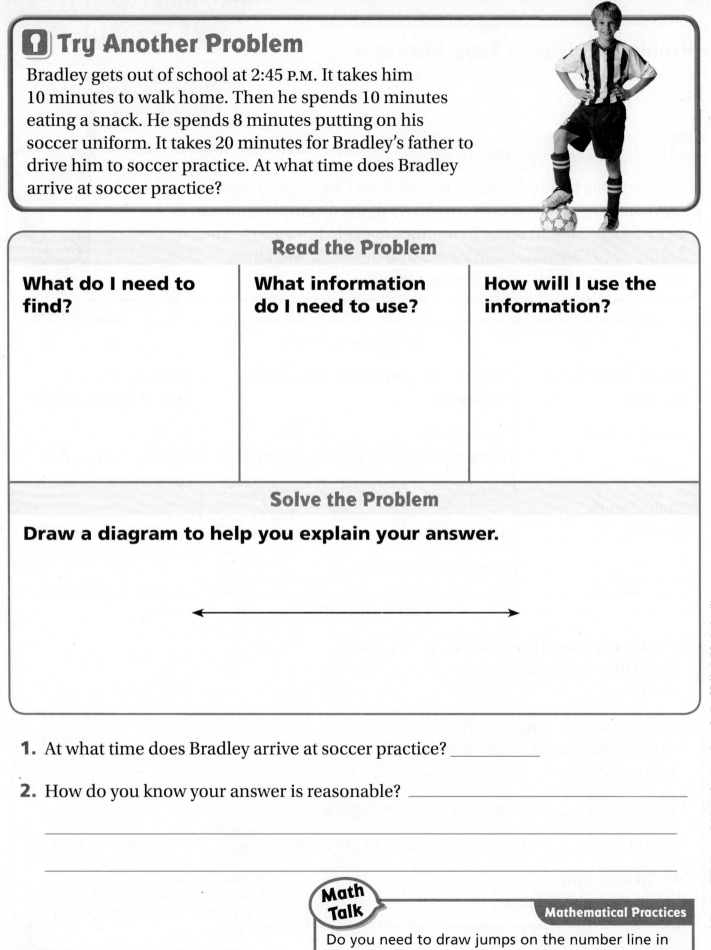

1. At what time does Bradley arrive at soccer practice? _____

2. How do you know your answer is reasonable? _____

_____

_____

Math Talk

Mathematical Practices

Do you need to draw jumps on the number line in the same order as the times in the problem? **Explain.**

© Houghton Mifflin Harcourt Publishing Company • Image Credits: ©Rubberball Productions/Alamy

Name _____

Unlock the Problem

✓ Circle the question.
✓ Underline important facts.
✓ Choose a strategy you know.

Share and Show

1. Patty went to the shopping mall at 11:30 A.M.
   She shopped for 25 minutes. She spent 40 minutes
   eating lunch. Then she met a friend at a movie.
   At what time did Patty meet her friend?

   First, begin with _____ on the number line.

   Then, count forward _____ and _____.

   Think: I can break apart the times into shorter amounts of time
   that make sense.

   ←————————|————————————————————→

   11:30 A.M.

   So, Patty met her friend at _____ _____M.

2. What if Patty goes to the mall at 11:30 A.M. and meets a
   friend at a movie at 1:15 P.M.? Patty wants to shop and have
   45 minutes for lunch before meeting her friend. How much
   time can Patty spend shopping?

   _____

3. Avery got on the bus at 1:10 P.M. The trip took 90 minutes.
   Then she walked for 32 minutes to get home. At what time
   did Avery arrive at home?

   _____

On Your Own

4. **Go DEEPER** Kyle and Josh have a total of 64 CDs. Kyle has
   12 more CDs than Josh. How many CDs does each boy
   have?

   _____

© Houghton Mifflin Harcourt Publishing Company

5. Jamal spent 60 minutes using the computer. He spent a half hour of the time playing games and the rest of the time researching his report. How many minutes did Jamal spend researching his report?

_____

6. **THINK SMARTER** When Caleb got home from school, he worked on his science project for 20 minutes. Then he studied for a test for 30 minutes. He finished at 4:35 P.M. At what time did Caleb get home from school?

Math on the Spot

_____

7. **MATHEMATICAL PRACTICE 6** Miguel played video games each day for a week. On Monday, he scored 83 points. His score went up 5 points each day. On what day did Miguel score 103 points? **Explain** how you found your answer.

_____

_____

8. **THINK SMARTER** When Laura arrived at the library, she spent 40 minutes reading a book. Then she spent 15 minutes reading a magazine. She left the library at 4:15 P.M.

Circle the time that makes the sentence true.

Laura arrived at the library at

| 3:20 P.M. |
| 3:35 P.M. |
| 5:10 P.M. |

© Houghton Mifflin Harcourt Publishing Company

FOR MORE PRACTICE:
Standards Practice Book

✓ Mid-Chapter Checkpoint

Vocabulary

Choose the best term from the box.

Vocabulary
A.M.
minute
P.M.

1. In one _____ , the minute hand moves from one mark to the next on a clock. (p. 407)

2. The times after noon and before midnight are written

   with _____ . (p. 412)

Concepts and Skills

Write the time for the activity. Use A.M. or P.M. (3.MD.1)

3. play ball	4. eat breakfast	5. do homework	6. sleep

_____	_____	_____	_____

Find the elapsed time. (3.MD.1)

7. Start: 10:05 A.M.   End: 10:50 A.M.

   ←——————————————→

   10:05

   _____

8. Start: 5:30 P.M.
   End: 5:49 P.M.

   _____

Find the starting time or the ending time. (3.MD.1)

9. Starting time: _____
   Elapsed time: 50 minutes
   Ending time: 9:05 A.M.

   ←——————————————→

   9:05 A.M.

10. Starting time: 2:46 P.M.
    Elapsed time: 15 minutes

    Ending time: _____

© Houghton Mifflin Harcourt Publishing Company

11. Veronica started walking to school at 7:45 A.M. She arrived at school 23 minutes later. At what time did Veronica arrive at school? (3.MD.1)

_____

12. The clock shows the time the art class ends. At what time does it end? (3.MD.1)

_____

13. Matt went to his friend's house. He arrived at 5:10 P.M. He left at 5:37 P.M. How long was Matt at his friend's house? (3.MD.1)

_____

14. Brenda's train leaves at 7:30 A.M. She needs to arrive 10 minutes early to buy her ticket. It takes her 20 minutes to get to the train station. At what time should Brenda leave her house? (3.MD.1)

_____

15. Write the time you get home from school. (3.MD.1)

_____

© Houghton Mifflin Harcourt Publishing Company

Name _____

Measure Length

Essential Question How can you generate measurement data and show the data on a line plot?

Measurement and Data—3.MD.4
MATHEMATICAL PRACTICES
MP.4, MP.5, MP.6

CONNECT You have learned how to measure length to the nearest inch. Sometimes the length of an object is not a whole unit. For example, a paper clip is more than 1 inch but less than 2 inches.

You can measure length to the nearest half inch or fourth inch. The half-inch markings on a ruler divide each inch into two equal parts. The fourth-inch markings divide each inch into four equal parts.

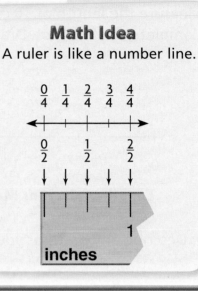

Math Idea
A ruler is like a number line.

$\frac{0}{4}$ $\frac{1}{4}$ $\frac{2}{4}$ $\frac{3}{4}$ $\frac{4}{4}$

$\frac{0}{2}$ $\frac{1}{2}$ $\frac{2}{2}$

inches

Unlock the Problem · Real World

Example 1 Use a ruler to measure the glue stick to the nearest half inch.

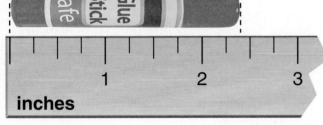

- Line up the left end of the glue stick with the zero mark on the ruler.

- The right end of the glue stick is between the half-inch marks for

  _____ and _____.

- The mark that is closest to the right end of the glue stick is for _____ inches.

So, the length of the glue stick to the

nearest half inch is _____ inches.

Example 2 Use a ruler to measure the paper clip to the nearest fourth inch.

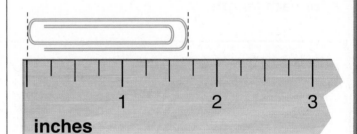

- Line up the left end of the paper clip with the zero mark on the ruler.

- The right end of the paper clip is between the fourth-inch marks for

  _____ and _____.

- The mark that is closest to the right end of the paper clip is for _____ inches.

So, the length of the paper clip to the

nearest fourth inch is _____ inches.

© Houghton Mifflin Harcourt Publishing Company

🔑 Activity · Make a line plot to show measurement data.

Materials ■ inch ruler ■ 10 crayons

Measure the length of 10 crayons to the nearest half inch.
Complete the line plot. Draw an ✗ for each length.

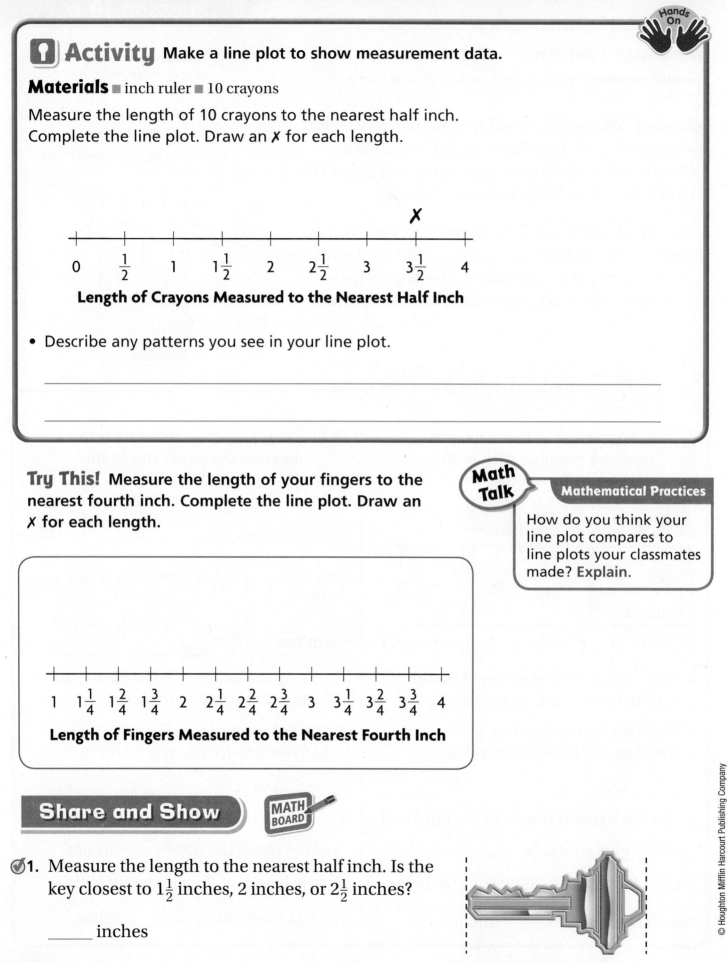

✗

$$0 \quad \frac{1}{2} \quad 1 \quad 1\frac{1}{2} \quad 2 \quad 2\frac{1}{2} \quad 3 \quad 3\frac{1}{2} \quad 4$$

Length of Crayons Measured to the Nearest Half Inch

• Describe any patterns you see in your line plot.

_____

_____

Try This! Measure the length of your fingers to the
nearest fourth inch. Complete the line plot. Draw an
✗ for each length.

$$1 \quad 1\frac{1}{4} \quad 1\frac{2}{4} \quad 1\frac{3}{4} \quad 2 \quad 2\frac{1}{4} \quad 2\frac{2}{4} \quad 2\frac{3}{4} \quad 3 \quad 3\frac{1}{4} \quad 3\frac{2}{4} \quad 3\frac{3}{4} \quad 4$$

Length of Fingers Measured to the Nearest Fourth Inch

Math Talk · **Mathematical Practices**

How do you think your
line plot compares to
line plots your classmates
made? **Explain.**

Share and Show MATH BOARD

✓**1.** Measure the length to the nearest half inch. Is the
key closest to $1\frac{1}{2}$ inches, 2 inches, or $2\frac{1}{2}$ inches?

_____ inches

430

© Houghton Mifflin Harcourt Publishing Company

Name _____

Measure the length to the nearest fourth inch.

2.  ____ inches

On Your Own

Use the lines for 3–4.

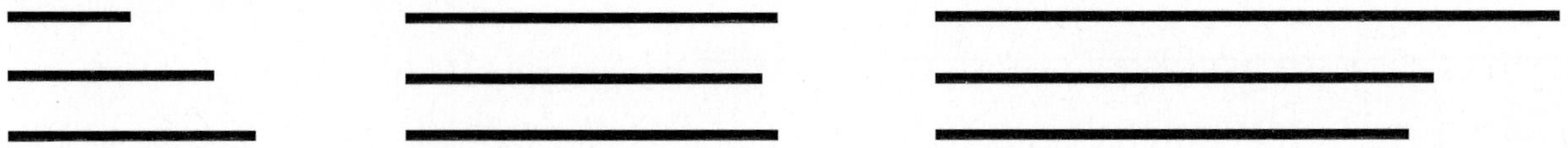

3. Measure the length of the lines to the nearest half inch and make a line plot.

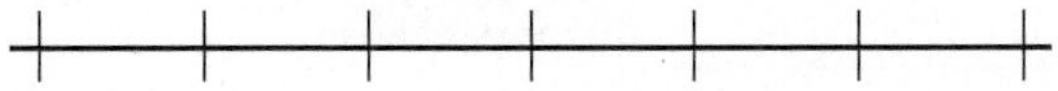

4. Measure the length of the lines to the nearest fourth inch and make a line plot.

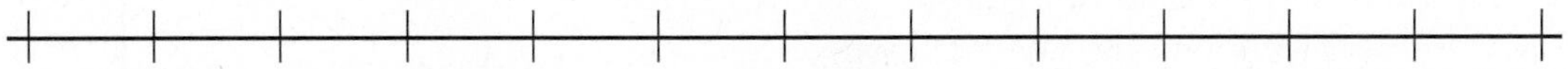

© Houghton Mifflin Harcourt Publishing Company • Image Credits: ©Stockbyte/Getty Images

Problem Solving • Applications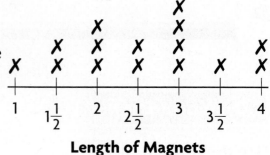

Use the line plot for 5–7.

5. **GO DEEPER** Tara has a magnet collection from places she visited. She measures the length of the magnets to the nearest half inch and records the data in a line plot. Are more magnets longer than $2\frac{1}{2}$ inches or shorter than $2\frac{1}{2}$ inches? Explain.

Length of Magnets

_____

_____

_____

6. **THINK SMARTER** How many magnets measure a whole number of inches? How many magnets have a length between two whole numbers?

_____

_____

7. **MATHEMATICAL PRACTICE ⑥** **Explain** why you think the line plot starts at 1 and stops at 4.

_____

_____

_____

8. **THINK SMARTER** What is the length of the pencil to the nearest half inch?

_____ inches

Explain how you measured the pencil.

_____

_____

FOR MORE PRACTICE:
Standards Practice Book

© Houghton Mifflin Harcourt Publishing Company

Name _____

Estimate and Measure Liquid Volume

Essential Question How can you estimate and measure liquid volume in metric units?

Measurement and Data—3.MD.2
MATHEMATICAL PRACTICES
MP.4, MP.5, MP.6

Unlock the Problem Real World

Liquid volume is the amount of liquid in a container. The **liter (L)** is the basic metric unit for measuring liquid volume.

Activity 1

Materials ■ 1-L beaker ■ 4 containers ■ water ■ tape

STEP 1 Fill a 1-liter beaker with water to the 1-liter mark.

STEP 2 Pour 1 liter of water into a container. Mark the level of the water with a piece of tape. Draw the container below and name the container.

STEP 3 Repeat Steps 1 and 2 with three different-sized containers.

Container 1 _____

Container 2 _____

Math Talk **Mathematical Practices**

What can you say about the amount of liquid volume in each container?

Container 3 _____

Container 4 _____

1. How much water did you pour into each container? _____

2. Which containers are mostly full? Describe them.

_____

3. Which containers are mostly empty? Describe them.

_____

© Houghton Mifflin Harcourt Publishing Company

Compare Liquid Volumes

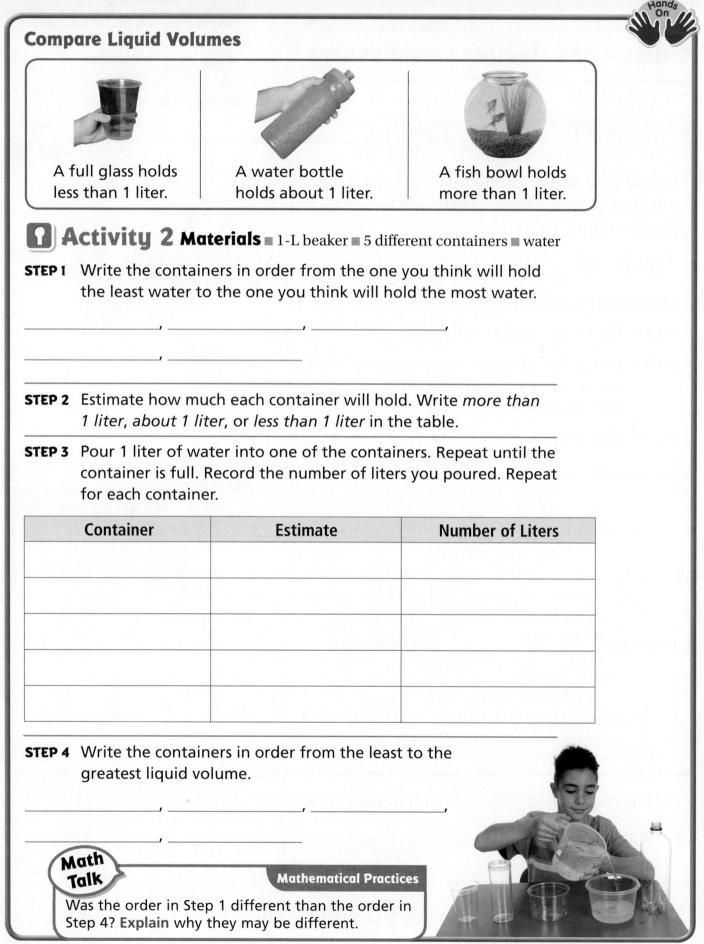 A full glass holds less than 1 liter.	A water bottle holds about 1 liter.	A fish bowl holds more than 1 liter.

🔒 Activity 2 Materials ▪ 1-L beaker ▪ 5 different containers ▪ water

STEP 1 Write the containers in order from the one you think will hold the least water to the one you think will hold the most water.

_____, _____, _____,

_____, _____

STEP 2 Estimate how much each container will hold. Write *more than 1 liter*, *about 1 liter*, or *less than 1 liter* in the table.

STEP 3 Pour 1 liter of water into one of the containers. Repeat until the container is full. Record the number of liters you poured. Repeat for each container.

Container	Estimate	Number of Liters

STEP 4 Write the containers in order from the least to the greatest liquid volume.

_____, _____, _____,

_____, _____

Math Talk

Mathematical Practices

Was the order in Step 1 different than the order in Step 4? **Explain** why they may be different.

© Houghton Mifflin Harcourt Publishing Company • Image Credits: (tr) ©PhotoDisc/Getty Images

Name _____

© Houghton Mifflin Harcourt Publishing Company • Image Credits: (tc) ©C Squared Studios/Getty Images; (bc) ©NiKreationS / Alamy; (tcr) ©Stockbyte/Getty Images

Share and Show

1. The beaker is filled with water. Is the amount *more than 1 liter, about 1 liter,* or *less than 1 liter*?

_____

Estimate how much liquid volume there will be when the container is filled. Write *more than 1 liter, about 1 liter,* or *less than 1 liter*.

2. cup of tea	✅ 3. kitchen sink	✅ 4. teapot

_____	_____	_____

On Your Own

Estimate how much liquid volume there will be when the container is filled. Write *more than 1 liter, about 1 liter,* or *less than 1 liter*.

> **Math Talk** **Mathematical Practices**
> **Explain** how you could estimate the liquid volume in a container.

5. pitcher	6. juice box	7. punch bowl
_____	_____	_____

Use the pictures for 8–10. Rosario pours juice into four bottles that are the same size.

8. Did Rosario pour the same amount into each bottle? _____

9. Which bottle has the least amount of juice? _____

10. Which bottle has the most juice? _____

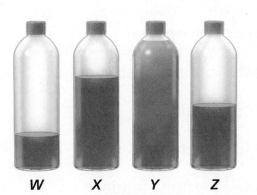

W   X   Y   Z

Problem Solving • Applications Real World

Use the containers for 11–13. Container _A_ is full when 1 liter of water is poured into it.

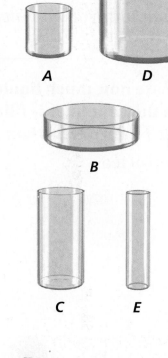

A   **D**

B

11. **GO DEEPER** Estimate how many liters will fill Container _C_ and how many liters will fill Container _E_. Which container will hold more water when filled?

_____

_____

12. **MATHEMATICAL PRACTICE ⑥** Name two containers that will be filled with about the same number of liters of water. **Explain.**

_____

_____

_____

C   **E**

13. **THINK SMARTER** **What's the Error?** Samuel says that you can pour more liters of water into Container _B_ than into Container _D_. Is he correct? Explain.

_____

_____

_____

Personal Math Trainer

14. **THINK SMARTER ✚** The bottle of tea holds about 1 liter. For numbers 14a–14e, choose Yes or No to tell whether it will hold more than 1 liter.

14a. teacup   ○ Yes   ○ No

14b. kitchen trash can   ○ Yes   ○ No

14c. small pool   ○ Yes   ○ No

14d. fish tank   ○ Yes   ○ No

14e. perfume bottle   ○ Yes   ○ No

© Houghton Mifflin Harcourt Publishing Company

FOR MORE PRACTICE:
Standards Practice Book

Name _____

Estimate and Measure Mass

Essential Question How can you estimate and measure mass in metric units?

Measurement and Data— 3.MD.2

MATHEMATICAL PRACTICES
MP.4, MP.5, MP.6, MP.7

Unlock the Problem Real World

🔑 Pedro has a dollar bill in his pocket. Should Pedro measure the mass of the dollar bill in grams or kilograms?

The **gram (g)** is the basic metric unit for measuring **mass**, or the amount of matter in an object. Mass can also be measured by using the metric unit **kilogram (kg)**.

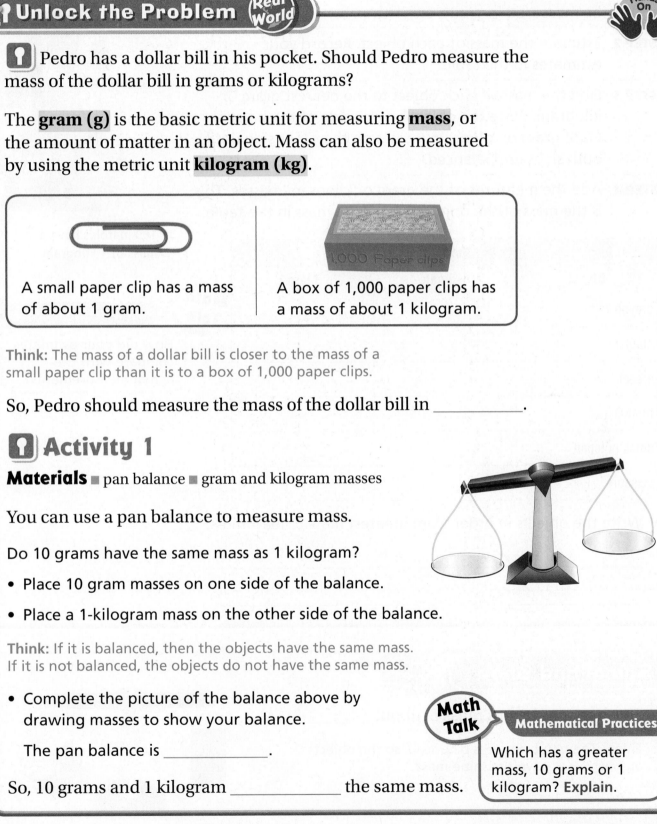

A small paper clip has a mass of about 1 gram.

A box of 1,000 paper clips has a mass of about 1 kilogram.

Think: The mass of a dollar bill is closer to the mass of a small paper clip than it is to a box of 1,000 paper clips.

So, Pedro should measure the mass of the dollar bill in _____.

🔑 Activity 1

Materials ▪ pan balance ▪ gram and kilogram masses

You can use a pan balance to measure mass.

Do 10 grams have the same mass as 1 kilogram?

• Place 10 gram masses on one side of the balance.

• Place a 1-kilogram mass on the other side of the balance.

Think: If it is balanced, then the objects have the same mass. If it is not balanced, the objects do not have the same mass.

• Complete the picture of the balance above by drawing masses to show your balance.

The pan balance is _____.

So, 10 grams and 1 kilogram _____ the same mass.

Math Talk **Mathematical Practices**

Which has a greater mass, 10 grams or 1 kilogram? **Explain.**

© Houghton Mifflin Harcourt Publishing Company

Activity 2

Materials ■ pan balance ■ gram and kilogram masses ■ classroom objects

STEP 1 Use the objects in the table. Decide if the object should be measured in grams or kilograms.

STEP 2 Estimate the mass of each object. Record your estimates in the table.

STEP 3 Find the mass of each object to the nearest gram or kilogram. Place the object on one side of the balance. Place gram or kilogram masses on the other side until both sides are balanced.

STEP 4 Add the measures of the gram or kilogram masses. This is the mass of the object. Record the mass in the table.

▲ 189 marbles have a mass of 1 kilogram.

Mass		
Object	**Estimate**	**Mass**
crayon		
stapler		
eraser		
marker		
small notepad		
scissors		

Math Talk

Mathematical Practices

How did your estimates compare with the actual measurements?

• Write the objects in order from greatest mass to least mass.

_____ , _____ , _____ ,

_____ , _____ , _____

Share and Show   MATH BOARD

1. Five bananas have a mass of about _____.

Think: The pan balance is balanced, so the objects on both sides have the same mass.

© Houghton Mifflin Harcourt Publishing Company

Name _____

Choose the unit you would use to measure the mass.
Write *gram* or *kilogram*.

2. strawberry

✓3. dog

> **Math Talk**
>
> **Mathematical Practices**
>
> **Explain** how you decided which unit to use to measure mass.

_____

Compare the masses of the objects. Write
is less than, *is the same as*, or *is more than*.

4.

The mass of the bowling pin

_____ the mass of
the chess piece.

✓5.

The mass of the erasers

_____ the mass of
the clips.

On Your Own

Choose the unit you would use to measure the mass.
Write *gram* or *kilogram*.

6. chair

7. sunglasses

8. watermelon

Compare the masses of the objects. Write
is less than, *is the same as*, or *is more than*.

9.

The mass of the pen _____
the mass of the paper clips.

10.

The mass of the straws _____
the mass of the blocks.

© Houghton Mifflin Harcourt Publishing Company • Image Credits: tc ©GK Hart/Vikki Hart/Getty Images; (bl) ©Ryan McVay/Getty Images; (bc) ©comstock/Getty Images; (br) ©artville/Getty Images

Problem Solving • Applications

11. **GO DEEPER** Put the sports balls shown at the right in order from greatest mass to least mass.

_____

_____

Golf ball

Table tennis ball

Bowling ball

12. **MATHEMATICAL PRACTICE ④ Use Diagrams** Choose two objects that have about the same mass. Draw a balance with one of these objects on each side.

13. **MATHEMATICAL PRACTICE ④ Use Diagrams** Choose two objects that have different masses. Draw a balance with one of these objects on each side.

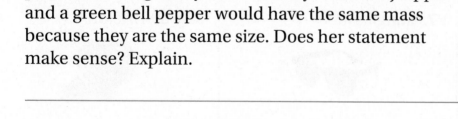

Baseball

Tennis ball

14. **THINK SMARTER Pose a Problem** Write a problem about the objects you chose in Exercise 13. Then solve your problem.

_____

_____

15. **THINK SMARTER Sense or Nonsense?** Amber is buying produce at the grocery store. She says that a Fuji apple and a green bell pepper would have the same mass because they are the same size. Does her statement make sense? Explain.

_____

_____

_____

16. **THINK SMARTER** Select the objects with a mass greater than 1 kilogram. Mark all that apply.

Ⓐ skateboard   Ⓓ egg

Ⓑ laptop computer   Ⓔ desk

Ⓒ cell phone   Ⓕ pencil

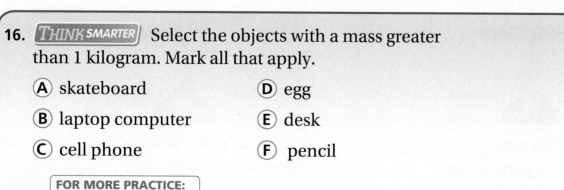

© Houghton Mifflin Harcourt Publishing Company • Image Credits: (tl) ©Image Club Graphics/Eyewire/Getty Images; (tr) ©Stockbyte/Getty Images; (br) ©photonic 3/Alamy Images

Solve Problems About Liquid Volume and Mass

Measurement and Data—3.MD.2
Also 3.OA.7, 3.NBT.2
MATHEMATICAL PRACTICES
MP.1, MP.2, MP.4, MP.7

Essential Question How can you use models to solve liquid volume and mass problems?

🔑 Unlock the Problem Real World

A restaurant serves iced tea from a large container that can hold 24 liters. Sadie will fill the container with the pitchers of tea shown below. Will Sadie have tea left over after filling the container?

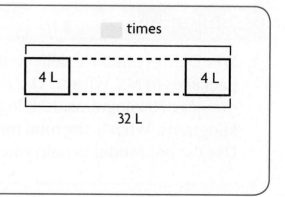

🔓 Example 1 Solve a problem about liquid volume.

_____ L   _____ L   _____ L   _____ L

Since there are _____ equal groups of _____ liters, you can multiply.

_____ ⃝ _____ = _____

Circle the correct words to complete the sentences.

_____ liters is *greater than / less than* 24 liters.

So, Sadie *will / will not* have tea left over.

Try This! Use a bar model to solve.

Raul's fish tank contains 32 liters of water. He empties it with a bucket that holds 4 liters of water. How many times will Raul have to fill the bucket?

_____ ⃝ _____ = _____

So, Raul will have to fill the bucket _____ times.

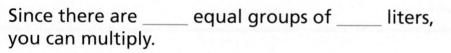

times

| 4 L | - - - - - - - | 4 L |

32 L

© Houghton Mifflin Harcourt Publishing Company • Image Credits: ©Ted Foxx/Alamy Images

🔒 Activity Solve a problem about mass.

Materials ■ pan balance ■ glue stick ■ gram masses

Jeff has a glue stick and a 20-gram mass on one side of a balance and gram masses on the other side. The pan balance is balanced. What is the mass of the glue stick?

STEP 1 Place a glue stick and a 20-gram mass on one side of the balance.

STEP 2 Place gram masses on the other side until the pans are balanced.

STEP 3 To find the mass of the glue stick, remove 20 grams from each side.

Think: I can remove 20 grams from both sides and the pan balance will still be balanced.

STEP 4 Then add the measures of the gram masses on the balance.

The gram masses have a measure of _____ grams.

So, the glue stick has a mass of _____ .

Math Talk **Mathematical Practices**

What equation can you write to find the mass of the glue stick? Explain.

Try This! Use a bar model to solve.

A bag of peas has a mass of 432 grams.
A bag of carrots has a mass of 263 grams.
What is the total mass of both bags?

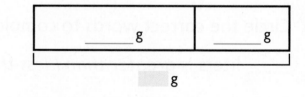

_____ ◯ _____ = _____

So, both bags have a total mass of _____ grams.

Share and Show 📋 MATH BOARD ✎

1. Ed's Delivery Service delivered three packages to Ms. Wilson. The packages have masses of 9 kilograms, 12 kilograms, and 5 kilograms. What is the total mass of the three packages? Use the bar model to help you solve.

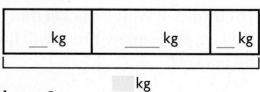

_____

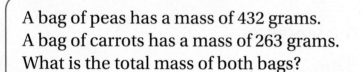

442

© Houghton Mifflin Harcourt Publishing Company

Name _____

Write an equation and solve the problem.

2. Ariel's recipe calls for 64 grams of apples and 86 grams of oranges. How many more grams of oranges than apples does the recipe call for?

_____ ◯ _____ = _____ _____

3. Dan's Clams restaurant sold 45 liters of lemonade. If it sold the same amount each hour for 9 hours, how many liters of lemonade did Dan's Clams sell each hour?

_____ ◯ _____ = _____ _____

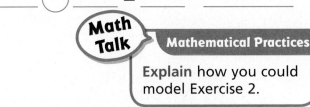

Math Talk **Mathematical Practices**

Explain how you could model Exercise 2.

On Your Own

MATHEMATICAL PRACTICE ④ Write an Equation **Write an equation and solve the problem.**

4. Sasha's box holds 4 kilograms of napkins and 29 kilograms of napkin rings. What is the total mass of the napkins and napkin rings?

_____ ◯ _____ = _____ _____

5. Josh has 6 buckets for cleaning a restaurant. He fills each bucket with 4 liters of water. How many liters of water are in the buckets?

_____ ◯ _____ = _____ _____

6. **THINK SMARTER** Ellen will pour water into Pitcher B until it has 1 more liter of water than Pitcher A. How many liters of water will she pour into Pitcher B? Explain how you found your answer.

Pitcher A   Pitcher B

_____

_____

7. **Practice: Copy and Solve** Use the pictures to write two problems. Then solve your problems.

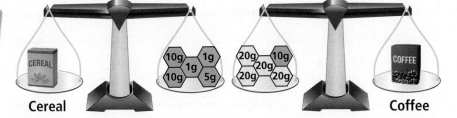

Grape Juice   Apple Juice   Cereal   Coffee

© Houghton Mifflin Harcourt Publishing Company

Unlock the Problem (Real World)

8. Ken's Café serves fruit smoothies. Each smoothie has 9 grams of fresh strawberries. How many grams of strawberries are in 8 smoothies?

a. What do you need to find? _____

b. What operation will you use to find the answer? _____

c. **MATHEMATICAL PRACTICE ②** **Use Diagrams** Draw a diagram to solve the problem.

d. Complete the sentences.

There are _____ smoothies with _____ grams of strawberries in each.

Since each smoothie is an _____ group, you can _____.

_____ ◯ _____ = _____

So, there are _____ grams of strawberries in 8 smoothies.

9. **Go DEEPER** Arturo has two containers, each filled with 12 liters of water. Daniel has two containers, each filled with 16 liters of water. What is the total liquid volume of the boys' containers?

_____

10. **THINK SMARTER** A deli makes its own salad dressing. A small jar has 3 grams of spices. A large jar has 5 grams of spices. Will 25 grams of spices be enough to make 3 small jars and 3 large jars? Show your work.

© Houghton Mifflin Harcourt Publishing Company

FOR MORE PRACTICE:
Standards Practice Book

1. Yul and Sarah's art class started at 11:25 A.M. The class lasted 30 minutes. Yul left when the class was done. Sarah stayed an extra 5 minutes to talk with the teacher and then left.

   Write the time that each student left. Explain how you found each time.

   _____

   _____

2. Julio measured an object that he found. It was about $\frac{3}{4}$ inch wide.

   For numbers 2a–2d, choose Yes or No to tell whether the object could be the one Julio measured.

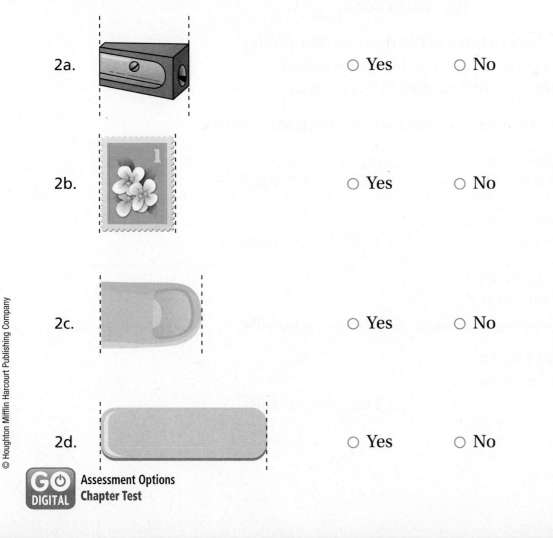

2a. ○ Yes   ○ No

2b. ○ Yes   ○ No

2c. ○ Yes   ○ No

2d. ○ Yes   ○ No

© Houghton Mifflin Harcourt Publishing Company

GO DIGITAL   Assessment Options
Chapter Test

3. Dina started swimming at 3:38 P.M. She swam until 4:15 P.M. How long did Dina swim?

_____ minutes

4. Rita's class begins social studies at ten minutes before one in the afternoon. At what time does Rita's class begin social studies? Circle a time that makes the sentence true.

Rita's class begins social studies at

1:10 A.M.
1:10 P.M.
12:50 A.M.
12:50 P.M.

5. Select the objects with a mass greater than 1 kilogram. Mark all that apply.

(A) bicycle   (C) eraser

(B) pen   (D) math book

6. A chicken dish needs to bake in the oven for 35 minutes. The dish needs to cool for at least 8 minutes before serving. Scott puts the chicken dish in the oven at 5:14 P.M.

For numbers 6a–6d, select True or False for each statement.

6a. Scott can serve the dish at 5:51 P.M.   ○ True   ○ False

6b. Scott can serve the dish at 5:58 P.M.   ○ True   ○ False

6c. Scott should take the dish out of the oven at 5:51 A.M.   ○ True   ○ False

6d. Scott should take the dish out of the oven at 5:49 P.M.   ○ True   ○ False

© Houghton Mifflin Harcourt Publishing Company

7. Anthony's family went out to dinner. They left at the time shown on the clock. They returned home at 6:52 P.M.

Part A

How long was Anthony's family gone?

_____ hour _____ minutes

Part B

Explain how you found your answer.

_____

_____

_____

8. Tran checked the time on his watch after he finished his daily run.

Select the time that Tran finished running. Mark all that apply.

Ⓐ 14 minutes before nine   Ⓒ quarter to nine

Ⓑ eight forty-six   Ⓓ nine forty-six

9. Cara uses a balance scale to compare mass.

Circle a symbol that makes the comparison true.

The mass of the blocks ⎡ < ⎤ the mass of the
erasers. ⎣ > ⎦
⎣ = ⎦

© Houghton Mifflin Harcourt Publishing Company

10. A large bottle of water holds about 2 liters.

For numbers 10a–10e, choose Yes or No to tell whether the container will hold all of the water.

10a. kitchen sink   ○ Yes   ○ No

10b. water glass   ○ Yes   ○ No

10c. ice cube tray   ○ Yes   ○ No

10d. large soup pot   ○ Yes   ○ No

10e. lunchbox thermos   ○ Yes   ○ No

11. Select the items that would be best measured in grams. Mark all that apply.

(A) watermelon

(B) lettuce leaf

(C) grape

(D) onion

12. Samir made a list of what he did on Tuesday. Write the letter for each activity next to the time he did it.

(A) Get out of bed.   ☐ 8:05 A.M.

(B) Walk to school.   ☐ 6:25 P.M.

(C) Eat lunch.   ☐ 3:50 P.M.

(D) Go to guitar lesson
     after school.   ☐ 11:48 A.M.

(E) Eat dinner at home.   ☐ 6:25 A.M.

© Houghton Mifflin Harcourt Publishing Company

Name _____

13. Amy has 30 grams of flour. She puts 4 grams of flour in each pot of chowder that she makes. She puts 5 grams of flour in each pot of potato soup that she makes. She makes 4 pots of chowder. Does Amy have enough flour left over to make 3 pots of potato soup?

14. Use an inch ruler to measure.

Part A

What is the length of the leaf to the nearest fourth inch?

_____

Part B

Explain what happens if you line up the left side of the object with the 1 on the ruler.

_____

_____

15. Mrs. Park takes the 9:38 A.M. train to the city. The trip takes 3 hours and 20 minutes. What time does Mrs. Park arrive in the city?

_____

16. Hector buys two bags of gravel for his driveway. He buys a total of 35 kilograms of gravel. Select the bags he buys.

15 kg	17 kg	18 kg	19 kg
○	○	○	○

© Houghton Mifflin Harcourt Publishing Company

17. Ashley measures the shells she collects. She records the measurements in a chart.

Number of Shells	Length in Inches
1	1
2	$2\frac{1}{2}$
3	$1\frac{1}{2}$
1	2

Part A

Ashley found a razor clam shell this long. Use an inch ruler to measure. Record the measurement in the chart.

_____ inches

Part B

Complete the line plot to show the data in the chart. How many shells are longer than 2 inches? Tell how you know.

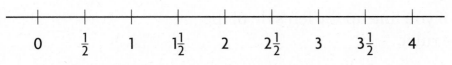

0    $\frac{1}{2}$ 1 $1\frac{1}{2}$ 2 $2\frac{1}{2}$ 3 $3\frac{1}{2}$ 4

Length of Shells Measured to the Nearest Half Inch

_____

_____

18. Lucy fills a bathroom sink with water. Is the amount of water *more than 1 liter, about 1 liter, or less than 1 liter*? Explain how you know.

_____

_____

_____

© Houghton Mifflin Harcourt Publishing Company

Perimeter and Area

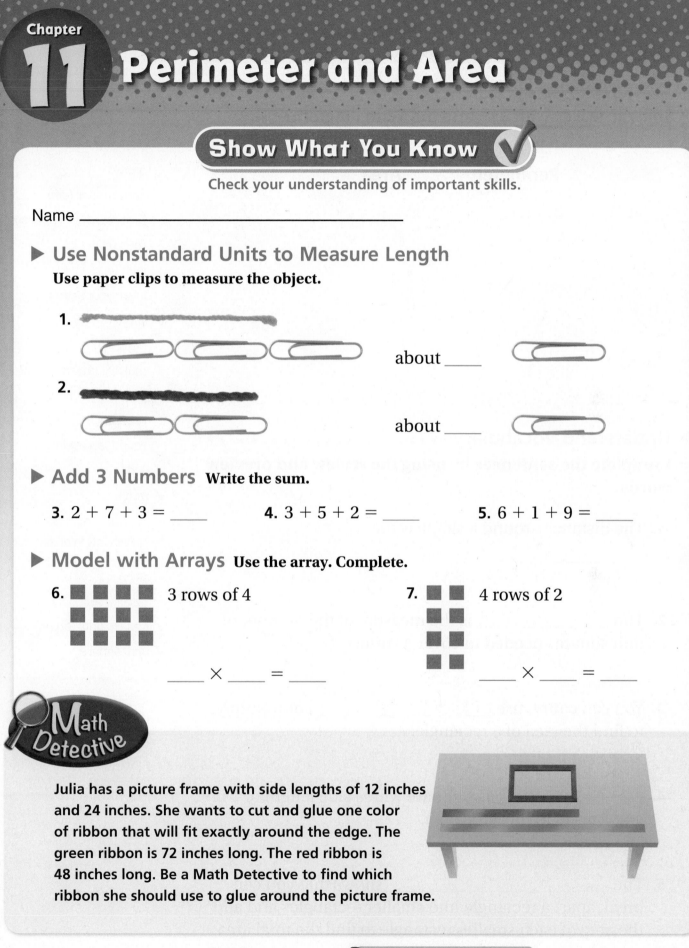

Show What You Know ✓

Check your understanding of important skills.

Name _____

▶ **Use Nonstandard Units to Measure Length**

Use paper clips to measure the object.

1. about ____

2. about ____

▶ **Add 3 Numbers** Write the sum.

3. $2 + 7 + 3 =$ ____ **4.** $3 + 5 + 2 =$ ____ **5.** $6 + 1 + 9 =$ ____

▶ **Model with Arrays** Use the array. Complete.

6. 3 rows of 4

____ $\times$ ____ = ____

7. 4 rows of 2

____ $\times$ ____ = ____

Math Detective

Julia has a picture frame with side lengths of 12 inches and 24 inches. She wants to cut and glue one color of ribbon that will fit exactly around the edge. The green ribbon is 72 inches long. The red ribbon is 48 inches long. Be a Math Detective to find which ribbon she should use to glue around the picture frame.

© Houghton Mifflin Harcourt Publishing Company

Personal Math Trainer
Online Assessment and Intervention

Vocabulary Builder

▶ **Visualize It** •

Sort the words with a ✔ into the Venn diagram.

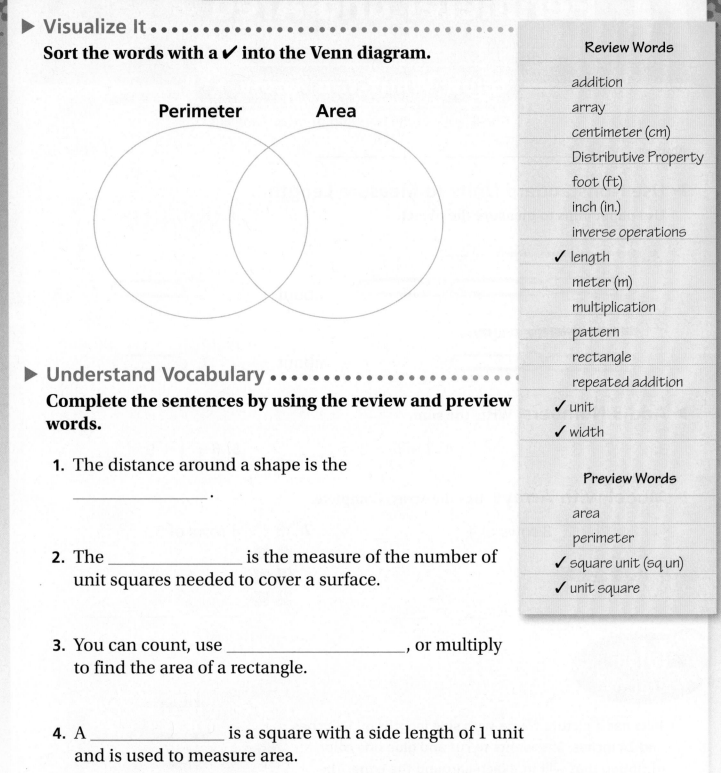

Perimeter   Area

Review Words
addition
array
centimeter (cm)
Distributive Property
foot (ft)
inch (in.)
inverse operations
✓ length
meter (m)
multiplication
pattern
rectangle
repeated addition
✓ unit
✓ width

Preview Words
area
perimeter
✓ square unit (sq un)
✓ unit square

▶ **Understand Vocabulary** •

Complete the sentences by using the review and preview words.

1. The distance around a shape is the
   _____ .

2. The _____ is the measure of the number of
   unit squares needed to cover a surface.

3. You can count, use _____, or multiply
   to find the area of a rectangle.

4. A _____ is a square with a side length of 1 unit
   and is used to measure area.

5. The _____ shows that you can
   break apart a rectangle into smaller rectangles and add
   the area of each smaller rectangle to find the total area.

• **Interactive Student Edition**
• **Multimedia eGlossary**

© Houghton Mifflin Harcourt Publishing Company

Name _____

Model Perimeter

Essential Question How can you find perimeter?

Measurement and Data—
3.MD.8
MATHEMATICAL PRACTICES
MP.1, MP.3, MP.4, MP.7

Investigate

Perimeter is the distance around a figure.

Materials ■ geoboard ■ rubber bands

You can find the perimeter of a rectangle on a geoboard or on dot paper by counting the number of units on each side.

A. Make a rectangle on the geoboard that is 3 units on two sides and 2 units on the other two sides.

B. Draw your rectangle on this dot paper.

← 1 Unit

C. Write the length next to each side of your rectangle.

D. Add the number of units on each side.

_____ + _____ + _____ + _____ = _____

E. So, the perimeter of the rectangle

is _____ units.

• How would the perimeter of the rectangle change if the length of two of the sides was 4 units instead of 3 units?

_____

_____

© Houghton Mifflin Harcourt Publishing Company

Draw Conclusions

1. Describe how you would find the perimeter of a rectangle that is 5 units wide and 6 units long.

   _____

2. **THINK SMARTER** A rectangle has two pairs of sides of equal length. Explain how you can find the unknown length of two sides when the length of one side is 4 units, and the perimeter is 14 units.

   _____

   _____

3. **MATHEMATICAL PRACTICE ①** **Evaluate** Jill says that finding the perimeter of a figure with all sides of equal length is easier than finding the perimeter of other figures. Do you agree? Explain.

   _____

   _____

Make Connections

Math Talk Mathematical Practices

If a rectangle has a perimeter of 12 units, how many units wide and how many units long could it be? Explain.

You can also use grid paper to find the perimeter of figures by counting the number of units on each side.

Start at the arrow and trace the perimeter. Begin counting with 1. Continue counting each unit around the figure until you have counted each unit.

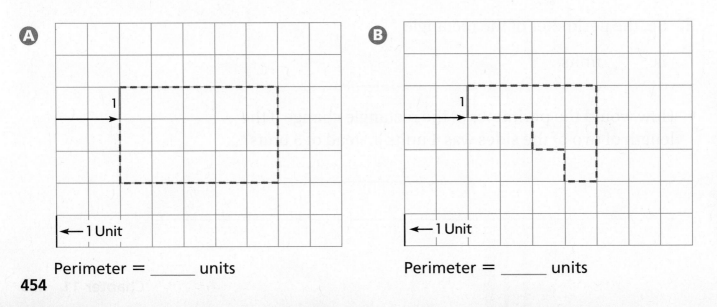

Ⓐ

←— 1 Unit

Perimeter = _____ units

Ⓑ

←— 1 Unit

Perimeter = _____ units

© Houghton Mifflin Harcourt Publishing Company

Name _____

Find the perimeter of the figure. Each unit is 1 centimeter.

1.
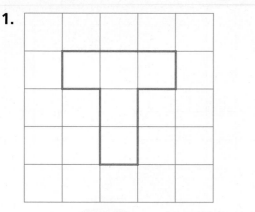

_____ centimeters

2.
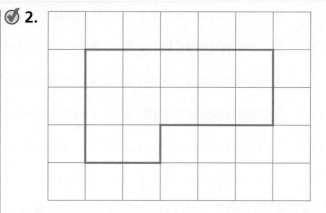

_____ centimeters

3.
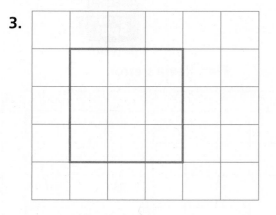

_____ centimeters

4.
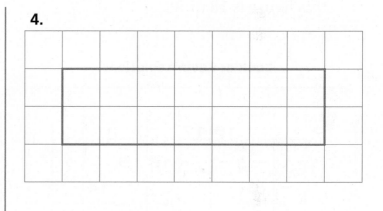

_____ centimeters

Find the perimeter.

5. A figure with four sides that measure 4 centimeters, 6 centimeters, 5 centimeters, and 1 centimeter

_____ centimeters

6. A figure with two sides that measure 10 inches, one side that measures 8 inches, and one side that measures 4 inches

_____ inches

Problem Solving • Applications Real World

7. **MATHEMATICAL PRACTICE 6** **Explain** how to find the length of each side of a triangle with sides of equal length, and a perimeter of 27 inches.

_____

_____

© Houghton Mifflin Harcourt Publishing Company

8. **THINK SMARTER** Luisa drew a rectangle with a perimeter of 18 centimeters. Select the rectangles that Luisa could have drawn. Mark all that apply. Use the grid to help you.

(A) 9 centimeters long and 2 centimeters wide

(B) 6 centimeters long and 3 centimeters wide

(C) 4 centimeters long and 4 centimeters wide

(D) 5 centimeters long and 4 centimeters wide

(E) 7 centimeters long and 2 centimeters wide

9. **THINK SMARTER** **What's the Error?** Kevin is solving perimeter problems. He counts the units and says that the perimeter of this figure is 18 units.

Look at Kevin's solution. **Find Kevin's error.**

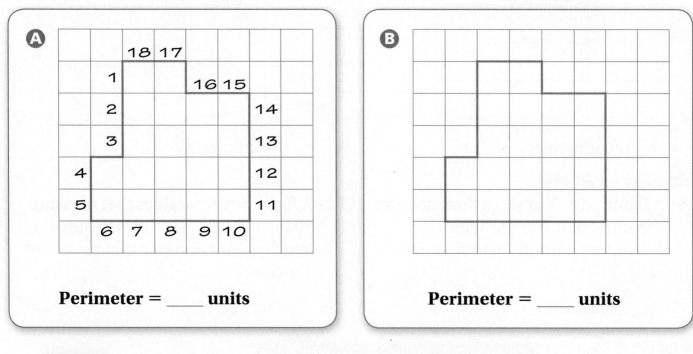

Perimeter = _____ units

Perimeter = _____ units

• **GO DEEPER** Describe the error Kevin made. Circle the places in the drawing of Kevin's solution where he made an error.

_____

_____

© Houghton Mifflin Harcourt Publishing Company

FOR MORE PRACTICE:
Standards Practice Book

Name _____

Find Perimeter

Essential Question How can you measure perimeter?

Measurement and Data—
3.MD.8 *Also 3.NBT.2, 3.MD.4*
MATHEMATICAL PRACTICES
MP.4, MP.5, MP.6, MP.7

You can estimate and measure perimeter in standard units, such as inches and centimeters.

⚷ Unlock the Problem Real World   Hands On

Find the perimeter of the cover of a notebook.

🔑 Activity   Materials ▪ inch ruler

STEP 1 Estimate the perimeter of a notebook in inches. Record your estimate.   _____ inches

STEP 2 Use an inch ruler to measure the length of each side of the notebook to the nearest inch.

STEP 3 Record and add the lengths of the sides measured to the nearest inch.

_____ + _____ + _____ + _____ = _____

So, the perimeter of the notebook cover measured

to the nearest inch is _____ inches.

Math Talk   **Mathematical Practices**

Explain how your estimate compares with your measurement.

Try This! Find the perimeter.

Use an inch ruler to find the length of each side.

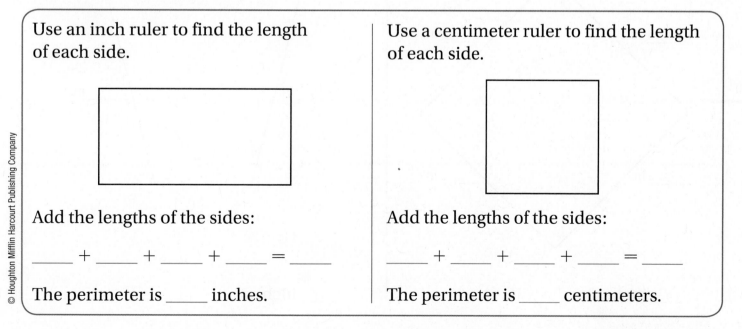

Add the lengths of the sides:

____ + ____ + ____ + ____ = ____

The perimeter is _____ inches.

Use a centimeter ruler to find the length of each side.

Add the lengths of the sides:

____ + ____ + ____ + ____ = ____

The perimeter is _____ centimeters.

© Houghton Mifflin Harcourt Publishing Company

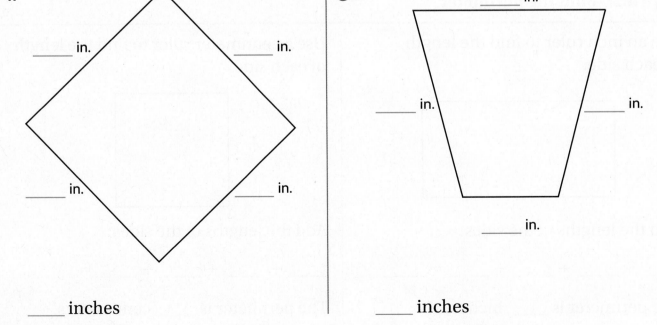

Share and Show

MATH BOARD

1. Find the perimeter of the triangle in inches.

_____ in. _____ in.   **Think:** How long is each side?

_____ in.

_____ inches

Math Talk **Mathematical Practices**

Explain how many numbers you add together to find the perimeter of a figure.

Use a centimeter ruler to find the perimeter.

2.

_____ cm

_____ cm   _____ cm

_____ cm

_____ centimeters

☑3.

_____ cm

_____ cm   _____ cm

_____ cm   _____ cm

_____ centimeters

Use an inch ruler to find the perimeter.

4.

_____ in.   _____ in.

_____ in.   _____ in.

_____ inches

☑5.

_____ in.

_____ in.   _____ in.

_____ in.

_____ inches

© Houghton Mifflin Harcourt Publishing Company

Name _____

On Your Own

Use a ruler to find the perimeter.

6.

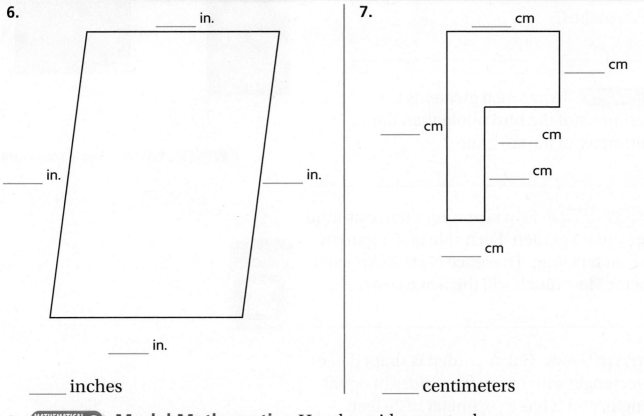

_____ in.

_____ in.   _____ in.

_____ in.

_____ inches

7.

_____ cm

_____ cm

_____ cm   _____ cm

_____ cm

_____ cm

_____ centimeters

8. **MATHEMATICAL PRACTICE ④** **Model Mathematics** Use the grid paper to draw a figure that has a perimeter of 24 centimeters. Label the length of each side.

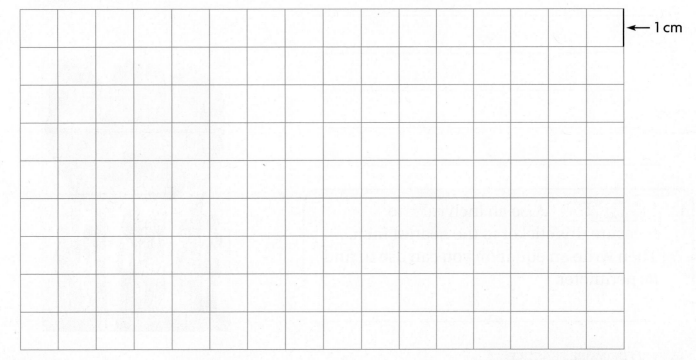

← 1 cm

© Houghton Mifflin Harcourt Publishing Company

Problem Solving • Applications

Use the photos for 9–10.

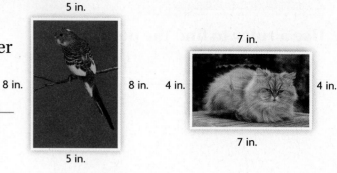

5 in.

8 in.   8 in.   4 in.

5 in.

7 in.

4 in.

7 in.

9. Which of the animal photos has a perimeter of 26 inches?

_____

10. **GO DEEPER** How much greater is the perimeter of the bird photo than the perimeter of the cat photo?

_____

WRITE ▸ Math • **Show Your Work**

11. **THINK SMARTER** Erin is putting a fence around her square garden. Each side of her garden is 3 meters long. The fence costs $5 for each meter. How much will the fence cost?

_____

12. **WRITE** ▸ Math Gary's garden is shaped like a rectangle with two pairs of sides of equal length, and it has a perimeter of 28 feet. Explain how to find the lengths of the other sides if one side measures 10 feet.

_____

_____

_____

_____

13. **THINK SMARTER** Use an inch ruler to measure this sticker to the nearest inch. Then write an equation you can use to find its perimeter.

_____

© Houghton Mifflin Harcourt Publishing Company • Image Credits: (tl) ©Comstock Images/Getty Images; (tr) ©Maria Meester/Shutterstock

Name _____

Algebra • Find Unknown Side Lengths

Essential Question How can you find the unknown length of a side in a plane figure when you know its perimeter?

Measurement and Data—
3.MD.8 *Also 3.NBT.2*
MATHEMATICAL PRACTICES
MP.1, MP.4, MP.7, MP.8

Unlock the Problem (Real World)

Chen has 27 feet of fencing to put around his garden. He has already used the lengths of fencing shown. How much fencing does he have left for the last side?

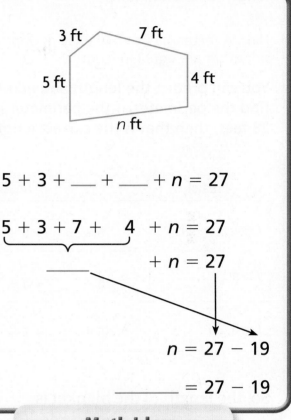

3 ft   7 ft
5 ft   4 ft
n ft

 Find the unknown side length.

Write an equation for the perimeter.

Think: If I knew the value of *n*, I would add all the side lengths to find the perimeter.

Add the lengths of the sides you know.

Think: Addition and subtraction are inverse operations.

Write a related equation.

So, Chen has _____ feet of fencing left.

$5 + 3 + \underline{} + \underline{} + n = 27$

$5 + 3 + 7 + \underline{4} + n = 27$

$\underline{} + n = 27$

$n = 27 - 19$

$\underline{} = 27 - 19$

> **Math Idea**
> A symbol or letter can stand for an unknown side length.

Try This!

The perimeter of the figure is 24 meters. Find the unknown side length.

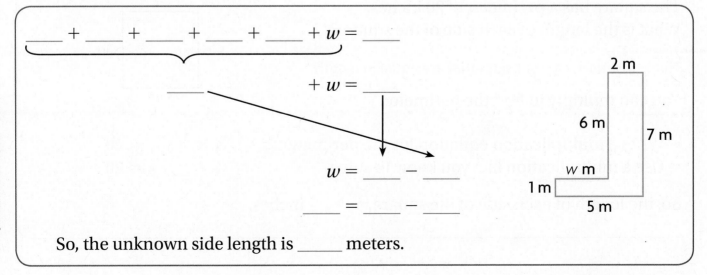

$\underline{} + \underline{} + \underline{} + \underline{} + \underline{} + w = \underline{}$

$\underline{} + w = \underline{}$

$w = \underline{} - \underline{}$

$\underline{} = \underline{} - \underline{}$

2 m
6 m   7 m
w m
1 m   5 m

So, the unknown side length is _____ meters.

© Houghton Mifflin Harcourt Publishing Company

🔑 Example Find unknown side lengths of a rectangle.

Lauren has a rectangular blanket. The perimeter is 28 feet. The width of the blanket is 5 feet. What is the length of the blanket?

Hint: A rectangle has two pairs of opposite sides that are equal in length.

You can predict the length and add to find the perimeter. If the perimeter is 28 feet, then that is the correct length.

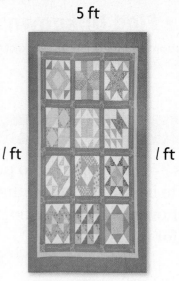

5 ft

l ft   *l* ft

5 ft

Predict	Check	Does it check?
l = 7	5 + ____ + 5 + ____ = ____	**Think:** Perimeter is not 28 feet, so the length does not check.
l = 8	5 + ____ + 5 + ____ = ____	**Think:** Perimeter is not 28 feet, so the length does not check.
l = 9	5 + ____ + 5 + ____ = ____	**Think:** Perimeter is 28 feet, so the length is correct. ✓

So, the length of the blanket is _____ feet.

Try This! Find unknown side lengths of a square.

The square has a perimeter of 20 inches. What is the length of each side of the square?

Think: A square has four sides that are equal in length.

You can multiply to find the perimeter.

- Write a multiplication equation for the perimeter.   4 × *s* = 20
- Use a multiplication fact you know to solve.   4 × ____ = 20

So, the length of each side of the square is _____ inches.

s in.

s in.   *s* in.

s in.

© Houghton Mifflin Harcourt Publishing Company • Image Credits: ©D. Hurst/Alamy

Name _____

Find the unknown side lengths.

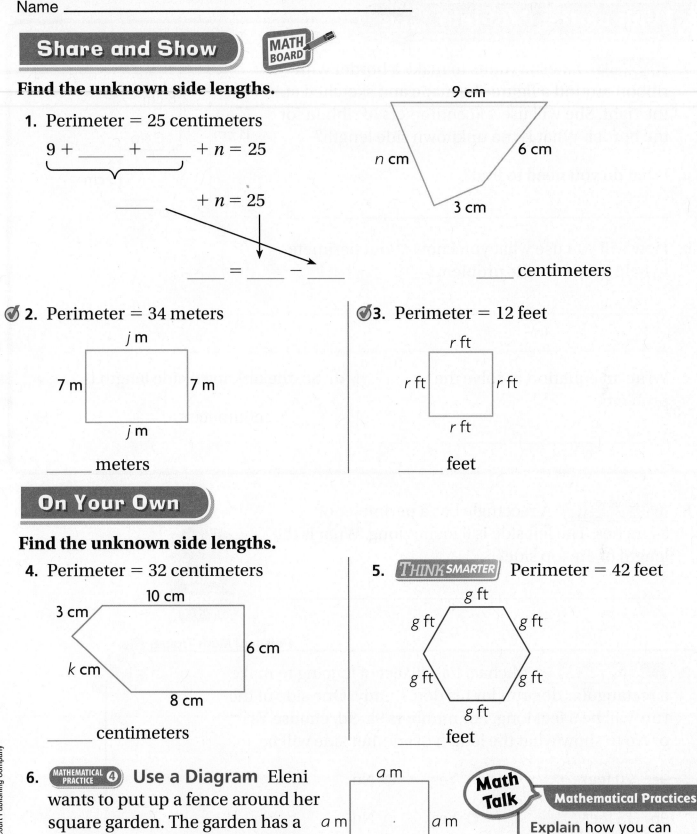

1. Perimeter = 25 centimeters

9 + _____ + _____ + n = 25

_____ + n = 25

_____ = _____ − _____

_____ centimeters

✓2. Perimeter = 34 meters

j m

7 m   7 m

j m

_____ meters

✓3. Perimeter = 12 feet

r ft

r ft r ft

r ft

_____ feet

On Your Own

Find the unknown side lengths.

4. Perimeter = 32 centimeters

10 cm
3 cm
6 cm
k cm
8 cm

_____ centimeters

5. THINK SMARTER Perimeter = 42 feet

g ft
g ft g ft
g ft g ft
g ft

_____ feet

6. MATHEMATICAL PRACTICE ④ **Use a Diagram** Eleni wants to put up a fence around her square garden. The garden has a perimeter of 28 meters. How long will each side of the fence be? Explain.

a m

a m a m

a m

Math Talk **Mathematical Practices**

Explain how you can use division to find the length of a side of a square.

_____

_____

© Houghton Mifflin Harcourt Publishing Company

Unlock the Problem · Real World

7. **GO DEEPER** Latesha wants to make a border with ribbon around a figure she made and sketched at the right. She will use 44 centimeters of ribbon for the border. What is the unknown side length?

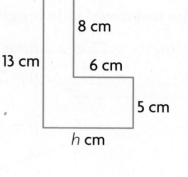

3 cm
8 cm
13 cm
6 cm
5 cm
h cm

a. What do you need to find?

_____

b. How will you use what you know about perimeter to help you solve the problem?

_____

_____

c. Write an equation to solve the problem.

_____

d. So, the unknown side length is

_____ centimeters.

8. **THINK SMARTER** A rectangle has a perimeter of 34 inches. The left side is 6 inches long. What is the length of the top side?

Math on the Spot

_____

Personal Math Trainer

9. **THINK SMARTER +** Michael has 40 feet of fencing to make a rectangular dog run for his dog, Buddy. One side of the run will be 5 feet long. For numbers 9a–9d, choose Yes or No to show what the length of another side will be.

9a. 20 feet ○ Yes ○ No

9b. 15 feet ○ Yes ○ No

9c. 10 feet ○ Yes ○ No

9d. 8 feet ○ Yes ○ No

FOR MORE PRACTICE: Standards Practice Book

© Houghton Mifflin Harcourt Publishing Company

Name _____

Understand Area

Essential Question How is finding the area of a figure different from finding the perimeter of a figure.

Measurement and Data—
3.MD.5, 3.MD.5a *Also 3.MD.5b,*
3.MD.6, 3.MD.8
MATHEMATICAL PRACTICES
MP.2, MP.4, MP.5, MP.6

🔑 Unlock the Problem (Real World)

CONNECT You learned that perimeter is the distance around a figure. It is measured in linear units, or units that are used to measure the distance between two points.

Area is the measure of the number of unit squares needed to cover a flat surface. A **unit square** is a square with a side length of 1 unit. It has an area of 1 **square unit (sq un)**.

Unit Square

1 unit

1 unit   1 unit

1 unit

Perimeter

1 unit + 1 unit + 1 unit +
1 unit = 4 units

Area

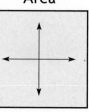

1 square unit

Math Idea

You can count the number of units on each side of a figure to find its perimeter. You can count the number of unit squares inside a figure to find its area in square units.

🔓 Activity **Materials** ■ geoboard ■ rubber bands

Hands On

A Use your geoboard to form a figure made from 2 unit squares. Record the figure on this dot paper.

· · · · · ·

· · · · · ·

· · · · · ·

· · · · · ·

· · · · · ·

What is the area of this figure?

Area = _____ square units

B Change the rubber band so that the figure is made from 3 unit squares. Record the figure on this dot paper.

· · · · · ·

· · · · · ·

· · · · · ·

· · · · · ·

· · · · · ·

What is the area of this figure?

Area = _____ square units

Math Talk **Mathematical Practices**

For B, did your figure look like your classmate's figure? **Explain.**

© Houghton Mifflin Harcourt Publishing Company

Try This! Draw three different figures that are each made from 4 unit squares. Find the area of each figure.

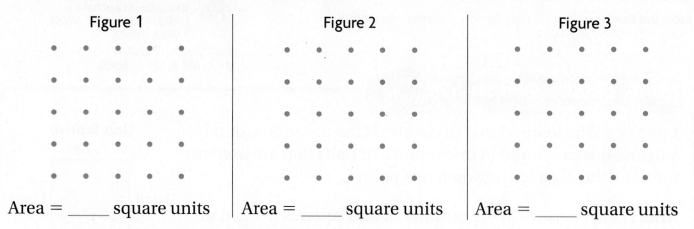

Figure 1   Figure 2   Figure 3

Area = _____ square units | Area = _____ square units | Area = _____ square units

- How are the figures the same? How are the figures different?

Share and Show MATH BOARD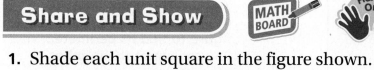

1. Shade each unit square in the figure shown. Count the unit squares to find the area.

   Area = _____ square units

Count to find the area of the figure.

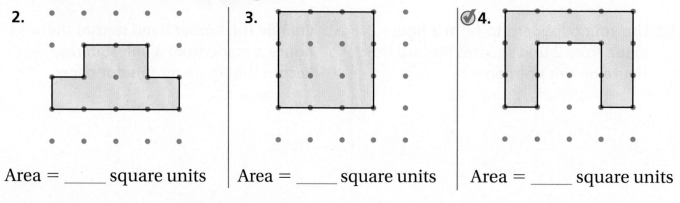

2.   3.   ✔4.

Area = _____ square units | Area = _____ square units | Area = _____ square units

Write *area* or *perimeter* for the situation.

5. buying a rug for a room

_____

✔6. putting a fence around a garden

_____

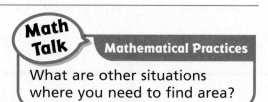

Math Talk **Mathematical Practices**

What are other situations where you need to find area?

© Houghton Mifflin Harcourt Publishing Company

Name _____

Count to find the area of the figure.

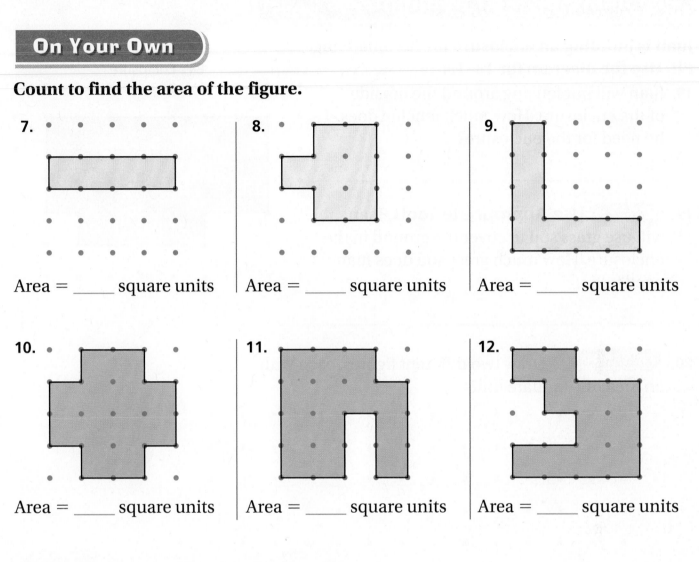

7.

Area = _____ square units

8.

Area = _____ square units

9.

Area = _____ square units

10.

Area = _____ square units

11.

Area = _____ square units

12.

Area = _____ square units

Write *area* or *perimeter* for the situation.

13. painting a wall

_____

14. covering a patio with tiles

_____

15. putting a wallpaper border around a room

_____

16. gluing a ribbon around a picture frame

_____

17. **GO DEEPER** Nicole's mother put tiles on a section of their kitchen floor. The section included 5 rows with 4 tiles in each row. Each tile cost $2. How much money did Nicole's father spend on the tiles?

_____

© Houghton Mifflin Harcourt Publishing Company

Problem Solving • Applications Real World

Juan is building an enclosure for his small dog, Eli. Use the diagram for 18–19.

Eli's Enclosure

18. Juan will put fencing around the outside of the enclosure. How much fencing does he need for the enclosure?

_____

19. **MATHEMATICAL PRACTICE 5 Use Appropriate Tools** Juan will use grass sod to cover the ground in the enclosure. How much grass sod does Juan need?

_____

20. _THINK SMARTER_ Draw two different figures, each with an area of 10 square units.

Math on the Spot

21. _THINK SMARTER_ What is the perimeter and area of this figure? Explain how you found the answer.

Perimeter _____ units

Area _____ square units

_____

_____

_____

© Houghton Mifflin Harcourt Publishing Company

FOR MORE PRACTICE:
Standards Practice Book

Measure Area

Essential Question How can you find the area of a plane figure?

Measurement and Data—
3.MD.5b, 3.MD.6 *Also 3.MD.5,
3.MD.5a, 3.MD.7, 3.MD.7a*
MATHEMATICAL PRACTICES
MP.2, MP.4, MP.5, MP.6

🔑 Unlock the Problem

Jaime is measuring the area of the rectangles with 1-inch square tiles.

1 square inch

🔒 Activity 1 Materials ▪ 1-inch grid paper ▪ scissors

Cut out eight 1-inch squares. Use the dashed lines as guides to place tiles for *A–C*.

Ⓐ Place 4 tiles on Rectangle *A*.

• Are there any gaps? _____

• Are there any overlaps? _____

• Jaime says that the area is 4 square inches. Is Jaime's measurement correct? _____

So, when you measure area, there can be no space between the tiles, or no gaps.

Ⓑ Place 8 tiles on Rectangle *B*.

• Are there any gaps? _____

• Are there any overlaps? _____

• Jaime says that the area is 8 square inches. Is Jaime's measurement correct? _____

So, when you measure the area, the tiles cannot overlap.

Ⓒ Place 6 tiles on Rectangle *C*.

• Are there any gaps? _____

• Are there any overlaps? _____

• Jaime says that the area is 6 square inches. Is Jaime's measurement correct? _____

So, the area of the rectangles is

_____ square inches.

Rectangle *A*

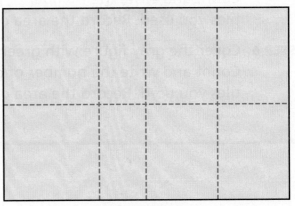
Rectangle *B*

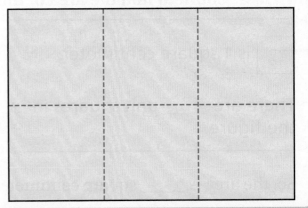
Rectangle *C*

© Houghton Mifflin Harcourt Publishing Company

Activity 2 Materials ■ green and blue paper ■ scissors

ERROR Alert

Be sure that there are no gaps or overlaps when you use square tiles to find area.

STEP 1 Estimate the number of blue square tiles it will take to cover the gray figure.

_____ blue square tiles

STEP 2 Estimate the number of green tiles it will take to cover the gray figure.

_____ green square tiles

STEP 3 Trace the blue square pattern ten times and cut out the squares.

STEP 4 Trace the green square pattern thirty-six times and cut out the squares.

STEP 5 Cover the gray figure with blue square tiles. Count and write the number of blue square tiles you used. Record the area of the figure.

_____ blue square tiles

Area = _____ blue square units

STEP 6 Cover the gray figure with green square tiles. Count and write the number of green square tiles you used. Record the area of the figure.

_____ green square tiles

Area = _____ green square units

Math Talk

Mathematical Practices

Explain why the number of green square tiles needed to cover the figure is different than the number of blue square tiles needed.

Try This! Count to find the area of the figure.

☐ is 1 square centimeter.

There are _____ unit squares in the figure.

So, the area is _____ square centimeters.

© Houghton Mifflin Harcourt Publishing Company

Name _____

1. Count to find the area of the figure. Each unit square is 1 square centimeter.

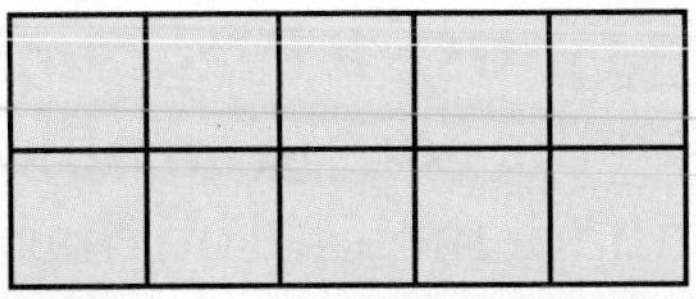

   Think: Are there any gaps? Are there any overlaps?

   There are _____ unit squares in the figure.

   So, the area is _____ square centimeters.

Count to find the area of the figure.
Each unit square is 1 square centimeter.

Math Talk **Mathematical Practices**

Explain how you can use square centimeters to find the area of the figures in Exercises 2 and 3.

2.

   Area = _____ square centimeters

3.

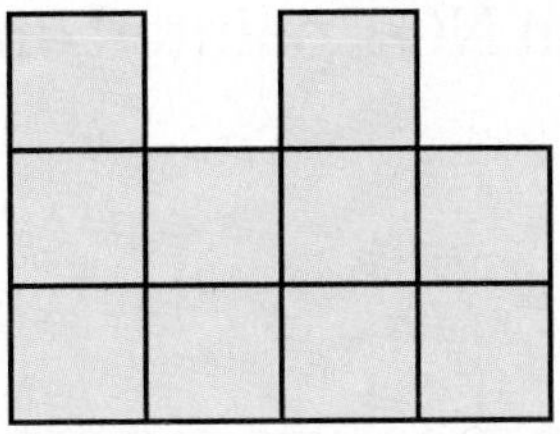

   Area = _____ square centimeters

On Your Own

Count to find the area of the figure.
Each unit square is 1 square inch.

4.

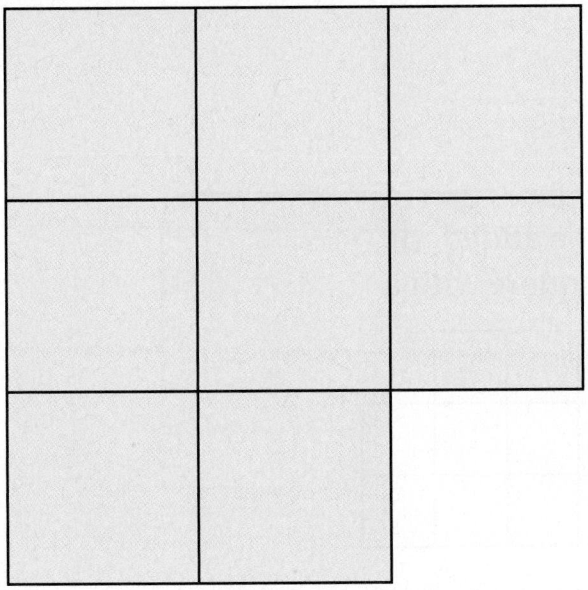

   Area = _____ square inches

5.

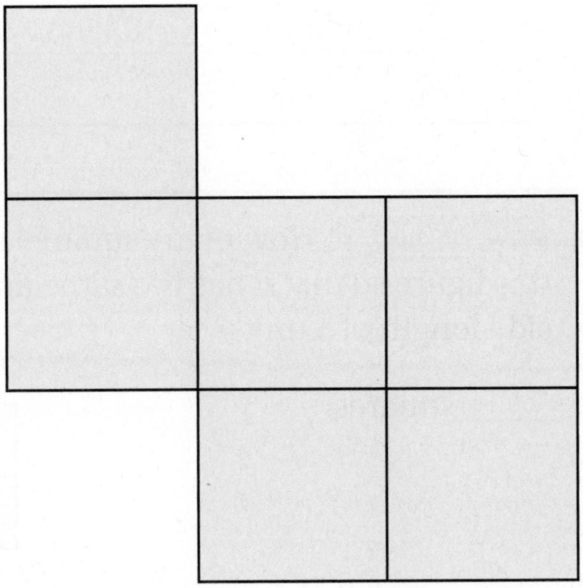

   Area = _____ square inches

© Houghton Mifflin Harcourt Publishing Company

Problem Solving • Applications

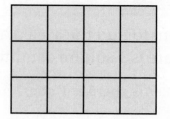

6. **MATHEMATICAL PRACTICE ④ Use a Diagram** Danny is placing tiles on the floor of an office lobby. Each tile is 1 square meter. The diagram shows the lobby. What is the area of the lobby?

_____

7. **GO DEEPER** Angie is painting a space shuttle mural on a wall. Each section is one square foot. The diagram shows the unfinished mural. How many more square feet has Angie painted than NOT painted on her mural?

_____

Rectangle A

8. **THINK SMARTER** You measure the area of a table top with blue unit squares and green unit squares. Which unit square will give you a greater number of square units for area? **Explain.**

_____

_____

_____

9. **THINK SMARTER** How many squares need to be added to this figure so that it has the same area as a square with a side length of 5 units?

_____ squares

© Houghton Mifflin Harcourt Publishing Company

Name _____

Use Area Models

Essential Question Why can you multiply to find the area of a rectangle?

Measurement and Data—3.MD.7, 3. MD.7a *Also 3.MD.5, 3.MD.5a, 3.MD.5b, 3.MD.6, 3.MD.7b, 3.OA.3, 3.OA.7, 3.NBT.2*
MATHEMATICAL PRACTICES
MP.1, MP.3, MP.6, MP.8

Unlock the Problem Real World

Cristina has a garden that is shaped like the rectangle below. Each unit square represents 1 square meter. What is the area of her garden?

• Circle the shape of the garden.

One Way   Count unit squares.

Count the number of unit squares in all.

There are _____ unit squares.

So, the area is _____ square meters.

Other Ways

A Use repeated addition.

Count the number of rows. Count the number of unit squares in each row.

_____ rows of _____ = ■

Write an addition equation.

So, the area is _____ square meters.

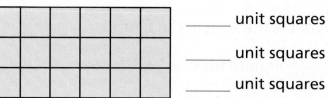

_____ unit squares

_____ unit squares

_____ unit squares

_____ + _____ + _____ = _____

B Use multiplication.

Count the number of rows. Count the number of unit squares in each row.

_____ rows of _____ = ■

This rectangle is like an array. How do you find the total number of squares in an array?

_____

Write a multiplication equation.

So, the area is _____ square meters.

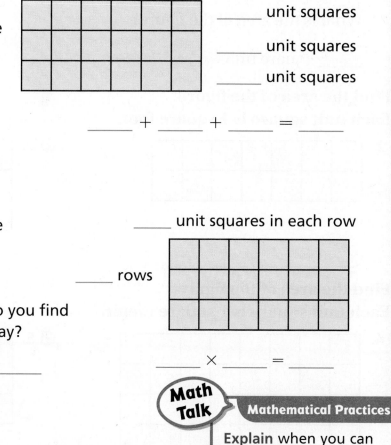

_____ unit squares in each row

_____ rows

_____ × _____ = _____

Math Talk   **Mathematical Practices**

Explain when you can use different methods to find the same area.

© Houghton Mifflin Harcourt Publishing Company

Try This!

**Find the area of the figure.
Each unit square is 1 square foot.**

Think: There are 4 rows of 10 unit squares.

_____ × _____ = _____

So, the area is _____ square feet.

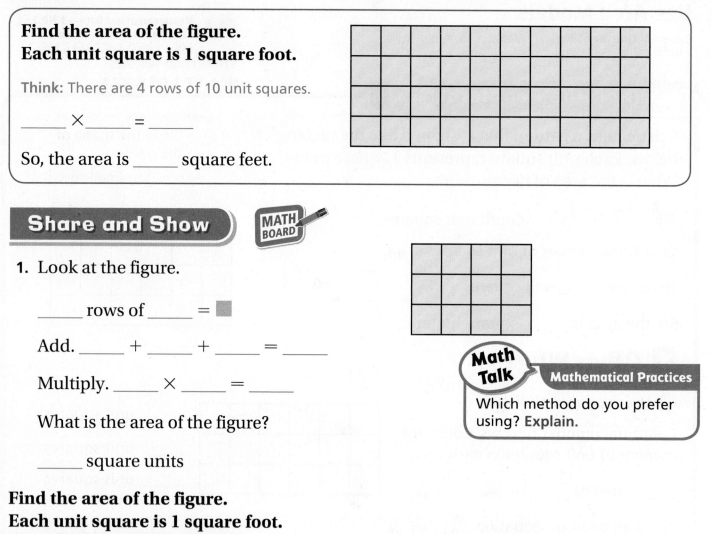

Share and Show MATH BOARD

1. Look at the figure.

_____ rows of _____ = ▨

Add. _____ + _____ + _____ = _____

Multiply. _____ × _____ = _____

What is the area of the figure?

_____ square units

Math Talk **Mathematical Practices**

Which method do you prefer using? **Explain.**

**Find the area of the figure.
Each unit square is 1 square foot.**

2.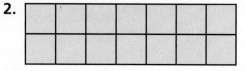

_____

✓ 3.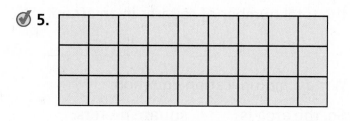

_____

**Find the area of the figure.
Each unit square is 1 square meter.**

4.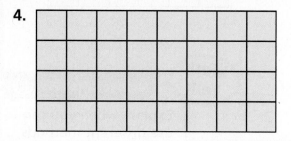

_____

✓ 5.

_____

© Houghton Mifflin Harcourt Publishing Company

Name _____

Find the area of the figure.
Each unit square is 1 square foot.

6.

_____

7.

_____

Find the area of the figure.
Each unit square is 1 square meter.

8.

_____

9.

_____

10. **MATHEMATICAL PRACTICE ④ Use Diagrams** Draw and shade three rectangles with an area of 24 square units. Then write an addition or multiplication equation for each.

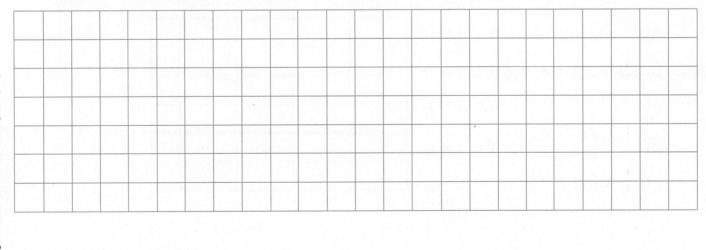

_____

_____

© Houghton Mifflin Harcourt Publishing Company

Problem Solving • Applications Real World

11. **GO DEEPER** Compare the areas of the two rugs at the right. Each unit square represents 1 square foot. Which rug has the greater area? Explain.

_____

_____

_____

12. **THINK SMARTER** A tile company tiled a wall using square tiles. A mural is painted in the center. The drawing shows the design. The area of each tile used is 1 square foot.

Write a problem that can be solved by using the drawing. Then solve your problem.

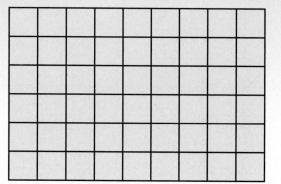

Math on the Spot

_____

_____

_____

13. **THINK SMARTER** Colleen drew this rectangle. Select the equation that can be used to find the area of the rectangle. Mark all that apply.

(A) $9 \times 6 = n$

(B) $9 + 9 + 9 + 9 + 9 + 9 = n$

(C) $9 + 6 = n$

(D) $6 \times 9 = n$

(E) $6 + 6 + 6 + 6 + 6 + 6 = n$

© Houghton Mifflin Harcourt Publishing Company

Mid-Chapter Checkpoint

Vocabulary

Choose the best term from the box.

Vocabulary
area
perimeter
square unit

1. The distance around a figure is the _____. (p. 453)

2. The measure of the number of unit squares needed to cover a figure with no gaps or

   overlaps is the _____. (p. 465)

Concepts and Skills

Find the perimeter of the figure. Each unit is 1 centimeter. (3.MD.8)

3.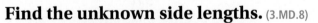

_____ centimeters

4.

_____ centimeters

Find the unknown side lengths. (3.MD.8)

5. Perimeter = 33 centimeters

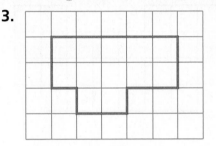

10 cm

4 cm

6 cm

g cm

10 cm

_____ centimeters

6. Perimeter = 32 feet

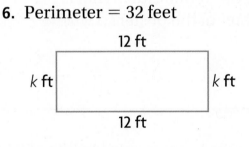

12 ft

k ft   k ft

12 ft

_____ feet

Find the area of the figure. Each unit square is 1 square meter.

(3.MD.5, 3.MD.5a, 3.MD.5b, 3.MD.6, 3.MD.7, 3.MD.7a)

7.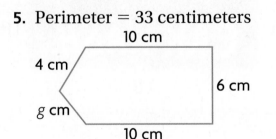

_____ square meters

8.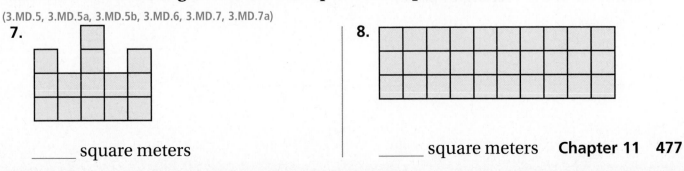

_____ square meters

© Houghton Mifflin Harcourt Publishing Company

9. Ramona is making a lid for her rectangular jewelry box. The jewelry box has side lengths of 6 centimeters and 4 centimeters. What is the area of the lid Ramona is making? (3.MD.7, 3.MD.7a)

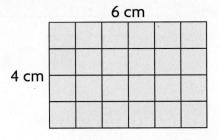

_____

10. Adrienne is decorating a square picture frame. She glued 36 inches of ribbon around the edge of the frame. What is the length of each side of the picture frame? (3.MD.8)

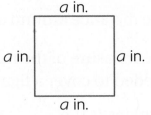

_____

11. Margo will sweep a room. A diagram of the floor that she needs to sweep is shown at the right. What is the area of the floor? (3.MD.5b, 3.MD.6)

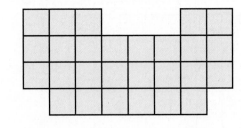

_____

12. Jeff is making a poster for a car wash for the Campout Club. What is the perimeter of the poster? (3.MD.8)

_____

13. A rectangle has two side lengths of 8 inches and two side lengths of 10 inches. What is the perimeter of the rectangle? (3.MD.8)

_____

© Houghton Mifflin Harcourt Publishing Company

Name _____

Problem Solving • Area of Rectangles

Essential Question How can you use the strategy *find a pattern* to solve area problems?

Measurement and Data—3.MD.7b
Also 3.OA.3, 3.OA.7, 3.OA.9
MATHEMATICAL PRACTICES
MP.1, MP.2, MP.6, MP.7

? Unlock the Problem Real World

Mr. Koi wants to build storage buildings, so he drew plans for the buildings. He wants to know how the areas of the buildings are related. How does the area change from the area of Building *A* to the area of Building *B*? How does the area change from the area of Building *C* to the area of Building *D*?

Use the graphic organizer to help you solve the problem.

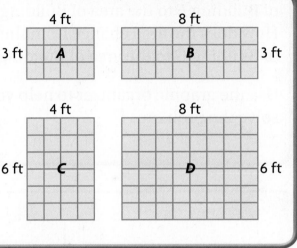

Read the Problem

What do I need to find?	**What information do I need to use?**	**How will I use the information?**
I need to find how the areas will change from *A* to *B* and from _____ to _____.	I need to use the _____ and _____ of each building to find its area.	I will record the areas in a table. Then I will look for a pattern to see how the _____ will change.

Solve the Problem

I will complete the table to find patterns to solve the problem.

	Length	Width	Area		Length	Width	Area
Building *A*	3 ft			Building *C*		4 ft	
Building *B*	3 ft			Building *D*		8 ft	

I see that the lengths will be the same and the widths will be doubled.

The areas will change from _____ to _____ and from _____ to _____.

So, when the lengths are the same and the widths are doubled,

the areas will be _____.

© Houghton Mifflin Harcourt Publishing Company

ⓘ Try Another Problem

Mr. Koi is building more storage buildings. He wants to know how the areas of the buildings are related. How does the area change from the area of Building *E* to the area of Building *F*? How does the area change from the area of Building *G* to the area of Building *H*?

Use the graphic organizer to help you solve the problem.

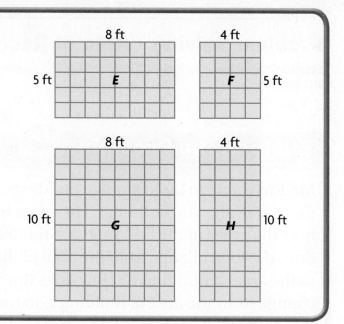

Read the Problem

What do I need to find?	**What information do I need to use?**	**How will I use the information?**

Solve the Problem

	Length	Width	Area		Length	Width	Area
Building *E*				Building *G*			
Building *F*				Building *H*			

- How did your table help you find a pattern?

_____

_____

_____

© Houghton Mifflin Harcourt Publishing Company

Math Talk

Mathematical Practices

What if the length of both sides is doubled? How would the areas change?

Name _____

Use the table for 1–2.

1. Many pools come in rectangular shapes. How do the areas of the swimming pools change when the widths change?

   First, complete the table by finding the area of each pool.

   Think: I can find the area by multiplying the length and the width.

   Then, find a pattern of how the lengths change and how the widths change.

   The _____ stays the same. The widths

   _____.

   Last, describe a pattern of how the area changes.

   The areas _____ by ____ square feet.

Swimming Pool Sizes			
Pool	Length (in feet)	Width (in feet)	Area (in square feet)
A	8	20	
B	8	30	
C	8	40	
D	8	50	

2. What if the length of each pool was 16 feet? Explain how the areas would change.

   _____

On Your Own

3. **MATHEMATICAL PRACTICE 7** **Look for a Pattern** If the length of each pool in the table is 20 feet, and the widths change from 5, to 6, to 7, and to 8 feet, describe the pattern of the areas.

   _____

   _____

© Houghton Mifflin Harcourt Publishing Company

4. **MATHEMATICAL PRACTICE ①** **Analyze Relationships** Jacob has a rectangular garden with an area of 56 square feet. The length of the garden is 8 feet. What is the width of the garden?

_____

5. **GO DEEPER** A diagram of Paula's bedroom is at the right. Her bedroom is in the shape of a rectangle. Write the measurements for the other sides. What is the perimeter of the room? (Hint: The two pairs of opposite sides are equal lengths.)

_____

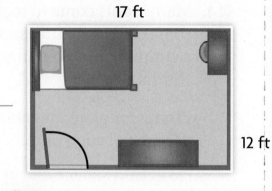

17 ft

12 ft

6. **THINK SMARTER** Elizabeth built a sandbox that is 4 feet long and 4 feet wide. She also built a flower garden that is 4 feet long and 6 feet wide and a vegetable garden that is 4 feet long and 8 feet wide. How do the areas change?

_____

_____

_____

_____

7. **THINK SMARTER** Find the pattern and complete the chart.

Total Area (in square feet)	50	60	70	80	
Length (in feet)	10	10		10	
Width (in feet)	5	6	7		

How can you use the chart to find the length and width of a figure with an area of 100 square feet?

_____

_____

FOR MORE PRACTICE:
Standards Practice Book

© Houghton Mifflin Harcourt Publishing Company

Name _____

Area of Combined Rectangles

Essential Question How can you break apart a figure to find the area?

Measurement and Data—
3.MD.7c, 3.MD.7d
Also 3.MD.5, 3.MD.5a, 3.MD.5b, 3.MD.7b, 3.OA.3, 3.OA.5, 3.OA.7, 3.NBT.2
MATHEMATICAL PRACTICES
MP.1, MP.3, MP.4, MP.6, MP.7

Unlock the Problem · Real World

Anna's rug has side lengths of 4 feet and 9 feet. What is the area of Anna's rug?

Activity Materials ■ square tiles

Remember

You can use the Distributive Property to break apart an array.

$3 \times 3 = 3 \times (2 + 1)$

STEP 1 Use square tiles to model 4×9.

STEP 2 Draw a rectangle on the grid paper to show your model.

STEP 3 Draw a vertical line to break apart the model to make two smaller rectangles.

The side length 9 is broken into _____ plus _____.

STEP 4 Find the area of each of the two smaller rectangles.

Rectangle 1: _____ × _____ = _____

Rectangle 2: _____ × _____ = _____

STEP 5 Add the products to find the total area.

_____ + _____ = _____ square feet

STEP 6 Check your answer by counting the number of square feet.

_____ square feet

So, the area of Anna's rug is _____ square feet.

Math Talk Mathematical Practices

Did you draw a line in the same place as your classmates? **Explain** why you found the same total area.

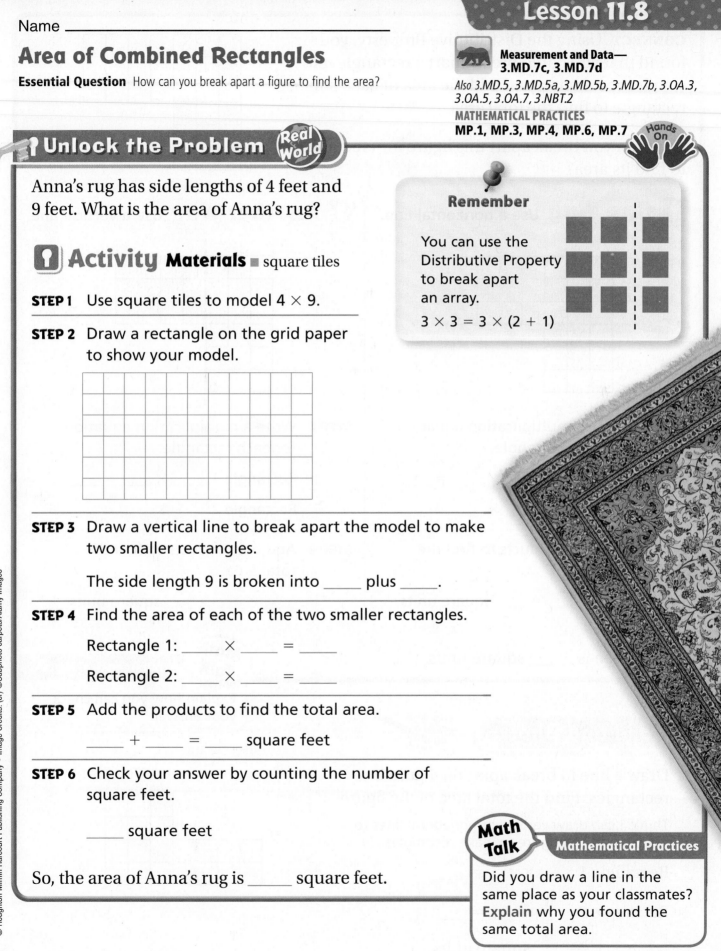

© Houghton Mifflin Harcourt Publishing Company • Image Credits: (cr) ©Sdbphoto carpets/Alamy Images

CONNECT Using the Distributive Property, you found that you could break apart a rectangle into smaller rectangles, and add the area of each smaller rectangle to find the total area.

How can you break apart this figure into rectangles to find its area?

One Way Use a horizontal line.

STEP 1 Write a multiplication equation for each rectangle.

Rectangle 1: ___ × ___ = ___

Rectangle 2: ___ × ___ = ___

STEP 2 Add the products to find the total area.

___ + ___ = ___ square units

Another Way Use a vertical line.

STEP 1 Write a multiplication equation for each rectangle.

Rectangle 1: ___ × ___ = ___

Rectangle 2: ___ × ___ = ___

STEP 2 Add the products to find the total area.

___ + ___ = ___ square units

So, the area is _____ square units.

Math Talk **Mathematical Practices**

Explain how you can check your answer.

Share and Show

MATH BOARD

1. Draw a line to break apart the figure into rectangles. Find the total area of the figure.

   Think: I can draw vertical or horizontal lines to break apart the figure to make rectangles.

   Rectangle 1: ___ × ___ = ___

   Rectangle 2: ___ × ___ = ___

   ___ + ___ = ___ square units

© Houghton Mifflin Harcourt Publishing Company

Name _____

Use the Distributive Property to find the area. Show your multiplication and addition equations.

✓ 2.

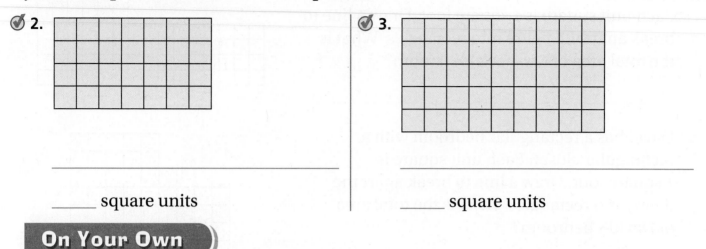

_____

_____ square units

✓ 3.

_____

_____ square units

On Your Own

Use the Distributive Property to find the area. Show your multiplication and addition equations.

4.

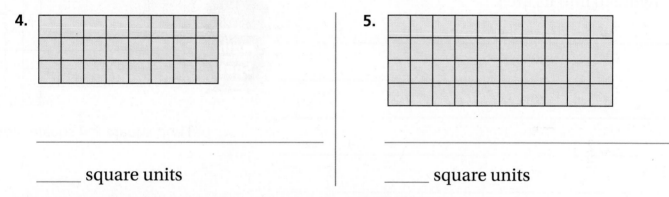

_____

_____ square units

5.

_____

_____ square units

Draw a line to break apart the figure into rectangles. Find the area of the figure.

6.

Rectangle 1: ____ × ____ = ____

Rectangle 2: ____ × ____ = ____

____ + ____ = ____ square units

7. **GO DEEPER**

Rectangle 1: ____ × ____ = ____

Rectangle 2: ____ × ____ = ____

Rectangle 3: ____ × ____ = ____

____ + ____ + ____ = ____ square units

© Houghton Mifflin Harcourt Publishing Company

Problem Solving • Applications

8. A model of Ms. Lee's classroom is at the right. Each unit square is 1 square foot. Draw a line to break apart the figure into rectangles. What is the total area of Ms. Lee's classroom?

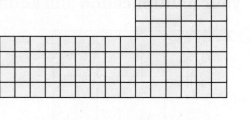

_____

9. David has a rectangular bedroom with a rectangular closet. Each unit square is 1 square foot. Draw a line to break apart the figure into rectangles. What is the total area of David's bedroom?

_____

10. **THINK SMARTER** **Explain** how to break apart the figure to find its area.

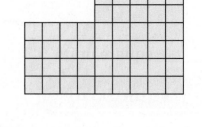

_____

_____

_____

_____

1 unit square = 1 square meter

11. **MATHEMATICAL PRACTICE ④ Interpret a Result** Use the Distributive Property to find the area of the figure at the right. Write your multiplication and addition equations.

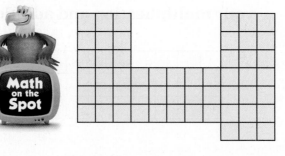

_____

_____

1 unit square = 1 square centimeter

© Houghton Mifflin Harcourt Publishing Company

Personal Math Trainer

12. **THINK SMARTER +** Pete drew a diagram of his backyard on grid paper. Each unit square is 1 square meter. The area surrounding the patio is grass.

How much more of the backyard is grass than patio? Show your work.

_____ more square meters

FOR MORE PRACTICE: Standards Practice Book

Same Perimeter, Different Areas

Essential Question How can you use area to compare rectangles with the same perimeter?

Measurement and Data—3.MD.8
Also 3.MD.5, 3.MD.5a, 3.MD.5b, 3.MD.7b, 3.0A.3, 3.0A.7, 3.NBT.2.
MATHEMATICAL PRACTICES
MP.1, MP.3, MP.4, MP.7

Unlock the Problem Real World

Toby has 12 feet of boards to put around a rectangular sandbox. How long should he make each side so that the area of the sandbox is as large as possible?

- What is the greatest perimeter Toby can make for his sandbox?

_____

Activity

Materials ■ square tiles

Use square tiles to make all the rectangles you can that have a perimeter of 12 units. Draw and label the sandboxes. Then find the area of each.

Sandbox 1

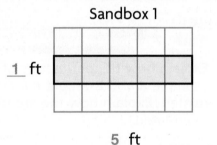

_1_ ft

_5_ ft

Sandbox 2

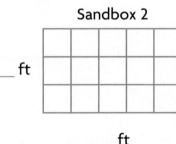

__ ft

__ ft

Sandbox 3

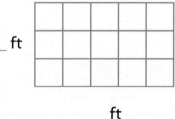

__ ft

__ ft

Find the perimeter and area of each rectangle.

	Perimeter	Area
Sandbox 1	_5_ + _1_ + _5_ + _1_ = _12_ feet	_1_ × _5_ = ___ square feet
Sandbox 2	___ + ___ + ___ + ___ = ___ feet	___ × ___ = ___ square feet
Sandbox 3	___ + ___ + ___ + ___ = ___ feet	___ × ___ = ___ square feet

The area of Sandbox ____ is the greatest.

So, Toby should build a sandbox that is

____ feet wide and ____ feet long.

Math Talk **Mathematical Practices**

How are the sandboxes alike? How are the sandboxes different?

© Houghton Mifflin Harcourt Publishing Company

Examples Draw rectangles with the same perimeter and different areas.

A Draw a rectangle that has a perimeter of 20 units and an area of 24 square units.

The sides of the rectangle measure

_____ units and _____ units.

B Draw a rectangle that has a perimeter of 20 units and an area of 25 square units.

The sides of the rectangle measure

_____ units and _____ units.

> **Math Talk** **Mathematical Practices**
>
> **Explain** how the perimeters of Example *A* and Example *B* are related. **Explain** how the areas are related.

Share and Show MATH BOARD

1. The perimeter of the rectangle at the right is

_____ units. The area is _____ square units.

2. Draw a rectangle that has the same perimeter as the rectangle in Exercise 1 but with a different area.

3. The area of the rectangle in Exercise 2 is

_____ square units.

☑ 4. Which rectangle has the greater area?

_____

5. If you were given a rectangle with a certain perimeter, how would you draw it so that it has the greatest area?

_____

> **Math Talk** **Mathematical Practices**
>
> **Explain** how you knew what the rectangle for Exercise 5 would look like.

© Houghton Mifflin Harcourt Publishing Company

Name _____

Find the perimeter and the area. Tell which rectangle has a greater area.

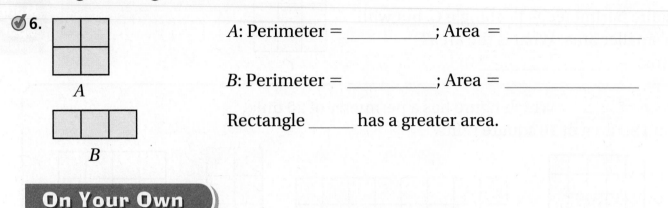

6.

A

B

A: Perimeter = _____; Area = _____

B: Perimeter = _____; Area = _____

Rectangle _____ has a greater area.

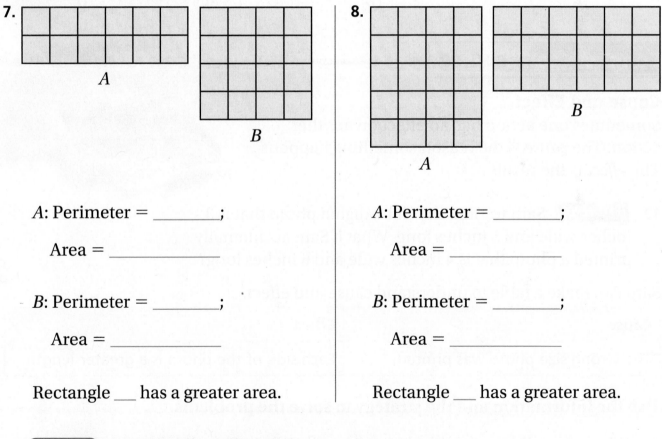

On Your Own

Find the perimeter and the area. Tell which rectangle has a greater area.

7.

A

B

A: Perimeter = _____;

Area = _____

B: Perimeter = _____;

Area = _____

Rectangle ___ has a greater area.

8.

A

B

A: Perimeter = _____;

Area = _____

B: Perimeter = _____;

Area = _____

Rectangle ___ has a greater area.

9. **MATHEMATICAL PRACTICE ⑥ Use Math Vocabulary** Todd's flower garden is 4 feet wide and 8 feet long. If the answer is 32 square feet, what is the question?

_____

© Houghton Mifflin Harcourt Publishing Company

Problem Solving • Applications

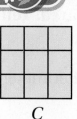

10. **THINK SMARTER** Draw a rectangle with the same perimeter as Rectangle *C*, but with a smaller area. What is the area?

Area = _____

C

11. **THINK SMARTER** Which figure has a perimeter of 20 units and an area of 16 square units?

Ⓐ   Ⓑ   Ⓒ   Ⓓ

Connect to Reading

Cause and Effect

Sometimes one action has an effect on another action. The *cause* is the reason something happens. The *effect* is the result.

12. **GO DEEPER** Sam wanted to print a digital photo that is 3 inches wide and 5 inches long. What if Sam accidentally printed a photo that is 4 inches wide and 6 inches long?

Sam can make a table to understand cause and effect.

Cause	Effect
The wrong size photo was printed.	Each side of the photo is a greater length.

Use the information and the strategy to solve the problems.

a. What effect did the mistake have on the perimeter of the photo?

_____

_____

b. What effect did the mistake have on the area of the photo?

_____

_____

© Houghton Mifflin Harcourt Publishing Company • Image Credits: (cr) ©Elizabeth Whiting & Associates/Alamy

FOR MORE PRACTICE:
Standards Practice Book

Name _____

Same Area, Different Perimeters

Essential Question How can you use perimeter to compare rectangles with the same area?

Measurement and Data—3.MD.8
Also 3.MD.5, 3.MD.5a, 3.MD.5b,
3.MD.7b, 3.OA.3, 3.OA.7, 3.NBT.2
MATHEMATICAL PRACTICES
MP.2, MP.3, MP.4

🔑 Unlock the Problem Real World   Hands On

Marcy is making a rectangular pen to hold her rabbits. The area of the pen should be 16 square meters with side lengths that are whole numbers. What is the least amount of fencing she needs?

• What does the least amount of fencing represent?

_____

🔒 Activity Materials ■ square tiles

Use 16 square tiles to make rectangles. Make as many different rectangles as you can with 16 tiles. Record the rectangles on the grid, write the multiplication equation for the area shown by the rectangle, and find the perimeter of each rectangle.

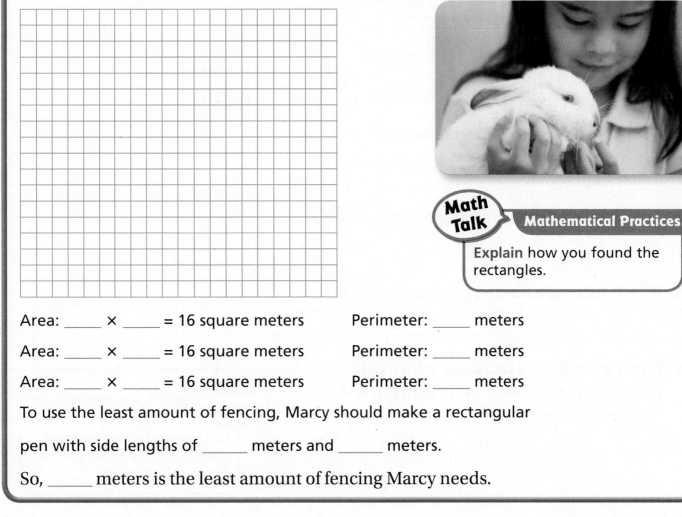

Math Talk **Mathematical Practices**

Explain how you found the rectangles.

Area: _____ × _____ = 16 square meters   Perimeter: _____ meters

Area: _____ × _____ = 16 square meters   Perimeter: _____ meters

Area: _____ × _____ = 16 square meters   Perimeter: _____ meters

To use the least amount of fencing, Marcy should make a rectangular

pen with side lengths of _____ meters and _____ meters.

So, _____ meters is the least amount of fencing Marcy needs.

© Houghton Mifflin Harcourt Publishing Company • Image Credits: (tr) © somos/veer/Getty Images

Try This!

Draw three rectangles that have an area of 18 square units on the grid. Find the perimeter of each rectangle. Shade the rectangle that has the greatest perimeter.

Share and Show

1. The area of the rectangle at the right is

   _____ square units. The perimeter is _____ units.

2. Draw a rectangle that has the same area as the rectangle in Exercise 1 but with a different perimeter.

3. The perimeter of the rectangle in Exercise 2 is

   _____ units.

✓ 4. Which rectangle has the greater perimeter?

   _____

5. If you were given a rectangle with a certain area, how would you draw it so that it had the greatest perimeter?

   _____

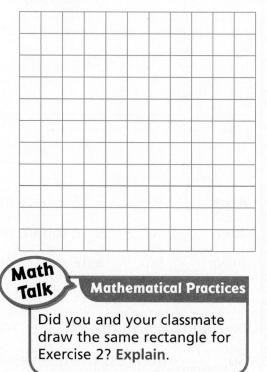

Math Talk **Mathematical Practices**

Did you and your classmate draw the same rectangle for Exercise 2? **Explain.**

© Houghton Mifflin Harcourt Publishing Company

Name _____

Find the perimeter and the area. Tell which rectangle has a greater perimeter.

6.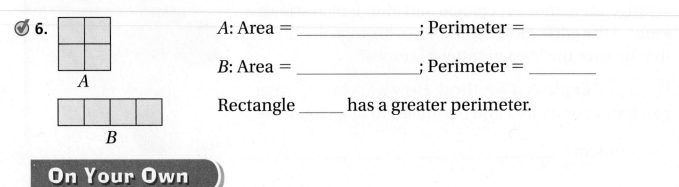

A: Area = _____; Perimeter = _____

B: Area = _____; Perimeter = _____

Rectangle _____ has a greater perimeter.

On Your Own

Find the perimeter and the area. Tell which rectangle has a greater perimeter.

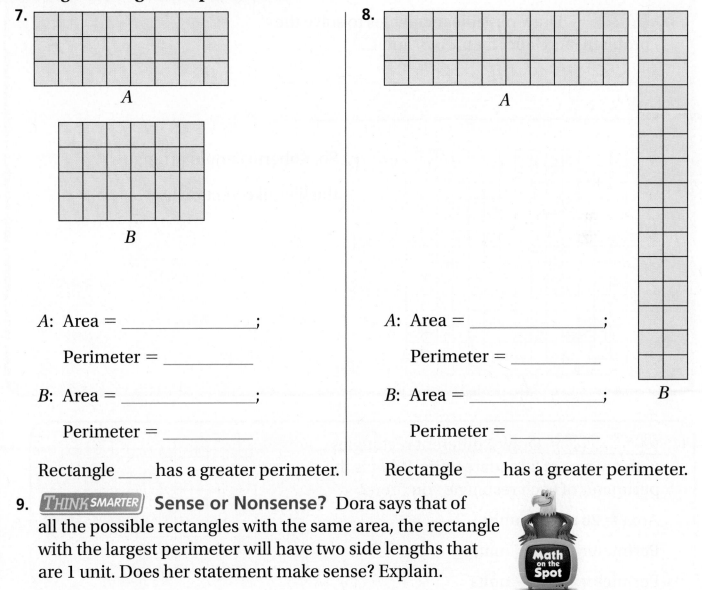

7.

A: Area = _____;

Perimeter = _____

B: Area = _____;

Perimeter = _____

Rectangle _____ has a greater perimeter.

8.

A: Area = _____;

Perimeter = _____

B: Area = _____;

Perimeter = _____

Rectangle _____ has a greater perimeter.

9. **THINK SMARTER** **Sense or Nonsense?** Dora says that of all the possible rectangles with the same area, the rectangle with the largest perimeter will have two side lengths that are 1 unit. Does her statement make sense? Explain.

_____

© Houghton Mifflin Harcourt Publishing Company

🔑 Unlock the Problem (Real World)

10. Roberto has 12 tiles. Each tile is 1 square inch. He will arrange them into a rectangle and glue 1-inch stones around the edge. How can Roberto arrange the tiles so that he uses the least number of stones?

a. **MATHEMATICAL PRACTICE 6** **Explain a Method** How will you use what you know about area and perimeter to help you solve

the problem? _____

_____

_____

b. **GO DEEPER** Draw possible rectangles to solve the problem, and label them *A*, *B*, and *C*.

_____

_____

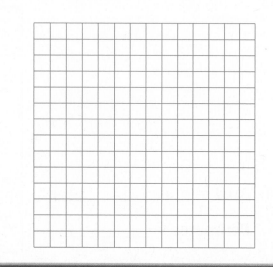

c. So, Roberto should arrange

the tiles like Rectangle _____.

11. **THINK SMARTER** Draw 2 different rectangles with an area of 20 square units. What is the perimeter of each rectangle you drew?

Area = 20 square units

Perimeter = _____ units

Perimeter = _____ units

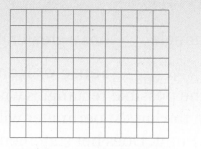

© Houghton Mifflin Harcourt Publishing Company • Image Credits: (tr) ©george doyle/Getty Images; ©Rosemary Calvert/Getty Images

Chapter 11 Review/Test

1. Find the perimeter of each figure on the grid. Identify the figure that have a perimeter of 14 units. Mark all that apply.

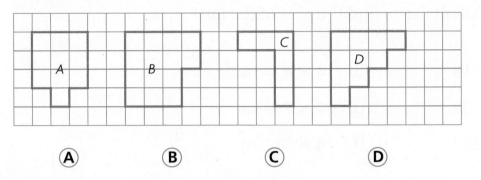

Ⓐ   Ⓑ   Ⓒ   Ⓓ

2. Kim wants to put trim around a picture she drew. How many centimeters of trim does Kim need for the perimeter of the picture?

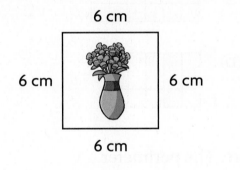

_____ centimeters

3. Sophia drew this rectangle on dot paper. What is the area of the rectangle?

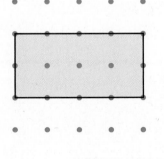

_____ square units

© Houghton Mifflin Harcourt Publishing Company

Assessment Options
Chapter Test

4. The drawing shows Seth's plan for a fort in his backyard. Each unit square is 1 square foot.

Which equations can Seth use to find the area of the fort? Mark all that apply.

(A) $4 + 4 + 4 + 4 = 16$

(D) $4 \times 4 = 16$

(B) $7 + 4 + 7 + 4 = 22$

(E) $7 \times 7 = 49$

(C) $7 + 7 + 7 + 7 = 28$

(F) $4 \times 7 = 28$

5. Which rectangle has a number of square units for its area equal to the number of units of its perimeter?

(A)

(C)

(B)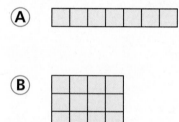

(D)

6. Vanessa uses a ruler to draw a square. The perimeter of the square is 12 centimeters. Select a number to complete the sentence.

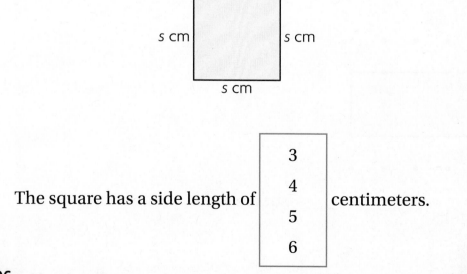

The square has a side length of

| 3 |
| 4 |
| 5 |
| 6 |

centimeters.

© Houghton Mifflin Harcourt Publishing Company

Name _____

7. Tomas drew two rectangles on grid paper.

Circle the words that make the sentence true.

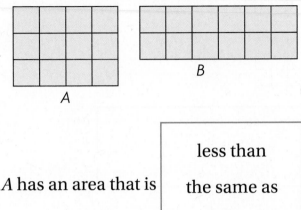

Rectangle *A* has an area that is
| less than |
| the same as |
| greater than |

the area of Rectangle *B*, and a perimeter that is

| less than |
| the same as |
| greater than |
the perimeter of Rectangle *B*.

8. Yuji drew this figure on grid paper. What is the perimeter of the figure?

_____ units

9. What is the area of the figure shown? Each unit square is 1 square meter.

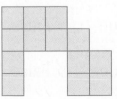

_____ square meters

© Houghton Mifflin Harcourt Publishing Company

10. Shawn drew a rectangle that was 2 units wide and 6 units long. Draw a different rectangle that has the same perimeter but a different area.

11. Mrs. Rios put a wallpaper border around the room shown below. She used 72 feet of wallpaper border.

What is the unknown side length? Show your work.

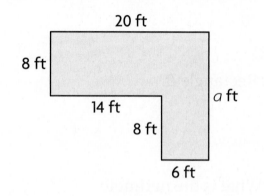

_____ feet

12. Elizabeth has two gardens in her yard. The first garden is 8 feet long and 6 feet wide. The second garden is half the length of the first garden. The area of the second garden is twice the area of the first garden. For numbers 12a–12d, select True or False.

12a.	The area of the first garden is 48 square feet.	○ True ○ False
12b.	The area of the second garden is 24 square feet.	○ True ○ False
12c.	The width of the second garden is 12 feet.	○ True ○ False
12d.	The width of the second garden is 24 feet.	○ True ○ False

© Houghton Mifflin Harcourt Publishing Company

13. Marcus bought some postcards. Each postcard had a perimeter of 16 inches. Which could be one of the postcards Marcus bought? Mark all that apply.

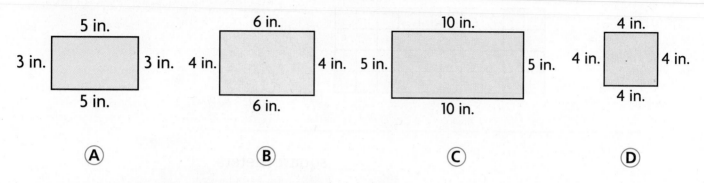

5 in.

3 in.   3 in.

5 in.

Ⓐ

6 in.

4 in.   4 in.

6 in.

Ⓑ

10 in.

5 in.   5 in.

10 in.

Ⓒ

4 in.

4 in.   4 in.

4 in.

Ⓓ

14. Anthony wants to make two different rectangular flowerbeds, each with an area of 24 square feet. He will build a wooden frame around each flowerbed. The flowerbeds will have side lengths that are whole numbers.

Part A

Each unit square on the grid below is 1 square foot. Draw two possible flowerbeds. Label each with a letter.

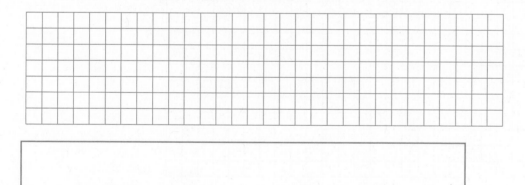

Part B

Which of the flowerbeds will take more wood to frame? Explain how you know.

_____

_____

_____

© Houghton Mifflin Harcourt Publishing Company

15. Keisha draws a sketch of her living room on grid paper. Each unit square is 1 square meter. Write and solve a multiplication equation that can be used to find the area of the living room in square meters.

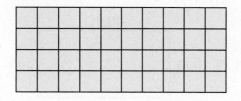

_____

_____ square meters

16. Mr. Wicks designs houses. He uses grid paper to plan a new house design. The kitchen will have an area between 70 square feet and 85 square feet. The pantry will have an area between 4 square feet and 15 square feet. Draw and label a diagram to show what Mr. Wicks could design. Explain how to find the total area.

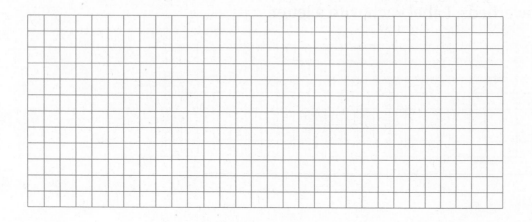

_____

_____

© Houghton Mifflin Harcourt Publishing Company

© Houghton Mifflin Harcourt Publishing Company

Critical Area Geometry

CRITICAL AREA Describing and analyzing two-dimensional shapes

Students at Dommerich Elementary helped design and construct a mosaic to show parts of their community and local plants and animals.

Make a Mosaic

Have you ever worked to put puzzle pieces together to make a picture or design? Pieces of paper can be put together to make a colorful work of art called a mosaic.

Get Started

Materials ■ construction paper ■ glue ■ ruler ■ scissors

Work with a partner to make a paper mosaic. Use the Important Facts to help you.

- Draw a simple pattern on a piece of paper.

- Cut out shapes, such as rectangles, squares, and triangles of the colors you need from construction paper. The shapes should be about 1 inch on each side.

- Glue the shapes into the pattern. Leave a little space between each shape to make the mosaic effect.

Describe and compare the shapes you used to make your mosaic.

Important Facts

- Mosaics is the art of using small pieces of materials, such as tiles or glass, to make a colorful picture or design.
- Mosaic pieces can be small plane shapes, such as rectangles, squares, and triangles.
- Mosaic designs and patterns can be anything from simple flower shapes to common objects found in your home or patterns in nature.

Completed by _____

© Houghton Mifflin Harcourt Publishing Company

Show What You Know ✓

Check your understanding of important skills.

Name _____

▶ **Plane Shapes**

1. Color the triangles blue.

2. Color the rectangles red.

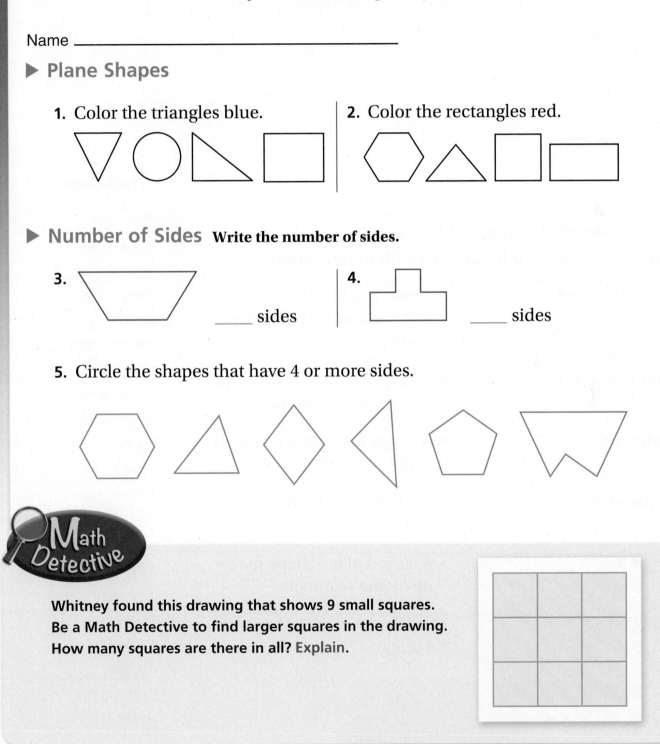

▶ **Number of Sides** Write the number of sides.

3. _____ sides

4. _____ sides

5. Circle the shapes that have 4 or more sides.

© Houghton Mifflin Harcourt Publishing Company

Math Detective

Whitney found this drawing that shows 9 small squares.
Be a Math Detective to find larger squares in the drawing.
How many squares are there in all? Explain.

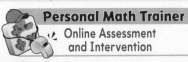

Personal Math Trainer
Online Assessment
and Intervention

Vocabulary Builder

▶ **Visualize It** ••

Complete the tree map by using the words with a ✓.

polygon

▶ **Understand Vocabulary** ••••••••••••••••••••••••••

Draw a line to match the word with its definition.

1. closed shape •

         • A part of a line that includes two endpoints and all the points between them

2. line segment •

         • A shape formed by two rays that share an endpoint

3. right angle •

         • A shape that starts and ends at the same point

4. hexagon •

         • An angle that forms a square corner

5. angle •

         • A closed plane shape made up of line segments

6. polygon •

         • A polygon with 6 sides and 6 angles

Preview Words

angle
closed shape
hexagon
intersecting lines
line
line segment
open shape
parallel lines
perpendicular lines
point
polygon
✓ quadrilateral
ray
✓ rectangle
✓ rhombus
right angle
✓ square
✓ trapezoid
✓ triangle
Venn diagram
vertex

© Houghton Mifflin Harcourt Publishing Company

• **Interactive Student Edition**
• **Multimedia eGlossary**

Name _____

Describe Plane Shapes

Essential Question What are some ways to describe two-dimensional shapes?

Geometry—3.G.1

MATHEMATICAL PRACTICES
MP.5, MP.6, MP.7

🔑 Unlock the Problem · Real World

An architect draws plans for houses, stores, offices, and other buildings. Look at the shapes in the drawing at the right.

A **plane shape** is a shape on a flat surface. It is formed by points that make curved paths, line segments, or both.

point • is an exact position or location	point	**line** • is a straight path • continues in both directions • does not end	
endpoints • points that are used to show segments of lines	endpoints	**line segment** • is straight • is part of a line • has 2 endpoints	

ray
• is straight   • is part of a line   • has 1 endpoint   • continues in one direction

Some plane shapes are made by connecting line segments at their endpoints. One example is a square. Describe a square using math words.

Think: How many line segments and endpoints does a square have?

A square has ____ line segments. The line

segments meet only at their _____.

Math Talk **Mathematical Practices**

Explain why you cannot measure the length of a line.

© Houghton Mifflin Harcourt Publishing Company

Plane shapes have length and width but no thickness, so they are also called **two-dimensional shapes**.

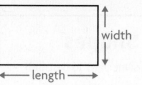
width

length

Try This! Draw plane shapes.

Plane shapes can be open or closed.

A **closed shape** starts and ends at the same point.

In the space below, draw more examples of closed shapes.

An **open shape** does not start and end at the same point.

In the space below, draw more examples of open shapes.

Math Talk **Mathematical Practices**

Explain whether a shape with a curved path must be a closed shape, an open shape, or can be either.

• Is the plane shape at the right a closed shape or an open shape? Explain how you know.

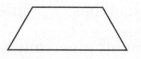

_____

_____

506

© Houghton Mifflin Harcourt Publishing Company

Share and Show

MATH BOARD

1. Write how many line segments

   the shape has. _____

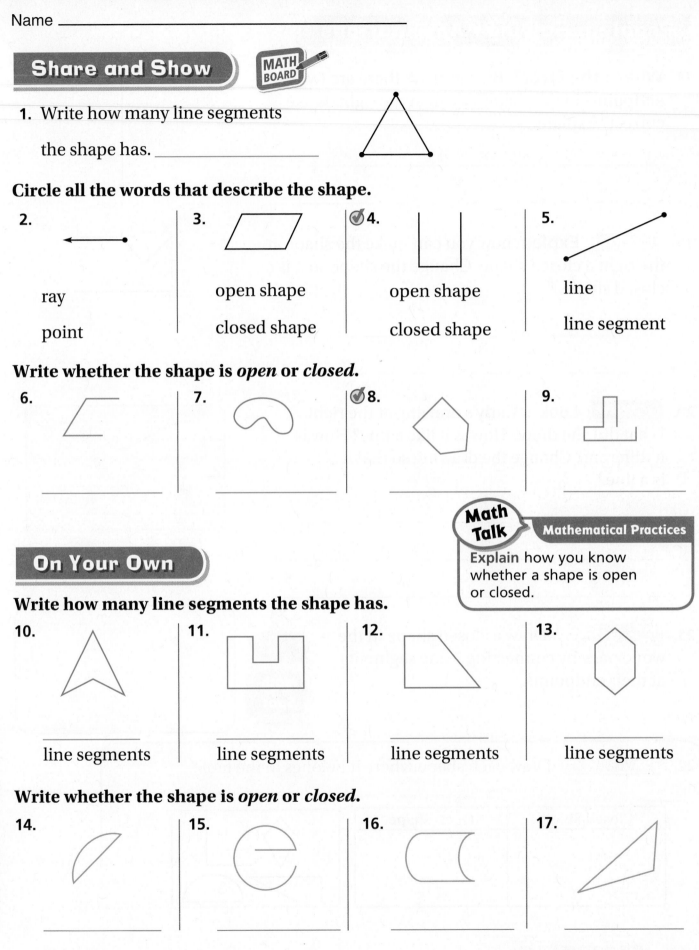

Circle all the words that describe the shape.

2.

   ray

   point

3.

   open shape

   closed shape

✓4.

   open shape

   closed shape

5.

   line

   line segment

Write whether the shape is *open* or *closed*.

6. _____

7. _____

✓8. _____

9. _____

Math Talk **Mathematical Practices**

Explain how you know whether a shape is open or closed.

On Your Own

Write how many line segments the shape has.

10.

   _____
   line segments

11.

   _____
   line segments

12.

   _____
   line segments

13.

   _____
   line segments

Write whether the shape is *open* or *closed*.

14. _____

15. _____

16. _____

17. _____

© Houghton Mifflin Harcourt Publishing Company

Problem Solving • Applications

18. What's the Error? Brittany says there are two endpoints in the shape shown at the right. Is she correct? Explain.

_____

_____

19. **MATHEMATICAL PRACTICE 6** **Explain** how you can make the shape at the right a closed shape. Change the shape so it is a closed shape.

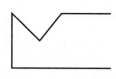

_____

_____

20. **GO DEEPER** Look at Carly's drawing at the right. What did she draw? How is it like a line? How is it different? Change the drawing so that it is a line.

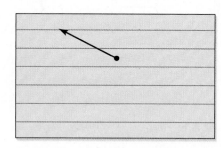

_____

_____

21. **THINK SMARTER** Draw a closed shape in the workspace by connecting 5 line segments at their endpoints.

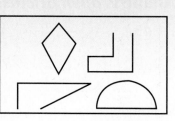

22. **THINK SMARTER** Draw each shape where it belongs in the table.

Closed Shape	Open Shape

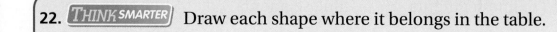

© Houghton Mifflin Harcourt Publishing Company

Describe Angles in Plane Shapes

Essential Question How can you describe angles in plane shapes?

Unlock the Problem (Real World)

An **angle** is formed by two rays that share an endpoint. Plane shapes have angles formed by two line segments that share an endpoint. The shared endpoint is called a **vertex**. The plural of *vertex* is *vertices*.

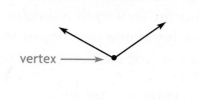

vertex →

Jason drew this shape on dot paper.

• How many angles are in Jason's shape?

_____

Look at the angles in the shape that Jason drew.

How can you describe the angles?

Describe angles.

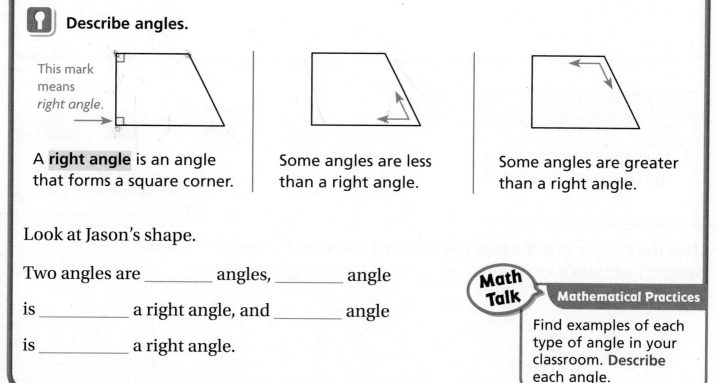

This mark means *right angle.* →

A **right angle** is an angle that forms a square corner.

Some angles are less than a right angle.

Some angles are greater than a right angle.

Look at Jason's shape.

Two angles are _____ angles, _____ angle

is _____ a right angle, and _____ angle

is _____ a right angle.

Math Talk **Mathematical Practices**

Find examples of each type of angle in your classroom. **Describe** each angle.

© Houghton Mifflin Harcourt Publishing Company

Activity Model angles.

Materials ■ bendable straws ■ scissors ■ paper ■ pencil

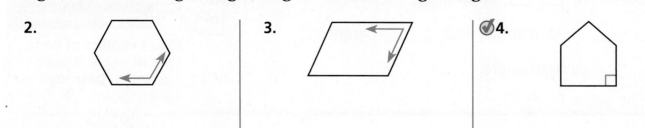

- Cut a small slit in the shorter section of a bendable straw. Cut off the shorter section of a second straw and the bendable part. Insert the slit end of the first straw into the second straw.

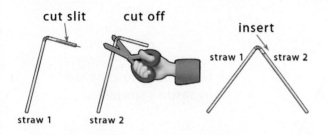

cut slit   cut off

insert

straw 1   straw 2

straw 1   straw 2

- Make an angle with the straws you put together. Compare the angle you made to a corner of the sheet of paper.

- Open and close the straws to make other types of angles.

In the space below, trace the angles you made with the straws. Label each *right angle, less than a right angle,* or *greater than a right angle.*

Share and Show

 MATH BOARD

1. How many angles are in the triangle at the right?

_____

Math Talk — **Mathematical Practices**

Explain how you know an angle is greater than or less than a right angle.

Use the corner of a sheet of paper to tell whether the angle is a *right angle, less than a right angle,* or *greater than a right angle.*

2.

3.

✓4.

_____   _____   _____

© Houghton Mifflin Harcourt Publishing Company

Name _____

Write how many of each type of angle the shape has.

5.

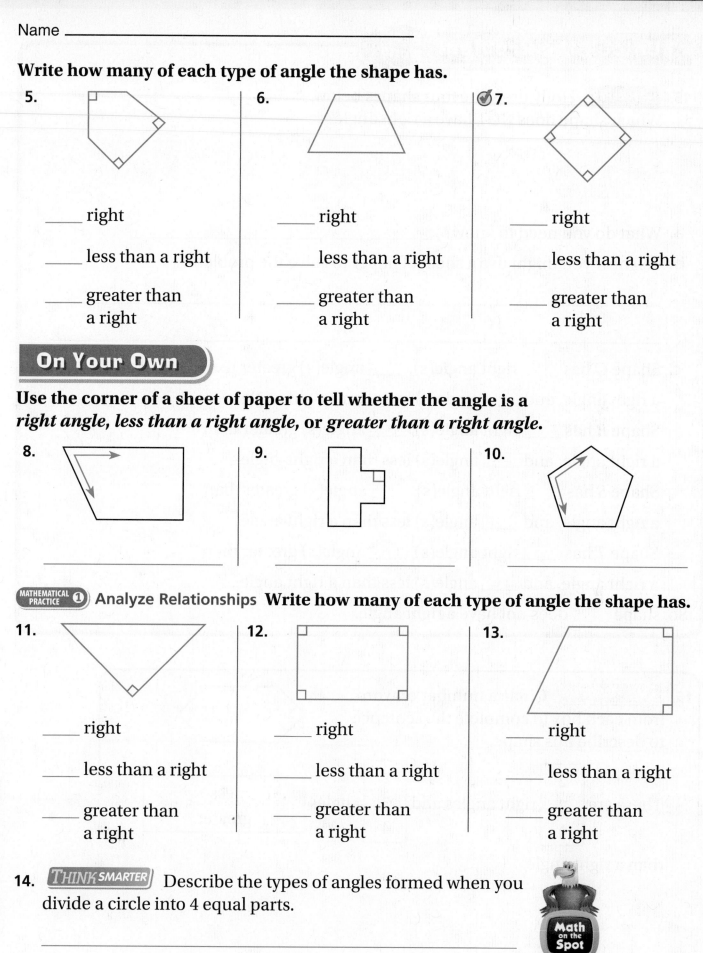

____ right

____ less than a right

____ greater than
a right

6.

____ right

____ less than a right

____ greater than
a right

7.

____ right

____ less than a right

____ greater than
a right

On Your Own

Use the corner of a sheet of paper to tell whether the angle is a
right angle, less than a right angle, **or** *greater than a right angle.*

8.

_____

9.

_____

10.

_____

MATHEMATICAL PRACTICE ① Analyze Relationships **Write how many of each type of angle the shape has.**

11.

____ right

____ less than a right

____ greater than
a right

12.

____ right

____ less than a right

____ greater than
a right

13.

____ right

____ less than a right

____ greater than
a right

14. THINK **SMARTER** Describe the types of angles formed when you
divide a circle into 4 equal parts.

_____

© Houghton Mifflin Harcourt Publishing Company

🔑 Unlock the Problem (Real World)

15. **GO DEEPER** Holly drew the four shapes below.
Which shape does NOT have a right angle?

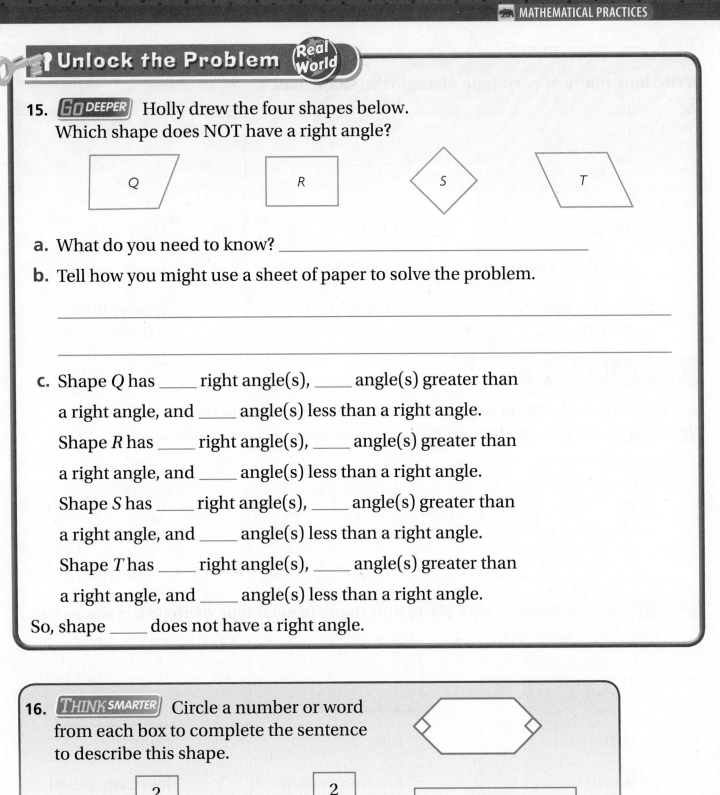

a. What do you need to know? _____

b. Tell how you might use a sheet of paper to solve the problem.

_____

_____

c. Shape *Q* has _____ right angle(s), _____ angle(s) greater than
a right angle, and _____ angle(s) less than a right angle.

Shape *R* has _____ right angle(s), _____ angle(s) greater than
a right angle, and _____ angle(s) less than a right angle.

Shape *S* has _____ right angle(s), _____ angle(s) greater than
a right angle, and _____ angle(s) less than a right angle.

Shape *T* has _____ right angle(s), _____ angle(s) greater than
a right angle, and _____ angle(s) less than a right angle.

So, shape _____ does not have a right angle.

16. **THINK SMARTER** Circle a number or word
from each box to complete the sentence
to describe this shape.

There are
| 2 |
| 3 |
| 4 |
right angles and
| 2 |
| 3 |
| 4 |
angles
| less |
| greater |

than a right angle.

© Houghton Mifflin Harcourt Publishing Company

FOR MORE PRACTICE:
Standards Practice Book

Name _____

Identify Polygons

Essential Question How can you use line segments and angles to make polygons?

Geometry—3.G.1

MATHEMATICAL PRACTICES
MP.2, MP.6, MP.7

CONNECT In earlier lessons, you learned about line segments and angles. In this lesson, you will see how line segments and angles make polygons.

A **polygon** is a closed plane shape that is made up of line segments that meet only at their endpoints. Each line segment in a polygon is a **side**.

> **Math Idea**
> All polygons are closed shapes. Not all closed shapes are polygons.

🔑 Unlock the Problem (Real World)

Circle all the words that describe the shape.

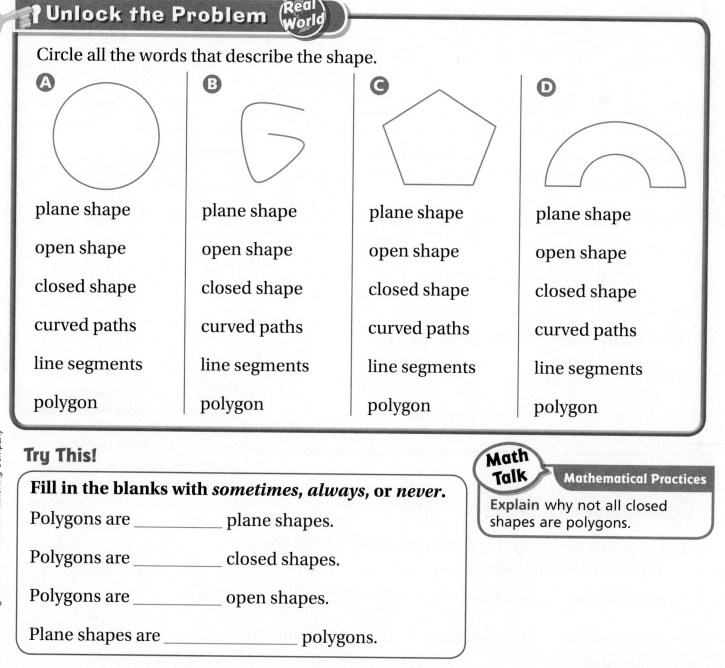

A	B	C	D
plane shape	plane shape	plane shape	plane shape
open shape	open shape	open shape	open shape
closed shape	closed shape	closed shape	closed shape
curved paths	curved paths	curved paths	curved paths
line segments	line segments	line segments	line segments
polygon	polygon	polygon	polygon

Try This!

Fill in the blanks with *sometimes*, *always*, or *never*.

Polygons are _____ plane shapes.

Polygons are _____ closed shapes.

Polygons are _____ open shapes.

Plane shapes are _____ polygons.

> **Math Talk** Mathematical Practices
> **Explain** why not all closed shapes are polygons.

© Houghton Mifflin Harcourt Publishing Company

Name Polygons Polygons are named by the number of sides and angles they have.

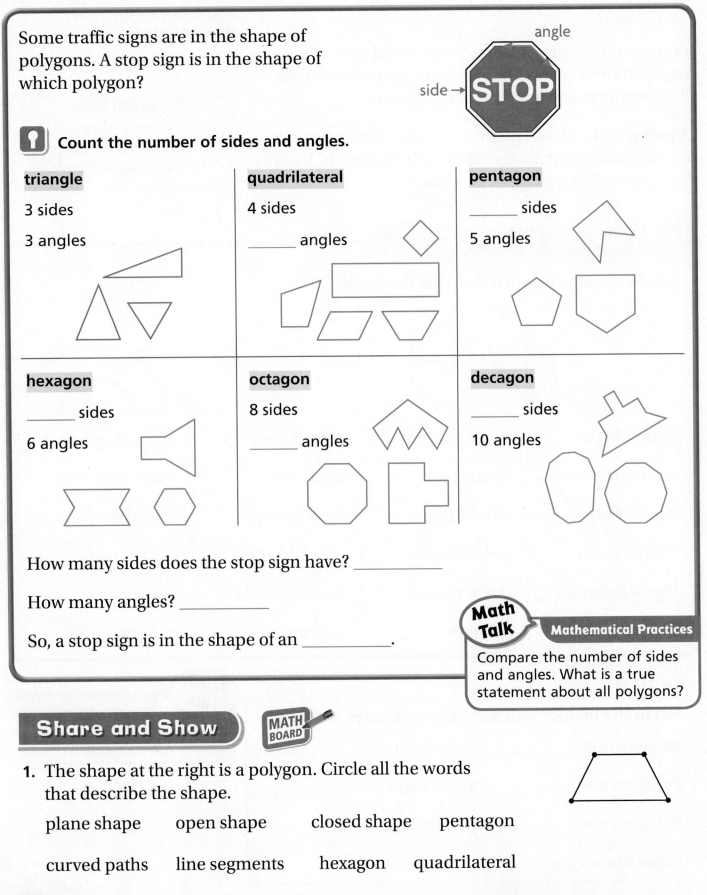

Some traffic signs are in the shape of polygons. A stop sign is in the shape of which polygon?

angle

side → STOP

🔑 **Count the number of sides and angles.**

triangle

3 sides

3 angles

quadrilateral

4 sides

_____ angles

pentagon

_____ sides

5 angles

hexagon

_____ sides

6 angles

octagon

8 sides

_____ angles

decagon

_____ sides

10 angles

How many sides does the stop sign have? _____

How many angles? _____

So, a stop sign is in the shape of an _____.

Math Talk **Mathematical Practices**

Compare the number of sides and angles. What is a true statement about all polygons?

Share and Show MATH BOARD

1. The shape at the right is a polygon. Circle all the words that describe the shape.

   plane shape   open shape   closed shape   pentagon

   curved paths   line segments   hexagon   quadrilateral

© Houghton Mifflin Harcourt Publishing Company

Name _____

Is the shape a polygon? Write *yes* or *no*.

2.

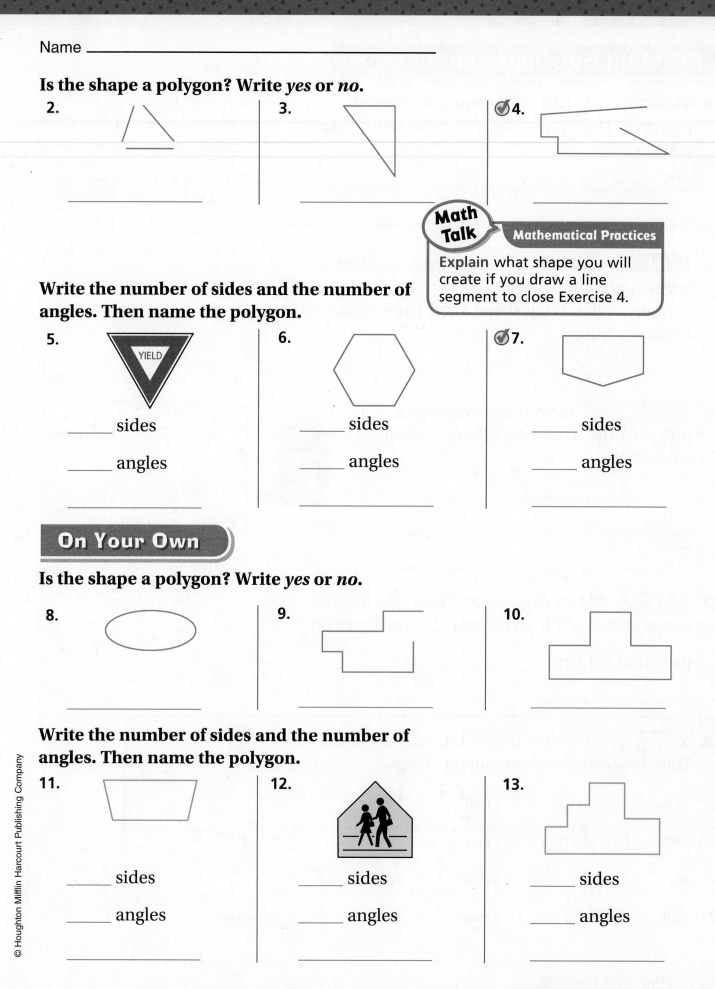

3.

✓4.

Math Talk **Mathematical Practices**

Explain what shape you will create if you draw a line segment to close Exercise 4.

Write the number of sides and the number of angles. Then name the polygon.

5.

YIELD

_____ sides

_____ angles

_____

6.

_____ sides

_____ angles

_____

✓7.

_____ sides

_____ angles

_____

On Your Own

Is the shape a polygon? Write *yes* or *no*.

8.

9.

10.

Write the number of sides and the number of angles. Then name the polygon.

11.

_____ sides

_____ angles

_____

12.

_____ sides

_____ angles

_____

13.

_____ sides

_____ angles

_____

© Houghton Mifflin Harcourt Publishing Company

Problem Solving • Applications

14. **WRITE** ▸*Math* Jake said Shapes *A—E* are all polygons. Does this statement make sense? Explain your answer.

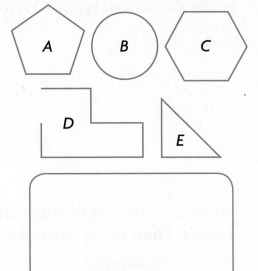

_____

_____

15. **GO DEEPER** I am a closed shape made of 6 line segments. I have 2 angles less than a right angle and no right angles. What shape am I? Draw an example in the workspace.

_____

16. **THINK SMARTER** Is every closed shape a polygon? Use a drawing to help explain your answer.

_____

_____

_____

17. **MATHEMATICAL PRACTICE ③** **Make Arguments** Ivan says that the shape at the right is an octagon. Do you agree or disagree? Explain. _____

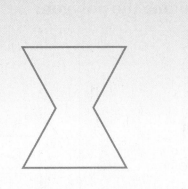

_____

18. **THINK SMARTER** For numbers 18a–18d, select True or False for each description of this shape.

18a.	polygon	○ True	○ False
18b.	open shape	○ True	○ False
18c.	hexagon	○ True	○ False
18d.	pentagon	○ True	○ False

© Houghton Mifflin Harcourt Publishing Company

Describe Sides of Polygons

Essential Question How can you describe line segments that are sides of polygons?

Geometry—3.G.1

MATHEMATICAL PRACTICES
MP.1, MP.4, MP.8

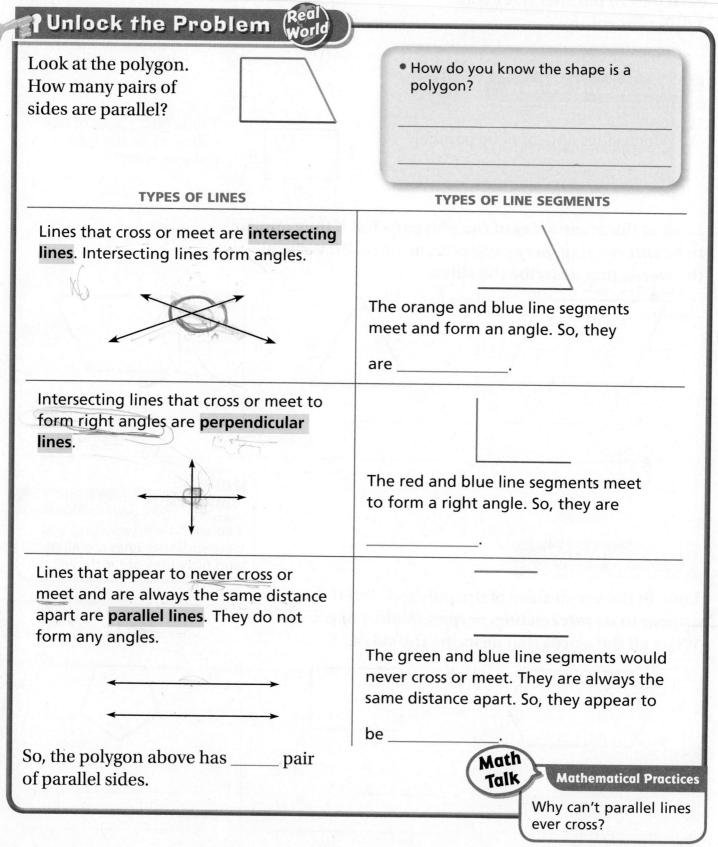

Unlock the Problem (Real World)

Look at the polygon. How many pairs of sides are parallel?

- How do you know the shape is a polygon?

_____

_____

TYPES OF LINES

Lines that cross or meet are **intersecting lines**. Intersecting lines form angles.

Intersecting lines that cross or meet to form right angles are **perpendicular lines**.

Lines that appear to never cross or meet and are always the same distance apart are **parallel lines**. They do not form any angles.

TYPES OF LINE SEGMENTS

The orange and blue line segments meet and form an angle. So, they

are _____.

The red and blue line segments meet to form a right angle. So, they are

_____.

The green and blue line segments would never cross or meet. They are always the same distance apart. So, they appear to

be _____.

So, the polygon above has _____ pair of parallel sides.

Math Talk

Mathematical Practices

Why can't parallel lines ever cross?

© Houghton Mifflin Harcourt Publishing Company

Try This! Draw a polygon with only 1 pair of parallel sides. Then draw a polygon with 2 pairs of parallel sides. Outline each pair of parallel sides with a different color.

Share and Show

1. Which sides appear to be parallel?

_____

c

b   *d*

a

Think: Which pairs of sides appear to be the same distance apart?

Look at the green sides of the polygon. Tell if they appear to be *intersecting, perpendicular,* or *parallel.* Write all the words that describe the sides.

2.

_____

_____

✓ 3.

_____

_____

✓ 4.

_____

_____

Math Talk   **Mathematical Practices**

Explain how intersecting and perpendicular lines are alike and how they are different.

On Your Own

Look at the green sides of the polygon. Tell if they appear to be *intersecting, perpendicular,* or *parallel.* Write all the words that describe the sides.

5.

_____

_____

6.

_____

_____

7.

_____

_____

© Houghton Mifflin Harcourt Publishing Company

Name _____

Problem Solving • Applications

Use pattern blocks *A–E* for 8–11.

Chelsea wants to sort pattern blocks by the types of sides.

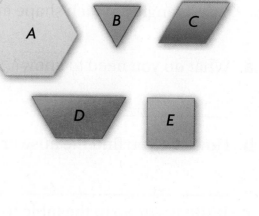

8. Which blocks have intersecting sides?

_____

9. Which blocks have parallel sides?

_____

10. Which blocks have perpendicular sides?

_____

11. Which blocks have neither parallel nor perpendicular sides?

_____

12. **Go DEEPER** How many pairs of perpendicular line segments are in the box at the right?

_____

13. **THINK SMARTER** Can the same two lines be parallel, perpendicular, and intersecting at the same time? Explain your answer.

▲ The red line segments show 1 pair of perpendicular line segments.

_____

_____

_____

© Houghton Mifflin Harcourt Publishing Company

Unlock the Problem

14. **MATHEMATICAL PRACTICE ③** **Compare Representations** I am a pattern block that has 2 fewer sides than a hexagon. I have 2 pairs of parallel sides and 4 right angles. Which shape am I?

a. What do you need to know? _____

_____

b. How can you find the answer to the riddle? _____

_____

c. Write *yes* or *no* in the table to solve the riddle.

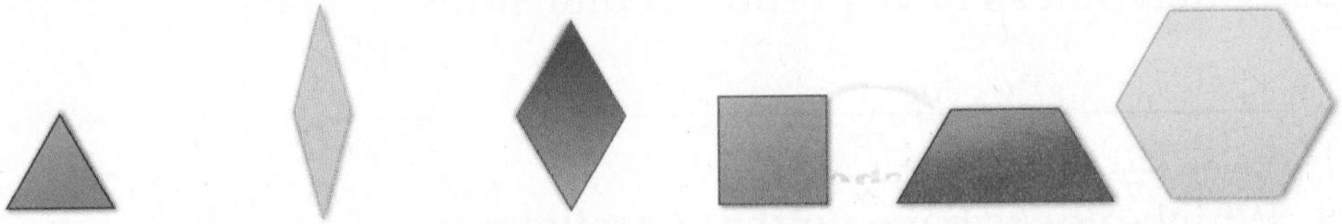

2 fewer sides than a hexagon						
2 pairs of parallel sides						
4 right angles						

So, the _____ is the shape.

15. **THINK SMARTER** Select the shapes that have at least one pair of parallel sides. Mark all that apply.

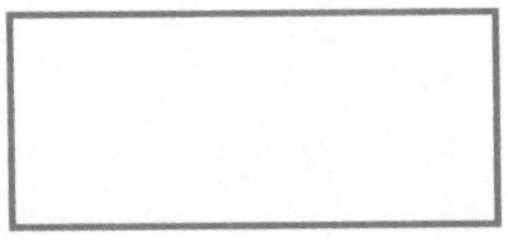

Ⓐ

Ⓒ

Ⓑ

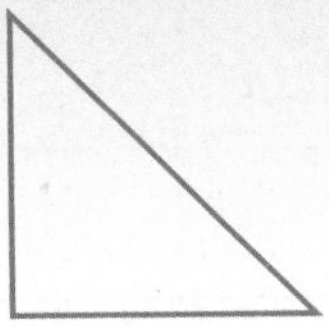

Ⓓ

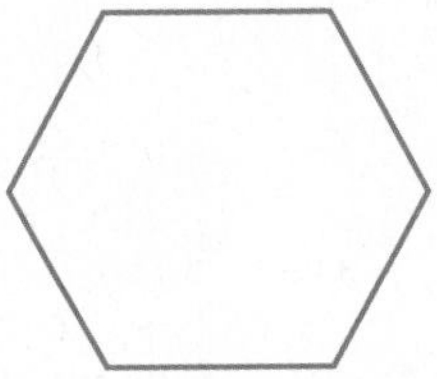

FOR MORE PRACTICE:
Standards Practice Book

© Houghton Mifflin Harcourt Publishing Company

Name _____

Mid-Chapter Checkpoint

Vocabulary

Choose the best term from the box to complete the sentence.

Vocabulary
angle
point
polygon
right angle

1. An _____ is formed by two rays that share an endpoint. (p. 509)

2. A _____ is a closed shape made up of line segments. (p. 513)

3. A _____ forms a square corner. (p. 509)

Concepts and Skills

Use the corner of a sheet of paper to tell whether the angle is a *right angle, less than a right angle,* or *greater than a right angle.* (3.G.1)

4.
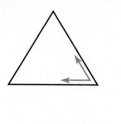
_____

5.
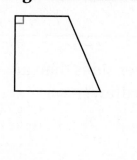
_____

6.
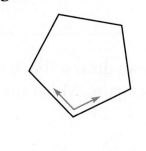
_____

Write the number of sides and the number of angles. Then name the polygon. (3.G.1)

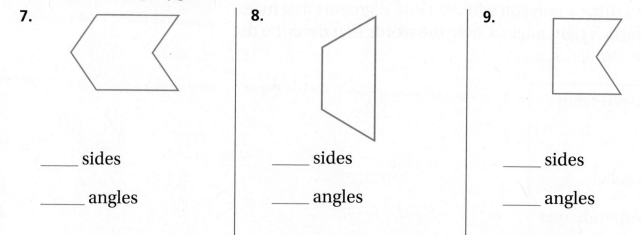

7.

____ sides

____ angles

_____

8.

____ sides

____ angles

_____

9.

____ sides

____ angles

_____

© Houghton Mifflin Harcourt Publishing Company

10. Anne drew the shape at the right. Is her shape an open shape or a closed shape? (3.G.1)

_____

11. This sign tells drivers there is a steep hill ahead. Write the number of sides and the number of angles in the shape of the sign. Then name the shape. (3.G.1)

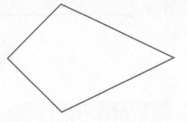

_____

12. Why is this closed plane shape NOT a polygon? (3.G.1)

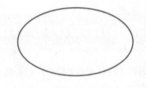

_____

_____

13. Sean drew a shape with 2 fewer sides than an octagon. Which shape did he draw? (3.G.1)

_____

14. John drew a polygon with two line segments that meet to form a right angle. Circle the words that describe the line segments. (3.G.1)

intersecting

curved

parallel

perpendicular

© Houghton Mifflin Harcourt Publishing Company

Name _____

Classify Quadrilaterals

Essential Question How can you use sides and angles to help you describe quadrilaterals?

Geometry—3.G.1

MATHEMATICAL PRACTICES
MP.2, MP.4, MP.6

Unlock the Problem (Real World)

Quadrilaterals are named by their sides and their angles.

Describe quadrilaterals.

quadrilateral

_____ sides

_____ angles

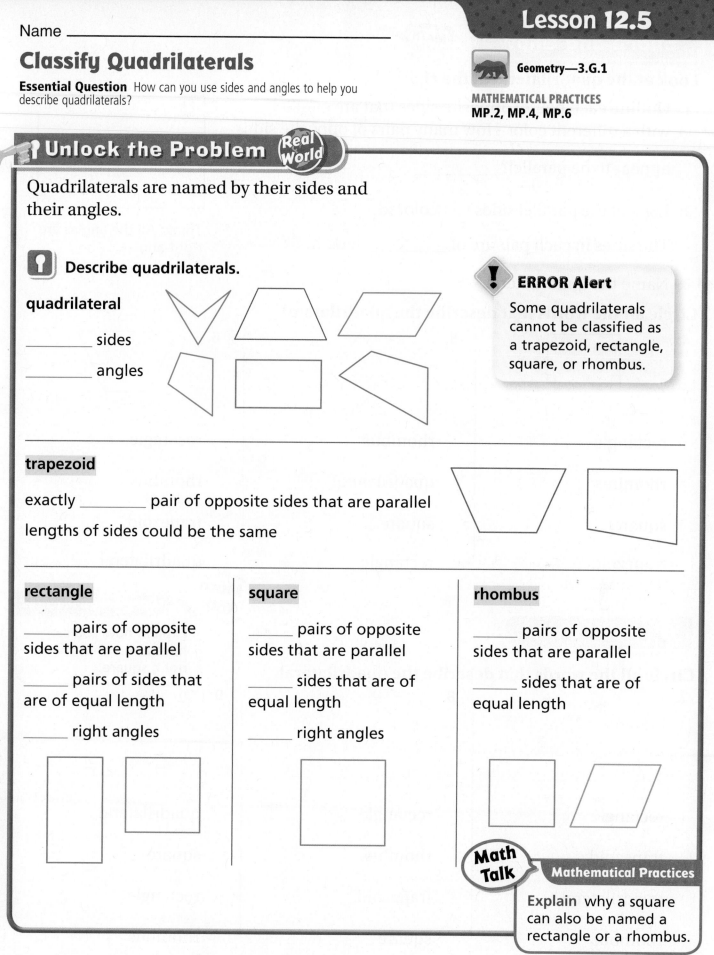

! ERROR Alert
Some quadrilaterals cannot be classified as a trapezoid, rectangle, square, or rhombus.

---

trapezoid

exactly _____ pair of opposite sides that are parallel

lengths of sides could be the same

---

rectangle

_____ pairs of opposite sides that are parallel

_____ pairs of sides that are of equal length

_____ right angles

square

_____ pairs of opposite sides that are parallel

_____ sides that are of equal length

_____ right angles

rhombus

_____ pairs of opposite sides that are parallel

_____ sides that are of equal length

Math Talk — **Mathematical Practices**

Explain why a square can also be named a rectangle or a rhombus.

© Houghton Mifflin Harcourt Publishing Company

Look at the quadrilateral at the right.

1. Outline each pair of opposite sides that are parallel with a different color. How many pairs of opposite sides appear to be parallel? _____

2. Look at the parallel sides you colored.

   The sides in each pair are of _____ length.

3. Name the quadrilateral. _____

Think: All the angles are right angles.

Circle all the words that describe the quadrilateral.

4.

rectangle

rhombus

square

trapezoid

5.

rhombus

quadrilateral

square

rectangle

6.

rectangle

rhombus

trapezoid

quadrilateral

On Your Own

Math Talk **Mathematical Practices**

Explain how you can have a rhombus that is not a square.

Circle all the words that describe the quadrilateral.

7.

rectangle

trapezoid

quadrilateral

rhombus

8.

rectangle

rhombus

trapezoid

square

9.

quadrilateral

square

rectangle

rhombus

© Houghton Mifflin Harcourt Publishing Company

Name _____

Problem Solving • Applications

Use the quadrilaterals at the right for 10–12.

10. Which quadrilaterals appear to have 4 right angles?

_____

11. Which quadrilaterals appear to have 2 pairs of opposite sides that are parallel?

_____

12. Which quadrilaterals appear to have no right angles?

_____

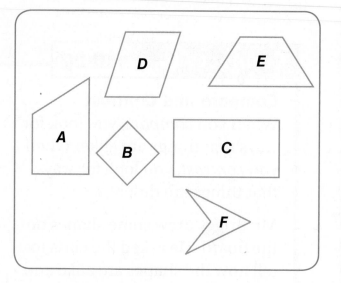

Write *all* or *some* to complete the sentence for 13–18.

13. The opposite sides of _____ rectangles are parallel.

14. _____ sides of a rhombus are the same length.

15. _____ squares are rectangles.

16. _____ rhombuses are squares.

17. _____ quadrilaterals are polygons.

18. _____ polygons are quadrilaterals.

19. **MATHEMATICAL PRACTICE ⑥** Circle the shape at the right that is not a quadrilateral. **Explain** your choice.

_____

_____

_____

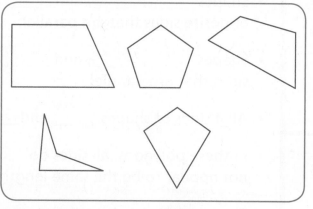

20. **THINK SMARTER** I am a polygon that has 4 sides and 4 angles. At least one of my angles is less than a right angle. Circle all the shapes that I could be.

quadrilateral   rectangle   square   rhombus   trapezoid

© Houghton Mifflin Harcourt Publishing Company

Chapter 12 • Lesson 5   525

21. **THINK SMARTER** Identify the quadrilateral that can have two pairs of parallel sides and no right angles.

(A) rhombus   (B) square   (C) trapezoid

Connect to Reading

Compare and Contrast

When you *compare*, you look for ways that things are alike. When you *contrast*, you look for ways that things are different.

Mr. Briggs drew some shapes on the board. He asked the class to tell how the shapes are alike and how they are different.

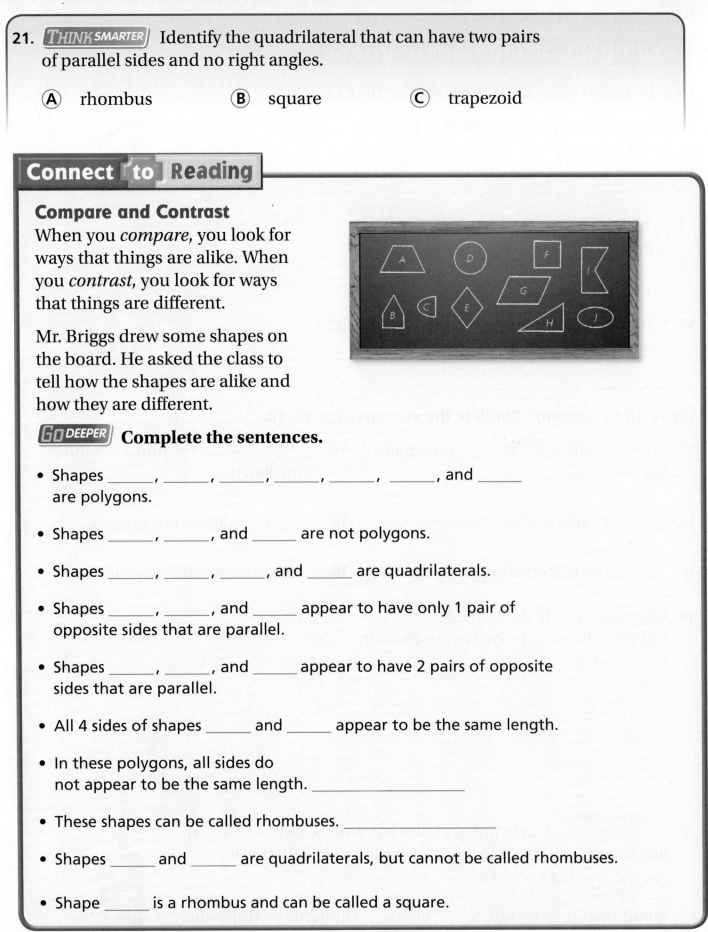

GO DEEPER **Complete the sentences.**

• Shapes _____, _____, _____, _____, _____, _____, and _____ are polygons.

• Shapes _____, _____, and _____ are not polygons.

• Shapes _____, _____, _____, and _____ are quadrilaterals.

• Shapes _____, _____, and _____ appear to have only 1 pair of opposite sides that are parallel.

• Shapes _____, _____, and _____ appear to have 2 pairs of opposite sides that are parallel.

• All 4 sides of shapes _____ and _____ appear to be the same length.

• In these polygons, all sides do not appear to be the same length. _____

• These shapes can be called rhombuses. _____

• Shapes _____ and _____ are quadrilaterals, but cannot be called rhombuses.

• Shape _____ is a rhombus and can be called a square.

FOR MORE PRACTICE:
Standards Practice Book

© Houghton Mifflin Harcourt Publishing Company

Name _____

Draw Quadrilaterals

Essential Question How can you draw quadrilaterals?

🔑 Unlock the Problem

CONNECT You have learned to classify quadrilaterals by the number of pairs of opposite sides that are parallel, by the number of pairs of sides of equal length, and by the number of right angles.

How can you draw quadrilaterals?

🔓 Activity 1 Use grid paper to draw quadrilaterals.

Materials ■ ruler

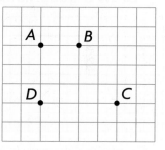

• Use a ruler to draw line segments from points A to B, from B to C, from C to D, and from D to A.

• Write the name of your quadrilateral.

_____

🔓 Activity 2 Draw a shape that does not belong.

Materials ■ ruler

Ⓐ Here are three examples of a quadrilateral. Draw an example of a polygon that is not a quadrilateral.

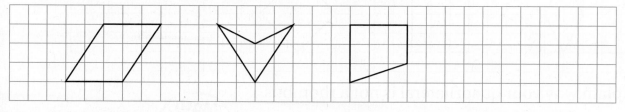

• Explain why your polygon is not a quadrilateral.

_____

_____

© Houghton Mifflin Harcourt Publishing Company

B Here are three examples of a square.
Draw a quadrilateral that is not a square.

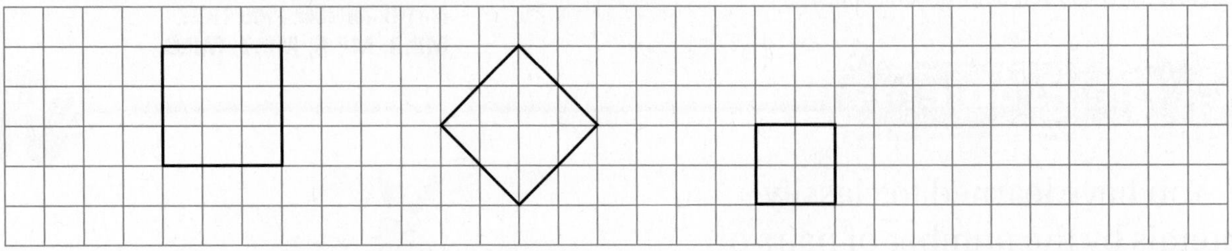

- Explain why your quadrilateral is not a square.

_____

_____

C Here are three examples of a rectangle.
Draw a quadrilateral that is not a rectangle.

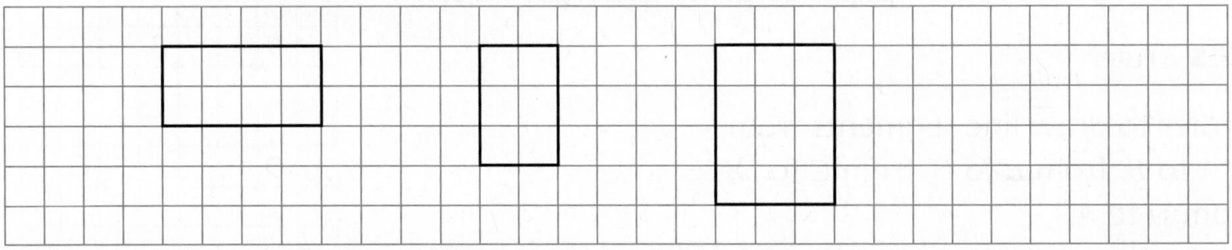

- Explain why your quadrilateral is not a rectangle.

_____

_____

D Here are three examples of a rhombus.
Draw a quadrilateral that is not a rhombus.

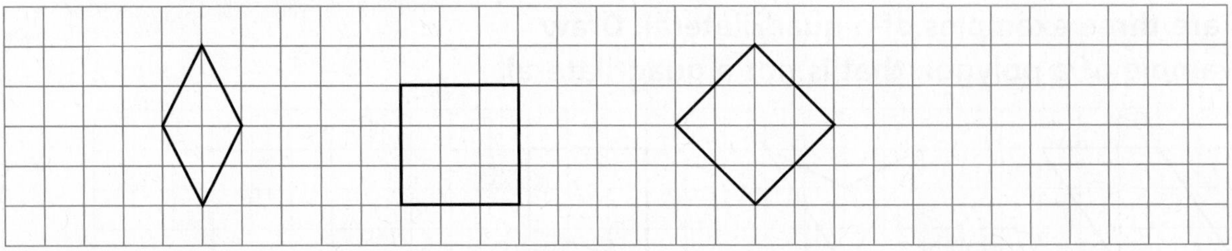

- Explain why your quadrilateral is not a rhombus.

_____

_____

Math Talk **Mathematical Practices**

Compare your drawings with your classmates. **Explain** how your drawings are alike and how they are different.

© Houghton Mifflin Harcourt Publishing Company

Name _____

1. Choose four endpoints that connect to make a rectangle.

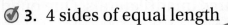

   Think: A rectangle has 2 pairs of opposite sides that are parallel, 2 pairs of sides of equal length, and 4 right angles.

Draw a quadrilateral that is described.
Name the quadrilateral you drew.

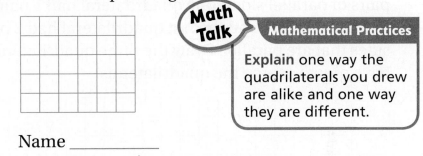

2. 2 pairs of equal sides

Name _____

3. 4 sides of equal length

Name _____

Math Talk

Mathematical Practices

Explain one way the quadrilaterals you drew are alike and one way they are different.

On Your Own

Practice: Copy and Solve Use grid paper to draw a quadrilateral that is described. Name the quadrilateral you drew.

4. exactly 1 pair of opposite sides that are parallel

5. 4 right angles

6. 2 pairs of sides of equal length

Draw a quadrilateral that does not belong. Then explain why.

7.

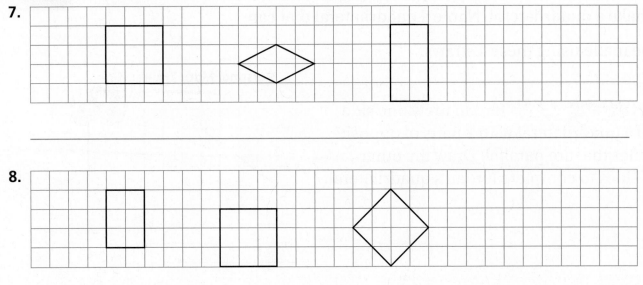

8.

Problem Solving • Applications (Real World)

9. (MATHEMATICAL PRACTICE ③) **Make Arguments** Jacki drew the shape at the right. She said it is a rectangle because it has 2 pairs of opposite sides that are parallel. Describe her error.

_____

_____

10. Go DEEPER Adam drew three quadrilaterals. One quadrilateral had no pairs of parallel sides, one quadrilateral had 1 pair of opposite sides that are parallel, and the last quadrilateral had 2 pairs of opposite sides that are parallel. Draw the three quadrilaterals that Adam could have drawn. Name the quadrilaterals.

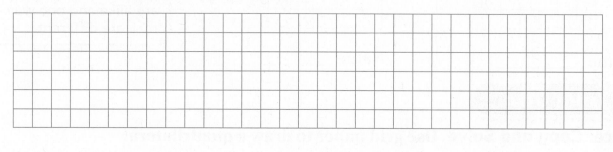

_____ _____ _____

11. THINK SMARTER Amy has 4 straws of equal length. Name the quadrilaterals that can be made using these 4 straws.

_____ Amy cuts one of the straws in half. She uses the two halves and two of the other straws to make a quadrilateral. Name a quadrilateral that can

be made using these 4 straws. _____

Personal Math Trainer

12. THINK SMARTER ➕ Jordan drew one side of a quadrilateral with 2 pairs of opposite sides that are parallel. Draw the other 3 sides to complete Jordan's quadrilateral.

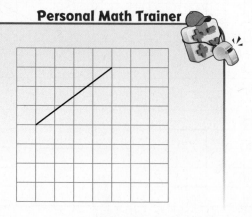

© Houghton Mifflin Harcourt Publishing Company

FOR MORE PRACTICE:
Standards Practice Book

Name _____

Describe Triangles

Essential Question How can you use sides and angles to help you describe triangles?

 Geometry—3.G.1

MATHEMATICAL PRACTICES
MP.4, MP.5, MP.7, MP.8

🔑 Unlock the Problem Real World

Hands On

How can you use straws of different lengths to make triangles?

🔒 Activity Materials ▪ straws ▪ scissors ▪ MathBoard

STEP 1 Cut straws into different lengths.

STEP 2 Find straw pieces that you can put together to make a triangle. Draw your triangle on the MathBoard.

STEP 3 Find straw pieces that you cannot put together to make a triangle.

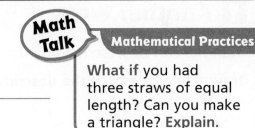

---

1. Compare the lengths of the sides. Describe when you can make a triangle.

_____

_____

Math Talk **Mathematical Practices**

What if you had three straws of equal length? Can you make a triangle? **Explain.**

2. **MATHEMATICAL PRACTICE ❶** **Describe** when you cannot make a triangle.

_____

_____

_____

3. Explain how you can change the straw pieces in

Step 3 to make a triangle. _____

_____

© Houghton Mifflin Harcourt Publishing Company

Ways to Describe Triangles

What are two ways triangles can be described?

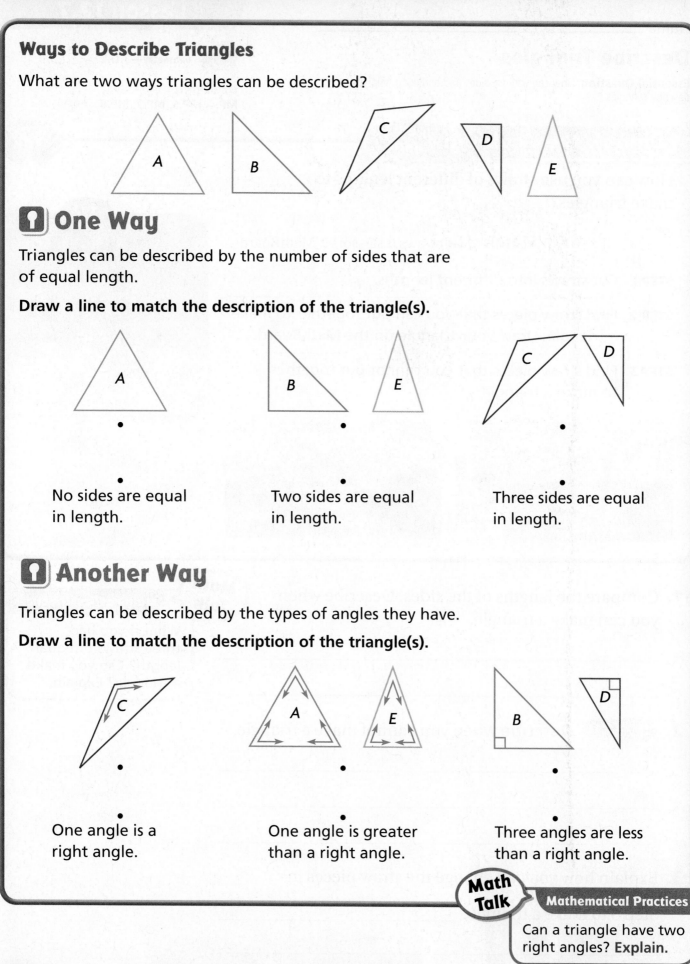

🔒 One Way

Triangles can be described by the number of sides that are of equal length.

Draw a line to match the description of the triangle(s).

No sides are equal in length.

Two sides are equal in length.

Three sides are equal in length.

🔒 Another Way

Triangles can be described by the types of angles they have.

Draw a line to match the description of the triangle(s).

One angle is a right angle.

One angle is greater than a right angle.

Three angles are less than a right angle.

Math Talk

© Houghton Mifflin Harcourt Publishing Company

Mathematical Practices

Can a triangle have two right angles? **Explain.**

Name _____

1. Write the number of sides of equal length the triangle appears to have.

_____

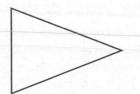

Use the triangles for 2–4. Write *F*, *G*, or *H*.

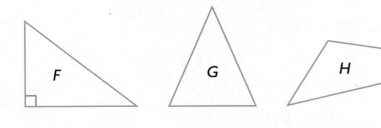

2. Triangle _____ has 1 right angle.

✓3. Triangle _____ has 1 angle greater than a right angle.

✓4. Triangle _____ has 3 angles less than a right angle.

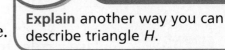
Math Talk **Mathematical Practices**

Explain another way you can describe triangle *H*.

On Your Own

**Use the triangles for 5–7. Write *K*, *L*, or *M*.
Then complete the sentences.**

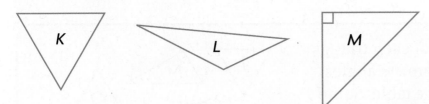

5. Triangle _____ has 1 right angle and appears to have

_____ sides of equal length.

6. Triangle _____ has 3 angles less than a right angle and

appears to have _____ sides of equal length.

7. Triangle _____ has 1 angle greater than a right angle and

appears to have _____ sides of equal length.

© Houghton Mifflin Harcourt Publishing Company

Problem Solving • Applications 🌎Real World

8. **MATHEMATICAL PRACTICE ①** **Make Sense of Problems** Martin said a triangle can have two sides that are parallel. Does his statement make sense? Explain.

_____

_____

9. **GO DEEPER** Compare Triangles *R* and *S*. How are they alike? How are they different?

_____

_____

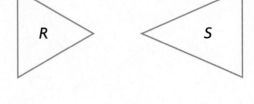

10. **THINK SMARTER** Use a ruler to draw a straight line from one corner of this rectangle to the opposite corner. What shapes did you make? What do you notice about the shapes?

_____

_____

11. **THINK SMARTER** Write the name of each triangle where it belongs in the table. Some triangles might belong in both parts of the table. Some triangles might not belong in either part.

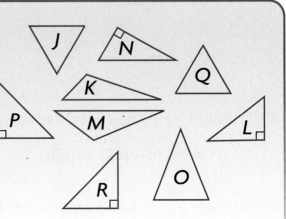

Has 1 Right Angle	Has at Least 2 Sides of Equal Length

© Houghton Mifflin Harcourt Publishing Company

FOR MORE PRACTICE:
Standards Practice Book

Name _____

Problem Solving • Classify Plane Shapes

Essential Question How can you use the strategy *draw a diagram* to classify plane shapes?

Geometry—3.G.1

MATHEMATICAL PRACTICES
MP.1, MP.2, MP.4, MP.7

🔑 Unlock the Problem (Real World)

A **Venn diagram** shows how sets of things are related. In the Venn diagram at the right, one circle has shapes that are rectangles. Shapes that are rhombuses are in the other circle. The shapes in the section where the circles overlap are both rectangles and rhombuses.

What type of quadrilateral is in both circles?

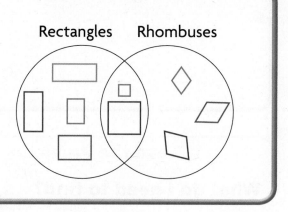

Rectangles   Rhombuses

Read the Problem	Solve the Problem
What do I need to find? _____ _____	What is true about all quadrilaterals? _____ Which quadrilaterals have 2 pairs of opposite sides that are parallel? _____
What information do I need to use? the circles labeled _____ and _____	Which quadrilaterals have 4 sides of equal length? _____ Which quadrilaterals have 4 right angles? _____
How will I use the information? _____ _____ _____	The quadrilaterals in the section where the circles overlap have _____ pairs of opposite sides that are parallel, _____ sides of equal length, and _____ right angles. So, _____ are in both circles.

Math Talk

Mathematical Practices

Does a △ fit in the Venn diagram? Explain.

© Houghton Mifflin Harcourt Publishing Company

🔒 Try Another Problem

The Venn diagram shows the shapes Andrea used to make a picture. Where would the shape shown below be placed in the Venn diagram?

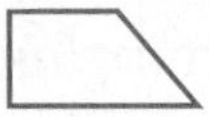

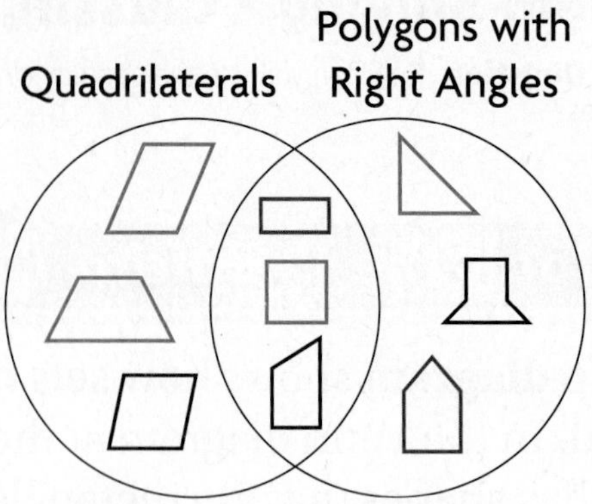

Quadrilaterals   Polygons with Right Angles

Read the Problem	Solve the Problem
What do I need to find?	**Record the steps you used to solve the problem.**
What information do I need to use?	
How will I use the information?	

1. How many shapes do not have right angles?

   _____

2. How many red shapes have right angles but are

   not quadrilaterals? _____

3. **MATHEMATICAL PRACTICE ② Reason Abstractly** What is a different way to sort the shapes?

   _____

   _____

Math Talk

Mathematical Practices

What name can be used to describe all the shapes in the Venn diagram? **Explain** how you know.

© Houghton Mifflin Harcourt Publishing Company

Name _____

Use the Venn diagram for 1–3.

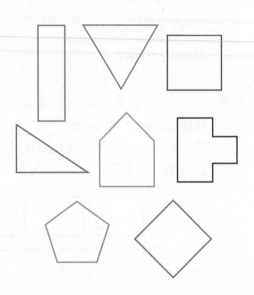

✅ 1. Jordan is sorting the shapes at the right in a Venn diagram. Where does the ◇ go?

First, look at the sides and angles of the polygons.

Next, draw the polygons in the Venn diagram.

The shape has _____ sides of equal length

and _____ right angles.

So, the shape goes in the

_____.

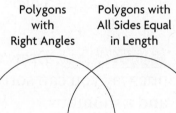

Polygons with Right Angles   Polygons with All Sides Equal in Length

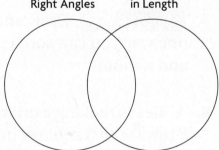

✅ 2. Where would you place a ▱?

_____

3. What if Jordan sorted the shapes by Polygons with Right Angles and Polygons with Angles Less Than a Right Angle? Would the circles still overlap? Explain.

_____

_____

4. **GO DEEPER** Eva drew the Venn diagram below. What labels could she have used for the diagram?

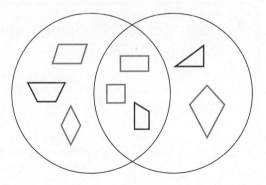

_____   _____

_____   _____

© Houghton Mifflin Harcourt Publishing Company

On Your Own

5. Ben and Marta are both reading the same book. Ben has read $\frac{1}{3}$ of the book. Marta has read $\frac{1}{4}$ of the book. Who has read more? _____

6. 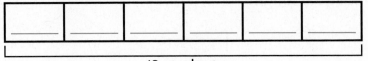 **Represent a Problem** There are 42 students from 6 different classes in the school spelling bee. Each class has the same number of students in the spelling bee. Use the bar model to find how many students are from each class.

$$\boxed{}\boxed{}\boxed{}\boxed{}\boxed{}\boxed{}$$

42 students

_____ students ÷ _____ classes = _____ students

7. **THINK SMARTER** Draw and label a Venn diagram to show one way you can sort a rectangle, a square, a trapezoid, and a rhombus.

8. Ashley is making a quilt with squares of fabric. There are 9 rows with 8 squares in each row. How many squares of fabric are there?

_____

Personal Math Trainer

9. **THINK SMARTER +** Sketch where to place these shapes in the Venn diagram.

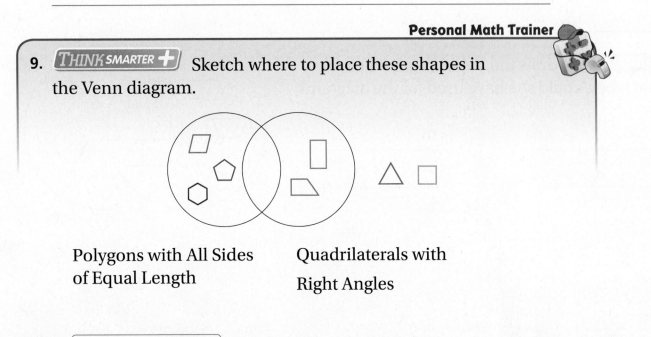

Polygons with All Sides of Equal Length

Quadrilaterals with Right Angles

© Houghton Mifflin Harcourt Publishing Company

Name _____

Relate Shapes, Fractions, and Area

Essential Question How can you divide shapes into parts with equal areas and write the area as a unit fraction of the whole?

Geometry—3.G.2
Also 3.NF.1, 3.NF.3d, 3.MD.5
MATHEMATICAL PRACTICES
MP.4, MP.6, MP.7, MP.8

Investigate

Materials ■ pattern blocks ■ color pencils ■ ruler

CONNECT You can use what you know about combining and separating plane shapes to explore the relationship between fractions and area.

A. Trace a hexagon pattern block.

B. Divide your hexagon into two parts with equal area.

C. Write the names of the new shapes. _____

D. Write the fraction that names each part of the whole

you divided. _____
Each part is $\frac{1}{2}$ of the whole shape's area.

E. Write the fraction that names the whole area. _____

> **Math Idea**
>
> Equal parts of a whole have equal area.

Draw Conclusions

1. Explain how you know the two shapes have the same area.

_____

_____

2. Predict what would happen if you divide the hexagon into three shapes with equal area. What fraction names the area of each part of the divided hexagon? What fraction names the whole area?

_____

3. [THINK SMARTER] Show how you can divide the hexagon into four shapes with equal area.

Each part is _____ of the whole shape's area.

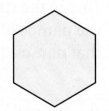

© Houghton Mifflin Harcourt Publishing Company

Make Connections

The rectangle at the right is divided into four parts with equal area.

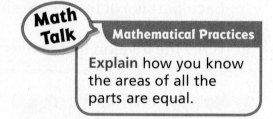

- Write the unit fraction that names each part of the divided whole. _____

- What is the area of each part? _____

- How many $\frac{1}{4}$ parts does it take to make one whole? _____

- Is the shape of each of the $\frac{1}{4}$ parts the same? _____

- Is the area of each of the $\frac{1}{4}$ parts the same? Explain how you know.

_____

_____

Divide the shape into equal parts.

Draw lines to divide the rectangle below into six parts with equal area.

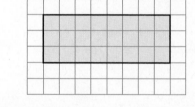

Math Talk

Mathematical Practices

Explain how you know the areas of all the parts are equal.

- Write the fraction that names each part of the divided whole. _____

- Write the area of each part. _____

- Each part is _____ of the whole shape's area.

Share and Show

1. Divide the trapezoid into 3 parts with equal area. Write the names of the new shapes. Then write the fraction that names the area of each part of the whole.

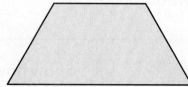

_____

© Houghton Mifflin Harcourt Publishing Company

Name _____

Draw lines to divide the shape into equal parts that show the fraction given.

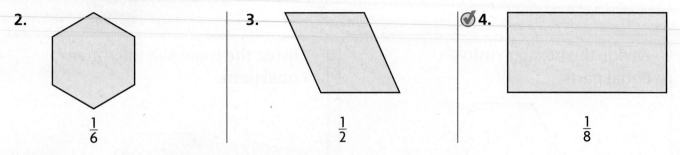

2.

$\dfrac{1}{6}$

3.

$\dfrac{1}{2}$

✓4.

$\dfrac{1}{8}$

**Draw lines to divide the shape into parts with equal area.
Write the area of each part as a unit fraction.**

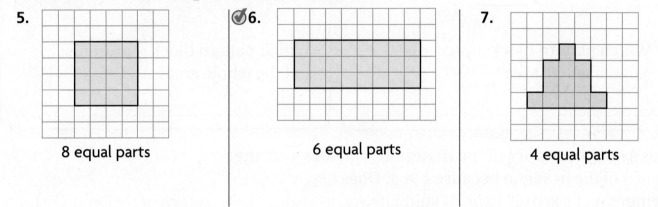

5.

8 equal parts

✓6.

6 equal parts

7.

4 equal parts

Problem Solving • Applications Real World

8. **MATHEMATICAL PRACTICE ②** **Use Reasoning** If the area of three ◇ is equal to the area of one ⬡, the area of how many ◇ equals four ⬡? Explain your answer.

_____

9. **THINK SMARTER** Divide each shape into the number of equal parts shown. Then write the fraction that describes each part of the whole.

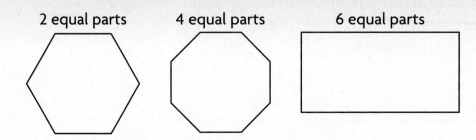

2 equal parts   4 equal parts   6 equal parts

_____   _____   _____

© Houghton Mifflin Harcourt Publishing Company

10. **THINK SMARTER** **Sense or Nonsense?**

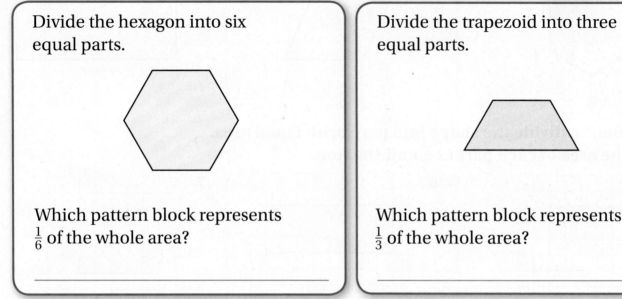

Divide the hexagon into six equal parts.

Which pattern block represents $\frac{1}{6}$ of the whole area?

_____

Divide the trapezoid into three equal parts.

Which pattern block represents $\frac{1}{3}$ of the whole area?

_____

Alexis said the area of $\frac{1}{3}$ of the trapezoid is greater than the area of $\frac{1}{6}$ of the hexagon because $\frac{1}{3} > \frac{1}{6}$. Does her statement make sense? Explain your answer.

_____

_____

_____

_____

- Write a statement that makes sense.

_____

_____

- **GO DEEPER** What if you divide the hexagon into 3 equal parts? Write a sentence that compares the area of each equal part of the hexagon to each equal part of the trapezoid.

_____

_____

© Houghton Mifflin Harcourt Publishing Company

FOR MORE PRACTICE:
Standards Practice Book

Name _____

1. Which words describe this shape? Mark all that apply.

   (A) polygon

   (B) open shape

   (C) pentagon

   (D) quadrilateral

2. Umberto drew one side of a quadrilateral with 4 equal sides and no right angles. Draw the other 3 sides to complete Umberto's shape.

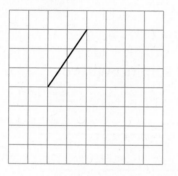

3. Mikael saw a painting that included this shape.

   For numbers 3a–3d, select True or False for each statement about the shape.

   3a. The shape has no   ○ True   ○ False
        right angles.

   3b. The shape has 2 angles   ○ True   ○ False
        greater than a right angle.

   3c. The shape has 2 right angles.   ○ True   ○ False

   3d. The shape has 1 angle   ○ True   ○ False
        greater than a right angle.

© Houghton Mifflin Harcourt Publishing Company

Assessment Options
Chapter Test

4. Fran used a Venn Diagram to sort shapes.

Part A

Draw another plane shape that belongs inside the left circle of the diagram but NOT in the section where the circles overlap.

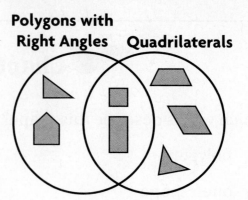

Polygons with
Right Angles   Quadrilaterals

Part B

How can you describe the shapes in the section where the circles overlap?

_____

_____

5. Match each object in the left column with its name in the right column.

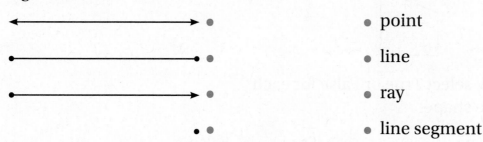

- point

- line

- ray

- line segment

6. Describe the angles and sides of this triangle.

_____

© Houghton Mifflin Harcourt Publishing Company

Name _____

7. Which words describe this shape. Mark all that apply.

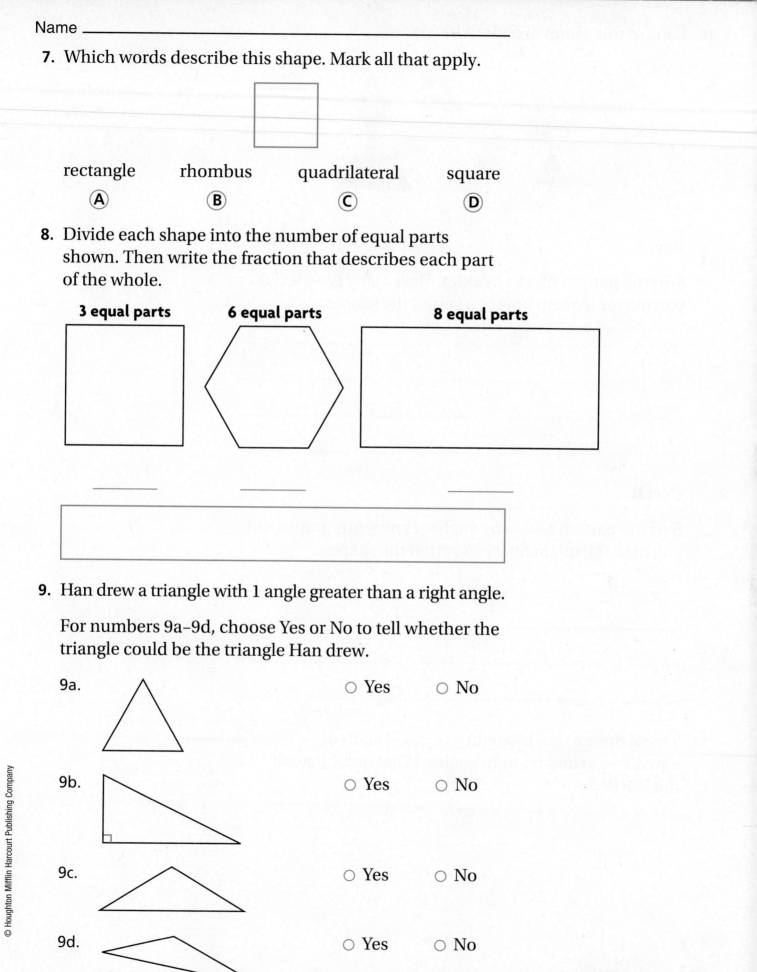

rectangle   rhombus   quadrilateral   square
Ⓐ   Ⓑ   Ⓒ   Ⓓ

8. Divide each shape into the number of equal parts shown. Then write the fraction that describes each part of the whole.

3 equal parts   **6 equal parts**   **8 equal parts**

_____   _____   _____

9. Han drew a triangle with 1 angle greater than a right angle.

For numbers 9a–9d, choose Yes or No to tell whether the triangle could be the triangle Han drew.

9a.   ○ Yes   ○ No

9b.   ○ Yes   ○ No

9c.   ○ Yes   ○ No

9d.   ○ Yes   ○ No

© Houghton Mifflin Harcourt Publishing Company

10. Look at this group of pattern blocks.

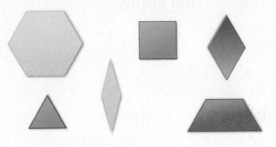

Part A

Sort the pattern blocks by sides. How many groups did you make? Explain how you sorted the shapes.

_____

_____

_____

_____

Part B

Sort the pattern blocks by angles. How many groups did you make? Explain how you sorted the shapes.

_____

_____

_____

_____

11. Teresa drew a quadrilateral that had 4 sides of equal length and no right angles. What quadrilateral did she draw?

_____

© Houghton Mifflin Harcourt Publishing Company

Name _____

12. Rhea used a Venn diagram to sort shapes. What label could she use for circle *A*?

Polygons with All
A   Sides of Equal Length

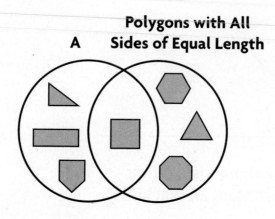

13. Colette drew lines to divide a rectangle into equal parts that each represent $\frac{1}{6}$ of the whole area. Her first line is shown. Draw lines to complete Colette's model.

14. Brad drew a quadrilateral. Select the pairs of sides that appear to be parallel. Mark all that apply.

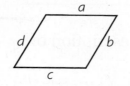

(A)   *a* and *b*   (C)   *c* and *a*

(B)   *b* and *d*   (D)   *d* and *c*

© Houghton Mifflin Harcourt Publishing Company

15. Give two reasons that this shape is **not** a polygon.

_____

16. A triangle has 1 angle greater than a right angle. What must be true about the other angles? Mark all that apply.

Ⓐ At least one must be less than a right angle.

Ⓑ One could be a right angle.

Ⓒ Both must be less than a right angle.

Ⓓ One must be greater than a right angle.

17. Ava drew a quadrilateral with 2 pairs of opposite sides that are parallel. The shape has at least 2 right angles. Draw a shape that Ava could have drawn.

18. For 18a–18d, select True or False for each description of a ray.

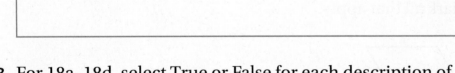

18a.	straight	○ True	○ False
18b.	has 2 endpoints	○ True	○ False
18c.	part of a line	○ True	○ False
18d.	continues in 1 direction	○ True	○ False

© Houghton Mifflin Harcourt Publishing Company

Glossary

Pronunciation Key

a	add, map	f	fit, half	n	nice, tin
ā	ace, rate	g	go, log	ng	ring, song
â(r)	care, air	h	hope, hate	o	odd, hot
ä	palm, father	i	it, give	ō	open, so
b	bat, rub	ī	ice, write	ô	order, jaw
ch	check, catch	j	joy, ledge	oi	oil, boy
d	dog, rod	k	cool, take	ou	pout, now
e	end, pet	l	look, rule	o͝o	took, full
ē	equal, tree	m	move, seem	o͞o	pool, food

p	pit, stop	û(r)	burn, term
r	run, poor	yo͞o	fuse, few
s	see, pass	v	vain, eve
sh	sure, rush	w	win, away
t	talk, sit	y	yet, yearn
th	thin, both	z	zest, muse
th	this, bathe	zh	vision, pleasure
u	up, done		
u̇	pull, book		

ə the schwa, an unstressed vowel representing the sound spelled *a* in *above*, *e* in *sicken*, *i* in *possible*, *o* in *melon*, *u* in *circus*

Other symbols:
- • separates words into syllables
- ′ indicates stress on a syllable

addend [a′dend] **sumando** Any of the numbers that are added in addition
Examples: $2 + 3 = 5$
      ↑   ↑
  addend   addend

addition [ə•dish′ən] **suma** The process of finding the total number of items when two or more groups of items are joined; the opposite operation of subtraction

A.M. [ā•em] **a.m.** The time after midnight and before noon

analog clock [an′ə•log kläk] **reloj analógico** A tool for measuring time, in which hands move around a circle to show hours and minutes
Example:

angle [ang′gəl] **ángulo** A shape formed by two rays that share an endpoint
Example:

Word History

When the letter *g* is replaced with the letter *k* in the word **angle**, the word becomes *ankle*. Both words come from the same Latin root, *angulus*, which means "a sharp bend."

area [âr′ē•ə] **área** The measure of the number of unit squares needed to cover a surface
Example:

Area = 6 square units

© Houghton Mifflin Harcourt Publishing Company

Glossary H1

array [ə•rā′] **matriz** A set of objects arranged in rows and columns
Example:

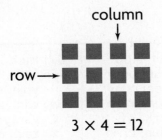

$3 \times 4 = 12$

Associative Property of Addition [ə•sō′shē•āt•iv präp′ər•tē əv ə•dish′ən] **propiedad asociativa de la suma** The property that states that you can group addends in different ways and still get the same sum
Example:
$$4 + (2 + 5) = 11$$
$$(4 + 2) + 5 = 11$$

Associative Property of Multiplication [ə•sō′shē•āt•iv präp′ər•tē əv mul•tə•pli•kā′shən] **propiedad asociativa de la multiplicación** The property that states that when the grouping of factors is changed, the product remains the same
Example:
$$(3 \times 2) \times 4 = 24$$
$$3 \times (2 \times 4) = 24$$

bar graph [bär graf] **gráfica de barras** A graph that uses bars to show data
Example:

capacity [kə•pas′i•tē] **capacidad** The amount a container can hold
Example:
1 liter = 1,000 milliliters

cent sign (¢) [sent sīn] **símbolo de centavo** A symbol that stands for *cent* or *cents*
Example: 53¢

centimeter (cm) [sen′tə•mēt•ər] **centímetro (cm)** A metric unit that is used to measure length or distance
Example:

1 cm

circle [sûr′kəl] **círculo** A round closed plane shape
Example:

closed shape [klōzd shāp] **figura cerrada** A shape that begins and ends at the same point
Examples:

Commutative Property of Addition [kə•myōōt′ə•tiv präp′ər•tē əv ə•dish′ən] **propiedad conmutativa de la suma** The property that states that you can add two or more numbers in any order and get the same sum
Example: $6 + 7 = 13$
$7 + 6 = 13$

Commutative Property of Multiplication [kə•myōōt′ə•tiv präp′ər•tē əv mul•tə•pli•kā′shən] **propiedad conmutativa de la multiplicación** The property that states that you can multiply two factors in any order and get the same product
Example: $2 \times 4 = 8$
$4 \times 2 = 8$

compare [kəm•pâr′] **comparar** To describe whether numbers are equal to, less than, or greater than each other

compatible numbers [kəm•pat′ə•bəl num′bərz] **números compatibles** Numbers that are easy to compute with mentally

© Houghton Mifflin Harcourt Publishing Company

cone [kōn] **cono** A three-dimensional, pointed shape that has a flat, round base
Example:

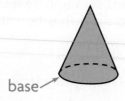
base

counting number [kount´ing num´bər] **número natural** A whole number that can be used to count a set of objects (1, 2, 3, 4 . . .)

cube [kyo͞ob] **cubo** A three-dimensional shape with six square faces of the same size
Example:

cylinder [sil´ən•dər] **cilindro** A three-dimensional object that is shaped like a can
Example:

D

data [dāt´ə] **datos** Information collected about people or things

decagon [dek´ə•gän] **decágono** A polygon with ten sides and ten angles
Example:

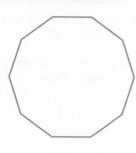

decimal point [des´ə•məl point] **punto decimal** A symbol used to separate dollars from cents in money
Example: $4.52
⌐ decimal point

denominator [dē•näm´ə•nāt•ər] **denominador** The part of a fraction below the line, which tells how many equal parts there are in the whole or in the group
Example: $\frac{3}{4}$ ← denominator

difference [dif´ər•əns] **diferencia** The answer to a subtraction problem
Example: 6 − 4 = 2
⌐difference

digital clock [dij´i•təl kläk] **reloj digital** A clock that shows time to the minute, using digits
Example:

digits [dij´its] **dígitos** The symbols 0, 1, 2, 3, 4, 5, 6, 7, 8, and 9

dime [dīm] **moneda de 10¢** A coin worth 10 cents and with a value equal to that of 10 pennies; 10¢
Example:

Distributive Property [di•strib´yo͞o•tiv präp´ər•tē] **propiedad distributiva** The property that states that multiplying a sum by a number is the same as multiplying each addend by the number and then adding the products
Example: 5 × 8 = 5 × (4 + 4)
5 × 8 = (5 × 4) + (5 × 4)
5 × 8 = 20 + 20
5 × 8 = 40

divide [də•vīd´] **dividir** To separate into equal groups; the opposite operation of multiplication

dividend [div´ə•dend] **dividendo** The number that is to be divided in a division problem
Example: 35 ÷ 5 = 7
⌐dividend

© Houghton Mifflin Harcourt Publishing Company

division [də•vizh′ən] **división** The process of sharing a number of items to find how many groups can be made or how many items will be in a group; the opposite operation of multiplication

divisor [de•vī′zər] **divisor** The number that divides the dividend
Example: 35 ÷ 5 = 7

↑__divisor

dollar [däl′ər] **dólar** Paper money worth 100 cents and equal to 100 pennies; $1.00
Example:

 E

edge [ej] **arista** A line segment formed where two faces meet

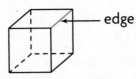

—— edge

eighths [ātths] **octavos**

These are eighths

elapsed time [ē•lapst′ tīm] **tiempo transcurrido** The time that passes from the start of an activity to the end of that activity

endpoint [end′point] **extremo** The point at either end of a line segment

equal groups [ē′kwəl grōōpz] **grupos iguales** Groups that have the same number of objects

equal parts [ē′kwəl pärts] **partes iguales** Parts that are exactly the same size

equal sign (=) [ē′kwəl sīn] **signo de igualdad** A symbol used to show that two numbers have the same value
Example: 384 = 384

equal to (=) [ē′kwəl tōō] **igual a** Having the same value
Example: 4 + 4 is equal to 3 + 5.

equation [ē•kwā′zhən] **ecuación** A number sentence that uses the equal sign to show that two amounts are equal
Examples:
3 + 7 = 10
4 − 1 = 3
6 × 7 = 42
8 ÷ 2 = 4

equivalent [ē•kwiv′ə•lənt] **equivalente** Two or more sets that name the same amount

equivalent fractions [ē•kwiv′ə•lənt frak′shənz] **fracciones equivalentes** Two or more fractions that name the same amount
Example:

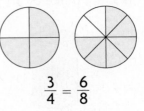

$$\frac{3}{4} = \frac{6}{8}$$

estimate [es′tə•māt] *verb* **estimar** To find about how many or how much

estimate [es′tə•mit] *noun* **estimación** A number close to an exact amount

even [ē′vən] **par** A whole number that has a 0, 2, 4, 6, or 8 in the ones place

expanded form [ek•span′did fôrm] **forma desarrollada** A way to write numbers by showing the value of each digit
Example: 721 = 700 + 20 + 1

experiment [ek•sper′ə•mənt] **experimento** A test that is done in order to find out something

© Houghton Mifflin Harcourt Publishing Company

F

face [fās] **cara** A polygon that is a flat surface of a solid shape

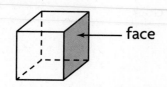

factor [fak′tər] **factor** A number that is multiplied by another number to find a product
Examples: 3 × 8 = 24

factor   factor

foot (ft) [fo͝ot] **pie** A customary unit used to measure length or distance;
1 foot = 12 inches

fourths [fôrths] **cuartos**

These are fourths

fraction [frak′shən] **fracción** A number that names part of a whole or part of a group
Examples:

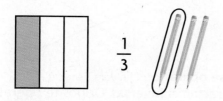

$\frac{1}{3}$

Word History

Often, a *fraction* is a part of a whole that is broken into pieces. *Fraction* comes from the Latin word *frangere*, which means "to break."

fraction greater than 1 [frak′shən grāt′ər than wun] **fracción mayor que 1** A number which has a numerator that is greater than its denominator
Examples:

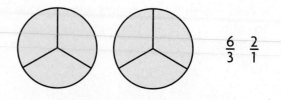

$\frac{6}{3}$ $\frac{2}{1}$

frequency table [frē′kwən•sē tā′bəl] **tabla de frecuencia** A table that uses numbers to record data
Example:

Favorite Color	
Color	**Number**
Blue	10
Green	8
Red	7
Yellow	4

G

gram (g) [gram] **gramo (g)** A metric unit that is used to measure mass;
1 kilogram = 1,000 grams

greater than (>) [grāt′ər than] **mayor que** A symbol used to compare two numbers when the greater number is given first
Example:
Read 6 > 4 as "six is greater than four."

Grouping Property of Addition [gro͞op′ing präp′ər•tē əv ə•dish′ən] **propiedad de agrupación de la suma** *See* Associative Property of Addition.

Grouping Property of Multiplication [gro͞op′ing präp′ər•tē əv mul•tə•pli•kā′shən] **propiedad de agrupación de la multiplicación** *See* Associative Property of Multiplication.

© Houghton Mifflin Harcourt Publishing Company

H

half dollar [haf dol'ər] **moneda de 50¢**
A coin worth 50 cents and with a value
equal to that of 50 pennies; 50¢
Example:

half hour [haf our] **media hora** 30 minutes
Example: Between 4:00 and 4:30 is one
half hour.

halves [havz] **mitades**

These are halves

hexagon [hek'sə•gän] **hexágono** A polygon
with six sides and six angles
Examples:

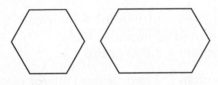

horizontal bar graph [hôr•i•zänt'l bär graf]
gráfica de barras horizontales A bar graph
in which the bars go from left to right
Examples:

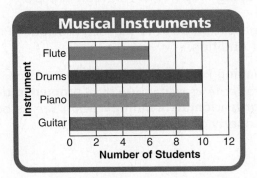

hour (hr) [our] **hora (h)** A unit used to measure
time; in one hour, the hour hand on an analog
clock moves from one number to the next;
1 hour = 60 minutes

hour hand [our hand] **horario** The short hand on
an analog clock

I

Identity Property of Addition [ī•den'tə•tē
präp'ər•tē əv ə•dish'ən] **propiedad de
identidad de la suma** The property that
states that when you add zero to a number,
the result is that number
Example: 24 + 0 = 24

Identity Property of Multiplication [ī•den'tə•tē
präp'ər•tē əv mul•tə•pli•kā'shən] **propiedad de
identidad de la multiplicación** The property
that states that the product of any number
and 1 is that number
Examples: 5 × 1 = 5
1 × 8 = 8

inch (in.) [inch] **pulgada (pulg.)** A customary
unit used to measure length or distance
Example:

intersecting lines [in•tər•sekt'ing līnz] **líneas
secantes** Lines that meet or cross
Example:

inverse operations [in'vûrs äp•ə•rā'shənz]
operaciones inversas Opposite operations,
or operations that undo one another, such
as addition and subtraction or multiplication
and division

K

key [kē] **clave** The part of a map or graph
that explains the symbols

kilogram (kg) [kil'ō•gram] **kilogramo (kg)**
A metric unit used to measure mass;
1 kilogram = 1,000 grams

© Houghton Mifflin Harcourt Publishing Company

length [lengkth] **longitud** The measurement of the distance between two points

less than (<) [les <u>than</u>] **menor que** A symbol used to compare two numbers when the lesser number is given first
Example:
Read 3 < 7 as "three is less than seven."

line [līn] **línea** A straight path extending in both directions with no endpoints
Example:

←—————————→

Word History

The word *line* comes from *linen*, a thread spun from the fibers of the flax plant. In early times, thread was held tight to mark a straight line between two points.

line plot [līn plät] **diagrama de puntos** A graph that records each piece of data on a number line
Example:

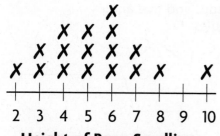

Height of Bean Seedlings to the Nearest Centimeter

line segment [līn seg′mənt] **segmento** A part of a line that includes two points, called endpoints, and all of the points between them
Example:

●—————————●

liquid volume [lik′wid väl′yo͞om] **volumen de un líquido** The amount of liquid in a container

liter (L) [lēt′ər] **litro (L)** A metric unit used to measure capacity and liquid volume;
1 liter = 1,000 milliliters

mass [mas] **masa** The amount of matter in an object

meter (m) [mēt′ər] **metro (m)** A metric unit used to measure length or distance;
1 meter = 100 centimeters

midnight [mid′nīt] **medianoche** 12:00 at night

milliliter (mL) [mil′i•lēt•ər] **mililitro (mL)** A metric unit used to measure capacity and liquid volume

minute (min) [min′it] **minuto (min)** A unit used to measure short amounts of time; in one minute, the minute hand on an analog clock moves from one mark to the next

minute hand [min′it hand] **minutero** The long hand on an analog clock

multiple [mul′tə•pəl] **múltiplo** A number that is the product of two counting numbers
Examples:

$$\begin{array}{cccc} 6 & 6 & 6 & 6 \\ \times\,1 & \times\,2 & \times\,3 & \times\,4 \\ \hline 6 & 12 & 18 & 24 \end{array}$$

← counting numbers
← multiples of 6

multiplication [mul•tə•pli•kā′shən] **multiplicación** The process of finding the total number of items in two or more equal groups; the opposite operation of division

multiply [mul′tə•plī] **multiplicar** To combine equal groups to find how many in all; the opposite operation of division

nickel [nik′əl] **moneda de 5¢** A coin worth 5 cents and with a value equal to that of 5 pennies; 5¢
Example:

noon [no͞on] **mediodía** 12:00 in the day

© Houghton Mifflin Harcourt Publishing Company

number line [num′bər līn] **recta numérica**
A line on which numbers can be located
Example:

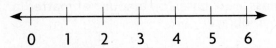

number sentence [num′bər sent′ns] **enunciado numérico** A sentence that includes numbers, operation symbols, and a greater than symbol, a less than symbol, or an equal sign
Example: 5 + 3 = 8

numerator [noō′mər•āt•ər] **numerador** The part of a fraction above the line, which tells how many parts are being counted
Example: $\frac{3}{4}$ ← numerator

octagon [äk′tə•gän] **octágono** A polygon with eight sides and eight angles
Examples:

odd [od] **impar** A whole number that has a 1, 3, 5, 7, or 9 in the ones place

open shape [ō′pən shāp] **figura abierta** A shape that does not begin and end at the same point
Examples:

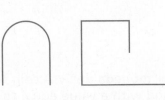

order [ôr′dər] **orden** A particular arrangement or placement of numbers or things, one after another

order of operations [ôr′dər əv äp•ə•rā′shənz] **orden de las operaciones** A special set of rules that gives the order in which calculations are done

Order Property of Addition [ôr′dər präp′ər•tē əv ə•dish′ən] **propiedad de orden de la suma** See Commutative Property of Addition.

Order Property of Multiplication [ôr′dər präp′ər•tē əv mul•tə•pli•kā′shən] **propiedad de orden de la multiplicación** See Commutative Property of Multiplication.

parallel lines [pâr′ə•lel līnz] **líneas paralelas** Lines in the same plane that never cross and are always the same distance apart
Example:

pattern [pat′ərn] **patrón** An ordered set of numbers or objects in which the order helps you predict what will come next
Examples:
2, 4, 6, 8, 10

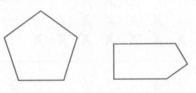

pentagon [pen′tə•gän] **pentágono** A polygon with five sides and five angles
Examples:

perimeter [pə•rim′ə•tər] **perímetro** The distance around a shape
Example:

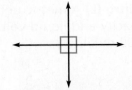

perpendicular lines [pər•pən•dik′yoō•lər līnz] **líneas perpendiculares** Lines that intersect to form right angles
Example:

© Houghton Mifflin Harcourt Publishing Company

picture graph [pik'chər graf] **gráfica con dibujos** A graph that uses pictures to show and compare information
Example:

How We Get to School	
Walk	✹ ✹ ✹
Ride a Bike	✹ ✹ ✹ ✹
Ride a Bus	✹ ✹ ✹ ✹ ✹ ✹
Ride in a Car	✹ ✹
Key: Each ✹ = 10 students.	

place value [plās val'yoo] **valor posicional** The value of each digit in a number, based on the location of the digit

plane [plān] **plano** A flat surface that extends without end in all directions
Example:

plane shape [plān shāp] **figura plana** A shape in a plane that is formed by curves, line segments, or both
Example:

P.M. [pē•em] **p.m.** The time after noon and before midnight

point [point] **punto** An exact position or location

polygon [päl'i•gän] **polígono** A closed plane shape with straight sides that are line segments
Examples:

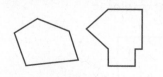

polygons   not polygons

© Houghton Mifflin Harcourt Publishing Company

Word History

Did you ever think that a ***polygon*** looks like a bunch of knees that are bent? This is how the term got its name. *Poly-* is from the Greek word *polys*, which means "many." The ending *-gon* is from the Greek word *gony*, which means "knee."

product [präd'əkt] **producto** The answer in a multiplication problem
Example: $3 \times 8 = 24$
product

Q

quadrilateral [kwäd•ri•lat'ər•əl] **cuadrilátero** A polygon with four sides and four angles
Example:

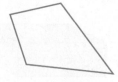

quarter [kwôrt'ər] **moneda de 25¢** A coin worth 25 cents and with a value equal to that of 25 pennies; 25¢
Example:

quarter hour [kwôrt'ər our] **cuarto de hora** 15 minutes
Example: Between 4:00 and 4:15 is one quarter hour.

quotient [kwō'shənt] **cociente** The number, not including the remainder, that results from division
Example: $8 \div 4 = 2$
quotient

R

ray [rā] **semirrecta** A part of a line, with one endpoint, that is straight and continues in one direction
Example:

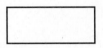

rectangle [rek´tang·gəl] **rectángulo** A quadrilateral with two pairs of parallel sides, two pairs of sides of equal length, and four right angles
Example:

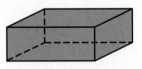

rectangular prism [rek·tang´gyə·lər priz´əm] **prisma rectangular** A three-dimensional shape with six faces that are all rectangles
Example:

regroup [rē·grōōp´] **reagrupar** To exchange amounts of equal value to rename a number
Example: 5 + 8 = 13 ones or 1 ten 3 ones

related facts [ri·lāt´id fakts] **operaciones relacionadas** A set of related addition and subtraction, or multiplication and division, number sentences
Examples: $4 \times 7 = 28$ $28 \div 4 = 7$
$7 \times 4 = 28$ $28 \div 7 = 4$

remainder [ri·mān´dər] **residuo** The amount left over when a number cannot be divided evenly

results [ri·zults´] **resultados** The answers from a survey

rhombus [räm´bəs] **rombo** A quadrilateral with two pairs of parallel sides and four sides of equal length
Example:

right angle [rīt ang´gəl] **ángulo recto** An angle that forms a square corner
Example:

round [round] **redondear** To replace a number with another number that tells about how many or how much

S

scale [skāl] **escala** The numbers placed at fixed distances on a graph to help label the graph

side [sīd] **lado** A straight line segment in a polygon

sixths [siksths] **sextos**

These are sixths

skip count [skip kount] **contar salteado** A pattern of counting forward or backward
Example: 5, 10, 15, 20, 25, 30, . . .

solid shape [sä´lid shāp] **cuerpo geométrico** *See* three-dimensional shape.

sphere [sfir] **esfera** A three-dimensional shape that has the shape of a round ball
Example:

square [skwâr] **cuadrado** A quadrilateral with two pairs of parallel sides, four sides of equal length, and four right angles
Example:

© Houghton Mifflin Harcourt Publishing Company

square unit [skwâr yoo′nit] **unidad cuadrada**
A unit used to measure area such as square
foot, square meter, and so on

standard form [stan′dərd fôrm] **forma normal**
A way to write numbers by using the digits
0–9, with each digit having a place value
Example: 345 ← standard form

subtraction [səb•trak′shən] **resta** The process of
finding how many are left when a number of
items are taken away from a group of items;
the process of finding the difference when two
groups are compared; the opposite operation
of addition

sum [sum] **suma o total** The answer to an
addition problem
Example: 6 + 4 = 10

⬑—sum

survey [sûr′vā] **encuesta** A method of gathering
information

tally table [tal′ē tā′bəl] **tabla de conteo** A table
that uses tally marks to record data
Example:

Favorite Sport	
Sport	**Tally**
Soccer	|||| |||
Baseball	|||
Football	||||
Basketball	||||	

thirds [thûrdz] **tercios**

These are thirds

three-dimensional shape [thrē də•men′shə•nəl shāp]
figura tridimensional A shape that has length,
width, and height
Example:

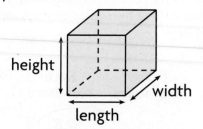

time line [tīm līn] **línea cronológica**
A drawing that shows when and in what
order events took place

trapezoid [trap′i•zoid] **trapecio**
A quadrilateral with exactly one pair of
parallel sides
Example:

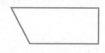

triangle [trī′ang•gəl] **triángulo** A polygon with
three sides and three angles
Examples:

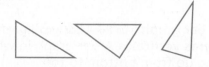

two-dimensional shape [too də•men′shə•nəl shāp]
figura bidimensional A shape that has only
length and width
Example:

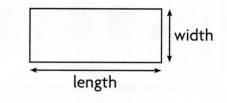

unit fraction [yoo′nit frak′shən] **fracción
unitaria** A fraction that has 1 as its top
number, or numerator
Examples: $\frac{1}{2}$ $\frac{1}{3}$ $\frac{1}{4}$

unit square [yoo′nit skwâr] **cuadrado de una unidad**
A square with a side length of 1 unit, used to
measure area

© Houghton Mifflin Harcourt Publishing Company

Venn diagram [ven dī'ə•gram] **diagrama de Venn** A diagram that shows relationships among sets of things
Example:

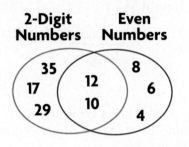

vertex [vûr'teks] **vértice** The point at which two rays of an angle or two (or more) line segments meet in a plane shape or where three or more edges meet in a solid shape
Examples:

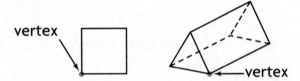

vertical bar graph [vûr'ti•kəl bär graf] **gráfica de barras verticales** A bar graph in which the bars go up from bottom to top

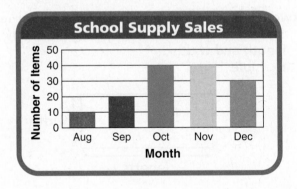

whole [hōl] **entero** All of the parts of a shape or group
Example:

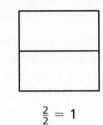

$\frac{2}{2} = 1$

This is one whole.

whole number [hōl num'bər] **número entero** One of the numbers 0, 1, 2, 3, 4, . . . The set of whole numbers goes on without end

word form [wûrd fôrm] **en palabras** A way to write numbers by using words
Example: The word form of 212 is two hundred twelve.

Zero Property of Multiplication [zē'rō präp'ər•tē əv mul•tə•pli•kā'shən] **propiedad del cero de la multiplicación** The property that states that the product of zero and any number is zero
Example: $0 \times 6 = 0$

© Houghton Mifflin Harcourt Publishing Company

Correlations

Standards You Will Learn		Student Edition Lessons
Mathematical Practices		
MP.1	Make sense of problems and persevere in solving them.	Lessons 1.1, 2.1, 2.4, 5.3, 6.4, 7.2, 9.1, 10.3, 11.3
MP.2	Reason abstractly and quantitatively.	Lessons 1.4, 1.5, 3.7, 5.2, 6.8, 7.2, 10.9, 11.4, 12.8
MP.3	Construct viable arguments and critique the reasoning of others.	Lessons 2.6, 4.7, 5.3, 7.5, 9.1, 10.4, 10.5, 11.1, 12.6
MP.4	Model with mathematics.	Lessons 1.12, 2.2, 3.2, 5.2, 6.1, 8.2, 10.3, 11.3, 12.2
MP.5	Use appropriate tools strategically.	Lessons 1.2, 2.1, 4.1, 5.2, 7.1, 7.3, 9.1, 11.4, 12.7
MP.6	Attend to precision.	Lessons 1.3, 2.1, 2.3, 5.2, 6.6, 7.1, 9.4, 10.1, 12.6
MP.7	Look for and make use of structure.	Lessons 1.1, 2.4, 3.2, 5.1, 6.5, 8.2, 9.3, 10.9, 12.3
MP.8	Look for and express regularity in repeated reasoning.	Lessons 1.5, 2.2, 3.6, 5.5, 6.8, 7.2, 9.2, 11.3, 12.4
Domain: Operations and Algebraic Thinking		
Represent and solve problems involving multiplication and division.		
3.OA.1	Interpret products of whole numbers, e.g., interpret 5×7 as the total number of objects in 5 groups of 7 objects each.	Lessons 3.1, 3.2
3.OA.2	Interpret whole-number quotients of whole numbers, e.g., interpret $56 \div 8$ as the number of objects in each share when 56 objects are partitioned equally into 8 shares, or as a number of shares when 56 objects are partitioned into equal shares of 8 objects each.	Lessons 6.2, 6.3, 6.4

© Houghton Mifflin Harcourt Publishing Company

Domain: Operations and Algebraic Thinking		
Represent and solve problems involving multiplication and division.		
3.OA.3	Use multiplication and division within 100 to solve word problems in situations involving equal groups, arrays, and measurement quantities, e.g., by using drawings and equations with a symbol for the unknown number to represent the problem.	Lessons 3.3, 3.5, 4.1, 4.2, 4.3, 6.1, 6.5, 6.6, 7.1, 7.3, 7.8
3.OA.4	Determine the unknown whole number in a multiplication or division equation relating three whole numbers.	Lessons 5.2, 7.8
Understand properties of multiplication and the relationship between multiplication and division.		
3.OA.5	Apply properties of operations as strategies to multiply and divide. *Examples: If $6 \times 4 = 24$ is known, then $4 \times 6 = 24$ is also known (Commutative property of multiplication.) $3 \times 5 \times 2$ can be found by $3 \times 5 = 15$, then $15 \times 2 = 30$, or by $5 \times 2 = 10$, then $3 \times 10 = 30$. (Associative property of multiplication.) Knowing that $8 \times 5 = 40$ and $8 \times 2 = 16$, one can find 8×7 as $8 \times (5 + 2) = (8 \times 5) + (8 \times 2) = 40 + 16 = 56$. (Distributive property.)*	Lessons 3.6, 3.7, 4.4, 4.6, 6.9
3.OA.6	Understand division as an unknown-factor problem.	Lesson 6.7
Multiply and divide with 100.		
3.OA.7	Fluently multiply and divide within 100, using strategies such as the relationship between multiplication and division (e.g., knowing that $8 \times 5 = 40$, one knows $40 \div 5 = 8$) or properties of operations. By the end of Grade 3, know from memory all products of two one-digit numbers.	Lessons 4.5, 4.8, 4.9, 6.8, 7.2, 7.4, 7.5, 7.6, 7.7, 7.9

© Houghton Mifflin Harcourt Publishing Company

Domain: Operations and Algebraic Thinking		
Solve problems involving the four operations, and identify and explain patterns in arithmetic.		
3.OA.8	Solve two-step word problems using the four operations. Represent these problems using equations with a letter standing for the unknown quantity. Assess the reasonableness of answers using mental computation and estimation strategies including rounding.	Lessons 1.12, 3.4, 4.10, 7.10, 7.11
3.OA.9	Identify arithmetic patterns (including patterns in the addition table or multiplication table), and explain them using properties of operations.	Lessons 1.1, 4.7, 5.1
Domain: Number and Operations in Base Ten		
Use place value understanding and properties of operations to perform multi-digit arithmetic.		
3.NBT.1	Use place value understanding to round whole numbers to the nearest 10 or 100.	Lessons 1.2, 1.3
3.NBT.2	Fluently add and subtract within 1000 using strategies and algorithms based on place value, properties of operations, and/or the relationship between addition and subtraction.	Lessons 1.4, 1.5, 1.6, 1.7, 1.8, 1.9, 1.10, 1.11
3.NBT.3	Multiply one-digit whole numbers by multiples of 10 in the range 10–90 (e.g., 9×80, 5×60) using strategies based on place value and properties of operations.	Lessons 5.3, 5.4, 5.5

© Houghton Mifflin Harcourt Publishing Company

Domain: Number and Operations—Fractions		
Develop understanding of fractions as numbers.		
3.NF.1	Understand a fraction $1/b$ as the quantity formed by 1 part when a whole is partitioned into b equal parts; understand a fraction a/b as the quantity formed by a parts of size $1/b$.	Lessons 8.1, 8.2, 8.3, 8.4, 8.7, 8.8, 8.9
3.NF.2	Understand a fraction as a number on the number line; represent fractions on a number line diagram.	
	a. Represent a fraction $1/b$ on a number line diagram by defining the interval from 0 to 1 as the whole and partitioning it into b equal parts. Recognize that each part has size $1/b$ and that the endpoint of the part based at 0 locates the number $1/b$ on the number line.	Lesson 8.5
	b. Represent a fraction a/b on a number line diagram by marking off a lengths $1/b$ from 0. Recognize that the resulting interval has size a/b and that its endpoint locates the number a/b on the number line.	Lesson 8.5

© Houghton Mifflin Harcourt Publishing Company

Domain: Number and Operations—Fractions

Develop understanding of fractions as numbers.

3.NF.3	Explain equivalence of fractions in special cases, and compare fractions by reasoning about their size.	
	a. Understand two fractions as equivalent (equal) if they are the same size, or the same point on a number line.	Lesson 9.6
	b. Recognize and generate simple equivalent fractions, e.g., 1/2 = 2/4, 4/6 = 2/3). Explain why the fractions are equivalent, e.g., by using a visual fraction model.	Lesson 9.7
	c. Express whole numbers as fractions, and recognize fractions that are equivalent to whole numbers.	Lesson 8.6
	d. Compare two fractions with the same numerator or the same denominator by reasoning about their size. Recognize that comparisons are valid only when the two fractions refer to the same whole. Record the results of comparisons with the symbols >, =, or <, and justify the conclusions, e.g., by using a visual fraction model.	Lessons 9.1, 9.2, 9.3, 9.4, 9.5

© Houghton Mifflin Harcourt Publishing Company

Domain: Measurement and Data

Solve problems involving measurement and estimation of intervals of time, liquid volumes, and masses of objects.

3.MD.1	Tell and write time to the nearest minute and measure time intervals in minutes. Solve word problems involving addition and subtraction of time intervals in minutes, e.g., by representing the problem on a number line diagram.	Lessons 10.1, 10.2, 10.3, 10.4, 10.5
3.MD.2	Measure and estimate liquid volumes and masses of objects using standard units of grams (g), kilograms (kg), and liters (l). Add, subtract, multiply, or divide to solve one-step word problems involving masses or volumes that are given in the same units, e.g., by using drawings (such as a beaker with a measurement scale) to represent the problem.	Lessons 10.7, 10.8, 10.9

Represent and interpret data.

3.MD.3	Draw a scaled picture graph and a scaled bar graph to represent a data set with several categories. Solve one- and two-step "how many more" and "how many less" problems using information presented in scaled bar graphs.	Lessons 2.1, 2.2, 2.3, 2.4, 2.5, 2.6
3.MD.4	Generate measurement data by measuring lengths using rulers marked with halves and fourths of an inch. Show the data by making a line plot, where the horizontal scale is marked off in appropriate units—whole numbers, halves, or quarters.	Lessons 2.7, 10.6

© Houghton Mifflin Harcourt Publishing Company

Domain: Measurement and Data

Geometric measurement: understand concepts of area and relate area to multiplication and to addition.

3.MD.5	Recognize area as an attribute of plane figures and understand concepts of area measurement.	Lesson 11.4
	a. A square with side length 1 unit, called "a unit square," is said to have "one square unit" of area, and can be used to measure area.	Lesson 11.4
	b. A plane figure which can be covered without gaps or overlaps by *n* unit squares is said to have an area of *n* square units.	Lesson 11.5
3.MD.6	Measure areas by counting unit squares (square cm, square m, square in, square ft, and improvised units).	Lesson 11.5
3.MD.7	Relate area to the operations of multiplication and addition.	Lesson 11.6
	a. Find the area of a rectangle with whole-number side lengths by tiling it, and show that the area is the same as would be found by multiplying the side lengths.	Lesson 11.6
	b. Multiply side lengths to find areas of rectangles with whole-number side lengths in the context of solving real world and mathematical problems, and represent whole-number products as rectangular areas in mathematical reasoning.	Lesson 11.7
	c. Use tiling to show in a concrete case that the area of a rectangle with whole-number side lengths *a* and *b* + *c* is the sum of *a* × *b* and *a* × *c*. Use area models to represent the distributive property in mathematical reasoning.	Lesson 11.8
	d. Recognize area as additive. Find areas of rectilinear figures by decomposing them into non-overlapping rectangles and adding the areas of the non-overlapping parts, applying this technique to solve real world problems.	Lesson 11.8

© Houghton Mifflin Harcourt Publishing Company

Domain: Measurement and Data

Geometric measurement: recognize perimeter as an attribute of plane figures and distinguish between linear and area measures.

3.MD.8	Solve real world and mathematical problems involving perimeters of polygons, including finding the perimeter given the side lengths, finding an unknown side length, and exhibiting rectangles with the same perimeter and different areas or with the same area and different perimeters.	Lessons 11.1, 11.2, 11.3, 11.9, 11.10

Domain: Geometry

Reason with shapes and their attributes.

3.G.1	Understand that shapes in different categories (e.g., rhombuses, rectangles, and others) may share attributes (e.g., having four sides), and that the shared attributes can define a larger category (e.g., quadrilaterals). Recognize rhombuses, rectangles, and squares as examples of quadrilaterals, and draw examples of quadrilaterals that do not belong to any of these subcategories.	Lessons 12.1, 12.2, 12.3, 12.4, 12.5, 12.6, 12.7, 12.8
3.G.2	Partition shapes into parts with equal areas. Express the area of each part as a unit fraction of the whole.	Lesson 12.9

© Houghton Mifflin Harcourt Publishing Company

Index

© Houghton Mifflin Harcourt

© Houghton Mifflin Harcourt

© Houghton Mifflin Harcourt

© Houghton Mifflin Harcourt

© Houghton Mifflin Harcourt

© Houghton Mifflin Harcourt

© Houghton Mifflin Harcourt

© Houghton Mifflin Harcourt

© Houghton Mifflin Harcourt

6. Attend to precision. In many lessons. Some examples are: 13, 63, 71, 193, 241, 265, 379, 407, 527

7. Look for and make use of structure. In many lessons. Some examples are: 5, 77, 105, 189, 235, 325, 375, 441, 513

8. Look for and express regularity in repeated reasoning. In many lessons. Some examples are: 21, 67, 123, 207, 249, 269, 371, 461, 517

© Houghton Mifflin Harcourt

© Houghton Mifflin Harcourt

Number lines
add and subtract minutes, 415, 420
adding with, 17–20, 415–418, 419
comparing fractions on, 372–373
counting back on, 39, 236–238, 269–272, 273–277, 278
counting up on, 274–275
dividing with, 235–238, 269, 273–276, 278
elapsed time. *See* Time
fractions greater than 1, 357–361
fractions on, 337–340
multiplying with, 109–112, 143–146, 169, 203–206
number line for hours in a day, 411
round numbers and, 9–12
skip counting, 109–112
   by eights, 169
   by fives, 143–144
   by sixes, 109
   by tens, 143–144
   time intervals. *See* Time
   by twos, 140
subtracting with, 39–42
take away tens and ones, 39–42
use to represent
   distances, 337–340
   elapsed time, 415–417, 419–422, 423–426
whole numbers on, 337–340, 343–346

Number patterns, 5–8, 165–168, 174, 189–192

Numbers
compatible, 13–16, 18–19, 35–38
counting, 203, 408, 316, 453
even, 5–8, 165–168, 169–170
expanded form of, 18, 25–28, 30, 40
fractions, 321–324, 325–328, 315–318, 329–332, 337–340, 343–346, 347–350, 351–354, 355–358, 367–370, 371–374, 375–378, 379–382, 385–388, 389–392, 393–396
hundreds, 9–12, 14–16, 25–28, 29–32, 36–38, 40–41, 43–46, 47–50, 203–206, 207–210
odd, 5–8, 165–168, 169–172
ones, 17–20, 21–24, 25–28, 29–32, 36–38, 39–42, 43–46, 47–50, 127–130, 253–256
ordering, 385–388
rounding, 9–12, 13–16
standard form of, 26
tens, 9–12, 17–20, 21–24, 25–28, 29–32, 39–42, 43–46, 47–50, 143–146, 207–210

unknown, 45, 141, 145, 163, 193–196, 267, 282–283, 286–287, 292–293, 296–297, 301, 309
zero, 127–130, 253–256

Numerators, 333
comparing fractions with same, 375–378, 379–382
defined, 333
fractions greater than 1, 344–346
ordering fractions with same, 385–388

O

Octagons
angles of, 513–516
sides of, 513–516

Odd numbers, 5–8, 165–168, 169–170

Ones, 10–12, 17–20, 21–24, 25–28, 29–32, 36–38, 39–42, 43–46, 47–50, 127–130, 207–210

On Your Own, In most lessons. Some examples are: 7, 31, 275, 297, 529, 538

Open shapes, 506–508

Ordering
fractions, 385–388
fraction strips, 385–388
liquid volume, 434
mass, 438

Order of operations, 307–310

Organize data, 63–66

P

Parallel lines, 517–520

Partitioning
fractions, 321–324, 325–328
shapes, 539–542

Patterns
addition, 5–8, 189–192
on the addition table, 5–8
arithmetic, 5–8, 165–168, 189–192
defined, 5
describing, 189–192
explaining using properties, 5–8, 165–168, 170
finding, 479–482
multiplication, 165–168, 174, 189–192
on the multiplication table, 165–168
with nine, 173–176

© Houghton Mifflin Harcourt

© Houghton Mifflin Harcourt

© Houghton Mifflin Harcourt

© Houghton Mifflin Harcourt

© Houghton Mifflin Harcourt

Table of Measures

METRIC	CUSTOMARY
Length	

METRIC	CUSTOMARY
1 centimeter (cm) = 10 millimeters (mm)	
1 decimeter (dm) = 10 centimeters (cm)	1 foot (ft) = 12 inches (in.)
1 meter (m) = 100 centimeters	1 yard (yd) = 3 feet, or 36 inches
1 meter (m) = 10 decimeters	1 mile (mi) = 1,760 yards, or 5,280 feet
1 kilometer (km) = 1,000 meters	

Capacity and Liquid Volume

METRIC	CUSTOMARY
1 liter (L) 5 1,000 milliliters (mL)	1 pint (pt) = 2 cups (c)
	1 quart (qt) = 2 pints
	1 gallon (gal) = 4 quarts

Mass/Weight

METRIC	CUSTOMARY
1 kilogram (kg) = 1,000 grams (g)	1 pound (lb) = 16 ounces (oz)

TIME

1 minute (min) = 60 seconds (sec)	1 year (yr) = 12 months (mo), or about 52 weeks
1 hour (hr) = 60 minutes	1 year = 365 days
1 day = 24 hours	1 leap year = 366 days
1 week (wk) = 7 days	1 decade = 10 years
	1 century = 100 years

MONEY

1 penny = 1 cent (¢)
1 nickel = 5 cents
1 dime = 10 cents
1 quarter = 25 cents
1 half dollar = 50 cents
1 dollar ($) = 100 cents

SYMBOLS

< is less than
> is greater than
= is equal to

© Houghton Mifflin Harcourt Publishing Company